THE MORMON CHURCH ON TRIAL

Reed Smoot portrait by William Henry Taggert.
Courtesy Reed Smoot, a grandson, Provo, Utah

THE MORMON CHURCH ON TRIAL

Transcripts of the Reed Smoot Hearings

Michael Harold Paulos, editor

with an introduction by
Harvard S. Heath

Signature Books • Salt Lake City • 2008
A Smith-Pettit Foundation Book

To Kim, Addison, Brandon, Cardon,
and the Billies for their love and support
and in memory of Heath Tad Briggs

Jacket design by Ron Stucki

©2007 Signature Books. All rights reserved. Signature Books
is a registered trademark of Signature Books Publishing, LLC.

The Mormon Church on Trial: Transcripts of the Reed Smoot Hearings
was printed on acid-free paper and was composed, printed, and
bound in the United States of America

www. signaturebooks.com

2012   2011   2010   2009   2008   5   4   3   2   1

LIBRARY OF CONGRESS CATALOGING-IN-PUBLICATION DATA
The Mormon Church on trial : transcripts of the Reed Smoot
hearings /edited by Michael Harold Paulos ; with an introduction
by Harvard S. Heath.
        p. cm.
    Includes bibliographical references and index.
    ISBN-13: 978-1-56085-152-3 (alk. paper)
    ISBN-10: 1-56085-152-X (alk. paper)
    1. Smoot, Reed, 1862-1941—Political and social views. 2. Smoot,
Reed, 1862-1941—Religion. 3. Smoot, Reed, 1862-1941—Trials,
litigation, etc. 4. Legislative hearings—United States. 5. United
States—Politics and government—1901-1909—Sources. 6. Religion and
politics—United States—History—20th century—Sources. 7. Mormon
Church—United States—History—20th century—Sources. 8. Religion
and politics—Utah—History—20th century—Sources. 9. Mormon
Church—Utah—History—20th century—Sources. I. Paulos, Michael H.

E664.S68M67 2007
328.73'092—dc22
                                        2007036646

Contents

Editor's Preface

DESPITE SOME VERY GOOD RECENT scholarship,[1] much of the daily drama of the Reed Smoot hearings, 1903-1906, remains untold if only because of the volume of official and supporting documentation. The hearings were conducted by a committee of the United States Senate to consider the suitability of newly elected Senator Reed Smoot (1862-1941) to represent the State of Utah. Because Smoot was an LDS apostle, the case attracted national and international attention. Newspapers ran sensational front-page stories as events unfolded. One can only imagine the frenzy a similar hearing would generate today in our information-saturated age—every nook and cranny of Mormonism scrutinized, "shocking" new revelations proclaimed daily.

The Smoot hearings impacted the direction of the Church of Jesus Christ of Latter-day Saints, whose doctrines and practices—not Smoot—emerged as the real focus of the hearings. In many ways, the controversy came to represent what historians today have termed the "transition" period of LDS development, when the church began to shed its rural, insular past and enter the larger mainstream of American religious culture. The present one-volume abridgement of the official record is an attempt to spotlight this important collision between the United States and Mormonism at the dawn of the twentieth century. The historical background for the hearings is treated in Harvard S. Heath's knowledgeable introduction to this volume.

Although the hearings may have been inevitable and useful in the long term, they were painful in the short term. Smoot's correspondence during the years of the hearings speaks directly to the anxiety, stress, and pressure he and others lived with. (Unfortunately, Smoot's diaries for this period have not survived.) At one especially difficult moment, he wrote, "I must admit that it is the hardest thing that I have had to meet in life. I have thought a great deal over the situation, it has worried me until I can hardly sleep, I have prayed over it and have received no an-

---

1. See Harvard S. Heath, "Reed Smoot: First Modern Mormon," Ph.D. diss., Brigham Young University, 1990; Kathleen Flake, *The Politics of American Religious Identity: The Seating of Senator Reed Smoot, Mormon Apostle* (Chapel Hill: University of North Carolina Press, 2004).

swer to my prayers satisfactory to myself ..."[2] Given the uncertain reper-
cussions of the testimony against him and fragile political alliances he
managed to secure, it was easy for Smoot to wax pessimistic: "It is true
that at times the clouds look very dark and seem to hang very low, but as
the days pass by the sunshine again appears, and I find that the friends
that I have made in the past are generally standing by me."[3]

My introduction to Senator Smoot and his turbulent first term in office came while I was serving a full-time proselytizing mission for the
LDS Church in Florida from 1994 to 1996. My next exposure occurred
in mid-1999 while enrolled in a history class taught by Susan Easton
Black at Brigham Young University. The class lectures touched gingerly
upon the hearings and LDS Church President Joseph F. Smith's testimony before a sometimes combative committee.

Beginning in the summer of 2004, I tried to spend almost every available moment working on this abridgement even though it was a challenge to fend off other distractions. My reading of the documents
helped to stimulate an interest in public policy and informed my evolv-
ing political and religious views. Gradually, I began to see connections
between Smoot's day and my own—an illuminating experience, to say
the least.

The full title of the official published record is *Proceedings before the
Committee on Privileges and Elections of the United States Senate in the Matter
of the Protests against the Right of Hon. Reed Smoot, a Senator from the State of
Utah, to Hold His Seat.*[4] It is abbreviated in the present abridgement as
Smoot Hearings, followed by volume and page numbers. The hearings, including initial protests to Smoot's election, spanned three and a half
years from January 26, 1903, to June 11, 1906, and covered in detail topics ranging from LDS involvement in politics and business to the
church's temple endowment ceremony, plural marriage, the 1890 Wilford Woodruff Manifesto, and other public and private beliefs and practices. Most witnesses traveled to Washington, D.C., from Utah or Idaho,
and each person's testimony was colored by his or her standing in the

---

2. Smoot to Joseph F. Smith, Mar. 23, 1904, Reed Smoot Papers, L. Tom Perry Special Collections, Harold B. Lee Library, Brigham Young University, Provo, Utah. Unless
otherwise noted, all correspondence cited throughout this book may be found in the
Smoot Papers at BYU.

3. Smoot to Joseph F. Smith, Apr. 9, 1904.

4. The proceedings were published by the Government Printing Office in four volumes, 1904-06, as Senate Report No. 486, 59th Congress, 1st Session. The total page
count is 3,432.

LDS Church—very few straddling the fence. Witnesses included high-level church officials, so-called "apostates," and non-Mormons.

As I combed through the hearings, I was most struck by the testimony of LDS Church President Joseph F. Smith and of Reed Smoot himself. I found their interrogations interesting and revealing; in fact, many of the topics they tackled continue to figure in contemporary LDS Church debates and controversies. Where I included testimony from other witnesses, their statements usually appeared within the context of the topics raised in the examination of the other two witnesses. I have tried, where appropriate, to balance testimony favorable to the LDS Church with testimony that was not.

In the footnotes I have added information from primary sources such as letters, newspaper articles, and diary entries that explain and contextualize the testimony or provide a glimpse into the interpretation the national and Utah media gave to the proceedings. In Salt Lake City, especially, the newspaper commentaries, both pro and con, were vociferous. My decisions about what additional material readers might find helpful reflect my own interests as well as a sense of what others might find obscure. In the reader's interest, I also silently corrected obvious typographical errors in the transcripts and supplemental material.

I was otherwise guided in my choices about what testimony to include and what further information to place in the notes by the following:

1. At Brigham Young University, the Harold B. Lee library contains J. Reuben Clark's marked-up copy of the hearings. Clark, who would come to serve in the church's First Presidency from 1933 to 1961, highlighted sections of Joseph F. Smith's testimony in the first volume. I note where such overlapping occurs between my abridgement and Clark's markings. Ironically, Clark joined the First Presidency the same year as Smoot lost his Senate seat.

2. Upon completion of the hearings, separate reports were issued by committee members both for and against Smoot. The majority report ran thirty-two pages, the minority report forty-three pages. These two documents included analysis, relevant testimony, and supporting documentation bolstering each side. My abridgement sometimes follows the excerpts the committee members found relevant or otherwise includes text from their reports, in which case I note the sources.

3. Closing arguments before the committee occurred on January 26-27, 1905, but the case was reopened a year later on February 6, 1906. An additional fifteen witnesses testified, followed by a second round of closing arguments. This additional material seemed significant, includ-

ing again portions of the record the attorneys chose to cite in their closings. Where the abridgement includes such material, I include a note to that effect.

4. Smoot's case was eventually decided by the Senate on February 20, 1907. This was a full eight months after an adverse recommendation by the investigating committee. The measure to disqualify Smoot, which required a two-thirds majority to pass, failed by a vote of 42-28. Between when the committee issued its report and the full Senate voted, eight senators, including Smoot himself, delivered speeches for or against him. Where they cited testimony from the hearings, I have noted this in my abridgement.

A project like this is possible only with help and encouragement from friends and associates. My wife, Kim, spent many hours proofing the text as well as humoring my obsession. My sons, Addison and Brandon, were patient, and I'm sure they find it a little strange to discover their father now at home on Saturdays. Tom Kimball deserves all the credit, as well as blame, for introducing me to this project; Kathleen Flake improved its focus and structure. Brothers Alex, Pete, Matty, Andy, and Tim helped out, on demand, with a variety of miscellaneous tasks. Parents Harold and Tina became involved, if only in the interest of their quirky son. Other supporters were Bruce Quick, Stephen Wood, Robert Holland, Heath and Colleen Briggs, and Kelly Ball. I must also acknowledge members of both the Reed Smoot and Carl Badger families (Badger was Smoot's personal secretary during the hearings), including great-grandson and namesake Reed Smoot, Kathryn Egan, Ethan Kawasaki, and Alice Quinn. Others deserving of thanks are Scott Kenney, Will Bagley, Jim Harris, John Murphy, and Russ Taylor.

My encounter with the Smoot Hearings changed me forever. The day I turned this project over to others was bittersweet.

Introduction

Harvard S. Heath

I T IS DOUBTFUL LDS OFFICIALS ANTICIPATED the furor that erupted with Reed Smoot's election to the U.S. Senate by the Utah state legislature in 1903. Perhaps church authorities thought that with the elections of other Mormons in 1896 and 1900, Apostle Smoot's election posed no serious problem because he was not a polygamist and was largely removed from the rancor of an earlier era of persecution and prosecution. The unsuccessful seating of B. H. Roberts was almost a dim memory at this juncture. Besides, Roberts had been a polygamist and Democrat—two things Smoot was not. LDS leaders expected opposition from Democrats, a few disgruntled Republicans, and assorted non-Mormons but did not sense the simmering groundswell of indignation over the appointment to national public office of a high-ranking LDS Church general authority.[1]

Before proceeding further, it may be helpful to understand the place and significance of the Smoot debacle in the context of previous hearings. A systematic study of the years 1791 to 1903 indicates that 107 such hearings occurred which questioned or contested the right of an elected Senator to be seated. To appreciate the magnitude of petitions sent to Washington, D. C., opposing Smoot, it is helpful to know that a petition could come from a single individual or from literally thousands of people. With this qualification in mind, the 3,482 petitions regarding the seating of Smoot represented a significant number of outraged citizens whose moral indignation had been aroused.

The initial salvo against Smoot was unleashed by the Salt Lake Minis-

HARVARD S. HEATH is former curator of the Utah and American West Archives, L. Tom Perry Special Collections, Harold B. Lee Library, Brigham Young University. He edited *In the World: The Diaries of Reed Smoot* and contributed to the reprint edition of *The House of the Lord* by James E. Talmage. He is currently preparing for publication the diaries of LDS Church President David O. McKay.

1. For a detailed discussion of the Smoot hearings, with complete source citations, see my "Reed Smoot: First Modern Mormon," Ph.D. diss., Brigham Young University, 1990, esp. chapter 2 on the hearings, 84-197. The standard biography is Milton R. Merrill, *Reed Smoot: Apostle in Politics* (Logan: Utah State University Press, 1990).

terial Association, led by Edward B. Critchlow, a Salt Lake City attorney, and an array of critics of the LDS Church. Although Critchlow authored, and William M. Paden, pastor of the First Presbyterian Church of Salt Lake City, provided research for the original petition opposing Smoot, it was John L. Leilich, Superintendent of Missions for the Methodist Church, who fanned the early flames by accusing Smoot of being a polygamist—which he wasn't. This erroneous allegation haunted the prosecution throughout the hearings. Smoot learned of the association's petition while visiting an LDS stake (diocese) conference in Fillmore, Utah, on November 25, 1902. Smoot was a visiting church dignitary at the conference, having been ordained an apostle in 1900. Incensed at what he learned, and in the heat of the moment, he composed a draft telegram stating that his duty was to his country, first and foremost, and he was as capable of serving as any member of the ministerial association. Some associates, realizing the public relations mine field he was about to detonate, assisted him to tone down the substance of the telegram before sending it.

Prior to traveling to Washington, Smoot was already deluged with letters from across the country inquiring about what his victory would mean for the LDS Church and the country. In response, Smoot typically expressed appreciation for the writer's interest and briefly argued that Mormons had always been misunderstood and misrepresented. However, such replies belied the fact that Smoot was physically spent and emotionally upset over the prospect of facing the inevitable controversy. He met with the LDS First Presidency in February 1903 to consider how he should deal with the opposition to his election. Smoot asked for and received a blessing before embarking on what would become the most ambitious, tumultuous undertaking of his career.

After arriving in Washington, he was pleased to learn he would be formally presented and seated prior to his status being contested. Whether Smoot or LDS leaders felt more secure at this point is difficult to determine, although it appears many supporters believed this was going to be a brief tempest in a teapot and would soon blow over. Smoot shared with colleagues a cautious optimism over his prospects. Nevertheless, as the hearings progressed, his attitude became punctuated by wild emotional swings, and he was subject to alternating bouts of jubilant optimism and dire depression.

The Senate Committee on Privileges and Elections was charged with investigating the ministerial association's allegations. It appointed nine Republicans and five Democrats to conduct the initial hearings. Their

findings and recommendations would be reported to the full body of
the Senate. Although the committee's composition changed from beginning to end, the original membership comprised nine northern Republicans, including chair Julius C. Burrows from Michigan, four southern Democrats, and one western Democrat, Fred T. Dubois of Idaho.
(See brief biographies of committee members below.)

Newspapers found the controversy not only newsworthy but titillat-
ing for their readership, especially among the Eastern press which
would consistently track the proceedings. The Salt Lake City newspapers ran daily stories. The non-LDS *Salt Lake Tribune* provided a service,
which Smoot found annoying, of sending the newspaper to all members
of the committee and all government department heads. Known to be
antagonistic toward the LDS Church, the *Tribune* took pleasure in adding to Smoot's woes with investigative stories containing as much sensational and salacious material as could be found.

At the outset of the hearings, it was unclear just who was on
trial—Smoot or the LDS Church. A reading of the proceedings reveals
that the focus fluctuated. However, it is apparent that the church's practices and policies were to receive substantially more attention than
Smoot's personal life or qualifications, although it is hard to separate
the two as discrete issues.

From March through September 1903, optimism still reigned in
Smoot's camp. Charges had been leveled, but to this point no serious
damage had yet been done to the junior Senator's cause. Then as Congress reconvened in the fall of 1903, the case took a turn for the worse,
and for the next two months Smoot's prior optimism turned to deep
concern for the future. The first major problem occurred on November
4 when Apostle Heber J. Grant said he would take more than two wives if
the government allowed it. Smoot struggled to explain this remark to his
fellow Senators. The second problem was the anti-Mormon proclivity of
Senator Dubois, who traveled to Salt Lake City on a fact-finding mission.
Dubois was intent on proving the allegations against Smoot and docu-
menting vigilantism and treason against the U.S. government. The Senator initiated the impetus that led to the disfranchisement of all of
Idaho's Mormons in the 1880s and it was reported that Dubois also
wanted to organize anti-Mormon newspapers in Idaho and Montana.

By late 1903, aware of the fight that was brewing, LDS leaders decided to seek competent legal counsel. Previously, the First Presidency
had designated Franklin S. Richards to represent church interests as an
in-house attorney. Smoot eventually settled on Augustus S. Worthing-

ton, a non-Mormon lawyer with experience handling Constitutional cases in the nation's capital, and Waldemar Van Cott, based in Salt Lake City. Through November and December 1903, while attorneys prepared, witnesses subpoenaed by the prosecution began arriving in Washington and newspapers flocked to them for interviews. Smoot tried to keep church officials apprised of developments through letters and coded telegrams. To prevent the contents from falling into unfriendly hands, he was soon using intermediaries to deliver his correspondence with the First Presidency.

Smoot's attorneys were aware of the tack the prosecution would take. The Senator's critics intended to argue that (1) he was a polygamist, (2) he had taken an oath against the State of Utah and the U.S. government, (3) he would do whatever church officials asked, and (4) he condoned the continued practice of polygamy including unlawful cohabitation. Smoot had hoped to keep the church on the sidelines through his ordeal, but it became painfully apparent that the committee wanted to explore Mormon practices and doctrines and intended to subpoena its leaders. By February 1904, Smoot was contemplating what he had wrought upon his church. He knew some friends at home thought his election was a mistake and that the price to be exacted for his seat was scarcely worth the problems it posed. He was aware that some fellow members of the Quorum of the Twelve Apostles were less than enthusiastic about what was transpiring, leading him to consider resigning from the Senate. On the other hand, he had the unqualified support of sixty-five-year-old church president Joseph F. Smith, which would eventually prove decisive.

Following some preliminary negotiations, the committee was ready to proceed on March 2, 1904. The subpoenas had been sent out; the first witness, Joseph F. Smith, was called to testify. What he said startled the committee and gave the press a field day. For instance, he admitted he had cohabited with all of his five wives during the period after the 1890 Wilford Woodruff Manifesto, the ostensible end to plural marriage. President Smith said he felt this was entirely within the law as he *understood* it. The church no longer contracted plural marriages, he said, but those already involved in the practice were not expected to abandon their wives and children. He stressed that he had no intention of leaving his wives and the eleven children borne to him after 1890. The mental picture of this articulate, bearded gentleman living with five wives caused an uproar in Washington as many observers interpreted his testimony to be confirmation of the allegations against Smoot.

Apostle Francis M. Lyman, the next LDS authority to testify, responded similarly, explaining that he too felt obligated to care for and be with his plural wives and children. Other subpoenaed apostles—Marriner Wood Merrill and George Teasdale—were excused because of illness. John Henry Smith was ill but agreed to appear at a later date. However, the witnesses the prosecution most wanted to question were two younger apostles, John W. Taylor and Matthias F. Cowley, both of whom had fled the country or maintained the necessary anonymity to avoid being subpoenaed.

Testimonies by Smith and Lyman gave the prosecution hope. By contrast, they dampened Smoot's spirits, especially when he saw the unexpected public reaction. The press emphasized that the church leadership continued in their unlawful cohabitation and made this the central issue for the American public. Senators who were previously friendly to Smoot informed him that they were receiving up to 2,000 letters a day requesting that the Mormon be denied his seat. Given the sensational exposures of recent testimony, they wanted to know what other unsavory details future witnesses might reveal.

In the April 1904 general conference in Salt Lake City, President Joseph F. Smith issued what has become known as the Second Manifesto reiterating the church's opposition to polygamy and threatening excommunication to those who entered into new marriages. Smoot felt this declaration was imperative. He had come to learn all too well that if he stood back and compared the theoretical discontinuance of polygamy with the actual facts on the ground, the perception was of duplicity. In Washington, the Second Manifesto was considered to be too little, too late, and there were more calls for Apostles Taylor and Cowley to make an appearance.

Smoot breathed a sigh of relief when committee decided to recess in May, while feeling demoralized by the fact the case was not yet over. Congress reconvened that fall and Smoot's counsel decided to try to push the matter into January 1905 to give them time to prepare and to let the rage of the previous spring subside as much as possible. It was apparent the chair would have nothing to do with this postponement and pushed for the committee to reconvene some time in December 1904. Smoot was pleased to find he had the continuing support of some Senators. However, once again there were ominous signs on the horizon when a well-known Mormon baiter, Charles Mostyn Owen, agreed to expose to the world the secret rituals of Mormon temples, including the so-called "oath of vengeance" against the United States. The prosecution was going to argue, Smoot learned, that these rites seriously impaired the Senator's ability to function effectively and independently and might be grounds to preclude him from holding office.

Smoot continued to be inundated by questions about LDS theology and practice, matters in which he had never been very knowledgeable. Church leaders provided him with documentation to authoritatively establish doctrine and urged him and his counsel not to make any missteps on these points. When the investigation continued in December 1904, it became obvious that Smoot was going to be judged on the church's doctrine, as LDS leaders had predicted. Because the holidays were approaching, the hearings continued only three weeks before recessing. Nevertheless, testimony was presented to show the church had not been sincere or above board in its statements about polygamy.

When the hearings re-opened in January 1905, the Washington press and the Senate committee lingered for a time over the church's assumed duplicity regarding polygamy and its involvement in directing political activities in Utah and other states. However, having seen substantial progress by the defense while he was vacationing in Salt Lake City, Smoot arrived feeling sanguine about the upcoming sessions. His counsel tried to anticipate what the witnesses might say and prepare appropriately. Joseph F. Smith let it be known that those in or out of the church who opposed Smoot's right to be seated were traitors and warned against associating with them. Church leaders admonished members to conduct themselves in a way that would not incur suspicion or condemnation from those seeking to attack the church at the hearings.

For the next seventeen days, forty-two witnesses appeared for and against Smoot. The majority were defense witnesses intended to offset the prejudicial testimony from the prosecution. The defense wanted to sprinkle in enough prominent non-Mormons, or "gentiles," to dispel the idea that Mormons had a monolithic hold on Utah and surrounding regions. While the witnesses did not offer anything startling, they typically lauded Mormons for their contributions to society and sought to create a favorable impression of the Mormon people. It was difficult to determine how these testimonies affected the committee members and other Senators. The press coverage continued searching for and reporting on sensational and spectacular disclosures and ignored the mundane to keep readers interested in the case.

On January 18, 1905, the defense put LDS educator James E. Talmage on the stand. He had spent six months compiling material for his discussion of the church's tenets in order to refute the witnesses who had preceded him. Two days later, Smoot was unexpectedly called to the stand. Aware that his testimony would be crucial, perhaps the deciding factor in his case, he walked the tightrope of trying not to offend the enemy and not embarrass or criticize his church. According to observers, Smoot was "cautious" and "evasive." Realizing the necessity of distancing him from the startling testimony of some of the church's leaders, the defense gave Smoot every opportunity to present himself as a rational, intelligent individual lacking the fanaticism and fervor that had marked some of the previous witnesses. The image Smoot projected was that of a new kind of Mormon—monogamous, business-oriented, civic-minded, and not given to the traditional world view that had characterized the older generation of Latter-day Saints. He sought to deflect accusations of disloyalty, law breaking, aberrant social and political behavior, and political interference from the priesthood. The cross-examination was predictably brutal. However, by January 28 the attorneys on both sides were ready to make concluding statements. Thereafter, no one knew what might come next and neither side was predicting how the case would be decided.

Smoot himself prepared for several possibilities including another continuance. In fact, when the committee decided to carry the investigation over, Smoot became extremely anxious that no untoward event would occur during the interim. His first concern was that something outrageous or irrational might occur at the April general conference, particularly with regard to Apostles Taylor and Cowley. For reasons that seem clear today, he chose not to attend that spring's conference, citing business commitments on the west coast, and excused himself from all sessions. No adverse action was taken against Taylor and Cowley. Both were sustained in their apostolic offices.

Additional protests occurred in the nation's capital in the fall of 1905. The National Congress of Mothers, claiming more than two million members, demanded that Smoot be sent home. When he arrived in Washington, he found hundreds of letters awaiting him, asking about positions that had been raised in his case. The most disturbing letters were those that suggested he resign his apostleship to keep his Senate seat or vice versa. When the committee reconvened in February 1906, Smoot was unsure of the mood of other Senators. He fretted over the reaction of U.S. President Theodore Roosevelt who, Smoot believed, was the key to his ultimate victory. He therefore undertook steps to reassure Roosevelt, beginning with his decision at the October 1905 general conference to refuse to sustain Apostles Taylor and Cowley as members of the Quorum of the Twelve. In less than a month, both apostles had privately resigned from their quorum, although President Smith decided not to announce their resignations until absolutely necessary.

The beginning of January 1906 was as inauspicious as the previous January. The previous spring, Smoot had exuded a new confidence that everything would soon be behind him. Then Senator Burrows, assisted by Charles Owen and others, introduced evidence that made Smoot once again apprehensive; they were determined to pursue the unresolved question about the temple endowment ritual. Principally they wanted to know if the ritual made the government subservient to the priesthood. After presenting witnesses—notably Walter M. Wolfe, a former Brigham Young University professor and participant in the controversial Cluff expedition to South America—Burrows intended to show that the endowment precluded Smoot from executing his oath as a Senator. Following Wolfe's seemingly damning testimony, Smoot's counsel portrayed Wolfe as a drunkard and apostate. Although the former BYU professor's testimony was distressing, Smoot's supporters concluded that it was not as damaging as it could have been.

By the time the proceedings ended, Smoot felt that if anything, he had gained ground during the session, the prosecution's vaunted witnesses not having produced the trouble Smoot's counsel had feared. Some Senators found aspects of the testimony disturbing, with regard to polygamy, government involvement, and church interference in politics, but there seemed to be nothing so startling that it would adversely affect the case any more than previous revelations already had. Smoot had initially leaned toward wanting to force a vote and be done with the matter, whatever the outcome. But as March and April passed, his colleagues sensed it would be prudent to have the hearings carry over until the next session. Those who were up for re-election were reluctant to anger constituents by voting in Smoot's favor.

The last issue that needed resolution was the status of Apostles Taylor and Cowley. The committee watched to see what might develop at the church's upcoming general conference of April 1906. For about six months, the resignations had been sitting on the First Presidency's desk. By March, President Smith concluded it was time to accept the resignations because Smoot's situation had made it imperative. A painful decision involving the sacrifice of two apostles, the resignations strengthened Smoot's case but dealt a devastating blow to Taylor and Cowley and their families.

A decision was made in May 1906 to carry the full Senate vote over until the next year. Smoot's attorneys, the Republican Party, and the LDS Church favored a delay. However, in resolving the matter in the committee on June 6, the resolution that "Reed Smoot is not entitled to his seat as a United States Senator from the State of Utah" passed by a vote of seven to five. By June 11, two committee reports were filed with the Senate: a majority report opposing Smoot and the minority view supporting him. The majority argued that as a Mormon officer, he was not entitled to high government office because the Mormon Church practiced and promoted polygamy and sought to direct, influence, and dominate social, political, and economic affairs in Utah, which the Senators considered to be un-American. The minority report argued that Smoot was qualified and duly elected, that he had done nothing to indicate he was unable to function as a competent, productive, and loyal public servant.

In January 1907, Smoot's political friends were confident of a favorable outcome. One factor supporting this optimism was Senator Dubois's resounding defeat in Idaho in the 1906 elections, which led LDS leaders to sense public opinion might be turning. Meanwhile, Smoot impatiently awaited Senator Burrows's decision to introduce Resolution 142 to the Senate floor. This was done on February 20. After debate, a vote was called at 4:00 p.m. on the following wording: "Resolved that Reed Smoot is not entitled to his seat as a United States Senator from the State of Utah[;] two thirds of the Senators concurring therein." When the votes were tallied, the resolution failed by a vote of forty-two to twenty-eight, five votes shy of the two-thirds majority required for passage of the measure.

Even though it was an equivocal vote of confidence for Smoot, it nevertheless confirmed his right to represent the State of Utah. Of greater significance was that for the first time in its history, the LDS Church had achieved political legitimacy. This should not be misinterpreted as social and cultural acceptance or an indication that American opinion had been magically transformed over night. That process had only begun, but it was a process the Smoot hearings had accelerated. The church desperately needed a victory in this case to gain the respect and stature it needed to be recognized as a bonafide member of American society. Throughout the next two decades, church leaders would look back to the hearings as a crucial turning point in the church's acceptance nationally and later internationally.

With the unswerving support of Joseph F. Smith and backing of Republican friends, Smoot would go on to re-election for four more terms.

Along with the influence Smoot would come to wield in national politics, often to the church's benefit, these electoral victories confirmed to
President Smith that he had done the right thing to assist Smoot in this
watershed moment in Mormon history. The church sought respectabil-
ity, and this was embodied in the influence Smoot came to project.
More than any other man of his time, he helped his state and church out
of nineteenth-century isolation into the modern twentieth century. No
doubt, the church would have reached the same destination by another
road had the hearings not occurred. Even so, it is doubtful the transfor-
mation would have happened with the rapidity and distinction Smoot
brought to that process.

Senate Committee
on Privileges and Elections

Joseph Weldon Bailey (1862-1929), D-Texas; elected to two terms in Senate, 1901-13; five-term Congressman, 1891-1901; resigned near end of second Senate term; unsuccessful candidate for Texas governor, 1920; son (Joseph Weldon Bailey Jr.) served in Congress (D-Texas), 1933-34; admitted to bar, 1883; served on Committee on Privileges and Elections through entire Smoot hearings, attending fifteen days of testimony.

Albert Jeremiah Beveridge (1862-1927), R-Indiana; elected to two terms in Senate, 1899-1911; unsuccessful Progressive candidate for Indiana governor, 1912, Senate 1914; unsuccessful Republican candidate for Senate, 1922; admitted to bar, 1887; later freelance historian; served on Committee on Privileges and Elections through entire Smoot hearings, attending fourteen days of testimony.

Julius Caesar Burrows (1837-1915), R-Michigan; elected to three terms in Senate, 1895-1911; nine-term Congressman, 1873-95; resigned from Congress to fill open Senate seat; admitted to bar, 1859; spoke for abolition during Lincoln campaigns; served as chair of the Committee on Privileges and Elections through entire Smoot hearings, attending fifty-two days of testimony.

James Paul Clarke (1854-1916), D-Arkansas; elected to three terms in Senate, 1903-16, died in office; served as Senate president pro tempore, 1914-15; governor of Arkansas, 1895-96; admitted to bar, 1879; served on Committee on Privileges and Elections from beginning of Smoot case until he resigned on January 31, 1906, not having heard any testimony; replaced by Patterson.

Chauncey Mitchell Depew (1834-1928), R-New York; elected to two terms in Senate, 1899-1911; unsuccessful candidate for Senate, 1881; unsuccessful candidate for U.S. presidential nomination, 1888; admitted to bar, 1858; served on Committee on Privileges and Elections through entire Smoot hearings, attending six days of testimony.

William Paul Dillingham (1843-1923), R-Vermont; elected to four terms as Senator, 1900-23, died in office; admitted to bar, 1867; governor of Vermont, 1888-90; served on Committee on Privileges and Elections through entire Smoot hearings, attending twenty-five days of testimony.

Jonathan Prentiss Dolliver (1858-1910), R-Iowa; elected to two terms in Senate, 1900-10, died in office; six-term Congressman, 1889-1900; resigned from Congress to fill open Senate seat; admitted to bar, 1878; served on Committee on Privileges and Elections beginning in late 1905, replacing McComas, attending two days of testimony.

Fred Thomas Dubois (1851-1930), D-Idaho; served two terms in Senate, 1891-97, 1901-07, as Republican, independent "Silver Republican," and Democrat; previously delegate from Territory of Idaho, 1887-90; U.S. Marshal of Idaho, 1882-86; used anti-Mormonism as main political platform; served on Committee on Privileges and Elections through entire Smoot hearings, attending forty-three days of testimony.

Joseph Benson Foraker (1846-1917), R-Ohio; elected to two terms in Senate, 1897-1909; governor of Ohio, 1885-89; unsuccessful Republican candidate for Ohio governor, 1883, 1889; admitted to bar, 1869; fought in Civil War; served on Committee on Privileges and Elections through entire Smoot hearings, attending twenty-four days of testimony.

James Beriah Frazier (1856-1937), D-Tennessee; elected to one term in Senate, 1905-11; governor of Tennessee, 1903-05; admitted to bar, 1881; son (James Beriah Frazier Jr.) a seven-term Congressman (D-Tennessee), 1949-63; replaced Patterson on Committee on Privileges and Elections, February 12, 1906, attending three days of testimony.

George Frisbie Hoar (1826-1904), R-Massachusetts; elected to five terms in Senate, 1877-1904, died in office; four-term Congressman, 1869-77; admitted to bar, 1849; helped conduct impeachment proceedings against William W. Belknap, 1876; served on Committee on Privileges and Elections until death on September 30, 1904, having attended ten days of testimony, replaced by Knox.

Albert Jarvis Hopkins (1846-1922), R-Illinois; elected to one term in Senate, 1903-09; nine-term Congressman, 1885-1902; admitted to bar,

1871; served on Committee on Privileges and Elections through entire Smoot hearings, attending twenty-two days of testimony.

Philander Chase Knox (1853-1921), R-Pennsylvania; elected to two terms in Senate, 1904-09, 1917-21, died in office; resigned first term to become U.S. Secretary of State; appointed U.S. Attorney General, 1901-04; admitted to bar, 1875; credited with being most widely read, "brainiest" man in Senate; served on Committee on Privileges and Elections from late 1904 through end of Smoot hearings, replacing Hoar, attending fifteen days of testimony.

Louis Emory McComas (1846-1907), R-Maryland; elected to one term in Senate, 1899-1905; four-term Congressman, 1883-90; unsuccessful candidate, 1876, 1890; appointed Associate Justice of Supreme Court of District of Columbia, 1892; admitted to bar, 1868; served on Committee on Privileges and Elections until retirement, March 1905, having attended twenty-four days of testimony, replaced by Dolliver.

Lee Slater Overman (1854-1930), D-North Carolina; elected to five terms in Senate, 1903-30, died in office; unsuccessful Senate candidate, 1895; admitted to bar, 1878; served on Committee on Privileges and Elections through entire Smoot hearings, attending forty days of testimony.

Thomas MacDonald Patterson (1839-1916), D-Colorado; elected to one term in Senate, 1901-07; two-term Congressman, 1875-78 (as Delegate, then Representative); twice unsuccessful Democratic candidate for Colorado governor; admitted to bar, 1867; served on Committee on Privileges and Elections from January 31, 1906, to February 12, 1906, not having heard any testimony, replaced by Frazier.

Edmund Winston Pettus (1821-1907), D-Alabama; elected to two terms in Senate, 1901-07, died in office; served as lieutenant in Mexican War, for Confederacy in Civil War; admitted to bar, 1842; served on Committee on Privileges and Elections through entire Smoot hearings, attending twenty-seven days of testimony.

Smoot Hearings Chronology

1903

Jan. 26   William M. Paden and seventeen others formally submit complaint regarding seating Reed Smoot as U.S. Senator from Utah.

Feb. 25   John L. Leilich adds to the above complaint.

1904

Jan. 4   Reed Smoot answers complaint.

Jan. 16   Senate Committee on Privileges and Elections convenes at 10:30 a.m. to begin hearings. Present Senators Bailey, Beveridge, Burrows, Dillingham, Dubois, Hopkins, McComas, Overman, Pettus, and Smoot. Opening statements from Thomas P. Stevenson and Robert W. Tayler for the complainants, Waldemar Van Cott and Augustus S. Worthington for the respondent, also from Reed Smoot. Executive session, 1:20 p.m.

Mar. 1   The committee meets briefly at 10:30 a.m. Present Senators Bailey, Burrows, Dillingham, Dubois, Foraker, Hopkins, McComas, Overman, Pettus, and Smoot, with John G. Carlisle and Robert W. Tayler for the complainants, Van Cott and Worthington for the respondent.

Mar. 2   The committee meets at 10:00 a.m. Present Senators Bailey, Beveridge, Burrows, Depew, Dillingham, Dubois, Foraker, Hoar, Hopkins, McComas, Overman, Pettus, and Smoot, with attorneys Carlisle, Tayler, Van Cott, and Worthington. Joseph F. Smith is first witness. The committee recesses from 11:45 a.m. until 2:00 p.m. Smith testifies again. The committee recesses for ten minutes. Smith's testimony continues. The committee meets in executive session at 4:05 p.m.

Mar. 3   The committee meets at 10:30 a.m. Present Senators
            Beveridge, Burrows, Dillingham, Dubois, Foraker, Hoar,
            Hopkins, Overman, Pettus, and Smoot, with attorneys
            Tayler, Van Cott, Worthington, and (for Joseph F. Smith)
            Franklin S. Richards. Smith's testimony continues. The
            committee recesses from 11:55 a.m. until 2:00 p.m.
            Smith's testimony continues afterward. The committee
            adjourns at 4:20 p.m.

Mar. 4   The committee meets at 10:30 a.m. Present Senators
            Bailey, Beveridge, Burrows, Dillingham, Dubois, Foraker,
            Hoar, Hopkins, McComas, Overman, Pettus, and Smoot,
            with attorneys Richards, Tayler, Van Cott, and
            Worthington. Smith's testimony continues. The commit-
            tee recesses from 11:55 a.m. until 2:00 p.m., after which
            Smith's testimony resumes. The committee adjourns at
            4:35 p.m.

Mar. 5   The committee meets at 10:30 a.m. Present Senators
            Bailey, Burrows, Dillingham, Dubois, Foraker, Hoar,
            Hopkins, Overman, Pettus, and Smoot, with attorneys
            Richards, Tayler, Van Cott, and Worthington. Smith's tes-
            timony continues. The committee adjourns at 11:55 a.m.

Mar. 7   Committee meets at 10:30 a.m. Present Senators Bur-
            rows, Dillingham, Dubois, Foraker, Hoar, McComas,
            Overman, Pettus, and Smoot, with attorneys Richards,
            Tayler, Van Cott, and Worthington. Smith's testimony
            continues. The committee recesses from 11:55 a.m. until
            2:00 p.m. Smith returns, followed by Clara Mabel Barber
            Kennedy. The committee adjourns at 4:08 p.m.

Mar. 8   The committee meets at 10:30 a.m. Present Senators Bur-
            rows, Dubois, Foraker, Hoar, Hopkins, Overman, Pettus,
            and Smoot, with attorneys Richards, Tayler, Van Cott,
            and Worthington. Kennedy continues, followed by
            Charles E. Merrill, Emma Mathews, and Francis M.
            Lyman. The committee recesses from 11:55 a.m. until
            2:00 p.m. Lyman resumes his testimony. The committee
            adjourns at 4:30 a.m.

Mar. 9   The committee meets at 10:30 a.m. Present Senators Bur-
            rows, Depew, Dillingham, Dubois, Foraker, Hoar,

McComas, Overman, Pettus, and Smoot, with attorneys
Richards, Tayler, Van Cott, and Worthington. Joseph F.
Smith returns. The committee recesses from noon until
2:00 p.m. Andrew Jenson testifies, followed by Lorin
Harmer, Hyrum M. Smith, Thomas Merrill, and Alma
Merrill. The committee adjourns at 3:55 p.m.

Mar. 10   The committee meets at 10:30 a.m. Present Senators
Beveridge, Burrows, Depew, Dillingham, Dubois, Foraker,
Hoar, Hopkins, McComas, Overman, Pettus, and Smoot,
with attorneys Richards, Tayler, Van Cott, and
Worthington. Jenson returns. The committee goes into
executive session at 11:45 a.m. and afterward recesses un-
til 2:00 p.m. Jenson continues, followed by E. B.
Critchlow. The committee adjourns at 4:10 p.m.

Mar. 11   The committee meets at 10:30 a.m. Present Senators
Beveridge, Burrows, Dillingham, Foraker, Hoar, Hopkins,
Overman, and Smoot, with attorneys Richards, Tayler,
Van Cott, and Worthington. Critchlow continues. The
committee recesses from 11:55 a.m. until 2:00 p.m.
Critchlow returns. The committee adjourns at 4:10 p.m.

Mar. 12   The committee meets at 10:30 a.m. Present Senators Burrows, Dillingham, Hoar, McComas, Overman, and Smoot,
with attorneys Richards, Tayler, Van Cott, and
Worthington. Critchlow continues. The committee recesses from 12:50 p.m. until 2:00 p.m. Critchlow returns,
followed by Ogden Hiles. The committee adjourns at
4:25 p.m.

Apr. 20   The committee meets at 10:30 a.m. Present Senators
Bailey, Beveridge, Burrows, Depew, Dubois, Hopkins,
Overman, Pettus, and Smoot, with attorneys Richards,
Tayler, Van Cott, and Worthington. B. H. Roberts testi-
fies. The committee recesses from 11:50 a.m. until 2:00
p.m. Roberts continues, followed by Edward H. Barthell.
The committee adjourns at 4:10 p.m.

Apr. 21   The committee meets at 10:30 a.m. Present Senators
Beveridge, Burrows, Dubois, McComas, Overman, Pettus,
and Smoot, with attorneys Carlisle, Richards, Tayler, Van
Cott, and Worthington. Roberts is recalled, followed by

Calvin Cobb. The committee recesses at 11:55 a.m. until 2:00 p.m. Cobb continues. Next is Angus M. Cannon. The committee adjourns at 3:35 p.m.

Apr. 22   The committee meets at 10:30 a.m. Present Senators Bailey, Burrows, Dubois, Foraker, Hopkins, McComas, Overman, Pettus, and Smoot, with attorneys Richards, Tayler, Van Cott, and Worthington. Orlando W. Powers testifies. The committee recesses from 11:55 a.m. until 2:00 p.m. Powers continues. The committee adjourns at 4:10 p.m.

Apr. 23   The committee meets at 10:30 a.m. Present Senators Bailey, Burrows, Dubois, Hopkins, McComas, Overman, Pettus, and Smoot, with attorneys Richards, Tayler, Van Cott, and Worthington. Powers continues. The committee recesses from 11:55 a.m. until 2:00 p.m. Powers resumes. The committee adjourns at 3:55 p.m.

Apr. 25   The committee meets at 10:00 a.m. Present Senators Bailey, Burrows, Dillingham, Dubois, McComas, Overman, and Smoot, with attorneys Richards, Tayler, Van Cott, and Worthington. Powers continues, followed by Moses Thatcher. The committee adjourns at 11:50 a.m.

Apr. 26   The committee meets at 10:30 a.m. Present Senators Bailey, Burrows, Depew, Dillingham, Dubois, Foraker, Hopkins, Overman, Pettus, and Smoot, with attorneys Richards, Tayler, Van Cott, and Worthington. Thatcher continues. The committee goes into executive session at 11:25 a.m.

Apr. 27   The committee meets at 10:30 a.m. Present Senators Burrows, Dillingham, Dubois, Overman, and Smoot, with attorneys Richards, Tayler, Van Cott, and Worthington. L. E. Abbott testifies. The committee adjourns at 11:20 a.m.

May 2   The committee meets at 12:30 p.m. Present Senators Burrows, Dubois, McComas, and Smoot, with attorneys Richards, Tayler, and Worthington. Angus M. Cannon, Jr., testifies. The committee adjourns at 3:45 p.m.

Dec. 12   The committee meets at 10:30 a.m. Present Senators Burrows, Dubois, Foraker, Overman, Pettus, and Smoot, with attorneys Richards, Tayler, Van Cott, and Worthington. Rev. J. M. Buckley and George Reynolds testify. The committee recess from 11:50 until 2:00 p.m. Reynolds continues, followed by John H. Hamlin. The committee adjourns at 4:30 p.m.

Dec. 13   The committee meets at 10:00 a.m. Present Senators Burrows, Dubois, McComas, Overman, and Smoot, with attorneys Richards, Tayler, Van Cott, and Worthington. The following testify: J. H. Wallis Sr., George H. Brimhall, and Josiah Hickman. The committee recesses from 11:55 a.m. until 2:00 p.m. Hickman resumes, followed by Margaret Geddes and Arthur Morning. The committee adjourns at 3:15 p.m.

Dec. 14   The committee meets at 10:00 a.m. Present Senators Burrows, Dubois, and Smoot, with attorneys Richards, Tayler, Van Cott, and Worthington. Reynolds is recalled, followed by Wilhelmina C. Ellis. Wallis is recalled, followed by August W. Lundstrom. The committee adjourns at 3:00 p.m.

Dec. 15   The committee meets at 10:00 a.m. Present Senators Burrows, Dubois, McComas, Overman, and Smoot, with attorneys Richards, Tayler, Van Cott, and Worthington. Lundstrom is recalled, followed by John Nicholson. Wallis is recalled. The committee recesses from 11:40 a.m. until 1:30 p.m. Lundstrom continues. The committee adjourns at 2:00 p.m.

Dec. 16   The committee meets at 10:00 a.m. Present Senators Burrows, Dubois, Foraker, McComas, Overman, and Smoot, with attorneys Richards, Tayler, Van Cott, and Worthington. Annie Elliott and Charles H. Jackson testify. The committee adjourns at noon.

Dec. 17   The committee meets at 10:00 a.m. Present Senators Burrows, Dubois, McComas, Overman, Pettus, and Smoot, with attorneys Richards, Tayler, Van Cott, and Worthington. Jackson continues; Nicholson and Hickman are recalled. The committee recesses from 12:55 p.m. until 2:00 p.m. Charles W. Penrose testifies. Ellis is recalled, followed by William Budge and John Henry Smith. The committee adjourns at 4:30 p.m.

Dec. 19   The committee meets at 10:00 a.m. Present Senators Bur-
            rows, Dubois, Pettus, and Smoot, with attorneys Richards,
            Tayler, Van Cott, and Worthington. Smith continues, fol-
            lowed by Isaac Birdsall. The committee recesses from
            1:55 p.m. until 2:00 p.m. Birdsall, Budge, and Smith all
            continue, followed by William Balderston and A. C. Nel-
            son. The committee adjourns at 4:10 p.m.

Dec. 20   The committee meets at 10:00 a.m. Present Senators Bur-
            rows, Dubois, Pettus, and Smoot, with attorneys Richards,
            Tayler, Van Cott, and Worthington. Smith is recalled, fol-
            lowed by Benjamin B. Heywood, Annie C. Thurber, and
            Charles Mostyn Owen. The committee recesses from
            12:50 p.m. until 1:30 p.m. Balderston, Owen, and Penrose
            all continue. Afterward the chair rules that such testi-
            mony "tend[s] to prove the doctrines of the organiza-
            tion," and the committee adjourns at 3:55 p.m.

1905

Jan. 10   The committee meets briefly at 10:00 a.m., then ad-
            journs. Present Senators Burrows, Knox, Overman, and
            Smoot, with attorney Tayler.

Jan. 11   The committee meets at 10:00 a.m. Present Senators Bur-
            rows, Dillingham, Dubois, Knox, McComas, Overman,
            Pettus, and Smoot, with attorneys Tayler, Van Cott, and
            Worthington. William J. McConnell testifies. The com-
            mittee recesses at 11:55 a.m. until 2:00 p.m. McConnell
            resumes, followed by Burton Lee French. The committee
            adjourns at 4:25 p.m.

Jan. 12   The committee meets at 10:00 a.m. Present Senators Bur-
            rows, Dubois, Foraker, Knox, and Smoot, with attorneys
            Tayler, Van Cott, and Worthington. F. H. Holzheimer tes-
            tifies. The committee recesses from noon until 1:30 p.m.
            Frank Martin, James H. Brady, and J. W. N. Whitecotton
            testify. The committee adjourns at 5:00 p.m.

Jan. 13   The committee meets at 10:00 a.m. Present Senators Bev-
            eridge, Burrows, Dubois, Foraker, Hopkins, Knox, Over-
            man, and Smoot, with attorneys Tayler, Van Cott, and

Worthington. Whitecotton resumes his testimony. The committee recesses from 11:55 a.m. until 1:30 p.m. Whitecotton continues, followed by Hiram E. Booth and Arthur Pratt. The committee adjourns at 5:05 p.m.

Jan. 14   The committee meets at 10:00 a.m. Present Senators Burrows, Dubois, Foraker, Knox, McComas, Overman, and Smoot, with attorneys Tayler, Van Cott, and Worthington. The following all testify: James E. Lynch, Hugh M. Dougall, Alonzo Arthur Noon, and William Hatfield. The committee recesses from 11:55 a.m. until 1:30 p.m. In the afternoon, James H. Brady, William McConnell, and William Hatfield continue, followed by John P. Meakin, Robert T. Burton Jr., Samuel N. Cole, James A. Miner, and W. D. Candland. The committee adjourns at 4:00 p.m.

Jan. 16   The committee meets at 10:00 a.m. Present Senators Burrows, Dubois, Foraker, Overman, and Smoot, with attorneys Tayler, Van Cott, and Worthington. James A. Miner resumes, followed by Elias A. Smith, and William P. O'Meara. The committee recesses from 11:50 a.m. until 1:30 p.m. O'Meara continues, followed by Charles W. Morse, William M. McCarty, and A. S. Condon. The committee adjourns at 5:15 p.m.

Jan. 17   The committee meets at 10:00 a.m. Present Senators Burrows, McComas, Overman, and Smoot, with attorneys Tayler, Van Cott, and Worthington. William M. McCarty is recalled, followed by Richard W. Young. The committee recesses from noon until 2:00 p.m. Young resumes, followed by E. D. R. Thompson, Charles De Mosey, F. S. Fernstrom, C. V. Anderson, H. J. Hayward, Jens Christian Neilsen, and William Langton. The committee adjourns at 4:40 p.m.

Jan. 18   The committee meets at 10:00 a.m. Present Senators Burrows, Hopkins, Overman, and Smoot, with attorneys Tayler, Van Cott, and Worthington. James A. Miner is recalled, followed by James E. Talmage. The committee recesses from 11:45 a.m. until 1:30 p.m. Talmage resumes his testimony. The committee adjourns at 4:45 p.m.

Jan. 19   The committee meets at 10:00 a.m. Present Senators Burrows, Dubois, Overman, and Smoot, with attorneys Tayler, Van Cott, and Worthington. Talmage continues his testimony. The committee recesses from noon until 1:30 p.m. Young and Langton are recalled, followed by Glen Miller, John W. Hughes, Mary G. Coulter, and Mrs. W. H. Jones. The committee adjourns at 4:25 p.m.

Jan. 20   The committee meets at 10:00 a.m. Present Senators Burrows, Dubois, Knox, and Smoot, with attorneys Tayler, Van Cott, and Worthington. Smoot testifies. The committee recesses from noon until 2:00 p.m. Smoot resumes his testimony. The committee adjourns at 4:30 p.m.

Jan. 21   The committee meets at 10:00 a.m. Present Senators Bailey, Beveridge, Burrows, Dillingham, Dubois, Foraker, Knox, Overman, Pettus, and Smoot, with attorneys Tayler, Van Cott, and Worthington. Smoot continues his testimony. The committee adjourns at 11:55 a.m.

Jan. 23   The committee meets at 10:00 a.m. Present Senators Bailey, Burrows, Dillingham, Dubois, Foraker, Hopkins, McComas, Overman, and Smoot, with attorneys Tayler, Van Cott, and Worthington. Smoot continues his testimony. The committee recesses from noon until 1:30 p.m. Smoot resumes, followed by Moroni Gillespie, John M. Whitaker, Oleen N. Stohl, and J. U. Eldredge Jr. The committee adjourns at 4:13 p.m.

Jan. 24   The committee meets at 10:00 a.m. Present Senators Burrows, Depew, Dubois, Foraker, Hopkins, Knox, McComas, and Overman, with attorneys Tayler, Van Cott, and Worthington. Frank B. Stephens testifies. The committee recesses from noon until 1:30 p.m. Stephens resumes, followed by Z. T. Sowers, James E. Talmage, Oleen N. Stohl, William Langton, and David Eccles. The committee adjourns at 5:05 p.m.

Jan. 25   The committee meets from 10:00 a.m. until 10:30 a.m. Present Senators Burrows, Dubois, and Knox, with attorneys Tayler, Van Cott, and Worthington.

Jan. 26   The committee meets at 10:00 a.m. Present Senators

Bailey, Beveridge, Burrows, Dillingham, Dubois, Knox, McComas, Overman, Pettus, and Smoot, with attorneys Tayler, Van Cott, and Worthington. Taylor begins his closing argument opposing Smoot. The committee recesses from 11:30 a.m. until 2:00 p.m. Tayler resumes his argument. The committee adjourns at 4:30 p.m.

Jan. 27   The committee meets at 10:00 a.m. Present Senators Bailey, Beveridge, Burrows, Dillingham, Dubois, Foraker, Hopkins, Knox, McComas, Overman, Pettus, and Smoot, with attorneys Tayler, Van Cott, and Worthington. Tayler continues his argument, followed by Van Cott in Smoot's defense. The committee recesses from 11:55 a.m. until 2:00 p.m. Van Cott resumes, followed by Worthington, also in Smoot's defense. Tayler closes.

1906

Feb. 6   The committee meets briefly from 10:00 a.m. until 10:30 a.m. Present Senators Burrows, Dillingham, Hopkins, Pettus, and Smoot, with attorneys Carlisle and Worthington.

Feb. 7   The committee meets at 10:00 a.m. Present Senators Beveridge, Burrows, Depew, Dillingham, Hopkins, Knox, Overman, Pettus, and Smoot, with attorneys Carlisle, Van Cott, and Worthington. Walter M. Wolfe testifies. The committee goes into executive session at 12 noon, then adjourns.

Feb. 8   The committee meets at 10:00 a.m. Present Senators Beveridge, Burrows, Dillingham, Hopkins, Knox, and Overman. Wolfe continues, followed by William Jones Thomas, John P. Holmgren, and Charles A. Smurthwaite. The committee recesses from noon until 2:00 p.m. Henry W. Lawrence and Charles Mostyn Owen testify. The committee adjourns at 3:35 p.m.

Feb. 9   The committee meets at 10:00 a.m. Present Senators Beveridge, Burrows, Dillingham, Hopkins, Knox, and Overman. Smurthwaite continues. The committee adjourns at 11:20 a.m.

Mar. 26   The committee meets at 10:20 a.m. Present Senators Burrows, Dubois, Frazier, and Smoot, with attorneys Carlisle and Worthington. Robert J. Shields and James H. Linford testify. The committee recesses from 12:20 p.m. until 2:00 p.m. Charles E. Marks, Stephen H. Love, James Clove, and William K. Henry testify. The committee adjourns at 4:02 p.m.

Mar. 27   The committee meets at 10:00 a.m. Present Senators Burrows and Dubois, with attorney Worthington, who introduces some letters and affidavits. William K. Henry continues, followed by Joseph Geoghegan. The committee adjourns at 11:55 a.m.

Apr. 12   The committee meets at 10:00 a.m. Present Senators Bailey, Burrows, Dillingham, Foraker, Dolliver, Dubois, Frazier, Knox, Overman, Pettus, and Smoot, with attorneys Carlisle and Worthington. Carlisle summarizes the prosecution's case. The committee adjourns at 11:55 a.m.

Apr. 13   The committee meets at 10:00 a.m. Present Senators Burrows, Dillingham, Foraker, Dolliver, Dubois, Frazier, Knox, and Pettus, with attorney Worthington, who summarizes the respondent's case. The committee adjourns at 12:05 p.m.

June 11   Senator Burrows submits the final majority committee report to the U.S. Senate; dissenting members submit a minority report.

1907

Feb. 20   The Senate fails to sustain the resolution against Smoot, who retains his Senate seat.

I.
MID-JANUARY
1904

1.

The Committee

Saturday, January 16

"The first public hearing in the Smoot Trial ... was slimly attended by members of the committee and by the public. [Nevertheless] all [who were present] manifested keen interest in the case and all excepting Senators Dillingham and Overman asked many questions of Senator Smoot's council." —*Salt Lake Herald*, Jan. 16, 1904

THE CHAIRMAN.[1] The committee is advised that the protestants and the respondent in the pending matter are represented by counsel. The Chair will inquire if anyone appears for the protestants at this time.[2]

MR. ROBERT W. TAYLER.[3] I appear for the protestants.

---

1. The committee chair, Senator Julius Caesar Burrows, exploited the hearings for political gain, as Smoot described in a letter to LDS President Joseph F. Smith: "I called on President [Theodore] Roosevelt and asked him to use his influence as far as possible to have my case decided at as early a day as possible—He expressed a little fear about the position Senator Burrows would take, and stated that he was afraid that he would not be able to have very much influence with him." The reason for this was that Roosevelt had leaned on Burrows, a fellow Republican, to "go contrary to the wishes of the great majority of his constituents in voting for the Cuban Reciprocity Treaty." Burrows faced re-election, "and it may be that he will yield to public clamor and carry the investigation just as far as they demand" (Jan. 4, 1904). In an interesting sidebar, Harvard S. Heath noted that Burrows was a distant relative of Joseph F. Smith ("Reed Smoot: First Modern Mormon," Ph.D. diss. Brigham Young University, 1990, 102-03).

2. The prosecution submitted a twenty-six-page document on January 26, 1903, which charged that (1) the LDS priesthood had supreme authority in all things temporal and spiritual; (2) the First Presidency and twelve apostles were the supreme administrators of this authority; (3) the church's authorities had not "abandoned the principles and practice of political dictation," nor "abandoned belief in polygamy and polygamous cohabitation"; (4) the church's attitude was evidenced by its teachings; (5) "this body of officials, of whom Senator-elect Smoot is one," had "sought to pass a law nullifying enactments against polygamous cohabitation"; and (6) "protect and honor the violators of the laws against polygamy and polygamous cohabitation."

Not surprisingly, the *Salt Lake Tribune* considered "the election of an apostle to be unwise and adverse to the true interests of the State" (Jan. 21, 1903). The LDS Church-owned *Deseret News* defended Smoot, arguing that the opposition was "based on prejudice and false representations by persons envious of [his] success" (Jan. 21, 1903).

3. Robert W. Tayler (1852-1910) was lead attorney representing the complainants. He had served four terms as U.S. Representative from Ohio, 1895-1902, and was later appointed U.S. District Judge for northern Ohio.

THE CHAIRMAN. Who appears for the respondent, the junior Senator from Utah?

MR. A. S. WORTHINGTON.[4] I appear for him, Mr. Chairman, and so does Mr. Waldemar Van Cott.[5]

MR. THOMAS P. STEVENSON. Mr. Chairman, I appear for the National Reform Association, one of the organizations which has been protesting against the seating of Mr. Smoot.

THE CHAIRMAN. Do you represent the original protestants?

MR. STEVENSON. We are original.

THE CHAIRMAN. Do you speak for any of the signers to the protest now under consideration?

MR. STEVENSON. We filed a protest last spring, at the time Senator Smoot took his seat[6] ...

MR. TAYLER. Mr. Chairman and gentlemen of the committee, I represent the protestants who filed the first protest,[7] or the protest signed by W. M. Paden and others, that appears first in the printed document which the committee has issued.[8] I do not disavow, in so far as I would be able to do so, the representations of the party interested in the sup-

---

4. Augustus S. Worthington agreed to be lead attorney for Smoot after Charles J. Faulkner agreed to take the case for $5,000, then changed his mind. Smoot suspected "some influence at work to discourage the attorneys," perhaps by committee members in telling attorneys it would be a "long drawn out fight" (Smoot to Joseph F. Smith, Dec. 16, 1903).

5. Waldemar Van Cott (1859-1940) was born in Salt Lake City but was not Mormon.

6. Smoot was elected by the Utah state legislature on Tuesday, January 20, 1903, by a vote of ten of eighteen in the senate and thirty-six of forty-four in the house ("Smoot Is Now a Real Senator," *Deseret News,* Jan. 20, 1903). Following his swearing-in, the First Presidency wrote to Smoot: "The news of your taking your seat in the Senate reached us by associated press at the temple during our meeting there, and we need not tell you how exceedingly delightful and joyful it made us all feel. Our joy found expression in singing that beautiful hymn, 'Zion stands with the hills surrounded,' and offering thanksgiving to the Lord for the victory won" (Mar. 9, 1903).

7. The original complainants were C. E. Allen, Clarence T. Brown, J. J. Corum, E. B. Critchlow, W. Montgomery Ferry, C. C. Goodwin, George R. Hancock, Harry C. Hill, J. L. Leilich, Abill Leonard, S. H. Lewis, H. G. McMillan, W. A. Nelden, W. M. Paden, George M. Scott, Ezra Thompson, P. P. Williams, and E. W. Wilson. See *Smoot Hearings,* 1:26. Their complaint had to be filed within ten days after Smoot took his seat in the Senate. For a brief biography of each participant, see Critchlow's testimony in *Smoot Hearings,* 1:591-93.

8. A few days before the Salt Lake Ministerial Association filed its protest in 1903, a Salt Lake newspaper reported that the association intended to question Smoot's "credentials" and had "telegraphed to the proper persons in Washington" (*Salt Lake Telegram,* Jan. 22, 1903). For the entire protest, see *Smoot Hearings,* 1:1-26.

plemental protest.[9] I merely say, respecting the charge made in the supplemental protest, that I do not know, and therefore can not say to the committee, that proof will be made sustaining the charge of what is called the Leilich protest,[10] to the effect that Mr. Smoot is a polygamist.[11] I have no desire, and the committee, I gather, has no desire, to hear any argument, at this time at least upon the question of their power to act in a case of this sort, or the legal effect of the things which it is claimed will be proved. The Senators are as familiar as anybody could be with the provisions of the Constitution respecting the power of the Senate to judge of the elections, returns, and qualifications of its members, and also its power to expel. I need only say that there is absolutely no limit upon the right or the power of the Senate in regard to these two procedures, except that the exclusion of a member or the declaration of the vacancy of a seat, on account of a claim that the applicant is disqualified, must of course be sustained by a majority vote of the Senate, and his expulsion must be sustained by a vote of two-thirds of the members of the Senate. Beyond that there is no limit to the power of the Senate ...

---

9. The supplemental protest contained thirteen points, submitted on February 25, 1903, by John L. Leilich. Perhaps the most sensational was the thirteenth charge: "Reed Smoot is a polygamist, and ... since the admission of Utah in the union of States he ... having a legal wife, married a plural wife in the State of Utah in violation of the laws ... and since such plural or polygamous marriage the said Reed Smoot has lived and cohabited with both his legal wife and his plural wife in the State of Utah" (*Smoot Hearings*, 1:26-30). Leilich's protest was received with skepticism by the *Deseret News*, claiming that "the man who has been the forefront of the whole crusade stated ... today that he was afraid 'Brother Leilich had made a pretty mess of the whole business.'" ("Leilich Denounced as a Common Falsifier," *Deseret News*, Feb. 27, 1903).

10. In a letter to Smoot two weeks after Leilich's protest, the First Presidency explained, "We read the charge in company with Brother [Charles W.] Penrose [editor of the *Deseret News*], and concluded not to dignify it with a place in the columns of the News" (Mar. 9, 1903).

11. The twenty-six-page document included excerpts from LDS scripture, sermons, and newspaper articles, including this from the *Salt Lake Telegram*, January 16, 1903:

Apostle Smoot, who is in Provo, was cross-examined over the telephone by the telegram to-day. Here is what happened: "You state in a morning paper that you are not a polygamist, and as a Mormon and as an apostle have never been asked to practice polygamy preach it, or advise others to practice it. Will you answer another question? Do you believe in polyg—?"

"I will not. I will not. I won't," broke in Mr. Smoot before the reporter could finish the question.

"Will you not answer the plain question: Do you believe in polygamy?"

"I will not answer any question that is not submitted in writing. I have been misquoted and my statements misconstrued by Salt Lake papers, and thereby injured in Washington," the apostle declared, as he hung up his telephone.

First, then, the Mormon priesthood, according to the doctrine of that church and the belief and practice of its membership, is vested with, and assumes to exercise, supreme authority in all things temporal and, spiritual, civil and political. The head of the church claims to receive divine revelations, and these Reed Smoot, by his covenants and obligations, is bound to accept and obey, whether they affect things spiritual or things temporal. That is the first proposition ...

Second, the first presidency—

SENATOR BEVERIDGE. Is that the first proposition upon which you base your contest against the respondent?

MR. TAYLER. Yes, sir.

SENATOR BEVERIDGE. His membership in the Mormon Church?

MR. TAYLER. Yes, sir; exactly.

SENATOR BEVERIDGE. I am merely asking for information; but would or would it not mean that no member of the Mormon Church has a right to hold office.[12]

MR. TAYLER. I think that is true. Of course the committee will understand that as a practical and as a public question there is a very marked and proper distinction to be made between a layman in the Mormon Church and one who is in high official position, who is himself authorized to receive revelations and impart them to his inferiors, who must obey those revelations thus imparted.[13]

Second. The first presidency and twelve apostles, of whom Reed Smoot is one, are supreme in the exercise of this authority of the church and in the transmission of that authority to their successors. Each of them is called prophet, seer, and revelator ...

The [Utah] legislature, overwhelmingly Mormon, passed a law which provided that no prosecution should be instituted under the law forbidding polygamous cohabitation unless it was done "on complaint of the husband or wife, or a relative of the accused, within the first degree of consanguinity, or of the person with whom the unlawful act is alleged to have been committed, or of the father or mother

---

12. Beveridge was making the indirect point that since statehood, Utah had elected Frank J. Cannon, a Mormon, to the Senate. Cannon (1859-1933), son of LDS authority George Q. Cannon, subsequently left the church and was later officially expelled. He regularly attacked Smoot and Joseph F. Smith in the editorial pages of the *Salt Lake Tribune* and especially in his 1911 book, *Under the Prophet in Utah*. See also Michael H. Paulos, "Political Cartooning and the Reed Smoot Hearings," *Sunstone*, Dec. 2006, 36-40.

13. This entire section was cited by Van Cott in his closing argument for Smoot (*Smoot Hearings*, 3:628).

of said person; and no prosecution for unlawful cohabitation shall be
commenced except on complaint of the wife or alleged plural wife of
the accused ..."[14]

Now that law, which passed the two houses of the legislature by an
overwhelming majority, passed without protest,[15] without a sign of a
ripple on the surface of the Mormon sea officially; but the governor,
himself a Mormon, assigning the reason why he did it, that it would
arouse public sentiment in this country so vigorously against the Mormon people that it would destroy them, vetoed the bill.[16]

SENATOR BEVERIDGE. What has the respondent to do with that law?

MR. TAYLER. The respondent?

SENATOR BEVERIDGE. What has that law to do with the respondent?

MR. TAYLER. I have said only that the respondent—

SENATOR BEVERIDGE. What has he to do with the passage of that law?

MR. TAYLER. I have said only that the respondent was one of the ruling officers of the church, and that he entered no protest against nor did he
undertake to prevent this nullification of the law.

SENATOR BEVERIDGE. You do not assert that he had anything to do with
the passage of the law, one way or the other?

MR. TAYLER. Oh, no.

SENATOR McCOMAS. I understand Senator Smoot was an apostle at that
time—1901.[17]

MR. TAYLER. Yes, sir. He was an apostle at that time.

---

14. According to the *Deseret News* (Mar. 15, 1901), this language was used in other
states (Iowa, Michigan, Minnesota, North Dakota, and Oregon), where "the crime of
adultery could only be prosecuted on the complaint of the husband or wife of the accused."

15. In fact, the bill was vigorously debated by the state senate before passing eleven
to seven ("Evans Bill Passes Senate," *Deseret News,* Mar. 8, 1901). The opposition editorialized that "the Evans bill would be more effective in stirring up eastern wrath against
the dominant church in Utah than any public or private measure that could be devised"
("Senator Evans' Bill," *Salt Lake Herald,* Mar. 9, 1901).

16. The Evans bill passed in the Utah House on March 11, 1901, by a vote of 25-17.
Utah Governor Daniel M. Wells vetoed the bill on March 14, stating that if allowed to become law, it would be "employed as a most effective weapon against the very classes
whose condition it is intended to ameliorate. Furthermore, I have every reason to believe its enactment would be the signal for a general demand upon the National Congress for a constitutional amendment directed solely against certain social conditions
here" ("Disapproves of the Evans Bill," *Deseret News,* Mar. 15, 1901).

17. McComas was one of eight Republicans on the committee. Although from the
same party as Smoot, they were "men whom I have been a little afraid of, and I am still of
the opinion that if I have any serious opposition, it will come from the [Republican]
members of this committee" (Smoot to Joseph F. Smith, Nov. 18, 1903).

SENATOR BEVERIDGE. You do not charge that he personally advocated the passage of the law, or anything of that kind?[18]

MR. TAYLER. No, I do not know that he did. Now, gentlemen, those are the things we expect to prove, and upon them ask the opinion of the committee and the Senate as to its duty.

SENATOR MCCOMAS. Before you take your seat, I wish to ask you a question. Was any other legislation in that direction either attempted or enacted thereafter?

MR. TAYLER. No, I think not.

SENATOR OVERMAN. When was that legislation passed?

MR. TAYLER. In 1901.

SENATOR MCCOMAS. March 8, 1901.

MR. TAYLER. Mr. Smoot became an apostle in 1900.[19]

SENATOR BEVERIDGE. Do you charge the respondent himself with violating the law of the United States in reference to polygamy?

MR. TAYLER. No ...

MR. WORTHINGTON. Mr. Chairman and gentlemen, it will be perceived that the formal statement of the charges which are here made against Senator Smoot, as they have been reduced to writing and read by my friend, Mr. Tayler, differs very materially from the statement of the charges against the Senator made in the protest itself. While we are prepared now to respond in a general way to those charges and to [inform] the committee as to what we have to say about them, we will ask the privilege of the committee, within a few days, of reducing to writing our answer to this formal statement, so that the committee may have it for consideration in connection with the statement itself.

SENATOR MCCOMAS. I trust that will be done.

THE CHAIRMAN. If there is no objection, it will be so ordered.

SENATOR SMOOT. Two days will be plenty. We can answer it by Monday, if the committee wants it.[20]

MR. WORTHINGTON. First, as to the questions of law which will arise here, and as to which Mr. Tayler has said very little. He refers to the general language of the Constitution in reference to the expulsion of Sena-

---

18. Shortly before Wells vetoed the Evans bill, the *Salt Lake Tribune* asked several LDS leaders for their opinion of it. Smoot demurred, saying he had "every confidence in Gov. Well's ability to handle the matter to the best interests of the State." Church President Lorenzo Snow said, "I don't know why I should say anything about it." Joseph F. Smith, on the other hand, believed Wells should sign the bill "as it was in the best interests of the state." See "Evans Bill Condemned," *Salt Lake Tribune,* Mar. 13, 1901.

19. Smoot was ordained an apostle on April 8, 1900.

20. Smoot submitted a ten-page reply (*Smoot Hearings,* 1:31-40).

tors and Members of the House, and says there is no limit to the power. I agree with him, Mr. Chairman, that there is no limit to the power of the Senate in that regard. I do not agree with him that there is no limit to the jurisdiction of the Senate. I think it will be shown, when we come to investigate these questions of law, that the proposition is well settled at both ends of the Capitol that neither House has jurisdiction to consider a charge made against a Senator or a Member of the House as to any offense alleged to have been committed by him before he was elected, unless it is something which relates to the election itself, as that it was obtained by bribery or something of that kind. It so happens that that question—

SENATOR PETTUS. Do you maintain that no moral quality in a Senator or Member would authorize either body to expel him or refuse him a seat?

MR. WORTHINGTON. No, Senator, I did not say that. I say for offenses committed before he was elected.

SENATOR PETTUS. I mean before he was elected.

MR. WORTHINGTON. Yes.

SENATOR PETTUS. Your proposition, as I understand, is that no matter what a man may have done or said prior to his election, his election purified him so far as that body is concerned?

MR. WORTHINGTON. That is exactly the proposition. I was about to say that that question was most thoroughly considered in the House of Representatives when Mr. [Brigham H.] Roberts was sent here as a Representative from the State of Utah [in 1898]. It was charged that he was a polygamist, not in theory only, but in practice; that he was defying the laws of the State and the compact under which the State was admitted into the Union. He was not allowed to take his seat, and the question of his qualification was referred to a committee, of which my friend, the gentleman from Ohio, was chairman. A very elaborate and able report was prepared and submitted by the majority of the committee, including Mr. Tayler, in which all the precedents are gone over and in which that conclusion was reached, and that conclusion was sustained by the House of Representatives by a very large majority.[21]

A minority of the committee, composed of two of the nine members who reported on the matter, stated that in their opinion the House was bound to admit Mr. Roberts because he possessed the constitutional qualifications—he had the requisite age, the requisite citi-

---

21. When Tayler was a U.S. Congressman, he chaired the Committee on Elections, 1898-99, that ousted B. H. Roberts from the Congress.

zenship, and he was an inhabitant of the State—and that was all you could look into; that they must admit him, and after being admitted they could turn him out, and he ought to be turned out. So the question was fairly presented, and it was conceded by everybody—I think there was no dissent in the House or in the committee—that he could not occupy his seat because he was a polygamist; but it was decided by the committee and by the majority of the House that if they seated him they could not expel him, because the charge involved something that had been committed in the past, and that therefore he must be prevented from taking his seat ...

MR. VAN COTT. Mr. Chairman and gentlemen of the committee, I am sorry I was not able to grasp the entire meaning of Mr. Tayler's statement and to remember it, so as to give the committee the benefit of replying to it at this time. However, we will do so in writing Monday. There are some things that I carry in mind and to which I can refer very briefly.

Mr. Tayler said there was a bill introduced in the [Utah] legislature providing in regard to polygamy, that the complaint could only be made by the husband or wife of the party who was wronged or relatives within the first degree of consanguinity; that the legislature was overwhelmingly Mormon, which is true, and that it passed without a ripple. In that statement Mr. Tayler, not having been in Utah, is violently mistaken. It did make a ripple. It made big waves, and there was a great deal of talk, not only by Mormons but by Gentiles, over any such proposed legislation. It was not a ripple; it was violent.[22]

The act went to a Mormon governor. He vetoed it. It went back to the Mormon legislature. They could have passed it over his veto. They sustained his veto. If we go into that question in the evidence there will [be] reasons shown, which I would rather not state now, as to why probably that act was introduced. I will say this briefly from my standpoint. In the Mormon Church there are men who are wise and men who are very unwise, just as there are in other churches, just as there are in all parties and in all bodies. The Mormon Church is by no means free of its foolish men, and from my standpoint that was an exceedingly foolish measure. But if we go into the matter it will be found that Senator Smoot had nothing to do with it ...

Now, the question is, should this committee investigate cases of unlawful cohabitation or simply cases of polygamy? As a matter of

22. Presumably Van Cott's reference to "violence" is to hostility in tone evinced by the Evans Bill, not to actual violence.

propriety, I say they should investigate only cases of polygamy and not of polygamous cohabitation, with one proviso, which I will state a little later. I want to state the reason why the committee, I think, as a matter of propriety, should do that. It is this: In the enabling act—and I will have to furnish the committee later with those references if it desires, because I see the books are not here, so that I can refer to them—in the constitutional convention, and I will start there, because that is the natural place to begin, there was present Mr. C. S. Varian, a very prominent Gentile. He had been assistant United States district attorney and also United States district attorney in the prosecution of polygamy cases and unlawful cohabitation cases, and had been very vigorous and had been very successful. I have no doubt it was largely through his efforts that the condition came about where the Gentiles united with the Mormons. He was in the constitutional convention. When the proposed constitution was reported to the convention, the language of the constitution was simply like the language of the enabling act—"polygamous or plural marriages are forever prohibited." That is all there was in the proposed constitution, and that is just like the enabling act.

I wish to call your attention to the significance of it. It is not "unlawful cohabitation and polygamous cohabitation and polygamy are forever prohibited," but that "polygamy is forever prohibited in the State of Utah." When that was reported to the convention Mr. Varian called attention to the fact that that provision was not self-executing; that it would take legislation for the purpose of backing it up, and therefore he proposed an amendment to the effect that a certain act of the legislature of Utah, which punished polygamy, be engrafted right into the constitution, so that it would be self-executing in its provisions.

In the discussion of that, Mr. Varian called attention to the act. He said it should be engrafted into the constitution so far as polygamy was concerned, but so far as unlawful polygamous cohabitation was concerned, adultery was concerned, and those things, they should not go into the constitution[23] ...

SENATOR OVERMAN. Let me ask you a question for information.

---

23. On January 17, 1904, Smoot's secretary Carl Badger confided in his journal: "The first hearing came off yesterday (16th). The Senator thinks that Van Cott made too many admissions" (in Rodney J. Badger, *Liahona and Iron Rod: The Biography of Carl A. and Rose J. Badger* [Bountiful, Utah: Family History Publishers, 1985], 210). Badger's journals and correspondence span the duration of the hearings and provide a behind-the-scenes view of the inner machinations and scuttlebutt.

MR. VAN COTT. Certainly.

SENATOR OVERMAN. What do you mean by "polygamous cohabitation?" Is there any difference between that and the usual crime of fornication, denounced in the States as "fornication" and "adultery?"

MR. VAN COTT. It is just the same with one exception, if you will let me explain. In Washington and other places, I suppose, there is not a man who comes up and says that he has two wives. So, if he lives with a woman not his wife, he is guilty of fornication or adultery. In Utah a man comes out and says: "A is my wife; B is my wife; C is my wife."

SENATOR OVERMAN. He announces it publicly. That is the difference?

MR. VAN COTT. Practically.

SENATOR PETTUS. I ask if marriage is not a part of "polygamous cohabitation?"

MR. VAN COTT. Do you mean polygamous marriage?

SENATOR PETTUS. Is not marriage a part of the definition of "polygamous cohabitation?"

MR. VAN COTT. Yes, sir; exactly.

SENATOR PETTUS. A second marriage?

MR. VAN COTT. Yes, sir; it presupposes the marriage. That is the difference ...

MR. WORTHINGTON. I am requested by Senator Smoot to interrupt Mr. Van Cott for a moment to say that the chairman assumes what Senator Smoot understands is not the fact at all; that is, that the apostles are a part of the governing body of the church.

THE CHAIRMAN. Omitting that, take the three individuals constituting the presidency, and the twelve making up the apostles, what is expected to be shown in answer to the charge that any or all of those people are to-day living in polygamy?

MR. VAN COTT. Answering you Mr. Chairman, when you said the "governing body"—

THE CHAIRMAN. I omit that.

MR. VAN COTT. I understood you; and I was going to pass that over without making any correction, because I understood the meaning. In regard to the others mentioned, frankly speaking, I know nothing about whether they are living in polygamy or not. I have inquired. Of the first presidency, composed of Joseph F. Smith, John R. Winder, and Anthon H. Lund, I will say that Anthon H. Lund, one of the first presidency, I have always understood, was a monogamist; that he has never gone into polygamy; that he has never advised it or encouraged it. In regard to John R. Winder—

THE CHAIRMAN. I do not care about the details. What, if anything, do you propose to show upon that point generally?

MR. VAN COTT. I am stating it because I can not answer yes or no.

THE CHAIRMAN. Very well.

MR. VAN COTT. In regard to John R Winder, I understand without a doubt—I know him intimately—that he is a monogamist. He is not practicing unlawful cohabitation.

SENATOR DUBOIS. That is admitted by Mr. Tayler. There is no contention over that at all. I listened very attentively to his statement—

MR. TAYLER. My understanding is that two first councilors to the president of the church are not polygamists. At least we make no such claim and make no proof of it.

SENATOR DUBOIS. But that a majority of the apostles are?

THE CHAIRMAN. How about the president [Joseph F. Smith]?

MR. VAN COTT. I was coming to him. As to the president, I understand by repute, and I believe it, that he is a polygamist. I inquired, long before I was connected with this case, as to whether he was living in polygamy, and I have been informed both ways. I have been told that he was not obeying the law. I have been told that he was. As to that I have no proof, and I do not know, and Senator Smoot does not know, and if he did I should give the information to the committee.

THE CHAIRMAN. May I ask you a question in this connection?

MR. VAN COTT. Certainly.

THE CHAIRMAN. How many wives is it reputed he has?

MR. VAN COTT. I do not remember, and could not state.

THE CHAIRMAN. Now as to the apostles.

MR. VAN COTT. In regard to the apostles, I know several of them, and my present recollection is that there are six or seven who are polygamists, and the others never have been polygamists.

MR. WORTHINGTON. What do you mean by "polygamists"—living with polygamous wives?

MR. VAN COTT. I say "polygamists." I mean by that that they had married more than one wife.

MR. WORTHINGTON. It does not mean polygamy.

MR. VAN COTT. In regard to polygamous cohabitation, there is not one of these apostles that I know of who is living in polygamous cohabitation. I have heard, as to several, that they have obeyed the law strictly ever since the manifesto of President [Wilford] Woodruff in 1890. If there is one of them who has been living in polygamous cohabitation since the manifesto I have not personal knowledge of it, and I do not know of it, so far as the proof is concerned ...

THE CHAIRMAN. Is a man by the name of Heber J. Grant one of the apostles?

MR. VAN COTT. Yes, sir.

THE CHAIRMAN. Where is he?

MR. VAN COTT. I suppose from the newspapers that he has gone to England in connection with the Mormon Church.[24]

THE CHAIRMAN. Do you know whether he is a polygamist?

MR. VAN COTT. I know that he is a polygamist. Whether he is living in polygamous cohabitation I only know from the newspapers. They say he is, but outside of that I do not know ...

SENATOR McCOMAS. Do you expect to prove that six apostles and the president are now practicing unlawful cohabitation?[25]

MR. TAYLER. More than that. I say that the first president and five of the apostles now practicing polygamy signed the prayer to the President of the United States for amnesty.[26]

THE CHAIRMAN. Did Apostle Grant sign it?

MR. TAYLER. He did.

---

24. Speaking to the University of Utah, Grant bragged of having plural wives. The result was that a warrant was issued for his arrest; but before Sheriff Frank Emery could deliver the warrant to the apostle's house. Grant was tipped off and was already "speeding eastward":

> The Herald was informed last evening that on Tuesday evening Apostle Grant got on the Rio Grande train from the west side of the yards, catching the smoking car as the train pulled out. The train was an hour late out of Salt Lake ... "I had not the slightest idea he would try to escape" said Sheriff Emery ... "I supposed he would submit to a warrant without question" (*Salt Lake Herald,* Nov. 12, 1903).

25. Smoot filed an "additional answer" after the opening statements:

> I deny that either the president or any of the apostles of the church has taken a polygamous wife since the manifesto of 1890. I deny that either the president or any of the twelve apostles has at any time practiced polygamy or polygamous cohabitation, with my countenance or with my knowledge, except as herein above set forth ... I deny that any plural marriage ceremony has been performed by any apostle of the church since the manifesto of 1890, and deny that many or any bishops or other high officials of the church have taken plural wives since that time. I deny, except as herein above admitted, in the answer to this third specification, that all or any of the first presidency or the twelve apostles encourage, countenance, conceal, or connive at polygamy or polygamous cohabitation. I deny that the first presidency or the twelve apostles honor or reward by any office or preferment those who most persistently and defiantly violate the law of the land (*Smoot Hearings,* 1:74-77).

26. Pursuant to legislation against polygamy in 1880s, LDS leaders were actively pursued by federal officials. Once the Manifesto was in effect, church leaders desired amnesty for those who contracted plural marriages prior to 1890. Their prayer for amnesty was presented in late 1891 to U.S. President Benjamin Harrison, who granted it on January 4, 1893.

THE CHAIRMAN. Where is he?

MR. TAYLER. I understand he is a fugitive from justice. At any rate a warrant is out for him for a violation of this law.

THE CHAIRMAN. Is he one of the apostles?

MR. TAYLER. Yes, sir; he is one of the apostles ...

II.
FIRST WEEK OF MARCH
1904

2.

Joseph F. Smith

Wednesday, March 2

Six Methodists, two Congregationalists, two Presbyterians, an Episcopalian, a Baptist, and a Unitarian compose the tribunal before which the Mormon Church is on trial at Washington. Four years ago the precedent was laid down that a polygamist should not sit in Congress. That was the first test since the Statehood of Utah of the relations of Mormonism to the United States government. The second test is the Reed Smoot case. If he is unseated it must be on grounds which would apply equally to any member of the Mormon hierarchy." —*Harper's Weekly*, Mar. 26, 1904[1]

Joseph F. Smith,[2] having duly affirmed,[3] testified as follows:
MR. TAYLER. Where do you live, Mr. Smith?[4]

---

1. The hearings had been scheduled to begin a day earlier. However, Van Cott asked Senator Burrows "for a postponement ... until to-morrow morning, ... [as] Mr. Worthington unexpectedly is compelled to be in the court of appeals of this District." Tayler said he did not want to appear "ungracious" but said he also knew "the witnesses who have been subpoenaed to come from Utah are not yet here" (*Smoot Hearings*, 1:79).

2. Joseph F. Smith (1838-1918), president of LDS Church, was a practicing polygamist. On February 2, 1904, Carl Badger had recorded:

> President Jos. F. Smith says let the investigation come; we have been trying to preach our faith for seventy years and do not now shrink from telling a Congressional committee what we believe and what we have done. It is the answer of a warrior. The Senator [Smoot] calls it an approval of his [Smoot's] course. I have understood that the Senator has been trying to shield President Smith from an investigation, certainly he has reportedly said that he "worries" not about himself, but the disposition on the part of the Committee to take a broad scope in the investigation—the Church and its leaders" (in Rodney J. Badger, *Liahona and Iron Rod: The Biography of Carl A. and Rose J. Badger* [Bountiful, Utah: Family History Publishers, 1985], 210).

3. Smith opted to "affirm" rather than "swear" an oath to tell the truth. He explained: "We believe in the Scriptures, 'swear not at all'" (*Smoot Hearings*, 1:387). Three others followed his example: Smoot, Joseph F. Smith's son Hyrum, and Charles W. Penrose.

4. A few days earlier, the *Deseret News* quoted Senator Clark of Wyoming on the "great willingness" of Joseph F. Smith and others to appear in Smoot's behalf. According to Clark, if they "expected that the evidence would prejudice the case of Mr. Smoot they would scarcely be eager to testify"; therefore, "the prospect that Senator Smoot will retain his seat" was "very bright" ("Another Delay in Smoot Case," *Deseret News*, Feb. 27, 1904).

MR. SMITH. I live in Salt Lake City.

MR. TAYLER. How long have you lived there?

MR. SMITH. Since 1848.

MR. TAYLER. I believe you were born of parents who were members of the Mormon Church?[5]

MR. SMITH. Yes, sir.

MR. TAYLER. So that all your life you have been in that church?

MR. SMITH. Yes, sir.

MR. TAYLER. What official position do you now hold in the church?

MR. SMITH. I am now the president of the church.

MR. TAYLER. Is there any other description of your title than mere president?

MR. SMITH. No, sir; not that I know of.

MR. TAYLER. Are you prophet, seer, and revelator?

MR. SMITH. I am so sustained and upheld by my people.

MR. TAYLER. Do you get that title by reason of being president or by reason of having been an apostle?

MR. SMITH. By reason of being president.

MR. TAYLER. Are not all the apostles also prophets, seers, and revelators?

MR. SMITH. They are sustained as such at our conferences.

MR. TAYLER. They all have that title now, have they not?

MR. SMITH. Well, they are so sustained at the conferences.

MR. TAYLER. I want to know if they do not have that title now.

MR. SMITH. I suppose if they are sustained they must have that title.

MR. TAYLER. Are they sustained as such now?

MR. SMITH. I have said so twice, sir.

MR. TAYLER. Who were your predecessors in office as president of the church?

MR. SMITH. My immediate predecessor was Lorenzo Snow.

MR. TAYLER. And his predecessor?

MR. SMITH. Wilford Woodruff.

MR. TAYLER. And his?

MR. SMITH. John Taylor.

MR. TAYLER. Yes; go on back through the line.

MR. SMITH. Brigham Young.

MR. TAYLER. Yes.

MR. SMITH. And Joseph Smith.

MR. TAYLER. You are possessed of the same powers that they were possessed of?

---

5. Smith's parents were Hyrum Smith and Mary Fielding Smith.

Mr. Smith. Yes, I am supposed to be possessed of the same authority that they were.

Mr. Tayler. You believe yourself to be, do you not?

Mr. Smith. I think I do believe so.

Mr. Tayler. I do not know that there is any significance in your use of the word "think," Mr. Smith, but one hardly thinks that he has a belief. He either knows or does not know that he has a belief.

Mr. Smith. I think I do. ...

Mr. Tayler. Is the "Deseret News" the organ of the Church?

Mr. Smith. Well, I suppose it is in some sense the organ of the church. It is not opposed to the church, at least.

Mr. Tayler. It is not opposed to it?

Mr. Smith. No, sir.

Mr. Tayler. It has for years published, has it not, at the head of its columns, that it is the organ of the church, or the official organ of the church?

Mr. Smith. Not that I know of.

Mr. Tayler. Not that you know of?

Mr. Smith. No, sir. It has been called that. It is styled that.

Mr. Tayler. It is styled that, but you do not recall ever having seen, at the head of any page or on any page, in a conspicuous place in the "Deseret News," the statement that it was the organ of the church, or the official organ of the church?

Mr. Smith. I do not recall that I ever saw it.

Mr. Tayler. You read that paper regularly, do you?

Mr. Smith. As much as I have time to read it.

Mr. Tayler. I can appreciate now the significance of that answer. How long have you been reading the "Deseret News"?

Mr. Smith. I think it was started in 1851 or 1852; somewhere along there. I believe it was established somewhere along in the early fifties, and I have read it more or less ever since.[6]

Mr. Tayler. Do you know who owns it?

Mr. Smith. How is that?

Mr. Tayler. Do you know who owns it?

Mr. Smith. I know who owns the building that it is in.

Mr. Tayler. Who owns the building in which it is published?

Mr. Smith. The church.

Mr. Tayler. The church?

Mr. Smith. Yes, sir.

---

6. The *Deseret News* was first published on June 15, 1850.

MR. TAYLER. Tell us what you know about the owners of that newspaper.

MR. SMITH. It has been for a number of years past owned by a company—an incorporated company.

MR. TAYLER. What is the name of the company?

MR. SMITH. The Deseret News Publishing Company.

MR. TAYLER. Do you know who its officers are?

MR. SMITH. Now, it is not owned by that company.

MR. TAYLER. Oh, it is not?

MR. SMITH. No; it is not.

MR. TAYLER. What do you know—

MR. SMITH. But I say for years it was owned by a company of that kind.

MR. TAYLER. What do you know about its present ownership?

MR. SMITH. I presume that the present ownership is the church.

MR. TAYLER. You suppose the present owner is the church?

MR. SMITH. Yes, sir; the church.

MR. TAYLER. Mr. Smith, we have referred to the work of Doctor [James E.] Talmage[7] and its origin. Was Orson Pratt[8]—

THE CHAIRMAN. Mr. Tayler, before you go to that subject, it was impossible to hear what Mr. Smith said in relation to the ownership of the "Deseret News."

MR. CARLISLE.[9] He says the church owns it now.

---

7. James E. Talmage (1862-1933) was a Utah educator and theologian. The *Deseret News* reported on a Sunday sermon Talmage delivered the week prior to President Smith's testimony:

> Referring to the investigation about to be opened up at Washington, Elder Talmage expressed the hope that it would be thorough and searching, for he felt that there was no better way of preaching "Mormonism" to the nation. He believed that the hearing decided upon by the senate of the United States, was for the best good of this people, and when it was all over the Latter-day Saints would have just cause to be thankful that it had been brought forth (Feb. 29, 1904).

Talmage wrote essentially the same in his journal (Mar. 2, 1904, L. Tom Perry Special Collections, Harold B. Lee Library, Brigham Young University, Provo, Utah).

8. Orson Pratt (1811-81) was a member of the church's Quorum of Twelve Apostles.

9. John G. Carlisle (1834-1910) was one of two attorneys employed by the prosecution. He had served as a Democratic U.S. Senator, 1890-93, and resigned to become Secretary of the Treasury under President Grover Cleveland, 1893-97. In a letter to Smoot, the First Presidency advised Smoot that in light of "the fact that Mr. Carlysle has been employed to represent the protestants,"

> we think that some lawyer of equally high standing in the profession should be employed to represent you before the committee. He should be a constitutional lawyer of national repute, ... he should also be a Republican ... Do not understand that this suggestion implies that the matter of your defense should be left entirely to such counsel as we have suggested. Our experience in the past has demonstrated that

THE CHAIRMAN. Was that your answer?

MR. BEVERIDGE. The paper and the building both.

MR. WORTHINGTON. His exact answer was, "I presume the church owns it."

THE CHAIRMAN. I wanted to get the answer. Is that your answer, Mr. Smith?

MR. SMITH. Yes, sir.

THE CHAIRMAN. That you presume—

MR. SMITH. It is the present owner of the "Deseret News."

MR. TAYLER. I do not want to have any misconstruction put upon your use of the word "presume." Do you use the word "presume" because you do not know that it is so owned?

MR. SMITH. I really do not know so that I could tell you positively.

MR. TAYLER. Who would know?

MR. SMITH. I presume I could find out.

MR. TAYLER. Could you find out before you leave Washington?

MR. SMITH. Perhaps so.

MR. TAYLER. Perhaps so?

MR. SMITH. Yes.

MR. TAYLER. Is there anybody in Washington who knows?

MR. SMITH. I do not know if anybody, unless my counsel can tell you.

MR. TAYLER. Was Orson Pratt an authoritative writer in the church?

MR. SMITH. He was in some things, and in some things he was not.

MR. TAYLER. Is Brigham H. Roberts[10] an authoritative writer in the church?

MR. SMITH. Well—

MR. TAYLER. Of course, I understand that no man who writes of his own

---

outside attorneys have but little conception of the real inwardness of our affairs, and, in order to be of service to us, they require to be carefully posted and prompted by persons familiar with the issues, and, at the same time, possessing a deeper interest in the matter than any merely hired attorney can have. For that reason we would expect to have Brother [Franklin S.] Richards go down and advise with such counsel as might be employed, and give him the full benefit of his knowledge and experience, but, we think it would be wise and more effective to have Brother Franklin act in this capacity than to have him appear openly as your attorney (Nov. 17, 1903).

A Salt Lake newspaper sarcastically suggested that Charles W. Penrose, editor of the *Deseret News*, be retained as Smoot's attorney because "he has been practicing on the kind of defense needed by the Apostle, for thirty years. What [Smoot] needs are bold assertions that have an honest look on their face, but which, when analyzed ... are found to be but 'sound and fury signifying nothing,' mere 'sounding brass or tinkling symbols'" ("The Smoot Answer," *Goodwin's Weekly*, Jan. 16, 1904).

10. Roberts (1857-1933) was a member of the First Council of the Seventy.

motion, however truly he may write, thereby becomes authority.

Mr. Smith. No.

Mr. Tayler. But has he been constituted, in any work that he has written, authority?

Mr. Smith. No, sir; not that I know of.

Mr. Tayler. Has he written anything which is in terms sanctioned by the church as declaring its doctrine and policy?

Mr. Smith. I have never heard any of B. H. Roberts's writings called in question by the church.

Mr. Tayler. I would not want to intimate that that answer is not candid, Mr. Smith, but I put the question in another form: Whether or not some of his writings have not been, in terms, approved by the Mormon hierarchy, if I may use that expression?

Mr. Smith. I do not think so.

Mr. Tayler. Do you recall a book entitled "Mormonism; [I]ts Origin and History," by B. H. Roberts?

Mr. Smith. I do. That is his own work.

Mr. Tayler. That is his own work?

Mr. Smith. Yes, sir.

Mr. Tayler. By whom was it published?

Mr. Smith. I think by the "Deseret News," but I am not sure.

Mr. Tayler. Was it not published by the church?

Mr. Smith. No, sir; not that I know of.

Mr. Tayler. Was it not copyrighted by Joseph F. Smith?

Mr. Smith. I think likely it was, because we bought his copyright from him.

Mr. Tayler. Was it not copyrighted by Joseph F. Smith for the Church of Jesus Christ of Latter-Day Saints?

Mr. Smith. My recollection is the church bought the copyright of Roberts.

Mr. Tayler. And published the book?

Mr. Smith. The "Deseret News" published the book.

Mr. Tayler. Did the church publish it? The "Deseret News" may have printed it; but did not the church publish it?

Mr. Smith. Well, perhaps it did. I am not posted.

Mr. Tayler. Let me read you the title page of this book.

Mr. Smith. All right.

Mr. Tayler. I will read it: "Mormonism. The relation of the church to Christian sects. Origin and history of Mormonism. Doctrines of the church. Church organization. Present status. By B. H. Roberts. Published by the church. Deseret News printer. Salt Lake City." On the other side of this sheet: "Copyrighted by Joseph F. Smith, for the Church of Jesus Christ of Latter-Day Saints." Both of those inscriptions which I have read correctly recite the facts?

MR. SMITH. So far as I am aware they do.

MR. TAYLER. And, Mr. Smith, the opening sentence of this little work is as follows: "This brochure is issued under the authority of the Church of Jesus Christ of Latter-Day Saints." Is that correct.

MR. SMITH. I think it is. If it says so, it is correct.

MR. TAYLER. The next sentence is: "It is therefore an authoritative utterance upon that subject of which it treats—the relation of the church to Christian sects; its origin; its history; its doctrines; its organization; its present status." That is true, is it not?

MR. SMITH. Yes, sir; I think likely it is.

MR. TAYLER. Then this work is to be distinguished, is it not, as respects its authority, from all other works that have been written by other persons unless they were such as were written under inspiration or other revelation?

MR. SMITH. Yes, sir. ...

SENATOR McCOMAS. I should like to ask one question. You say that the councilors are appointed by the president of the church. How are the apostles selected?

MR. SMITH. In the first place they were chosen by revelation. The council of the apostles have had a voice ever since in the selection of their successors.

SENATOR McCOMAS. Had a voice?

MR. SMITH. Yes, sir.

SENATOR McCOMAS. Have they had the election of their successors to perpetuate the body of apostles since the first revelation?

MR. SMITH. I do not know that I understand your question.

SENATOR McCOMAS. You say the first apostles were selected in accordance with revelation.

MR. SMITH. Yes, sir.

SENATOR McCOMAS. Revelations to whom?

MR. SMITH. To Joseph Smith.[11]

SENATOR McCOMAS. And the twelve apostles were then first named?

MR. SMITH. Yes, sir.

SENATOR McCOMAS. When vacancies occurred thereafter, by what body were the vacancies in the twelve apostles filled?

---

11. Smith (1804-44) was founder and first president of the LDS Church.

Mr. Smith. Perhaps I may say in this way: Chosen by the body by the twelve themselves, by and with the consent and approval of the first presidency.

Senator Hoar. Was there a revelation in regard to each of them?

Mr. Smith. No, sir; not in regard to each of them. Do you mean in the beginning?

Senator Hoar. I understand you to say that the original twelve apostles were selected by revelation?

Mr. Smith. Yes, sir.

Senator Hoar. Through Joseph Smith?

Mr. Smith. Yes, sir; that is right.

Senator Hoar. Is there any revelation in regard to the subsequent ones?

Mr. Smith. No, sir; it has been the choice of the body.

Senator McComas. Then the apostles are perpetuated in succession by their own act and the approval of the first presidency?

Mr. Smith. That is right.[12]

Mr. Tayler. Mr. Smith, will you state—

Senator Bailey. Mr. Tayler, before you proceed I should like to ask the witness a question.

Mr. Tayler. Certainly.

Senator Bailey. Could the first president prevent a selection which had been made by the apostles to fill a vacancy in their number?

Mr. Smith. I think the twelve would be very reluctant to insist upon the election of a man to whom the president was opposed.

Senator Bailey. I would understand that as a matter looking to harmonious relations between the first president and the apostles. But it is not a question of that. It is a question of power. If the apostles choose to do so, could they elect a man over the protest of the president?[13]

Mr. Smith. I presume they could; but I do not think they would.

Senator Bailey. But they have the power?

Mr. Smith. They have the power if they chose to do it; but I do not think they would do it. ...

Senator Hoar. I do not quite understand one kind of phrase which recently appears in Mr. Smith's answers. He says "I presume," "My understanding is," "I believe," "Not that I know of," "So far as I am

---

12. The previous seven questions and answers were included in the report submitted by Burrows opposing Smoot; see *Smoot Hearings*, 4:474.

13. J. Reuben Clark's copy of the hearings highlighted some of this exchange in purple ink.

aware," "I think likely." Now, I wish to understand if in regard to these matters of faith as to which you have been asked you mean to express yourself doubtfully, as an ordinary man might, or whether they are things which you yourself know to be true by divine revelation.[14]

MR. SMITH. If you please, when I speak in reference to defined principles and doctrines of the church I speak from my heart, without any uncertainty on my part.

SENATOR HOAR. As of knowledge?

MR. SMITH. But when I speak of things that I may be at fault about in memory, that I may not be thoroughly posted about, I may be excused, perhaps, if I use the words "I presume," etc. But on principles of the doctrines of the church I think—now I say I think—I do think I can speak positively.

SENATOR HOAR. You know?

MR. SMITH. I know as well as any man can know; at least as well as I can know. I do not wish—

SENATOR HOAR. For instance, on being asked whether one of the presidents, perhaps the second president, was appointed by a divine revelation, you replied that you were not present, but you thought so. Is that one of the things of which you have an ordinary, human knowledge, or is it a thing of which you have an inspired knowledge—that the president of the body was chosen by revelation?

MR. SMITH. To me it is a matter of certainty. I believe it with all my heart.

SENATOR HOAR. I do not wish to interpose in the examination, but this has been said so often that I desired to understand whether Mr. Smith's form of language meant to imply doubt. I do not mean doubt in the human sense, for there are a great many things that we all feel confident of in our religious faith, whatever it is, or in our political faith, or any other faiths. But I want to understand if, in regard to what you have told us or are about to tell us is the religious faith of your church, you mean to express doubt in the sense that you may possibly be mistaken and that other men are likely to be as right as you are, or if you mean to have us understand that you know from divine inspiration? I understand you now that in all matters in regard

---

14. Kathleen Flake has noted the nuances in Smith's testimony. As she observed, a good lawyer gives a witness "two choices, you can either make an admission against your interest or you can perjure yourself." But a sophisticated witness knows how to "split the difference" ("Does It Matter How We Remember the Abandonment of Plural Marriage?" presented at the Salt Lake Sunstone Symposium, Aug. 13, 2004, Tape SL0426); see also Kathleen Flake, *The Politics of American Religious Identity: The Seating of Senator Reed Smoot, Mormon Apostle* (Chapel Hill: University of North Carolina Press, 2004).

to the faith of your church you, its president, speak from an inspired knowledge?

Mr. Smith. I believe—yes, sir; I do.

Mr. Tayler. With reference to your power as president of the church, let me ask you if you believe that it is stated as it is in verse 4, section 68, of the Doctrine and Covenants? Let me paraphrase it to apply to you.

Mr. Worthington. What page is that?

Mr. Tayler. Page 248. "That whatsoever you shall speak when moved upon by the Holy Ghost shall be scripture, shall be the will of the Lord, shall be the mind of the Lord, shall be the word of the Lord, shall be the voice of the Lord, and the power of God unto salvation."

Mr. Smith. Yes, sir; I believe that doctrine, and it does not apply only to me, but it applies to every elder in the church with equal force.

Mr. Tayler. With equal force?

Mr. Smith. Yes, sir.

Mr. Tayler. That applies only when moved upon by the Holy Ghost?

Mr. Smith. That is correct.

Mr. Tayler. Do you understand that that is intended to cover the case of inspiration or revelation?

Mr. Smith. Yes, sir.

Mr. Tayler. Is every elder of the church, according to the belief and practice of your organization, likely to receive revelations directly from God?

Mr. Smith. When he is inspired by the Holy Ghost; yes.

Mr. Tayler. I am coming to the subject of revelation in a moment. But does anybody, except the head of the church, have what you call revelations binding upon the church?

Mr. Smith. Yes, sir; everybody is entitled to revelations.

Mr. Tayler. Has any person, except a first president of the church, ever received a revelation which was proclaimed and became binding upon the church?

Mr. Smith. No, sir.

Mr. Tayler. No?

Mr. Smith. No, sir. The revelations for the government and guidance of the church come only through the head.[15] But every elder of the church and every member of the church is entitled to the spirit of revelation.

---

15. J. Reuben Clark's copy of the hearings underlined the majority of the questions and answers in this exchange.

MR. TAYLER. I suppose—

SENATOR OVERMAN. Do you mean entitled from God or through the presidency?

MR. SMITH. From God.

SENATOR OVERMAN. To receive it direct from God?

MR. SMITH. From God.

SENATOR OVERMAN. Has any revelation ever been received from God to the members or elders of the church except through the president?

MR. SMITH. Yes, sir. Let me say that we hold, that every member of the church receives a witness of the spirit of God of the truth of the doctrine that he embraces and he receives it because of the testimony of the spirit to him, which is the spirit of revelation.

MR. TAYLER. Then any elder in the church may receive a revelation?

MR. SMITH. For his own guidance.

MR. TAYLER. For his own guidance?

MR. SMITH. For his own guidance.

MR. TAYLER. Then Mr. Smoot may do so?

MR. SMITH. For his own guidance.

MR. TAYLER. For his own guidance?

MR. SMITH. Yes, sir.

MR. TAYLER. He may then come into direct contact with God in the form of a revelation to him for his own guidance?

MR. SMITH. Yes, sir.

THE CHAIRMAN. What was the answer to the question?

MR. SMITH. Yes, sir; the same as any other member of the church.

MR. TAYLER. I do not know that there is any significance in your use of the word "member" now and the word "elder" then. Are all members of the church elders?

MR. SMITH. Pretty nearly all. All the male members are—nearly all of them; I would not say all of them were.

MR. TAYLER. You have already touched upon the subject of revelation, and if you have anything further to say about it I think this would be as good a time as any, as to the method in which a revelation is received and its binding or authoritative force upon the people.

MR. SMITH. I will say this, Mr. Chairman, that no revelation given through the head of the church ever becomes binding and authoritative upon the members of the church until it has been presented to the church and accepted by them.[16]

MR. WORTHINGTON. What do you mean by being presented to the church?

---

16. J. Reuben Clark's copy underlined this answer.

MR. SMITH. Presented in conference.

MR. TAYLER. Do you mean by that that the church in conference may say to you, Joseph F. Smith, the first president of the church, "We deny that God has told you to tell us this?"

MR. SMITH. They can say that if they choose.

MR. TAYLER. They can say it?

MR. SMITH. Yes, sir; they can. And it is not binding upon them as members of the church until they accept it.

MR. TAYLER. Until they accept it?

MR. SMITH. Yes, sir.

MR. TAYLER. Were the revelations to Joseph Smith, jr., all submitted to the people?[17]

MR. SMITH. Yes, sir.

SENATOR OVERMAN. Does it require a majority to accept or must it be the unanimous voice?

MR. SMITH. A majority. Of course only those who accept would be considered as in good standing in the church.[18]

MR. TAYLER. Exactly. Has any revelation made by God to the first president of the church and presented by him to the church ever been rejected?

MR. SMITH. I do not know that it has; not that I know of.

SENATOR HOAR. That answer presents precisely the question I put to you a little while ago. "Not that I know of," you replied. Do you know, as the head of the church, what revelations to your predecessors are binding upon the church?

MR. SMITH. I know, as I have stated, that only those revelations which are submitted to the church and accepted by the church are binding upon them. That I know.

SENATOR HOAR. Then the counsel asked you if any revelation of the head of the church had been rejected.

MR. SMITH. Not that I know of. I do not know of any that have been rejected.

SENATOR HOAR. Do you mean to reply doubtfully upon that question, whether some of the revelations are binding and some are not?

MR. SMITH. There may have been; I do not know of any.

SENATOR HOAR. That then is not a matter in which you have an inspired knowledge?

---

17. In fact, at first Joseph Smith's revelations were distributed privately at his discretion and many were never submitted to the general membership.

18. J. Reuben Clark's copy underlined this exchange and noted it in the margins.

MR. SMITH. No, sir.

THE CHAIRMAN. But you do not know of any instance where the revelation so imparted to the church has been rejected?

MR. SMITH. No, sir; not by the whole church. I know of instances in which large numbers of members of the church have rejected the revelation, but not the body of the church.

SENATOR OVERMAN. What became of those people who rejected it?

MR. SMITH. Sir?

SENATOR OVERMAN. What became of the people who rejected the divine revelation; were they unchurched?

MR. SMITH. They unchurched themselves.

SENATOR OVERMAN. Oh, yes. They were outside the pale of the church then?

MR. SMITH. Yes, sir.

THE CHAIRMAN. They unchurched themselves by not believing?

MR. SMITH. By not accepting.

MR. TAYLER. Then if you had a revelation and presented it to your people, all who did not accept it would thereby be unchurched?

MR. SMITH. Not necessarily.

MR. TAYLER. Not necessarily?

MR. SMITH. No, sir.

MR. TAYLER. I should like to have you distinguish between this answer and the one you just gave.

MR. SMITH. Our people are given the largest possible latitude for their convictions, and if a man rejects a message that I may give to him but is still moral and believes in the main principles of the gospel and desires to continue in his membership in the church, he is permitted to remain and he is not unchurched. It is only those who on rejecting a revelation rebel against the church and withdraw from the church at their own volition.[19]

SENATOR HOAR. Mr. Smith, the revelations given through you and your predecessors have always been from God?

MR. SMITH. I believe so.

SENATOR HOAR. Very well. As I understand, those persons who you say reject one of your revelations but still believe in the main principles of the church are at liberty to remain in the church. Do I understand you to say that any revelation coming from God to you is not one of the main principles of the church? Does not the person who rejects it reject the direct authority of God.

---

19. J. Reuben Clark's copy has a marginal bracket around this entire answer.

MR. SMITH. Yes, sir; no doubt he does.

SENATOR HOAR. And still he remains a member of the church?

MR. SMITH. Yes, sir.

SENATOR HOAR. In good standing, if a moral man?

MR. SMITH. Yes, sir.

SENATOR HOAR. Although disobeying the direct commandment of God?

MR. SMITH. Would you permit me to say a few words?

SENATOR HOAR. Certainly. We shall be glad to hear you.

MR. SMITH. I should like to say to the honorable gentlemen that the members of the Mormon Church are among the freest and most independent people of all the Christian denominations. They are not all united on every principle. Every man is entitled to his own opinion and his own views and his own conceptions of right and wrong so long as they do not come in conflict with the standard principles of the church. If a man assumes to deny God and to become an infidel we withdraw fellowship from him. If a man commits adultery we withdraw fellowship from him. If men steal or lie or bear false witness against their neighbors or violate the cardinal principles of the Gospel, we withdraw our fellowship. The church withdraws its fellowship from that man and he ceases to be a member of the church. But so long as a man or a woman is honest and virtuous and believes in God and has a little faith in the church organization, so long we nurture and aid that person to continue faithfully as a member of the church, though he may not believe all that is revealed.

I should like to say this to you, in point, that a revelation on plural marriage is contained in that book [Doctrine and Covenants]. It has been ascertained by actual count that not more than perhaps 3 or 4 per cent of the membership of the Church of Jesus Christ of Latter-Day Saints ever entered into that principle. All the rest of the members of the church abstained from that principle and did not enter into it, and many thousands of them never received it or believed it; but they were not cut off from the church. They were not disfellowshipped and they are still members of the church; that is what I wish to say.[20]

SENATOR DUBOIS. Did I understand you to say that many thousands of them never believed in the doctrine of plural marriage?

---

20. Recent studies have found much higher rates. See Kathryn M. Daynes, *More Wives than One* (Urbana: University of Illinois Press, 2001); Larry M. Logue, *A Sermon in the Desert: Belief and Behavior in Early St. George, Utah* (Urbana: University of Illinois Press, 1988).

MR. SMITH. Yes, sir—

SENATOR DUBOIS. You misunderstand me. I do not undertake to say that they practiced it. I accept your statement on that point. But do you mean to say that any member of the Mormon Church in the past or at the present time says openly that he does not believe in the principle of plural marriages?

MR. SMITH. I know that there are hundreds, of my own knowledge, who say they never did believe in it and never did receive it, and they are members of the church in good-fellowship. Only the other day I heard a man, prominent among us, a man of wealth, too, say that he had received all the principles of Mormonism except plural marriage, and that he never had received it and could not see it. I myself heard him say it within the last ten days.

SENATOR HOAR. Is the doctrine of the inspiration of the head of the church and revelations given to him one of the fundamental or non-fundamental doctrines of Mormonism?

MR. SMITH. The principle of revelation is a fundamental principle to the church.

SENATOR HOAR. I speak of the revelations given to the head of the church. Is that a fundamental doctrine of Mormonism?

MR. SMITH. Yes, sir.

SENATOR HOAR. Does or does not a person who does not believe that a revelation given through the head of the church comes from God reject a fundamental principle of Mormonism?

MR. SMITH. He does; always if the revelation is a divine revelation from God.

SENATOR HOAR. It always is, is it not? It comes through the head of the church?

MR. SMITH. When it is divine, it always is; when it is divine, most decidedly.

THE CHAIRMAN. I do not quite understand that—"when it is divine." You have revelations, have you not?

MR. SMITH. I have never pretended to nor do I profess to have received revelations. I never said I had a revelation except so far as God has shown to me that so-called Mormonism is God's divine truth; that is all.[21]

---

21. President Smith later clarified his remarks:

President Joseph F. Smith, alluding to his testimony on the subject of revelation, which was given on the occasion of the Reed Smoot investigation in Washington, and over which much controversy had arisen, declared that while he had never received from God a revelation on some new doctrine or commandment, to be writ-

THE CHAIRMAN. You say that was shown to you by God?

MR. SMITH. By inspiration.

THE CHAIRMAN. How by inspiration; does it come in the shape of a vision?

MR. SMITH. "The things of God knoweth no man but the spirit of God;" and I can not tell you any more than that I received that knowledge and that testimony by the spirit of God.

MR. TAYLER. You do not mean that you reached it by any process of reasoning or by any other method by which you reach other conclusions in your mind, do you?

MR. SMITH. When I have reached principles; that is, I have been confirmed in my acceptance and knowledge of principles that have been revealed to me, shown to me, on which I was ignorant before, by reason and facts.

MR. TAYLER. I do not know that I understand your answer. Mr. Stenographer, will you please read it.

SENATOR BAILEY. Before we proceed any further, I assume that all these questions connected with the religious faith of the Mormon Church are to be shown subsequently to have some relation to civil affairs. Unless that is true I myself object to going into the religious opinions of these people. I do not think Congress has anything to do with that unless their religion connects itself in some way with their civil or political affairs.

Now, if that is true, if it is proposed to establish that later on, then of course it is entirely pertinent.

SENATOR HOAR. I suppose you will make your statement with this qualification or explanation, that unless what we might think merely civil or political they deem religious matters.

SENATOR BAILEY. Then of course it would be a matter addressing itself to us with great force.

THE CHAIRMAN.[22] The chair supposed that this was preliminary.

---

ten and preserved and handed down as a law to the Church, he had been guided, from the day of his baptism to the present, by divine influence, and had been aided time and again by the spirit of God in his work in the ministry, and strongly expressed the wish that if, in his day, some new revelation should be needed by the Church, he might be worthy to receive it" (in Salt Lake High Council Minutes, Mar. 19, 1905, excerpt in editor's possession).

22. In a letter to Joseph F. Smith, Smoot described his relationship to Burrows:

There is scarcely a day that Senator Burrows does not profess friendship, but I know positively that he is very bitter indeed. Senator Foraker told me yesterday just how he feels, and to what limits he would like to go. ... At the meeting Saturday Senator Burrows had an armful of anti-Mormon literature, and desired to read extracts from

MR. TAYLER. Undoubtedly.

SENATOR BAILEY. I have assumed that it was and have said nothing up to this time. But so far as concerns what they believe, it does not concern me unless it relates to their conduct in civil and political affairs.

MR. TAYLER. Undoubtedly, that is correct. Mr. Smith, in what different ways did Joseph Smith, jr., receive revelations?

MR. SMITH. I do not know, sir; I was not there.

MR. TAYLER. Do you place any faith at all in the account of Joseph Smith, jr., as to how he received those revelations?

MR. SMITH. Yes, sir; I do.

MR. TAYLER. How does he say he got them?

MR. SMITH. He does not say.

MR. TAYLER. He does not?

MR. SMITH. Only by the spirit of God.

MR. TAYLER. Only by the spirit of God?

MR. SMITH. Yes, sir.

MR. TAYLER. Did Joseph Smith ever say that God or an angel appeared to him in fact?

MR. SMITH. He did.

MR. TAYLER. That is what I asked you a moment ago.

MR. SMITH. He did.

MR. TAYLER. Did Joseph Smith contend that always there was a visible appearance of the Almighty or of an angel?

MR. SMITH. No sir; he did not.

MR. TAYLER. How otherwise did he claim to receive revelations?

MR. SMITH. By the spirit of the Lord.

MR. TAYLER. And in that way, such revelations as you have received, you have had them?

MR. SMITH. Yes, sir [23] ...

---

the same for the information of the committee, but the Committee decided that it was not proper at this executive session, but Senator Burrows insisted that each one of the Committee read [them] (Jan. 26, 1904).

23. Shortly after this testimony, the committee recessed for an hour and fifteen minutes. The *Salt Lake Herald* noted that during the recess

Belva Lockwood, the noted woman's rights advocate, gave an enthusiastic welcome to President Joseph F. Smith ... [who] seemed greatly please[d] with the words of Mrs. Lockwood, especially when, with beaming face, she made the following declaration: "Two per cent is a very small proportion of the members of the Mormon church to practice plural marriage. It is the smallest percentage found among members of any Christian church." Miss Marilla Young Richer, a descendant of Brigham Young, lecturer and writer of Chicago, a masculine looking woman, also extended cordial greetings to ... Smith, and she and ... Lockwood sat with Smoot and his

MR. TAYLER. And do you remember when the Supreme Court of the United States declared that [anti-bigamy] law constitutional?[24] ...

MR. WORTHINGTON. Mr. Chairman, why should we take up time in discussing when a decision of the Supreme Court of the United States was rendered? That decision was rendered in 1878 and did hold the law to be constitutional. What is the use of taking up time with it?

MR. TAYLER. It enables us to get along very much more easily—and I am doing it in the interest of speed—if we understand these historical facts. I am glad we get it from the mouth of counsel, anyhow.

Did the church accept that decision of the Supreme Court as controlling their conduct?

MR. SMITH. It is so on record.

MR. TAYLER. Did it?

MR. SMITH. I think it did, sir.

MR. TAYLER. That is to say, no plural marriages were solemnized in the church after October, 1878?

MR. SMITH. No; I can not say as to that.

MR. TAYLER. Well, if the church solemnized marriages after that time it did not accept that decision as conclusive upon it, did it?

MR. SMITH. I am not aware that the church practiced polygamy, or plural marriages, at least, after the manifesto [of 1890].

MR. TAYLER. Yes, I know; but that was a long, long time after that. I am speaking now of 1878, when the Supreme Court decided the law to be constitutional.

MR. SMITH. I will say this, Mr. Chairman, that I do not know of any marriages occurring after that decision ...

MR. TAYLER. ... I will ask you this: We have fixed the date of this decision as the fall of 1878; am I correct in my understanding of your statement that, so far as you are aware, no polygamous marriage has been performed with the sanction of the church since the fall of 1878?

MR. SMITH. No, sir; I do not wish to be understood that way. I said after—

MR. TAYLER. What is the fact?

MR. SMITH. What I wish to be understood as saying is that I know of no marriages occurring after the final decision of the Supreme Court of

friends and counsel during the hearing ("Belva Beamed upon the Mormon Leader," *Salt Lake Herald*, Mar. 2, 1904).

24. Tayler refers to the 1862 Morrill Anti-Bigamy Act which made plural marriage a crime in U.S. territories. See Sarah Barringer Gordon, *The Mormon Question: Polygamy and Constitutional Conflict in Nineteenth-Century Utah* (Chapel Hill: University of North Carolina Press, 2002), 81-83.

the United States on that question, and it was accepted by our people as the decision of the Supreme Court of the United States.

MR. TAYLER. Then you do know of marriages occurring after the decision of 1878 in the Reynolds case?

MR. SMITH. I think likely I do.

THE CHAIRMAN. You mean, Mr. Tayler, plural marriages?

MR. TAYLER. Of course I refer to plural marriages.

MR. SMITH. Yes, sir.

SENATOR FORAKER. What is the date of the final decision [Manifesto], 1889?

MR. WORTHINGTON. The final decision was in 1890.

SENATOR FORAKER. January, 1890?

MR. WORTHINGTON. No; I have the exact date here. It was May 19, 1890.

MR. TAYLER. I want to interpolate here, in regard to final decision. Of course there was lots of litigation, but the word "final" has no significance at all. In 1878 the Supreme Court of the United States declared the law—

MR. SMITH. The law of 1862.

MR. TAYLER. Which made plural marriages unlawful[, the law of 1862 being ruled] constitutional in every respect.

SENATOR FORAKER. I understand; but the witness said he knew of no plural marriages subsequent to the final decision and the acceptance of it by his church.

MR. SMITH. That is right.

SENATOR FORAKER. I only wanted to know the date of the acceptance. Did that follow immediately after this decision of May 19, 1890?

MR. SMITH. Soon after. ...

MR. TAYLER. ... The orthodox members of the Mormon Church had accepted the [1843] revelation of Joseph Smith respecting plural marriages as laying down a cardinal and fundamental doctrine of the church, had they not?

MR. SMITH. Yes, sir.

SENATOR DUBOIS.[25] Not Joseph Smith?

---

25. Senator Dubois infrequently interjects a question, but Smoot's Nov. 1903 letter to the First Presidency indicates that he knew of Dubois's behind-the-scenes antagonism:

I have been told in the strictest confidence, that a political combination has been formed by Senator Kearns [of Utah], Dubois, and Clark of Montana, the object of which is the control of the politics in Utah, Idaho, and Montana. They tried to purchase the Boise "Statesman," but the price asked was greater than they would stand. It is now stated that Fred Dubois will start an anti-Mormon paper in Idaho (Nov. 14, 1903).

Mr. Tayler. I mean Joseph Smith, jr.

Mr. Smith. That is right.

Mr. Tayler. And as is often stated in these papers, plural marriages in consequence of that had been entered into?

Mr. Smith. Yes, sir.

Mr. Tayler. This manifesto was intended to reach through all the world wherever the Mormon Church operated, was it not?

Mr. Smith. It is so stated.

Mr. Tayler. It is so stated?

Mr. Smith. Yes, sir.

Mr. Tayler. Well, where?

Mr. Smith. In the investigation that followed.

Mr. Tayler. Then the fact is—

Mr. Smith. Before the master of chancery, I suppose.

Mr. Worthington. Let him finish his answer, Mr. Tayler.

Mr. Tayler. It is not an answer to say that it is stated somewhere, unless it is stated in some document.

Mr. Smith. It is stated in a document.

Mr. Tayler. Is that the fact?

Mr. Smith. Let me hear your question.

Mr. Tayler. That the suspension of the law commanding polygamy operated everywhere upon the Mormon people, whether within the United States or without?

Mr. Smith. That is our understanding, that it did.

Mr. Tayler. Did this manifesto and the plea for amnesty affect also the continuance of cohabitation between those who had been previously married?

Mr. Smith. It was so declared in the examination before the master in chancery.[26]

Mr. Tayler. I am asking you.

Mr. Smith. Well, sir; I will have to refresh my memory by the written word. You have the written word there, and that states the fact as it existed.

Mr. Tayler. I want to ask you for your answer to that question.

Mr. Smith. What is the question?

---

26. On March 3, 1887, Congress escheated all property held by the LDS Church. Following the Manifesto, Wilford Woodruff, Joseph F. Smith, and others sought to restore the property by testifying on October 19-20, 1891, before Judge C. F. Loofbourow, master in chancery, who subjected the church leadership to a rigorous examination about the exact meaning of the Manifesto. Extracts from the testimony were included in the initial complaint against Smoot (*Smoot Hearings*, 1:20-22).

MR. TAYLER. The stenographer will read it.

The stenographer read as follows: "Did this manifesto and the plea for amnesty affect also the continuance of cohabitation between those who had been previously married?"

MR. SMITH. It was so understood.

MR. TAYLER. And did you so understand it?

MR. SMITH. I understood it so; yes, sir.

MR. TAYLER. The revelation which Wilford Woodruff received [Manifesto], in consequence of which the command to take plural wives was suspended, did not, as you understand it, change the divine view of plural marriages, did it?

MR. SMITH. It did not change our belief at all.

MR. TAYLER. It did not change your belief at all?

MR. SMITH. Not at all, sir.

MR. TAYLER. You continued to believe that plural marriages were right?

MR. SMITH. We do. I do, at least. I do not answer for anybody else. I continue to believe as I did before.[27]

MR. TAYLER. You stated what were the standard inspired works of the church, and we find in the Book of Doctrine and Covenants the revelation made to Joseph Smith in 1843 respecting plural marriages. Where do we find the revelation suspending the operation of that command?

MR. SMITH. Printed in our public works.

MR. TAYLER. Printed in your public works?

MR. SMITH. Printed in pamphlet form. You have a pamphlet of it right there.

MR. TAYLER. It is not printed in your work of Doctrine and Covenants?

MR. SMITH. No, sir; nor a great many other revelations, either.[28]

MR. TAYLER. Nor a great many other revelations?

MR. SMITH. Yes, sir.

MR. TAYLER. How many revelations do you suppose—

MR. SMITH. I could not tell you how many.

MR. TAYLER. But a great many?

MR. SMITH. A great many.

---

27. The three previous questions and answers were used by Burrows on the Senate floor in support of the resolution to deny Smoot his seat, also in the majority report opposing Smoot (*Smoot Hearings*, 4:482).

28. The Manifesto was issued as a press release and published in newspapers, including the *Deseret News*. It was added to the Doctrine and Covenants in 1908. See Robert J. Woodford, "The Historical Development of the Doctrine and Covenants," Ph.D. diss, Brigham Young University, 1974, 3:1825-33.

MR. TAYLER. Why have they not been printed in the Book of Doctrine and Covenants?

MR. SMITH. Because it has not been deemed necessary to publish or print them.

MR. TAYLER. Are they matters that have been proclaimed to the people at large?

MR. SMITH. No, sir; not in every instance.

MR. TAYLER. Why not?

MR. SMITH. Well, I don't know why not. It was simply because they have not been.

MR. TAYLER. Is it because they are not of general interest, or that all of the people need to know of?

MR. SMITH. A great many of these revelations are local.

MR. TAYLER. Local?

MR. SMITH. In their nature. They apply to local matters.

MR. TAYLER. Yes, exactly.

MR. SMITH. And these, in many instances, are not incorporated in the general revelations, and in the Book of Doctrine and Covenants.

MR. TAYLER. For instance, what do you mean by local?

MR. SMITH. Matters that pertain to local interests of the church.

MR. TAYLER. Of course the law or revelation suspending polygamy is a matter that does affect everybody in the church.

MR. SMITH. Yes.

MR. TAYLER. And you have sought to inform them all, but not by means of putting it within the covers of one of your inspired books?

MR. SMITH. Yes.

MR. TAYLER. The various revelations that are published in the Book of Doctrine and Covenants covered twenty-five or thirty years, did they not?

MR. SMITH. Yes, sir.

MR. TAYLER. And as new revelations were given they were added to the body of the revelations previously received?

MR. SMITH. From time to time they were, but not all.

MR. TAYLER. No; but I mean those that are published in that book?

MR. SMITH. Yes, sir.

MR. TAYLER. You have, I suppose, published a great many editions of the Book of Doctrine and Covenants?

MR. SMITH. Yes, sir.

MR. TAYLER. And as recently as 1903 you have put out an edition of that book?

Mr. Smith. Well, I can not say that from memory.

Mr. Tayler. No; but within the last year, or two, or three?

Mr. Smith. Yes; I think, likely, it is so.

Mr. Tayler. As the head of the church, have you given any instruction to put within that book of Doctrine and Covenants any expression that the revelation of Joseph Smith has been qualified?

Mr. Smith. No, sir.

Mr. Tayler. The revelation of Joseph Smith respecting plural marriages remains in the book?

Mr. Smith. Yes, sir.

Mr. Tayler. And in the last editions just as it did when first promulgated?

Mr. Smith. Yes, sir.

Mr. Tayler. And it remains now without expurgation or note or anything to show that it is not now a valid law?

Mr. Smith. In the book?

Mr. Tayler. In the book; exactly.

Mr. Smith. Yes, sir.

Mr. Tayler. And in connection with the publication of the revelation itself.

Mr. Smith. But the fact is publicly and universally known by the people.

The Chairman. There is one thing I do not understand that I want to ask about. This manifesto suspending polygamy, I understand, was a revelation and a direction to the church?

Mr. Smith. I understand it, Mr. Chairman, just as it is stated there by President Woodruff himself. President Woodruff makes his own statement. I can not add to nor take anything from that statement.

The Chairman. Do you understand it was a revelation the same as other revelations?

Mr. Smith. I understand personally that President Woodruff was inspired to put forth that manifesto.

The Chairman. And in that sense it was a revelation?

Mr. Smith. Well, it was a revelation to me.

The Chairman. Yes.

Mr. Smith. Most emphatically.

The Chairman. Yes; and upon which you rely. There is another revelation directing plural marriages, I believe, previous to that?

Mr. Smith. Yes.

The Chairman. And I understand you to say now that you believe in the former revelation directing plural marriages in spite of this later revelation for a discontinuance?

MR. SMITH. That is simply a matter of belief on my part. I can not help my belief.

THE CHAIRMAN. Yes; you adhere to the original revelation and discard the latter one.

MR. SMITH. I adhere to both. I adhere to the first in my belief. I believe that the principle is as correct a principle to-day as it was then.

THE CHAIRMAN. What principle?

MR. SMITH. The principle of plural marriage. If I had not believed it, Mr. Chairman, I never would have married more than one wife.

THE CHAIRMAN. That is all. ...

MR. TAYLER. Did you know, in his lifetime, Abram H. or Abram M. Cannon?

MR. SMITH. Abraham H. Cannon[29]—I knew him well.

MR. TAYLER. What official position did he occupy?

MR. SMITH. He was one of the twelve.

MR. TAYLER. Was he a polygamist?

MR. SMITH. I believe he was. I do not know much about his family relations.

MR. TAYLER. You do not know whether he had more than one wife or not?

MR. SMITH. I could not say that I know that he had, but I believe that he had.

MR. WORTHINGTON. At what time are you speaking of?

MR. TAYLER. During his lifetime, of course.

MR. WORTHINGTON. That would be highly probable. The question is whether it was before or after the manifesto.

SENATOR FORAKER. When did he die?

MR. TAYLER. He died in 1896, I believe. Did you know any of his wives?

MR. SMITH. I have known some of them by sight. ...

MR. TAYLER. ... Lillian Hamlin. Did you know her?

MR. SMITH. I know her by sight; yes.

MR. TAYLER. Do you know her now?

MR. SMITH. Yes; I know her now.

MR. TAYLER. Was she his wife?

MR. SMITH. That is my understanding, that she was his wife.

MR. TAYLER. Do you know when he married her?

MR. SMITH. No, sir; I do not.

MR. TAYLER. Did you marry them?

---

29. Abraham H. Cannon (1859-96), son of George Q. Cannon of the First Presidency, was ordained an apostle on October 7, 1889, by Joseph F. Smith.

MR. SMITH. No, sir; I did not.

MR. TAYLER. How long did you know her?

MR. SMITH. My first acquaintance with her was in June. The first time I ever saw her was in June, 1896, I believe, as near as I can recall.

MR. TAYLER. What year, Mr. Smith?

MR. SMITH. In 1896. Some time in June, 1896.

MR. TAYLER. Where was she living then?

MR. SMITH. I am not aware of where she was living. I think her home was in Salt Lake City.

MR. TAYLER. Is that where she was when you became acquainted with her?

MR. SMITH. That is where I first saw her, in Salt Lake City.

MR. TAYLER. Did you see her after that?

MR. SMITH. Yes, sir.

MR. TAYLER. Where?

MR. SMITH. I have seen her a number of times since then, in Provo, in Salt Lake City, and elsewhere.

MR. TAYLER. You did not see her in California about that time?

MR. SMITH. I did, most distinctly.

MR. TAYLER. Where?

MR. SMITH. In Los Angeles.

MR. TAYLER. With whom was she there?

MR. SMITH. She was with Abraham Cannon.

MR. TAYLER. Was she married to him then?

MR. SMITH. That is my understanding, sir.

MR. TAYLER. Was she married to him when you saw her shortly before that?

MR. SMITH. That is my belief. That is, I do not know anything about it, but that is my belief, that she was his wife ...

MR. TAYLER. How intimately had you known Abraham H. Cannon before this? For years you had known him well, had you?

MR. SMITH. I had known him a great many years.

MR. TAYLER. When did you first learn that Lillian Hamlin was his wife?

MR. SMITH. The first that I suspected anything of the kind was on that trip, because I never knew the lady before.

MR. TAYLER. Now, if Lillian Hamlin, within a year or two years prior to June, 1896, was an unmarried woman, how could she be married to Abraham H. Cannon or Abraham M. Cannon?

MR. VAN COTT. Mr. Chairman, we object to the assumption that Mr. Tayler makes in that question. I think it is improper that he should make any assumption in putting the question. I ask to have the question read.

MR. SMITH. I can say that I do not know anything about it.

MR. VAN COTT. If he knows nothing about it, I expect that does away with the objection.

MR. TAYLER. Do you know that Lillian Hamlin was not his wife in 1892?

MR. SMITH. I do not know anything about it, sir. I did not know the lady, and never heard of her at all until that trip.

MR. TAYLER. Did you know that she was engaged to be married to Abraham H. Cannon's brother?[30]

MR. SMITH. No, sir; I did not know that.

MR. TAYLER. Do you know George Teasdale?

MR. SMITH. Yes, sir; I know George Teasdale.

MR. TAYLER. How long have you known him?

MR. SMITH. I have known him ever since 1863.

MR. TAYLER. He is one of the apostles?

MR. SMITH. Yes, sir.

MR. TAYLER. How long has he been one of them?

MR. SMITH. That I could not tell you from memory.[31]

MR. TAYLER. Well, about how long?

MR. SMITH. I should think over twenty years.

MR. TAYLER. How often do the first presidency and the apostles meet?

MR. SMITH. We generally meet once a week.

MR. TAYLER. Was he a polygamist?

MR. VAN COTT. Mr. Chairman, we object to this question for the reason that it is entirely immaterial and irrelevant in the inquiry affecting Mr. Smoot's right to be a Senator, as to any offense that may have been committed by any other person. Of course this objection was one that was mooted at the time of the preliminary matter. Our position was stated by us, and as I remember at that time Mr. Tayler stated his position. There are several Senators around the table at this time who were not present at that time, and in making the objection I wish to refer just briefly to the matter, so as to bring the history up to this time.

The chairman at that time stated that he would like our views on certain matters. One of them that was mooted and discussed at some little length was whether it was material to inquire into anything except what affected Reed Smoot. Reed Smoot is claiming his seat as

---

30. Abraham's deceased brother was David Hoagland Cannon (1871-92).

31. Teasdale (1831-1907) was ordained to the Quorum of Twelve Apostles on October 16, 1882.

United States Senator. If he has committed any offense, as polygamy, if he has taken any oath that is inconsistent with good citizenship, of course that can be inquired into; but it was claimed by counsel for the protestants at that time that they would go into offenses that they alleged had been committed by other persons than Reed Smoot, and the question is whether that is material. It was discussed at that time before some of the Senators present, but not decided, it being announced afterwards, as I understood, that that matter would be decided and passed upon when we came to the introduction of testimony. At that time I made the statement, and I repeat it, that if this were in a court of justice, to introduce testimony tending to show that A, B, and C were guilty of an offense for the purpose of convicting Reed Smoot would not be thought of nor offered by any attorney and would not be received by any court, because it would be opposed to our fundamental sense of justice to introduce any such testimony or consider any such testimony in a court. As Senator Hopkins said at that time, this is not a court; but I know there are many eminent lawyers here, who are Senators, at this table and on this committee listening to the testimony. From my standpoint, I see no more distinction as to its being in opposition to fundamental justice to introduce testimony as to Teasdale, as to A[braham]. H. Cannon, and as to A, B, and C for the purpose of affecting Reed Smoot than it would be in a court of justice. Suppose that the testimony should be introduced, and the committee should receive it that A, B, and C have violated the law of the marriage relation. When it is received, are you going to deny Reed Smoot a seat in the United States Senate on that proof? If you are, then you might as well stop here, because the answer admits that some people who were polygamists before the manifesto have kept up their relations; that is, the relation of living with more than one wife, so that it is unnecessary to go on if that is all that is required. If, on the other hand, that class of testimony is not going to deny Mr. Smoot a seat in the Senate, then it is immaterial and irrelevant and should not be received here. The Senators will observe that when they pick up this protest and read through all these charges, there is not, from cover to cover, one charge in it except academic questions. There is not one charge in it that the voters in Utah were not free to vote as they pleased. There is the academic question whether theoretically the church might not have controlled some of those votes; but there is no charge that the church did control them or did attempt to control them.

So, in the same way, when you look through those charges, there is

not one charge nor one hint nor one insinuation that the election of
Reed Smoot to the Senate of the United States was not the result of
the free expression of voters. If that is true, it seems to me utterly il-
logical to say that this class of testimony can go in unless the committee is going to say that, that Reed Smoot is going to be charged with
and convicted of something that A, B, and C have done.

SENATOR HOAR. Suppose this were the charge. I do not wish to be understood now, by putting a question, to mean that a particular answer to
it ought to be made. I do it in order to bring a matter to your attention. Suppose that Mr. Smoot belonged to an association of counterfeiters. I will not say Mr. Smoot particularly, but suppose some other
member of the Senate were charged with belonging to an association
of counterfeiters and it were proved that he was one of a body of
twelve men, frequently meeting, certain to be very intimate with each
other from the nature of their relation, all of whom except himself
had formerly believed that counterfeiting was not only lawful but, under certain circumstances under which they stood, was duty, and it
was sought to be proved that all these persons whose opinion, way of
life, and practice he was likely to know continued in the practice of
counterfeiting down to the present time; would or would not that be
one step in proof that he himself thought counterfeiting lawful, and,
connected with other testimony which might be introduced hereafter, that he practiced it?[32] ...

32. To add more tumult to Smoot's life, his oldest sister, Anna Christine Smoot Taylor, died at 4 a.m. on Wednesday, March 2. See "Senator Smoot's Sister Dies at Provo,"
Deseret News, Mar. 2, 1904.

3.

Joseph F. Smith

Thursday, March 3

"So great has become the interest in the investigation ... that it was necessary today to post a policeman at the door of the room of the committee ... where the hearings are progressing. All persons except those directly interested were kept out of the room, though outside the door it was impossible almost to maintain a passageway through the corridor of the Capitol." —*Evening Star,* Washington, D.C., Mar. 3, 1904

"When chairman Burrows ... announced the adjournment ... this evening the consensus of opinion was that it would have been better for Mr. Smoot had President Smith ... not appeared before the committee. In other words, had he been conveniently absent from the country ... or hidden away somewhere, the junior Senator's position would have been better." —*Salt Lake Tribune,* Mar. 3, 1904

Joseph F. Smith,[1] having previously affirmed, was examined, and testified as follows ...

MR. TAYLER. Before proceeding with the line of questioning respecting Apostle George Teasdale, Mr. Smith, I desire to recur for a moment to the subject of Abraham H. Cannon. At the time of his death he was an apostle?

MR. SMITH. Yes, sir.

MR. TAYLER. How long had he been an apostle, or about how long?

MR. SMITH. I do not know.

MR. TAYLER. Had he been for some time; some years?

MR. SMITH. Yes; some years.[2]

---

1. The *Washington Post* described Smith's physical appearance during the day's testimony:

> All eyes were upon President Smith, who proved what the lawyers call a "frank witness," and who in personal appearance was more than once during the day referred to by the onlookers as strongly resembling ex-Senator Peffer of Kansas. He has a patriarchal beard, wears gold-rimmed glasses, and has a rather thin voice, which nevertheless is sufficiently strong to be distinctly heard. Senator Smoot sat near, but was the object of much less attention than the head of the church ("Probe of Mormon Faith," Mar. 3, 1904).

2. At the time of his death, Cannon had served as an apostle for almost seven years.

MR. TAYLER. At the time of his death he was a polygamist, you stated, I believe?

MR. SMITH. That is my understanding, sir.

MR. TAYLER. You knew several of his wives?

MR. SMITH. Well, I can not say I knew them, except that I have seen them.

MR. TAYLER. You have seen them?

MR. SMITH. Yes, sir; and they were reputed to be his wives.

MR. TAYLER. And they were reputed to be his wives?

MR. SMITH. I do not know anything about it.

MR. TAYLER. Prior to June, 1896, you had never heard of Lillian Hamlin being his wife?

MR. SMITH. No, sir.

MR. TAYLER. Nor had you known her prior to that time?

MR. SMITH. No, sir.

MR. TAYLER. Did you see them at Los Angeles?

MR. SMITH. Yes, sir.

MR. TAYLER. Were you out in a boat from there?

MR. SMITH. Yes, sir.

THE CHAIRMAN. I did not understand the date.

MR. TAYLER. June, 1896.

THE CHAIRMAN. 1896?

MR. TAYLER. Yes.

THE CHAIRMAN. Proceed.

MR. TAYLER. Where did you go with them in a boat?

MR. SMITH. We went to Catalina Island.[3]

---

3. In a letter to Smoot, Joseph F. Smith responded to charges that he performed the plural marriage between Cannon and Hamlin on a boat to Catalina Island:

> I can only say that if Lillian H. Cannon [said] ... she "was married to Abram H. Cannon by President Jos. F. Smith, at Sea &c." She simply lied! I dislike to say that any lady would lie. And I am loath to believe that Mrs. Cannon ever told anybody any such thing, for I cannot conceive what object she could have in making such a statement if she made it at all. I have been told by one of her most intimate friends that she herself denies ever having told such a story. To you, I will say that my wife accompanied me on that trip. I cannot recall a moment when I was in the presence of Mrs. Cannon that my wife was not with us. My wife was seasick while crossing the channel to Catalina Island, and I was with her during the voyage which did not occupy more than two hours and scarcely that long I think. The boat was filled with excursionists and we all took Deck passage. The day was lovely, clear and warm, and we enjoyed the trip except that Mrs. Smith was seasick. Hugh J. Cannon, a brother of Abrams, was also in our party, and was a witness to all our past time and enjoyments. He as well as Mrs. Smith ought to be able to testify to every incident of the trip as well as I could. Still I would not care to have Mrs. Smith called down there on *your* case" (April 9, 1904).

The ceremony did take place (see note 4 below), but the only post-Manifesto polygamous marriage performed by Joseph F. Smith, according to D. Michael Quinn, was for

MR. TAYLER. Did you go from there anywhere out in the water?

MR. SMITH. No, sir.

MR. TAYLER. Your journey through the water was merely from the mainland to Catalina Island?

MR. SMITH. That is correct.

MR. TAYLER. Was there any talk, or did anything occur while you were aboard that boat, respecting the marriage relations of Abraham H. Cannon—

MR. SMITH. No, sir.

MR. TAYLER. And his wife?

MR. SMITH. No, sir.

MR. TAYLER. No reference was made to the subject at all?

MR. SMITH. Not to me.

MR. TAYLER. Not to you?

MR. SMITH. No, sir.

MR. TAYLER. To whom was any reference made?

MR. SMITH. I do not know.

MR. TAYLER. Nothing was said in your presence or to your knowledge about that subject?

MR. SMITH. No, sir. The first I heard of it was years afterwards through the public prints.

MR. TAYLER. Through the public prints?

MR. SMITH. Yes, sir.

MR. TAYLER. That is, that you had married them aboard that vessel?

MR. SMITH. That is what I heard in the public prints.

MR. TAYLER. That is what you heard?

MR. SMITH. Yes, sir.

MR. TAYLER. Did you have any talk on that journey or after you left Salt Lake—after you first heard or learned that Lillian Hamlin was the wife of Abraham Cannon—as to when they were married?

MR. SMITH. No, sir.

MR. TAYLER. Did you have any talk with either of them?

MR. SMITH. Not in the least.

MR. TAYLER. Not in the least?

Abraham H. Cannon's deceased brother, performed in the Salt Lake Temple a few days prior to the Catalina Island episode ("LDS Church Authority and New Plural Marriage, 1890-1904," *Dialogue: A Journal of Mormon Thought* 18 [Spring 1985]: 84). Another scholar believes Abraham Cannon's plural marriage was probably performed by his father, George Q. Cannon (B. Carmon Hardy, *Solemn Covenant: The Mormon Polygamous Passage* [Urbana: University of Illinois Press, 1992], 220).

MR. SMITH. Not in the least, sir; and no one ever mentioned to me that they were or were not married. I simply judged they were married because they were living together as husband and wife.[4]

MR. TAYLER. Exactly.

MR. SMITH. That is all I know about it.

MR. TAYLER. And your knowledge of any status which may have existed between them was not due to anything they told you?

MR. SMITH. No, sir; not at all.

SENATOR FORAKER. Before he gets away from that subject, is there any objection to stating what he read in the newspapers—the story to which you have referred?

MR. TAYLER. I did put that in. I asked him if he had married them aboard the steamer.

SENATOR FORAKER. That is what you saw in the newspaper?

MR. SMITH. That is what I read in the newspaper.

SENATOR FORAKER. And there was no truth in that?

MR. SMITH. No, sir. ...

MR. TAYLER. Is the law of the church, as well as the law of the land, against the taking of plural wives?

MR. SMITH. Yes, sir; I will say—

MR. TAYLER. Is that the law?

MR. SMITH. I would substitute the word "rule" of the church.

MR. TAYLER. Rule?

MR. SMITH. Instead of law; as you put it.

MR. TAYLER. Very well. Then to take a plural wife would be a violation of a rule of the church?

MR. SMITH. It would.

MR. TAYLER. Would it be such a violation of the rule of the church as would induce the church authorities to take it up like the violation of any other rule would do?

MR. SMITH. It would.[5]

---

4. Tayler used this entire excerpt in his closing argument (*Smoot Hearings*, 3:546-48). When interviewed by the *Deseret News* in 1911, Lillian Hamlin affirmed that

Joseph F. Smith did not perform the marriage ceremony between Abram H. Cannon and myself. Other than this I do not care to make any statement. You might just say, however, that if anybody else should ever be accused, wrongfully, of performing the ceremony which united Abram H. Cannon and myself in plural marriage, I will also, if asked, exonerate that person, but until such a time comes, if it ever does, I have nothing more to say ("Lillian Hamlin Says Jos. F. Smith Did Not Perform the Ceremony," Mar. 2, 1911).

5. The five previous questions and answers were used by Hopkins on the Senate floor in defense of Smoot.

MR. TAYLER. Is the cohabitation with one who is claimed to be a plural wife a violation of the law or rule of the church, as well as of the law of the land?[6]

MR. SMITH. If the committee will permit me, I could not answer the question yes or no.

MR. TAYLER. You can not answer it yes or no?

MR. SMITH. No, sir. I should like to explain that matter.[7]

MR. TAYLER. I surely have no objection myself to your doing so.

MR. SMITH. Mr. Chairman, may I be permitted?

THE CHAIRMAN. Certainly; but be as brief as you can. You have a right to make your own answer.

MR. SMITH. In regard to the status of polygamists at the time of the manifesto, it was understood for some time, according to the investigation before the master in chancery, that they would abstain from associations with their families, and I think as a rule—of course I am not familiar with it and could not say from my own knowledge—that was observed. But at the time, at the passage of the enabling act for the admission of the Territory as a State, the only provision that was made binding for the admission of the State was that plural marriages should cease, and there was nothing said in the enabling act prohibiting the cohabitation of a man with his wives at that time.[8]

SENATOR HOAR. I do not want to interrupt you, but you mean, I suppose, with wives previously married?

MR. SMITH. That is what I mean. It was understood that plural marriages had ceased. It has been the continuous and conscientious practice and rule of the church ever since the manifesto to observe that mani-

---

6. J. Reuben Clark's copy of the hearings underlined this exchange.

7. On October 19-20, 1891, Smith answered questions before the master in chancery in Utah:

Q. Do you understand that the manifesto applies to cohabitation of men and women in plural marriage where it had already existed?

A. I can not say whether it does or not.

Q. It does not in terms say so, does it?

A. No. I think, however, the effect of it is so. I don't see how the effect of it can be otherwise" (in *Smoot Hearings*, 1:22).

8. In testimony before the master in chancery in Utah the same days as Joseph F. Smith (see note 7 above), Church President Wilford Woodruff was asked whether church members were told to discontinue existing relationships, if "polygamous relations already formed before [the Manifesto] should not be continued—that is, there should be no association with plural wives—in other words, that unlawful cohabitation, as it is named and spoken of, should also stop, as well as future polygamous marriages," to which Woodruff answered, "Yes, sir; that has been my view" (in *Smoot Hearings*, 1:21).

festo with regard to plural marriages and from that time till to-day there has never been, to my knowledge, a plural marriage performed in accordance with the understanding, instruction, connivance, counsel, or permission of the presiding authorities of the church, or of the church, in any shape or form; and I know whereof I speak, gentlemen, in relation to that matter.[9]

MR. TAYLER. That is all of your answer?

MR. SMITH. What was your question?

THE CHAIRMAN. Now let the reporter repeat the question.

MR. SMITH. Excuse me; I think I have the thread: Was it contrary to the rule of the church? It was.

MR. WORTHINGTON. What was?

MR. SMITH. That is, the association of a man, having married more than one wife previous to the manifesto, abstaining from association with them.

THE CHAIRMAN. I do not think you understand the question. Let the reporter read it.

THE REPORTER READ AS FOLLOWS: "Mr. Tayler. Is the cohabitation with one who is claimed to be a plural wife a violation of the law or rule of the church, as well as of the law of the land?"

MR. SMITH. That was the case, and is the case, even to-day.[10]

MR. TAYLER. What was the case; what you are about to say?

MR. SMITH. That is contrary to the rule of the church and contrary as well to the law of the land for a man to cohabit with his wives.[11]

But I was placed in this position. I had a plural family, if you please; that is, my first wife was married to me over thirty-eight years ago, my last wife was married to me over twenty years ago, and with these wives I had children, and I simply took my chances preferring to meet the consequences of the law rather than to abandon my children and their mothers; and I have cohabited with my wives—not openly,[12]

---

9. The claim that the church did not officially permit any new plural marriages after the Manifesto is one Smith would reiterate throughout his testimony.

10. Two other LDS leaders testified in October 1891 before the master in chancery in Utah. Lorenzo Snow stated that "the intention and scope of that manifesto was ... that the law should be observed in all matters concerning plural marriage, embracing the present condition of those who had previously entered into marriage." Although the Manifesto did not "explicitly state" that men should leave their current plural wives, Anthon H. Lund acknowledged that the church president had said as much (in *Smoot Hearings,* 1:21-22).

11. The previous two questions and answers were included in the majority report submitted by Senator Burrows on June 11, 1906 (*Smoot Hearings,* 4:480).

12. J. Reuben Clark's copy of the hearings marked this answer in brackets.

that is, not in a manner that I thought would be offensive to my neighbors—but I have acknowledged them; I have visited them. They have borne me children since 1890, and I have done it knowing the responsibility and knowing that I was amenable to the law. Since the admission of the State there has been a sentiment existing and prevalent in Utah that these old marriages would be in measure condoned. They were not looked upon as offensive; as really violative of law; they were, in other words, regarded as an existing fact, and if they saw any wrong in it they simply winked. In other words, Mr. Chairman, the people of Utah, as a rule, as well as the people of this nation, are broad-minded and liberal-minded people, and they have rather condoned than otherwise, I presume, my offense against the law. I have never been disturbed.[13] Nobody has ever called me in question, that I know of, and if I had, I was there to answer to the charge; or any charge that might have been made against me, and I would have been willing to submit to the penalty of the law, whatever it might have been.[14]

MR. TAYLER. So that obedience to the law is perfectly satisfied, according to your view of it, if one is ready to pay the penalty for its violation?

MR. SMITH. Not at all. I should like to draw a distinction between unlawful cohabitation and polygamy. There is a law prohibiting polygamy, plural marriages.[15]

SENATOR HOAR. You mean now a law of the State of Utah?

MR. SMITH. I mean the law of the State, and I mean that this is in the constitution of our State. It is required by the enabling act. That law, gen-

---

13. On January 16, 1905, Tayler read into the record a "petition or remonstrance that was received by the Senate" from "law-abiding citizens of Utah" who found in Smith's testimony reason to bring criminal charges against him: "We also most earnestly protest against the continuance of the state of degradation and immoral living the testimony referred to discloses, and demand that the laws against this crime shall be enforced with such vigor as to compel the defiant transgressors to come within the law and keep good faith with our generous nation" (*Smoot Hearings*, 2:926).

14. Carl Badger's journal for March 26, 1904, reads: "Senator Burrows took the Senator [Smoot] into his room and gave him a lecture about the 'beastly practices' of President Smith" (in Rodney J. Badger, *Liahona and Iron Rod: The Biography of Carl A. and Rose J. Badger* [Bountiful, Utah: Family History Publishers, 1985], 214).

15. In a letter to Reed Smoot one month after this testimony, President Smith fumed:

It is astonishing how the mind of man, of ordinary intelligence, cannot grasp the situation out here, and see the difference between the offense under the law called "unlawful cohabitation," and the graver offense, under the law, called "polygamous marriage." "There are none so blind as those who will not see, nor so deaf as those who will not hear." When men pronounce the "Mormon" people insincere, they simply lie or are deceived (Apr. 9, 1904).

tlemen, has been complied with by the church; that law has been kept by the church; and there never has been a plural marriage by the consent or sanction or knowledge or approval of the church since the manifesto.[16]

The law of unlawful cohabitation is another law entirely, and relates to the cohabitation of a man with more than one wife. That is the law which I have presumed to face in preference to disgracing myself and degrading my family by turning them off and ceasing to acknowledge them and to administer to their wants—not the law in relation to plural marriage. That I have not broken. Neither has any man broken it by the sanction or approval of the church.[17]

Mr. Tayler. You say that there is a State law forbidding unlawful cohabitation?

Mr. Smith. That is my understanding.

Mr. Tayler. And ever since that law was passed you have been violating it?

Mr. Smith. I think likely I have been practicing the same thing even before the law was passed.

Mr. Tayler. Yes.

Mr. Smith. Long years before it was passed.

Mr. Tayler. You have not in any respect changed your relations to these wives since the manifesto or since the passage of this law of the State of Utah. I am not meaning to be unfair in the question, but only to understand you. What I mean is, you have been holding your several wives out as wives, not offensively, as you say. You have furnished them homes. You have given them your society. You have taken care of the children that they bore you, and you have caused them to bear you new children—all of them.

Mr. Smith. That is correct, sir.[18]

---

16. Notice it is the "church," rather than individual leaders, that has not given consent to post-Manifesto plural marriages, as pointed out by Kathleen Flake, *The Politics of American Religious Identity: The Seating of Senator Reed Smoot, Mormon Apostle* (Chapel Hill: University of North Carolina Press, 2004), 76.

17. J. Reuben Clark's copy of the hearings marked this entire answer with brackets.

18. In a letter to Smith three weeks after this testimony, Smoot wrote:

I feel it my duty to write to you and let you know as near as possible the conditions as they exist here in Washington, especially among the senators, since the testimony given before the Committee ... Of course, you are aware that the public press, that is, the great daily papers of the nation have had some vicious and bitter articles directed particularly against the Church and based upon your testimony and that of Apostle Lyman. Many of the papers are continuing the same class of articles, but along a different line than those that first appeared. The first impression or shock was when

Mr. Tayler. That is correct?

Mr. Smith. Yes, sir.

Mr. Tayler. Now, since that was a violation of the law, why have you done it?

Mr. Smith. For the reason I have stated. I preferred to face the penalties of the law to abandoning my family.

Mr. Tayler. Do you consider it an abandonment of your family to maintain relations with your wives except that of occupying their beds?

Mr. Smith. I do not wish to be impertinent, but I should like the gentleman to ask any woman, who is a wife, that question.

Mr. Tayler. Unfortunately, or fortunately, that is not the status of this examination at this point.

Mr. Smith. All the same; it is my sentiment.

Senator Foraker. I do not see how investigation along that line is going to give us any light. What we want are facts. The witness has testified to the fact. This is all a matter of argument and discussion—the effect of it, or what his opinion is about it. It is our opinion we are concerned about[19] ...

---

they learned that polygamy, (as they call it) was still practiced in Utah, and their editorials were directed against polygamy and the practice of polygamy by the Mormon Church. It seems impossible to make the American people believe that there is any difference between polygamy and unlawful cohabitation. I cannot even make the Senators understand it, for they claim that it is the act of unlawful cohabitation that makes polygamy, ... I call their attention to the fact that Congress, itself, at the time of the passage of the Edmunds Act ... understood the difference ... On second thought and further consideration of the evidence, the daily papers are writing editorials against us from a much more serious point of view, according to my opinion; and such articles, I am afraid, will have a greater weight with the thinking class of people and create a more bitter feeling of antagonism against us than all the articles they could write against the belief or practice of polygamy. Thousand of editorials are appearing now branding the Mormon leaders as liars, covenant breakers, violators of the laws of man and the law of God, and the Mormon people as religious dupes and religious fanatics. It is this class of articles that has a great deal of weight with the Senators and they are beginning to question the sincerity of the Mormon people and discussion [of] what they term the broken pledges made to the Government by the leaders of the Mormon Church. My particular friends in the Senate have stated to me over and over again that the testimony that has been given in my case can have but one effect, ... to show to the American people and the world that the Mormon people are not sincere and are not honest when it comes to a question of religion. ... This sentiment of insincerity has permeated the whole Senate, and a great many Senators have brought me the testimony and asked for an explanation, and I must admit that it is the hardest thing that I have had to meet in life. I have thought a great deal over the situation, it has worried me until I can hardly sleep, I have prayed over it and have received no answer to my prayers satisfactory to myself" (Mar. 23, 1904).

19. This entire section was used by Tayler in his closing argument for the prosecution (*Smoot Hearings*, 3:566-69).

MR. TAYLER. Mr. Smith, how many children have been born to your several wives since the manifesto of 1890?

MR. WORTHINGTON.[20] I object to that. He professes that he has been living with them. What difference does it make whether it is one child or three?

MR. TAYLER. Of course it will be important as showing how continuous, how notorious, how offensive, has been his conduct in this respect.

SENATOR FORAKER. The committee must necessarily infer from what the witness stated that this cohabitation has been continuous and uninterrupted.

SENATOR BEVERIDGE. He so stated.

MR. TAYLER. Precisely; but not how well advertised, how offensive, how instructive it has been to his people; how compelling.

SENATOR BEVERIDGE. I understood the witness to say that he had children born to him since that time.

MR. TAYLER. Precisely.

SENATOR BEVERIDGE. That has already been stated.

MR. TAYLER. But it makes a great difference whether it is 2 or 22.

THE CHAIRMAN. Mr. Smith, I wish to ask you a question preliminarily. I understood you, in response to a question of counsel, to state that you married your first wife at such a time, and the second wife at such a time, both before 1890?

MR. SMITH. Yes, sir.

THE CHAIRMAN. The last wife, I mean. Were there any intermediate marriages?

MR. SMITH. Yes, sir.

THE CHAIRMAN. How many?

MR. SMITH. There were three besides the first and the last.

THE CHAIRMAN. Then you have five wives?

MR. SMITH. I have.

THE CHAIRMAN. Mr. Tayler, what is your question?

MR. TAYLER. My question is, How many children have been born to him by these wives since 1890?

---

20. Carl Badger wrote in his journal on March 3, 1904:

Mr. Worthington to-night referred to President Smith as "the grand old man," and said that a friend, once a lawyer, now a minister, moved away from him [Worthington] in the street car in mock horror and said that he would have nothing to do with a defender of a "Mormon." When Mr. Worthington got off the car, the man said that he was glad they had met, and that he would have done just as Mr. Smith had done with his wives if he had been in the same position (Badger, *Liahona and Iron Rod*, 212).

THE CHAIRMAN. The chair thinks that question is competent.

MR. SMITH. I have had 11 children born since 1890.

MR. TAYLER. Those are all the children that have been born to you since 1890?

MR. SMITH. Yes, sir; those are all.

MR. TAYLER. Were those children by all of your wives; that is, did all of your wives bear children?

MR. SMITH. All my wives bore children.

MR. TAYLER. Since 1890?

MR. SMITH. That is correct.

THE CHAIRMAN. I understand, since 1890.

MR. SMITH. Since 1890. I said that I have had born to me 11 children since 1890, each of my wives being the mother of from 1 to 2 of those children.[21]

THE CHAIRMAN. Mr. Tayler, proceed.

MR. TAYLER. None of them has borne more than two children to you?

MR. SMITH. None that I recollect now. I could not tell you without I referred to the dates.[22]

---

21. Following the day's testimony, the *Deseret News* editorialized:

President Smith's frankness seemed to surprise several members of the committee, who seemed prepared to expect evasions and excuses. ... In the meantime interest in the hearing grows. There were twice as many women in the room this morning as attended the hearing yesterday, and fully 20 members of the house stood against the walls. At times, the trend of questions indicated that counsel for the protestants proposed to lift the bed curtains in the homes of every official of the Church, but this line of questioning was stopped for the time being, at least. The indications are that the testimony will fill several volumes ("A Frank, Honest Declaration," Mar. 3, 1904).

The next day, the *Salt Lake Tribune* agreed that it had been "an epoch-making occasion" due to the "frankness and candor" of President Smith's answers, for which the *Tribune* felt he was "emphatically to be commended." It was "decidedly refreshing to see such testimony as this, giving exact truth," as well as "a complete surprise to us." It was in "direct contrast" to efforts to "conceal or evade" that had characterized "the sort of testimony that has usually been given in the courts of Utah when matters of this kind have been under investigation" ("President Smith's Testimony," Mar. 4, 1904).

The previous five questions and answers were included in the report submitted to the Senate by Chairman Burrows (*Smoot Hearings*, 4:480).

22. Smith's wives and children were: 1. Levira Annett Clark (1842-88), married Smith 1859, no children, separated 1866, later divorced; 2. Julina Lambson (1849-1936), married Smith 1866—children Edward Arthur (1858-1911), Mercy Josephine (1867-70), Mary Sophronia (1869-1948), Donnette (1872-1961), Joseph Fielding (1876-1972), David Asael (1879-1952), George Carlos (1881-1931), Julina Clarissa (1884-1923), Elias Wesley (1886-1970), Emily Jane (1888-1982), Rachael Jane (1888-1982), Edith Eleanor (1894-1987), and unknown; 3. Sarah Ellen Richards (1850-1915), married Smith 1868—children Sarah Ellen (1869), Leonora (1871-1907), Joseph Richards (1873-1954), Heber John (1876-77), Rhoda Ann (1878-79), Leonora (1871-1907), Minerva (1880-1958), Alice

THE CHAIRMAN. I do not think that is material.

MR. TAYLER. That was not intended for information so much as it was for my guidance with respect to another question which I do not care to ask.

SENATOR FORAKER. It is very evident that there must have been two children by four of the wives, and three by one, which would make eleven.

MR. TAYLER. That is very true. You of course understand that I might have difficulty in locating the mother of some of the children, as Mr. Smith himself is not quite sure—

MR. SMITH. You will not have any difficulty so far as I am concerned.[23]

MR. TAYLER. I have no doubt if you could recall the particular situation, but you said you were not sure but that one might have borne you three children.

MR. SMITH. I rather think she has.

MR. TAYLER. You rather think?

MR. SMITH. Yes. I could tell you a little later by referring. I can not say that I remember the dates of births of my children—all of them. ...

SENATOR OVERMAN. Did Senator Smoot ever advise you to desist from polygamous cohabitation with your plural wives?

MR. SMITH. Not that I know of. I do not think that Mr. Smoot has ever attempted to interfere with my family relations. I do not know that he knows anything about them, except what I have told you here to-day.

(1882-1901), Willard Richards (1884-1972), Franklin Richards (1888-1967), Jeanetta (1891-1932), and Asenath (1896-1982); 4. Edna Lambson (1851-1926), married Smith 1871—children Hyrum Mack (1872-1918), Alvin Fielding (1874-1948), Alfred Jason (1876-1978), Edna Melissa (1879-1958), Albert Jesse (1881-83), Robert Smith (1883-86), Emma (1888-1969), Zina (1890-1915), Ruth (1893-98), and Martha (1897-1977); 5. Mary Taylor Schwartz (1865-1956), married Smith 1884—children John Schwartz (1888-89), Calvin Schwartz (1890-1966), Samuel Schwartz (1892-1983), James Schwartz (1894-1950), Agnes (1897-1966), Silas Schwartz (1900-83), and Royal Grant (1906-71); and 6. 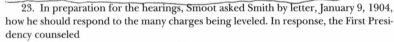Alice Ann Kimball (1858-1946), married Smith 1883—children Lucy Mack (1890-1933), Andrew Kimball (1893-1951), Jesse Kimball (1896-1953), and Fielding Kimball (1900-74).

23. In preparation for the hearings, Smoot asked Smith by letter, January 9, 1904, how he should respond to the many charges being leveled. In response, the First Presidency counseled

> In your letter you say that the President is accused of living in polygamous relations. That he does not forsake or repudiate his wives is admitted, but who can prove that he violates the law of the land? You certainly have no knowledge of his doing so. You suggest that you might say that you could not vote for him for a secular office. We do not think you will gain anything by this, as the senators, knowing the strong regard the leaders of the Church have for one another, would hardly believe it. We know what a difficult position you are placed in, and how guarded and careful you must be in all admissions you make, and hence we do not feel to criticise your answer, but simply suggest that you be on your guard (Jan. 20, 1904).

SENATOR OVERMAN. Did he ever discuss the matter with you in any way?

MR. SMITH. Never to my knowledge. I should like to repeat, in connection with this question, that it is a well-known fact throughout all Utah, and I have never sought to disguise that fact in the least, or to disclaim it, that I have five wives in Utah. My friends all know that—Gentiles and Jews and Mormons. They all knew that I had five wives.

MR. TAYLER. I do not doubt it at all.

MR. SMITH. Whether they knew that I was living with them or not I can not say. I did not inform them of that. I did not acknowledge it to them, because they never asked me nor interrogated me on that point at all.

THE CHAIRMAN. Mr. Tayler, proceed.

SENATOR OVERMAN. Are the apostles your advisers?

MR. SMITH. Mr. Senator, I receive advice and counsel from any and every good man.

SENATOR OVERMAN. Do they have any special authority?

MR. SMITH. No more than any other member of the church, except as a body or a council of the church.

SENATOR OVERMAN. Did any of the apostles ever advise you or ask you to desist from this conduct?

MR. SMITH. No, sir.

THE CHAIRMAN. Mr. Smith, just one question. Do you know whether Mr. Smoot has visited at your house or houses?

MR. SMITH. I do not believe he ever did. I have no recollection whatever that he was ever in my house.

THE CHAIRMAN. Or any one of your residences?

MR. SMITH. Or anyone of them. I will modify that if you will allow me, please?

THE CHAIRMAN. Certainly.

MR. SMITH. I will say that I met Mr. Smoot in my present residence, my official residence, if you please, some two or three times, I think. He dropped in to talk with me about something, some private matters, in my present residence.

MR. WORTHINGTON. Where you live with your first wife?

MR. SMITH. Yes, sir; where I live with my first wife.

THE CHAIRMAN. Proceed, Mr. Tayler.

MR. TAYLER. Now, referring to George Teasdale, is he a polygamist?

MR. VAN COTT. Just a moment. I object to the question unless you mean now, Mr. Tayler.

MR. TAYLER. The word "is" has a present tense, of course.

MR. VAN COTT. If it is confined to the present I have no objection to make.

MR. SMITH. He is not now a polygamist.

MR. TAYLER. Has he been within recent years?

MR. WORTHINGTON. I object, unless it is confined to the date of the manifesto.

MR. TAYLER. Since 1890?

MR. SMITH. I do not know.

THE CHAIRMAN. What was the question?

MR. SMITH. I have been twice in all my life in the residence of George Teasdale, and but twice. He lives at Nephi, a hundred and some odd miles south of Salt Lake City, and I do not visit at his home. I am not familiar with his family relations, and never have been. All I know is that Mr. Teasdale is a member of the council of the twelve, and we meet together, not with his family, but as an individual and as a member of the council. I do not know anything about his polygamous status or the status of his family. ...

MR. TAYLER. Who is John W. Tayler?[24]

MR. SMITH. With what reference do you ask the question? Who is he? What do you mean?

MR. TAYLER. Is he one of the apostles?

MR. SMITH. Yes, sir.

MR. TAYLER. Has he been an apostle for many years?

MR. SMITH. Yes; for many years; a number of years.

MR. TAYLER. He seems to be the fifth in order on the list. Would that indicate the chronological order of his elevation as an apostle the order in which the names are generally given?

MR. SMITH. No, sir; I think not.

MR. TAYLER. Is he a polygamist?

MR. SMITH. Well, now; he is reputed, I think, to be a polygamist.

MR. TAYLER. He is reputed to be a polygamist?

MR. SMITH. Yes, sir. I could not say to you that he was. Of my own knowledge I could not say that he is a polygamist.

MR. TAYLER. Have you the slightest doubt of it?

MR. SMITH. I have not very much doubt of it.

MR. TAYLER. Where is he now?

MR. SMITH. I do not know, sir.

MR. TAYLER. I do not mean what, at this particular instant, his location is, but I mean officially he is away somewhere.

---

24. John W. Taylor (1858-1916), son of LDS Church President John Taylor, was ordained a member of the Quorum of Twelve Apostles on April 9, 1884.

MR. SMITH. The last I heard of him he was sent as a commissioner to investigate a certain tract of land which was offered for sale to our people by the Great Northern Railroad Company and that is some weeks ago. Since then I have not heard of him and I do not know where he is.[25] ...

SENATOR DUBOIS. Could an apostle be a polygamist without your knowledge?

MR. SMITH. I hardly think he could.

SENATOR DUBOIS. Then what is the use of saying "I think;" "I do not know?"

MR. SMITH. Because I never saw a woman married to him in my life.

SENATOR DUBOIS. Could an apostle be a polygamist without your knowledge? Can they go out and enter into polygamy without your knowledge?

MR. SMITH. No, sir; not that I know of. I say "not that I know of."

SENATOR DUBOIS. Then an apostle could not be a polygamist unless you knew it?

MR. SMITH. Unless he violated the rule of the church without my knowledge, and I do not think he would do that.

MR. TAYLER. Apostle M[arriner]. W[ood]. Merrill is one of your—

MR. SMITH. One of our twelve.[26]

MR. TAYLER. One of your twelve. Is he a polygamist?

MR. SMITH. He has that reputation.

MR. TAYLER. How many wives is he reputed to have?

---

25. Two weeks after this testimony, Smith wrote to Smoot:

I have not yet heard one word from John W. Taylor, nor from M[atthias]. F. Cowley ... I have written and telegraphed in various directions for them, but so far without avail. I wonder sometimes if I am indeed—"my brothers keeper." I have no doubt they will turn up somewhere ere-long. I am however half inclined to let the "imperious 'Czar'" hunt up his own witnesses. Altho[ugh] I believe the two Elders above named might fill their missions better before the anti-Mormon inquisition at Washington than they can do, or are doing in their legitimate mission fields ... I feel quite sure that these three men will make poor witnesses for "Julius Czar," Dubois, Taylor et al! I mean the anti-Mormon Church inquisitions ... not at all the honorable Senators and gentleman who are true Republicans with honest and impartial views and intentions (Mar. 20, 1904).

The third man referred to in the letter was Joseph M. Tanner of the church's general board of education. He was reputed to have taken plural wives after the Manifesto. Tanner never made it to Washington to testify and was quietly dropped from his position on the education board the same day Cowley's and Taylor's resignations from the Quorum of the Twelve were made public ("Church Drops J. M. Tanner," *Salt Lake Tribune,* Apr. 10, 1906).

26. Marriner Wood Merrill (1832-1906) was ordained to the Quorum of Twelve on October 7, 1889.

MR. SMITH. I do not know.

MR. TAYLER. Do you mean you have never heard?

MR. SMITH. I have never heard.

MR. TAYLER. He has a large number?

MR. SMITH. I do not know.

MR. TAYLER. Do you mean that you have no idea?

MR. SMITH. Not in the least—any more than you have, and perhaps not as good.

MR. TAYLER. Only that he is a polygamist?

MR. SMITH. That is all.[27]

THE CHAIRMAN. Where does he reside, Mr. Smith?

MR. SMITH. Mr. Merrill resides in Richmond, Cache County, in the northern part of the State of Utah.

MR. WORTHINGTON. How far from Salt Lake City?

MR. SMITH. In the neighborhood of a hundred miles I should judge, on an offhand guess. I do not know the exact distance, but it is nearly a hundred miles from Salt Lake City.

MR. TAYLER. Heber J. Grant is one of the twelve apostles?[28]

MR. SMITH. Yes, sir.

MR. TAYLER. Is he a polygamist?

MR. SMITH. He so acknowledged, I believe, a few weeks ago.

MR. TAYLER. He so acknowledged?

MR. SMITH. I believe so. It was so reported in the public prints.

MR. TAYLER. Is that all you know about it?

MR. SMITH. Well, I know that I have seen two ladies who are reputed to be his wives.

MR. TAYLER. You have stated that an apostle could not be a polygamist without your knowledge.

MR. SMITH. I have not denied that he was a polygamist.

MR. TAYLER. No.

MR. SMITH. Not in the least.

MR. WORTHINGTON. The witness said an apostle could not be a polygamist without his knowledge, unless he violated the rule of the church.

MR. TAYLER. Where is Heber J. Grant now?

MR. SMITH. He is in Europe.[29]

---

27. Merrill married a total of eight wives who bore him forty-six children. All of Merrill's wives were living at the time of this testimony.

28. Grant (1856-1945) was ordained to the Quorum of Twelve on October 12, 1882.

29. Adding fuel to an already blazing fire, Utah Governor Heber M. Wells, shortly after this testimony, appointed "fugitive" LDS mission president Heber J. Grant to rep-

MR. TAYLER. For the church?

MR. SMITH. Yes, sir.

MR. TAYLER. Do you call his mission an important and honorable one?

MR. SMITH. Yes, sir.

MR. TAYLER. Do you know which of his wives, if either, went with him.

MR. SMITH. I am not posted.

MR. TAYLER. You are not posted?

MR. SMITH. No, sir.

THE CHAIRMAN. You do not know, then?

MR. SMITH. Sir?

THE CHAIRMAN. You do not know which one of his wives went with him?

MR. SMITH. I could not say that I know positively, but I believe that it is his second wife.

MR. TAYLER. That is, you mean his second living wife?

MR. SMITH. That is what I mean.

THE CHAIRMAN. Do you know how many wives he has?

MR. SMITH. Who?

THE CHAIRMAN. Grant.

MR. SMITH. Mr. Grant?

THE CHAIRMAN. Yes.

MR. SMITH. I think he had at one time three, but his first wife, then living, died.[30]

THE CHAIRMAN. How many has he now?

MR. SMITH. Only two that I know of.

THE CHAIRMAN. Only two?

MR. SMITH. Only two. Pardon me for saying "that I know of," Mr. Chairman. I am like all other men; I only know what I know.

---

resent Utah at the First International Hygiene Congress in Nuremberg, Germany, April 1904. Of this appointment, a Salt Lake newspaper editorialized:

> Governor Wells' appointment of Heber J. Grant ... was a most amazing indiscretion, to put the case as mildly as possible. The governor much credit[s] the people of Utah and the nation with surprisingly short memories. Perhaps, though, it is the memory of the governor that is at fault ... [to] find some absconding embezzler to represent Utah at the next international convention of bankers. ... Perhaps he really doesn't care whether Senator Smoot loses his seat or not" ("Our Indiscreet Governor," *Salt Lake Herald,* Mar. 5, 1904).

30. Grant's wives and children were: 1. Lucy Stringham (1858-93), married Grant 1877—children Susan Rachel (1878-1969), Lucy (1880-1966), Florence (1883-1977), Edith (1885-1947), Anna (1886-70), and Heber Stringham (1888-96); 2. Hulda Augusta Winters (1856-1952), married Grant 1884, no children; and 3. Emily Harris Wells (1857-1908), married Grant 1884—children Martha Deseret (1886-1970), Grace (1888-73), Daniel Wells (1891-95), Emily (1896-1929), and Francis Marion (1899-1995).

THE CHAIRMAN. Oh, the committee understand.

MR. TAYLER. John Henry Smith is an apostle?[31]

MR. SMITH. Yes, sir.

MR. TAYLER. Is he a polygamist?

MR. SMITH. He has two wives. I am pretty well acquainted with his folks. He is a kinsman of mine.[32]

THE CHAIRMAN. Is he one of the apostles?

MR. SMITH. Yes, sir.

MR. TAYLER. You, as the head of the church, never undertook to apply any more rigid rule of conduct to him than you applied to yourself?

MR. SMITH. I certainly could not condemn him when I was in the same practice.

MR. TAYLER. I suppose not.

THE CHAIRMAN. Where does he reside, Mr. Smith?

MR. SMITH. He resides in Salt Lake City.

THE CHAIRMAN. With his two wives?

MR. SMITH. Yes, sir.

MR. TAYLER. Do you know whether he has had children by these wives since the manifesto?

MR. SMITH. I could not tell you about that. I do not know anything about it.[33]

MR. TAYLER. You do not know anything about whether he has had children since—

MR. SMITH. No, sir.

MR. WORTHINGTON. You said he lived in Salt Lake City. You do not mean in the same household with his wives?

MR. SMITH. Oh, no; they each have their home ...

MR. TAYLER. M[atthias]. F. Cowley is one of the apostles?[34]

---

31. John Henry Smith (1848-1911) was ordained to the Quorum of Twelve on October 27, 1880.

32. The Smiths were second cousins.

33. John Henry Smith's wives and children were: 1. Sarah Farr (1849-1921), married Smith 1866—children John Henry (1868), George Albert (1870-1951), Lorin Farr (1872), Don Carlos (1874-1927), Ezra Chase (1876-1951), Charles Warren (1879), Winslow Farr (1881-1966), Nathaniel Libby (1883-1935), Nancy Clarabell (1886-1961), Tirzah Priscille (1888-1951), and Elsie Louise (1891-1926); 2. Josephine Groesbeck (1857-1948), married Grant 1887—children Sarah Ann (1878-1938), Nicholas Groesbeck (1881-1945), Joseph Harmon (1884-1942), Lucy (1887-1900), Elizabeth (1890-1973), Glenn Groesbeck (1893-1970), Arzella (1895-1969), and Josephine (1898-1973).

34. Matthias F. Cowley (1858-1940) was ordained to the Quorum of Twelve on October 7, 1897.

MR. SMITH. Yes, sir.

MR. TAYLER. Is he a polygamist?

MR. SMITH. He is reputed to have two wives.[35]

MR. TAYLER. Where does he live?

MR. SMITH. He lives in Salt Lake City.

MR. TAYLER. Where is he now?

MR. SMITH. I do not know, sir.

MR. TAYLER. I mean in a general way.

MR. SMITH. In a general way, the last I heard of him he was making a tour of the northern missions of the church in Idaho and Montana and Oregon; that he started out some weeks ago on that line. I do not know where he is to-day.[36]

MR. TAYLER. What information have you as to his children, born to a plural wife since the manifesto?

MR. SMITH. I have no knowledge of his family at all. I never was in his house.

MR. TAYLER. Have you any information respecting it?[37]

---

35. Cowley's wives and children were: 1. Abigail Abbie Hyde (1863-1931), married Cowley 1884—children Matthias Hyde (1885), Sarah Abbie (1886-1950), Anna Leona (1888-1966), Moses Foss (1892-1929), William Hyde (1895-1968), Matthew (1897-1953), Carol Elizabeth (1899-1980), and Charles Floyd (1901-70); 2. Luella Smart Parkinson (1870-1962), married Cowley 1889—children Joseph (1884-?), Laura (1886-?), Laura Parkinson (1893-1976), Samuel Parkinson (1899-1934), Elna Parkinson (1901-?), Heber Carter (1901-18), and unknown; and 3. Nora Taylor (1862-?), married Cowley 1904, children unknown.

36. Two days after this testimony, a Salt Lake newspaper reported:

Apostle Cowley was in Portland as late as last Wednesday [Mar. 2], and addressed a meeting there Tuesday evening [Mar. 1]. In his remarks he talked of the Smoot case[:] ... "With reference to the agitation concerning Reed Smoot, I want to remind you that senators and politics are no part of our religious services, and that as a senator Mr. Smoot does not represent any church or any class of people. ... We do not use church influence in politics. ... The church has no concern about the retention of his seat in the senate. It had nothing to do with his election. If the senate casts him out, it will not retard the progress of the church in the least degree. The church depends on God to promote her interest upon the earth, and not upon a United States senator. ... This talk about polygamy comes from the same source that has always misrepresented and persecuted our church" ("Cowley Located in Portland, Ore.," *Salt Lake Herald,* Mar. 5, 1904).

37. A few weeks later on March 22, 1904, Carl Badger noted in his journal:

I heard Pres. Smith say he would find out where the missing witnesses were—I sent the telegrams to Pres. [John R.] Winder to locate them—and if they had not been guilty of performing new marriages, he would have them come. It showed that he did not know and did not think it impossible. In the event of their having performed new marriages, the Senator said to-day, that he volunteered "if the President thought best" to resign his seat in the Senate, rather than bring the Senate on the Apostles, the wrongly married people, and the Church. Apostle [Francis M.]

MR. SMITH. No, sir.

MR. TAYLER. What?

MR. SMITH. No, sir.

MR. TAYLER. None at all?

MR. SMITH. No, sir.

MR. TAYLER. Rudger Clawson is an apostle?[38]

MR. SMITH. Yes, sir.

MR. TAYLER. Is he a polygamist?

MR. SMITH. No, sir.

MR. TAYLER. How do you know?

MR. SMITH. Because he was at one time, but his wife left him, and he has but one wife.[39]

MR. TAYLER. When was that?

MR. SMITH. When did his first wife leave him?

MR. TAYLER. Yes.

MR. SMITH. I could not tell you as to the date. I think it was sometime in the eighties.[40]

MR. TAYLER. You mean that he has not had two wives since the manifesto?

MR. SMITH. No, sir; he has not.

MR. TAYLER. You are positive of that?

MR. SMITH. I am quite positive of it. I am quite intimate with him.

MR. TAYLER. Is your information to the effect that men are not polygamists so much more definite than that they are polygamists—

MR. SMITH. No, sir.

Lyman wrote Richard [R. Lyman, his son,] "that they [Cowley and Taylor] were at their wits ends to know what to answer." Dick wrote back that any guilty man would be (Badger, *Liahona and Iron Rod,* 213).

38. Rudger Clawson (1857-1943) was ordained to the Quorum of Twelve on October 10, 1898.

39. Following passage of the Edmunds Anti-Polygamy Act of 1882, Clawson, a polygamist, became the test case to challenge this law. He was convicted and served three years in prison. Several months after his testimony in the Smoot hearings, Clawson married another plural wife on August 3, 1904, in a ceremony performed by Matthias Cowley.

40. Clawson married Florence Ann Dinwoody on August 12, 1882. The couple's engagement was tumultuous, based on Rudger's intention to enter plural marriage. Less than a year later, he married Lydia Elizbeth Spencer (born 1883). On November 4, 1884, he was convicted and began serving his prison sentence. While there, he learned his first wife intended to divorce him, which she did in 1885. See David S. Hoopes and Roy Hoopes, *The Making of a Mormon Apostle: The Story of Ruder Clawson* (Lanham, New York: Madison Books, 1990); Stan Larson, ed., *Prisoner for Polygamy: The Memoirs and Letters of Rudger Clawson at the Utah Territorial Penitentiary, 1884-87* (Urbana: University of Illinois Press, 1993).

Mr. Tayler. That you can use language of such positiveness in the one case and not in the other?

Mr. Smith. I happen, sir, to be very well acquainted with Rudger Clawson. At one time he was the second councilor to President Snow with myself. He lives as a neighbor to me, and we sit in the same office together from day to day, and I am very intimate with Rudger Clawson and with his family.

Mr. Tayler. F[rancis]. M. Lyman is an apostle?[41]

Mr. Smith. Yes, sir.

Mr. Tayler. What position does he hold respecting the apostles.

Mr. Smith. He is the president of the twelve.

Mr. Tayler. The president?

Mr. Smith. Yes, sir.

Mr. Tayler. And is, according to the experience of the church, in the line of succession to you?

Mr. Smith. That is the understanding.

Mr. Tayler. That is the understanding?

Senator Overman. What is his name?

Mr. Worthington. Lyman.

Mr. Smith. F[rancis]. M. Lyman.

Mr. Tayler. Is he a polygamist?

Mr. Smith. Mr. Chairman, as Mr. Lyman is here, would it not be proper for him to answer the question himself?

The Chairman. If you know you had better answer it.

Mr. Smith. I know only by reputation. He is reputed to have two wives.[42]

Senator Beveridge. Mr. Smith, I should like to ask you a question, with the permission of the chairman.

The Chairman. Certainly.

---

41. Francis M. Lyman (1840-1916) was ordained to the Quorum of Twelve on October 27, 1880, and sustained as president of the Twelve on October 6, 1903.

42. Lyman's wives and children were: 1. Clara Caroline Callister (1850-92), married Lyman 1869—children Richard Roswell (1870-1963), George Albert (1873-1906), Lucy Smith (1876-1971), Ida (1878-1968), John Callister (1880-1951), Amy (1882-1975), and Don Callister (1886-1992); 2. Susan Delilah Callister (1863-1945), married Lyman 1884—children Clark (1891), Waldo Wilcken (1893-1971), Grant Herbert (1896-1918), Florence (1898-1977), Rudger Clawson (1900-09), and Helen Mar (1904-?); 3. Clara Caroline Callister (1850-92), married Lyman 1869, no children; and 4. Rhoda Ann Taylor (1840-1917), married Cowley 1857—children Rhoda Alice (1859-1942), Ellen Taylor (1861-81), Francis Marion (1863-1957), Edna Jane (1866-1932), Louisa Ann (1868-1906), Mary Crisman (1871-1965), Lois Victoria (1876-1966), Ada Alta (1878-81), and Hila Olive (1881-82). For Lyman's testimony, see *Smoot Hearings,* 1:426-74.

SENATOR BEVERIDGE. Has any of these men about whom Mr. Tayler has asked you married plural wives since the manifesto?

MR. SMITH. No, sir; not one of them.

SENATOR BEVERIDGE. Then the wives that you refer to were wives married before the manifesto?

MR. SMITH. Before the manifesto for years.

SENATOR PETTUS. They were married before?

SENATOR BEVERIDGE. I was asking whether any have taken wives since.

MR. SMITH. Let me say to you, Mr. Senator—I have said it, but I repeat it—there has not any man, with the consent or knowledge or approval of the church, ever married a plural wife since the manifesto.[43]

THE CHAIRMAN. Proceed, Mr. Tayler.

MR. TAYLER. Now, Mr. Smith, do you remember a few years ago the death of the wife of George Teasdale?

MR. SMITH. I have some recollection of being at a funeral.

MR. TAYLER. Was that the funeral of Marion Scoles?[44]

MR. SMITH. I believe it was, although I was not acquainted with the lady.

MR. TAYLER. George Teasdale was an apostle?

MR. SMITH. Yes, sir.

MR. TAYLER. You are the head of the church?

MR. SMITH. I am now, but at that time I was not.

MR. TAYLER. No. I am making your knowledge now the predicate for this question which I want to ask you in good faith. If Marion Scoles never heard of George Teasdale or saw him, and lived in another country prior to 1893, how could she have become his wife if he had another wife living at that time?

MR. VAN COTT. Just a moment, Mr. Smith. Mr. Chairman, I object to the question. The witness is asked a hypothetical question on something that is entirely immaterial and irrelevant. If Mr. Smith knows any facts, ask him about the facts, but do not ask him a question of this kind. I should like to have the stenographer read the question. It is entirely immaterial to ask him to give his opinion in a matter of this kind.

THE CHAIRMAN. The question asked him was how a certain person could become this party's wife—I suppose the counsel means under the practice of the church; how that could be done.

MR. TAYLER. Yes.

---

43. This was technically true since permission had come from individual church officials and not from the church as a whole.

44. Scoles was Teasdale's fifth wife, thirty-four years his junior.

THE CHAIRMAN. When she was in another country.

MR. VAN COTT. I should like to have the question read, just to show that it is a supposition instead of asking for a fact.

SENATOR HOAR. In the first place, the witness has stated his belief about this gentleman; then he stated that no person, with the knowledge of the authorities of the church, with their consent or approval, has contracted a plural marriage since the manifesto. Now, it seems to me fair, as testing the accuracy of Mr. Smith's understanding, to call his attention to this condition and ask him how it could have been brought about. ...

MR. SMITH. I do not know anything about the lady. I do not know whether she lived in another country or not; I never saw the lady but once before her funeral in my life. I do not know anything about his marrying her—when or where or in what way.

SENATOR HOAR. The question, as I understand it, is whether there is any way known to the witness by which a person not in this country prior to 1893 could have been married to the party inquired of before the manifesto. That is the substance of the question.

MR. SMITH. I do not know of any way by which it could have been done. May I state this, Mr. Chairman?

THE CHAIRMAN. That answers the question, but if you wish to proceed you may do so.

MR. SMITH. That answers the question. I wish to clear up one point, so far as my understanding goes.

THE CHAIRMAN. All right.

MR. SMITH. That is, at the time, whenever it may have been, as I have heard Mr. Teasdale say, when he married Marion Scoles he did not understand that he had any wife living at all. ...

SENATOR HOAR. I merely wish to ask him this question for my own personal information. When your agents meet, converse with, or solicit persons to join your church, in other parts of the world than Utah, do they not urge, as you understand it, the rightfulness of polygamy from a religious point of view?

MR. SMITH. Never.

SENATOR HOAR. To-day?

MR. SMITH. To-day, never. Only when they are forced into a defense of their belief. They do not advocate nor teach the doctrine nor inculcate it in any way, shape, or form.[45]

---

45. J. Reuben Clark's copy of the hearings placed the majority of questions and answers in this exchange within brackets.

SENATOR HOAR. That is, if anybody should raise the question, which has been applied to you, with the agent, the agent would answer as you have answered, perhaps. But what I want to know is, whether if you employ a man to go to England or to Massachusetts, or anywhere else, to solicit converts or adherents to the Mormon Church, to come to Utah and join you, whether or not those agents are instructed now, to-day, to preach—I do not speak of its lawfulness in regard to the statutes or acts of Congress—the rightfulness of polygamy as from a religious point of view. I understand you to [be] negative [to] that in the fullest degree?

MR. SMITH. In the fullest degree?

SENATOR HOAR. Yes.

MR. SMITH. And let me add, Mr. Senator, that in every instance our elders who are sent out to preach the gospel are instructed not to advocate plural marriage in their ministrations. It is a thing of the past. ...

THE CHAIRMAN. The committee will now take a recess until 2 o'clock. ...

MR. TAYLER. Mr. Smith, just before the recess of the committee you were asked a question by Senator Hoar, as to whether your missionaries, and those who were sent out by you to preach your doctrines, inculcated or declared the doctrine of polygamy. Somewhat in substance I think that was the inquiry, and you answered that they did not.

MR. SMITH. I did answer that they did not, and I further said that they were invariably instructed, before they left their homes, not to teach that doctrine and not to engage, if they could avoid it, in any discussions of that doctrine; and I would add to that that they do not enter into any discussion of that doctrine except where they are compelled to defend their belief.[46]

MR. TAYLER. The belief of your missionaries is that polygamy is a divinely ordained relation?

MR. SMITH. I can not say what the belief of our elders is on that subject.

MR. TAYLER. You can not?

MR. SMITH. No, sir; they have their own individual beliefs.

MR. TAYLER. Are you familiar with a little book published by the "Deseret News" entitled "Ready References; a Compilation of Scripture Texts," etc.?

MR. SMITH. Yes, sir.

---

46. Seventeen days later, Smith informed Smoot: "We have taken every pains we could to caution our Elders against making any allusions to your 'Case', so called. We have said teach the 1st principles of the gospel and let politics severely alone. We will continue to do so" (Mar. 20, 1904).

MR. TAYLER. "Designed especially for the use of missionaries and Scripture students?"

MR. SMITH. I am acquainted with it.

MR. TAYLER. That is a book that is used by your missionaries?

MR. SMITH. I suppose it is used more or less by them.

MR. TAYLER. Well, it is correctly described on its title page as designed for their use, is it not?

MR. SMITH. Yes.

MR. TAYLER. Is there a chapter in that on the subject of polygamy?

MR. SMITH. Yes, sir.

MR. TAYLER. An argument in favor of polygamy and its propriety?[47]

MR. SMITH. Yes, sir.

MR. TAYLER. Is there any qualification within the covers of that book of that doctrine and belief in plural marriage?

MR. SMITH. Not that I know of. That book, I may say, was published, as will be seen if you will give the date, a great many years ago.

MR. TAYLER. Yes.

MR. SMITH. And it has been in existence a great many years. I do not know anything about recent editions of it, whether that has been continued in it or not.

MR. TAYLER. I notice this, in the preface of the third edition—

SENATOR DILLINGHAM.[48] What is the date of that edition, Mr. Tayler?

MR. TAYLER. I am about to read it so as to get in its order as it is. The latter part of this preface is as follows: "Some improvement has been made in the arrangement of the references, and a few passages have been

---

47. The sections of the "Ready Reference" dealing with polygamy were entered into the official hearings (1:216-26).

48. Dillingham was a friend of Smoot and at times provided him with insider information about the committee. For instance, Smoot wrote to Joseph F. Smith:

This afternoon I had a long talk with Senator Dillingham, and asked him to tell me just what happened at the Committee meeting last Saturday [Jan. 9, 1904]. ... [Dillingham explained] he [Burrows] commenced to read a letter stating that it was from a very dear friend of his ... He then began to read the letter to the Committee, and it contained a most bitter attack upon the Mormon Church. He had not proceeded very far when ... Dillingham interrupted him and asked if the letter was a personal one, and ... Burrows answered that it was. Dillingham asked ... Burrows if he intended to use the letter in the case, and if ... Smoot would be given a chance to read it and answer it. Burrows remarked that I would not be permitted to see it as it was written to him as a personal letter. Dillingham remarked that this was manifestly unfair and that the Chairman certainly knew it. Burrows did not answer him, but put up the letter and commenced to explain his position. From the remarks made, every one on the Committee knew that he was very bitter and is going to do all in his power to draw the Church into the investigation" (Jan. 11, 1904).

added. Otherwise this edition is similar to the former. That the work may prove acceptable to the public and great good result from its more extensive publication is the earnest desire of the publishers. Salt Lake City, October 12, 1902." Do you recall the statement in this little book, under the head of "Patriarchal marriage," the declaration, "Polygamy implied in the Savior's promise?"

MR. WORTHINGTON. What is the page, Mr. Tayler?

MR. TAYLER. Page 135.

MR. SMITH. My recollection—

MR. TAYLER. Do you recollect that? I do not want to interfere with any statement you want to make.

MR. SMITH. Not specifically; no. I would like to say that that chapter in the book is devoted entirely to Scriptural references and historical references with reference to the principle of plural marriage, extending back in the days of Judea, and all the way down—simply Bible references and historical references in respect to that principle. That is my recollection of it.

MR. TAYLER. There are a large number of references here besides those taken from the Bible.

MR. SMITH. I understand; from history.

MR. TAYLER. Quite a discussion of the subject.

MR. SMITH. Yes, sir.

MR. TAYLER. Following the extracts from the Bible?

MR. SMITH. Yes.

MR. TAYLER. Running down to modern times. Do you recall the marginal description of the text in these words, "Polygamy right in the sight of God?"

MR. SMITH. From a scriptural standpoint, yes. I would like to add that according to my best understanding the use of that book by our elders is almost entirely abandoned, it having been set forth to them that it is better for them to take the Bible and the standard works of the church as they are, independent of all auxiliary writings or books. ...

MR. TAYLER. In 1892, Mr. Smith, how many wives did you have?

MR. SMITH. In 1892?

MR. TAYLER. Yes.

MR. SMITH. I had five.[49]

MR. TAYLER. Who was your first wife? You spoke of her this morning.

MR. SMITH. Mrs. J. L. Smith.

---

49. The previous two questions and answers were included in Burrows's majority report to the Senate (*Smoot Hearings,* 4:489).

MR. TAYLER. Mrs. J. L. Smith?

MR. SMITH. Yes, sir.

MR. TAYLER. What was her name?

MR. SMITH. Her name was Lamson.

MR. TAYLER. What was her first name?

MR. SMITH. Julina.

MR. TAYLER. Did you have a wife Levira?

MR. SMITH. Yes.

MR. TAYLER. When did she die?

MR. SMITH. Many years ago.

MR. TAYLER. Many years ago?

MR. SMITH. Yes, sir.

MR. TAYLER. How many years ago?

MR. SMITH. I could not tell you that.

MR. TAYLER. You can not remember the year in which she died?

MR. SMITH. No, sir.

MR. TAYLER. She is the only one of your wives who has died, is she?

MR. SMITH. She is the only one who has died.

MR. TAYLER. And have you no idea when it was she died?

MR. SMITH. No, sir; I have not, for this reason: I will state before the committee that she was divorced from me many years before she died, and I lost track of her.

MR. TAYLER. How was she divorced?

MR. SMITH. By the fourth judicial district court of San Francisco, I believe, as near as I recollect.

MR. TAYLER. Had you obtained a church divorce from her?

MR. SMITH. I had.

MR. TAYLER. Prior to that time?

MR. SMITH. No, sir; she obtained a church divorce from me prior to that time.[50]

MR. WORTHINGTON. This seems to have been twenty years or more prior to 1890, the date of the manifesto?

MR. SMITH. It was a long time before the manifesto, Mr. Chairman.

THE CHAIRMAN. Yes; the Chair understands that. What is the purpose of this, Mr. Tayler?

---

50. Brigham Young performed the ceremony in his office on April 5, 1859, joining Joseph F. Smith (age twenty) to Levira Clark (age sixteen). This was Smith's first marriage. It ended seven years later when on October 4, 1866, Smith found her with another man. A few months earlier (May 5), Smith had married his second wife, Julina. Soon thereafter, on July 1, he was secretly ordained an apostle by Young. There was not a vacancy at the time in the Quorum of the Twelve.

SENATOR BEVERIDGE. Inasmuch as the witness has testified to this extent, I think he should be allowed to speak further.

THE CHAIRMAN. There is no objection, then.

MR. SMITH. I would like to say, Mr. Chairman, if you please, that it is very embarrassing and trying to me to publicly announce my private domestic affairs before this committee.

MR. TAYLER. As far as I am concerned, I do not care so much about that. You can proceed as you please.

MR. SMITH. I do it very reluctantly, simply because I am required to do so by this honorable committee. I regret it very much, and I wish to say that much to the committee, because my statements and testimony here are going to the world, and I do not want it understood, being compelled, as I have been, to give information and to make statements of opinion in relation to my friends, that I am in any sense a spotter or an informer. If there is anything, gentleman, that I despise it is an infamous spotter and informer,[51] and I am not one of those. I wish to state that in order that it may go down on record.

THE CHAIRMAN. Very well. Proceed, Mr. Tayler.

MR. TAYLER. One of the often-declared principles of your church is, "Mind your own business," is it not?[52]

MR. SMITH. You are correct.

MR. TAYLER. Now, did you not, along about 1896 or 1897, claim that Levira had not been divorced from you and that you were entitled to share in the property of which she was possessed at the time of her death?

MR. SMITH. I will make a statement of that fact.

MR. TAYLER. I would like to have you answer categorically, if you can.

MR. SMITH. I prefer not to say yes or no.

MR. TAYLER. Well, proceed.

MR. SMITH. An attorney, a friend of mine—

MR. TAYLER. As I stated, to find out if he did not have six wives instead of five at the time of the manifesto.

MR. SMITH. Mr. Chairman, she was divorced from me many years before that in California.

---

51. Smith is alluding to Charles Mostyn Owen, a well-known anti-Mormon. Owen made a career spying on polygamous Mormon households. For Owen's full testimony before the committee, see *Smoot Hearings,* 2:395-405, 412-38.

52. This oft-quoted phrase was known in LDS circles as the "Mormon Creed" or "Eleventh Commandment" and was placed in the masthead of John Taylor's newspaper, *The Mormon.*

The Chairman. That seems to dispose of the matter, so far as that is concerned. ...

The Chairman. One moment, Mr. Smith. How is it as to the property you hold in trust?

Mr. Smith. The property I hold in trust belongs to the church, and when I am no more the title to the property that I hold in trust for the church will go to my successor as trustee in trust. My individual holdings—

The Chairman. That is, to the next president?

Mr. Smith. To the next president or the next trustee in trust. It does not follow always that the president is the trustee in trust.[53]

Senator Dillingham. Does that property on the books of the corporation stand in the name of the church or in the name of an individual as trustee?

Mr. Smith. It stands in the name of an individual as trustee in trust.

Mr. Tayler. In what form does your church have title to the Deseret News property?

Mr. Smith. It owns the deed.

Mr. Tayler. I am speaking now of the newspaper, not the building.

Mr. Smith. The press; yes. I would like to state that when I was asked that question before, Mr. Tayler, I was not aware of the fact that I have since learned from my counsel here that during the trusteeship of Lorenzo Snow the "Deseret News" plant was transferred from the Deseret News Company to Lorenzo Snow, trustee, in trust. I was not aware of the fact, Mr. Chairman, when that question was asked me yesterday, I believe it was. I have since learned that that is the fact and that my counsel, who is here, made out the papers for the transfer.

The Chairman. That correction will appear, of course.

Mr. Smith. Thank you.

Mr. Tayler. So that it is in you as trustee in trust?

Mr. Smith. Now I own it as trustee in trust. Furthermore, I will say that I have discovered since yesterday that there is published on the second or third page of the "Deseret News" the statement that it is the organ of the Church of Jesus Christ of Latter-Day Saints, and it is such in this capacity that when the church has any proclamation to make public they print it in the "Deseret News." The business department of the "Deseret News" is run precisely on the same business principles that any and every other newspaper enterprise is run upon.

---

53. J. Reuben Clark's copy of the hearings has a check mark in the margin next to this answer from Smith.

SENATOR BEVERIDGE. Are its editorials supposed to be an expression of the church opinion?

MR. SMITH. Not at all; and the church is not responsible for the editorial expressions unless they are issued over the signatures of the presidency of the church.

SENATOR BEVERIDGE. If any editorial appears in that paper advising the leaders to take a certain political course is that in any wise an authority of the church?

MR. SMITH. Not in the least. It is as independent as any newspaper in Utah in its expressions and publications.

MR. TAYLER. As independent as any newspaper could be of its owner.[54]

MR. SMITH. As independent as any paper in Utah, sir. I make no exception whatever.

THE CHAIRMAN. Mr. Smith, who is the editor of the paper?

MR. SMITH. Charles W. Penrose.

THE CHAIRMAN. Is he connected with your church?

MR. SMITH. Yes, sir; he is an elder in the church.

SENATOR BEVERIDGE. Is he a polygamist?

THE CHAIRMAN. He is not one of the apostles.

MR. SMITH. No, sir.

THE CHAIRMAN. Is he a polygamist?

MR. SMITH. I understand that he is.

MR. TAYLER. Is he one of the first presidents of the seventies?

MR. SMITH. No, sir; he is not.

MR. TAYLER. What is he besides what you have described him to be, if anything, officially?

MR. SMITH. He has been until recently the second councilor to the president of the Salt Lake Stake of Zion. ...

MR. TAYLER. The prophet, Joseph Smith, jr., received a great many revelations pertaining to temporal affairs, did he not?

MR. SMITH. I would hardly say a great many, but he did receive some revelations with regard to temporal affairs.

MR. TAYLER. They were received by the people, were they?

MR. SMITH. They were accepted generally by the members of the church.

MR. TAYLER. And they are recognized now as having been revelations from Almighty God, are they not?

MR. SMITH. Yes, sir.

MR. TAYLER. Just as binding upon the conscience of those who receive them as any other revelation that Joseph Smith received?

---

54. J. Reuben Clark's copy of the hearings marked this exchange with brackets.

Mr. Smith. Just as binding on the conscience of members of the church as baptism for the remission of sins and the laying on of hands for the Holy Ghost.

Mr. Tayler. And polygamy?

Mr. Smith. And I will say to the gentlemen of the committee that there is not, and can not be, any possible restraint held over the members of the Church of Jesus Christ of Latter-Day Saints except the restraint which people themselves voluntarily give. Every man and woman and member of the church is as free to belong to the church or to withdraw from it as any other man or woman in the world, and there is no restraint over them except their voluntary wish.

Mr. Tayler. Then the Almighty does not speak by revelations directly to them?

Mr. Smith. Yes, sir; but men obey it or not as they please. They are at liberty to obey or not, just as they please.[55]

Mr. Tayler. Exactly.

Mr. Smith. And they disobey if they wish with perfect impunity.

Mr. Tayler. In your conception of God, then, He is not omnipotent and omniscient?

Mr. Smith. Oh, yes; I think He is.

Mr. Tayler. But do you mean to say you, at your pleasure, obey or disobey the commands of Almighty God?

Mr. Smith. Yes, sir.

Mr. Tayler. Communicated to you?

Mr. Smith. I obey or disobey at my will.

Mr. Tayler. Just as you please?

Mr. Smith. Just as I please.

Mr. Tayler. And that is the kind of a God you believe in?

Mr. Smith. That is exactly the kind of a God I believe in ...

Senator Hoar. Let me ask one question right there. When was that official consent, if ever, given to Mr. Smoot to come here as Senator of the United States? How; in what form?

Senator Beveridge. Did he have to get your consent?

Mr. Smith. He did. He applied to his associates for their consent for him to become a candidate before the legislature for Senator of the United States.

The Chairman. Whom do you mean by his associates?

Mr. Smith. His associates, the apostles.

---

55. J. Reuben Clark's copy of the hearings has check marks in the margins of Smith's last three answers in this exchange.

THE CHAIRMAN. The twelve?

MR. SMITH. The twelve apostles; yes, sir.

MR. TAYLER. And the first presidency?

MR. SMITH. And the first presidency; and he obtained their unanimous consent to become a candidate if he chose.[56]

MR. TAYLER. Did anybody else obtain their unanimous consent to become a candidate at that time for that office?

MR. SMITH. I do not know that any official member of the church was a candidate at that time.

MR. TAYLER. Then nobody else whose duty it was to obtain consent to run for that office asked?

MR. SMITH. There was no one else a candidate who was an official member of the church.

SENATOR BEVERIDGE. Under what conditions was that consent given?

MR. SMITH. Under what conditions?

SENATOR BEVERIDGE. Were any conditions attached to the consent?

MR. SMITH. None whatever. We simply released him from his duty as one of our number to become a candidate and to attend to the duties of the Senatorship if he was elected.

SENATOR BEVERIDGE. I understand you then to say he does not attend to the duties of the apostolate?

MR. SMITH. Not while he is here; he can not.

SENATOR DUBOIS. Did anyone else ask your consent to be a candidate for the United States Senate at that time?

MR. SMITH. Not at that time, because there was no official member of the church a candidate at that time.

SENATOR DUBOIS. No one else of either party or any other citizen of Utah received your consent, except Apostle Smoot, to become a candidate for the United States Senate?[57]

---

56. J. Reuben Clark's copy of the hearings has a check mark in the margin next to this answer by Smith.

57. Almost a year later, Dubois spoke to the Mothers' Congress in Washington, D.C., on "The Purity of the Home" and declared that

Mormonism is a decided, if not the greatest, single menace which confronts us as a people. ... The political strength of this organization has vastly increased, until now, in addition to absolutely controlling Utah, [they have] the balance of power in Idaho and Wyoming, and are spreading over and through Oregon and Nevada and have a following of no inconsiderable importance in other western states. Their great aim is political power so as to protect them in their polygamous practices. It is impossible to elect a senator from Utah, Idaho or Wyoming who will oppose the methods and practices and governing power of the Mormon church. I do not mean to be understood by this statement that the Mormon hierarchy is strong enough to select

MR. SMITH. I wish to be understood that no one else, so far as my knowledge extends, who was a candidate for that position was an official member of the church. That is what I wish to convey.

THE CHAIRMAN. Mr. Smith, I desire to ask you who made this request; Mr. Smoot himself?

MR. SMITH. Mr. Smoot himself.

THE CHAIRMAN. Was it in writing?

MR. SMITH. No, sir.

THE CHAIRMAN. Was it at a meeting of the apostles and the president?

MR. SMITH. I think not. If I mistake not, he asked these people individually.

SENATOR OVERMAN. Were any minutes kept of the meeting where he was released?

MR. SMITH. No, sir; not that I am aware of.

SENATOR BEVERIDGE. It is not as formal a matter as that, then?

MR. SMITH. No, sir; it is simply a consent on the part of his associates to yield their claim upon his services in the church to become a candidate before the legislature.[58]

MR. WORTHINGTON. Is it anything more than a leave of absence?

MR. SMITH. That is all. It is practically that.

SENATOR BEVERIDGE. One or two questions were asked you by Senator Dubois, Mr. Smith, which suggest something to me. Did the fact that you gave consent to Mr. Smoot to be a candidate for the United States

---

the senators in Idaho and Wyoming, but I do say that they are sufficiently powerful to defeat any one for the United States senate in either of those states if they desire to ... Notwithstanding the testimony which Joseph [F.] Smith gave before the senate committee, no one has the temerity in Utah to undertake and to prosecute him, and it is utterly impossible to enforce the laws of Utah against him. ... I ought to close, but I must say a few words about the Mormon people, the followers. Most of them practice the virtues of industry, thrift, sobriety, honesty, and, outside of polygamy, personal virtue. Their articles of faith seem to them to represent to them all the morality, and the revelations which their leaders proclaim from time to time seem to them to set them above all other peoples of the world ("Senator Dubois to the Mothers," *Salt Lake Herald*, Mar. 15, 1905).

Following this speech, Utah's junior Senator, George Sutherland, responded: "I was elected to the senate without the support in any way, shape or manner of the 'Mormon' Church. ... I did not have directly or indirectly the aid of the 'Mormon Church or any of its leaders.' ... My judgment is that ... Joseph F. Smith, ever since he has been the head of the Church, has absolutely kept his hands out, and the Church clear of politics. ... If Senator Dubois asserts the contrary, he simply does not know what he is talking about. In regard to polygamy, the conditions are greatly exaggerated ("Sutherland and Dubois," *Deseret News*, Mar. 16, 1905).

58. J. Reuben Clark's copy of the hearings has two checkmarks in the margins next to this question and answer.

Senate in any wise interfere with your giving consent to any other member of the apostolate, if they had asked it?

MR. SMITH. Not in the least.

SENATOR BEVERIDGE. Would you have given consent to more than one?

MR. SMITH. Yes, sir; if they had asked it.

SENATOR HOAR. Was a similar consent given to Mr. Cannon when he came to the Senate?

MR. SMITH. How is that?

SENATOR HOAR. Was Mr. Cannon, when he came to the Senate, given official consent?

MR. SMITH. Let me ask you which Cannon you mean.

SENATOR HOAR. The only one who came to the Senate.

MR. VAN COTT. Frank J. Cannon.[59]

MR. SMITH. He is not and never has been an official member, of the church, in any sense or form.[60] ...

MR. TAYLER. Your quorums are generally in harmony?

MR. SMITH. They are generally in harmony.

MR. TAYLER. It is very rare, indeed, that you are not a unit?

MR. SMITH. I am very happy to say, sir, that is the fact.

MR. TAYLER. And that all the twelve and the three agree, as a rule?

MR. SMITH. Yes, sir; as a rule.

MR. TAYLER. And it is seldom it has ever been otherwise?

MR. SMITH. Quite so; although, let me add, Mr. Tayler, it has been so. It has not always been unanimous. There are exceptions to that rule.

MR. TAYLER. Exactly. Can you give us a recent exception to that rule?

MR. SMITH. Yes, sir.

MR. TAYLER. In what case?

---

59. J. Reuben Clark's copy of the hearings has a checkmark in the margin next to this answer. Frank J. Canon, son of George Q. Cannon, was editor of the *Salt Lake Tribune*. Carl Badger wrote to his wife on March 15, 1904: "The [Washington] Post this morning has a picture of Frank J. Cannon, accompanying a telegraphic announcement of his excommunication. I am told that the reason that Frank was cut off at this time was that he and others contemplated charging President Smith with apostasy at the coming Conference. I do not know that this is true" (Badger, *Liahona and Iron Rod*, 262). Prior to Cannon's excommunication, he published two especially inflammatory editorials in the *Tribune*, followed by an open letter defending his statement that "Joseph F. Smith was a false prophet and was leading the people astray" ("F. J. Cannon Finally Excommunicated," *Salt Lake Herald*, Mar. 15, 1905).

60. As evidenced by this quote, there was no love lost between Smith and Cannon. In 1911, Cannon would write a scathing attack on Smith entitled *Under the Prophet in Utah*.

MR. SMITH. In the case of Moses Thatcher.[61]

MR. TAYLER. What was the trouble with him?

MR. SMITH. He was not in harmony with his council for a great many years.

SENATOR FORAKER. Did he remain an apostle all the while?

MR. SMITH. All the while.

MR. TAYLER. He did not remain all the while, did he?

MR. SMITH. He remained all the while for years.

MR. TAYLER. Yes; until—

MR. SMITH. Until final action was taken on his case by his quorum.

MR. TAYLER. And they deposed him?

MR. SMITH. They deposed him.

MR. TAYLER. Did he have a formal trial?

MR. SMITH. Yes, sir.

MR. TAYLER. He was present?

MR. SMITH. That is to say, let me say to you, a time, an appointment for a trial was set, and he was urged to appear, and notified to appear by his council.

MR. TAYLER. Yes.

SENATOR BEVERIDGE. What was the occasion of his being out of harmony with his quorum?

SENATOR HOAR. Let him finish his answer.

SENATOR BEVERIDGE. Very well.

MR. SMITH. And he refused to appear, and absented himself from the council, declining to answer or respond to the call to be there.[62]

MR. TAYLER. Were charges formulated against him?

MR. WORTHINGTON. He has not yet finished his answer.

MR. TAYLER. Very well, I thought he had.

MR. SMITH. And long prior to this circumstance he had been out of harmony with the other members of the quorum, and had absented himself from their meetings many times in succession.[63] ...

MR. TAYLER. Mr. Smith, what was the immediate occasion of the controversy with Moses Thatcher at the time of his deposition?

---

61. Thatcher (1842-1909) was ordained to the Quorum of Twelve Apostles on April 7, 1879.

62. For more on this, see Edward Leo Lyman, "The Alienation of an Apostle from His Quorum: The Moses Thatcher Case," *Dialogue: A Journal of Mormon Thought* 18 (Summer 1985): 67-91; Kenneth W. Godfrey, "Moses Thatcher in the Dock: His Trials, the Aftermath, and His Last Days," *Journal of Mormon History* 24 (Spring 1988): 54-88. For Thatcher's full testimony, see *Smoot Hearings,* 1:936-1050.

63. J. Reuben Clark's copy of the hearings marked this exchange with brackets.

MR. SMITH. The immediate, that is, the principal, circumstance which led to the final investigation of his status was his becoming a candidate for a political office without consulting with his associates. That was the beginning of the investigation.

SENATOR DUBOIS. What office was that did you say?

MR. SMITH. I could not tell you now what office it was. I think he was a candidate for Senator, or something or that kind.

MR. TAYLER. United States Senator?

MR. SMITH. I am not sure, but I think that was the case.

MR. TAYLER. Mr. Smith, do you recall a document published by the "Deseret News," entitled "The Thatcher episode: A concise statement of the facts in the case. Interesting letters and documents and review of M. Thatcher's claims, pleas, and admissions"?

MR. SMITH. Yes; I recollect the journal.[64]

MR. TAYLER. Published in 1896?

MR. SMITH. I remember.

MR. TAYLER. That was intended, was it not, to give the church's side of that controversy?

MR. SMITH. The church had nothing to do with it.

MR. TAYLER. I understood you to say that Moses Thatcher—

MR. SMITH. With the publication of this book, I mean.

MR. TAYLER. It was published by the "Deseret News," was it not?

MR. SMITH. That is very true, but it was done for the author.

MR. TAYLER. Do you know who was the author?

MR. SMITH. There was one pamphlet of that character published by C[harles]. W. Penrose, and there was another one also on that same order published by a man by the name of Nelson,[65] and they were their own personal views.

MR. TAYLER. Exactly. C[harles]. W. Penrose is the C[harles]. W. Penrose of whom you have spoken?

MR. SMITH. Yes.

MR. TAYLER. And the editor of the "Deseret News"?

MR. SMITH. Yes.

MR. TAYLER. Do you know whether the document I have and now show you is the one Mr. Penrose prepared?

MR. SMITH. I could not tell you.

----

64. The entire pamphlet was entered into the record as part of Smith's testimony (1:247-86).

65. Nels L. Nelson, *An Open Letter to Hon. Moses Thatcher* (Feb. 16, 1897).

Mr. TAYLER. Can you tell me, Mr. Van Cott? I do not want to get any confused statement.

Mr. VAN COTT. I do not know. I could find out for you this evening, probably.

Mr. TAYLER. All right.

Mr. SMITH. Is there no title to it?

Mr. TAYLER. There is no signature.

Mr. SMITH. I rather think, sir, that C[harles]. W. Penrose is the author of that, but I do not know. ...

THE CHAIRMAN. Mr. Smith, I want to ask a question. To go back a little, you were inquired of in relation to an occasion when you were in Los Angeles and went out to an island.

Mr. SMITH. Yes, sir.

THE CHAIRMAN. What I want to inquire of you is whether there was any ceremony of any kind performed by you?

Mr. SMITH. No, sir.

THE CHAIRMAN. None whatever.

Mr. SMITH. None whatever.

THE CHAIRMAN. Now, one other question. You have said that you know of no instance of plural marriages since 1890?

Mr. SMITH. Yes.

THE CHAIRMAN. Performed in the State of Utah?

Mr. WORTHINGTON. By the church, of course?

Mr. SMITH. Yes.

SENATOR FORAKER. Or with their approval.

THE CHAIRMAN. I so understood you.

Mr. SMITH. Yes, sir.[66]

THE CHAIRMAN. Will you state whether you have performed any plural marriages outside the State of Utah?

Mr. SMITH. No, sir; I never have.

THE CHAIRMAN. Either in Mexico or—

Mr. SMITH. Nowhere on earth, sir.

THE CHAIRMAN. Do you know of any such?

Mr. SMITH. No, sir; I do not.

THE CHAIRMAN. That is all.

Mr. SMITH. I wish to say again, Mr. Chairman, that there have been no plural marriages solemnized by and with the consent or by the knowl-

---

66. This was technically true since the church itself did not officially approve or perform any post-Manifesto plural marriage.

edge of the Church of Jesus Christ of Latter-Day Saints by any man. I
do not care who he is.

THE CHAIRMAN. I understood that.

MR. WORTHINGTON. Since the manifesto?

MR. SMITH. I mean that, of course. I understand that this investigation
comes in after the manifesto.

SENATOR DUBOIS. If an apostle of the church had performed such a ceremony within or without the jurisdiction of the United States, would
you consider that being with the authority of your church?

MR. SMITH. If any apostle or any other man claiming authority should do
any such thing as that, he would not only be subject to prosecution
and heavy fine and imprisonment in the State under the State law,
but he would also be subjected to discipline and excommunication
from the church by the proper tribunals of the church.

SENATOR FORAKER. As for the excommunication from the church, that
would be imposed upon him no matter whether it were performed inside the United States or outside?

MR. SMITH. I do not know any different. It is contrary to the rules of the
church.

SENATOR FORAKER. That was the question asked you—whether or not, if
performed without the United States, these penalties would be imposed.

MR. SMITH. Well, it would be all the same. If any complaint was made of
any such thing as that and proof had, the man doing it would not only
be subject to prosecution under the law, but he would be subject to
discipline in the church.

SENATOR FORAKER. The point I wish to call your attention to is that, if performed without the United States, he could not be prosecuted for it in
Utah?

MR. SMITH. Oh, no.

SENATOR FORAKER. It would not be an offense against the laws of Utah?

MR. SMITH. To be sure.

SENATOR FORAKER. But would the church, nevertheless, impose its penalty of excommunication?[67]

MR. SMITH. It would. Mr. Senator, if any complaint of that kind was made
and proven.

---

67. Referring to exchanges like this, Smith later spoke positively of the courtesy
shown him by Senators Dillingham and Foraker, whom he characterized as "the only
members of the Committee who seemed to have a particle of human sympathy for us
while there in the crucial test to which I was subjected and I love them for their humanity" (Smith to Smoot, May 18, 1906).

THE CHAIRMAN. You say permission was given to Senator Smoot, I understand, to be a candidate for the Senate?[68]

MR. SMITH. Yes.

THE CHAIRMAN. Suppose permission had been denied by the president and the apostles and associates, and he was commanded not to be a candidate and he had persisted in being a candidate, what action would have been taken?

MR. SMITH. His associates would have considered him out of harmony with them.

THE CHAIRMAN. Out of harmony?

MR. SMITH. Yes; out of harmony.

THE CHAIRMAN. And when they found it was not in harmony, then what?

MR. SMITH. I do not know that any action would follow that; except that he would not be in good fellowship with his associates.[69]

THE CHAIRMAN. Would he still continue as an apostle?

MR. SMITH. Unless he committed some overt act of unchristian-like conduct, or rebellion, I may say—or at least I use the word rebellion—against the church. ...

THE CHAIRMAN. Have you anything further with this witness, Mr. Tayler?

MR. TAYLER. I wanted to ask a question or two. Do you make any distinction, when you speak of marriage and marriage ceremony, between marriage and sealing or sealing in marriage?

MR. SMITH. No difference, sir.

MR. TAYLER. The church now performs the ordinary marriage ceremonies, of course, Mr. Smith?

MR. SMITH. Yes, sir.

MR. TAYLER. And they are in form as they were when plural marriages were celebrated, are they?

MR. SMITH. The same form exactly.

MR. TAYLER. And do you have as many different kinds of marriage now as formerly?

MR. SMITH. We have as many different kinds of marriage now as formerly.[70]

MR. TAYLER. Let me call your attention to what I mean, because it will

---

68. J. Reuben Clark's copy of the hearings marked this question and answer with brackets.

69. J. Reuben Clark's copy of the hearings marked this question and answer with brackets.

70. J. Reuben Clark's copy of the hearings marked this exchange with brackets.

save time: Sealing for time only, sealing for time and eternity, and sealing for eternity only.

MR. SMITH. Yes, sir.

MR. TAYLER. Do you have those?

MR. SMITH. Yes, sir.

MR. TAYLER. All three of them.

MR. SMITH. All three of them.

MR. TAYLER. In all respects, except as to the solemnization of plural marriages, the practice and form of the church are the same as formerly?

MR. SMITH. The same as formerly.

MR. TAYLER. Do you keep records of all marriages?

MR. SMITH. We keep records of all marriages, I believe, as far as I know.

MR. TAYLER. Who is the custodian of those records?

MR. SMITH. Well, there are different persons.

MR. TAYLER. Do you mean they are at different places?

MR. SMITH. At different places; yes, sir.

MR. TAYLER. At what different places are they?

MR. SMITH. They are distributed at all the temples.

MR. TAYLER. How many temples are there in Utah, for instance?

MR. SMITH. There are four.

MR. TAYLER. Where?

MR. SMITH. At Logan, at Salt Lake City, at Manti, in Sanpete County, and at St. George, Washington County.

MR. TAYLER. Where in Utah may marriages be solemnized?

MR. SMITH. At these temples.

MR. TAYLER. And only at those temples?

MR. SMITH. Oh, no; any elder of the church can perform marriage ceremonies.

MR. TAYLER. Any elder of the church?

MR. SMITH. Any elder of the church.

MR. TAYLER. That is to say, practically any adult male inhabitant in the Mormon Church in Utah—

MR. SMITH. No.

MR. TAYLER. Can perform the marriage ceremony?

MR. SMITH. No; you are quite wrong. ...

SENATOR HOAR. Is there any State law for recording them?

MR. SMITH. Recording marriages? Yes, sir.

SENATOR HOAR. What is that?

MR. SMITH. It is, that no person is eligible to marriage without they are of a certain age—

SENATOR HOAR. No; about recording them.

MR. SMITH. That they must apply to the court for a license to marry, and a certificate of marriage that must be signed by the person officiating is handed to the person, to the woman generally, who is married, and the certificate, or license, rather, is returned to the court.

SENATOR HOAR. You do not answer, still, the one point I have in mind, which is the recording of the marriage itself. What is the State law when A B has been married lawfully, however that may be, to C D? Is there any law where that record shall be preserved?

MR. SMITH. In the courts.

SENATOR HOAR. In the courts?

MR. SMITH. Yes, sir.

SENATOR HOAR. Suppose, for instance, a person being a member of your communion applies to the proper authority, an elder or apostle, or anybody, and gets married, he has got first to get the license from the civil authority you speak of?

MR. SMITH. He has; yes.

SENATOR HOAR. And then after the marriage is solemnized, am I correct in understanding you that the certificate [indicates] that it has been solemnized by the officiating person—

MR. SMITH. Minister.

SENATOR HOAR. The minister, or whoever it is, is also recorded with the civil authority?

MR. SMITH. It is returned to the court, or to the clerk of the court, and is recorded.

SENATOR HOAR. The court which issues the license?

MR. SMITH. Yes, sir.

SENATOR HOAR. Is it true, then, that all Mormon marriages in recent years—I will not go back into old times, but to-day—are recorded by the civil tribunals of Utah?

MR. SMITH. Yes, sir.

SENATOR HOAR. That is what I wanted to know.

MR. VAN COTT. Mr. Tayler, might I ask a question just on that line referred to by Senator Hoar, to just clear this? Would you pardon it?

MR. TAYLER. That is all right.

SENATOR HOAR. Let me understand one thing. Would your church recognize as valid, or would your social life recognize as a lawfully married woman, a person whose marriage was not so authorized and recorded?

MR. SMITH. Yes, sir.

SENATOR HOAR. You would?

MR. SMITH. Yes sir.

MR. VAN COTT. Did you understand the question?

MR. SMITH. I do not know whether I did.

SENATOR HOAR. I want you to understand this carefully. I want to know whether, in case a person did not comply with this civil law?

MR. SMITH. Oh, I beg your pardon.

SENATOR HOAR. I do not mean in the case of some accidental omission, but in the case of a person who is not married according to that civil law; do you Mormons recognize that person, whether a member of your communion or not, as lawfully married?

MR. SMITH. No, sir.

MR. VAN COTT. The question I want to ask you along the line of Senator Hoar's questions, is this: Are any marriages performed by elders or in the temples unless they bring along this certificate from the clerk?

MR. SMITH. No.

SENATOR HOAR. Of course, the point of my question is, to know whether the Mormons, as a practice, are in the habit of performing secret marriages, or marriages unknown to the world outside?

MR. SMITH. No, sir; they do not do it.

THE CHAIRMAN. If parties were married in the temple, for instance, upon a license, would that marriage be recorded in the temple?

MR. SMITH. Yes, sir.

THE CHAIRMAN. It would be recorded in the temple?

MR. SMITH. It would be recorded in the temple.

THE CHAIRMAN. Would it also be recorded in the civil courts?

MR. SMITH. Yes, sir.

SENATOR DUBOIS. Is any outsider or Gentile ever admitted to any of these four temples you speak of?

MR. SMITH. No; nor a great many Mormons, either.

MR. TAYLER. Do you suppose there is any record of Abraham Cannon's marriage to Lillian Hamlin?

MR. SMITH. I do not know anything about it, sir.

MR. TAYLER. Of course there naturally would not be records of plural marriages now, would there?

MR. SMITH. No, sir. Well, there is no such thing.

MR. TAYLER. I say if anybody should happen to do that?

MR. SMITH. If they do I do not think they would dare to keep a record of it. ...

4.
Joseph F. Smith
Friday, March 4

"Very nearly the same party of women spectators adorned the walls as on each of the previous days. But the ladies had evidently passed the word to their friends that the hearing afforded great interest to all who like to pry into the family affairs of the neighbors. ... The afternoon session began minutes after 2 with several members of the committee absent. There were, however, five or six senators, not members [of the committee,] who found places among the spectators. The corridor leading to the committee room was more crowded than ever, men and women elbowing each other in their efforts to secure a sight of the witnesses who have been summoned. The room will seat about 75 people, aside from members of the committee and counsel. At least 500 have attempted to secure entrance during the day." —*Deseret News*, Mar. 4, 1904

Joseph F. Smith, having previously affirmed, was examined and testified as follows ...

SENATOR HOAR. Mr. Smith, I should like to ask one question. I am not sure that it has a direct bearing on this inquiry, and that is whether, in your church, in ecclesiastical or religious matters, women are recognized as in all respects the equals of men in rights and privileges?

MR. SMITH. As voters, they are recognized as equal with men. In the matter of the holding of priestly authority, they are not regarded as on the same plane that men are.

SENATOR HOAR. Are they admitted to hold what you call priestly authority?

MR. SMITH. Sir?

SENATOR HOAR. Are they admitted to hold what you call priestly authority?

MR. SMITH. I just remarked that in that respect they are not regarded as equal with men.

SENATOR HOAR. But that does not quite answer my question, you will see.

MR. SMITH. I beg pardon.

SENATOR HOAR. It may be, while not being regarded as the equals of men, they might hold some authority.

MR. SMITH. They do hold authority in all matters pertaining to their sex.

SENATOR HOAR. Are they eligible to any of the church offices of which you have given us a list—the apostles, and the first presidency, and the councilors, etc.?

MR. SMITH. No, sir. The office of presidency, and apostles, and councilors, and general authorities of the church are confined to males.

SENATOR HOAR. What priestly authority, then, is vested in women, and how is it exercised? You say that priestly authority in matters affecting their own sex is vested in them.

MR. SMITH. We have an organization called the Woman's Relief Society, which exists throughout the entire church, and it is organized in stake and also in ward capacities.

SENATOR HOAR. Woman's Relief Society?

MR. SMITH. Yes, sir.

SENATOR HOAR. Does that mean a society for the relief of women who need relief, or a society for relief to be administered by women to anybody who needs relief?

MR. SMITH. To anybody and everybody. It is purely a charitable organization.

SENATOR HOAR. For the relief of poverty and sickness?

MR. SMITH. Yes, sir; poverty and sickness, and orphans, and the aged, and all needing assistance.

SENATOR HOAR. Is there any other? What makes that a priestly authority? You give that as an example of the priestly authority to which women are admitted?

MR. SMITH. Yes. They receive their authority, of course, from the church.

SENATOR HOAR. But there is nothing priestly in the office, is there, or what you would term priestly?

MR. SMITH. Yes; in the nature of the office. They hold their meetings—

SENATOR HOAR. Do you regard that as a priestly authority—the exercise of charity to the sick and poor?

MR. SMITH. Yes, sir; I think we do.

SENATOR HOAR. I ought not to delay this hearing by a discussion of that question.

MR. SMITH. Senator, if you please—

SENATOR HOAR. Yes.

MR. SMITH. We regard this organization as one of the most essential organizations of the church. It was brought into existence in the days of Joseph Smith, and is one of the oldest institutions of the church.

SENATOR HOAR. But what is there in it in the nature of authority?

MR. SMITH. They have authority to preach the gospel; they have authority to teach correct principles—the principles of our religion—and to
inculcate those principles in their example as well as in their teaching
throughout the church and throughout the world.[1]

SENATOR HOAR. But do you understand that that preaching or teaching
or setting a good example comes properly within the definition of
the term ecclesiastical or priestly authority?

MR. SMITH. We do, when they receive that authority from those holding
the priesthood.

SENATOR HOAR. Is there any person in your church who is not authorized
to set a good example, whether by the leave of the priesthood or not?

MR. SMITH. Certainly not; but this organization is especially called to that
labor, and it is its particular duty.

SENATOR HOAR. Do you not understand by the word "authority," control
over other persons? Now, what control do these persons exercise
which would be termed priestly authority?

MR. SMITH. If I could have one of our books here—

MR. TAYLER. Which one?

MR. SMITH. Doctrine and Covenants. If I may be permitted, I should like
to read from it. I should like to give you the authority itself. May I read
it, sir?

SENATOR HOAR. Read.[2] ...

---

1. In a letter to Smoot, Joseph F. Smith wrote of the proselyting opportunity the
hearings presented, noting that the church had sent out thousands of missionaries and
spent "hundreds of thousands of dollars in endeavoring to expose" the church message
"and bring it to the notice of the world." He therefore advised Smoot against evasion:
"Don't shrink from the issue, tell them to come ahead, invite them to make a most thorough investigation, the more thorough the better in all and everything that belongs to
us" (Jan. 28, 1904).

2. President Smith read D&C 121:34-44:

Behold, there are many called, but few are chosen. And why are they not chosen?

Because their hearts are set so much upon the things of this world, and aspire to
the honors of men, that they do not learn this one lesson—

That the rights of the priesthood are inseparably connected with the powers of
heaven, and that the powers of heaven cannot be controlled nor handled only upon
the principles of righteousness.

That they may be conferred upon us, it is true; but when we undertake to cover
our sins, or to gratify our pride, our vain ambition, or to exercise control or dominion
or compulsion upon the souls of the children of men, in any degree of unrighteous-
ness, behold, the heavens withdraw themselves; the Spirit of the Lord is grieved; and
when it is withdrawn, Amen to the priesthood or the authority of that man.

Behold, ere he is aware, he is left unto himself, to kick against the pricks, to per-
secute the saints, and to fight against God.

We have learned by sad experience that it is the nature and disposition of almost

MR. SMITH. This is the authority they exercise.

SENATOR HOAR. With the exception of the authority as you have defined it, exercised by the charitable organization for the relief of the poor and sick, do women exercise any other priestly authority in your church?

MR. SMITH. May I, if you please, explain to you that we do not ordain women to the priesthood.

SENATOR HOAR. And they do not hold these offices?

MR. SMITH. Yes; they hold offices in the church.

SENATOR HOAR. No; I mean they do not hold the offices of which you have spoken just now.

MR. SMITH. We do not ordain them as elders and high priests.

SENATOR HOAR. Or as presidents and councilors?

MR. SMITH. They are presidents over their various organizations.

SENATOR HOAR. Do I understand they vote?

MR. SMITH. They vote, just the same as men do.

SENATOR HOAR. In all places of assembly—is that a proper use of the word?

MR. WORTHINGTON. At conferences.

SENATOR HOAR. They vote equally with men?

MR. SMITH. In all our conferences. There is not a woman in the church whose vote on the acceptance or on the rejection of any officer of the church is not equal to my own.

SENATOR HOAR. That is what I wanted to know. ...

THE CHAIRMAN. Do you obey the law in having five wives at this time, and having them bear to you eleven children since the manifesto of 1890?

MR. SMITH. Mr. Chairman, I have not claimed that in that case I have obeyed the law of the land.

THE CHAIRMAN. That is all.

---

all men, as soon as they get a little authority, as they suppose, they will immediately begin to exercise unrighteous dominion.

Hence many are called, but few are chosen.

No power or influence can or ought to be maintained by virtue of the priesthood, only by persuasion, by long-suffering, by gentleness and meekness, and by love unfeigned;

By kindness, and pure knowledge, which shall greatly enlarge the soul without hypocrisy, and without guile—

Reproving betimes with sharpness, when moved upon by the Holy Ghost; and then showing forth afterwards an increase of love toward him whom thou hast reproved, lest he esteem thee to be his enemy;

That he may know that thy faithfulness is stronger than the cords of death.

Mr. Smith. I do not claim so, and I have said before that I prefer to stand my chances against the law.[3]

The Chairman. Certainly.

Mr. Smith. Rather than to abandon my children and their mothers. That is all there is to it.

Senator Beveridge. That leads necessarily to another question. I understood you yesterday to say why it was you continued that, that you were willing to take the chances as an individual. My question was directed to this: That, as head of the church, whatever your beliefs may be, it is your practice and the practice of the church to obey the law of the land, in teaching, notwithstanding what your opinion may be. Is that correct or not?

Mr. Smith. That is correct, and I wish to assert that the church has obeyed the law of the land, and that it has kept its pledges with this Government; but I have not, as an individual, and I have taken that chance myself. ...

Senator Dubois.[4] To start out with, Mr. Smith has now several times stated that only three or four per cent were in polygamy. That has gone without challenge. My judgment is that three or four per cent were convicted. I think the prosecution will be able to show that much more than three or four per cent were in the polygamous relations. I am almost willing to hazard the guess that three or four per cent were actually convicted.

Senator Foraker. In so far as I made use of the term "three or four per cent," I took it from the witness. I have no knowledge on the subject.

Senator Dubois. I understand. I do not undertake to give the percentage, but it will be given. However, I make my statement in contradiction to that of the president.

Mr. Worthington. Do you refer to three or four per cent of the whole membership of the Mormon church or only the marriageable males?

Senator Dubois. Ah, you do not consider the women in polygamy?

Mr. Worthington. I did not know—

Senator Dubois. You mean that the women are not in polygamy?

---

3. The short exchange above was included in the majority report submitted by Senator Burrows on June 11, 1906 (*Smoot Hearings*, 4:480).

4. Prior to this question, at Foraker's request, Tayler entered the 1843 revelation on plural married (D&C 132) into evidence (*Smoot Hearings*, 1:202-208). Carl Badger wrote in his journal, "The reading of the Section on Marriage from the D&C was a horrible experience ... it sounded terrible" (in Rodney J. Badger, *Liahona and Iron Rod: The Biography of Carl A. and Rose J. Badger* [Bountiful, Utah: Family History Publishers, 1985], 212).

MR. WORTHINGTON. I merely wanted to know whether you meant 3 or 4 per cent of the whole church population or that percentage of the marriageable males.

SENATOR DUBOIS. I will state at the proper time what I mean. We will accept your statement, Mr. Smith, that a small percentage are in polygamy. How many presidents of the church from the beginning have been monogamists?

MR. SMITH. How many?

SENATOR DUBOIS. Yes.

MR. SMITH. How many presidents have been monogamists? I think that all of the first presidents of the church down to myself have had plural wives.

SENATOR DUBOIS. I understood from the testimony here yesterday that the heir to the throne is also a polygamist—the head of the quorum of apostles now, who under the rule and precedents, should he survive you, will be the president of the church. I understood that he is also a polygamist.

MR. SMITH. I should like to correct the Senator by saying that we have no heir to the throne.[5]

SENATOR DUBOIS. He is the head of the quorum of the apostles, and there has been a line of unbroken precedents that the head of the quorum of the apostles succeeds to the office of president.

MR. SMITH. That is correct.

SENATOR DUBOIS. If the term "heir to the throne" is offensive, I will withdraw it.

MR. SMITH. If you please.

SENATOR DUBOIS. But apparently, following the precedents of the church, he will succeed to the office of president. Now, of course you could not state, but has it not been a fact that the great majority of the high ecclesiastical positions in the church have been filled by polygamists?

MR. SMITH. I could not state that from positive knowledge, but I will say this frankly, that a large number of them have been polygamists. The fact of the matter is, that the most prominent men, the most influential men, the men who have stood highest in business and in social circles in Utah among the Mormon people, have been men who had more than one wife.

---

5. The "heir to the throne" referred to Francis M. Lyman, president of the Quorum of Twelve Apostles. Lyman would be a witness in the hearings on March 8 (*Smoot Hearings*, 1:426-74).

SENATOR DUBOIS. That is a satisfactory answer to me. I simply wanted to show that this very small percentage are very influential.

SENATOR HOAR. I should like to ask a question merely to understand what I did not get at heretofore. I understood the question to be put whether this revelation to Joseph Smith, promulgated and made public by Brigham Young, in regard to polygamy, was permissive or obligatory. I understood—and I am not sure I understood you aright—that it was permissive, but did you mean to say that or do you mean to say that it is obligatory, so far as a general principle of conduct is concerned, but not mandatory under the circumstances? Now I will illustrate what I mean by the injunction of our scripture—what we call the New Testament.

MR. SMITH. Which is our scripture also.

SENATOR HOAR. Which is your scripture also?

MR. SMITH. Yes, sir.

SENATOR HOAR. The apostle says that a bishop must be sober and must be the husband of one wife.

MR. SMITH. At least.

SENATOR HOAR. We do not say that. (Laughter.) The bishop must be sober and must be the husband of one wife. I suppose that is generally construed to enjoin upon bishops the marriage relation. But I have known several bishops, two in my own State, of great distinction, who were bachelors. I suppose they would say, if you asked them, that that was an obligation to sustain by their example the marriage relation, but that it did not apply under all circumstances and upon all occasions, and that the ordinary element of human illness and poverty, or any other special reason, exempted them from it. I gather from your general answer that that is what you mean by your answer whether it is permissive or mandatory; that the principle is mandatory, but that it is not of universal application under all circumstances.[6]

MR. SMITH. I think, Senator, I can accept of your statement without any criticism at all.

SENATOR HOAR. That is what I wanted to know.

MR. SMITH. I should like to be permitted to call the attention of the honorable Senator to the fact that this injunction was made to the church in Judea in the midst of a polygamous people, and that all of the people believed in the practice of polygamy at that time.

SENATOR HOAR. You mean the ancients?

---

6. J. Reuben Clark's copy of the hearings bracketed with purple ink this entire question from Hoar.

Mr. Smith. Yes, sir; the Jews at that time. But it was made obligatory upon the bishop that he should have one wife, because the duties of a bishop require an experienced man.

Senator McComas. You said that the revelation of polygamy promulgated by Brigham Young was permissive and not mandatory.

Mr. Smith. Begging pardon, I said that it is so construed by our people.

Senator McComas. So construed, and your church so construes it?

Mr. Smith. It is so construed by our people.

Senator McComas. To be permissive and not mandatory?

Mr. Smith. In the sense of saying that as a principal it was a vital principle at the time, but it was not mandatory, from the very fact that only a very small percentage engaged in it, and, with all deference to the Senator who has expressed himself, I still maintain that the estimate of 3 per cent of the Mormon people who entered into polygamy is based upon figures that were produced at the time the announcement was made.

Senator McComas. I will not require you to repeat the statement you have made, although you have repeated part of it.

Mr. Smith. Thank you.

Senator McComas. You said, if I understand you, that the [1890] manifesto of President Woodruff was construed by you and by your church as mandatory.

Mr. Smith. Yes, sir.

Senator McComas. As mandatory?

Mr. Smith. Yes, sir.

Senator McComas. Apart from your personal belief as a man, in your office as president of the church, have you often or ever or repeatedly rebuked those who have, after President Woodruff's manifesto, urged the practice of plural marriage, when they did so in your presence or to your knowledge or when it has been brought to your attention?

Mr. Smith. I should say that I have never heard anybody advocate it or encourage or recommend it in any shape or form since the manifesto.

Senator McComas. Have you ever—

Mr. Smith. Only in the sense that has been read here to-day; that is, in a little social gathering I announced my own belief in it and at the same time announced the fact that it was not practiced and was stopped.

Senator McComas. Have you ever heard or have you read addresses made by apostles of your church encouraging plural marriages since the manifesto?

Mr. Smith. No, sir; never.

SENATOR MCCOMAS. You have never seen them reported in the newspapers?

MR. SMITH. No, sir

SENATOR MCCOMAS. Not in any instance?

MR. SMITH. No; unless you can construe what I said there—

SENATOR MCCOMAS. What you said? I am talking about the statements of others.

MR. SMITH. I have not heard anybody else.

SENATOR MCCOMAS. Apostle [Heber J.] Grant, for instance, and others?

MR. SMITH. I understood that Apostle Grant[7] merely announced the fact that he had two wives and that he had contributed $300 to a certain class in the University of Utah in honor of his two wives—$150 each. He announced it publicly. The anti-Mormon press of Salt Lake City took it up and made a great big hubbub about it.[8]

SENATOR MCCOMAS. I understood you to say that you have never heard in any public place any apostle or elder of the church encourage the practice of plural marriages or defend it after the Woodruff manifesto?[9]

MR. SMITH. I will say truly as to both forms of your question, I have never heard them advocate it; I have never heard them defend it in public.

SENATOR MCCOMAS. And you have never read of it?

---

7. Here and elsewhere during the hearings, allusions to Elder Grant were a reminder that Grant had left the country to avoid being subpoenaed. Joseph F. Smith later wrote to Smoot:

> To say I was surprised at the as[s]umption of the zealous Senator would be putting it milde. I had never before heard that Heber J. Grant was wanted as a witness, and neither he nor Moses Thatcher had ever been suggested to me as among those Mr. Tayl[e]r expressed a desire that I would persuade to appear before the Committee. Is it possible to enlighten the Senator on the point of my obligation to furnish witnesses for Messrs. Tayl[e]r, [Charles] Owen, and the Ministerial Association in this so called "Smoot investigation"? Please inform the worthy Senator for me, and save me the task, that I made no promise whatever to the Committee, not even to Mr. Tayler either on or off the witness chair to furnish any witnesses at all (Apr. 20, 1904).

8. Prior to the hearings, President Theodore Roosevelt told Smoot "it was very unfortunate that Mr. Grant made the remarks that he did at the State University." Soon thereafter, the president had "delegations wait upon him calling his attention to the remarks, and claiming [Grant's speech] disclosed the true attitude of the Church toward the Government, that the people were still defiant and law-breakers." Nevertheless, Roosevelt told the concerned visitors "Reed Smoot should not be held responsible for the statements of other men simply because he was a member of the church that they belonged to" (Smoot to Joseph F. Smith, Jan. 8, 1904).

9. The *Salt Lake Herald* had editorialized on Grant's blunder:

> The Second James must have known that some centuries after his own body had moldered Heber J. Grant would inhabit the earth, or he would never have written so positively that "the tongue no man can tame; it is an unruly evil, full of deadly poi-

MR. SMITH. But I have said this, if you please, Mr. Senator, that if the principle in the abstract is attacked by opponents, it is very, very likely that we will defend it, from a scriptural view point.

SENATOR McCOMAS. I am not asking you what you would do. I want to know what you have done.

MR. SMITH. We have not done anything of the kind.

SENATOR McCOMAS. Have you read in the newspapers in Salt Lake City reports that appear to be authentic of any apostle or elder who has thus defended the practice of polygamy? And if so, I desire to know if you have ever in your place as president of the church in any manner called him to account for violating the Woodruff manifesto, which you say is mandatory upon the members of the church.

MR. SMITH. There are some papers very bitterly anti-Mormon published in Salt Lake City.[10]

SENATOR McCOMAS. I am only asking you with respect to those which seem to be fair and authoritative reports.

MR. SMITH. I have never seen any fair, authoritative, or reliable reports of that kind.

SENATOR McCOMAS. You never have?

MR. SMITH. I never have.

MR. WORTHINGTON. Not since the manifesto?

MR. SMITH. Not in the papers.

---

son." Apostle Grant rarely talks in public without violating the proprieties, which is a mild way of putting it. Mr. Grant talked on Wednesday to the young men and young women students at the University of Utah. ... Apostle Grant ... has about as much discretion as a 2-year old child, and his faculty for getting himself and his church into hot water is limited only by the number of his opportunities. Grant is the Mormon Burchard, with quite a good deal to spare" ("Grant Needs Muzzle," Nov. 6, 1903).

The allusion to speaking without thinking was to the Reverend Samuel D. Burchard, who famously endorsed James G. Blaine for president in 1884. In doing so, Burchard charged that Democrats were the party of "rum, Romanism, and rebellion," which alienated most Irish-American voters.

10. The day of this testimony, the *Deseret News* complained about its rival *Salt Lake Tribune*:

The old anti-"Mormon" gall and wormwood and sinuous prevarication and abuse in the Tribune, oozes out in acrid volume mingled with a pretended half-eulogy, half sarcasm, about the testimony of President Smith before the committee. But it matters little. The protestors and their organ will elicit much more than they want in the examination and will fall in other directions. The country will learn the facts, and the rational and sensible will perceive the true situation, and whether prejudice prevail against Senator Smoot or not, the result will be the spread of "Mormonism" throughout the world. But we advise the antis not to shout too loudly or too soon ("Law and Testimony," Mar. 4, 1904).

SENATOR McCOMAS. You have never heard any in public?

MR. SMITH. No, sir; I never have. ...

MR. WORTHINGTON. Now I come to a line of inquiry as to which Senator Hoar made inquiry a moment ago. Prior to 1862 there was, I believe, no law in force in Utah against either polygamy or polygamous cohabitation?

MR. SMITH. No, sir.

MR. WORTHINGTON. And your people arrived there from Nauvoo [Illinois] about 1847?

MR. SMITH. Yes, sir.

MR. WORTHINGTON. So that they had been there about fifteen years?

MR. SMITH. That is correct.

MR. WORTHINGTON. The formal public proclamation of polygamy as an article of faith and practice was made by Brigham Young in 1852?

MR. SMITH. Yes, sir.

MR. WORTHINGTON. So it was publicly proclaimed and practiced for ten years before Congress did any thing?

MR. SMITH. Yes, sir.

MR. WORTHINGTON. Then, in 1862 there was passed an act which made bigamy an offense?

MR. SMITH. Yes, sir.

MR. WORTHINGTON. That act, however, I believe, did not in any way relate to polygamous cohabitation?

MR. SMITH. No, sir.

MR. WORTHINGTON. It punished only the offense of a man taking another wife?

MR. SMITH. That is right.

MR. WORTHINGTON. And as to those who had already taken wives, it did not make it unlawful for them to continue to live with them and each of them as husband and wife?

MR. SMITH. That was our understanding.

MR. WORTHINGTON. Then that act was declared constitutional in 1878.

SENATOR HOAR. By what authority?

MR. WORTHINGTON. By the Supreme Court of the United States, in what is called the Reynolds case, which is here. Then, in 1882 there was passed a law, which is called the Edmunds law.

MR. SMITH. Yes, sir.

MR. WORTHINGTON. And that, for the first time, made polygamous cohabitation an offense?

MR. SMITH. That is according to my understanding.

MR. WORTHINGTON. So that your people had been living there and practicing polygamous cohabitation or plural cohabitation for thirty years before there was any law passed making it an offense?

MR. SMITH. Yes, sir.

MR. WORTHINGTON. In the meantime you had acquired several wives, I believe?

MR. SMITH. Yes, sir.

MR. WORTHINGTON. And many others of your people had?

MR. SMITH. Yes, sir.

MR. WORTHINGTON. Then there were other decisions of the Supreme Court, beginning in 1885 and beginning down to 1889, which related to that law and other subsequent laws?

MR. SMITH. That is my understanding.

MR. WORTHINGTON. The last of which decisions was made in May, 1890?

MR. SMITH. Yes, sir.

MR. WORTHINGTON. And then came the proclamation, or manifesto, as it is called here?

MR. SMITH. That is correct.

MR. WORTHINGTON. The acts of Congress then had made a clear distinction between polygamy—

SENATOR HOAR. What is the date of the manifesto? That will make my notes complete.

MR. WORTHINGTON. September 26, 1890, is the date of the manifesto, and the date of the submission of it to the conference for approval was the 6th of October, 1890. I think you said after the manifesto your people, as a general rule, ceased polygamous cohabitation even?

MR. SMITH. That is correct, sir.

MR. WORTHINGTON. And finally the State was admitted in 1896, under the enabling act of 1894?

MR. SMITH. Yes, sir.

MR. WORTHINGTON. And the enabling act made it a condition of Utah coming into the Union that polygamy should be forbidden, but did not prohibit polygamous cohabitation or make forbearance from that offense a condition?

MR. SMITH. That is a correct statement.

MR. WORTHINGTON. Then your people adopted the constitution which has been read here, in which they did make it an offense, and provided that the clause should be irrevocable without the consent of the United States that polygamy or plural marriages should be forever prohibited?

MR. SMITH. Yes, sir.

MR. WORTHINGTON. And there was nothing in the constitution prohibiting polygamous cohabitation?

MR. SMITH. That is correct.

MR. WORTHINGTON. Continuing to live with wives already married?

MR. SMITH. Yes, sir.

MR. WORTHINGTON. If I remember rightly, you said that seemed to you to
be an implication by the Congress of the United States that perhaps
you people who had married in these old times might continue to live
with your wives and nothing would be said about it?

MR. SMITH. But that is a fact, and also the liberal sentiment that was exhibited by all people, both Mormons and Gentiles.

MR. WORTHINGTON. Is it a fact—it has been stated here several times—that
the great majority of the inhabitants of Utah belong to the Mormon
Church?

MR. SMITH. Yes, sir.

MR. WORTHINGTON. It has been so during all these years?

MR. SMITH. All these years.

MR. WORTHINGTON. And it has been said here that the body of 15 men
who are charged here with being conspirators control the church?

MR. SMITH. That is the charge, I believe.

MR. WORTHINGTON. You have told us your view as to their authority?

MR. SMITH. Yes, sir.

MR. WORTHINGTON. What I want to know is, if Congress had decided that
Utah might come into the Union on the condition solely that they
would not have any more plural marriages, and there is a law there
which makes polygamous cohabitation a crime also, where did that
come from?

MR. SMITH. It was passed by the Utah legislature. In other words, the
Edmunds-Tucker bill was enacted by the legislature of the Territory
or of the State.

MR. WORTHINGTON. That was in 1892, was it?

MR. SMITH. Counsel [Franklin S.] Richards[11] says it was first enacted under the Territorial statute, and then it was continued or reenacted under the State government.

MR. WORTHINGTON. Is this, then, the law which makes polygamous cohabitation an offense? Section 4209 has already been read by Mr. Tayler,

---

11. Franklin S. Richards (1849-1934) served as legal counsel for Smith, Smoot, and
other witnesses. The son of LDS Apostle Franklin D. Richards, he was a devout Mormon
but a monogamist. For his reminiscence of the hearings, see the epilogue in this volume.

but I will read it here: "If any male person hereafter cohabits with more than one woman, he shall be guilty of a misdemeanor, and on conviction thereof shall be punished by a fine of not more than three hundred dollars or by imprisonment in the county jail for not more than six months, or by both said punishments, in the discretion of the court." That is the only law, then, is it, that makes polygamous cohabitation an offense in Utah?

MR. SMITH. In force in Utah.

MR. WORTHINGTON. And that law was passed by a legislature which was—

MR. SMITH. Largely Mormon.

MR. WORTHINGTON. Overwhelmingly Mormon?

MR. SMITH. Yes, sir.[12] ...

SENATOR HOAR. Now, between 1882 and 1885 and 1890 which was binding upon the conscience of the members of the Mormon Church, the old revelation or the statute?

MR. SMITH. I think the leading authorities of the church felt that the statute was binding.

SENATOR HOAR. Over the revelation?

MR. SMITH. Over the revelation, because it had become the confirmed law of the land. In other words, the constitutional law of the land, having been so declared by the Supreme Court; but younger fellows like myself, Senator, were a little more difficult to control, I suppose—

SENATOR HOAR. You may say that, if you like. I did not put that with a view to going into any inconsistency.

MR. SMITH. I presume I am the greatest culprit.

SENATOR HOAR. I put that question not with any view to inquire into your personal conduct or anybody's, but you will see in a moment that it has a very particular and important significance on this question. That is, suppose in regard to a matter of personal conduct, like polygamy, the revelation stands on one side unrepealed and the law of the land on the other, which, in your judgment, is binding upon the consciences of your people?

MR. SMITH. If you please, I will state, having been intimate with these gentlemen, that President Woodruff and George Q. Cannon and President Lorenzo Snow, who afterwards succeeded Wilford Woodruff in the presidency of the church, absolutely obeyed the law of the land.

SENATOR HOAR. That does not fully answer the question.

---

12. For a history of these anti-polygamy acts, see Sarah Barringer Gordon, *The Mormon Question: Polygamy and Constitutional Conflict in Nineteenth-Century America* (Chapel Hill: University of North Carolina Press, 2002).

Mr. Smith. Excuse me, then. I perhaps do not understand it.

Senator Hoar. You are the head of the Mormon Church?

Mr. Smith. To-day.

Senator Hoar. I will not use the word "Mormon" if you do not like it.

Mr. Smith. That is all right. I will accept that, Senator.

Senator Hoar. You are the head of your church, and I ask you, as the most authoritative and weighty exponent of its doctrine and belief, when, in regard to personal conduct, the law of the land comes in conflict with the divine revelation received through you or your predecessor, which is binding upon the conduct of the true son of the church.

Mr. Smith. In this case—and I think, perhaps, you will accept it as the answer to your question—under the manifesto of President Woodruff the law of the land is the binding law on the consciences of the people.

Senator Hoar. Before the manifesto of Mr. Woodruff, is my question.

Mr. Smith. We were in something of a state of chaos about that time.

Senator Hoar. That is not the point. The point is, which, as a matter of obligation, is the prevalent authority, the law of the land or the revelation?

Mr. Smith. Well, perhaps the revelation would be paramount.

Senator Hoar. Perhaps?

Mr. Smith. I am simply expressing a view.

Senator Hoar. Do you think "perhaps" is an answer to that?

Mr. Smith. I am simply trying to illustrate it.

Senator Hoar. Yes; I will not interrupt you.

Mr. Smith. With another man the law would be accepted, and this was the condition the people of the church were in until the manifesto settled the question.

Mr. Worthington. Let me ask you a question in that connection.

Senator Hoar. I had not quite gotten through, Mr. Worthington.

Mr. Worthington. I beg your pardon, Senator.

Mr. Smith. Does that answer the question, Senator?

Senator Hoar. I think it does, so far; but I want to go a little farther. Suppose you should receive a divine revelation, communicated to and sustained by your church, commanding your people to-morrow to do something forbidden by the law of the land. Which would it be their duty to obey?

Mr. Smith. They would be at liberty to obey just which they pleased. There is absolutely no compulsion.

MR. WORTHINGTON. Have you finished your answer to that question, Mr. Smith?

MR. SMITH. I do not think I have quite. One of the standard principles of our faith, and one that has been read here to-day, is that we shall be obedient to the law. This is the word: "Let no man break the laws of the land, for he that keepeth the laws of God hath no need to break the laws of the land. Wherefore, be subject to the powers that be until He reigns whose right it is to reign, and subdues all enemies under His feet. Behold the laws which ye have received"—this is speaking to the church—"from my hand are the laws of the Church, and in this light ye shall hold them forth."[13] Not in conflict with the laws of the land, but simply as the laws of the church.[14]

SENATOR BEVERIDGE. Suppose them to be in conflict, Mr. Smith, which would control the conduct of the member of your church, the law of the land or the revelation?[15]

MR. SMITH. I think under the discipline that we have had for the last twenty years our people would obey the law of the land.

THE CHAIRMAN. Which would control you?

MR. SMITH. I should try with all my might, Mr. Chairman, to obey the law of the land, but I would not like to be put in a position where I would

---

13. See D&C 58:21-23.

14. In a letter to Smoot, President Smith elaborated:

You may tell Senator Hoar for me, if you choose, that I have never broken a law of God to my knowledge in my life, and that I did not testify that I had. And I never to my knowledge broke but one law of my country. And that law is against my conscience and against good morals, so far as I am concerned. That is the law against living with my family, whom I took before the law was enacted. I never said in my testimony that for disregarding that law I expected to ask for or receive mercy. I plainly said that I would rather face the penalties of that law than the more dreadful consequences of abandoning my children and their mothers (Apr. 9, 1905).

15. Speaking in LDS general conference thirty-three years later, Smoot said he had recently re-read President Smith's testimony and surmised something about Senator Beveridge's questions:

This young man [Beveridge] at the time was a very popular Senator of the United States, and as I read the hearings in my case, and his questions that were asked President Joseph F. Smith, when the latter was a witness before the Privileges and Elections Committee, I felt in my soul then, and you couldn't help it if any one of you were to read the proceedings, that what Senator Beveridge wanted to know was why and how the Church of Jesus Christ of Latter-day Saints held together so well, and why its members were willing to sacrifice so much of their time and their substance, and were willing to give their lives for the Church, if necessary, as shown by the testimonies given, and he felt in his soul that there was something greater than the thoughts of man; that there must be some power in the Church and that power was manifested in its representatives who testified in this case. (*LDS Conference Reports* [Salt Lake City: Church of Jesus Christ of Latter-day Saints, Apr. 1937], 106).

have to abandon my children. I could not do that very well. I would rather stand anything than to do that.

SENATOR HOAR. I was not referring in my question to that particular thing. I would like to ask one question which is flatly curiosity, for this is a most interesting matter. Did I understand you correctly that there has been no revelation since this revelation of Woodruff's for the general government of the church?

MR. WORTHINGTON. He said there have been none for twenty-one years except that. That is the only one in twenty-one years.

SENATOR HOAR. Then there has been none since, so that you have received no revelation yourself?

MR. SMITH. No, sir.

SENATOR HOAR. Now, if this question is in the least trespassing on any delicacy in your mind I do not want to press it. I ask it solely for curiosity. If a revelation were to come to you, or if you have a belief it would come to you, in what way does it come? By an inward light, by an audible voice, by a writing, or in what way? Have you anything you can tell us about that?

MR. SMITH. It might come by an audible voice or it might come by an inspiration known and heard only by myself.

SENATOR HOAR. Or by writing, I suppose, as in the case of Joseph Smith?

MR. SMITH. In the case of the Book of Mormon; yes, sir.

SENATOR HOAR. That is all.

SENATOR BAILEY. One word about this document which you call the manifesto. As a matter of fact, that does not purport to have been a revelation at all, if what I have before me is a correct copy of it. It seems to have been provoked—I do not use that in any offensive sense—by a report made to the Congress of the United States, in which report it was charged that the church continues the practice of polygamy and that they have found something like 40 cases; and in response to the press dispatches conveying a copy of that report, the president of the church issues an official declaration. That, I take it, is what you call the manifesto?

MR. WORTHINGTON. Yes; that is it.

MR. SMITH. But the manifesto really—that is, the estoppel of plural marriages—was issued before that.

MR. RICHARDS. He is talking of the manifesto.

MR. SMITH. Oh, yes; the manifesto.

SENATOR BAILEY. When you speak of the manifesto, you speak of this document?

MR. SMITH. I speak of that; yes, sir.

SENATOR BAILEY. That is the manifesto (handing witness a pamphlet).

MR. SMITH. This contains the manifesto.

SENATOR BAILEY. The pamphlet contains it, but the particular document, the form of words to which I have called attention there, is the manifesto itself, is it not?

MR. SMITH. The form of words that contains the manifesto, or is the manifesto, is a declaration by Wilford Woodruff, the head of the church, that he will abstain from plural marriages and use his influence to prevent all others from entering into it.

SENATOR BAILEY. I think, if I correctly read it, it declares that he has not encouraged it, but, on the contrary, has reproved those who taught it. But what I am trying to do is to draw, at least in my own mind, the distinction between the manifesto and a revelation. A revelation, as I understand it, comes from on high. That manifesto seems to have been merely a way of reaching and denying a report made to the American Congress; and while it does establish a code of conduct, I do not understand that to be religious in its character at all.

MR. SMITH. It was essentially religious for the reason that it was a specific estoppel of plural marriages by the head of the church.

SENATOR BAILEY. Well, in obedience of the law. Of course, it might have been communicated to the secret conferences or to the conferences of the church that he had prayed for light and had received a revelation.

MR. SMITH. That is it.

SENATOR BAILEY. But so far as that document is concerned, it nowhere indicates that there has been any light from heaven on the subject. It appears that it is in obedience to the law, and I rather think it puts the responsibility for discontinuing the practice of polygamy on the law of the land. I would not be sure, but I think maybe the concluding sentence indicates that it is a pure matter of obedience to the law; and while obeying the law is commendable, and I have no criticism about it, I am simply trying to—

MR. SMITH. It is certainly in pursuance of the decision of the Supreme Court declaring the law against plural marriages and against unlawful cohabitation constitutional, that the church was brought to the adoption of the rule of the church not to allow or permit any further plural marriages.[16]

---

16. J. Reuben Clark's copy of the hearings underlined the sentence "that the church

4. JOSEPH F. SMITH

SENATOR BAILEY. I understand; but that is a matter of law and not of religion.

MR. SMITH. Oh, no; it is a matter of religion.

SENATOR BAILEY. At this time that the official declaration was made, it was not even the law of the church, I believe, until it was what you call sustained.

MR. SMITH. It was submitted to the entire church.

SENATOR BAILEY. I was going to say, it could not have been the law, because on the next page I find that President Lorenzo Snow offered the following, which seems to have been a written resolution, approving and adopting this manifesto.[17]

MR. SMITH. Before the whole conference; yes, sir.

SENATOR BAILEY. Yes. The very last sentence of it is: "And I now publicly declare that my advice to the Latter-day Saints is to refrain from contracting any marriage forbidden by the law of the land." He does not say that he has received a revelation that changes the law of the church. He simply says that he has come to a resolution to obey the law of the land.

MR. SMITH. Does he not say that he has prayed and obtained light?

SENATOR BAILEY. I think not, in this.

MR. RICHARDS. Mr. Chairman, may I make a word of explanation?

SENATOR BAILEY. I should be glad to have it.

MR. RICHARDS. I see Mr. Smith is confused about the contents of this instrument and other instruments. It does appear in other instruments, in a sermon delivered by President Woodruff, and in a petition to the President of the United States, and also, I think, in some of the testimony that was given before the master in chancery, what the circumstances were under which this document was promulgated, and by reason of which he claimed it to have been the force of inspiration and revelation; but it does not appear here.[18]

MR. TAYLER. Does the divine origin of it appear in this manifesto you send out?

MR. RICHARDS. No, sir; it does not, and that is why I say the witness is confused. He is cognizant of its appearing somewhere, but he is confused as to whether it is in that paper.

---

was brought to the adoption of the rule of the church not to allow or permit any further plural marriages."

17. J. Reuben Clark's copy bracketed this question by Bailey.

18. For a reprint of Wilford Woodruff's testimony on the Manifesto, see *Smoot Hearings*, 1:21.

SENATOR BAILEY. The instrument itself negat[es] that idea. The paragraph of it preceding the one from which I read the concluding sentence of the document is this: "Inasmuch as laws have been enacted
by Congress forbidding plural marriages, which laws have been pronounced constitutional by the court of last resort, I hereby declare my
intention to submit to those laws, and to use my influence with the
members of the church over which I preside to have them do likewise." Now, I take it, if it had been a revelation, he would have used
the language of a prophet rather than the language of a lawyer, and
instead of declaring that inasmuch as Congress had passed laws forbidding this he would have declared he had received a revelation.

SENATOR DILLINGHAM. May I be permitted, Senator Bailey, to call your attention to the record here, on page 18. The petition to the President
of the United States contains this clause: "According to our creed, the
head of the church receives from time to time revelations for the religious guidance of his people"—

MR. WORTHINGTON. It is signed by Woodruff.

SENATOR DILLINGHAM. Yes. "In September, 1890, the present head of the
church in anguish and prayer cried to God for help for his flock, and
received permission to advise the members of the Church of Jesus
Christ of Latter-Day Saints that the law commanding polygamy was
henceforth suspended."

MR. SMITH. Now permit me to say that the presentation of this to the general conference of the church, and the resolution that was adopted by
the entire church made this binding upon the whole church.[19]

SENATOR BAILEY. Yes; I understand that. I have no disposition to engage
in any debate as to matters of faith. I hardly consider myself competent for that kind of discussion; and if it were made a matter of inspiration I would feel foreclosed against any argument. But so far as this
question is concerned—so far as this official declaration is concerned—it is purely a question of law and not of conscience. Now, one
other question, and that other question is suggested by that idea. I noticed in response to Senator Hoar's question, Mr. Smith, you said as
between a conflicting law and a conflicting revelation, the law would
be binding on some and the revelation on others?

MR. SMITH. It might be, I said.

SENATOR BAILEY. Do you mean by that that it would be binding as a matter of conduct or as a matter of conscience?

MR. SMITH. As a matter of conscience.

---

19. J. Reuben Clark's copy bracketed this entire answer by Smith.

SENATOR BAILEY. I can not understand how a man who has any Christian faith can yield his conscience to the law, though I do understand how he can conform his conduct to it. I can not quite understand how, if the revelation comes from on high, you could, as a matter of conscience, yield it to a law that is made by ordinary, every-day lawmakers, either in Utah or at Washington, though I understand perfectly well that as a question of good citizenship you would, in temporal affairs, yield to the law of the land. I would like to know, for my own satisfaction—and it is not a matter with which this committee has much concern, but just for my own satisfaction—would your church people make any distinction between conforming as a matter of law and nonconforming as a matter of conscience?

MR. SMITH. I tried to illustrate that some time ago, and I will repeat my idea. To my conscience the revelation conflicting with the law might appeal and be paramount, but to my brother and to my associate member of the church it might not appeal to his conscience, and he would not be affected by it at all.

SENATOR BAILEY. I did not make myself entirely plain, evidently, from your answer. I can conceive easily how a man's conscience might remain the same, although his conduct would differ. I could conceive how you and your associates in the first presidency might have precisely the same conscience in respect to a matter, and yet your conduct might differ. You might feel that you could not yield your conscience to the law, and they might feel that, reserving to themselves the same conscientious regard for institutions, still they would yield it to the commands of the State; and what I was trying to ascertain was whether your people as a church would still adhere to their conscientious beliefs in a given institution, although, as a matter of law, they might yield it.

MR. SMITH. Yes, sir; I think that is correct. I think they would do that as a general thing.

THE CHAIRMAN. You think what, Mr. Smith?

MR. SMITH. I think that our people—the Mormon people—would as a rule, while they might retain their convictions or their conscience, conform to the law; that is, their acts.

SENATOR HOAR. May I put one question right there, Mr. Bailey?

SENATOR BAILEY. Certainly.

SENATOR HOAR. Could a man remain in good standing as an apostle, who, if the divine command were in conflict with the command of the human lawgiver, disobeyed God and obeyed man?

MR. SMITH. I did not catch the last, Senator.

SENATOR HOAR. Could a man, in your judgment, remain in good standing as an apostle, who, if the divine command by revelation enjoined one thing and the human law the contrary, disobeyed God and obeyed man?

MR. SMITH. Would he remain in good standing?

SENATOR HOAR. Yes. Would he remain in good standing?

MR. SMITH. I rather think he would be considered as a little out of harmony with his associates if he did that.

SENATOR BEVERIDGE.[20] Mr. Smith, as a matter of conduct, where there is a conflict between revelation—or by whatever term it is called—and the law of the land, which, as a church matter, does your church direct the members to obey?

MR. SMITH. To obey the law of the land. That is what we have done absolutely.

SENATOR DUBOIS. I would like to ask one question.

SENATOR DILLINGHAM. It is half past 4. I move the committee adjourn.

SENATOR DUBOIS. I will ask this question, and I will stop there for the time being. I want to supplement the question made by Senator Hoar. You said that if you received a revelation your people could obey it or not, as they saw fit. Now, presume that revelation had been submitted to your people and all of them in their conference had held up their hands. Do you still think it would not be the duty of your people to obey that revelation, and that they would not obey that revelation?

MR. SMITH. That they would not obey that revelation?

SENATOR DUBOIS. Yes.

MR. SMITH. I think that when the people hold up their hands to accept a principle, and they do accept a principle, they are honest enough to carry it out.

SENATOR DUBOIS. They will all carry it out?

MR. SMITH. I think so.

SENATOR DUBOIS. They would accept your revelation then?

MR. SMITH. Yes.

SENATOR DUBOIS. Some of them would and some would not?

---

20. Nineteen days later, Smoot mentioned that "Senator Beveridge is receiving from one to two thousand letters a day, and other Senators are being deluged with requests to vote to unseat me. The plan now is to have every American who can write send letters to their Senators demanding that they listen to the voice of the American people, and unseat me no matter what the testimony may be" (Smoot to Joseph F. Smith, Mar. 23, 1904).

MR. SMITH. Some would and some would not, to be sure.

SENATOR DUBOIS. Would it not be obligatory upon every member of your organization to accept that revelation, if sustained by the holding up of hands?

MR. SMITH. No, sir; only those who were disposed to do it would do it. Those who were not disposed to do it would not do it.

SENATOR DUBOIS. Then, of course, anyone is at liberty to refuse a revelation?

MR. SMITH. That is right.

SENATOR DUBOIS. It is not binding at all upon any of your people?

MR. SMITH. How is that?

SENATOR DUBOIS. It is not binding at all upon any of your people?

MR. SMITH. Not at all; only the binding of conscience. It never was.

SENATOR DUBOIS. It has no effect or force or authority which must be obeyed according to your church organization and laws?

MR. SMITH. Not in the least. There is not a man in the Church of Jesus Christ of Latter-Day Saints that is under any more obligation to obey the doctrines of the church and the laws of the church than you are, Senator—not one particle.[21]

SENATOR DUBOIS. When promulgated by the head of the church?

MR. SMITH. Yes, sir.

SENATOR DUBOIS. You promulgate, then, a revelation to your apostles to start with, and they do not have to accept it?

MR. SMITH. Not unless they choose.

SENATOR DUBOIS. Then, if they impart that in turn to their people—

MR. SMITH. Excuse me. I say not unless they choose.

SENATOR DUBOIS. They are not under any sort of obligation, then, to obey?

MR. SMITH. Not unless they choose to. They have their volition, their free agency, and the church does not interfere with the conscience or the free agency of men at all.

SENATOR BAILEY. Could you not make use of a better word and say "unchurched" if they refuse to obey the ordinances of the church?

MR. SMITH. Oh, yes.

---

21. The editor of the *Salt Lake Herald* did not appreciate these kinds of parsed answers: "The evasions of the President are but a repetition of the old trickery and phraseology which has been trilled into the ears of the unwary ever since the ill-starred days of the first of the prophets. Also such elusive and barren sophisms place the President of the powerful Mormon organization in an extremely pathetic and undignified attitude" ("The President's Evasion," Mar. 5, 1904).

SENATOR BAILEY. I think they do that with the Baptist Church and the Methodist Church and all the rest of them.

MR. SMITH. Yes; we do that.

SENATOR BAILEY. If they did not receive it, you would withdraw membership, or fellowship, as you call it?

MR. SMITH. That would depend on whether they committed overt acts of unchristianlike conduct.

SENATOR BAILEY. The rejection of the creed is, in the eyes of the church, I suppose, unchristianlike, is it not? Of course, you understand about the creeds of the other churches. Suppose a member of the Baptist Church should reject, say, the doctrine of baptism. I suppose they would unchurch him, would they not? Would not your organization—your church would be the better term—do the same?

MR. SMITH. Certainly.

[SENATOR] BAILEY. So would you not do an exact obedience to your doctrine that far?[22]

MR. SMITH. Permit me to put it this way, if you please, with exact language: We preach our doctrine. We submit it to the judgment of men. They either receive it or reject it on their own volition. If they receive it and are initiated into the church as members of the church, then they are amenable to the laws and rules of the church; and if they do not obey the laws and observe the rules of the church after becoming members of it, and commit overt acts or transgress the laws of the church, then they are dealt with for their fellowship in the church, and the hand of fellowship is withdrawn from them unless they repent.[23] ...

---

22. Carl Badger recorded in his journal on March 5, 1904:

Yesterday Dr. Edward Everett Hale, the venerable chaplain of the Senate, sat on the "Mormon side" of the room, between the Senator and [Apostle] Hyrum Smith. A stranger would have taken him for a typical Mormon. The doctor asked for a copy of the hearings in the case and the Senator promised them to him, and turned to me and asked me to make a note of the same. I asked to be introduced to him, and he said something perfunctory, and gave me a nerveless grasp of the hand" (in Badger, *Liahona and Iron Rod*, 212).

23. J. Reuben Clark's copy bracketed this entire answer.

5.
Joseph F. Smith
Saturday, March 5

"The sensational headlines which some of the local papers are printing, for the purpose of inflaming the public mind over the senatorial investigation at Washington, are very misleading and intentionally so, because not warranted by the information that follows. That however is one of the tricks of the trade known as 'yellow journalism.' The testimony of President Joseph F. Smith has disclosed nothing in the shape of a 'skeleton' nor anything in the nature of a 'mystery.'" —*Deseret News,* Mar. 5, 1904

"The smallest of rural chapels is larger than the chamber picked out for this investigation about which the people of this country have read more in the last month than on any other topic except the war in the Orient. Crowding every available inch of space, sixty chairs can be placed in the room. ... The hearings, in Congressional parlance, are 'public,' but a seat within earshot has been a rarely obtained privilege." —*Harper's Weekly,* Mar. 26, 1904.

Joseph F. Smith, having previously affirmed, was examined, and testified as follows ...

MR. WORTHINGTON. There has been a good deal said here about the proportion of polygamists to the Mormon population. Have you any statistics on that subject?

MR. SMITH. I have not any in my possession, but some years ago the facts were published, and I think they were reached by the Utah Commission, and as near, Mr. Chairman, as my recollection goes—it is a long time ago and it is a matter which has not been brought to my attention since, although I have some recollection of it—when the Utah Commission was created and sent to Utah to administer the government there, they excluded all polygamists from the elective franchise, and as women held the elective franchise the same as men they were excluded of course as well as the men.

MR. WORTHINGTON. The women who were in polygamy?

MR. SMITH. All women were voters in Utah. Afterwards, however, the women were disfranchised by act of Congress, I believe, in the Territory. But I understand that the commissioners, after excluding all polygamists, ascertained that there had been excluded some 12,000 in the neighborhood of that, I would not say just what—out of a population of some 250,000 or 300,000. Of course these were polygamists, including the men and the women; and as it took two women to one man to make polygamy, two-thirds of that number of the population excluded from voting would be women, leaving only one-third, or practically about 4,000 men. And reckoning that it takes a man specially to create the status of plural marriage, it was supposed that thus 4,000 male voters represented the actual polygamists of the church, which was something less, I believe, in reality, than 2 per cent of the entire membership of the church.

Now, Mr. Chairman, this statement of mine may be subject to some correction from the record. I do not pretend to state it as absolutely correct, but that is my recollection of it, to the best of my understanding. ...

MR. WORTHINGTON. In the answer of Reed Smoot, found on the bottom of page 38 of the record, it is set forth that the returns of subordinate officers of the church show the number of polygamists at certain times. Do you have records of that kind?

MR. SMITH. I have.

MR. WORTHINGTON. Have you any information—

SENATOR DUBOIS. I beg your pardon, but I rather think it is my right—

MR. WORTHINGTON. Certainly, Senator, it is your right.

SENATOR DUBOIS. And I think it is a courtesy due to the president and myself that I should make my statement here. I am willing to accept the statement which the president has made. I think it is altogether likely that we reason from different premises, and, of course, if we do we will reach different conclusions.

THE CHAIRMAN. What is the point.

SENATOR DUBOIS. As to the proportion of polygamists?

THE CHAIRMAN. Do you desire to question him at this point?

SENATOR DUBOIS. I desire to make a statement. He says that by the Utah commission there were 12,000 polygamists excluded from voting, and he assumes there are 2 women to each man. There must of necessity have been 2 women to each man.

MR. WORTHINGTON. At least 2.

SENATOR DUBOIS. At least 2.

MR. SMITH. Yes, sir.

SENATOR DUBOIS. I should think very likely the percentage would be larger than 2. In his calculation he includes suckling babes. How can a child 2 years old be in polygamy?

MR. SMITH. I beg pardon, I am talking about voters.

SENATOR DUBOIS. There were about 220,000 persons in Utah of voting age. Now, how many of those were gentiles?

MR. SMITH. At that time, I do not know.

SENATOR DUBOIS. Well, about a third to a fourth?

MR. SMITH. I would, at a guess, at that time—that was in—

SENATOR DUBOIS. We will have the full statistics pretty soon.

MR. SMITH. I would not wish to undertake to make a guess at it. I would rather refer right to the statistics themselves.

SENATOR DUBOIS. We will say a fourth.

MR. SMITH. No, sir; I do not think there was a fourth at that time.

SENATOR DUBOIS. Say a fifth.

MR. SMITH. I could not say anything about it because I do not know, but I do not think there was a fourth.

SENATOR DUBOIS. All right. Then I will assume that there were 50,000 gentiles in Utah. That would leave 170,000?

MR. TAYLER. Of all ages.

SENATOR DUBOIS. A hundred and seventy thousand Mormons of all ages.

MR. SMITH. I wish to state, Mr. Chairman, to the chairman and to the Senators, that I suppose you mean by all ages, infants.

SENATOR DUBOIS. I beg pardon.

MR. SMITH. Infants?

SENATOR DUBOIS. Infants.

MR. SMITH. We never take any account of any child under 8 years old, so far as our church records are concerned—that is, as being reckoned a part of our church membership.

SENATOR DUBOIS. I know; but there were 12,000 male polygamists—

MR. SMITH. No, sir.

SENATOR DUBOIS. Twelve thousand polygamists excluded.

MR. SMITH. No, sir; I did not intend to convey that idea. That was a supposition. It was ascertained that there were about 12,000—

SENATOR DUBOIS. I thought you accepted that statement?

MR. SMITH. I said if that was the case at least two-thirds of that number would be women. That is a supposition. That would leave, of course, but one-third males. Now, I contend, if I have permission to contend with the Senator—

SENATOR DUBOIS. Certainly.

MR. SMITH. I do not wish to be disrespectful in any way.

SENATOR DUBOIS. Not at all. The controversy between you and me is because you include all and I include only those of sufficient age.

MR. SMITH. I would be rather inclined to think that at that time probably
three women to one man might have been the average. I could not
say.

THE CHAIRMAN. Right there, at what date was that?

MR. SMITH. That was in 1882.

SENATOR DUBOIS. Then you would have had 12,000—

MR. WORTHINGTON. One-fourth would have been men.

SENATOR DUBOIS. Twelve thousand polygamists out of a Mormon population, including everybody, of 170,000.

MR. SMITH. There were over 200,000, considerably.

SENATOR DUBOIS. There is a discrepancy, but we will figure it at 200,000.
Now, with the large families in Utah, I think it would be fair to assume
that there were four children to each family. I think there are seven
children to a family in Minnesota and some of those other States. Ordinarily I think it is one to five. But here there are plural wives. Taking
it all together, I should think, including the polygamous families and
all, there were four children to a family. What would you say to that?

MR. SMITH. I have no objection to that.

SENATOR DUBOIS. Then you would exclude from the 170,000 as being below the age of 18 considerably more than one-half, of necessity? I am
getting at it roughly. Of necessity you would exclude considerably
more than one-half. You can not count children as being in polygamy.

MR. WORTHINGTON. Do the census returns give the number of Mormons,
males and females?

SENATOR DUBOIS. Yes.

MR. WORTHINGTON. I think it is a matter we can get at, then.

SENATOR DUBOIS. I want to put this in here.

SENATOR DILLINGHAM.[1] Senator, you had better make your statement of
what you claim, so that we will have both statements on the record.

---

1. In a letter to Joseph F. Smith, Smoot wrote:

You and Brother [Francis M.] Lyman must have had a jolly good laugh on your way
home between Washington and Chicago. Senator Dillingham received a letter from
a young lady who occupied the berth in the Pullman car just opposite yours, giving
him a description of what happened on the train and what was said by you and
Brother Lyman ... There was one thing that she did not understand, or was unable to
catch your idea: In reading the testimony you laughed very heartily over some answers made by you that "put Burrows in a hole." She wanted to know from Senator
Dillingham what it was, as she was very curios to find out, so as to have the whole
story complete. I told Dillingham I could not imagine what it was (Mar. 23, 1904).
A few weeks later, President Smith responded:

Senator Dubois. I stated the other day that in my judgment the convictions showed that there were more than 2 or 3 percent, and that in my judgment there were a great many more than 3 or 4 per cent in polygamy at this time. ... That is my statement. I can put in the more exact figures if necessary. I did not want that statement to go to the country unchallenged. The difference between the president and myself is that we were reasoning from different premises. He included all the members of the church. I exclude, of course, those who are not in condition to be in polygamy. I do not question the veracity of the president's statement at all. I simply wish to call attention to the fact that our premises being so totally at variance, of course, our conclusions would be very much at variance.[2] ...

Mr. Worthington. When President [Lorenzo] Snow died, or just prior to his death; what office did you hold?

Mr. Smith. I was his second councilor.

Mr. Worthington. Who was the first councilor?

Mr. Smith. George Q. Cannon when living, but he was then dead. He had died previously.

Mr. Worthington. Was no other councilor living at the time President Snow died?

Mr. Smith. I do not quite understand your question.

You mention[ed] a letter sent to Senator Dillingham, by a young lady, in which F[rancis]. M. L[yman] and I were said to have had a "jolly laugh" ... This lady is said to have occupied the births opposite ours ... from Washington to Chicago. This is very strange. From Washington to Chicago we all ... occupied the Drawing room from which we did not go out, only to meals. There must be some mistake about this matter. I could not say that we did smile or laugh when we wanted to do so, but I cannot recall anything said about Senator Burrows. I read over Elder Lyman's testimony, and I remember that we had a good laugh at his expense, where the sly old Fox, Senator Hoar, got him tangled on the Senators favorite theme—"revelation". We thought the shrude old lawyer rather got Lyman into the hole. But you and Senator Dillingham can rest assured that there was no lady accompanying any berth opposite or near us from Washington to Chicago. But from Chicago to Omaha and from there home we had berths in the open car (Apr. 9, 1904).

2. Anthon H. Lund of the LDS First Presidency discussed this exchange between Senator Dubois and President Smith in a letter to Apostle Heber J. Grant:

You have seen the scheme of Dubois. He wants to disfranchise all the Mormons, and hopes to buil[d] up an anti-mormon party in Idaho that will carry him back to the Senate. He is one of the most cunning and unscrupulous men found. Pres. Smith said that when he was at Washington [D.C.] Dubois had just been brought out of a brothel, and could hardly talk to make himself understood until he got over the effects of his revelry, and yet the temperance women and the virtuous school marms hold him up as a defender of the purity of the home!" (Sept. 12, 1904, typescript in the D. Michael Quinn Papers, Special Collections, Beinecke Library, Yale University, New Haven, Connecticut).

MR. WORTHINGTON. I mean just at the time of his death.

MR. SMITH. At the time of his death he had chosen me as first councilor, and he had chosen Rudger Clawson his second councilor.

MR. WORTHINGTON. Was Mr. Clawson a polygamist?

MR. SMITH. No, sir.

MR. WORTHINGTON. He was a monogamist?

MR. SMITH. He was a monogamist.

MR. WORTHINGTON. So, at the time Lorenzo Snow died a majority of the first presidency, the highest tribunal in your church, were polygamists?

MR. SMITH. Yes, sir; that is right.

MR. WORTHINGTON. I want to find out what you did about having that body constituted—the first presidency. Who became your councilor?

MR. SMITH. I selected Hon. John R. Winder as my first councilor.[3]

MR. WORTHINGTON. Is he a polygamist or a monogamist?

MR. SMITH. A monogamist.

MR. WORTHINGTON. Who was your second councilor?

MR. SMITH. My second councilor was Anthon H. Lund.[4]

MR. WORTHINGTON. What was his status as to the marriage relation?

MR. SMITH. He is reputed to have but one wife, and that he never had any other.

MR. WORTHINGTON. Have those gentlemen remained your councilors?

MR. SMITH. Yes, sir.

MR. WORTHINGTON. So that from the time you became president a majority of the highest tribunal have been monogamists?

MR. SMITH. Yes, sir.

MR. WORTHINGTON. Now, what vacancies, if any, have been filled in the twelve since you became president?

MR. SMITH. Since I became president there have been two vacancies filled in the council of twelve.

MR. WORTHINGTON. How were they filled; by whom were they filled?

MR. SMITH. They were filled in the usual manner by the nomination or suggestion of members of the council and confirmation by the presidency of the church.

MR. WORTHINGTON. Who are the persons who were selected?

MR. SMITH. Who were the persons selected?

3. Winder was appointed first counselor to Smith on October 17, 1901, but was never ordained an apostle.

4. Lund was appointed second counselor to Smith on October 17, 1901, having been ordained an apostle in 1889.

MR. WORTHINGTON. Yes, sir.

MR. SMITH. My son, Hyrum M. Smith.[5]

MR. WORTHINGTON. You have already said that he is a man with but one wife?

MR. SMITH. Yes, sir.

MR. WORTHINGTON. He never had but one wife?

MR. SMITH. Yes, sir; that is correct. And the second was George A[lbert]. Smith, who is also a monogamist, and always has been a monogamist.[6]

SENATOR OVERMAN. Is he any relation to you?

MR. SMITH. He is my cousin's son. He is the son of John Henry Smith, and his father is my cousin.

MR. TAYLER. He is an apostle?

MR. SMITH. Yes, sir.

SENATOR DUBOIS. Who is John Henry Smith? What official position in the church does he hold?

MR. SMITH. He is one of the twelve.

MR. WORTHINGTON. Have I asked you whether he is a polygamist or monogamist?

MR. SMITH. Which—George A.?

MR. WORTHINGTON. I mean those who filled the vacancies.

MR. SMITH. George A. Smith is a monogamist and always has been.

MR. WORTHINGTON. Then, if I understand you correctly, you have appointed since you became president two councilors and two of the twelve apostles?

MR. SMITH. Yes, sir.

MR. WORTHINGTON. And all have been monogamists and are?

MR. SMITH. Yes, sir; all of them. ...

SENATOR BAILEY. Before you leave that,[7] if you do not intend yourself to

---

5. Hyrum M. Smith (1872-1918) was ordained to the Quorum of Twelve Apostles on October 24, 1901.

6. George Albert Smith (1879-1951) was ordained to the Quorum of Twelve Apostles on October 8, 1903, and would become church president on May 21, 1945.

7. Just prior to this statement by Bailey, Worthington entered into the record a sermon delivered by Wilford Woodruff in Logan, Utah, on November 1, 1891, which read in part:

The Lord showed me by vision and revelation exactly what would take place if we did not stop this practice [of plural marriage] ... all ordinances would be stopped through the land of Zion. Confusion would reign throughout Israel, and many men would be made prisoners. This trouble would have come upon the whole church, and we would have been compelled to stop the practice. ...

I know there are a good many men, and probably some leading men, in this ask any further questions about it, I would like to ask a question. The sermon says these 10,000 members of the church were moved upon by a revelation. I do not still see that the head of the church declares that he received a revelation. He does say that he went to God in anguish and prayer; just as Christians of various denominations do when their duty is not plain, and they rise from it more or less instructed. But that was an instruction to obey the law. I, myself, think a Christian would go to the stake before he would abandon his creed; and if that is a revelation, contradicting a former revelation.

MR. SMITH. It is not contradicting it.

SENATOR BAILEY. I think it is. The former revelation undoubtedly permitted plural marriages, if it did not command them, and this revelation forbids them.

MR. SMITH. It simply forbids the practice.

SENATOR BAILEY. That is a distinction without a difference—

MR. SMITH. Oh, no.

SENATOR BAILEY. Because the other undoubtedly permitted its practice. This forbids the practice. Now, if there is not a conflict between these two I am unable to comprehend what a conflict is. Under one state of the case they were permitted to enter into plural marriage and in another state of the case they were forbidden to do it. Now, from what I can understand—

MR. SMITH. Will the Senator please allow me to say a word just there?

THE CHAIRMAN. Let the Senator complete his statement.

MR. SMITH. I beg your pardon.

SENATOR BAILEY. I will pause to hear the witness.

THE CHAIRMAN. Very well.

MR. SMITH. The one is no more emphatic than the other. President Woodruff declares that he himself will stop and that he will use all his influence to have all the people stop the continuance of plural marriages, and all the people assembled in conference agreed with him that they would stop the practice of plural marriage.

Church who have been tried and felt as though President Woodruff had lost the spirit of God and was about to apostatize. Now, I want you to understand that he has not lost the Spirit, nor is he about to apostatize. The Lord is with him and with his people. He told me exactly what to do and what the result would be if we did not do it. I have been called upon by friends outside of the church and urged to take some steps with regard to this matter. They knew the course which the Government was determined to take. This feeling has also been manifested more or less by the members of the church. I saw exactly what would come to pass if there was not something done. I have had the spirit upon me for a long time (*Smoot Hearings,* 1:330-32).

SENATOR BAILEY. That does not touch the question which I have in mind.

MR. SMITH. All right.

SENATOR BAILEY. I will say to you very frankly that I do not have much patience with a doctrine which does not receive a revelation until there is a statute and where the revelation happens to conform to the statute. What I have been trying to fix in my mind is whether you taught that this was a revelation or merely a submission to the law. If it were a submission to the law, then it would be a question whether the Christian would submit to the laws of the land or to the laws of God. I do not pretend to judge about that, but when a sect teaches that an inspiration comes just after a statute has been passed and a report made to Congress, I do not quite understand that anybody is required to accept it as a revelation.

SENATOR FORAKER. All of that is a matter of opinion.

SENATOR BAILEY. Hardly, if the Senator please.

SENATOR FORAKER. I mean so far as the sense of duty is concerned.

SENATOR BAILEY. Not precisely that. I have been compelled to submit to many a law that I thought a vicious one, and which I would have voted to repeal, but as a good citizen I submitted to it. But just how far I would have submitted if I had been otherwise commanded by a revelation from God is a question that I am not now deciding.

MR. SMITH. May I please try to explain this matter a little to the Senator? I will try to be brief.

SENATOR BAILEY. Very well.

MR. SMITH. Mr. Senator, the facts are these: When the laws against plural marriage were passed by the Congress of the United States we held to the idea that they were unconstitutional laws. We are compelled by our doctrines—the doctrines of our church—to obey and observe the constitutional laws of our land.[8]

SENATOR BAILEY. I have heard such a statement read here.

MR. SMITH. We fought the validity of those laws in court all the way from the first and lower court to the highest court of our land, and when the subject finally came before the Supreme Court of the United States and was settled and the law was sustained as a constitutional law, then we, to be obedient to our own doctrines and faith, we are naturally, inclined to obey the law.

But we had a revelation on our statute books, commanding us, or at least not commanding us—yes, commanding us to enter into a cer-

---

8. J. Reuben Clark's copy of the hearings bracketed this answer by Smith.

tain covenant for eternity as well as for time, which is mandatory, with reference to the blessings that are promised in the law; they can not be received without it; and, with reference to the plural part of it, permissive, and we had the alternative before us as to whether we should observe even the constitutional law of the land that was so pronounced by the Supreme Court of the United States or to continue to practice the law of the church.[9]

President Woodruff, as president of the church, entitled, as we hold, as you may not hold, and as everybody is free to have his own opinion about it, to receive revelations and inspiration from Almighty God for the guidance of the church and that he is the final arbitrator for the church on matters of doctrine, sought to the Lord, and, as he says himself in the language which has been read here, the Lord made manifest to him clearly that it was his duty to stop plural marriages, and he received that revelation and that commandment from the Lord to stop it. He published it; announced it. It was submitted first to the officials of the church and accepted by them and then it was submitted to the entire church in conference assembled and it was accepted by them, and thus it became binding upon the church; and the church has from that day to this kept the law so far as plural marriages are concerned.

I should like to draw a distinction in the Senator's mind that there is a great difference in our judgment, in our feelings, between the law prohibiting plural marriages and the law prohibiting what is termed in the law unlawful cohabitation—a very great difference. Plural marriage has stopped; but I choose, rather than to abandon my children and their mothers, to run my risks before the law. I want to say, too, that it is the law of my State—it is not the law of Congress—under which I am living and by which I am punishable. It is the law of my State, and the courts of my State have competent jurisdiction to deal with me in my offenses against the law, and the Congress of the United States has no business with my private conduct any more than it has with the private conduct of any citizen of Utah or any other State. It is the law of my State to which I am amenable, and if the officers of the law have not done their duty toward me I can not blame them. I think they have some respect for me.

THE CHAIRMAN. I wish to ask you a question right here. You speak of your unwillingness to abandon your children.

MR. SMITH. Yes, sir.

---

9. J. Reuben Clark's copy of the hearings bracketed this paragraph by Smith.

THE CHAIRMAN. Why is it necessary, in order to support your children, educate, and clothe them, that you should continue to have children by a multiplicity of wives?

MR. SMITH. Because my wives are like everybody else's wife.

THE CHAIRMAN. I am not speaking of them.

MR. SMITH. I understand.

THE CHAIRMAN. I am speaking of the children now in existence born to you.

MR. SMITH. Yes.

THE CHAIRMAN. Why is it necessary to continue to have issue by wives in order to support and educate the children already in existence? Why is it necessary?

MR. SMITH. It is only to the peace and harmony and good will of myself and my wives; that is all.

THE CHAIRMAN. Then you could educate your children and clothe them and feed them without having new issue?

MR. SMITH. Well, yes; I possibly could, but that is just exactly the kernel in the nut.

THE CHAIRMAN. Yes.

MR. SMITH. I have chosen not to do that, Mr. Chairman.

THE CHAIRMAN. You have chosen not to do it?

MR. SMITH. That is it. I am responsible before the law for my action.

THE CHAIRMAN. And in not doing it, you are violating the law?[10]

MR. SMITH. The law of my State?

THE CHAIRMAN. Yes.

MR. SMITH. Yes, sir.

SENATOR OVERMAN. Is there not a revelation published in the Book of Covenants here that you shall abide by the law of the State?

---

10. Smoot called upon President Roosevelt often regarding Burrows's seemingly relentless assault. The year 1904 was a presidential election year. Describing one meeting with the president, Smoot explained to Joseph F. Smith:

Please do not have this letter read at council meeting, as it is intended for you and your [private] council. I feel it my duty to inform you just how things stand politically in Washington, and have asked Mr. Doremus to carry this letter direct to you, for I do not wish to trust it by mail. ... I have had several conversations with the President [Roosevelt] and have come to an understanding with him relative to the politics of the State of Utah. I have told him that I am for his reelection ... I believe that the President is doing all that he can consistently do to help me in my fight. I know he had Burrows at the White House last Saturday in relation to the case; but Roosevelt expressed to me after the interview, as he has done several times before, that he was very doubtful that anything could be done to change the course mapped out by Burrows. Burrows reelection comes this fall, and last Saturday he expressed to me that he has the fight of his life before him, and that it is very doubtful weather he will be successful" (Smoot to Joseph F. Smith, February 5, 1904).

MR. SMITH. It includes both unlawful cohabitation and polygamy.

SENATOR OVERMAN. Is there not a revelation that you shall abide by the laws of the State and land?

MR. SMITH. Yes, sir.

SENATOR OVERMAN. If that is a revelation, are you not violating the laws of God?

MR. SMITH. I have admitted that, Mr. Senator, a great many times here.[11]

SENATOR OVERMAN. I did not know that you had.

MR. SMITH. And I am amenable to the law for it. But I see the point of the Senator's question. Gentlemen, you have shown a great deal of leniency in permitting me to express my views here, and I do not wish to be offensive and I do not wish to take more time than I need to. But the church itself—I understand your point, that the church forbids me to violate the law, certainly it does—but the church gave me those wives, and the church can not be consistent and compel me to forsake them and surrender them.[12]

SENATOR BAILEY. "The Lord giveth and the Lord taketh away," and when the Lord gave this second revelation forbidding it—

MR. SMITH. He did not forbid it.

SENATOR BAILEY. Well, he did, if the manifesto is based upon a revelation, because the manifesto declares against it.

MR. SMITH. The manifesto declares positively the prohibition of plural marriages, and in the examination before the master in chancery the president of the church and other leading members of the church agreed before the master in chancery that the spirit and meaning of that revelation applied to unlawful cohabitation as well as to plural marriages.[13]

SENATOR BAILEY. That is what I was coming to now, Mr. Smith. Then, as I understand you, both plural marriage and unlawful cohabitation are

---

11. The previous twelve questions and answers would be cited in the Senate debate in 1907, also by Senator Dubois's wife in a 1905 speech to the Woman's Home Missionary Association, where she stated:

> Today I come to you ... on account of this testimony and the outrageous indifference of that answer. I would not enter the arena to help the Mormon women of Utah, for these women sustained President Smith when he returned from Washington, but I am pleading for children who come into the world outcasts. I am pleading for assistance to break the influence of the powerful hierarchy that threatens to overturn the government and break down the lofty ideals of childhood, pure motherhood and noble womanhood, and destroy the bulwark of our nation [, the] American home" ("Strong Address of Mrs. Dubois," *Salt Lake Herald,* Apr. 12, 1905).

12. J. Reuben Clark's copy of the hearings bracketed this answer.

13. J. Reuben Clark's copy of the hearings bracketed this answer.

forbidden by the statutes of Utah and by the revelations of God. Is that true?

Mr. Smith. That is the spirit of it, sir.

Senator Bailey. And yet you, as the head of the church, are defying both—

Mr. Smith. Oh, no.

Senator Bailey. The statute of Utah and the ordinance of the church—

Mr. Smith. Not the ordinance at all.

Senator Bailey. Perhaps; you have another and better expression to describe them?

Mr. Smith. If you say the manifesto—

Senator Bailey. I should say that a revelation once communicated to the church and sustained by the church would become an ordinance of the church.

Mr. Smith. If the Senator please—

Senator Bailey. If you will provide me with a better expression than that I shall be glad to adopt it. We will call it the law of the church.

Mr. Smith. No, sir; call it the rule.[14]

Senator Bailey. Does not a revelation become the law of the church?

Mr. Smith. Call it the rule of the church, and I will understand.

Senator Bailey. Law, after all, is but a rule of conduct prescribed by the supreme power. What I am trying now to emphasize is that the manifesto is a revelation, or that it is based upon a revelation; that the revelation—

Mr. Smith. If the Senator will permit me, it is inspired. It is the same thing. I admit what you say.

Senator Bailey. I do not know quite so much about these nice distinctions in the gospel as I hope I do in the law. I am amenable to correction on those. But at any rate, it is a revelation forbidding alike plural marriage and unlawful cohabitation; and that revelation from the Lord is supplemented and reinforced by the statutes of the State of Utah.

Mr. Smith. Yes.

Senator Bailey. I agree with you entirely, that for your individual conduct you are amenable to the State of Utah and not to the Federal Government. I concur in that statement; but is it true that the head of the church in Utah is living in open and proclaimed defiance of the statutes of that State, and also in defiance of a revelation received by

---

14. J. Reuben Clark's copy of the hearings bracketed this answer and the question that preceded it.

your predecessor—not your immediate predecessor, I believe, but a predecessor—and communicated to the church and sustained by it? Am I correct in that?

MR. SMITH. You are correct so far—that I have confessed here openly, and it has gone to the world—that I have not observed the law against cohabitation with my wives. That is all there is to it.

SENATOR BAILEY. What I am trying to make clear is that it is a law not only of the State of Utah but also a law of the church.

MR. SMITH. It is a rule of the church.

SENATOR BAILEY. That is what I want to make clear.

MR. SMITH. Yes.

SENATOR OVERMAN. There is one question I wish to ask. You may have stated it before. This manifesto, which was published, I understand you to say is sent [out as a] broad[sheet]?

MR. SMITH. Yes.

SENATOR OVERMAN. What I want to know is this: This manifesto does not tell about how the revelation came or that it is a revelation. Is this revelation published in any of your standard works?

MR. SMITH. I informed the committee yesterday that it has been an oversight, that it had not been published in the latest edition of the Doctrine and Covenants, and that I would see to it that it should be published in the next edition of the Doctrine and Covenants to meet this objection.[15]

THE CHAIRMAN. You are speaking of the manifesto?

MR. SMITH. Yes, sir.

THE CHAIRMAN. Pardon me a question right in the line of what Mr. Smith has been testifying about—speaking about the care of his children. Another statement you made is that you do not teach polygamy.

MR. SMITH. I do not understand the chairman.

THE CHAIRMAN. I understood you to say you were not teaching the doctrine of polygamy to your people.

MR. SMITH. That is right, and I should like to add in connection with the Senator's remarks, here that I am not openly and obnoxiously practicing unlawful cohabitation.

THE CHAIRMAN. Right in this connection—

MR. SMITH. I have avoided that.

THE CHAIRMAN. Right in this connection, you say you are not teaching polygamy?

---

15. The Manifesto was added to the Doctrine and Covenants in 1908. J. Reuben Clark's copy of the hearings bracketed this answer by Smith.

MR. SMITH. Yes, sir.

THE CHAIRMAN. How more forcibly could you teach it than by practicing it openly as the head of the church?

MR. SMITH. I am not practicing it openly.

THE CHAIRMAN. Are you practicing it secretly?

MR. SMITH. No, sir.[16]

THE CHAIRMAN. Then, how are you practicing it?

MR. SMITH. I am not practicing polygamy at all.

THE CHAIRMAN. You are not?

MR. SMITH. I have prohibited polygamy.

THE CHAIRMAN. You are not living in polygamous cohabitation?

MR. SMITH. Oh, yes; but not in polygamy. Polygamy means the marrying of more wives than one, but I am not living in polygamy. I am not practicing it or permitting it.

THE CHAIRMAN. Then your idea is, after the marriage is consummated, to live with a woman is not polygamy?

MR. SMITH. It is not polygamy inasmuch as the marriage occurred before the manifesto.[17] ...

---

16. This entire section would be used by Tayler in closing argument for the claimants (*Smoot Hearings,* 3:556-61).

17. Tayler used this exchange in his closing argument (ibid.).

III.
SECOND WEEK OF MARCH
1904

6.
Joseph F. Smith
Monday, March 7

"The second week of the Smoot hearing began this morning with
the usual double row of curious sensational seekers lined up on
the north side wall. There were not quite as many ribbons, feather
and millinery confections on exhibition, owing to the fact that the
morning opened with drizzling rain, which by 10 o'clock had developed into a steady downpour. ... Wedged firmly against the jamb of
the door was a negro at least six feet tall, who was the first colored
[of] many who has yet succeeded in getting his head inside the
door." —*Deseret News,* Mar. 7, 1904

"He [Joseph F. Smith] spoke as one having authority, to be sure,
but it was the authority of the specialist, the scholar, the man ac-
customed to handling terms of precision, rather than of one who
spoke with the tongues of men and of angels. His words were chosen deliberately and uttered slowly, his voice thin, and the tone in
which he answered questions so low that those at the other end of
the room found it hard to understand. His only gesture was an
up-and-down movement of a long forefinger. The elderly president
of a Western normal school, forced by circumstances to discuss his
private affairs before an unfriendly tribunal, would have borne himself much as did this head of a great religious body and of commercial enterprises so varied that they supply the people's wants with
everything from street-car rides, knit goods, and improving literature to theatricals and salt-water bathing. It was with an almost academic manner that President Smith made the declarations which
flashed to the ends of the earth" —*Harper's Weekly,* Mar. 26, 1904.

Joseph F. Smith, having previously affirmed, was examined, and testified as follows ...

MR. WORTHINGTON. ... You said something a moment ago about the apostles being consulted as advisers. I do not clearly understand whether
you said that they were the advisers of you in your official position, or
whether they are your personal advisers. Have they anything to do
with advising you as to your conduct personally any more than any
other member of the church has?

MR. SMITH. No, sir; not in the least.

MR. WORTHINGTON. At the time Senator Smoot became an apostle which was—I do not know whether it appears in the record—the 9th day of April, 1900, was it not?

MR. SMITH. The 9th or 10th; I am not sure which.

MR. WORTHINGTON. Let me ask you right there, while I think of it, when was your last child born? Do you remember the exact date?

MR. SMITH. I do not know that there is any particular coincidence about it. I think it was born on the day that he was sustained as one of the twelve. ...

MR. WORTHINGTON. You were not president at the time he became an apostle?

MR. SMITH. No, sir.

MR. WORTHINGTON. You became president on what day?

MR. SMITH. The 10th day of November, 1901.

MR. WORTHINGTON. Since that date, of course, he has not been present when the members of the first presidency have met officially.

MR. SMITH. No, sir.

MR. WORTHINGTON. And you have not been present, I presume, when the quorum of apostles met officially?

MR. SMITH. Since that time?

MR. WORTHINGTON. Yes; since you became president. The apostles are not present when the members of the first presidency hold their meetings?

MR. SMITH. No, sir.

MR. WORTHINGTON. And the members of the first presidency are not present when the Apostles hold their meetings?

MR. SMITH. No, sir.

MR. WORTHINGTON. But you are all present at the general councils which are held for prayer and advice?

MR. SMITH. Yes, sir.

MR. WORTHINGTON. Now, at any conference of that kind when you have been present, has the subject of your relations with reference to living with plural wives been touched upon in any way? Do you understand the question?

MR. SMITH. I hardly think I do.

MR. WORTHINGTON. The question is whether at any joint meetings which have been held of the first presidency and the twelve Apostles since you became president, and when you were present, has anything been said on this subject of your living and continuing to live in polygamous cohabitation with several wives?

Mr. Smith. Not that I know of.

Mr. Worthington. Have you any recollection?

Mr. Smith. No, sir; I have no recollection of anything having been said about it.

Mr. Worthington. So far as you know has there come up the subject whether members of the church should or should not, or were right or wrong in continuing to live in polygamous cohabitation?

Mr. Smith. I do not think anything has been said about it in any of our meetings. It has been generally conceded and generally understood, as I have frequently stated before, I think, that the plural marriages which occurred before the manifesto, many, many years ago in many instances, were not to be disturbed by the church; that the church was a party to the entering in of that marriage status, and that it would be inconsistent for the church to undertake to interrupt it, and the consequence has been that there has not been anything said to my knowledge against that principle. But I do know that when we have heard rumors; such as have been published by the anti-Mormon press, that there were marriages going on, the question has been broached many times in our councils, and invariably it has been resolved in our councils that all such things must stop, if they had not stopped, and so far as we were concerned, we knew of no such things occurring, and if anything of the kind did occur, it was without our knowledge or consent or approval. Those things have been mentioned.

Mr. Worthington. That is a digression, and something you have already stated several times.

Mr. Smith. I understand.

Mr. Worthington. What I want to know particularly, Mr. Smith, is whether at any of these joint meetings of the first presidency and the quorum of the apostles when you were present and since you became president this subject of polygamous cohabitation has been discussed at all?

Mr. Smith. I do not think it has.

Mr. Worthington. Either in the way of advisory talk or in taking official action?

Mr. Smith. I do not recall anything that has been said in relation to it.

Mr. Worthington. When you became president you were then, as I understand, living with your five wives, as you have stated here?

Mr. Smith. Yes, sir.

Mr. Worthington. And you had made up your mind long before that, that you would continue to do it, as I understand?

MR. SMITH. Yes, sir.

MR. WORTHINGTON. So that when Reed Smoot became an apostle, and you became president, your status in that respect had been fixed?

MR. SMITH. It had been fixed long years before.

MR. WORTHINGTON. Had Senator Smoot anything to do with that status?

MR. SMITH. No, sir.

MR. WORTHINGTON. Or with bringing you to that conclusion?

MR. SMITH. No, sir.

MR. WORTHINGTON. Or did he advise you—

MR. SMITH. No, sir.

MR. WORTHINGTON. Or encourage you?

MR. SMITH. No, sir.

MR. WORTHINGTON. Or connive at your sustaining that relation?

MR. SMITH. Not to my knowledge.

THE CHAIRMAN. Has he at any time protested to you against it?

MR. SMITH. No, sir; he never has had any conversation with me on the subject at all. ...

MR. WORTHINGTON. Mr. Chairman, before going on with the examination of the witness, I would like to say that just before the recess I made a remark which has been misinterpreted by some, and perhaps by the committee. I remarked, when Senator Dubois had, by accident, referred to me as counsel for the witness, that I was not his counsel, and I said if I were his counsel that there would have been some difference in his testimony, or something to that effect. I only meant by that to say that as I understood the law he had a right to refuse to answer a great many of the questions which have been asked him here, and if I had been in his place I would have refused to answer them.

I did not, in the slightest degree, of course, mean to reflect upon any person who may have advised him, because we all know he is represented here by very able, conscientious, and distinguished counsel. I am advised, however, that even, in so far as that is concerned, I was mistaken, because—and in this the witness can answer whether it is true or not—I am informed he was fully advised in the premises, and decided of his own motion that he would answer everything, whether he was compelled to answer it or not. How is that, Mr. Smith?

MR. SMITH. That is correct, sir.

THE CHAIRMAN. The statement of Mr. Worthington will go into the record.[1]

---

1. Worthington is apologizing for having said: "I am not counsel for Mr. Smith. I am

MR. WORTHINGTON. Mr. Smith, about the matter of rewarding those who have persistently violated the law by giving them high office. I want to ask a few questions bearing upon that charge. At the time of the manifesto President Woodruff was at the head of your church?

MR. SMITH. Yes, sir.

MR. WORTHINGTON. Let me ask you whether or not, so far as either your personal knowledge or the reputation of the matter goes, he complied with his own manifesto in the matter of polygamous cohabitation, as well as in the matter of polygamy proper?

MR. SMITH. He did, according to my best understanding.

MR. WORTHINGTON. How long did he live after the manifesto, about, and continue to be president?

MR. SMITH. He lived a number of years, quite a number of years. I could not tell you from memory.

MR. WORTHINGTON. His successor, you have told us, was [Lorenzo] Snow.

MR. SMITH. Yes, sir.

MR. WORTHINGTON. And what is the fact, as you understand it, as to whether or not he complied with the prohibition against polygamous cohabitation?

MR. SMITH. My understanding is that he complied strictly with it.

MR. WORTHINGTON. Then you succeeded him?

MR. SMITH. Yes, sir.

MR. WORTHINGTON. I wish you would explain a little more fully than you have about this matter of promotion—how it was you came to take the place of Lorenzo Snow. I think you have told us there has been a custom, at least, of promotion.

MR. SMITH. It has been the custom, since the death of Joseph Smith, that the president of the twelve succeeded to the presidency of the church.

MR. WORTHINGTON. That has been from the beginning—that has been a rule that has been followed?

MR. SMITH. It was the case with Brigham Young and his successors.

MR. WORTHINGTON. How is the apostle who becomes president of that quorum selected? Is that by selection or seniority, or how?

MR. SMITH. It is by seniority.

MR. WORTHINGTON. So that the last apostle takes the foot of the list?

MR. SMITH. Yes, sir.

MR. WORTHINGTON. And as vacancies occur he moves up?

MR. SMITH. Yes, sir.

---

counsel for Senator Smoot. If I were counsel for Mr. Smith the examination would be very different from what it is" (*Smoot Hearings,* 1:362).

MR. WORTHINGTON. Has there, so far as you know, from the beginning been any other rule followed?

MR. SMITH. No.

MR. WORTHINGTON. Or has that been universally followed?

MR. SMITH. That has been universally followed.

MR. WORTHINGTON. So that all the rewards that have come in that way have been by simply following the custom of the church?

MR. SMITH. That is correct, sir.

MR. WORTHINGTON. I understand you to say, however, that there is no law—no revelation or command—of the church in any way which requires that.

MR. SMITH. No; it is just simply a custom.[2]

MR. WORTHINGTON. And that if a vacancy should occur to-morrow it would be competent for any member of the church to be selected as president?

MR. SMITH. That is quite right. ...

MR. TAYLER. Mr. Smith, you testified on Friday or Saturday respecting the prevalence of polygamy in Utah, and of the number of polygamists there, using an interview which you had given out to the representative of the Associated Press.

MR. SMITH. Yes, sir.

MR. TAYLER. Did you have the interview, or a copy of it, in full in your hand at the time you testified?

MR. SMITH. I brought it with me.

MR. TAYLER. Was that the whole interview?

MR. SMITH. I think that was the whole interview at that time.

MR. TAYLER. Did not the interview that you gave out at that time and which was published in the "Deseret News," your church's newspaper, contain also a very strong declaration in favor of the election of Mr. Smoot as Senator?

MR. SMITH. I do not know of anything of the kind. Perhaps it did. I do not remember anything of that kind.[3]

---

2. J. Reuben Clark's copy of the hearings underlined in purple ink the majority of the questions and answers in this exchange.

3. The March 5, 1904, interview read: "Mr. Copp, local agent of the Associated Press, called upon President Smith this afternoon desiring information as to the status of polygamy, and the following questions and answers were put into form for that gentleman, at his request, for publication:

Q. Does the church solemnize or permit plural marriages?

A. Certainly not. The church does not perform, or sanction, or authorize marriage in any form that is contrary to the law of the land.

Mr. Tayler. You do not recall that, while the controversy was on respecting the election of a Senator, you put out this interview which you have described, saying that it was not true that polygamous marriage ceremonies had been performed in Utah by the church, and giving the figures showing the number of polygamists then in Utah, and then follow that with an argument in very vigorous terms in favor of the election of Mr. Smoot as Senator before the legislature that was about to convene?

Mr. Smith. No, sir—

Mr. Van Cott. Just a moment, Mr. Smith. Mr. Chairman, we suggest that the custom that was suggested the other day be followed, of showing Mr. Smith that interview, to refresh his recollection.

Mr. Worthington. Have you it here?

Mr. Tayler. I have it not right by me. I had it Saturday; but I wanted to know of the witness whether he gave out any interview of that sort, and I asked him if he had given us all of the interview.

Mr. Smith. I can tell the chairman and the committee that I have not given out any interview at all that I know of except that which I read here the other day.

The Chairman. Mr. Tayler asks you if you gave out the whole of the interview to the committee.

Q. Why then is it asserted that prominent Mormons practice polygamy?

A. That is done evidently to mislead the general public. Polygamy, under the law, is the marrying of a husband or wife while the legal husband or wife is living and undivorced. There is no such offence committed by sanction of the Mormon Church. But when the prohibition of polygamy was proclaimed by the president of the Mormon Church there were many persons who had contracted plural marriage, and that relation has been continued in many instances because the men in that position determined not to abandon their families, but to care for and provide for them and educate and cherish their children. This is erroneously construed as practicing "polygamy," and creates the impression that polygamous marriages are still permitted in and by the church.

Q. To what extent are these relations of polygamous families sustained?

A. It was ascertained by careful census in 1890, when President Woodruff issued his manifesto against further polygamous marriages, there were 2,451 such families belonging to the Church of Jesus Christ of Latter-Day Saints in the United States. In October, 1899, by another count, it was found that the number had been reduced, by death, 750; by removal beyond confines of the Republic, 63; by divorce, 95; leaving then but 1,543. In May, 1902, a complete and thorough inquiry showed that the original number in 1890 had been reduced 63 per cent, leaving then only 897, and the great majority of whom were of advanced age, and many of them have since departed this life. It is evident that with no addition to this total, but a rapid and continual decrease, the number of polygamous families will soon be reduced to zero" (*Smoot Hearings*, 1:323-24).

MR. SMITH. This is all that I know anything about. It was given to the associated press man. It was necessarily brief, as an associated press dispatch, and—

SENATOR HOAR. Did you give it to him in writing or did he take it down from your lips?

MR. SMITH. Who?

SENATOR HOAR. The man to whom you gave it.

THE CHAIRMAN. The correspondent?

MR. SMITH. He was there, and he asked the questions and I answered his questions, and furnished him the data that is contained—

SENATOR HOAR. All I want to know is this. Sometimes a person comes to a public man for an interview, and he [the public figure] writes down what he wants to say, and hands it to him for greater certainty. Did you give him what you gave him in writing, or did he report it, you giving it orally?

MR. SMITH. We gave it to him together. We sat down together, he and I, and we made out that report from the data we had.

SENATOR HOAR. You do not answer my question yet. I want to know whether you gave him a manuscript which he took, or whether you spoke to him and he took down the substance of your conversation. That is all.

MR. SMITH. He was in our office, Senator, if you please. A gentleman called upon us in our office—

SENATOR HOAR. That does not answer the question.

MR. SMITH. We sat down together.

MR. WORTHINGTON. Did you write the paper or did he write it?

MR. SMITH. We wrote it together. He wrote his questions to me and I wrote my replies.

THE CHAIRMAN. You wrote the answers yourself?

MR. SMITH. I wrote the answers myself.

THE CHAIRMAN. After the paper was completed, did you examine it?

MR. SMITH. I did.

MR. TAYLER. Mr. Critchlow had the paper, and he is not here to-day. That is why I haven't it.

MR. WORTHINGTON. You mean the newspaper.

MR. TAYLER. I have a "Deseret News" interview, verbatim ad literatim, what Mr. Smith read, save and except this endorsement of Mr. Smoot.

MR. WORTHINGTON. I mean you have not here the paper which was written at that time?

MR. TAYLER. No; and, I do not intend to depend upon that. I will take the

"Deseret News" account of it. If that is not reliable, it is up to you to show it is not.

SENATOR FORAKER. Let me ask; before you pass from that, is there any doubt that the witness was in favor of Mr. Smoot's election to the Senate?

MR. TAYLER. Not the slightest.

MR. VAN COTT. I think Mr. Smith ought to answer the question. I do not think Mr. Tayler ought to furnish the information.

MR. TAYLER. The question was asked me, Mr. Van Cott, and I have no objection to answering questions.

SENATOR FORAKER. I was not addressing myself to anyone in particular, but rather to the witness. I did not know but that some question had arisen. I have not been here in attendance all the while. I understood he favored the election of Mr. Smoot as Senator.

MR. SMITH. I never had any question in my mind in regard to it.

THE CHAIRMAN. That does not answer the question directly, Mr. Smith. Did you favor his election, is the question?

MR. SMITH. I gave my consent as an individual and a fellow-laborer to him that he should become a candidate if he chose. I certainly had no objections. If I had I would have made them known to him.[4]

MR. TAYLER. Does that answer your question satisfactorily, Senator?

SENATOR FORAKER. Yes; I was simply led to believe by this question that there might possibly have been something said when I was out that had given rise to a question as to whether or not he did favor his election to the Senate. I wanted to clear that up.

MR. TAYLER. I hope you feel it is cleared up, Senator.

SENATOR FORAKER. It was clear in my mind until you asked the question. It is now clear, just as it was before.

---

4. Recently Smoot had thanked Smith for his unwavering support:

I hasten to acknowledge the receipt of you letter of January 28, 1904, and sincerely thank you for the same. I assure you it has taken a load from my shoulders. ... I must acknowledge that I have had feelings that some of the brethren have taken the position that I was to blame for all this unpleasantness and trouble brought upon the Church through my personal ambition. ... I have never worried one second over myself or what may happen to me in this investigation, but I have laid awake nights thinking how I could protect you and your counselors from being brought into the fight. There has never been a time since the question of my running for ... Senator was first discussed that I would not have willingly withdrawn if you had even intimated that it was best to do so. ... I have read your letter over and over again and it appeals to me stronger each time I read it, and I thank the Lord that we have a Presidency that cannot be easily frightened. ... I sometimes think it would be a good thing to let the President and some of our particular friends in the Senate read you letter and understand your position, but, of course, I would not do so without your sanctions (Feb. 5, 1904).

THE CHAIRMAN. I want to ask you this, Mr. Smith, to make that clear. You say you gave your consent to Mr. Smoot to be a candidate for the United States Senate. Did you do anything toward his election beyond that?

MR. SMITH. No more than you did, Senator.

THE CHAIRMAN. That is not the question.

MR. SMITH. Well, I did not then, if you please.

THE CHAIRMAN. You did nothing, then?

MR. SMITH. I did nothing.

THE CHAIRMAN. Well, why did you regard your consent as necessary?

MR. SMITH. Because he was one of our general authorities, and the rule of the church is that one of our general authorities desiring to engage in any business contrary to the business he is strictly engaged in as general authority of the church comes to his associates and asks their permission to thus engage in something else ...

THE CHAIRMAN. Mr. Smith, is there an organization known as the Reform Church of Jesus Christ of Latter-day Saints?

MR. SMITH. I do not know of any organization of that name.

THE CHAIRMAN. I may be mistaken in the name. There is a Mormonism organization, separate from the organization to which you belong?

MR. SMITH. Yes, sir.

THE CHAIRMAN. What is that called?

MR. SMITH. It is called the Reorganized Church.

THE CHAIRMAN. Were you ever a member of that?

MR. SMITH. No, sir.

THE CHAIRMAN. Are you acquainted at Plano Ill[inois]?

MR. SMITH. Some twenty years ago I called there and visited with my cousin, who was then residing there, but he is not living there now.[5]

THE CHAIRMAN. Did this organization of which you speak have an existence in that place?

MR. SMITH. It did at that time. There was a branch of it at that time there.

THE CHAIRMAN. Who was at the head of that organization then?

MR. SMITH. Joseph Smith [III], my cousin.

THE CHAIRMAN. He was a cousin of yours?

MR. SMITH. Yes, sir.

THE CHAIRMAN. And is he living?

MR. SMITH. Yes, sir.

---

5. For more on the relationship between these cousins, see Linda King Newell, "Cousins in Conflict: Joseph Smith III and Joseph F. Smith," *Journal of the John Whitmer Historical Association* 9 (1989): 3-16.

THE CHAIRMAN. And a lineal descendant, I suppose, of Joseph Smith?

MR. SMITH. He is a son of Joseph Smith.

THE CHAIRMAN. Is he still at the head of that organization, do you know?

MR. SMITH. Yes, sir.

THE CHAIRMAN. I understood you to say that the prophet Joseph Smith—I mean the original revelator—

MR. SMITH. Yes.

THE CHAIRMAN. I understood you to say, somewhere in your testimony, that he was in his lifetime a polygamist?

MR. SMITH. Yes, sir.

THE CHAIRMAN. Can you name any person to whom he was married?

MR. SMITH. Yes, sir.

THE CHAIRMAN. Or any child born to him—

MR. SMITH. Oh, no; I can not tell you anything about the children. I can tell you one or two of his wives.

THE CHAIRMAN. If you will be kind enough to give them to me, I will be obliged to you.

MR. SMITH. Eliza R. Snow.[6]

THE CHAIRMAN. When did he marry her?

MR. SMITH. He married her in 1842, I think.

THE CHAIRMAN. Well, another?

MR. SMITH. Eliza Maria Partridge was one of his wives.[7]

THE CHAIRMAN. When was that?

MR. SMITH. Somewhere in the forties; I do not know just when; I could not tell from memory.

THE CHAIRMAN. Was his first wife alive at that time?

MR. SMITH. Yes, sir.

THE CHAIRMAN. Whom else, that you know of?[8]

---

6. For more on Snow, see Todd Compton, *In Sacred Loneliness: The Plural Wives of Joseph Smith* (Salt Lake City: Signature Books, 1997), 288-305.

7. For more on Partridge, see ibid., 396-432.

8. Notice the wide range of Senator Burrows's questions. Even in private conversation with Smoot, Burrows expressed contempt for Smoot and Latter-day Saints in general. For instance, the chairman withheld the prosecution's witness list from Smoot and his counsel so they would not tip off witnesses to go into hiding prior to being subpoenaed. Smoot elaborated in a letter to Joseph F. Smith:

I almost lost my temper with Senator Burrows last Saturday at the time he told me my case would not be heard until March first, and that he had agreed upon the witnesses to be subpoenaed for the protestants. I kindly asked him, if there was nothing wrong in so doing, to give me a list of the names of witnesses, as it would enable me to know about what class of testimony I would have to meet, and help me in making up my list of witnesses. He answered, "Oh, no. We could not do that, for if we

MR. SMITH. It would be very difficult for me to tell you who else from memory. ...

SENATOR OVERMAN. Let me ask a question for my own satisfaction. I have a little pamphlet which states that you teach that our Savior was a polygamist. Is that so?

MR. SMITH. We do not teach any such doctrine. We simply teach the historical fact that Jesus Christ descended through a line of polygamists from David and Abraham.

SENATOR OVERMAN. You do not teach that he had polygamous relations?

MR. SMITH. Oh, no, sir.[9] ...

---

did you would telegraph home, and they would get out of that way." This was a little more than I could stand without showing my disgust, and I told ... Burrows he need not worry about their going to run away, that his statement was uncalled for, and a reflection upon people who did not deserve it, and that it was without foundation (Feb. 9, 1904).

9. On this topic, Carl Badger wrote home to Utah on December 10, 1904: "There is to be a large mass-meeting to-morrow afternoon at the Tenth St. Congregational Church. ... Charles Mostyn Owen ... is going to assert that we teach in the religion classes that Mary and Martha were the wives of the Savior. Tell me candidly, is there the least suggestion of a truth in this? I know that the belief is quite general among our people that such was the case, but is there any truth that such is being taught in the religious classes?" (in Rodney J. Badger, *Liahona and Iron Rod: The Biography of Carl A. and Rose J. Badger* [Bountiful, Utah: Family History Publishers, 1985], 235). J. Reuben Clark's copy of the hearings underlined each of the questions and answers in this exchange.

7.

Clara Mabel Barber Kennedy,
Charles E. Merrill, and Francis M. Lyman

Monday & Tuesday, March 7-8

"The committee was late in getting together as usual. Even Atty. Tayler failed to appear until 10:40, and there were only five members of the committee in their seats when Mrs. Kennedy ... took the stand. ... Witnesses in the Smoot hearing learned today for the first time just what they are to receive in the way of fees. Mrs. Matthews and Mrs. Kennedy were each allowed railroad fare, meals, sleeping car fare, porterage and thirteen days at $3.00 a day each. They arrived only on Sunday, but ... were entitled to five days' pay each way ... This will be the basis of payment for all other witnesses." —*Deseret News,* Mar. 8, 1904

Mrs. Clara Mabel Barber Kennedy,[1] having been duly sworn, was examined and testified as follows ...

MR. TAYLER. Where do you live, Mrs. Kennedy?

MRS. KENNEDY. I live in Sevier County, Utah ...

MR. TAYLER. Where were you born?

MRS. KENNEDY. I was born in Albany, N[ew]. Y[ork].

MR. TAYLER. Did you go to Utah early in life?

MRS. KENNEDY. Yes, sir; at 2 years old.

MR. TAYLER. And your family was a Mormon family there?

MRS. KENNEDY. At Utah?

MR. TAYLER. Yes; in Utah.

MRS. KENNEDY. Yes; my father and mother are both Mormons.

MR. TAYLER. And later, while you were still young, did they move to Mexico?

MRS. KENNEDY. Yes, sir.

MR. TAYLER. Where in Mexico did you and your family live?

MRS. KENNEDY. At Diaz, Mexico.

MR. TAYLER. How old were you when you went there?

MRS. KENNEDY. About 10 years old—a little more than 10 years old.

---

1. Clara Mabel Barber Kennedy (1878-1966) was born in Albany, New York. She moved to Utah at age two, married a plural husband in Mexico at age seventeen, and later left her husband and the LDS Church, though she chose to remain in Utah.

MR. TAYLER. Was your mother a plural wife?

MRS. KENNEDY. Yes, sir.

MR. TAYLER. And you were taught the propriety of plural marriage, were you, during your early years?

MRS. KENNEDY. Yes, sir; I did not know any difference.

MR. WORTHINGTON. Did the witness give her age?

MR. TAYLER. No, she did not give her age. How old are you?

MRS. KENNEDY. I am 26 years old this coming June. ...

MR. TAYLER. When you were about 17 years old, were you married?

MRS. KENNEDY. Yes, sir.

MR. TAYLER. To whom were you married?

MRS. KENNEDY. James Francis Johnson.[2]

MR. TAYLER. Where was his home when you married him?

MRS. KENNEDY. At Mesa, Maricopa County, Ariz[ona].

MR. TAYLER. Was he at the time you married him a married man?

MRS. KENNEDY. Yes, sir.

MR. TAYLER. Did you know his wife; that is, did you meet his wife?

MRS. KENNEDY. Yes, sir.

MR. TAYLER. His first wife, I mean?

MRS. KENNEDY. Yes, sir.

MR. TAYLER. Where was she when you saw her first?

MRS. KENNEDY. At Diaz, Mexico.

MR. TAYLER. Was the subject of your marrying her husband talked over between you—among the three of you?

MRS. KENNEDY. Well, not exactly among the three of us, sir.

MR. TAYLER. Tell us what took place.

MRS. KENNEDY. It was between her and her husband, and I had a slight interview with his wife; not very lengthy.

MR. TAYLER. Did she know you were to marry him?

MRS. KENNEDY. Yes, sir; I think she did.

MR. TAYLER. Did she give her consent to it?

MRS. KENNEDY. I think she did. ...

MR. TAYLER. Where were you married?

MRS. KENNEDY. At [the home of the] president—well, he is not exactly president; he is among one of the first presidents of the stake.

MR. TAYLER. What day of the month and year was this?

MRS. KENNEDY. It was on the 19th evening of May.

---

2. James Francis Johnson (1856-1916) served in a stake presidency at the time of his marriage to Clara Kennedy. The couple had two children. Johnson's first wife, Rozina Richmond (1862-1949), gave birth to eighteen children.

Mr. Tayler. Of what year? What year was it you went there?

Mrs. Kennedy. I can not just recall.

Mr. Tayler. How old were you? That is the way to get at it.

Mrs. Kennedy. I was 17 years old.

Mr. Tayler. And you are now 26?

Mrs. Kennedy. Yes, sir.

Mr. Tayler. We can figure that out. 1896?

Mrs. Kennedy. Yes, sir.

Mr. Tayler. And who married you?

Mrs. Kennedy. Brother Young married me.

Mr. Tayler. Brother Brigham Young?

Mrs. Kennedy. Brother Brigham Young.[3]

Mr. Tayler. That is, the Apostle Brigham Young [Jr.]?

Mrs. Kennedy. I suppose so.[4]

Mr. Tayler. You have heard him so called?

Mrs. Kennedy. Yes, sir.

Mr. Tayler. How long did you live with Mr. Johnson?

Mrs. Kennedy. About five years from the time that I was married to him until I came back home. Of course, that would be just about five years. ...

Mr. Tayler. Had you seen Apostle Brigham Young before this time?

Mrs. Kennedy. Before I was married?

Mr. Tayler. Yes.

Mrs. Kennedy. Yes, sir.

Mr. Tayler. Where?

Mrs. Kennedy. At Diaz, Mexico.[5]

Mr. Tayler. You had been living there five or six years, I believe you said.

Mrs. Kennedy. Yes, sir.

Mr. Tayler. Will you look at that picture (exhibiting a book to the witness) and tell me if that is a picture of the man who married you?

Mrs. Kennedy. Well, now, I couldn't say as to that. It has been a number of years since I saw him, now. I couldn't say.

Mr. Tayler. You could not say from the picture?

---

3. Brigham Young Jr. (1836-1903) was sustained as one of the Twelve in October 1868 and president of the Twelve in October 1901.

4. J. Reuben Clark's copy of the hearings underlined with purple ink several questions and answers in this exchange. This is the only underlining in Clark's copy outside of Joseph F. Smith's testimony.

5. Tayler used this entire excerpt in his closing argument (*Smoot Hearings*, 3:540-42).

Mrs. Kennedy. I could not say from the picture whether that was him or not.[6] ...

Mr. Tayler. Who was Mr. Johnson? What place did he occupy in the church? That is the question I forgot to ask you.

Mrs. Kennedy. I think he was councilor to the stake president.

Mr. Tayler. At Mesa, Ariz[ona]?

Mrs. Kennedy. Yes, sir.

Mr. Tayler. After you married him and were living with him what official position did he have?

Mrs. Kennedy. He held the same for a while, I think. I do not know how long.

Mr. Tayler. He was constantly in an official position of some kind in the church, was he?

Mrs. Kennedy. In the stake.

Mr. Tayler. In the stake; yes.

Mrs. Kennedy. Yes, sir.

Senator Foraker. What has become of Mr. Johnson?

Mrs. Kennedy. That I could not say. I do not know where he is.

Senator Foraker. How did you come to separate? Under what circumstances and for what cause?

Mrs. Kennedy. Well, because I just couldn't stand the pressure any longer. That was all.

Senator Foraker. You left him or he left you?

Mrs. Kennedy. I left him.

Senator Foraker. At what place?

Mrs. Kennedy. I left him—do you mean when I came to Utah?

Senator Foraker. Whenever you left him. ... Where was he when you left him; in Utah?

Mrs. Kennedy. He was in Arizona.

Senator Foraker. How long did you live at Diaz after you married him?

Mrs. Kennedy. I lived there about three or four months.

---

6. In Worthington's first closing argument, he would state the following regarding this issue:

> It is claimed that that marriage ceremony was performed by a man who was then an apostle, Brigham Young, jr., but who has long since died. The testimony shows that when they went before that man, whoever he was, so far as the woman knows (and she is the only witness to the occurrence who was examined), she did not tell him that Johnson already had a wife, and so far as she knows nobody told him. She was shown ... a photograph which we have proved to be a good photograph of Apostle Young, and she said that she could not identify it as the picture of the man who married her. Now that is the one case in which they have proved a plural marriage. They have not proved it was done by anybody who was an officer of the church who ever had authority (*Smoot Hearings,* 3:746-47).

SENATOR FORAKER. Then where did you go?

MRS. KENNEDY. I went to Arizona. ...

MR. WORTHINGTON. How often had you seen Brigham Young [Jr.] before he married you to Johnson?

MRS. KENNEDY. Not very often.

MR. WORTHINGTON. Well, approximately; half a dozen times—a dozen?

MRS. KENNEDY. Oh, no; not more than maybe twice.

MR. WORTHINGTON. And on the other occasions where had you seen him?

MRS. KENNEDY. I had seen him once—I had seen him twice, I think, in Mexico.

MR. WORTHINGTON. But where in Mexico?

MRS. KENNEDY. At both Diaz and Juarez.

MR. WORTHINGTON. When you saw him in Diaz, where was he in Diaz?

MRS. KENNEDY. That I could not say, where he was. ...

MR. WORTHINGTON. You do not remember anything about where you saw him?

MRS. KENNEDY. I saw him in the town. I can not tell you just exactly where.

MR. WORTHINGTON. I do not ask for exactly where, but I ask under what circumstances, or whether it was in a house or in a church or in a wagon.

MRS. KENNEDY. It was in the church, I think, or in the meetinghouse.

MR. WORTHINGTON. Then why did you say, if it was in a meetinghouse, that you could not tell whether it was in a building or on the street? Well, it was in a church, was it not? Do you settle down on that?

MRS. KENNEDY. Yes, sir.

MR. WORTHINGTON. Did you hear him preach?

MRS. KENNEDY. No, sir.

MR. WORTHINGTON. Or did you see him present.

MRS. KENNEDY. I just saw him present.

MR. WORTHINGTON. How long were you in the same church where he was on that occasion?

MRS. KENNEDY. Not over a couple of hours.

MR. WORTHINGTON. Did you sit near him?

MRS. KENNEDY. No, sir.

MR. WORTHINGTON. How far from him?

MRS. KENNEDY. Back in the audience.

MR. WORTHINGTON. You saw his face?

MRS. KENNEDY. Yes, sir.

MR. WORTHINGTON. You had a good look at him?

MRS. KENNEDY. I do not know that I looked—

MR. WORTHINGTON. Mrs. Kennedy, I am not asking these questions fool-
ishly. We want to know whether the man who married you was really
Brigham Young [Jr.], if you were married at that time.

MRS. KENNEDY. That is what I was told—he was Brigham Young [Jr.].

MR. WORTHINGTON. I understand. You saw him in the church once at Diaz
before he married you?

MRS. KENNEDY. Yes, sir.

MR. WORTHINGTON. Did you see him more than once at Diaz before he
married you?

MRS. KENNEDY. Once or twice.

MR. WORTHINGTON. Where was it the other time?

MRS. KENNEDY. I think it was in the same capacity.

MR. WORTHINGTON. What do you mean by "in the same capacity?"

MRS. KENNEDY. In meeting, in the church.

MR. WORTHINGTON. Just as a church-goer. You simply went to church?

MRS. KENNEDY. Yes, sir.

MR. WORTHINGTON. He did not participate in the ceremonies?

MRS. KENNEDY. Well, he talked.

MR. WORTHINGTON. Oh, he did. How long did he talk?

MRS. KENNEDY. Well, not very long.

MR. WORTHINGTON. He had his face toward the audience, of course, when
he talked?

MRS. KENNEDY. Yes, sir.

MR. WORTHINGTON. And you had a good look at his face?

MRS. KENNEDY. Yes, sir.

MR. WORTHINGTON. You said you saw him before you were married, at
some other town or some other place besides Diaz. Where was that?

MRS. KENNEDY. Before we were married?

MR. WORTHINGTON. Yes. You said, a few moments ago, that before you
were married you had seen him at two different places, as I understood you, Diaz being one place and the other place I have forgotten.

MRS. KENNEDY. I saw him at Juarez.

MR. WORTHINGTON. How long before you were married?

MRS. KENNEDY. Just a few days—yes; just a few days.

MR. WORTHINGTON. A few days before he married you?

MRS. KENNEDY. Yes, sir.

MR. WORTHINGTON. And under what circumstances did you [see] him at
Juarez?

MRS. KENNEDY. In the meetinghouse.

MR. WORTHINGTON. Did he preach there?

MRS. KENNEDY. Yes, sir.

MR. WORTHINGTON. So that then you had a good opportunity see him?

MRS. KENNEDY. Yes, sir.

MR. WORTHINGTON. On the day he married you, how long were you in his presence?

MRS. KENNEDY. I should judge about an hour.

MR. WORTHINGTON. Now, from all these opportunities you had to see the man, I wish you would describe the man to the committee.

MRS. KENNEDY. Well, he was quite a large man. He was rather short. I think that he—I do not remember whether he wore a mustache or not. He had quite prominent features. That is all the description I could give of him. ...

MR. WORTHINGTON. Did you inform the person who performed this ceremony, whatever it was, that the man to whom he was marrying you had already a wife living?

MRS. KENNEDY. Please ask that question again.

MR. WORTHINGTON. I asked you whether you informed the man who married you that the man to whom he was marrying you already had a wife living?

MRS. KENNEDY. No, sir.

MR. WORTHINGTON. Do you know whether or not anybody so informed him?

MRS. KENNEDY. No, sir; I could not say.

MR. WORTHINGTON. Then, so far as you know, he may have supposed he was marrying Mr. Johnson to his first wife when he married you?

MRS. KENNEDY. I suppose so.

MR. WORTHINGTON. I understand from that, of course, that nothing was said in his hearing, to your knowledge, to inform him of the fact that Mr. Johnson already had a wife?

MRS. KENNEDY. No, sir.

MR. WORTHINGTON. Did you know, at any time, Apostle [George] Teasdale?

MRS. KENNEDY. Yes, sir.

MR. WORTHINGTON. Was he in that country at or about this time?

MRS. KENNEDY. Yes, sir.

MR. WORTHINGTON. Do you not know that application was made to him to perform this marriage ceremony and that he refused to do it or to authorize it?

MRS. KENNEDY. Yes, sir.

MR. WORTHINGTON. What do you know of that subject?

MRS. KENNEDY. Brother Teasdale refused positively; he said that it could not be done; said the thing could not be done.

MR. WORTHINGTON. How do you know that?

MRS. KENNEDY. Well, he told my mother that it could not positively be done. My mother interceded for me, and he told my mother that such a thing could not be done; it had all been done away with; it could not be done.[7]

MR. WORTHINGTON. Mrs. Kennedy, I asked you a few moments ago whether application had not been made to somebody else to perform this ceremony and that they had refused, and you said no. Your answers do not seem to stand together, and I merely mention it so that you may explain it. Did you understand my first question? I asked you a little while ago whether an effort had been made to get anybody else to perform this ceremony, and you said no.

MRS. KENNEDY. Not that I knew of.

MR. WORTHINGTON. Now you say that Apostle Teasdale had been asked to perform the ceremony and refused. Do you not see that those answers do not stand together. I am merely mentioning them so that you may make any explanation, if there is any.

MRS. KENNEDY. I do not know how—

---

7. Kennedy's mother testified as follows:

MR. WORTHINGTON. Before this drive to Juarez had you made any effort to have your daughter married at Diaz?

MRS. MATHEWS. I did.

MR. WORTHINGTON. To get the consent of any authority of the church?

MRS. MATHEWS. No; I could not get it.

MR. WORTHINGTON. How did you know?

MRS. MATHEWS. I applied to Brother Teasdale.

MR. WORTHINGTON. You mean Apostle Teasdale?

MRS. MATHEWS. Yes, sir; for the privilege.

MR. WORTHINGTON. What did he tell you?

MRS. MATHEWS. He told me it could not be done.

MR. WORTHINGTON. Did you urge it upon him?

MRS. MATHEWS. Yes, sir.

MR. WORTHINGTON. More than once?

MRS. MATHEWS. Yes.

MR. WORTHINGTON. What did he constantly reply?

MRS. MATHEWS. That it could not be done; simply impossible. ...

MR. WORTHINGTON. Where was Brother Teasdale, as you term him, when you made this application to him to have your daughter married?

MRS. MATHEWS. In Diaz, Mexico ...

MR. WORTHINGTON. Did he tell you that it was against the law of Mexico, or against the law of the church, or what?

MRS. MATHEWS. No; against the law of the church (*Smoot Hearings,* 1:422, 424).

MR. WORTHINGTON. I beg pardon.

MRS. KENNEDY. I have tried to forget those things. I have tried to put them away from me and to forget them all. They were not pleasant for me to think about, therefore I have put them aside. I have not thought of them. ...

MR. TAYLER. What you learned about Apostle Teasdale refusing to marry you you learned from your mother? You did not know it yourself, then?

MRS. KENNEDY. I did not know it myself. I simply knew it because my mother told me. ...

MR. WORTHINGTON. When was it your mother told you that? I do not like to press you about the matter.

MRS. KENNEDY. I could not just exactly tell when.

THE CHAIRMAN. What was the question?

MR. WORTHINGTON. When it was that her mother told her about Apostle Teasdale refusing to perform the ceremony. Was it before you were married to Mr. Johnson?

MRS. KENNEDY. Yes, sir.

MR. WORTHINGTON. She had tried to get Apostle Teasdale to do it, and he had said it could not be done.

MRS. KENNEDY. She asked for permission if such a thing could be done. Of course Ma will have to answer for herself.

MR. WORTHINGTON. I understand that. But it was after that that you took this 75-mile journey in a wagon to Juarez to get married?

MRS. KENNEDY. Yes, sir. ...

Charles E. Merrill,[8] being duly sworn, was examined and testified as follows ...

SENATOR PETTUS. Will you please explain why the last wife whom you married is your legal wife?

MR. MERRILL. Because she was married under the laws of the State of Utah. The laws of the State of Utah, as I understand them, did not make my wife a legal wife—my plural wife that I had in 1888—and I married this one under the laws of the Statue of Utah. I went to court and got a license to marry her.

THE CHAIRMAN. That is, the marriage of 1891?

MR. MERRILL. Yes, sir.

---

8. Merrill (1866-1931) was a son of LDS Apostle Marriner Wood Merrill, who was unable to testify due to poor health. Both father and son had taken an additional wife after the Manifesto (D. Michael Quinn, "LDS Church Authority and New Plural Marriages, 1890-1904," *Dialogue: A Journal of Mormon Thought* 18 [Spring, 1985], 72-73.

SENATOR DUBOIS. Have you that marriage certificate with you?[9]

MR. MERRILL. No; sir; I have not.

SENATOR DUBOIS. Can you get it?

MR. MERRILL. I think I could.

SENATOR DUBOIS. Will you get it?

MR. MERRILL. I will if you want it.

SENATOR DUBOIS. I should like to see it very much.

MR. VAN COTT. I will see that that is obtained, if there is one.

SENATOR DUBOIS. It was in March, 1891?

MR. MERRILL. Yes, sir.

SENATOR DUBOIS. When was the manifesto issued?

MR. MERRILL. It was in 1890, I think.

MR. WORTHINGTON. September 20, 1890—

THE CHAIRMAN. The record shows.

SENATOR OVERMAN. How were you married in 1888 to the plural wife?

MR. MERRILL. How was I married?

SENATOR OVERMAN. Yes; under the laws of the church?

MR. MERRILL. Yes, sir.

SENATOR OVERMAN. Who married you?

MR. MERRILL. N. C. Edlefson.

SENATOR OVERMAN. Did you have to have any record made of it?

MR. MERRILL. No, sir.

SENATOR OVERMAN. Were you married at the temple?

MR. MERRILL. No, sir; at his residence in Logan [Utah].

THE CHAIRMAN. Whose residence?

MR. MERRILL. N. C. Edlefson.

SENATOR OVERMAN. Who was Edlefson—an apostle?

MR. MERRILL. No, sir.

SENATOR OVERMAN. What official position did he hold?

MR. MERRILL. He was simply a worker in the temple.

SENATOR OVERMAN. He had a right to perform the marriage ceremony?

MR. MERRILL. Yes, sir; I so understood it.

SENATOR DUBOIS. Please describe that marriage ceremony.

MR. MERRILL. I can not do it.

SENATOR DUBOIS. You can not do it?

MR. MERRILL. No, sir.

SENATOR DUBOIS. Is there any certificate of that marriage?

MR. MERRILL. No, sir.

---

9. Merrill's father performed this sealing to Chloe Hendricks in the Logan temple, of which he was president.

SENATOR DUBOIS. Is there any record of that marriage?

MR. MERRILL. I did not keep any.

SENATOR DUBOIS. You have not a certificate of that marriage?

MR. MERRILL. No, sir.

THE CHAIRMAN. Who was present?

MR. MERRILL. I do not know the witnesses.

THE CHAIRMAN. Was anybody there?

MR. MERRILL. Yes, sir; there were two witnesses, I think.

THE CHAIRMAN. You do not know them?

MR. MERRILL. No, sir.

THE CHAIRMAN. You were there?

MR. MERRILL. Yes, sir.

SENATOR DUBOIS. You can not describe the ceremony?

MR. MERRILL. No, sir.

SENATOR DUBOIS. There was no music?

MR. MERRILL. No, sir.

SENATOR DUBOIS. No singing?

MR. MERRILL. No, sir.

SENATOR DUBOIS. Were any questions asked you?

MR. MERRILL. I do not remember now of any questions being asked.

MR. TAYLER. Was your first wife with you?

MR. MERRILL. No, sir.

SENATOR FORAKER. Was there any religious ceremony of any kind at all?

MR. MERRILL. Nothing more than the marriage ceremony.

SENATOR FORAKER. What was that?

THE CHAIRMAN. Yes; what was that?

MR. MERRILL. I could not tell you what it was—simply that the marriage ceremony was performed. I can not remember the words. I could not repeat one of them to you that I know of.

SENATOR OVERMAN. Did he read out of a book?

MR. MERRILL. I do not think so.

SENATOR HOAR. Do you not know what the ordinary form of marriage ceremony is in your church, or the substance of it?

MR. MERRILL. No, sir; I can not repeat it.

SENATOR HOAR. Or give the substance of it?

MR. MERRILL. The substance of it is that he pronounced us husband and wife.

THE CHAIRMAN. Did you join hands?

MR. MERRILL. Yes, sir.

SENATOR HOAR. You made some promises?

MR. MERRILL. Yes, sir.

SENATOR HOAR. Which you have forgotten?

MR. MERRILL. No, sir; not altogether.

SENATOR HOAR. If you have not forgotten them, will you state what they are?

MR. MERRILL. I do not know that I can state them in the language.

SENATOR HOAR. The substance?

MR. MERRILL. I promised to love and cherish her and support her. That is part of it.

SENATOR HOAR. Did you have the usual phrase in marriage ceremonies—"forsaking all others, cleave to her"—do you remember that?

MR. MERRILL. I do not remember that.

SENATOR HOAR. You do not know whether that was in or not?

MR. MERRILL. No, sir.

SENATOR HOPKINS. That would hardly be in such a ceremony, would it?

THE CHAIRMAN. There is one question right here. After your marriage to what you claim to be your legal wife, in 1891, have you continued to cohabit with the other woman?

MR. MERRILL. Yes, sir.

THE CHAIRMAN. And do now?

MR. MERRILL. Yes, sir—

SENATOR DUBOIS. I should like to ask Mr. Merrill a question. Do you still uphold the doctrine of polygamy?

MR. MERRILL. Do I still uphold it?

SENATOR DUBOIS. Yes.

MR. MERRILL. No, sir.

SENATOR DUBOIS. You practice it?

MR. MERRILL. I practice it.

SENATOR DUBOIS. But you do not uphold it?

MR. MERRILL. No, sir.

THE CHAIRMAN. He practices it, but disapproves of it.

SENATOR FORAKER. Like a prohibitionist who favors prohibition but is against enforcing the law.

SENATOR OVERMAN. You believe in keeping the divine law and disobeying the law of the land?

MR. MERRILL. I do not know that I can answer the question. ...

Francis Marion Lyman,[10] being duly sworn, was examined and testified as follows ...

---

10. President of the Quorum of Twelve Apostles, Francis M. Lyman (1840-1916)

MR. TAYLER. How long have you been an apostle?

MR. LYMAN. Since 1880.

MR. TAYLER. Have you always been in the church?

MR. LYMAN. Ever since I was baptized.

MR. TAYLER. I mean you were born—

MR. LYMAN. I was born of Latter-Day-Saint parents.

MR. TAYLER. That is what I mean. Are you the child of a plural wife?

MR. LYMAN. No, sir.

MR. TAYLER. How old are you?

MR. LYMAN. I was 64 years old the 12th day of last January.

MR. TAYLER. Are you a polygamist?

MR. LYMAN. Yes, sir.

MR. TAYLER. How many wives have you?

MR. LYMAN. Three.[11]

MR. TAYLER. Where do they live?

MR. LYMAN. One of them lives in Salt Lake City; one of them lives in Fillmore [Utah], and the other died about twelve years ago.

MR. TAYLER. You are living with two wives now?

MR. LYMAN. Yes, sir.

MR. TAYLER. Have you children by both of them?

MR. LYMAN. Yes, sir.

MR. TAYLER. Was the wife who died the first wife you married?

MR. LYMAN. No, sir; she was the second.

MR. TAYLER. So that one of your living wives is the one to whom you were married originally?

MR. LYMAN. In 1857.

---

was an imposing figure on the witness stand. According to the *New York Sun,* he was "a mountain of a man. He is broad in every dimension, with great shoulders, a barrel of a chest and a body big enough for a heavy-weight wrestler. He wears his grey hair brushed up in the pompadour style that is so much affected in the West, and his beard, which is as long as that of President Smith, is carefully trimmed and combed" ("Women Giggle at the Smoot Testimony," Mar. 9, 1904).

11. Lyman's three wives and twenty-two children were: 1. Rhoda Ann Taylor (1840-1917), married Lyman 1857—children Rhoda Alice (1859-1942), Ellen Taylor (1861-81), Francis Marion (1863-1957), Edna Jane (1866-1932), Mary Ann (1868-1906), Mary Crisman (1871-1965), Lois Victoria (1876-1966), Ada Alta (1878-81), and Hila Olive (1881-82); 2. Clara Caroline Callister (1850-92), married Lyman 1869—children Richard Roswell (1870-1963), George Albert (1873-1906), Lucy Smith (1876-1971), Ida (1878-1968), John Callister (1880-1951), Amy (1882-1975), and Don Callister (1886-1992); 3. Susan Delilah Callister (1863-1945), married Lyman 1884—children Clark (1891-91), Waldo Wilcken (1893-1971), Grant Herbert (1896-1918), Florence (1898-1977), Rudger Clawson (1900-09), and Helen Mar (1904-unknown).

MR. TAYLER. She was the only wife when you married her?

MR. LYMAN. In 1857.

MR. TAYLER. When were you married to your second wife—the one who is living, I mean—the present second wife?

MR. LYMAN. When was I married to her?

MR. TAYLER. Yes.

MR. LYMAN. On the 9th day of October 1884.

MR. TAYLER. Where were you married to her?

MR. LYMAN. Where?

MR. TAYLER. Yes.

MR. LYMAN. Salt Lake City.

MR. TAYLER. In the temple?

MR. LYMAN. In the endowment house.[12]

MR. TAYLER. You have children by her?

MR. LYMAN. Yes, sir.

MR. TAYLER. How many?

MR. LYMAN. Five.

MR. TAYLER. What are their ages?

MR. LYMAN. The first was born in 1891; the last was born in 1900.

MR. TAYLER. What time in 1891 was the first child born?

MR. LYMAN. On the 4th day of July.

MR. TAYLER. Were you a signer of the prayer for amnesty?[13]

MR. LYMAN. Yes, sir. ...

MR. TAYLER. And in that prayer for amnesty did you pledge yourself to obey the law?

MR. LYMAN. I do not remember exactly what the article contains. I pledged myself to all it says. I have not read it for a long time.

MR. TAYLER. Did you, as a matter of fact, pledge yourself, by that plea for amnesty, to obedience to the law, not only respecting the taking of plural wives, but the other laws respecting the plural marriage relation?

---

12. The Endowment House was a two-story adobe structure on the Salt Lake temple grounds and served the same purpose as a temple until the granite edifice was completed (James Dwight Tingen, "The Endowment House, 1855-1889," unpublished paper, written for a graduate-level history class, Brigham Young University, 1974, circulated privately, 31 pp.).

13. The prayer for amnesty, or amnesty proclamation, read in part: "To be at peace with the Government and in harmony with their fellow-citizens who are not of their faith, and to share in the confidence of the Government and people, our people have voluntarily put aside something [plural marriage] which all their lives they have believed to be a sacred principle. ... As shepherds of a patient and suffering people we ask amnesty for them and pledge our faith and honor for their future" (*Smooot Hearings*, 1:19).

MR. LYMAN. Whatever the article contains I signed.

MR. WORTHINGTON. I object, Mr. Chairman. It is asking the witness to give a construction to a paper which can be produced.

SENATOR FORAKER. Is it not the correct way to call his attention to what it says? He has stated that he signed the paper and that he pledged himself to everything that is in the paper.

MR. LYMAN. Yes, sir.

MR. TAYLER. I know; but the Senator will understand that all sorts of constructions have been given to this paper. We have heard the president of the church himself make a declaration on that subject, and I want to know whether this man claims that he did not understand he was to obey the law on other subjects than as to taking plural wives, or whether he agrees that he is violating the promise he then made.

THE CHAIRMAN. Suppose, Mr. Tayler, [will] you read to the witness that portion of the application for amnesty?

MR. WORTHINGTON. To that I have no objection, and then ask him how he construes it.

THE CHAIRMAN. And ask him in regard to it.

SENATOR FORAKER. The witness says he has not seen the paper or read it for a long time—

MR. TAYLER. But they are all pretty familiar with this paper.

SENATOR FORAKER. That is no reason why all the ordinary rules of examination should be violated.

MR. WORTHINGTON. Why do you say he is familiar with it?

THE CHAIRMAN. Read that portion of the petition to which you wish to call his attention.

MR. TAYLER. It is quite long, so that I do not wish to read it all.

THE CHAIRMAN. No.

MR. TAYLER. In this prayer for amnesty there is this sentence: "As shepherds of a patient, suffering people we ask amnesty for them and pledge our faith and honor for their future." Do you recall that statement?

MR. LYMAN. Yes, sir; I do.

MR. TAYLER. Did you interpret that as meaning that you would obey the law respecting polygamous cohabitation?

MR. LYMAN. I intended to do everything that was right in the observance of the law.

MR. TAYLER. Did you think it would be right to abstain from polygamous cohabitation with your plural wife?

MR. LYMAN. I think it would have been right.

MR. TAYLER. You did not do that, though?

MR. LYMAN. No, sir.

MR. TAYLER. Then you did wrong?

MR. LYMAN. Yes, sir; according to the law.

MR. TAYLER. According to the law?

MR. LYMAN. Yes, sir.

MR. TAYLER. It was wrong according to the church law as well?

MR. LYMAN. It was wrong according to the rule of the church.

MR. TAYLER. So you violated both laws?

MR. LYMAN. Yes, sir.

MR. TAYLER. The law of the land and the rule of the church?

MR. LYMAN. Yes, sir.

THE CHAIRMAN. I wish to ask a question right here. You are now continuing in this polygamous relation?

MR. LYMAN. Yes, sir.

THE CHAIRMAN. And intend to?

MR. LYMAN. I had thought of nothing else, Mr. Chairman.

THE CHAIRMAN. And you are the next in succession to the presidency?

MR. LYMAN. Yes, sir.

SENATOR HOAR. Let me see if I understand you. You used the phrase, or the counsel used the phrase, in the question which you answered affirmatively—

MR. LYMAN. Excuse me. I am a little hard of hearing.

SENATOR HOAR. You used the phrase, or the counsel used the phrase, which you accepted by an affirmative answer, "The rule of the church;" that you were violating a rule of the church, as you understand it. Do you understand the rule of the church to be the law of God?

MR. LYMAN. Yes, sir.

SENATOR HOAR. Very well. Then, do I understand you to say that you are living and intend to live in violation of the law of God and of the law of man, as you understand them?

MR. LYMAN. Mr. Chairman, I fully intend to be true to my obligations and covenants with the Lord and with my wives and children and to the Government of the United States. I have lived in all good conscience before the Lord and I have never done a thing willfully against the church nor my God nor my country.

If I may be allowed, Mr. Chairman, to make a remark, my case is possibly a little different from the case of other men generally. I was born in 1840. I can hardly remember when my father was not a polygamist. He married a number of wives in 1845, the next year after the death of [the] Prophet Joseph [Smith]. He was taught that doctrine by the prophet, and he was charged that it was important for him that he should embrace that principle. He was selected at one time as a councilor to the prophet. He entered into that principle and married six plural wives in 1845 and 1846, so that as my earliest recollections I remember my father's wives and families as I remember my father and my own mother.[14]

I was taught the truthfulness of that principle from the very beginning, and I lived in that plural family till I married and had a family of my own. I have never been able to see but that that principle is correct and true.

I have always felt that it was, in my heart and soul, and hence when I became a man I married, in 1857. I married again in 1869 and had families by both my wives. I married again in 1884 and I have greatly regretted—my soul has been very much pained—to find myself in opposition to the law of my country and the rule of my church. But I covenanted with those wives most solemnly to love and respect and revere them as my own heart and soul, and I felt I could not separate from them so long as they were true to me.

SENATOR HOAR. Now, I think I clearly understand; and I come back to the question. Do I not correctly understand you to say that the revelation requiring the future abstaining from polygamy by your people comes from God?

MR. LYMAN. I did not catch that question.

SENATOR HOAR. Do you not understand that the revelation requiring you to abstain from polygamy comes from God?

MR. LYMAN. Yes, sir.

SENATOR HOAR. Do you not understand that you are disobeying the commands of God in disobeying that revelation?

MR. LYMAN. So far, Mr. Chairman, as my disobeying the law in regard to polygamy is concerned, I have not. I have most earnestly and faithfully, from the adoption of the manifesto, done all in my power to prevent polygamous marriages in the church.

SENATOR HOAR. That is not my question.

MR. LYMAN. I have been most faithful in that.

---

14. Lyman's father, Amasa, had eight wives and thirty-eight children, having married Maria Louisa Tanner in 1835; Diontha Walker, 1843; Caroline Ely Partridge, 1844; Eliza Maria Partridge Smith, 1846; Paulina Eliza Phelps, 1846; Priscilla Rebecca Turley, 1846; Cornelia Eliza Leavitt, 1846; and Lydia Partridge, 1853. Amasa was ordained an apostle in August 1842, removed from the Quorum of the Twelve in 1867 for questioning the doctrine of blood atonement, and died in 1877.

SENATOR HOAR. I am not asking you about that. You have said more than once that in living in polygamous relations with your wives, which you do and intend to do, you knew that you were disobeying this revelation?

MR. LYMAN. Yes, sir.

SENATOR HOAR. And that in disobeying this revelation you were disobeying the law of God?

MR. LYMAN. Yes, sir.

SENATOR HOAR. Very well. So that you say that you, an apostle of your church, expecting to succeed, if you survive Mr. Smith, to the office in which you will be the person to be the medium of Divine revelations, are living and are known to your people to live in disobedience of the law of the land and of the law of God?

MR. LYMAN. Yes, sir.

SENATOR HOAR. He says "yes." That is all. ...

THE CHAIRMAN. You were married, I think you said, in the temple—I mean in the endowment house.

MR. LYMAN. In the endowment house.

THE CHAIRMAN. What is the difference between the endowment house and the temple?

MR. LYMAN. The endowment house was a temporary building for the purposes for which it was built—sacred purposes; but it was not a substantial building like the temple. It was just for the time being until we could build the temple. Our temple was forty years in building.

THE CHAIRMAN. This ceremony was performed in the endowment house?

MR. LYMAN. In the endowment house; yes, sir.

THE CHAIRMAN. You went through the endowment house, as it is commonly spoken of, did you?

MR. LYMAN. Yes, sir.

THE CHAIRMAN. Will you please state what the ceremony is in going through the endowment house?

MR. LYMAN. I could not do so. ... I could not do so if it was to save my life.

THE CHAIRMAN. You could not?

MR. LYMAN. No, sir.

THE CHAIRMAN. Can you state any portion of it?

MR. LYMAN. I might approximate something of it that I remember.

THE CHAIRMAN. As nearly as you can.

MR. LYMAN. I remember that I agreed to be an upright and moral man, pure in my life. I agreed to refrain from sexual commerce with any woman except my wife or wives as were given to me in the priesthood. The law of purity I subscribed to willingly, of my own choice, and to be true and good to all men. I took no oath nor obligation against any person or any country or government or kingdom or anything of that kind. I remember that distinctly.

THE CHAIRMAN. Of course the charge is made,[15] and I want to know the facts. You would know about it, having gone through the endowment house?

MR. LYMAN. Yes.

THE CHAIRMAN. There was nothing of that kind?

MR. LYMAN. Nothing of that kind.

THE CHAIRMAN. No obligation or oath?

MR. LYMAN. Not at all; no, sir.[16]

THE CHAIRMAN. Who was present at this ceremony?

MR. LYMAN. Daniel H. Wells—when I was married?

THE CHAIRMAN. Yes.

MR. LYMAN. Daniel H. Wells and others. I could not tell how many. Sometimes there are a hundred people go through and receive their endowments—a large company.

THE CHAIRMAN. Of course you do not know about that?

MR. LYMAN. No, sir.

THE CHAIRMAN. Is that all you can remember of the ceremony?

MR. LYMAN. Yes, sir. The marriage ceremony was performed by Daniel H. Wells.

THE CHAIRMAN. What position did he hold at that time?

MR. LYMAN. He was counselor.

THE CHAIRMAN. Yes.

MR. LYMAN. In fact, he married my three wives to me. He officiated in each case. The first time he was counselor to President Brigham Young—counselor in the presidency of the church. The last time I believe he was counselor to the twelve apostles.[17]

---

15. According to David John Buerger, beginning with the Nauvoo temple ceremony the oath of vengeance was required of all temple-goers. The oath reportedly called for each initiate to importune the heavens to avenge the blood of the prophets. See Buerger, *The Mysteries of Godliness: A History of Mormon Temple Worship* (San Francisco: Smith Research Associates, 1994), 133-72. The oath received significant coverage throughout the hearings. Some witnesses denied the oath's existence, others gave slightly different versions. For some of this testimony, see *Smoot Hearings*, 2:79, 148-49, 153, 189, 759, 774; 4:7, 69, 77, 108.

16. The previous seven questions and answers were included in the "View of the Minority" report submitted by Senator Foraker on June 11, 1906 (*Smoot Hearings*, 4:527).

17. Wells became an apostle and second counselor to Brigham Young on the same

THE CHAIRMAN. How long are these monthly meetings of the apostles? How long do they continue?

MR. LYMAN. The weekly meetings?

THE CHAIRMAN. Yes, sir.

MR. LYMAN. Two hours. ...

MR. TAYLER. Have the first presidency and the twelve apostles ever, to your knowledge, taken any action looking to the disciplining or prosecuting of persons who were charged with living in polygamous cohabitation?

MR. LYMAN. I think not.

MR. TAYLER. Do you mean you may have discussed whether you would or would not prosecute such persons?

MR. LYMAN. No, sir. ...

MR. WORTHINGTON. Have you known of any instance of any man being appointed or coming into high place in your church because he was a polygamist?

MR. LYMAN. Never.

MR. WORTHINGTON. By virtue of what is it they get into those offices?

MR. LYMAN. His merit and the designation of the Lord.

MR. WORTHINGTON. You have said the president of the church presides at the meetings of the apostles?

MR. LYMAN. That is the council, when we all meet together.

MR. WORTHINGTON. Do the apostles have meetings of their own?

MR. LYMAN. Yes, sir.

MR. WORTHINGTON. When the president is not there?

MR. LYMAN. Yes, sir.

MR. WORTHINGTON. That is what I understood from the president. How often do the apostles meet by themselves?

MR. LYMAN. Four times a year.

MR. WORTHINGTON. Only quarterly meetings?

MR. LYMAN. Quarterly meetings.

MR. WORTHINGTON. At any of those quarterly meetings, has this question of polygamous cohabitation been raised or discussed or acted upon?

MR. LYMAN. No, sir.

MR. WORTHINGTON. So far as you know, does Senator Smoot know, or has he known, that you have been living with more than one woman since he became an apostle?[18]

---

day of January 4, 1857. He was not a member of the Quorum of Twelve, although twenty years later, after Brigham Young's death, he was ordained a counselor to the Twelve.

18. A few months prior to this exchange, Smoot had written to Joseph F. Smith:

MR. LYMAN. He never knew.

THE CHAIRMAN. You say he never knew?

MR. LYMAN. He never knew; Apostle Smoot never knew that I was doing wrong.

MR. WORTHINGTON. These quarterly conferences are conferences of the stake, I believe?

MR. LYMAN. Yes, sir.

MR. WORTHINGTON. To what stake do you belong?

MR. LYMAN. Tooele [Utah] stake.

THE CHAIRMAN. Is that the same stake to which Senator Smoot belongs?

MR. LYMAN. No, sir.

MR. WORTHINGTON. When you say the apostles generally attend the meetings, do you mean all the apostles attend the quarterly meetings of all the stakes?

MR. LYMAN. They do, as nearly as they can; one at a time, or two, as the case may be.

MR. WORTHINGTON. Are the quarterly conferences held at the same time for the different stakes?

MR. LYMAN. Yes, sir; that is, there will be perhaps three or four on the same Saturday and Sunday.

MR. WORTHINGTON. So far as you know, since Senator Smoot became an apostle, has he ever been at any of those quarterly conferences where your wives were present?

MR. LYMAN. Never. ...

MR. WORTHINGTON. You have not been asked anything particularly to-day about the missionary work of the church. I understand that is the principal work of the apostles?

MR. LYMAN. Yes, sir.

MR. WORTHINGTON. And you are their head?

MR. LYMAN. Yes, sir.

MR. WORTHINGTON. I want to ask you as to the books which you use of late years. I will confine my inquiry on this subject to the time since Senator Smoot became an apostle, about four years ago. During that time,

---

To-day in the Cloak Room, Senator Hale [R-Maine] was talking to a number of the Senators, and among other things he said that he had read my answer and noticed that I denied ever having cohabited with any woman other than my wife, and remarked that he did not like that, for the reason that it brought into the Senate a class distinction. In explanation of what he meant by this, he said that eighty-nine of the Senators could not be classed in that category, and he hardly thought that it would be right for Smoot to stand out alone (Jan. 11, 1904).

what books have been used or have been most used by your church in
its missionary work?

MR. LYMAN. The Book of Mormon. We have taken pains to publish that
extensively in the United States and in foreign countries; and of the
commentaries, the "Articles of Faith," by [James E.] Talmage, is the
most popular work. If a man asks for a book, a comprehensive work,
from which to learn something of the doctrines of the Latter-day
Saints, we always recommend the "Articles of Faith."

MR. WORTHINGTON. That is the book that has been here?

MR. LYMAN. I do not know whether there has been one here or not. It has
been spoken of.

MR. WORTHINGTON. Yes; it has been identified.

MR. LYMAN. Yes.

MR. WORTHINGTON. That is the book which announces that polygamy was
prohibited in 1890, and refers to the manifesto?

MR. LYMAN. I believe it does.

MR. WORTHINGTON. You have not mentioned the Doctrine and Covenants.
Is that circulated, too?

MR. LYMAN. How is that?

MR. WORTHINGTON. You have not mentioned the Doctrine and Covenants.
Is that circulated, too?

MR. LYMAN. No; not so much.

MR. WORTHINGTON. In what proportion do you circulate the Doctrine and
Covenants and the Book of Mormon?

MR. LYMAN. Oh, the Doctrine and Covenants is not circulated as a book to
make converts with. It is not circulated at all. If anybody wants it—we
do not put it forward; but the Book of Mormon and the "Articles of
Faith." Then, there is the "Voice of Warning," by Parley P. Pratt, and
"Key to Theology," by Parley P. Pratt, and works of that kind.[19]

MR. WORTHINGTON. The Book of Mormon, I understand, was the original
book. It is the Mormon Bible, if I may use that expression?

MR. LYMAN. That is what it is called in the world; yes, sir.

MR. WORTHINGTON. It was first promulgated about 1820—

MR. LYMAN. 1830.

MR. WORTHINGTON. In that book polygamy was prohibited, I believe?

MR. LYMAN. Yes, sir; in that day. It is a history of ancient times.

MR. WORTHINGTON. In what proportion is the Doctrine and Covenants cir-

---

19. These two books are still in print. See Parley P. Pratt, *Key to the Science of Theology/
Voice of Warning* (Salt Lake City: Desert Book, 2002).

culated, compared with the "Articles of Faith," the Talmage book, which we have here?

MR. LYMAN. We do not look upon the Doctrine and Covenants as a book to circulate at all. It is a law of the church, the word of the Lord to the church, and the law and discipline, but for the doctrines of the church we take the commentaries more.

MR. WORTHINGTON. Now, say in the last four years, what has been the custom about instructing missionaries who go out on their work the last four years, since Senator Smoot became an apostle? I do not care to go back farther than that now.

MR. LYMAN. Of course, the last four years I have not been at home—that is, three years.[20]

MR. WORTHINGTON. Take the last fourteen years then, since the manifesto.

MR. LYMAN. We always instruct the elders that they are sent out to preach the first principles of the gospel.

MR. WORTHINGTON. Who instructs them?

MR. LYMAN. The twelve, and the first seven presidents of seventies.

MR. WORTHINGTON. They personally instruct them, do they?

MR. LYMAN. Yes, sir.

MR. WORTHINGTON. And do you participate in that instruction, so that you know what it is?

MR. LYMAN. Oh, yes, sir.

MR. WORTHINGTON. Just tell us what it is.

MR. LYMAN. We instruct them particularly to go into the world and preach the first principles of the gospel. That is what they are sent out for, and particularly to leave the mysteries alone. ...

MR. WORTHINGTON. To what extent, if at all, since 1890, in instructing your missionaries and sending them out to their work, have you told them to inculcate or encourage the practice of polygamy?

MR. LYMAN. They are always thoroughly warned, Mr. Chairman, to avoid the discussion of that subject, and prohibited from discussing it or advocating and defending or putting it forth, because we have yielded that requirement to the law and have ceased plural marriages entirely, and they never refer to it. They never advert to it at all unless they are approached and compelled to.

THE CHAIRMAN. And then what, if they are assailed?

MR. LYMAN. If they are compelled, we always advise that they should not listen, should not yield.

---

20. Lyman had been appointed to preside over the church's European Mission in February 1901. He was replaced by Heber J. Grant in 1903.

THE CHAIRMAN. But if compelled, then what?

MR. LYMAN. How is that?

THE CHAIRMAN. If compelled to, by an assault?

MR. LYMAN. I suppose they do, likely.

THE CHAIRMAN. Do what?

MR. LYMAN. I very much regret that they should answer at all in regard to it.

MR. WORTHINGTON. They do what?

THE CHAIRMAN. What do they do?

MR. LYMAN. They speak of the principle, I presume, when they are compelled.

THE CHAIRMAN. They denounce it or defend it?

MR. LYMAN. Defend it. They would not denounce it.

MR. WORTHINGTON. What are they instructed to say about the practice of it as distinguished from the theory?

MR. LYMAN. Forbid it entirely, and to instruct the people that nothing of the kind is tolerated in the church.

MR. WORTHINGTON. That is, you defend it as a belief?

MR. LYMAN. Yes.

MR. WORTHINGTON. But instruct that it is not to be pursued as a practice?

MR. LYMAN. They are entirely forbidden to handle it or do anything with it, and what they do of course I am unable to say.

MR. WORTHINGTON. Of course you can only say what they are told to do.

MR. LYMAN. Yes.

MR. WORTHINGTON. But so far as you personally are concerned, you can tell what you do? You go out as a missionary?

MR. LYMAN. And I always advise people that we are not practicing or teaching that doctrine at all.

THE CHAIRMAN. Right there just a moment. If your theory upon that is assailed in regard to polygamy, do you then defend it?

MR. LYMAN. How is that? If I am assailed?

THE CHAIRMAN. Yes; upon that doctrine; do you then defend it?

MR. LYMAN. If I was assailed, I should tell that we have let that doctrine go. We have let go of it.

THE CHAIRMAN. Do you, as a missionary, defend its rightfulness?

MR. LYMAN. Do I what?

THE CHAIRMAN. Do you defend its rightfulness?

MR. LYMAN. If I did anything, I would have to.

THE CHAIRMAN. You would have to do that?

MR. LYMAN. I would have to if I did anything.

MR. WORTHINGTON. Do you mean defend its rightfulness as a principle or as a practice?

MR. LYMAN. As a principle of faith.

MR. WORTHINGTON. I understand. You always instruct and tell everybody it is forbidden—the practice of it.

MR. LYMAN. Entirely; always. We never fail.

MR. WORTHINGTON. I was about to ask you if you knew President [Wilford] Woodruff, who issued the manifesto.

MR. LYMAN. I knew him well; yes, sir.

MR. WORTHINGTON. Was he the president in 1894?

MR. LYMAN. Yes, sir; I believe he was as late as 1894.

MR. WORTHINGTON. At the time of this alleged marriage of Mrs. Kennedy in Mexico, I mean?[21]

MR. LYMAN. Yes, sir.

MR. WORTHINGTON. He was the president?

MR. LYMAN. Yes, sir.

MR. WORTHINGTON. If any elder or preacher of the church had desired to have authority to perform a plural marriage ceremony at that time, from whom could he have obtained that authority?

MR. LYMAN. I am sure he could not have obtained it from anyone, but President Woodruff would have been the only man that could have given it.

MR. WORTHINGTON. Do you know what President Woodruff's instructions were at that time, and what he was doing about that?

MR. LYMAN. Yes, sir; he forbade it entirely.

SENATOR OVERMAN. Right. There; has the president power to confer that now upon any of the apostles?

MR. LYMAN. How is that?

SENATOR OVERMAN. Has the president now power to confer upon any of the apostles that right?

MR. LYMAN. Has he the power?

SENATOR OVERMAN. Yes.

MR. LYMAN. Oh, yes, sir; that is, he is the man who holds the keys, and the only man.

SENATOR OVERMAN. He holds the keys, and he has power now to confer upon the elders and apostles that right, notwithstanding the manifesto?

MR. LYMAN. He has all the power in that regard.

---

21. For the full text of Kennedy's testimony regarding her post-Manifesto marriage, see *Smoot Hearings*, 1:388-408.

SENATOR OVERMAN. Notwithstanding the manifesto, then, he has the right?

MR. LYMAN. He has the power.

SENATOR OVERMAN. He has the power to authorize elders to perform marriage with plural wives? Is that the way I understand you?

MR. LYMAN. He has that authority.

MR. WORTHINGTON. Why do you say he has the authority when the manifesto, which is a revelation, forbids it? I want to understand you.

MR. LYMAN. Because the authority is in abeyance just as the law is in abeyance.

MR. WORTHINGTON. You mean by that that he might receive another revelation commanding or authorizing him to allow it?

MR. LYMAN. No; not that, necessarily. His power has not been shortened and his authority has not been shortened.

MR. WORTHINGTON. I want to see that I understand you. I understand you all claim that the manifesto is a revelation?

MR. LYMAN. Yes. sir.

MR. WORTHINGTON. That is, a direction from the Almighty not to practice polygamy further?

MR. LYMAN. Yes, sir; that is what it is. ...

SENATOR OVERMAN. I understand you, Mr. Lyman, to state that this manifesto or revelation was only holding in abeyance the law as to plural marriages?

THE CHAIRMAN. Suspending it.

SENATOR OVERMAN. Suspending it for the time, but that the president still has the authority to confer that upon the elders and apostles?

MR. LYMAN. Yes; but he is not at liberty to exercise it.

SENATOR OVERMAN. He is not at liberty to exercise it?

MR. LYMAN. He is not at liberty to exercise it, because the Lord has forbidden it.

THE CHAIRMAN. If he had a revelation to suspend the suspension, then he would be authorized?

MR. LYMAN. I do not think there is any—I would not think there was any probability of that at all, Mr. Chairman.

THE CHAIRMAN. I am not speaking of the probabilities.

MR. LYMAN. No.

THE CHAIRMAN. Suppose the Lord should appear to him and direct him to suspend the suspension; he would then have to obey it?

MR. LYMAN. He has obeyed the law in—

THE CHAIRMAN. I say he would then have to obey that latest revelation?

MR. LYMAN. He has obeyed the law wherein the Lord forbade plural marriages.

THE CHAIRMAN. That revelation suspended it. That was the language?

MR. WORTHINGTON. Not in the manifesto, Mr. Chairman.

MR. LYMAN. Not in the manifesto.

MR. WORTHINGTON. The manifesto does not say "suspended."

SENATOR DUBOIS. Look at the revelation. Does not that say it?

MR. WORTHINGTON. No.

MR. TAYLER. What is the language?

MR. WORTHINGTON. The language of the manifesto is "prohibited," not
"suspended."

MR. TAYLER. Let us have the revelation.

THE CHAIRMAN. I think the language is "suspend."

MR. WORTHINGTON. No. You are mistaken, Mr. Chairman.

THE CHAIRMAN. I may be in error.[22] ... Is the apostleship within your
knowledge denied to any man because he is a polygamist?

MR. LYMAN. No, sir.

THE CHAIRMAN. That is no bar to apostleship?

MR. LYMAN. No, sir.

THE CHAIRMAN. On the contrary, is it a commendation?

MR. LYMAN. It would be nothing against him.

THE CHAIRMAN. You say that—

MR. LYMAN. That is, Mr. Chairman, would you allow me to explain, that
would be nothing against him if his marriage occurred before the
manifesto.

SENATOR DUBOIS. If it occurred after the manifesto, would it be anything
against him?

MR. LYMAN. Yes, sir. ...

THE CHAIRMAN. Just one word more. You say at these large gatherings of
the apostles the president and the apostles sit together?

MR. LYMAN. Yes, sir.

THE CHAIRMAN. In the temple?

MR. LYMAN. Yes, sir.

THE CHAIRMAN. There is a platform there?

MR. LYMAN. Yes, sir; in the tabernacle.

THE CHAIRMAN. In the tabernacle?

MR. LYMAN. Yes, sir.

THE CHAIRMAN. A platform or pulpit?

---

22. The Manifesto reads: "And I now publicly declare that my advice to the Latter-
day Saints is to refrain from contracting any marriage forbidden by the law of the land."

MR. LYMAN. It is a stand; yes, sir.

THE CHAIRMAN. And the first president and the apostles occupy that pulpit or stand together?

MR. LYMAN. Yes, sir.

THE CHAIRMAN. Have you seen Mr. Smoot there?

MR. LYMAN. Yes, sir.

THE CHAIRMAN. You say Mr. Smoot does not know you are a polygamist?

MR. LYMAN. No, sir.

THE CHAIRMAN. How do you know be does not know it?

MR. LYMAN. Because I do not know that he knows it. (Laughter.)

THE CHAIRMAN. You will not undertake to say what he knows or what he does not know, will you?

MR. LYMAN. I know some things; yes, sir.

THE CHAIRMAN. On that point?

MR. LYMAN. Yes; I think on that point I would be perfectly competent.

THE CHAIRMAN. You never discussed it with him, you say?

MR. LYMAN. Oh, never.

THE CHAIRMAN. Never in the world?

MR. LYMAN. No, sir.

THE CHAIRMAN. And still you know that he does not know that?

MR. LYMAN. I think I could prove it by him. (Laughter.)

THE CHAIRMAN. Undoubtedly; but you do not want to say, do you, that you know he does not know? You have said what the apostles are instructed to do, or the missionaries?

MR. LYMAN. Yes, sir.

THE CHAIRMAN. And they are instructed not to go into the mysteries?

MR. LYMAN. Yes, of the kingdom.

THE CHAIRMAN. Is polygamy one of the mysteries?

MR. LYMAN. Yes, sir; it would be now. (Laughter.)

THE CHAIRMAN. But if that doctrine is assailed, then you would be called upon to defend it as a faith would you?

MR. LYMAN. No; I do not think I would say anything about it. I would let them assail.

THE CHAIRMAN. You would let them assail and you would walk off?

MR. LYMAN. Yes.

THE CHAIRMAN. But you would defend the faith, would you not?

MR. LYMAN. No; I think I would let the faith take care of itself.

THE CHAIRMAN. But you would attend to the practice?

MR. LYMAN. No, sir. (Laughter.) ...

MR. TAYLER. ... Did I understand you correctly, Mr. Lyman, to say that the book of Doctrine and Covenants is rather kept in the background now?

Mr. Lyman. It is not used as a proselyting work at all.

Mr. Tayler. Do you not know that it is the one book that is so widely distributed that it has to have a fresh edition each year put out?

Mr. Lyman. It is not used as a proselyting book in this church, and has never been from the beginning.

Mr. Tayler. That is true. You have said that, but you have not answered my question. I will ask the reporter to read the question.

The reporter read the question as follows: "Mr. Tayler. Do you not know that that is the one book that is so widely distributed that it has to have a fresh edition each year put out?"

Mr. Lyman. No, sir; I do not know that.

Mr. Tayler. I understood you to say that some of your apostles have been chosen through revelations?

Mr. Lyman. Every one of them.

Mr. Tayler. Every one of them?

Mr. Lyman. Oh, yes.

Mr. Tayler. Mr. Smoot was chosen, then, through a revelation?

Mr. Lyman. Yes, sir.

Mr. Tayler. Who received that revelation?

Mr. Lyman. Lorenzo Snow—President Lorenzo Snow.

Mr. Tayler. What kind of a revelation was it?

Mr. Lyman. From the Lord.

Mr. Tayler. Was it written or—

Mr. Lyman. Oral. It was not written. It was the voice of the Lord to Lorenzo Snow.

Mr. Tayler. Speaking directly to him?

Mr. Lyman. To him.

Mr. Tayler. And specifically indicating Mr. Smoot?

Mr. Lyman. Yes, sir; it pointed him out exactly.

Mr. Tayler. You do not define it as being a desire of Lorenzo Snow?

Mr. Lyman. No, sir.

Mr. Tayler. To have Mr. Smoot one of the apostles, which he imagined would be approved by God?

Mr. Lyman. No, sir.

Mr. Tayler. But it is more specific and certain and substantive than that I have just stated.

Mr. Lyman. Yes, sir.

Senator Hoar. I would like to ask one question there. You say that Mr.

Smoot was selected as an apostle by the voice of the Lord to Lorenzo Snow?

Mr. Lyman. Yes, sir.

Senator Hoar. Do you know whether that voice was audible, in the sense of an ordinary sound?

Mr. Lyman. It was, no doubt, audible to him.

Senator Hoar. Audible as a sound rather than a light?

Mr. Lyman. Yes, sir.

Senator Hoar. How do you know?

Mr. Lyman. How do I know?

Senator Hoar. Yes.

Mr. Lyman. The Lord revealed it to me.

Senator Hoar. The Lord revealed it to you also?

Mr. Lyman. Yes; by his spirit.

Senator Hoar. How did He reveal it to you?

Mr. Lyman. By the spirit of the Lord.

Senator Hoar. Did He reveal it to you by an audible sound, as you hear the voice of an ordinary person speaking to you?

Mr. Lyman. He spoke to me by his spirit.

Senator Hoar. How?

Mr. Lyman. By his holy spirit.

Senator Hoar. How?

Mr. Lyman. To my soul.

Senator Hoar. How?

Mr. Lyman. And heart.

Senator Hoar. How?

Mr. Lyman. By the spirit of the Lord.

Senator Hoar. How did the spirit of the Lord speak by the spirit of the Lord to your soul? In what way was the speech made?

Mr. Lyman. I could tell you, Mr. Senator, how I obtained that spirit and testimony so that not only when Mr. Smoot has been chosen, but when every other apostle has been chosen, the spirit of the Lord has borne record to my spirit.

Senator Hoar. I understood Mr. Smith to testify that he had never had a revelation since he has been president of the church.[23]

Mr. Lyman. Yes.

_____

23. Senator Hoar is referring to President Smith's testimony from March 2: "I have never pretended to nor do I profess to have received revelations. I never said I had a revelation except so far as God has shown to me that so-called Mormonism is God's divine truth; that is all."

SENATOR HOAR. You have had some?

MR. LYMAN. What President [Joseph F.] Smith does as the president of this church he does by the direction of the spirit of the Lord, not a written revelation. Two of the apostles were chosen, and [no] revelation was written when George Teasdale was chosen, and Heber J. Grant, but—

SENATOR HOAR. Have you always obeyed those revelations in your actions about the selection of apostles?

MR. LYMAN. How is that?

SENATOR HOAR. Have you always obeyed those revelations?

MR. LYMAN. Yes, sir; in the selection.

SENATOR HOAR. Do you make any distinction in your mind between commands of the Lord, that you are at liberty to disobey, and commands that you are at liberty to obey?

MR. LYMAN. The commands of the Lord that I have disobeyed—that I presume the Senator refers to—in my life, I trust myself to the mercy of the Lord.

SENATOR HOAR. Have you repented of that disobedience?

MR. LYMAN. How is that?

SENATOR HOAR. Have you repented of that disobedience?

MR. LYMAN. Not yet; no, sir.

SENATOR HOAR. Not yet?

MR. LYMAN. Not yet. (Laughter.)

THE CHAIRMAN. You say that Mr. Smoot was chosen by revelation?

MR. LYMAN. Yes, sir.

THE CHAIRMAN. To Mr. [Lorenzo] Snow?

MR. LYMAN. Yes, sir.

THE CHAIRMAN. You voted for Mr. Smoot?

MR. LYMAN. Yes, sir.

THE CHAIRMAN. As an apostle?

MR. LYMAN. Yes, sir.

THE CHAIRMAN. Did you first communicate to Mr. Snow to ascertain what—

MR. LYMAN. Oh, yes, sir.

THE CHAIRMAN. And he told you what the Lord had told him?

MR. LYMAN. Yes, sir.

THE CHAIRMAN. When did you get your revelation about Mr. Smoot?

MR. LYMAN. When he made the revelation to me.

THE CHAIRMAN. Was it after Mr. Snow told you, or before?

MR. LYMAN. Oh, yes; after.

THE CHAIRMAN. You got your revelation after Snow got his and told you what it was?

MR. LYMAN. Yes, sir; the Lord did not tell me first.

SENATOR HOAR. I would like to ask one more question. Have you communicated to your associate apostles, or any of them, what you have stated to me, namely, that you disobeyed the commands of the Lord and that you have not yet repented?

MR. LYMAN. No; I have not told them.

SENATOR HOAR. Any of them?

MR. LYMAN. No; I have not told them.

SENATOR HOAR. So far as you know and believe, is not the fact of your disobedience, which has been spoken of, well known in that community?

MR. LYMAN. Yes, sir.

SENATOR HOAR. You have no reason to doubt it is known to your associate apostles?

MR. LYMAN. Oh, yes; I think so.

SENATOR HOAR. You think it is well known?

MR. LYMAN. I think it is generally understood.

SENATOR HOAR. You have no doubt it is well known to Mr. Smoot. Do you know whether they approve or disapprove?

MR. LYMAN. I am speaking of the people. I do not think Mr. Smoot knows in regard to the matter.

SENATOR HOAR. What makes you think that if the people generally know it, one of your associate apostles does not know it?

MR. LYMAN. He has never met one of my wives. ...

SENATOR HOAR. Have the people in general met one of your wives?

MR. LYMAN. How is that?

SENATOR HOAR. Have the people in general met your wives?

MR. LYMAN. They have met them some; yes, sir.

SENATOR HOAR. They have met them some?

MR. LYMAN. Yes, sir.

SENATOR HOAR. Do you mean to say, Mr. Lyman, that the fact that you are living in a state of polygamy is known to the people in general, as you believe, and yet that, as you believe, it is not known to Mr. Smoot, your associate apostle?[24]

---

24. In a letter to his mother on March 24, 1904, Carl Badger wrote:

The investigation has not been entirely pleasant for us, to say the least ... I entirely agree that President Smith and Apostles Lyman and [John Henry] Smith did the right thing but some of the truth was not pleasant to the ears of the country and pub-

MR. LYMAN. I mean that it is generally accepted as a fact. I do not—I perhaps ought not to have said that the people generally know it, but they generally accept it.

SENATOR HOAR. Do you mean to say that you believe that what the people generally accept as a fact on that subject is not known and accepted as a fact by Mr. Smoot, your associate apostle?

MR. LYMAN. I think it is accepted as a fact by Mr. Smoot, but I do not think he knows it. (Laughter.)

SENATOR HOAR. Well, in what sense do you declare you think that the people generally do know it, and at the same time declare that you think Mr. Smoot does not? What is the distinction between the general knowledge of the people and his, in your mind?

MR. LYMAN. I am so generally known, and my reputation is so wide that I think the church accept—

SENATOR HOAR. Are you not as well known to Mr. Smoot personally and by reputation as to the people in general?

MR. LYMAN. Yes, sir.

SENATOR HOAR. Then, why do you think he knows less about this matter than people in general?

MR. LYMAN. I think he knows just as much as they do. (Laughter.)

SENATOR HOAR. I wish to remind you that you have just said exactly the contrary of that. You have just said that you thought people in general did know it, and that you believed Mr. Smoot did not.

MR. LYMAN. I believe the people generally accept it as a fact, but they do not know it.

SENATOR HOAR. What did you mean just now when you said they did know it and Mr. Smoot did not? I asked you why, and you said because he had not met your wives.

MR. LYMAN. I presume they accept it as a fact, and I presume he does, but they do not know it.

SENATOR HOAR. You do not yet answer my question, which is why you said just now that you believed people in general did know it and that Mr. Smoot did not; and when I asked you why you thought your associate on the board of apostles did not know what the people knew, you said that he had not met your wives; and I asked you if the people generally

---

lic opinion is belaboring us over the head just at present. I do not feel too bad about this, but if Apostles Taylor and Cowley do not comply with the subpoena ... they are going to make things very unpleasant for us all" (in Rodney J. Badger, *Liahona and Iron Rod: The Biography of Carl A. and Rose J. Badger* [Bountiful, Utah: Family History Publishers, 1985], 216).

had, and you made the answer which you will recall. Do you take back what you said just now?

MR. LYMAN. I did, Mr. Senator.

SENATOR HOAR. You did take it back?

MR. LYMAN. I did take it back, yes; and I intended to say that the people generally know—the people accept it as a fact.

SENATOR HOAR. Do you not think, Mr. Apostle, that in this hearing it behooves you to be a little careful of your answers so that in so important a matter you do not have to take back in two or three minutes what you have said? Have you had any revelation or commandment in regard to the testimony you should give in this case?

MR. LYMAN. No, sir.

SENATOR HOAR. There is no inspiration of that or any part of it?

MR. LYMAN. As to the testimony I should give here?

SENATOR HOAR. As to the testimony you have given or are to give.

MR. LYMAN. No; I do not know that I have, particularly. I came here to answer the questions of the committee.

SENATOR HOAR. But I want to know whether you are answering them under the direction of the Lord, according to your belief, or merely, in your human and uninspired capacity?

MR. LYMAN. I believe I shall answer the questions that are asked me here as the spirit of the Lord directs me, and truthfully.

SENATOR HOAR. Do you mean to say that the spirit of the Lord directs you in your answers here?

MR. LYMAN. I believe so.

SENATOR HOAR. You believe so?

MR. LYMAN. Yes, sir.

SENATOR HOAR. Then in your belief, did the spirit of the Lord direct you to make the answer which you just took back and said was a mistake? Well, if you can not answer it I will not press it. That is all.[25] ...

---

25. Of Lyman's testimony, Smoot reported: "Brother Lyman did not do so well and you ask me what was the matter with him. The only thing that I can say is that Brother Lyman did not grasp the meaning of the questions asked him. It certainly was a very trying position for a man to be placed in and I suppose it would be wrong to judge a man too harshly under those conditions" (in Harvard Heath, "Reed Smoot: First Modern Mormon," Ph.D. diss., Brigham Young University, 1990, 122).

8.

Joseph F. Smith, Andrew Jenson, Lorin Harmer, and Hyrum M. Smith

Wednesday, March 9

"Members of the committee were later than ever in reaching the committee room this morning. ... The attorneys were all present except Carlisle, who has not been seen in the committee room since last Wednesday. It is understood that he has abandoned the case and that he returned to New York today. Nineteen women, ranged along one side of the room, gave a touch of color to the scene with their ribboned millinery, and three artists succeeded in squeezing into seats near the witness chair that they might again sketch President Smith and other principal witnesses ... The most conspicuous document in the room was a bound volume of the Deseret News, which was obtained from the library of Congress to enable Mr. Tayler to freshen the memory of Mr. Smith." —*Deseret News,* Mar. 9, 1904

Joseph F. Smith,[1] having previously affirmed, was examined and testified as follows ...

MR. TAYLER. Now, the church—I gather from your statement the officials of the church have been ever since 1890, and are now, very sensitive as to the charge that plural marriages have been solemnized.

MR. WORTHINGTON. Since the manifesto?

---

1. The *New York World* described Joseph F. Smith in its March 9, 1904, edition as:
... a man of five feet eight or nine, with broad shoulders, short neck and a general appearance of squattiness. Smith wears a black frock coat and a high cut waistcoat. His scraggly beard drops well down on his chest. In the lapel of his coat is a button an inch in diameter, on which is his own picture. His head seems small for his body. Its most prominent feature is the nose, which is large at both base and point and stands out beneath his gold-rimmed spectacles like a promontory on an otherwise flat and barren shore. His forehead is wide and low and slopes back abruptly. His eyes are small and shifty. They sparkle behind his glasses and are never still. His beard but partially conceals the lack of chin. Smith speaks like a preacher. His voice is sonorous. His words are well chosen. It is evident that he has had much practice in talking to the public. His temper is not well in hand, for at times he flares up and answers questions sharply. He rarely moves when other witnesses are on the stand. He watches each man closely, but betrays neither satisfaction at nor disapproval of the testimony. He looks like the solemn personage he is, impressed with his own authority, and evidently given to impressing others so far as he is able.

MR. TAYLER. Since the manifesto.

MR. SMITH. Yes; I think we have been very sensitive about that.

MR. TAYLER. Very sensitive?

MR. SMITH. Yes, sir.

MR. TAYLER. What inquiry did you make to find out whether Abraham H. Cannon, one of the twelve apostles of the church, had made a plural marriage?

MR. SMITH. I made no inquiry at all.

MR. TAYLER. Did you set on foot any inquiry?

MR. SMITH. No, sir; not myself.

MR. TAYLER. Did you have any interest in finding out whether there had been—

MR. SMITH. Not the least.[2]

MR. TAYLER. Not the least?

MR. SMITH. Not the least.

MR. TAYLER. So that the public charge that an apostle of the church had married a plural wife as late as 1896 did not concern you at all?

MR. SMITH. The public charge, or what you call a public charge, is simply the charge made by the bitterest anti-Mormon publication in Salt Lake City, and its charges are of such a vicious character that I pay no attention to them. If I were to undertake to answer one hundredth part of the vicious and vile charges that are made in the anti-Mormon papers against me and my people I would have nothing else to do in the world.

MR. TAYLER. Yes; but was not the charge respecting Abraham H. Cannon taking a plural wife made with much circumstance and detail?

MR. SMITH. Not that I know of, any more than it was newspaper talk.

MR. TAYLER. Was it not published in other papers outside of Utah?

MR. SMITH. Copied from the Salt Lake papers; yes; I presume it was. ...

MR. TAYLER. However that may be, you did not yourself make any investigation or set on foot any investigation?

MR. SMITH. None whatever.

MR. TAYLER. Did you hear it said that Abraham H. Cannon claimed that he had a right to marry Lillian Hamlin, because she had been betrothed to his dead brother.

MR. SMITH. I never heard anything of the kind; only what the papers stated.

---

2. The previous three questions and answers were used in the plenary debate when the full Senate voted on February 20, 1907.

Mr. Tayler. You also heard the charge made that George Teasdale had taken a plural wife?

Mr. Smith. Yes; in the papers.

Mr. Tayler. Yes.

Mr. Smith. I saw the account that was published in the papers; in some of them, at least. I do not know that I saw them all.

Mr. Tayler. He was and is an apostle of the church?

Mr. Smith. Yes, sir.

Mr. Tayler. Did you make any investigation as to that?

Mr. Smith. I did not feel called upon to do it.

The Chairman. The question is if you did it.

Mr. Smith. No, sir; I did not.

Mr. Tayler. Then you mean to say that as a general proposition, notwithstanding your sensitiveness on the subject of plural marriages having been authorized or performed under the sanction of the church, you do not investigate any charges that are made of that character.

Mr. Smith. It is not my business to investigate them. I have given to this honorable committee—

The Chairman. The question is, Did you make any investigation?

Mr. Smith. I have made the assertion and explanation here to this honorable committee that our courts of original jurisdiction in the church are the bishops' courts, and it is the duty of the bishops to inquire into the moral character and the moral standing and the good fellowship of members of the church who reside in the wards of the bishops. ...

Mr. Tayler. Did you not feel any duty laid upon you to investigate this, in the interest of the church, apart from any personal lapse?

Mr. Smith. No; not in the way that these reports and rumors came to me. They were the reports and rumors of malicious persons.

Mr. Tayler. Malicious persons?

Mr. Smith. Yes, sir.

Mr. Tayler. Sometimes malicious persons tell the truth.

Mr. Smith. That may be.

Mr. Tayler. Or is it your assumption that they never do?

Mr. Smith. We become habituated to hearing reports of malicious persons until we pay no attention to them, even if they do tell the truth.

Mr. Tayler. Suppose it were charged that Francis M. Lyman, president of the twelve apostles, who does not, I believe, live in your ward, had performed a plural-marriage ceremony at Provo; would that induce you to make any inquiry?

MR. SMITH. Mr. Chairman, I submit that it is not a supposable case.

THE CHAIRMAN. Would you make the inquiry? That is the question.

MR. SMITH. It is not a supposable case, and if it were the case I could not tell you—

THE CHAIRMAN. That is the only answer you desire to make?

MR. SMITH. It is the only answer I can give. It is not a supposable case. I suppose I am not required to answer suppositions. ...

THE CHAIRMAN. ... you have revelations ... frequently?

MR. SMITH. Yes, sir; that is correct.

MR. WORTHINGTON. I think from the answer, that the witness did not hear the last part of the question—that he has revelations frequently.

MR. SMITH. I did not hear that.

THE CHAIRMAN. He has already stated that the Lord revealed to him.

MR. WORTHINGTON. He has stated that there has been no revelation in the sense of a revelation for twenty-one years.

MR. TAYLER. He said written revelation.

MR. WORTHINGTON. He said no revelation.

SENATOR DUBOIS. Let me understand that.

MR. WORTHINGTON. He spoke of personal revelations to him—

SENATOR DUBOIS. I would rather have the witness interpret what he says than have the counsel do it.

MR. WORTHINGTON. I am not interpreting it. I am simply saying what he testified to.

SENATOR DUBOIS. I understand there has been no general revelation to the church received by you which the people have sustained?

MR. SMITH. I do not understand your question, sir.[3]

SENATOR DUBOIS. Have you received any revelation from God which has been submitted by you and the apostles to the body of the church in their semiannual conference, which revelation has been sustained by that conference through the upholding of their hands?

MR. VAN COTT. I object to that question, and I wish to take this opportunity of stating rather fully why I object to it, so as to be thoroughly understood in regard to what has gone before.

The Senator [Hoar] from Massachusetts last evening at the ad-

---

3. Responding to some of the patterns of questions, the *Deseret News* ran an excerpt from the *Nebraska State Journal*: "It would appear from the performances of the senate committee ... that a gentleman of the name of Smith, had also been elected to that body from Utah, and that the committee had him in hole. Either that or the committee is making itself quite ridiculous in its investigation of the private character and domestic habits of Mr. Smith ... The senate is skating on thin ice" (Mar. 8, 1904).

journment made a suggestion which on account of the short time that we were in session we deemed it inadvisable to reply to in any way. In substance it was this: That this was in one sense an investigation, and that the committee might even take hearsay testimony into consideration for the purpose of following it up and getting other information.

In the first place it occurred to me in this way: There must be, as I assume, a number of Senators—I do not mean in the committee, because I am not informed, but in the Senate—who are not lawyers. When all those Senators take this testimony and read it, how are they going to tell what is competent testimony and what is incompetent? It seems to me[4]—

SENATOR HOAR. Mr. Chairman, I think I must object to this discussion. I do not think we can, within the time allowed to us, listen to arguments calculated to overthrow the established custom of the Senate and of Senatorial committees for many years. The gentlemen who are engaged in this investigation I hope will do entire justice and act justly and reasonably; but we must in an investigation, unless we are going to spend twelve months or more, keep within certain limits. The counsel are here simply in aid of the inquiry of the Senate, and not as trying a case in an ordinary court; and while everything ought to be allowed to them I do not think that the old established usages or practices of the Senate in investigations of this kind ought to be open to very much discussion. I wish to say that with great respect to the gentleman, and with the very eager, earnest desire on my part that nothing shall happen that will do any substantial injustice to his client.

MR. VAN COTT. Senator Hoar—

SENATOR HOAR. I should like to have that settled by the committee before counsel proceeds.

MR. VAN COTT. I am not going to argue against that. I was stating that as a reason—

SENATOR HOAR. But you were arguing against it.

MR. VAN COTT. No, sir.

SENATOR HOAR. Mr. Chairman, I should like to have that matter settled.

MR. VAN COTT. I was giving the reason for what I was going to say. If it is desired that I shall stop, I do not wish to trespass upon the committee, but I think in justice to Mr. Smoot I ought to say—

---

4. Of the senators who sat on the Committee of Privileges and Elections during Smoot's case, Dubois was the only one who lacked legal training.

THE CHAIRMAN. You probably had better defer that until a later time.

MR. VAN COTT. In justice to my client I do not think I should, but if the committee desires it I will defer it.

THE CHAIRMAN. I think you had better do that. We want to get along with the case.

SENATOR DUBOIS. I do not think there is any difference between the president of the church and myself. I think he misapprehended my question.

THE CHAIRMAN. What is the question?

SENATOR DUBOIS. I wish to state that I am not a lawyer, and in addition to that I am trying to ask questions which the ordinary fellow, who is not a lawyer, would like to have answered. So, if I transgress the strict rules of law you must remember that I am a layman and am taking what laymen would consider a broad view of the case.

MR. VAN COTT. Senator Dubois, what I was going to say was simply with respect to one point. I was merely calling attention to the line of testimony for the purpose of showing in what sense this testimony was being received by the committee. That was all.

THE CHAIRMAN. What was the question, propounded by Senator Dubois?

SENATOR DUBOIS. Let the stenographer read it.

The reporter read as follows: "Senator Dubois. Have you received any revelation from God, which has been submitted by you and the apostles to the body of the church in their semiannual conference, which revelation has been sustained by that conference through the upholding of their hands?"

MR. SMITH. Since when?

SENATOR DUBOIS. Since you became president of the church.

MR. SMITH. No, sir; none whatever.

SENATOR DUBOIS. Individual members of the church can receive individual revelations, can they not?

MR. SMITH. If I may be permitted, the word "revelation" is used very vaguely here all the time. No man can get revelations at his will. If a man is prayerful and earnest in his desire and lives a righteous life and he desires information and intelligence, he will inquire of the Lord, and the Lord will manifest to him, through the presence and influence of his Spirit, his mind, and his will. That would be a revelation to that individual. ...

SENATOR DUBOIS. Have you received any individual revelations yourself, since you became president of the church under your own definition, even, of a revelation?

MR. SMITH. I can not say that I have.

SENATOR DUBOIS. Can you say that you have not?

MR. SMITH. No; I can not say that I have not.

SENATOR DUBOIS. Then you do not know whether you have received any such revelation as you have described, or whether you have not?

MR. SMITH. Well, I can say this: That if I live as I should in the line of my duties, I am susceptible, I think, of the impressions of the spirit of the Lord upon my mind at any time, just as any good Methodist or any other good church member might be. And so far as that is concerned, I say yes; I have had impressions of the Spirit upon my mind very frequently, but they are not in the sense revelations.

THE CHAIRMAN. Senator, do you think it is important to pursue that further?

SENATOR DUBOIS. No. ...

SENATOR HOAR. You said, ... if I understood you correctly, that the performing of a marriage which would be polygamous by a high officer of the church, like an apostle, since the manifesto is not a supposable case, and you did not like to be questioned about it.

MR. SMITH. It is not a supposable case.

SENATOR HOAR. How do you distinguish between that case being not supposable and the living in polygamy in defiance of the revelation of the Lord and the law of the land by such an official? Why, in your judgment, is one supposable and the other unsupposable?

MR. SMITH. For this reason, Mr. Senator. In the one case, in my case, we have felt that not only public opinion, but the constitution of our State and the general conditions that exist in Utah more or less justified me in pursuing the course I did. But, on the other hand, we have agreed that we will not solemnize any more plural marriages, and I do not believe that there is a member of the church, an official member of the church, in good standing, who would violate that promise. That is the reason.

Excuse me for being a little earnest about it, Mr. Senator. I am naturally a little emphatic in my nature. I do not mean to use any undue—

SENATOR HOAR. I think I will say now, for the information of everybody, that the putting of questions which might seem to imply in my mind, when I put them, a pretty strong sense of the inconsistency and delusion of the religious faith, so called, of the witness—and in saying that I suppose I may add that a great many members of different sects attribute both inconsistency and delusion to others—must not be taken to imply in my mind, as at present advised, any opinion one way or the other as to the right of the people who hold that religious faith, whether inconsistent or a delusion or even not sincere, to send one of that faith to the United States Senate under our Constitution and laws if the person so holding it has not violated law himself or is not engaged in an association which has for its object the violation of law. I do not wish to be taken by the public or counsel or anybody else, by putting the questions I have or any others which I may put, as indicating an opinion on that final question.[5]

MR. SMITH. Thank you. ...

THE CHAIRMAN. I should like to ask counsel if this witness will be needed further?

MR. VAN COTT. We are through with him.

MR. WORTHINGTON. Is it a final discharge?

THE CHAIRMAN. Yes.[6] ...

Andrew Jenson,[7] having been duly sworn, was examined and testified as follows ...

MR. TAYLER. What official position do you now hold?

MR. JENSON. I am one of the assistant historians in the church.

---

5. In a letter to Joseph F. Smith fourteen days later, Smoot wrote:

Senator Hoar yesterday in talking with me said that he did not object to the position taken by you in defending and caring for the wives and their children that you had taken before the Manifesto, but rather admired the stand you took; but he did unhesitatingly denounce your position in defying the laws of the land and breaking the laws of God, and also regretted to hear you answer that for so doing you expect to ask and receive mercy. "Moses Thatcher," said he, "was deposed because he was out of harmony with the Church, and being out of harmony was rightfully handled for it, but the President of the Church now acknowledges that he has broken one of the revelations of God, and he certainly must be out of harmony; and, why is it, if the Church is sincere, that Moses Thatcher was handled and deposed and received no mercy, while President Joseph F. Smith is sustained and honored." He also stated that he had understood in the past that any covenant, obligation, or agreement made by the Mormon people would honestly and conscientiously and strictly be adhered to by them. He expressed great sorrow to learn in this investigation that the agreement made by the leaders of the Mormon Church, and in behalf of the people of that Church, with the Government of the United States was violated by the very men who made the agreement, and who pledged their own honor and the honor of the Church and of the people that the agreement would be kept in good fai[t]h (Mar. 23, 1904).

6. On March 22, 1904, Carl Badger noted in his journal: "When President Smith had concluded his testimony one day[,] he left the Committee room saying over and over again to F[ranklin]. S. Richards, 'I am sorry for Reed,' 'I am sorry for Reed'" (in Rodney J. Badger, *Liahona and Iron Rod: The Biography of Carl A. and Rose J. Badger* [Bountiful, Utah: Family History Publishers, 1985], 213).

7. Jenson (1850-1941), the Assistant LDS Church Historian, lived in Salt Lake City and was a polygamist.

MR. TAYLER. Who is the chief historian?

MR. JENSON. Anthon H. Lund.[8]

MR. TAYLER. He is one of the counselors to the first president [Joseph F. Smith]?

MR. JENSON. Yes, sir.

MR. TAYLER. Are you practically the person in charge of the historical work of the church, or does Mr. Lund give constant attention to that?

MR. JENSON. His time does not permit him to do that, so I suppose I am the one that has charge.

MR. TAYLER. That was what I supposed. I called Mr. Smith's, or Mr. Lyman's, attention to a book entitled "The Church Chronology," compiled by Andrew Jenson, and dated 1899. That is an official publication of the church, is it not?

MR. JENSON. No, sir; you can not call it official. It is my own work.

MR. TAYLER. Just describe it. It is your own work.

MR. JENSON. It is my own work. I only am responsible for its contents.[9]

MR. TAYLER. It is published by the "Deseret News?"

MR. JENSON. Yes, sir.

MR. TAYLER. And this edition states that "Before printing, the copy was carefully read to a committee appointed by Historian Franklin D. Richards, consisting of Assistant Historians John Jaques and Charles W. Penrose and Elder A. Milton Musser. Great pains have been taken to make the work accurate and in all respects reliable as a work of reference, and as such it is respectfully presented to the public at large, and particularly to those who desire correct information in regard to the Latter-Day Saints and their most remarkable history." That is correct, is it?

MR. JENSON. Yes, sir; that is correct.

MR. TAYLER. So far as you know, this is a correct account of historical affairs as indicated in its pages?

MR. JENSON. Yes, sir; only we did discover a few inaccurate dates, but not of any importance.

---

8. Lund was installed as Church Historian on July 26, 1900.

9. Later in the hearing, James E. Talmage stated this in regard to Jenson's publications, including the *Church Chronology*: "They are in no sense authoritative as works by which the church can be bound; and, moreover, they are publications by Mr. Jenson put out partly as a commercial enterprise, as I understand. ... I had occasion to consult the Church Chronology soon after its first appearance, and I found two or three errors in it, and since then I have not consulted it further. It is not regarded as an authoritative work, and certainly not as a work by which the church or its members could be bound" (*Smoot Hearings*, 3:128-29).

MR. TAYLER. You have also published a book entitled "Latter-Day Saints' Biographical Encyclopedia?"

MR. JENSON. Yes, sir.

MR. TAYLER. Was that prepared by you?

MR. JENSON. Yes, sir.

MR. TAYLER. The edition that I have here is dated 1901 and published by the "Deseret News."

MR. JENSON. There has been only one edition.

MR. TAYLER. And in so far as you are able to learn, from the data at your command, this correctly represents events in the lives of the various Latter-Day Saints?

MR. JENSON. Yes, sir; so far as I have been able to obtain correct information. ...

Lorin Harmer,[10] having been duly sworn, was examined, and testified as follows ...

MR. TAYLER. Where do you live, Mr. Harmer?

MR. HARMER. Springville, Utah County, Utah.

MR. TAYLER. What official position do you hold in the church?

MR. HARMER. Not any.

MR. TAYLER. Have you had any official position in it?

MR. HARMER. Yes, sir.

MR. TAYLER. What?

MR. HARMER. I was bishop about five years, or six.

MR. TAYLER. When did you cease to be a bishop?

MR. HARMER. It was in 1899, I believe.

MR. TAYLER. How did you come to cease to be a bishop?

MR. HARMER. Well, I committed the crime of unchastity and lost my membership ...

MR. WORTHINGTON. Did you marry any wife since the manifesto?

MR. HARMER. No, sir.

MR. WORTHINGTON. Were you at any time married, or did you have any marriage ceremony between you and Ellen Anderson?

MR. HARMER. No, sir.

MR. WORTHINGTON. Have you held her out at any time as being your wife?

MR. HARMER. No, sir.

MR. WORTHINGTON. About your being punished and sent to the peniten-

---

10. Harmer (1854-1926), an excommunicated former LDS bishop, was living in Springville, Utah, at the time of the hearings.

tiary. Do you know whether Senator Smoot had anything to do with that?

Mr. Harmer. I think he did.

Mr. Worthington. What?

Mr. Harmer. Well, at that time, when I had the trouble with that woman, he was counselor to the president of the stake, and the president of the stake was quite sick at the time when I went over to Provo. I had a talk there with Mr. Smoot and he told me what the church was going to do right away, and I asked him to give me a little time that I might kindly prepare my folks for the worst.

Senator Beveridge. What was the church going to do right away?

Mr. Harmer. Well, they was going to take my bishopric from me, and the offices I then held in the church.

Senator Beveridge. What?

Mr. Harmer. I was bishop, and I was instructor of the priests' quorum, teachers' quorum, and deacons' quorum.

Senator Beveridge. Why were they going to take those things from you?

Mr. Harmer. Because I had committed a crime that the church could not allow.

Mr. Worthington. What crime? What was the conversation between you and the Senator, about what crime you had committed?

Mr. Harmer. Well, the crime of adultery, plainly speaking, and I got in my buggy and started home. Before I got home the county sheriff caught me, and I laid it to Mr. Smoot a-sending after me. They took me back to Provo, and I stayed there all that night in Provo; and I did not think it was hardly fair. I thought he ought to give me a little fairer chance, although it was a bad crime.

The Chairman. Let me ask you right there, if you will, what year was this?

Mr. Harmer. In 1899.

The Chairman. You said you laid it to Mr. Smoot. Do you know that he sent the officer after you?

Mr. Harmer. I do not know it, but it looked very much like it, you know.[11]

The Chairman. Have you anything further, Mr. Tayler.

Mr. Tayler. Nothing further.

The Chairman. You may stand aside, Mr. Harmer. Who is your next witness?

Mr. Tayler. Hyrum M. Smith.

---

11. Based on this testimony, one newspaper headlined: "Smoot Scores First Time in Senate Inquiry" (*Kansas City Journal*, Mar. 10, 1904).

SENATOR BEVERIDGE. Did I understand you to say you were also sent to the penitentiary for this crime, sir?

MR. HARMER. Yes, sir. ...

THE CHAIRMAN. Mr. Smith, will you be sworn?

MR. HYRUM M. SMITH.[12] I would prefer to affirm, Mr. Chairman.

Hyrum M. Smith,[13] having been duly affirmed, was examined and testified as follows ...

SENATOR DUBOIS. What happens to that individual who refuses persistently to obey the counsel which your officials choose to give him?

MR. HYRUM M. SMITH. Well, speaking for myself, I never had any of them refuse to obey counsel I have given.

SENATOR DUBOIS. You are not answering my question.

MR. HYRUM M. SMITH. Well, you said counsel I gave, and I have no such case.

SENATOR DUBOIS. You never counsel your people?

MR. HYRUM M. SMITH. Yes, sir.

SENATOR DUBOIS. Please read my question. I would like to have an answer.

The reporter read as follows: "Senator Dubois. What happens to that individual who refuses persistently to obey the counsel which your officials choose to give him?"

MR. HYRUM M. SMITH. If a person persistently refuses to receive the counsel which he is given, why, that individual would not be considered in full fellowship with those who give the counsel.

SENATOR DUBOIS. Would he be considered in full fellowship with the church?

MR. HYRUM M. SMITH. Not if that counsel was given by the church.

SENATOR DUBOIS. Suppose it was given by a high representative of the church like an apostle. Would not the apostle in that case be the representative of the church?

MR. HYRUM M. SMITH. Yes, sir; an apostle is a representative of the church.

---

12. A member of the Quorum of the Twelve Apostles, Smith (1872-1918) lived in Salt Lake City and was a monogamist.

13. The *New York World* described the witness as:

a smooth-faced man with a sharp, inquisitive nose ... foxy is the proper way to describe his face. Young Hiram is thirty-two, but he has been an apostle for three years and will some day be at the head of the Church. ... He talks like a man who has been trained by a professional elocutionist. His sentences roll out like the exhortations of a revivalist, but that is not strange, for he has been a missionary, spreading the creed of the Mormons in many lands. He is slight and bowed, carefully dressed and has much of the appearance of the prominent citizen who keeps the shoe store in the village in the West" ("Women Giggle at the Smoot Testimony," Mar. 9, 1904).

SENATOR DUBOIS. Then he would not be in fellowship with the church if he refused to obey the counsel which the apostle of the church gave him?

MR. HYRUM M. SMITH. Providing that counsel pertained to the church and to good fellowship in the church. He would cease to be in fellowship if he refused to obey that counsel[14] ...

SENATOR BEVERIDGE. I want to ask a question, Mr. Smith, as to this counsel addressed to members of your church. Did you ever give any of the members of your church any political counsel?

MR. HYRUM M. SMITH. No, sir.

SENATOR BEVERIDGE. Did you ever advise any of them how to vote on any question?

MR. HYRUM M. SMITH. No, sir. That is a matter, Mr. Senator, which I consider belongs to the right of every individual; and inasmuch as I myself consider that I am capable of using my own judgment in all political matters, even so do I not give counsel in that respect.

SENATOR BEVERIDGE. You spoke about good citizenship and one thing and another, and you said you counseled them to make good citizens in that respect. I was interested in knowing just how far your mind went in the counsel you give, which, in your view, would make them good citizens.

MR. HYRUM M. SMITH. Counsel to obey all of the statutes and ordinances of the municipality and the State, and no individual has to be at variance with any law, so far as I know, to be a good Latter-Day Saint, and that is what my counsel has been.

MR. WORTHINGTON. When you speak of advising your people about temporal affairs and their being out of fellowship if they do not take the advice, what do you mean by "temporal affairs"—what kind of affairs?

MR. HYRUM M. SMITH. When I speak of temporal affairs I mean being frugal, industrious, sustain one another, sustain home industries, build up their country, take care of their flocks and herds, properly fence their fields, and be frugal in sowing and planting, and taking care of machinery and outbuildings, and such things as that. That is what I mean by temporal advice. Those are temporal things, I believe. ...

MR. WORTHINGTON. Now, about the books you used. There was here this morning—you were here when that Book of Mormon was produced?

MR. HYRUM M. SMITH. Yes, sir.

---

14. This entire section above was used by Tayler in closing arguments for the claimants (*Smoot Hearings*, 3:497-98).

MR. WORTHINGTON. And you heard that condemnation of polygamy this morning?

MR. HYRUM M. SMITH. Yes, sir.

MR. WORTHINGTON. What use have you been making of that book in your apostolic work and missionary work?

MR. HYRUM M. SMITH. We make every effort we can to distribute that work among the people.

MR. WORTHINGTON. How does the extent to which that book is distributed among non-Mormons, where you are doing your missionary work, compare with the distribution of the book the Doctrine and Covenants?

MR. HYRUM M. SMITH. So far as I, myself, am concerned in missionary work, and those who immediately labored with me, we made no effort to circulate the Doctrine and Covenants among the people as a proselyting medium. The Book of Mormon was used extensively for that purpose.

MR. WORTHINGTON. How about this book of [James E.] Talmage's, the "Articles of Faith," which contains the substance of the manifesto? To what extent, if at all, has that been used in your mission work of late years?

MR. HYRUM M. SMITH. That book was not published when I, myself, filled a foreign mission, but I understand it is used extensively by the missionaries; and I, myself, have highly recommended it to missionaries about to depart for a mission.

MR. WORTHINGTON. Both it and the Book of Mormon are in common everyday use among those who are on missions?

MR. HYRUM M. SMITH. Yes, sir.

MR. WORTHINGTON. Something was asked of Mr. [Francis M.] Lyman the other day about the publication of frequent editions of the Doctrine and Covenants. Do you know anything about that?[15]

MR. HYRUM M. SMITH. No, I really do not know how frequently they are issued.

MR. WORTHINGTON. Among those who are members of the Mormon Church, out there in the inter-mountain States, is the Doctrine and Covenants commonly used as one of their household books, as well as the Book of Mormon?

MR. HYRUM M. SMITH. Yes, sir; it is practically the book of instruction in

15. Actually, this was Joseph F. Smith who was asked about the frequency of publication, the particular concern being Section 132, the revelation on plural marriage (*Smoot Hearings*, 1:108).

church government, and pertains more particularly to those who are members of the church than to those who are not members of the church.

Mr. Worthington. Then among those who are your members and who know all about the manifesto and this matter being forbidden by law, the Doctrine and Covenants is used a great deal more than it is among people who are not members and when you are doing missionary work?

Mr. Hyrum M. Smith. Yes, sir; and if I may be permitted to add here, I would like to do so in relation to the editions. I think it was relating to the Doctrine and Covenants that the question was asked, I believe, how it was that a number of editions had been issued recently.

Now, if I am not mistaken, and the Book of Doctrine and Covenants was referred to, I will say that, in my opinion, those books were purchased by the Latter-Day Saints themselves and not for distribution for proselyting purposes.

Mr. Worthington. One thing more about these apostle meetings, concerning which the chairman has asked you. You and Mr. Smoot have been present together at a number of these meetings?

Mr. Hyrum M. Smith. Yes, sir.

Mr. Worthington. At any meeting at which you were present and when he was present has the subject of polygamous cohabitation or polygamy been discussed, so far as you can remember?

Mr. Hyrum M. Smith. No, sir; not that I can remember.

Mr. Worthington. Can you tell me at any meeting while you were present, whether he was there or not, whether anything has been done looking to the advocating of polygamy or polygamous cohabitation?

Mr. Hyrum M. Smith. Looking to the advocating of it?

Mr. Worthington. Looking to it, one way or the other; and if so in what way?

Mr. Hyrum M. Smith. I have heard things occasionally. Of course the rumors that are rife come to our ears, as well as others; and on a number of occasions I have heard it most specifically given as instruction to those present that we must use our every effort to have these things stopped, if there was any truth whatever in the rumor, which we ourselves have not believed.

Mr. Worthington. To what rumors do you refer?

Mr. Hyrum M. Smith. That polygamy or the practice of plural marriage is being continued in the church.

Mr. Worthington. Then those rumors have been discussed and you have all agreed that everything must be done to stop it if it exists?

MR. HYRUM M. SMITH. Yes, sir.

MR. WORTHINGTON. What about polygamous cohabitation; that is, living with plural wives, as distinguished from taking them?

MR. HYRUM M. SMITH. I have never heard that question discussed at all.

MR. WORTHINGTON. If the meetings of the apostles, then, are in the nature of a conspiracy to carry on that sort of thing, you do not know about it and have not participated in it?

MR. HYRUM M. SMITH. No, sir. ...

SENATOR HOAR. Mr. Smith, the doctrine, when you were a missionary of the church, was a doctrine of opposition to polygamy, was it not—forbidding polygamy?

MR. HYRUM M. SMITH. That was a rule of the church; yes, sir.

SENATOR HOAR. Very well; I will use either the word "rule" or the word "doctrine."

MR. HYRUM M. SMITH. Yes, sir.

SENATOR HOAR. I suppose the rules of the church were based on its doctrine, and its doctrines are that the rules should be observed.

MR. HYRUM M. SMITH. Yes, sir.

SENATOR HOAR. However, that is a question I will not trouble you about. Did you as a missionary advocate or enforce that doctrine or rule [regarding plural marriage] and point out the reasonableness of it to your auditors?

MR. HYRUM M. SMITH. Yes, sir.

SENATOR HOAR. You argued against the rightfulness of polygamy, then, did you?

MR. HYRUM M. SMITH. I can hardly hear your question, Senator.

SENATOR HOAR. I asked you if you urged upon your converts, or persons you were trying to convert, the righteousness and rightfulness of the present doctrine of the church forbidding polygamy, as opposed to divine command?

MR. HYRUM M. SMITH. I hardly know how to answer your question.

SENATOR HOAR. When you undertook to win adherents to your church I suppose you commended the belief and practice of your people—the present belief and practice—did you not?

MR. HYRUM M. SMITH. Yes, sir.

SENATOR HOAR. Very well. In doing that did you commend and urge upon them the rightfulness of the present doctrine and rule of the church forbidding polygamy?

MR. HYRUM M. SMITH. I do not know that I remember. I remember distinctly in every case informing them that it was no longer a doctrine of the church, so far as our practice was concerned.

SENATOR HOAR. I am not asking whether you told them it was a doctrine no longer, but whether you argued and persuaded them that it was a religious and rightful doctrine.

MR. HYRUM M. SMITH. No, I did not argue. I have said that I avoided all argument on the question.

SENATOR HOAR. Well, if the rule of your church forbade polygamy, and you were trying to win converts to your faith, why did you omit from the things which you urged upon your converts the article of faith that polygamy was wrong?

MR. HYRUM M. SMITH. Well, I can not gather you, Senator Hoar.

SENATOR HOAR. Will you repeat that question, Mr. Reporter, so that the witness can hear it?

The reporter read the question as follows: "Senator Hoar. Well, if the rule of your church forbade polygamy, and you were trying to win converts to your faith, why did you omit from the things which you urged upon your converts the article of faith that polygamy was wrong?"

MR. HYRUM M. SMITH. I have always, in my ministrations among the people, urged the rightfulness of the commandments and the doctrines of the church, and I recognized that the practice of plural marriages had ceased, and the manifesto as a doctrine of the church I have frequently urged upon them.

SENATOR HOAR. And forbidden it? Well, my question is did you urge upon your converts that that was a rightful and true doctrine?

MR. HYRUM M. SMITH. Yes, sir.

SENATOR HOAR. That polygamy should be forbidden?

MR. HYRUM M. SMITH. Yes, sir.

SENATOR HOAR. As of right? I am not now speaking of it as merely resting on the divine authority but as being right in itself?

MR. HYRUM M. SMITH. That they should refrain from that?

SENATOR HOAR. Yes.

MR. HYRUM M. SMITH. Yes sir.

SENATOR HOAR. Then you did not refrain from discussing the subject of polygamy and its rightfulness in your ministrations, for you preached to your converts that it was wrong, did you not?

MR. HYRUM M. SMITH. Now, let me explain that, Senator Hoar. You place me in a false position, entirely.

SENATOR HOAR. I have only asked the question.

MR. HYRUM M. SMITH. I said I have avoided a discussion of that matter entirely. If it were to come up incidentally by a person who was favorably
disposed toward Mormonism, and who might be considered an inves-
tigator, and I were asked the question, I would answer his questions to
the best of my ability to the effect that while in times past plural marriages had been a doctrine and had been practiced by the church,
that it no longer was practiced by the church, nor should be; and to
that extent and no further have I gone in the discussion of the question.

SENATOR HOAR. Why did you confine yourself to the fact that the church
had now altered its rule, and not enter into the question of the rightfulness of the present rule?

MR. HYRUM M. SMITH. The principal reason for that is that with investiga-
tors of the doctrine of a church it is the first principles of the gospel
that are considered, and it is seldom polygamy is spoken of, either by
them or by the elders, and we have no particular occasion—

SENATOR HOAR. Then your answer is that it was not, in the mind of the
convert with whom you were dealing, a practical question at that
time?[16]

MR. HYRUM M. SMITH. That is my idea; yes, sir[17] ...

MR. TAYLER. Let me ask Mr. Joseph F. Smith a question, as to whether he
could get into communication with any of these apostles who have

---

16. Carl Badger noted in his diary on March 15, 1904, that "someone asked Senator
Hoar why he asked the questions of the witnesses. 'To keep Beveridge from joining the
Mormon Church,' he answered" (Badger, *Liahona and Iron Rod*, 212).

17. A year later, Hyrum Smith made the following public comment:

We believe that in President Roosevelt we have an unprejudiced friend; and we
know that in the Latter-day Saints President Roosevelt will find loyalty to the government and the greatest friendship toward him. There are no people in the nation
more friendly to him; and they will remain so just so long as he remains true to the
cause of humanity ... I believe he is a man who, so long as he believes our cause is just,
will be willing to do something for us. We assuredly will do all we can to sustain him,
and all other good men (in *LDS Conference Report* [Salt Lake City: Church of Jesus
Christ of Latter-day Saints, Apr. 1905], 97).

Carl Badger subsequently told his wife it was:

a foolish thing that Hyrum M. Smith said at conference, in reference to the Mormon
people having stood by President Roosevelt and that, therefore, the President would
stand by us. In the first place, the Mormon people, as a Mormon people did not
stand by the President, they did as Republicans, but it only adds fuel to the conflagra-
tion to make a remark which sounds mighty like the Church—the Mormon people as
Mormons—are in politics as supporters of the Republican party. This alienates Democrats at home and in national politics. But the most serious thing is that it compro-
mises the President. The President can deal us a stunning blow, and Hyrum almost
asked him to do it (in Badger, *Liahona and Iron Rod*, 268).

been subpoenaed and have not been reached, and whether any instruction from him would facilitate their coming here?

Mr. Joseph F. Smith. I presume I could find them in time, Mr. Tayler. I do not know how soon I could find them.[18]

Mr. Tayler. I would be obliged if you would give them such instruction as you can that we want them as soon as we can get them.

Mr. Van Cott. Which ones, Mr. Tayler?

Mr. Tayler. John W. Taylor, George Teasdale, M[atthias]. F. Cowley, John Henry Smith.[19]

Mr. Van Cott. You know he is very ill, and that Teasdale is very ill?

Mr. Worthington. They have been subpoenaed, and are not here simply because they are not well.

Mr. Joseph F. Smith. Mr. [Marriner Wood] Merrill has also been subpoenaed.

Mr. Tayler. I understood Mr. Merrill was quite ill. Of course a man who is physically incapable of coming or whose health would be affected by coming ought not be required to come. ...

---

18. Senator Burrows, whom President Smith referred to as the "Czar Committeeman," expected Smith to compel these apostles to testify. "I would suggest that the Senator take another look at the record and see what kind of a promise I made," Smith wrote to Smoot. "If I recall the fact, and I think I do, I made no such a promise. He will find what I said at the conclusion of Hyrum M's testimony. The imperious Caesar should speak from the record and not thro[ugh] his hat. An[d] yet, notwithstanding I ... did not intend to make such promise, I have done my best to find those ... men ... and persuade them to go to Washington" (Apr. 9, 1904).

19. Three weeks later, Senator Smoot reported to President Smith that "yesterday Julius Caesar asked me if I had heard from you. ... He asked me if I would not telegraph to you, and I suggested that he had better telegraph himself. He stated that he did not want to do that as he did not consider it proper. Every other day for the past two weeks he has wanted to know if those witnesses would be here, remarking that they were wanted and wanted bad, and also that the case would not be closed until they have testified" (Mar. 31, 1904).

9.

Andrew Jenson,
E. B. Critchlow, and Odgen Hiles

Thursday & Saturday, March 10, 12

"A bright afternoon brought out a big crowd to the Smoot hearing. In all about 85 or 90 persons, besides members of the committee, crowded into the room. This number included 15 or 20 newspaper men and artists, ... [and] no less than 32 women, ranging in age from the dowager of 70 to the school miss of 14. [Some have criticized] the committee for permitting children, boys and girls, to enter the room. At this writing, 3 o'clock p.m., there are in the corridor trying to force entrance through the crowd at the door, men and women, apparently respectable, with children at their sides five or six years old, and the Capitol officials make no attempt to keep them back." —*Deseret News,* Mar. 10, 1904

"At each senator's place at the table was a bundle of books containing copies of the Doctrine and Covenants, Book of Mormon, Articles of Faith and Pearl of Great Price. These were the volumes promised by President Smith and they will be carefully studied by most members of the committee during the recess next week" —*Deseret News,* Mar. 12, 1904

Andrew Jenson, having been previously sworn, was examined and testified as follows ...

MR. WORTHINGTON. You have testified that you are the author of this book which is called the "Latter-Day Saints' Biographical Encyclopedia?"

MR. JENSON. Yes, sir.

MR. WORTHINGTON. I wish to ask you, in making up your statements as to the lives of the different persons mentioned in that book, and especially as to the apostles and the first presidency—and I will confine myself to them—where you got the information that is there embodied?

MR. JENSON. About the early apostles I obtained my information from the public documents of the church; and as to the recent members I have copied some from Bishop Orson F. Whitney's sketches that he has prepared for the fourth volume of the "History of Utah," and also from M[atthias]. F. Cowley's "History of the Lives of the Leaders."

MR. WORTHINGTON. You made it up, then, from previous publications?

MR. JENSON. Yes, sir; partly so.

MR. WORTHINGTON. Let me ask you, as to Senator Smoot, whether, in the biography which refers to him, you consulted him at all or not?

MR. JENSON. No, sir; I could not reach Mr. Smoot. He was not found. He did not see it at all before it was published.

MR. WORTHINGTON. For instance, I note that you say in the very first sentence about Mr. Smoot, that he has been "a member of the council of twelve apostles since 1898." That is a mistake?

MR. JENSON. It is a typographical error. It ought to be 1900.

SENATOR FORAKER. It should be what?

MR. JENSON. 1900.

MR. WORTHINGTON. The next statement is: "Smoot, Reed, a member of the council of twelve apostles since 1898, is the son of Abraham O. Smoot and Anna Kirstine Mouritsen." M-o-u-r-i-t-s-e-n. Do you not know that his mother's name was Morrison?

MR. JENSON. This is the right name, I think.

MR. WORTHINGTON. This is the right name?

MR. JENSON. Yes. That is the original name—Mouritsen. She was born in a foreign land. That is the right spelling.

MR. WORTHINGTON. You did not get that from him, and you differ from him, perhaps?

MR. JENSON. I went back to the original. I know what the name is in the original language.

MR. WORTHINGTON. I merely mentioned that as an illustration.

MR. TAYLER. Where you used other publications, they were publications by officials of the church?

MR. JENSON. Not altogether.

MR. TAYLER. At least those that you named were.

MR. JENSON. Cowley's work was published by him, he being an apostle.

MR. TAYLER. And Whitney.

MR. JENSON. Whitney is also a writer; he is a historian. He is the author of the "History of Utah."

MR. TAYLER. Is he a Mormon?

MR. JENSON. Yes, sir.

MR. TAYLER. What official position did he hold?

MR. JENSON. He is also one of the assistant church historians now, but he was not at that time. ...

MR. WORTHINGTON. You have mentioned here, I think, for the first time in this hearing about the teachers, and I should like to have this record complete by having you tell us what are the duties of the teachers. They are ward officers?

MR. JENSON. Yes, sir; they are ward officers. Their business is only to assist the bishop in a local capacity; to visit with the people. ...

MR. WORTHINGTON. How often do they go around?

MR. JENSON. They should go around once a month.

MR. WORTHINGTON. So it is the business of the teacher to go to each household in the ward?

MR. JENSON. Yes, sir; and pray with them, and teach them the principles of the gospel.

MR. WORTHINGTON. What is their duty in relation to finding out whether anything wrong is going on; whether there is any violation of the church rules?

MR. JENSON. That is one of their duties, to see that there is no iniquity anywhere in the church.

MR. WORTHINGTON. That is done every week or two?

MR. JENSON. Every month.

MR. WORTHINGTON. And if a teacher ascertains that there is any violation of any rule of the church then it is his duty—

MR. JENSON. It is their duty.

MR. WORTHINGTON. To report it to the bishop?

MR. JENSON. To report it to the bishop, and for the bishop to take action upon it.

MR. WORTHINGTON. Then it is the duty of these people, if anyone is violating a rule of the church, to ferret it out, and bring it to the attention of the bishop?

MR. JENSON. Yes, sir. It almost invariably begins with the teachers. That is one of their special duties. ...

MR. WORTHINGTON. Suppose that the president of the church or one of the apostles resides—he resides in some ward, of course—in a ward, and suppose that he is violating a rule of the church, whose business is it to call him to account or to report him to the bishop?

MR. JENSON. He is no exception to the general rule. The teachers visit him just like a lay member of the church.

MR. WORTHINGTON. Suppose the president of the church is violating a rule of the church and an apostle knows it, is it, so far as your church organization is concerned, any more the duty of the apostle than it is the duty of anybody else in the ward to call attention to it?

MR. JENSON. No, sir. He would naturally say, "Why does not the teacher do his duty?"

MR. WORTHINGTON. If he came from some other ward or bailiwick and interfered in that matter he would be considered as going out of his jurisdiction?

MR. JENSON. Yes, sir; it is a rule that the general officers of the church
never interfere with local affairs.

MR. WORTHINGTON. When any member of the church, whether he is a
high officer or not, is violating a rule of the church, that is considered
a local affair?

MR. JENSON. Yes, sir; because he always belongs to some ward.

[SENATOR] HOAR. What?

MR. WORTHINGTON. He says it is a local affair and it is the business of the
teacher to call him to account.

MR. JENSON. As to moral conduct, there is no officer of the church, no
matter how high, the president not excepted, who is not amenable to
the bishops and the teachers. As an officer he is responsible to them. ...

E. B. Critchlow,[1] having been first duly sworn, was examined and testified as follows ...

MR. WORTHINGTON. ... I am told that Mr. [John L.] Leilich is a member of
this ministerial association. Is that true?

MR. CRITCHLOW. I think not now. I think he was at the time.

MR. WORTHINGTON. He was at that time a member of the ministerial association. He is one of the signers of both protests. He is one of the
nineteen, and then he also filed this individual protest of his own. So
there is a case of specific charges formally published against Senator
Smoot, published all over the country, which he [Smoot] has never
deigned to take notice of. And yet when we come to the facts of the
case we find that the charges are absolutely without foundation, and
that there is nobody who will come here and stand sponsor for them.[2]
If it is charged that Senator Smoot has made admissions to anybody,
let those person[s] be brought here. The subpoena of the committee
will reach them wherever they may be. Let us have their statements,
made under oath, with the opportunity to cross-examine—the two
sure tests of the weight of testimony.

1. At the time of the hearings, Edward B. Critchlow (1858-1920) lived in Salt Lake
City. Born in Mississippi, he attended Princeton University and Columbia Law School
before moving to Utah in 1883. He served as Assistant U.S. Attorney for three terms and
in the Utah State legislature for one term. He was one of nineteen signers of the original
protest against Smoot by the Salt Lake Ministerial Association.

2. For the full text of Leilich's protest, see the *Smoot Hearings,* 1:26-30. The charge
referenced here was "that said Senator-elect Smoot is a polygamist."

MR. TAYLER. Let me read the heart of this. This is the kind of a statement—

THE CHAIRMAN. I should like to ask a preliminary question before you do that. You speak of a certain publication?

MR. TAYLER. Yes, sir.

THE CHAIRMAN. In a Salt Lake paper?

MR. TAYLER. Yes, sir.

THE CHAIRMAN. Charging Mr. Smoot with certain things?

MR. TAYLER. No, sir.

THE CHAIRMAN. What is it?

MR. TAYLER. I will read it and you will see.

MR. WORTHINGTON. That will put it in the record. Let us see what it is.

MR. TAYLER. Let me read this.

MR. WORTHINGTON. I understand that this is not to go into the record, and yet the stenographer is taking it down.

SENATOR FORAKER. Let us pass on the question before anything is read.

MR. TAYLER. Let the stenographer not take it down.

SENATOR BEVERIDGE. Can you not tell us what it is?

SENATOR FORAKER. Tell us whether what you propose to put in the record would tend, by any other evidence, to bring it home to Mr. Smoot in such way as to charge him with responsibility for it. If so, it would be competent.

MR. TAYLER. Of course we will, but the committee will see at once that to a certain extent some responsibility may be laid upon Mr. Smoot by this very thing.

SENATOR BEVERIDGE. Go ahead and read it. That will be shorter and sweeter.

MR. WORTHINGTON. The reporter is still taking notes.

THE CHAIRMAN. The reporter will not take this down.

By direction or the chairman the reporter at this point ceased to report the proceedings for some minutes.

SENATOR FORAKER. Mr. Chairman, I do not believe in conducting an investigation with a stenographer to make a record and then keeping anything that is said out of the record. I think everything ought to go into the record. Something arises and some one suggests, "Now, do not take this down," and it is not five minutes until what you had the stenographer omit becomes absolutely essential to a proper understanding of what follows. Every word of this debate ought to have been in the record, and I supposed it was in the record.

MR. TAYLER. I supposed it all was being taken down except my quotation.

SENATOR FORAKER. No; that ought to have been put in the record, too. ...

SENATOR BEVERIDGE. You do not understand, then, that Mr. Smoot himself is a polygamist?

MR. CRITCHLOW. I have no understanding upon the question as a matter of fact at all.

SENATOR BEVERIDGE. Well, you understand he is not; do you not?

MR. CRITCHLOW. I would like to be precise upon that subject. My understanding is largely a matter of deduction. I have known Mr. Smoot fairly well for a number of years, and I never heard him charged with being a polygamist.

SENATOR BEVERIDGE. You have spoken quite freely here of general repute and general opinion and a whole lot of other things with which you seemed to be extremely familiar.

MR. CRITCHLOW. Yes, sir.

SENATOR BEVERIDGE. Is it of general repute that Mr. Smoot is a polygamist or not?

MR. CRITCHLOW. It is not of general repute that he is a polygamist.

THE CHAIRMAN. In that connection I wish to ask you, if it is not objectionable, you were one of the gentlemen who signed this remonstrance?

MR. CRITCHLOW. Yes, sir.

THE CHAIRMAN. Will you state to the committee who the other gentlemen are, if you know them?

MR. CRITCHLOW. I know them all.

THE CHAIRMAN. Just state in a general way who they are. The names are already before the committee, but I want to know where they live and who they are.

MR. CRITCHLOW. Dr. W. M. Paden is the pastor of the First Presbyterian Church of Salt Lake City, and has been for some three or four years. He formerly was pastor of the French Mission Church in the Latin quarter in Paris and of the Holland Memorial Church in Philadelphia. He is a graduate of Princeton University.

P. L. Williams is the general counsel of the Oregon Short Line Railroad Company in Utah and the Western States.

Mr. E. W. Wilson is the cashier of the Commercial National Bank and has been a resident of Salt Lake for twelve or fourteen years.

Mr. C. C. Goodwin was for some twenty years the editor of the "Salt Lake Tribune" and was formerly from California and Nevada.

Mr. W. A. Nelden is the president of the Nelden-Judson Drug Company, a wholesale drug company doing business in Utah and the Western States.

These gentlemen all reside at Salt Lake City, or did at that time.

Dr. Clarence T. Brown was at that time pastor of the Congregational Church at Salt Lake City; now at San Diego, Cal[ifornia].

Ezra Thompson is a native of Utah, a mining man, and has just concluded his second term as mayor of Salt Lake City. He was born in Utah, as I remember it.

J.J. Corum is a real estate man. He has been a resident of Utah for some sixteen years, and is a man whose business, I think, is largely concerned with real estate.

George R. Hancock is a mining superintendent and has resided in Utah since 1880.

W. Mont. Ferry is a nephew of the late Senator Thomas W. Ferry, of Michigan, and is a mining man.

J. L. Leilich was at that time, as I understand, the superintendent of the missions in Utah of the Methodist Episcopal Church. I understand he is now in California, but I know him very slightly.

MR. WORTHINGTON. He is the same man who put in a separate remonstrance charging polygamy?

MR. CRITCHLOW. He is; yes, sir.

Harry C. Hill was upon the staff of General Butler in the late war. He was a mining man and is now retired, a capitalist.

C. E. Allen is general manager or superintendent, I do not know which, of the United States Mining Company, a large mining corporation. Mr. Allen originally went to Utah as a professor.

MR. TAYLER. He was a member of Congress—the first Representative?

MR. CRITCHLOW. He was the first Representative to Congress under statehood.

Mr. George M. Scott is not now a resident of Salt Lake. He resides in San Francisco. He was for a great many years the head of George M. Scott & Co., a large wholesale and retail hardware establishment. I think he has retired from business.

S. H. Lewis was at one time an assistant United States attorney, and is now the standing master in chancery of the United States circuit court for our district.

THE CHAIRMAN. What was the last?

MR. CRITCHLOW. Mr. Samuel H. Lewis. He is the standing master in chancery of the United States circuit court for our district.

Mr. H. G. McMillan is a capitalist and mining man.

Abiel Leonard was, up to the time of his death, in November last, the bishop of the Protestant Episcopal Church, diocese of Utah.

SENATOR BEVERIDGE. Who got this protest up, Mr. Critchlow?

MR. CRITCHLOW. The material of it was supplied in large part by Doctor Paden, and it was written, so far as the form of it and the connecting matter, etc., was concerned, by myself.

SENATOR BEVERIDGE. Who got the signatures to it?

MR. CRITCHLOW. I did.

SENATOR BEVERIDGE. You got up the protest, then, practically?

MR. CRITCHLOW. Yes, sir: to the extent I have suggested.

SENATOR BEVERIDGE. You are a lawyer, are you not?

MR. CRITCHLOW. I am. ...

MR. VAN COTT. Mr. Critchlow, how many times did you meet with the ministerial association in preparing this protest?

MR. CRITCHLOW. Not once.

MR. VAN COTT. How many times did Doctor Paden?

MR. CRITCHLOW. With me?

MR. VAN COTT. Yes.

MR. CRITCHLOW. Many times.

MR. VAN COTT. Who was the first person who suggested this protest?

MR. CRITCHLOW. To me?

MR. VAN COTT. Yes.

MR. CRITCHLOW. Doctor Paden.

MR. VAN COTT. Then you worked with him a while on it?

MR. CRITCHLOW. I worked with him all the time on it.

MR. VAN COTT. All the while? When did you next or first take anyone into your confidence, if I may use that expression, in regard to the protest?

MR. CRITCHLOW. You mean myself personally?

MR. VAN COTT. Well, so far as you know?

MR. CRITCHLOW. I think the fact that Doctor Paden and I were preparing this protest was known to the committee that had been appointed by the ministerial association to draft it all the time.

MR. VAN COTT. Who were the committee that were appointed?

MR. CRITCHLOW. As I said, as I understood it, Doctor Paden, Doctor Brown, and Mr. J. L. Leilich.

MR. VAN COTT. That was the committee appointed by the ministerial association?

MR. CRITCHLOW. As I understood it.

MR. VAN COTT. So that, as you understood, before that the ministerial association had met and considered the matter and had appointed this committee?

MR. CRITCHLOW. That is what I understood.

MR. VAN COTT. About how long were you engaged in its preparation, Mr. Critchlow?

MR. CRITCHLOW. I should think about four or five days; that is, in such time as I could spare from my office to devote to it. ...

SENATOR OVERMAN. Was there any protest among the people generally, in addition to the formal protest gotten up by you?

MR. CRITCHLOW. You mean a protest expressed in words only?

SENATOR OVERMAN. I mean a protest among the public.

MR. CRITCHLOW. Very generally among the non-Mormon people; I might say almost universally, except among those who had particular reason—

SENATOR OVERMAN. I understand you reduced this to form?

MR. CRITCHLOW. I reduced this to what I supposed to be a proper form of protest.

SENATOR OVERMAN. And you say that expresses the general sentiment of the people?

MR. CRITCHLOW. Yes; I do.

MR. VAN COTT. As to this general sentiment that you have mentioned, did any of them come forward and volunteer to sign your protest?

MR. CRITCHLOW. No, sir. They knew nothing about it until they were asked to sign it.

MR. VAN COTT. And they never formed any affirmative movement to have a protest filed?

MR. CRITCHLOW. No, sir.

MR. VAN COTT. With the exception of the ministerial association?

MR. CRITCHLOW. That is all.

MR. VAN COTT. When you prepared this protest did these 19 protestants meet together?

MR. CRITCHLOW. No, sir.

MR. VAN COTT. You obtained signatures separately?

MR. CRITCHLOW. In large measure, separately. On one occasion four or five came together to my office and two or three of them took the protest home to read it. I remember Mr. P. L. Williams particularly took the protest and read it carefully and scanned it over. He had it overnight, as I remember it.

SENATOR BEVERIDGE. By the way, on that point will you let me interrupt you? Did anybody sign the protest without reading it, as they so often sign petitions?

MR. CRITCHLOW. I can not say about that, unless there is one instance. I think there is one man who did not read it in my presence, and I do not think had an opportunity of reading it at all. The substance of it was stated to him, and he signed it without its being read over. All the rest of them read it over carefully, so far as I know. ...

MR. VAN COTT. Which one of these was prepared first, Mr. Critchlow, the protest that you signed or the one that Leilich signed individually?

MR. CRITCHLOW. I know absolutely nothing about the Leilich protest. The first I heard of it was when it was filed at Washington [D.C.], whereupon, as perhaps the record shows, the protestants in Salt Lake disavowed the allegations of that protest.

MR. VAN COTT. And is it not a matter of current rumor—general report—believed by you, that Leilich did not file his protest until after yours was filed?

MR. CRITCHLOW. Yes, sir; that is my understanding of it, that he used the first protest as a basis for his, as I understand it.

MR. VAN COTT. And I call your attention to this, that the first protest, that is; the protest that is signed by the nineteen, is dated January 26, 1903, and the protest signed by Mr. Leilich alone is dated the 25th of February, 1903—about a month later. That would be about your judgment, would it, from what you know?

MR. CRITCHLOW. That is about my recollection of the relative dates when I heard of them and knew of them.

MR. VAN COTT. So that when Mr. Leilich signed this first protest and said in substance that the protestants accuse Mr. Smoot of no offense cognizable by law, Mr. Leilich had read over the protest?

MR. CRITCHLOW. Yes; he had, I know.

MR. VAN COTT. Then a month later, after signing a statement to that effect, under oath he states that Senator Smoot is a polygamist, and that he is advised by counsel that it is inexpedient at this time to give further particulars concerning such plural marriage and its results, or the place it was solemnized, or the maiden name of the plural wife. That is correct, is it?

MR. CRITCHLOW. Well, it is correct, as you state, that that was put into his protest; but perhaps I ought to say, Mr. Van Cott, that Mr. Leilich urged upon Mr. Paden and myself to put in many things which we refused to put in because we did not know of the absolute truth of them, and this subsequent protest of Mr. Leilich was, as I am informed, prepared and filed while Mr. Leilich was in Washington. I speak only from information on that point, however.[3]

_____

3. A couple years following this testimony, Smoot learned of the origin of Leilich's allegation. In a letter to Joseph F. Smith, he explained

MR. VAN COTT. Did Mr. Leilich give you that particular information that I have read?

MR. CRITCHLOW. That he was a polygamist?

MR. VAN COTT. Yes, sir. ...

MR. VAN COTT. ... In that pamphlet, "Nuggets of Truth," which you say you saw often during the campaign[4]—

MR. CRITCHLOW. Too often.

MR. VAN COTT. You saw it very often, anyway?

MR. CRITCHLOW. I did.

MR. VAN COTT. It was a little document that was issued for the purpose of converting the Mormon voters to Republicanism, was it not?

MR. CRITCHLOW. I assume that was the object. That was apparently the object of it.

MR. VAN COTT. Right on the front page of that little pamphlet there was a picture of Joseph Smith, the founder of the Mormon Church?

MR. CRITCHLOW. Well, it might as well have had it. If you suggest it as being there, I have no doubt of its being there.

MR. VAN COTT. I think it was there. It also had the name and picture of Brigham Young.

MR. CRITCHLOW. I have no doubt that it was there, if you suggest that it was.

Perhaps it would interest you to know how it came that John L Leilich made the charge of my being a polygamist, and as I get the information through parties [who were] interested in getting him to make the charge I give you the information as it comes to me and I have no doubt of its accuracy. Noble Warrum told Rev. Mr. Clemensen of Logan that I had a plural wife in Mexico, that he was positive of it for he was well acquainted with her. ... If Warrum denies this I think I can get affidavits to prove it. I understand this man Warrum is now employed by a company of which you are President (Dec. 12, 1905).

Warrum was an employee of the Utah Mexican Rubber Company. A prominent Democrat and Freemason, he had served as Salt Lake City recorder, a state senator, and probate judge. He would later become an editor at the *Salt Lake Tribune* and author of a respected four-volume history, *Utah Since Statehood*. In 1934 Church President Heber J. Grant would thank him publicly in general conference for his "wonderful" and "splendid" editorials at the deaths of Joseph F. Smith and Anthony W. Ivins (Jean Bickmore White, ed., *Church, State, and Politics: The Diaries of John Henry Smith* [Salt Lake City: Signature Books and Smith Research Associates, 1990], 600, 658; Mark Angus, *Salt Lake City Underfoot: Self-Guided Tours of Historic Neighborhoods* [Salt Lake City: Signature Books, 1993], 108; *Conference Report*, Oct. 1934).

4. The fourteen-page broadside, *Nuggets of Truth*, published by the Republican Territorial Committee in 1892, informed LDS members of their religious duty to vote Republican. When Republican candidate Frank J. Cannon learned the approach was backfiring, he had the pamphlet withdrawn (Edward Leo Lyman, *Political Deliverance: The Mormon Quest for Utah Statehood* [Urbana: University of Illinois Press, 1986], 201; *Smoot Hearings*, 1:828).

MR. VAN COTT. And Daniel H. Wells?

MR. CRITCHLOW. The same answer as to that.

MR. VAN COTT. And on the back, Frank J. Cannon?

MR. CRITCHLOW. The same answer as to that.

MR. VAN COTT. There was an argument made all the way through that these men were very ardent protectionists?[5]

MR. CRITCHLOW. Yes, sir.

MR. VAN COTT. And that the Mormon people should support Frank Cannon on the ground that all their leaders had been protectionists?

MR. CRITCHLOW. Yes, sir.

MR. VAN COTT. Now, you went on the stump advocating the election of Mr. Cannon?

MR. CRITCHLOW. Yes, sir.

MR. VAN COTT. And you knew that pamphlet was in circulation?

MR. CRITCHLOW. Yes, sir.

MR. VAN COTT. And I understood you also to say that you saw it too often?

MR. CRITCHLOW. Yes, sir.

MR. VAN COTT. Do I assume by that, that that particular kind of political proselyting did not have your approval?

MR. CRITCHLOW. It did not.

MR. VAN COTT. You knew it was used?

MR. CRITCHLOW. I knew it was used. It received our very severe disapprobation and the disapprobation of nearly every leader of the Republican party.

MR. VAN COTT. Did it not also have the emphatic disapproval and condemnation of Joseph F. Smith, who is now the president of the church?

MR. CRITCHLOW. It may have had.

MR. VAN COTT. And he is a strong Republican?

MR. CRITCHLOW. He is said to be. I think he is.

MR. VAN COTT. You know he is a strong Republican?

MR. CRITCHLOW. Yes, sir; I think he is. I have never talked with him on the subject or heard him make a speech. ...

MR. VAN COTT. You went out on the stump also, as late as 1894, with John Henry Smith?

MR. CRITCHLOW. Yes, sir.

MR. VAN COTT. He was a Mormon apostle?

---

5. The Republican Party during this time favored tariffs on imported goods. Smoot was an ardent protectionist, later co-authoring the famous 1930 Smoot-Hawley Tariff Act which contributed to the Great Depression.

MR. CRITCHLOW. Yes, sir.

MR. VAN COTT. Living in polygamy?

MR. CRITCHLOW. I think so.

MR. VAN COTT. I mean living in unlawful cohabitation.

MR. CRITCHLOW. Yes, sir.

MR. VAN COTT. You traveled with him disseminating Republican principles?

MR. CRITCHLOW. As best I knew how.

MR. VAN COTT. That was done for some time?

MR. CRITCHLOW. Yes, sir.

SENATOR BEVERIDGE. Let me ask you a question right here. Did you protest to him against his practices?

MR. CRITCHLOW. Against the practices of Mr. Smith?

SENATOR BEVERIDGE. Yes.

MR. CRITCHLOW. No, sir; except—

SENATOR BEVERIDGE. Did you admonish him?

MR. CRITCHLOW. No, sir; not at all.

SENATOR BEVERIDGE. When you were assistant United States district attorney did you admonish any of these gentlemen or warn them to
cease their practices?

MR. CRITCHLOW. Not at all.[6]

MR. TAYLER. Did you prosecute any of them?

SENATOR BEVERIDGE. He has answered that he did not.

MR. CRITCHLOW. I can not recollect. I think I did. I think I prosecuted a
number of them. I am very sure I did.[7] ...

Ogden Hiles,[8] having been first duly sworn, was examined and testified as follows ...

---

6. Carl Badger exulted in these admissions by Critchlow:

You will notice from the papers that Critchlow was compelled to admit that he
wanted the Senate to condemn ... Smoot for not doing exactly what he said he would
not do himself, that is failing to ... advise, admonish, and counsel ... the men who
have been living in violation of the law ... I, for one, felt like forgiving Critchlow for
all the meanness when he gave away his case with such readiness, he owned up like a
gentleman even though it knocked a hole in the bottom of his tongue, he had a
rather sickly smile on his face before he got through though (Badger to E. H.
Callister, Mar. 12, 1904, in Smoot Papers).

7. The *Salt Lake Tribune* called Critchlow's testimony "candid and fair," saying he
described events and circumstances "precisely as they existed" ("Mr. Critchlow's Testimony," Mar. 12, 1904).

8. Hiles (ca. 1847-1929) was a non-Mormon attorney from San Francisco who had
arrived in Utah as Assistant U.S. Attorney. He was elected to the Third Judicial District
Court in 1895 and served for five years.

MR. TAYLER. Now, Judge Hiles, we do not desire to go over the ground that Mr. Critchlow went over except in so far as you have special information respecting the field that he covered, nor do I want to arrest you by asking questions where it seems unnecessary. What special information have you respecting the condition of affairs there between 1883 or 1884, or the time you went there, and the manifesto?

MR. HILES. Well, as I have said, from 1886 to 1889 I was in the United States attorney's office as assistant.

MR. TAYLER. Yes.

MR. HILES. And during what were called the polygamy prosecutions I drew more indictments and prosecuted more cases under the Edmunds law and the Edmunds-Tucker law than any other officer. My duties called me from Ogden to Salt Lake, to Provo and to Beaver, in all parts of the [Utah] Territory; and, as I say, I drew more indictments and prosecuted more cases under those laws than any other officer. I examined hundreds and I may say thousands of witnesses during that time.

MR. TAYLER. Now proceed.

MR. WORTHINGTON. What time does that refer to, Judge?

MR. VAN COTT. 1886 to 1889.

MR. HILES. Yes. My first direct acquaintance with public affairs in Utah was, as I say, commenced in 1886, when I was appointed. At that time, under orders from the Attorney-General's office here in Washington, we were directed to proceed and prosecute offenders against these laws with as much vigor as we could, and we did proceed, commencing in the forepart of 1886. There had been some prosecutions in 1885. We had not proceeded far before it was made very clear as a general fact—it was already pretty well known in the community—that the people of Utah were living under a theocracy, under a government of priests. This state or condition was disclosed by the examination of witnesses before the grand juries by the examination of jurors touching their qualification to sit as jurors in polygamy cases, as they were called—

MR. TAYLER. Now tell us definitely what you mean by that—what answers were given?

MR. HILES. Invariably, if we would ask a Mormon whether he would obey the laws of the United States or the laws of the church, he would say that he would obey the law of the church. As stated by Mr. Critchlow yesterday, in every case—or in most every case the judge would offer the defendant who was convicted the clemency or suspension of judgment if he would agree to obey the law, and he would be asked whether he would in future obey the law. He would say no. "Why not?" "Well," he would say, "I choose to obey the law or God rather than man-made laws." If we suggested that the laws of the Republic were mild and that any lady or gentleman of standing might live under them without coming in hostility to them, he would say it made no difference. If we asked him what the law of God was, he said it was that which was revealed to them in their doctrine and covenants and in the Bible, and as expounded to them by the authorities—that is to say the authorities of the church[9] ...

---

9. Following ten days of testimony, the proceedings adjourned until April 21. In a letter to Joseph F. Smith describing the atmosphere in the capital, Smoot lamented that he was having:

> ... a pretty hard time to keep some of my former friends from deserting me, and also the Washington papers from making open warfare upon me. I have particularly noticed [Republican] Senator Platt, of Connecticut, is rather cool, and quite a number of my former Democratic friends. ... I have thought at times that my letters would give you the impression that I was exceedingly blue and downcast, but that is not the case. It is true that at times the clouds look very dark and seem to hang very low, but as the days pass by the sunshine again appears, and I find that the friends that I have made in the past are generally standing by me. From the expression I have heard the Senators make, I am positive that unless more evidence is presented and different from the evidence already given, I will not be unseated" (Apr. 9, 1904).

IV.
APRIL AND MAY
1904

10.

B. H. Roberts

Wednesday, April 20

"The following resolution [proposed in Washington, D. C.] ... was adopted by a standing vote [of the Daughters of the American Revolution], only one delegate ... dissenting: 'Whereas, The Mormon church teachers and many of its leaders defiantly practice polygamy, which is a crime against the Government and the United States and tends to the degradation of women, the destruction of the home, which is the bulwark of the Nation's safety, and the jeopardy of our sacred institutions ... We ... most earnestly protest against the continuance of an apostle of the Mormon church in an official position in the United States." —*Salt Lake Tribune,* Apr. 19, 1904

Brigham H. Roberts,[1] being first duly sworn, was examined, and testified as follows ...

MR. TAYLER.[2] ... When did you first enter politics in Utah?

MR. ROBERTS. I think it was about 1889. Pardon me. (A pause.) Well, I think likely that is about right, as nearly as I can fix it from recollection.

MR. TAYLER. Were you then elected to some office?

MR. ROBERTS. No, sir.

MR. TAYLER. What do you mean? I am not so particular about this, I think. But what do you mean by entering politics?

MR. ROBERTS. I began making political speeches and exercising an interest in political matters.

MR. TAYLER. When were you naturalized? Had that date anything to do with the date of your interest in politics?

---

1. At the time of his testimony, Roberts (1857-1933) lived in Centerville, Utah, and was one of the Seven Presidents of Seventies in the LDS hierarchy, with responsibility for the Young Men's auxiliary, as well as one of four Assistant LDS Church Historians. He was the author of *The Gospel; The Life of John Taylor; A New Witness for God; Outlines of Ecclesiastical History; The Rise and Fall of Nauvoo;* and *Succession in Presidency.* As his testimony will show, he had three wives, for which he was denied a seat in Congress after winning the Utah election in 1898.

2. Tayler chaired the Congressional committee that vacated Roberts's election to Congress in 1898.

MR. ROBERTS. I think not.

MR. TAYLER. When did you first become a candidate for office? That is what I had in mind when I asked the question.

MR. ROBERTS. 1894.

MR. TAYLER. What were you a candidate for then?

MR. ROBERTS. I was a candidate for member of the constitutional convention of our State.

MR. TAYLER. Were you elected?

MR. ROBERTS. I was elected. ...

MR. TAYLER. Were you a member of the constitutional convention which drafted the present constitution of Utah?

MR. ROBERTS. Yes.

MR. TAYLER. That was the constitution which was submitted to the people at the election of 1895?

MR. ROBERTS. Yes.

MR. TAYLER. Now, in 1895, you were a candidate for Congress?

MR. ROBERTS. I was.

MR. TAYLER. And were defeated at the polls by Mr. Allen, I believe.[3]

MR. ROBERTS. Yes, sir.

MR. TAYLER. Did you, with respect to that candidacy for Congress at that time, have differences with the church authorities?

MR. ROBERTS. Some differences.

MR. TAYLER. I wish you would describe what those differences were as well as you can.

MR. ROBERTS. If you will allow me to give the full history of that matter, if that is what you wish, I will do so.

MR. TAYLER. Yes.

MR. ROBERTS. Previous to my becoming a candidate for member of the constitutional convention, there had some unpleasantness arisen about men in high church standing having anything to do in politics, and the presidency of the church at that time decided that members of the quorum of apostles, members of my own council, the presidents of the seventy, and the presidents of the stakes, and the bishops of the wards, would better stay out of politics, and to that I consented or agreed. But during my brief absence from the State in the fall of 1894 I was nominated by our county convention to be a member of the constitutional convention, and on my return, being informed of the nomination, in conversation with some friends I stated that it

---

3. Clarence Elmir Allen (R-Utah) defeated Roberts in the 1895 election. He served one term in Congress and did not run for re-election.

was a nomination I could not accept owing to the previous arrangement that men of my standing in the church should not take part in
politics.

But I was informed that during my absence that order had been
somewhat changed, at least, and that it was thought there would be
too many men of standing in the community eliminated from so important a gathering as a constitutional convention, and that it had
been decided better that liberty be granted men of the character I
have described to enter into politics, and at least to accept these nominations. I inquired of the authorities of the church if that was correct,
and was informed that it was. ...

THE CHAIRMAN. You say you inquired of the authorities of the church. Of
whom did you inquire?

MR. ROBERTS. I inquired of one of the first presidents of the church.

THE CHAIRMAN. Of anybody else?

MR. ROBERTS. No, sir.

SENATOR DUBOIS. When you speak of the authorities of the church, do
you mean one of the first presidents?

MR. ROBERTS. Not necessarily.

MR. TAYLER. You mean somebody superior in authority to yourself, I assume?

MR. ROBERTS. Yes, sir.

MR. TAYLER. Such persons were to be found only in the body of the apostles or the first presidency?

MR. ROBERTS. Yes.

THE CHAIRMAN. Then you made this inquiry of the first presidency?

MR. ROBERTS. Yes; one of the presidents of the church. I asked him if the
rule with which I was acquainted had been altered, and he informed
me that it had been. This was in 1894.

THE CHAIRMAN. Who constituted the first presidency at that time?

MR. ROBERTS. Wilford Woodruff, George Q. Cannon, and Joseph F.
Smith.

THE CHAIRMAN. Of which one did you inquire?

MR. ROBERTS. Mr. Smith. In 1894 ... I stumped the State and was elected
to the convention. After the close of the constitutional convention I
was nominated by my party a candidate for Congress and took an active part in the campaign of that year. In the midst of the campaign, at
a meeting of the priesthood of the church in Salt Lake City, Mr. Smith
made some reference to Moses Thatcher and myself—

MR. TAYLER. You mean Joseph F. Smith?

Mr. Roberts. Yes; I mean Joseph F. Smith,[4] as having accepted these important nominations, which would take us away from our ecclesiastical duties, without consultation with any of the apostles or the first presidency; and his remarks were in the nature of a complaint of that conduct. Whereupon a number of men who had heard these remarks took it upon themselves to circulate the idea that Mr. Thatcher and myself were out of harmony with the church authorities, and that it would be agreeable to them to have us defeated. And very naturally we protested. I protested, and I think Mr. Thatcher also protested, against the action of these lesser authorities of the church making use of the casual remarks of Mr. Smith. The country was considerably agitated. Newspapers took it up; and that agitation resulted in the recon-

---

4. On the day of this testimony, Joseph F. Smith spoke words of encouragement in a letter to Smoot from Salt Lake City:

The matter as it now stands, appears to the judgment of thinking people, as an outrageous farce. Senator Burrows has fallen from the high and dignified position of Chairman of the Committee ... before whom, ostensibly, your right (the right of a brother Senator) to your seat in the Senate is to be determined by patient hearing of the evidence against such right. ... Is there no one to extend a friendly hand to ... the irate Senator, to save him from the ignominy he is rapidly bringing upon himself? Why should he prosecute a brother Senator? Why should he insist upon your furnishing witnesses for the Ministerial Association? ... Why should he be so set and determined to hunt up testimony against you? What is the matter with deluded old Senator any how? Has he caught the Anti Mormon rabies? He seemes to have caught it bad. What good will it do him? For 75 years every man who has fallen a prey to the disease has died with it.

I could give him a long list of fierce Anti Mormon monomaniacs who have spent their rage in furious attacks upon Mormonism, and now where are they? They may be sought for in vain on earth and in Heaven! To Stephen A. Douglas may be pointed as a lurid example of this fact. He was told by Joseph Smith what his fate would be if he raised his voice against the Mormon people. He did not heed it. He defied the prediction and he uttered that memorable, vindictive and senseless assertion, "That Mormonism was a loathsome ulcer on the body politic, and he would apply the knife to cut it out." That sentiment led him to his defeat and to his doom! But he is only one among hundreds and thousands of lesser lights who have gone the same road. And as God, Almighty Lives, the rest will follow sooner or later; if they do not repent. ...

We have received the News report of the proceeding this morning in the Committee room, with B. H. Roberts in the chair. We can not tell very much of the real thing by the Newspaper reports. I hope no harm will come to you by any testimony that may be given of the witnesses who are there, and who may come. I am surprised at the flimsy pretexts so far brought before the Committee as 'evidence in the Smoot Case'! My Dear boy they may have ignored you altogether of late and are trying to find some pretext to expel the Church from America! The poor deluded Ministers with their henchmen, Owen, Tayler, Critchlow, Hiles and Burrows et. al. do not comprehend the magnitude of the task they have undertaken. I expect to see Senator Burrows relegated to private life ere very long. The very thing he is doing will hasten it. ditto ... Dubois ... and any other man who falls into the egregious error into which they have fallen. "Fret not thy gizzard" (Apr. 20, 1904).

vening of the Democratic convention for the purpose of defining the attitude that the Democrats would take in that Issue.[5]

MR. TAYLER. What issue?

MR. ROBERTS. That is, of the alleged exercise of religious influence in a political contest.

THE CHAIRMAN. You have stated that your defeat would be "agreeable to them." Whom do you mean by them?

MR. ROBERTS. I mean that the parties who carried this report from the priesthood meeting represented that it would be agreeable to the first presidency and the apostles for us to be defeated. It was out of these circumstances that the friction counsel refers to arose between the authorities and myself. ...

MR. TAYLER. Tell us what took place at that convention.[6] ...

MR. ROBERTS. There was a long preamble reciting alleged interferences on the part of high church officials, followed by a declaration of principles, I think some eight or ten, or nine, in number. I do not now recall how many.

MR. TAYLER. That declaration of principles was confined, was it not, to the proposition that the church should keep its hands off from politics?

MR. WORTHINGTON. I think, certainly, if we are going into the matter of the preamble and the declaration of principles, we ought to have them instead of the witness recollection of their contents.

MR. TAYLER. Counsel misconceives the purpose of my question.

MR. WORTHINGTON. I do not know what the purpose is, Mr. Chairman, and I do not think it makes any difference. The purpose is to get before the Senate and the committee these documents, or their contents, and I see no reason why the statement of anybody as to what is in any of them should be admitted when the documents themselves are easily procurable and should be in the record if they are to be referred to at all.

THE CHAIRMAN. Read the question.

MR. TAYLER. I am dealing with the witness wholly and not with a matter of substantive proof.

THE CHAIRMAN. I suppose it is for identification.

---

5. Carl Badger noted in his journal on April 18, 1904, that the Senator [Smoot] seemed to think Roberts himself "might like to see him unseated" (in Rodney J. Badger, *Liahona and Iron Rod: The Biography of Carl A. and Rose J. Badger* [Bountiful, Utah: Family History Publishers, 1985], 219).

6. The proceedings of the state Democratic convention, held October 22, 1895, were entered into the official record (*Smoot Hearings*, 1:820-53).

MR. TAYLER. And as to the witness attitude respecting it.

THE CHAIRMAN. Let the reporter read the question.

The reporter read as follows: "Mr. Tayler. That declaration of principles was confined, was it not, to the proposition that the church should keep its hands off from politics?"

THE CHAIRMAN. Mr. Roberts, you may answer that. What is your answer?

MR. ROBERTS. Yes.

MR. TAYLER. You were in that convention?

MR. ROBERTS. Yes, sir.

MR. TAYLER. Did you speak in it?

MR. ROBERTS. I think I did.

MR. TAYLER. In that convention and through that campaign you, in very bitter terms, inveighed against this intrusion of the church into politics?

MR. ROBERTS. No, sir. I should like to disclaim any bitterness in the matter.

MR. TAYLER. I do not want to characterize improperly the language you used vigorously and most earnestly then?

MR. ROBERTS. Yes

MR. TAYLER. So vigorously and so earnestly that the higher authorities of the church assumed a similar attitude toward you—of vigorous and earnest opposition to your position?

MR. ROBERTS. I think that is right.

MR. TAYLER. And after the election, at which the Republican candidate was elected, the authorities of the church took up your recalcitrancy?

MR. ROBERTS. Yes, sir.

SENATOR OVERMAN. Was your opponent, Mr. Allen, who defeated you, a Mormon?

MR. ROBERTS. No, sir; he was a gentile.

MR. TAYLER. State what occurred between you and the authorities of the church with respect to your attitude in the campaign of 1895.

MR. ROBERTS. The authorities took the position—

THE CHAIRMAN. What do you mean by "the authorities?"

MR. ROBERTS. I mean the first presidency and the twelve. They took the position that my attitude during the campaign had misrepresented, before the people, their intentions and their wishes, and they desired to go over the matter with me, to consider it and, if possible, to bring about a reconciliation as between them and myself.[7]

---

7. Twelve days after this testimony, the *Salt Lake Herald* reported an interview with Dr. J. Wesley Hill, who had spent five years as pastor of the First Methodist Church of Ogden, Utah, and had since moved to Harrisburg, Pennsylvania. In this interview, Hill said:

SENATOR BEVERIDGE. In what respect did they say that your position had misrepresented their attitude?

MR. ROBERTS. They disclaimed many of the things that were recited in the preamble on which the democratic declaration of principles was made, disclaiming any intention or desire to interfere with the political rights or liberties of the people.[8] ...

MR. TAYLER. Wilford Woodruff at the time of your marriage[9] held what position?

MR. ROBERTS. He was president of the church. Pardon me. I think he was.

I visit the capital frequently. I was there three weeks ago and had considerable discussion with a number of the lawmakers in regard to the case of Senator Smoot. My best judgment is that he does not stand a ghost of a show of retaining his seat. Until the recent investigation there was a placidity in regard to the Mormon question in the minds of eastern people. They believed after the settlement of the Roberts case that Mormonism was being recast in the mould of modern evangelical Christianity and that polygamy was dying out. ... The churches all over the land took the matter up and the newspapers have condemned Mormonism as un-Christian and un-American. I have seen some of the most severe cartoons where it was represented as a devil-fish, as a destroyer of womanhood and as an influence of the most baneful character ... I do not believe that any lawmaking body or any political party will endeavor to stand up against this tremendous sentiment ("Smoot's Chances Very Poor," May 2, 1904).

8. The preamble contained the following principles or "Declaration of Truths":

I. That man may worship his Maker as his conscience dictates.

II. That no State nor political body has the right to interfere with this great privilege.

III. That man's first allegiance, politically, is to his country.

IV. That no church, ecclesiastical body, nor spiritual advisor should encroach upon the political rights of the individual.

V. That in a free country no man nor body of men can, with safety to the State, use the name or the power of any religious sect or society to influence or control the elective franchise.

VI. That a trust is imposed upon each citizen in a free country to act politically upon his own judgment and absolutely free from control or dictation, ecclesiastical or otherwise.

VII. That no political party can be required to obtain the consent of any church or the leader ther[e]of before selecting its candidate for public office.

VIII. That no citizen, by reason of his association with any church, can be absolved from his duty to the State, either in times of war or of peace without the consent of the State.

IX. That all men should be, and of right are, free to think, free to act, free to speak, and free to vote, without fear, molestation, intimidation, or undue influence (*Smoot Hearings*, 1:820).

9. The marriage referred to here was to Margaret Curtis Shipp. As one historian noted:

The 1890 date seems doubtful because of indications Dr. Shipp was yet living with her first husband until at least 1892. Not only is this inferred by the Salt Lake City Directory for those years, but Senator Smoot told Carl A. Badger he was reliably informed this was true. On the basis of the chronology of Mrs. Shipp's residences and

He may have been, however, president of the apostles. I can not recall that just now.

MR. TAYLER. If he was not president of the church, who was?

MR. ROBERTS. No one, if he was not.

MR. TAYLER. That is to say, if he was not, there was an interregnum?

MR. ROBERTS. Yes, sir.

MR. TAYLER. What relation did Daniel H. Wells sustain to Wilford Woodruff in April, 1890?

MR. ROBERTS. I could hardly define that. Daniel H. Wells was continued after the organization of the presidency as councilor to the apostles, and I do not know what relation would be thought to exist between a councilor to the apostles and the president of the church, though I should say it was nearly in the relationship of one of the members of the apostles to the presidency of the church.

MR. TAYLER. Did Daniel H. Wells in the first instance oppose marrying you to Mrs. Shipp?

MR. ROBERTS. No.

MR. TAYLER. How did you come to arrange with him? Did you go to him with Mrs. Shipp and say, "We want you to marry us," and he proceeded thereupon to marry you?

MR. ROBERTS. If you will allow me, the relationship between Mr. Daniel H. Wells and myself was very friendly. I had been an associate of his in the British mission a few years before, and closely associated with him, and had relations that were very friendly, and when I desired this marriage I went to him, as understanding that he had authority to perform the ceremony.

MR. TAYLER. When did he die?

MR. ROBERTS. I can not now recall the date, but I think it was about a year after that time, in 1891.

SENATOR OVERMAN. Was it necessary to get the consent of any of the authorities of the church to marry a plural wife?

MR. ROBERTS. It was necessary to get those who were understood to hold the authority to perform the ceremony.

SENATOR OVERMAN. Did your first wife or your second wife consent to your marrying the third wife?

MR. ROBERTS. No, sir.

SENATOR OVERMAN. Did they protest against it?

---

the beginning date for her use of the name Mrs. Roberts, Charles Mostyn Owen concluded the marriage occurred in the spring of 1894 (B. Carmon Hardy, *Solemn Covenant: The Mormon Polygamous Passage* [Urbana: University of Illinois Press, 1992], 247).

MR. ROBERTS. I do not hear the question.

SENATOR OVERMAN. Was there any protest on their part?

MR. ROBERTS. No, sir.

THE CHAIRMAN. Did they know of it at the time?

MR. ROBERTS. Not at the time.

MR. TAYLER. When did they learn of it?

MR. ROBERTS. I can not answer that question.

MR. TAYLER. I mean about when—how long afterwards?

MR. ROBERTS. Two or three years afterwards, I think.

MR. TAYLER. Did anybody know about it, so far as you know, until several years had elapsed?

MR. ROBERTS. No, sir.

SENATOR BEVERIDGE. How is that? I understand you to say, sir, that your marriage to your third wife was not known to any of your wives for three years.

MR. ROBERTS. No; I can not say when they knew it.

SENATOR BEVERIDGE. Well, for a considerable period?

MR. ROBERTS. Hardly that. There were a number of our friends who knew it.

SENATOR BEVERIDGE. But not your other two wives?

MR. ROBERTS. No, sir.

SENATOR BEVERIDGE. Other friends knew it, but not your two wives?

MR. ROBERTS. Yes, sir.

MR. TAYLER. Where did your third wife—I will speak of her as Mrs. Shipp, because that will identify her more easily, or Mrs. Maggie Roberts—

THE CHAIRMAN. May I ask a question right here?

MR. TAYLER. Certainly.

THE CHAIRMAN. Why did you conceal this third marriage from your other wives?

MR. ROBERTS. Chiefly for the purpose of relieving them from any embarrassment should the discovery of the marriage be made. Of course we understood that the marriage was illegal.

SENATOR BEVERIDGE. Then, how could they be embarrassed?

MR. ROBERTS. If called upon to testify, they would not wish to testify against me.

SENATOR BEVERIDGE. Oh!

THE CHAIRMAN. You understood at that time that the marriage was illegal?[10]

---

10. The chairman had little tolerance for this kind of disregard for the law and was

MR. ROBERTS. I did.

THE CHAIRMAN. Go on, Mr. Tayler.

MR. TAYLER. Where did Mrs. Maggie Roberts live from the time of your marriage on?

MR. ROBERTS. She lived in Salt Lake.

MR. TAYLER. In whose house?

MR. ROBERTS. She was a practicing physician and had both her own residence and office; that is, I mean to say, a hired residence.

MR. TAYLER. Her first husband was Doctor Shipp?

MR. ROBERTS. Yes, sir.

MR. TAYLER. Was she divorced from him?

MR. ROBERTS. She was.

MR. TAYLER. Where, and how?

MR. ROBERTS. In Salt Lake City.

MR. TAYLER. In the courts?

MR. ROBERTS. No, sir; she was a plural wife to him, and their marriage had no legal standing. The divorce, however, was sanctioned and approved by the church authorities.

MR. TAYLER. Do you know when she was divorced from Doctor Shipp?

MR. ROBERTS. Not precisely.

SENATOR OVERMAN. You say she had no divorce in the courts, but only a divorce by the church?

MR. ROBERTS. Yes, sir.

MR. WORTHINGTON. She could not have had any divorce from the courts, because she was not legally married to him.

SENATOR OVERMAN. Yes; it was an illegal marriage. ...

MR. TAYLER. ... Now, Mr. Roberts, you have characterized this manifesto of 1890 in such a way as to leave the impression upon my mind that you would not call it a specific and direct revelation, such as other rev-

---

feeling pressure from his home state of Michigan to do something about it. Smoot conveyed this to Joseph F. Smith on March 31, 1904:

Yesterday Burrows came to me white with rage, claiming that he had received letters from Michigan advising him that three girls had left Michigan with some Mormon elders for Utah, that their parents were heartbroken over the matter and requested that some action be taken by Congress. I asked him if he could give me the names and where the girls came from and I would try to find out if there was any truth in the matter. He stated that he had written for further information and would let me know as soon as he received it. He also stated that there would be a Constitutional amendment proposed prohibiting polygamy in the United States, and he believed that it would be passed. He is doing everything in his power to create a prejudice in the minds of Senators, but I think that he has carried his little game too far.

elations that the people of your church believe in. Was that inference of mine justified by your statement?

MR. ROBERTS. I think it was.

MR. TAYLER. Then, will you define the character that you attribute to that manifesto as a revelation or inspiration, its origin and its force?

MR. ROBERTS. I regard the manifesto as an administrative act of the president of the church, accepted by the church, and of binding force upon its members. But I regard it as an administrative act which President Woodruff, holding in his own hands the direct authority controlling that particular matter—that is, the matter of marriages—had a perfect right to make, and the acceptance of that action by the church makes that a positive binding law upon the church.

MR. TAYLER. And those who do not obey it are subject to the pains and penalties such as a church under its discipline may inflict upon its members who disobey it?

MR. ROBERTS. Yes, sir. ...

MR. VAN COTT. Now, calling your attention to 1895, have you stated the details of the conflict that was said to exist between you and the church in regard to this political rule?

MR. ROBERTS. I think I did not in detail.

MR. VAN COTT. You think you did not?

MR. ROBERTS. No, sir.

MR. VAN COTT. Calling your attention then to that subject, will you please state in chronological order just the facts about the dispute that arose, and state in detail, so that the committee will understand, the points of the conflict, if any, between you and the church and how they were finally fixed up and settled.

MR. ROBERTS. The commencement of the difficulty arose out of the remarks of Mr. Joseph F. Smith at a priesthood meeting in which he made complaint that Mr. Thatcher and I had accepted nominations for political office, which would take us from our religious duties, without leave of absence or without obtaining the consent to be released from our religious duties by the first presidency or any of the twelve.

In explanation of their insistence that that is what we ought to have done, they made declarations in the press and out of that, as I say, grew the general excitement of the campaign. After the close of the campaign they proposed to reduce to writing, to a written rule, the idea or the doctrine that men upon whose whole time the church had a claim should obtain leave of absence or permission in that sense to engage either in business that would take them away from their religious duties or in receiving political nominations.

I was unwilling at first to subscribe to that rule, for the reason that it had been charged in the prologue or preface to the Democratic declaration of principles that through that means they might seek to control the political affairs of the State. It was charged, I think, in speeches and in the papers, that they might give their consent, for instance, to one man to participate in politics and withhold it from another, or the people might be led to interpret their willingness to excuse one man from religious duties to mean that they favored both his nomination and his election and in this way bring their influence to bear upon the politics of the State.

It was upon that point especially that I made my contest against them. In the course of several meetings with them for the purpose of discussing these matters, however, they satisfied me that it was not their intention to control the politics of the State, but they sought only the management of their own ecclesiastical affairs; and in consequence of being convinced that that was their purpose I joined with them in signing the rule that hereafter men should not accept positions of any kind that would take them from the performance of their ecclesiastical duties without the consent of their superiors.[11] ...

SENATOR BAILEY. Mr. Roberts, suppose your fellow-citizens were to nominate you for a political office, without either consulting you or consulting your church associates, and after your nomination your church associates should refuse you permission to accept the nomination and make the race, would you consider it your duty to disregard the wishes of your party friends in a political matter in order to obey the wishes of your church associates in a political matter, or would you obey the church and refrain from engaging in politics and thus deny the claims of your fellow-citizens upon your services in a political way?

MR. ROBERTS. I think, Senator, that that perhaps would depend upon the circumstances. I can conceive the emergency arising, and perhaps it might be one's duty to respond to the wishes of his fellow citizens. I do not know as to that.

SENATOR BAILEY. Can there be any such thing as a religious obligation to deny your State your services in a political way, whether the occasion be a political emergency or not? Is not a man's duty as a citizen per-

---

11. For more on Roberts's experience in politics, see D. Craig Mikkelson, "The Politics of B. H. Roberts," *Dialogue: A Journal of Mormon Thought* 9 (Summer 1974): 26-40.

fectly consistent with any conception that exists in this country of his religious duty?

MR. ROBERTS. Well, I, perhaps, could not determine that offhand, Senator.

SENATOR BAILEY. Would you think it possible? I am not speaking about the religious phase of it. I am concerned here about the political phase. Do you think it consistent with good citizenship that you must secure permission of a nonpolitical organization before you are permitted to exercise your political rights as a citizen?

MR. ROBERTS. I regard this matter as I would those agreements that are sometimes entered into in business firms and law firms, and that if a man judged the emergency, the political emergency, of sufficient moment to call upon him to discharge the duties of his citizenship to his fellow-citizens, it would be his duty, perhaps, to resign either from the firm or from his official duties in a church organization.

SENATOR BAILEY. You are a lawyer, are you not, Mr. Roberts?

MR. ROBERTS. No; I am not a lawyer.

[SENATOR] BAILEY. I was going to ask you if you would regard a contract or agreement of that kind, made either by a lawyer with his associates in the practice of the law, or by a business man with his partner, as valid and binding. There could be no such thing in this country as a contract that denies a man the right to serve his fellow-citizens when they call on him for his services. I think such a contract would be void as against public policy. I express that opinion merely without examining the law, but I know that if the law in any State does countenance a contract that deprives a man of his political rights or denies him opportunity to meet his political obligations, that law ought to be changed, and I should say that a religious organization transcends its proper province when it undertakes to control the political action of its members.

MR. ROBERTS. You see, in this connection, it seems to me the matter is not so much political as it is religious. I think it would be necessary for a person who is in the obligation that I am in either to follow his agreement and obtain the approval of his associates for leave of absence, or else resign his position. Which I would do in any emergency I can not say. It would depend upon that emergency.

SENATOR BAILEY. Do I understand that under these rules a resignation is contemplated?

MR. ROBERTS. It could be so.

SENATOR BAILEY. Of course, a man might find it necessary to close his law

office in order to come to Congress, as most of us do, and it is for him
to determine, looking to all his relations and obligations, whether he
can afford to discontinue his business to come here in the public service. Such a consideration as that must, of course, address itself to everybody. I take it that a minister of any of the churches in this country
might consider that his duties as a pastor precluded him from engaging in a political contest, but if he were to sign an agreement with any
of his members that he would not offer himself for a nomination, or,
if nominated, offer himself for an election, without their consent,
that would be a line of conduct that I would regard as irreconcilable
with the duties of good citizenship. It seems to me a man must always
leave himself free to serve his country in any capacity where his country might require his services, and he must do that without agreeing
that he will first obtain the permission of any religious, industrial, or
business association.

Mr. Worthington. I will say, if the committee will pardon me, that this
rule does specially provide for the matter of resignation. It says on
page 171: "We hold that unless he is willing to consult with and obtain
the consent of his fellow-laborers and presiding officers in the priesthood he should be released from all obligations associated with the
latter before accepting any new position."

Senator Bailey. That is not a resignation. That is practically forcing him
out. That is simply admonishing him that he will be disestablished.

Mr. Roberts. Pardon me, Senator, we do not have any such understanding of it.

Senator Bailey. You do not?

Mr. Roberts. That is not my understanding of it. My understanding of it
is that this matter rests upon the same basis as the associations between lawyers who enter into the kind of political agreement about
which we have been speaking.

Senator Bailey. I had not looked at it before. It is a little worse than I
thought. It says: "Our position is that a man having accepted the honors and obligations of ecclesiastical office in the church can not properly, of his own volition, make these honors subordinate to, or even
coordinate with, new ones of an entirely different character."

I should regard any organization in this country—religious, industrial, or of any other character—as not to be tolerated if it teaches that
those who profess to follow it can not perform the duties of a good citizen. You are a man of great intelligence and you are thoroughly familiar with the subject, and I would like to hear what explanation—you
can give as good a one as any man connected with the church—they

have for declaring that a man can not be a good Christian and a good citizen at the same time, in effect.[12]

MR. ROBERTS. Of course I fail to recognize the "effect."

SENATOR BAILEY. You do, however, recognize that that declares that as long as he has any office in the church he can not perform his duties as an officer of the State, and that is certainly one of the duties of a citizen.

MR. ROBERTS. The plain understanding that we have of the matter is this, that one is not entitled to seek political preferment until he first obtains leave of absence or is excused from his official duties in the church. That is all. ...

SENATOR BAILEY. There is no obligation upon the average member, non-official, to seek permission, as I understand it, either in theory or in the practice of your church?

MR. ROBERTS. No, sir.

SENATOR BAILEY. But your prohibition rests upon those who are most apt to be sought by their fellow-citizens for public service. In other words, a man who is of ability and character sufficient to hold a prominent position in the church would be apt to be the very man designated by his fellow-citizens for a political service, and that very man who might be best able to serve the state is the man denied the right to serve it by this rule of the church, and he is denied the right upon the ground that the two are incompatible. Of course, as a matter of fact, nobody is ever forced to accept an office, and when they are elected, even without their consent, there are generally statutes that permit their resignation; but you readily recognize that the law might compel a man to accept an office. We have a provision in the Revised Statutes for the President resigning in case he does not want to serve. That is there to provide for contingencies that are never apt to arise, and so it might be that a man could be drafted into the civil as well as the military service of the Government. If that should happen you have an ordinance, rule, or regulation that forbids you to accept unless you sever your relations with the church, and we recognize that there is a conflict here between the church and the state.

MR. WORTHINGTON. Sever his relations with his office, Senator, not with the church.

SENATOR BAILEY. He severs the relation that exists at the time of his election, and assumes a new relation, that of a lay member. In other

---

12. Bailey is quoting from the LDS Church's "Political Manifesto" of 1896. For the entire document, see *Smoot Hearings*, 1:168-71.

words, they reduce him to the ranks. Now what I can not quite recon-
cile in my mind—and I have no prejudice about it either—is the idea
that there is a necessary conflict between your duty as an officer of
the church and your duty as a citizen.

MR. ROBERTS. In the event of such a crisis confronting one, I think you
would have to rely upon the patriotism and the judgment of the individual concerned.

SENATOR BAILEY. I never like to see a man's religion and patriotism in
conflict. That is the embarrassing thing to me. ...

SENATOR BAILEY. Mr. Roberts, I want to ask you a flat question. Is it not
true that in the politics of Utah the parties seek to enlist the favor of
the church, just as in other States we seek to enlist the sympathy and
support of the people by reason of their nationality or race or some
thing of that kind—for instance, as we appeal to the German vote in
Ohio, the Irish vote in New York—

MR. WORTHINGTON. The labor vote.

[SENATOR] BAILEY. Everywhere.

MR. ROBERTS. I think not, as to the parties. I believe there are individuals
who have sought to trim their sails according to those ideas.

SENATOR BAILEY. Utah has been rather impartial in bestowing her favors
on parties. She goes for one at one time and for the other the next
time.

MR. ROBERTS. Yes, sir.

SENATOR BAILEY. I suppose that is possible, but it is a little singular.

MR. ROBERTS. Would you permit me a word on that, Senator Bailey?

SENATOR BAILEY. Yes, sir.

MR. ROBERTS. I think that Senators ought to have before them in this investigation the fact that the people in Utah have occupied rather an
anomalous condition. I know that I grew up from boyhood to manhood without coming in contact with national politics, and was practically a stranger to both Democratic and Republican principles. Our
whole community grew up isolated, you may say, from the great national issues, and when we were brought in contact with them
through our efforts to obtain statehood, and our final obtaining of
statehood, you can understand that the people generally were un-
fixed in any substantial political convictions, and hence, I think, the
condition that you speak of. There was a very large element there un-
educated in matters of party politics, and I think that would account
for the fortunes and misfortunes of political parties in the State of
Utah to a large extent.

SENATOR BAILEY. I believe in your first election under the constitution the Republicans carried the legislature; in the next one the Democrats carried it, and probably in the next one the Republicans carried it?

MR. ROBERTS. Yes.

SENATOR BAILEY. I believe it is our time next.

MR. ROBERTS. I hope so, Senator.

SENATOR BAILEY. I am free to say that that condition, which had occurred to me, had been partially explained in my mind by the probability of church interference, and that whichever side prevailed was the side upon which the church cast its influence. That was the reason I wanted some explanation of the statement. I understand, of course, that it might happen without any fixed and definite political creed; they might veer from party to party; but it still appears to me that men might be a little more constant in their prejudices, even if not in their convictions, than to change every election. ...

THE CHAIRMAN. How many temples are there in Utah?

MR. ROBERTS. I believe there are four.[13]

THE CHAIRMAN. And the ceremony that used to be performed in the Endowment House is now performed in the temple?

MR. ROBERTS. Yes, sir.

MR. WORTHINGTON. He says he thinks it is. He does not know.

THE CHAIRMAN. Do you remember the ceremony?

MR. ROBERTS. No, sir; I do not remember the ceremonies distinctly.

THE CHAIRMAN. Do you remember any portion of it?

MR. ROBERTS. Only in a general way, Senator.

THE CHAIRMAN. Do you know, Mr. Roberts, of any change in the ceremony performed in the endowment house, and as it is performed to-day in the temple?

MR. ROBERTS. No sir.

THE CHAIRMAN. The ceremony is the same. Now, will you state to the committee what that ceremony was, or is, as nearly as you can?

MR. ROBERTS. Well, the ceremonies consist of what would be considered a series of ceremonies, I take it, of which I only have a general impression.

THE CHAIRMAN. You have something more than a general impression in your own case?

MR. ROBERTS. No; I think not.

---

13. These were located in Logan, Manti, St. George, and Salt Lake City.

THE CHAIRMAN. How many days did it take you to go through the Endowment House?

MR. ROBERTS. Well, part of one day.

THE CHAIRMAN. Who were present at the time? Do you remember?

MR. ROBERTS. I do not remember.

THE CHAIRMAN. Can you tell the committee any portion of that ceremony?

MR. ROBERTS. No, sir.

THE CHAIRMAN. Why not?

MR. ROBERTS. Well, for one reason, I do not feel at liberty to do so.

THE CHAIRMAN. Why not?

MR. ROBERTS. Because I consider myself in trust in relation to those matters, and I do not feel at liberty to make any disclosures in relation to them.

THE CHAIRMAN. It was then a secret?

MR. ROBERTS. Yes.

THE CHAIRMAN. Does this religious denomination have, as one of its ceremonies, secret obligations or covenants?

MR. ROBERTS. I think they could not be properly called secrets. Of course they are common to all worthy members of the church, and generally known by them.

THE CHAIRMAN. Well, secret from the world?

MR. ROBERTS. Secret from the world.

THE CHAIRMAN. The obligations and covenants, whatever they are, then, you are not at liberty to disclose?

MR. ROBERTS. No, sir. I would be led to regard those obligations as similar to those who perhaps have passed through Masonic fraternities, or are members of Masonic fraternities.

THE CHAIRMAN. Then your church organization in that particular is a sort of Masonic fraternity?

MR. ROBERTS. It is analogous, perhaps, in some of its features.

THE CHAIRMAN. You say you can remember, of course, what occurred, but you do not feel at liberty to disclose it, and for that reason you will not disclose it?

MR. ROBERTS. Not specifically. I do not wish, however, Senator, to be understood as being in any sense defiant in that matter.

THE CHAIRMAN. That is not so understood, Mr. Roberts, at all.

MR. ROBERTS. I do not wish to put myself in opposition or raise any issue here at all.

THE CHAIRMAN. The reason you have assigned is accepted. The obligation, whatever it is, taken in the Endowment House, is such that you do not feel at liberty to disclose it?

MR. ROBERTS. That is right.

THE CHAIRMAN. Should you do so, what would you expect as the result?

MR. ROBERTS. I would expect to lose caste with my people as betraying a trust. ...

THE CHAIRMAN. Have you ever been present at a marriage ceremony in the temple?

MR. ROBERTS. Yes, sir.

THE CHAIRMAN. Could you tell what that is?

MR. ROBERTS. I could not, only in a general way. The ceremony is of some length. I remember performing the ceremony in the case of my own daughter when she was married, and, not being familiar with the ceremony, a copy of it was placed in my hands and I read the ceremony, but I could only remember the general terms of it.

THE CHAIRMAN. If the members who have gone through the Endowment House, then, keep faith with the church, they will not disclose what occurred?[14]

MR. ROBERTS. No, sir.

SENATOR BAILEY. Do you feel at liberty, Mr. Roberts, to say whether or not there is anything in that ceremony that permits a man—I will adopt a different expression—that abridges a man's freedom of political action, or action in any respect, except in a religious way?

MR. ROBERTS. No, sir.

SENATOR BAILEY. I do not quite understand whether you mean by your answer to say that you do not feel free to answer that or that there is nothing?

MR. ROBERTS. I mean to say that there is nothing.

MR. TAYLER. When was the last time you witnessed this ceremony in the Endowment House?

MR. ROBERTS. You mean the marriage ceremony?

MR. TAYLER. Or in the temple when this obligation was taken?

MR. ROBERTS. Well, it is several years since.

MR. TAYLER. Is it many years?

MR. ROBERTS. It must be three or four years.

MR. WORTHINGTON. Are you referring, Mr. Tayler, to the marriage ceremony or the endowment?

---

14. Smoot reported that "Burrows has some nasty remark to make to me every day or so, and I sometimes wonder how it is that I can keep my mouth shut and avoid insulting him. I hope some day to be in a position where I can tell him what I think of him, and fully believe that day will come" (Smoot to Joseph F. Smith, Apr. 9, 1904).

MR. TAYLER. I mean whatever the ceremony was in this obligation of the Endowment House, which he says he does not care to disclose.

MR. WORTHINGTON. I so understood it, but I did not know whether the witness did or not.

MR. TAYLER. That ceremony and that obligation were the same in 1877 that they were when you saw it a few years ago?

MR. ROBERTS. Yes; as I remember it. ...

MR. TAYLER. Then it took Mr. [Daniel H.] Wells some time to marry you to Mrs. Shipp, did it?

MR. ROBERTS. Well, speaking of the length of the ceremony I should think likely that it would occupy, at a reasonable rate of reading, perhaps two minutes, or less even than that.

MR. TAYLER. How long were you marrying your daughter?

MR. ROBERTS. It took about that length of time to read the ceremony.

MR. TAYLER. Then the ceremony must be simple—not complicated, is it?

MR. ROBERTS. Oh, no. ...

SENATOR OVERMAN. You said the marriage ceremony took about two minutes to read—to read, you said. You emphasized that word. Is there any other thing in the ceremony except reading?

MR. ROBERTS. Oh, no. I think a person can read considerable of a ceremony in two minutes.

SENATOR OVERMAN. There is nothing else then, except just the reading of the ordinary ceremony?

MR. ROBERTS. That is all.

MR. VAN COTT. Mr. Roberts, are you a Mason?

MR. ROBERTS. No, sir.

MR. VAN COTT. Are you an Odd Fellow?

MR. ROBERTS. No, sir.

MR. VAN COTT. In any of these ceremonies that took place in the Endowment House or the temple, is there anything in any way that binds you to disobey the laws of the land, or to make any agreement against the Government, or its officers, or anything of the kind?

MR. ROBERTS. No, sir; absolutely nothing of the kind.

MR. VAN COTT. Or anything that is contrary to the discharge of all the duties of a good citizen?

MR. ROBERTS. No, sir.[15] ...

---

15. On April 21, 1904, Carl Badger wrote in his journal: "B. H. Roberts is the only witness who has been treated with entire respect" (in Badger, *Liahona and Iron Rod*, 219).

11.

Angus M. Cannon

Thursday, April 21

"Interest in the Smoot inquiry is decidedly on the wane. There was not a single member of the house or senate present this morning, except the bare quorum of the committee ... nor did the general public show that eagerness to hear the testimony which was so apparent during the first days of the hearing ... and the falling off in female attendance was marked. The reason for this is that all the evidence now being adduced is in line with that already brought out." —*Deseret News*, Apr. 21, 1904

Angus M. Cannon,[1] having been duly sworn, was examined and testified as follows ...

MR. TAYLER. Mr. Cannon, when were you first married?

MR. CANNON. On the 18th day of July, 1858.

MR. TAYLER. To whom were you then married?

MR. CANNON. Sarah Maria Mousley.

MR. TAYLER. To whom were you next married?

MR. CANNON. I would like to ask a question of the chairman, if you will permit, before I answer these questions.

MR. TAYLER. Certainly.

MR. CANNON. Mr. Chairman, with your permission I would like to say that I was brought into great trouble nineteen years ago and sent to prison for eight months because I paraded the mothers of my children before the community—acknowledged them, recognized them as my wives. My crime was said to consist in that I held them out as wives. I had the option given me to desert the mothers of my children, except one, or go to prison. I went to prison. I endured an eight-months' term. I remained there under sentence for six months, a term of eight months, to have that case advanced in the Supreme Court of the United States to test its legality.

---

1. At the time of his testimony, Cannon (1834-1915) was sixty-nine years old. The brother of a former counselor in the LDS First Presidency (George Q. Cannon), Angus presided over the Stake Lake Stake and served as stake patriarch. He was a polygamist.

Having been married before the passage of the antipolygamy law, known as the law of 1862, I felt that I could not desert the mothers of my children, who were married to me under those circumstances, and look them in the face with honest pride. Hence I went to prison. In prison I said to my associate prisoners: "You could not come here in honor; I could not stay out in honor." The Supreme Court confirmed the decision in my case. I was then led to be noncommunicative regarding my children and their mothers, and have dwelt quietly with them from that time to this. I have not paraded them, but with modest pride I have nourished them and cared for them, never having known any woman but the mothers of my own children.

Now, I have noticed in the public press that my president has been caricatured and his family has been caricatured throughout the United States and throughout the world. I am here to-day, and I would ask that I be protected against making a public exhibit of my family, that if I am imperiled in my liberties for acknowledging them, I would like, at least, to be made safe when I cease to parade them and I would ask that it be not made public here to-day. I will answer any questions that are put to me regarding our church, its influence, and its conduct, but I would ask that you permit me to be as modest now as I have been asked to be in the decision of the Supreme Court of the United States regarding the relationship that exists between the mothers of my children and myself. I do this in the interest of my family, for they [the public] have not been provoked by the marrying and multiplicity of wives, and parading them before them, but we have dwelt in tranquil peace, and existed with fellowship and love.

I would ask that I be favored, if you please to do so, as representing one of the highest tribunals that is a glory not only to this country but the crowning glory of the world, in the dignity that you represent.

MR. WORTHINGTON. Mr. Cannon, may I ask if you have any counsel to advise you about what your rights are?

MR. CANNON. I have no counsel; no, sir. I am here at your mercy.

MR. WORTHINGTON. Mr. Chairman, I think, in view of the statement of the witness, he ought to be informed that he is under no obligation to answer any questions that will incriminate himself.

MR. TAYLER. He can not incriminate himself before this committee.

THE CHAIRMAN. I suppose the statute of the United States protects him entirely.

MR. WORTHINGTON. No, Mr. Chairman, the statute of the United States does not protect him. While he is not my client, I think he ought to be informed of the law. The law, as decided by the Supreme Court of the United States, is that that statute to which you refer, section 180 of the Revised Statutes, is no protection, inasmuch as it simply says that the testimony that a witness shall give before a committee of Congress shall not be used against him. It does not provide, as a later statute does, in reference to proceedings by the Interstate Commerce Commission, that there shall be no prosecution for the offense. The Supreme Court has held that in the first case the witness can not be required to answer, because the statute does not protect him from a prosecution, and that it would be a vain thing to require him to give all the details of his alleged offense so that those who wish to prosecute him would know where to go for evidence, and simply say that what he had said here should not be used against him; but when the statute goes further, as it does in the Interstate Commerce Commission case, and says he shall never be prosecuted, then the Supreme Court has held that he can not he prosecuted either in the Federal courts or the State courts. That statute protects him everywhere, and then he must answer; but there is no statute which takes away the right to prosecute him in giving testimony before a Congressional committee, and the Supreme Court has decided that he is not required to answer, and they discharged a witness on a habeas corpus on that ground.

THE CHAIRMAN. The witness is at liberty to decline to answer any question.

MR. WORTHINGTON. He is not at liberty to decline to answer any question. If he declines to answer on the ground that the answer would incriminate him he is excused. If he refuses to answer any other question—a question which relates to the subject-matter which is before the committee—he is in contempt of the Senate and he commits an indictable offense.

THE CHAIRMAN. Certainly. Read the question, Mr. Reporter.

The reporter read as follows: "Mr. Tayler. To whom were you next married?"

THE CHAIRMAN. He stated his first marriage.

MR. TAYLER. I do not want him to admit before the committee that he committed an offense against a law forbidding polygamy, if that was done during the period over which the statute of limitations does not run.

THE CHAIRMAN. Can you answer that question, Mr. Cannon?

MR. CANNON. I would like to have the question read.

The question was again read by the reporter.

THE CHAIRMAN. What is your answer to that, Mr. Cannon?

MR. CANNON. I understand the Chair to decide that I shall answer that question?

THE CHAIRMAN. I think you should answer it.

MR. CANNON. I was married at the same time to Ann Amanda Mousley— the same hour.

THE CHAIRMAN. What did you say?

MR. CANNON. I was married in the same hour to Ann Amanda Mousley.

MR. TAYLER. By the same hour, do you mean by the same ceremony?

MR. CANNON. Yes, sir; at the same time.

THE CHAIRMAN. In 1858. Go on, Mr. Tayler.

MR. TAYLER. To whom were you next married?

MR. CANNON. I would ask, Mr. Chairman, if this is to be followed up, if I am to relate all my family matters. I was sent to prison because I did do it. Am I now to be placed in peril if I do not do it? I would ask that to be ruled upon.

SENATOR HOPKINS. You heard what the attorney has said, that certain questions you could decline to answer if you choose to. I think, perhaps, it might be well for him to designate some attorney.

MR. WORTHINGTON. He ought to have counsel of his own.

THE CHAIRMAN. You have stated your first marriage was in 1858, and named the person. Your second was in what year?

MR. CANNON. The same hour.

MR. WORTHINGTON. He married at the same time two sisters.

THE CHAIRMAN. At the same time you married another person. That was your second marriage. This question is, when were you next married?

MR. CANNON. My question is, am I to be placed in peril if I do not answer this question as I was placed in peril because I did parade the mothers of my children as my wives nineteen years ago?

THE CHAIRMAN. It is for you to answer or decline, as you prefer. These questions have been answered by all the witnesses, including the president of the church, frankly and openly. You can answer or decline, as you see proper.

MR. CANNON. Of course if you rule that I shall answer, I will answer. I will try to obey the law.

THE CHAIRMAN. I think the question is proper in this investigation.

MR. WORTHINGTON. Do I understand the Chair to rule that he thinks a witness is bound to answer a question that incriminates himself?

THE CHAIRMAN. I say the question is proper in this investigation. In view of the course to be pursued by the committee, the question is regarded as proper. Repeat the question, Mr. Reporter.

The reporter read as follows: "Mr. Tayler. To whom were you next married?"

MR. CANNON. I was next married to Mrs. Clara C. Mason.

MR. TAYLER. When were you married to her, Mr. Cannon?

MR. CANNON. I think it was in September, 1875. I would not be positive of it without having my record here.

MR. TAYLER. To whom were you next married?

MR. CANNON. I was next married to Martha Hughes.[2]

MR. TAYLER. And when were you married to her?

MR. CANNON. On the 6th day of October, 1884.

MR. TAYLER. To whom were you next married?

MR. CANNON. I was next married to Maria Bannion.

MR. TAYLER. When were you married to her?

MR. CANNON. On the 11th of March, 1886.

MR. TAYLER. To whom were you next married?

MR. CANNON. I was married to Johanna C. Danielson in the fall of 1886. I do not remember the date.

MR. TAYLER. To whom were you next married?

MR. CANNON. I have not been married since.

MR. TAYLER. Are all of your wives living?

MR. CANNON. They are. ...

MR. TAYLER. What effect has the manifesto had upon your relations with these six wives?

MR. CANNON. I say it has made me more modest in acknowledging them, and I have only been as attentive as I felt common humanity required me to be.

MR. TAYLER. You have not proclaimed them as your wives constantly and officiously, you mean by that, do you?

MR. CANNON. That is what I mean.

MR. TAYLER. You do not mean that they are any the less your wives now than before, do you?

MR. CANNON. I mean that I am more cold in my treatment of them than I should be. ...

MR. TAYLER. What was your understanding as to that manifesto? Did it do anything more than prohibit future plural marriages?

---

2. For more on this wife, see Constance L. Lieber and John Sillito, eds., *Letters from Exile: The Correspondence of Martha Hughes Cannon and Angus M. Cannon, 1886-1888* (Salt Lake City: Signature Books and Smith Research Associates, 1989).

MR. CANNON. That was the understanding I had of it when it was issued, that it prohibited future plural marriages.

THE CHAIRMAN. Was it your understanding, and the understanding of others, that it prohibited polygamous cohabitation?

MR. CANNON. I did not so understand it until I read President Woodruff's declaration, on the 1st day of November, in Logan [Utah], in 1891.

THE CHAIRMAN. Then you understood that it prohibited polygamous cohabitation?

MR. CANNON. I did.

THE CHAIRMAN. Since that time you have cohabited with these wives?

MR. CANNON. It has been my practice, if I can not live the law as the Lord gives it to me, I come as near to it as my mortal frailty will enable me to do.

THE CHAIRMAN. I understand that from statements. I only want to get at the fact, Mr. Cannon, that you have had three children born to you since the manifesto.

MR. CANNON. Yes, sir.

THE CHAIRMAN. And you understood its scope to prohibit polygamous cohabitation since 1891—these children were born to you since that date?[3]

MR. CANNON. I have understood so, but—

THE CHAIRMAN. Then you were living in violation of the manifesto, were you not?

MR. CANNON. I presume I come under the head of those that James spoke of.[4]

---

3. Ten days after this testimony, a socialist publication ran the following satirical story:

> Statistics have been gathered as to the number of Smoot's wives and the committee is shocked and horrified to find that he has several—a goodly flow of 'em—some young and some old crones. But they haven't found that he has any concubines; they have obtained no statistics of such. If the committee should investigate a lot of other congressmen, while they might find that none of them had more than one wife, they would find that a surprisingly large number of them had harems of varying size. They would find whole districts of the city set apart for congressional harems—harems that the police dare not to interfere with for fear of losing their jobs at the hands of angry congressmen with squads of concubines. ... The blasphemous mockery of the insane crusade against the Mormons is best appreciated when it is known that for a quarter of a century these same congressmen have been the protection, the support and the defenders of more than a hundred known brothels of the city. These are segregated in a district which adjoins the White House ground ("Congress and the Smoot Case," *Appeal to Reason*, May 1, 1904).

4. Cannon was probably referring to a biblical source such as James 5:16-20, which encourages those in the ministry to "confess their faults one to another," arguing that "if any of you do err from the truth, and one convert him; let him know, that he which

THE CHAIRMAN. Did you regard the manifesto, and do you regard it as of Divine origin?

MR. CANNON. I read that all Scripture comes as holy men of old were wrought upon to write and speak as dictated of the Holy Ghost, and I believe President Woodruff was dictated of the Holy Ghost.

THE CHAIRMAN. When he made this manifesto?

MR. CANNON. Yes, sir.

THE CHAIRMAN. Therefore you believe it was Divine?

MR. CANNON. I do.

THE CHAIRMAN. Then, in cohabiting with these wives since the manifesto, you have violated the law of God, have you not?

MR. CANNON. I know I can not live without violating His laws.

THE CHAIRMAN. Answer that question whether you have violated that particular law we are talking about.

MR. CANNON. I presume I did.

THE CHAIRMAN. Are you violating the laws of the United States in having children in polygamous cohabitation?

MR. CANNON. I presume it is so construed.

THE CHAIRMAN. Then you, as a patriarch, are violating both the law of your church and the law of the land.

MR. CANNON. Yes; I am only mortal.

THE CHAIRMAN. Was this violation known to the authorities and the president of the church when, three weeks ago, you were made a patriarch?

MR. CANNON. I am sure I do not know what the president of the church understood about my family relations. He knows I have been a very circumspect man. ...

SENATOR DUBOIS. When was the last general conference of the church held?

MR. CANNON. On the 6th of this present month.

SENATOR DUBOIS. Was Joseph F. Smith sustained at that conference?

MR. CANNON. He was sustained as president of the church.

SENATOR DUBOIS. Was there any opposition?

MR. CANNON. No, sir.

SENATOR DUBOIS. Was Mr. [Francis M.] Lyman, the president of the quorum of apostles, sustained at that conference?

MR. CANNON. He was.

SENATOR DUBOIS. Was there any opposition to him?

---

converteth the sinner from the error of his way shall save a soul from death, and shall hide a multitude of sins."

MR. CANNON. Not that I know of.

SENATOR DUBOIS. Was Brigham H. Roberts sustained at that conference?

MR. CANNON. He was.

SENATOR DUBOIS. Has he been sustained at previous conferences since the action of Congress in his case?

MR. CANNON. He has.

SENATOR DUBOIS. Has there ever been any opposition to his being sustained, that you know of?

MR. CANNON. I never knew of any.

SENATOR DUBOIS. Did your people in Utah have any idea of the testimony which President Smith and Mr. Lyman gave when they were down here?

MR. CANNON. I would like to hear that again.

SENATOR DUBOIS. Did you know anything about the testimony which Mr. Smith and Mr. Lyman gave here previous to the 6th of April?

MR. CANNON. I read it in the papers.

SENATOR DUBOIS. Did your people generally have any knowledge of the testimony which those gentlemen gave here?

MR. CANNON. I think probably they read it in the papers. I do not know.

SENATOR DUBOIS. Do you know whether any of your people complained about any of these men being sustained—complained in private?

MR. CANNON. I think the people sympathized with them in the position in which they were put.

SENATOR DUBOIS. And gladly sustained them?

MR. CANNON. Yes, sir.

THE CHAIRMAN. Then I understand you to say that since the president of the church testified before this committee as to his six wives and a number of children the church in the recent conference sustained him.

MR. CANNON. They did.

THE CHAIRMAN. And there was no criticism about it?

MR. CANNON. Well, they regretted that circumstances had conspired to bring him to occupy the position he did before this committee, knowing the trial he was going through, in sympathy with the mothers of his children, the obligations he had taken upon him with those mothers, and the obligations he was under to his country and to the church of God. That was their sympathy.

THE CHAIRMAN. In other words, they regretted the disclosure.

MR. CANNON. I will not say that. They were pleased that he disclosed the valor to tell the truth. They were pleased with that.

SENATOR DUBOIS. Did President Smith issue—not a manifesto, but an announcement to the church at the last conference in regard to polygamy?[5]

MR. CANNON. He did.

SENATOR DUBOIS. Did Mr. Lyman offer a resolution[6] embodying, I might say, the ideas advanced by Mr. Smith, to the conference?

MR. CANNON. There was something of that kind. I can not remember now exactly the form of it. I would like to see it. I could tell if that was it.

SENATOR DUBOIS. I am sorry that I haven't it here. I would like to have it put in the record. In that resolution and in the announcement which the president of the church made to the people it was stated that the church would deal with offenders against the law in regard to polygamy, was it not?

MR. CANNON. I can not now announce the sentiment that was in it. I failed to put a copy of it in my pocket.

MR. WORTHINGTON. It referred to plural marriages?

MR. CANNON. It related to any attempted plural marriages in the future and I was the one who seconded the resolution. ...

_____

5. According to the official conference report, President Smith said:

Now I am going to present a matter to you that is unusual and I do it because of a conviction which I feel that it is a proper thing for me to do. I have taken the liberty of having written down what I wish to present, in order that I may say to you the exact words which I would like to have conveyed to your ears, that I may not be misunderstood or misquoted. I present this to the conference for your action: OFFICIAL STATEMENT

'Inasmuch as there are numerous reports in circulation that plural marriages have been entered into contrary to the official declaration of President Woodruff, of September 26, 1890, commonly called the Manifesto, which was issued by President Woodruff and adopted by the Church at its general conference, October 6, 1890, which forbade any marriage violative of the law of the land;

'I, Joseph F. Smith, President of the Church of Jesus Christ of Latter-day Saints, hereby affirm and declare that no such marriages have been solemnized with the sanction, consent or knowledge of the Church of Jesus Christ of Latter-day Saints, and I hereby announce that all such marriages are prohibited, and if any officer or member of the Church shall assume to solemnize or enter into any such marriage he will be deemed in transgression against the Church and will be liable to be dealt with, according to the rules and regulations thereof, and excommunicated therefrom'" (in James R. Clark, ed., _Messages of the First Presidency of the Church of Jesus Christ of Latter-day Saints_ [Salt Lake City: Bookcraft, 1970], 4:84).

In a letter to Smoot a few days later, Smith wrote: "I hope the action taken at Conference was satisfactory. It [the response] was spontaneous and hearty" (Apr. 9, 1904).

6. Lyman stated: "Resolved that we, the members of the Church of Jesus Christ of Latter-day Saints, in General Conference assembled, hereby approve and endorse the statement and declaration of President Joseph F. Smith, just made to this Conference concerning plural marriages, and will support the courts of the Church in the enforcement thereof" (in Clark, _Messages of First Presidency_, 4:85).

THE CHAIRMAN. Mr. Cannon, I want to ask you a question right there. In this resolution passed at the conference, protesting against further plural marriages, was there anything said or any action taken in relation to future polygamous cohabitation?

MR. CANNON. I do not remember that there was. I do not remember the sentiment. That is why I would like to see it, if it had been here, that I could have read it.

THE CHAIRMAN. I read it hastily, and I thought you remembered it.

MR. TAYLER. There is nothing in it about polygamous cohabitation?

MR. CANNON. I do not think there is anything in it relating to polygamous cohabitation. If there had been, I would not have seconded it.

THE CHAIRMAN. You would not have seconded it if there had been a protest against that?

MR. CANNON. No, sir.

THE CHAIRMAN. Why not? Do you intend to continue polygamous cohabitation?

MR. CANNON. I will have to improve if I do not.

THE CHAIRMAN. Then, in other words, you intend to continue to violate the law of the land and the law of God, as you understand it?

MR. CANNON. I intend to try and be true to the mothers of my children until death deprives me of the opportunity.

THE CHAIRMAN. And the only way you can be true to them, I suppose, in your idea, is to live in polygamous cohabitation?

MR. CANNON. As near as I can, according to the dictates of my conscience and the requirements of the obligation I took upon me with them.

THE CHAIRMAN. Does your conscience, of which you now speak, control you more than the revelations from God and the laws of the land. ...

MR. CANNON. I can not say that it does, but I do say that I consider them, all—the obligations to the mothers of my children, the importance of obeying the manifesto, and regarding it as of Divine origin. Considering it all, I try to make my life conform to it, to satisfy my conscience the best I can.

THE CHAIRMAN. Is your conscience satisfied in disobeying the revealed will of God, as you say this manifesto was?

MR. CANNON. I never did a wrong in my life that I did not feel bad over it. ...

THE CHAIRMAN. That satisfies your conscience?

MR. CANNON. It satisfies me, just as it would to get an ox out of the mire on the Sabbath day, when I am told by the Lord I must not work.

THE CHAIRMAN. Then, this manifesto, or this command of God, is binding upon your conscience whenever you want it to be?

MR. CANNON. Whenever I feel that I can make my life to conform to the
will of the Lord. ...

THE CHAIRMAN. Do you remember the covenant you took when you went
through the endowment house?

MR. CANNON. Oh, yes.

THE CHAIRMAN. Could you state the ceremony?

MR. CANNON. I would not like to.

THE CHAIRMAN. Why not?

MR. CANNON. Because it is of a religious character, and it is simply an obligation that I enter into to be pure before my Maker, and worthy of the
attainment of my Redeemer, and the fellowship and love of my children and their mothers, my departed ancestry, and my coming descendants.

THE CHAIRMAN. What objection is there to making that public?

MR. CANNON. Because it is sacred.

THE CHAIRMAN. How sacred?

MR. CANNON. It is simply a covenant that I enter into with my Maker in
private.

THE CHAIRMAN. All the tenets of your religion are sacred, are they not?

MR. CANNON. Sir?

THE CHAIRMAN. They are all sacred, are they not—the teachings?

MR. CANNON. All of those are sacred—yes; all of those things.

THE CHAIRMAN. I do not quite understand why you should keep them
secret.

MR. CANNON. It is because it is necessary to keep them secret. If you will
permit me, Mr. Chairman, we admit only the purest of our people to
enter there.[7]

---

7. For more, see Edward L. Kimball, "The History of LDS Temple Admission Stan-
dards," *Journal of Mormon History* 24 (Spring 1998): 135-76. In the same month as this testimony, Joseph F. Smith addressed this topic of temple worthiness: "In regards to
recom[m]ends to the Temple the bishops should only give them to saints to receive their
first endowments and they should exercise more care and caution in giving same, as
some unworthy persons have been admitted to the Temple and even some who were not
members of the Church. One instance was when a detective who was out here and who
took such an interest in the people and sympathized with them so much that the bishop
recommended him to the Temple and he was endowed. ... [T]he press reports are such
that it shows that lies and misr[e]presentation are abroad and they are doing all they can
to injure us as a people therefore we should be discrete in our utterances and be as wise
as serpents but harmless as doves" (Thomas A. Clawson, Diary, Apr. 5, 1904, Utah State
Historical Society, Salt Lake City).

THE CHAIRMAN. People like you and the president of the church? I suppose the president of the church is admitted?

MR. CANNON. The presidency of the church, if he continues in good standing, and our people whoever are in good standing and deemed worthy to the proper recommends, are permitted to enter there.

THE CHAIRMAN. Do you enter into any obligation not to reveal these ceremonies?

MR. CANNON. I feel it would be very improper to reveal them.

THE CHAIRMAN. I say, do you enter into an obligation not to?

MR. CANNON. There are sacred obligations connected with all the higher ordinances of our church.

THE CHAIRMAN. In words, do you promise not to reveal?

MR. CANNON. I feel that that is the trust reposed in me, that I will not go and—

THE CHAIRMAN. I think you do not understand my question. Do you promise specifically not to reveal what occurs in the endowment house?

MR. CANNON. I would rather not tell what occurs there. I say this—

THE CHAIRMAN. I think, Mr. Cannon, you do not understand me. Do you promise not to reveal what occurs in the endowment house when you go through?

MR. CANNON. I feel that that is an obligation I take upon me when I do that.

THE CHAIRMAN. When you go through the endowment house do you take that obligation upon you in express terms?

MR. CANNON. I think I do.

THE CHAIRMAN. You know, do you know, whether you do or not? Why do you take that obligation not to reveal these things?

MR. CANNON. Because we are—I do not want to be disrespectful to this committee.

THE CHAIRMAN. I know you would not be.

MR. CANNON. The Lord gave us to understand that we should not make common the sacred things that he committed to his disciples. He told them they must not do that lest they trample them under their feet and rend them.

THE CHAIRMAN. Do you remember whether there was any penalty attached if they should reveal?

MR. CANNON. I do not remember that there is any penalty.

THE CHAIRMAN. None whatever?

MR. CANNON. I do not remember.

THE CHAIRMAN. Has there been any change in the ceremony of the endowment house since you went through in 1859, up to the present time, that you are aware of?

MR. CANNON. No.

THE CHAIRMAN. No change in the ceremony or obligations?

MR. CANNON. No.[8]

SENATOR OVERMAN. Could a person be an apostle without going through the endowment house?

MR. CANNON. Oh, yes.

SENATOR OVERMAN. Do you know whether the present twelve apostles have gone through the endowment house?

MR. CANNON. I presume they have.

SENATOR OVERMAN. You only presume they have?

MR. CANNON. Yes.

SENATOR OVERMAN. Have they or not; do you know?

MR. CANNON. I can not know a thing, only as I observe it, and I presume they have passed through those ordinances.

SENATOR OVERMAN. The twelve apostles, as they are now constituted, have all gone through?

MR. CANNON. I presume they have.

SENATOR HOPKINS. Do laymen in the church go through the endowments?

MR. CANNON. There are some that enter there.

SENATOR HOPKINS. Men and women both?

MR. CANNON. Yes, sir.

THE CHAIRMAN. Have you ever witnessed a marriage ceremony in the endowment house?

MR. CANNON. Yes, sir.

THE CHAIRMAN. Could you describe that to the committee?

MR. CANNON. Why, they simply take upon them the obligation to be true to each other, husband and wife, and the blessing of the Lord is pronounced upon them in their union by the officiating priest.

THE CHAIRMAN. Well, that is a very simple ceremony. That could be performed anywhere. Is that all there is of it?

MR. CANNON. That is all there is of it.

THE CHAIRMAN. It differs, then, in no way from an ordinary marriage in a private residence.

MR. CANNON. Well, it differs somewhat from some other marriages. I

---

8. This entire exchange was included in the minority report submitted by Foraker on June 11, 1906 (*Smoot Hearings*, 4:531-32).

find most of the denominations have their marriage ceremonies different, one from another.

MR. WORTHINGTON. I do not think the witness understands your question.

THE CHAIRMAN. We would like to have you state, if you can, what the ceremony is, if you feel at liberty to do so.

MR. CANNON. I do not remember it.

THE CHAIRMAN. You do not remember the ceremony?

MR. CANNON. I can not remember it.

THE CHAIRMAN. You were not married in the temple in any of your marriages? In any one of your six marriages, were you married in the temple?

MR. CANNON. No; not one of them.

THE CHAIRMAN. Were you married in the endowment house?

MR. CANNON. One.

THE CHAIRMAN. Which one?

MR. CANNON. I was married to Martha Hughes.[9] ...

---

9. The evening after his testimony, Cannon ate "a dish of oysters with [Franklin S.] Richards and at his expense drank a cocktail with [Waldemar] Van Cott. They with Senator Smoot expressed themselves satisfied with my testimony which I did not, as I felt like a donkey that had its ears cut off" (Cannon, Diary, Apr. 21, 1904, Archives, Church of Jesus Christ of Latter-day Saints, Salt Lake City).

12.

Orlando W. Powers

Saturday & Monday, April 23, 25

"On the whole there is not much fault to be found with [Judge Powers's testimony]. He has exaggerated the 'holdings' of the Church in the corporate institutions alluded to, and has failed to see a distinction between the Church as an organized body, and prominent members thereof in their business connections. This is a common error ... [but] the fuller account of the Judge's testimony placed it in a better light than the brief report in our regular dispatches."
—*Deseret News*, Apr. 27, 1904

Orlando W. Powers,[1] first duly sworn, was examined, and testified as follows ...

SENATOR McCOMAS. You are a very close observer of that community and of the State life generally. So far as you can give an opinion, I wish you would tell us how the younger Mormon men, married and unmarried, say under 40, regard the practice of polygamy.

MR. POWERS. I think I can safely say that the younger men and the younger women of the Mormon Church—

SENATOR McCOMAS. I was going to ask you about the women directly.

MR. POWERS. And I have talked with a great many of them upon the subject, are opposed to the practice, and strongly opposed to the practice. Although I have often been surprised at the power that the church has over its members, nevertheless, my opinion—my conscientious opinion—is that if the church was to attempt to reestablish polygamy, by revelation or otherwise, it would have trouble from those younger men and women.

SENATOR McCOMAS. Do you think they are strong enough to resist and overcome an attempt to reestablish the practice of polygamy?

MR. POWERS. I believe so.

SENATOR McCOMAS. Is it true that their attitude now is one of tolerance in

---

1. Powers was an attorney in Salt Lake City at the time of his testimony. He had moved to Utah from Michigan in 1885 when U.S. President Grover Cleveland appointed him an Associate Justice of the Utah Supreme Court. He sat for approximately one hundred cases involving polygamous cohabitation, including the trial that resulted in the conviction of LDS Apostle and future church president Lorenzo Snow.

respect of the existing conditions as to polygamy—the marriages of elder women to elder men—expecting that the practice will die out with that generation?

MR. POWERS. There exists this condition in that regard, as I have found from talking with my own friends and neighbors of the Mormon Church, of the younger generation. There is a feeling of toleration, with an idea that it will pass away. There is also—at least many of them had expressed to me—a feeling hostile to the continuance of polygamous cohabitation and to polygamy, and I know that there is that sentiment among many of the younger members of the church.[2]

SENATOR McCOMAS. Is it or not an increasing sentiment, in your opinion?

MR. POWERS. I hope so.

SENATOR McCOMAS. You have no definite belief.

MR. POWERS. I think so—

SENATOR McCOMAS. You think so—

MR. POWERS. And I hope so. At the same time, conditions are so peculiar out there, and we are so often mistaken with regard to men and things, that it is hard for one to give a definite conclusion as to the future.

SENATOR McCOMAS. In 1870, on a Sunday, I was in the [Salt Lake] tabernacle, and I heard Brigham Young appeal to the young men to marry and to marry often. He said the railroad had just come in, and that the competition with the Gentiles and the men who each had only one family would make it more difficult for the younger Mormons to support many families. But he said now the trial was upon them, and, as he expressed it, the Lord would be on their side. He seemed to be

---

2. One of the rising LDS generation who opposed plural marriage was Carl Badger, Smoot's secretary. In a letter of November 1, 1904, to his wife, he explained:

About my talking against polygamy; people can easily misunderstand me. I believe that polygamy is not the ideal system of marriage, that is all I have said; and I cannot say any less. It can be lived as clean physically and morally as monogamy but it is not ideal. As I love life, and what is more dear to me than life, my wife, I love those who gave me my life and my darling wife, but I cannot say therefore that I think polygamy ideal. I do not. I can not, and I will not say I do and can. You ask me to remain quiet. I do not seek occasion. (I am not sure that I can say that, for I like to discuss the question), and when it is offered or thrust upon me I cannot say anything that I do not believe. I do not deal irreverently with the subject; it is so closely connected with those whom I love that I cannot do that. Then, as I have said, the relation itself is sacred, but that does not make it ideal. I am afraid that I cannot give up the right to say what I believe in regard to polygamy. Now is the time, if there is ever to be a time, when something should be said about it. We cannot tamper with fire, and that is what we are doing when we preached that polygamy is divine. ... I am against the practice of polygamy, and I will fight it, now and always" (in Rodney J. Badger, *Liahona and Iron Rod: The Biography of Carl A. and Rose J. Badger* [Bountiful, Utah: Family History Publishers, 1985], 230).

right to the extent that they continued polygamy for some years after the railroad came in, and with the Gentile competition. Is not that difficulty ever present to the younger race of people—the men and women—that when a man has a number of families it is a harder proposition to make a living than it is for a man who has no family or only one family?

MR. POWERS. I think it is, and I also think another matter, which is of a purely social nature, enters into it somewhat. We [in the West] are growing there more like the rest of the world, and our women are growing like the women of the rest of the world, and they are becoming attracted to social matters, and they are beginning to desire to clothe themselves as beautifully as the women of the rest of the country. I think that will have some effect, too, because it increases the responsibilities if a man has a family who are going to dress—

SENATOR HOPKINS. Do I understand that even now a plural wife does not have the social standing that a first wife has?

MR. POWERS. I did not intend to say that as among the Mormon people. Yes; they have, I think, the same standing among the Mormon people.

SENATOR OVERMAN. Is there any growing hostility among the younger generation against church interference in politics?

MR. POWERS. Yes.

SENATOR McCOMAS. I was just coming to that. I beg your pardon, Senator.

SENATOR OVERMAN. I am through.

SENATOR McCOMAS. I was about to ask you how the incidents of which you have spoken ... affect the public opinion among the younger Mormons who do not care for polygamy. I want to know how, in your opinion, they—men and women—receive what you have stated to have been interferences and efforts by the church to control political action at elections and in the legislature and in conventions. Are they restive or not restive under this church control?

MR. POWERS. They are restive under the church control of our political affairs. ...

SENATOR McCOMAS. How do the Mormon people, so far as you observe, submit to dictation as to how they shall vote at the general election, the municipal election, and how they shall cast their votes for senators in the legislature; do they submit more or less readily to the church dictation, of which you have spoken, as the years go on?

MR. POWERS. Some submit regularly; some submit protesting against it, and some will not submit. ...

THE CHAIRMAN. Will you state why it is that those who live in polygamous cohabitation to-day are not prosecuted?

MR. POWERS. I will do so as well as I can, and I simply state here the views, as I know them, of what are termed the "old guard" of the Liberal party, Republicans and Democrats, who fought the church party in the days when it was a power.[3] Those [non-Mormon] men have felt, and still feel, that if the church will only stop new plural marriages and will allow this matter to die out and pass away, they will not inter-fere with them. First of all, of course, we want peace in Utah. We would like to be like the rest of the country. We want to make of it a State like the States of the rest of the Union. We want the Mormon people to be like the rest of the American people; but we realize that there is a condition there which the people of the East do not—and, I presume, can not—understand. You can not make people who have been brought up under our [American] system of Government and our system of marriage believe that folks can sincerely and honestly believe that it is right to have more than one wife, and yet those peo-ple believe it. They are a God-fearing people, and it has been a part of their faith and their life.

Now, to the eastern people their manner of living is looked upon as immoral. Of course it is, viewed from their standpoint. Viewed from the standpoint of a Mormon it is not. The Mormon wives are as sincere in their belief in polygamy as the Mormon men, and they have no more hesitation in declaring that they are one of several wives of a man than a good woman in the East has in declaring that she is the single wife of a man. There is that condition. There are those people—

SENATOR HOPKINS. Do you mean to say that a Mormon woman will as readily become a plural wife as she would a first wife?

MR. POWERS. Those who are sincere in the Mormon faith—who are good Mormons, so called—I think would just as readily become plural wives (that has been my experience) as they would become the first wife. That condition exists. There is a question for statesmen to solve. We have not known what was best to do. It has been discussed, and people would say that such and such a man ought to be prosecuted.

---

3. Prior to statehood, there were two political parties in Utah: the Mormon "Peoples Party" and non-Mormon "Liberal Party." Although these had been disbanded in favor of affiliation with national political parties, underlying sentiments still ran along the same fault line of Mormon vs. Gentile (see, e.g., John Sillito, "Democratic Party," in Allan Kent Powell, ed., *Utah History Encyclopedia* [Salt Lake City: University of Utah Press, 1994], 133-34).

Then they would consider whether anything would be gained; whether we would not delay instead of hastening the time that we hope to
live to see; whether the institution would not flourish by reason of
what they would term persecution. And so, notwithstanding a protest
has been sent down here to you, I will say to you the people have acquiesced in the condition that exists.

MR. VAN COTT. You mean the gentiles.

MR. POWERS. Yes; the gentiles.

THE CHAIRMAN. Have you any knowledge of the extent to which polygamous cohabitation exists in the State to-day?

MR. POWERS. I have tried not to know about it. When it has come under
my immediate observation I have known about it. I do not know to
what extent it exists. I want to see it pass away.

THE CHAIRMAN. Does it exist outside of the city of Salt Lake?

MR. POWERS. Oh, without doubt.

THE CHAIRMAN. Have you any idea as to the extent?

MR. POWERS. No; I could not give an idea as to the extent, because, as I tell
you, I have honestly tried not to know about it.[4]

SENATOR MCCOMAS. Have there been many polygamous marriages lately?
Of course polygamous marriages are forbidden, and it is difficult to
ascertain whether there have been.

MR. POWERS. If there are any polygamous marriages at the present time,
my opinion is they are sporadic cases. I have not since the time that I
have lived there believed it was the worst feature of Mormonism. Polygamy, I think, is bound in the course of our advance as a nation to
pass away. I do not believe it can exist any more than slavery could exist. I want to say—

SENATOR HOPKINS. Very well. On that basis, with the passing of this generation, polygamous marriages and polygamous cohabitation will
disappear. Now, you say, in your judgment that is not the worst feature
of that religion.

MR. POWERS. Yes.

SENATOR HOPKINS. What is there in that religion aside from that which
does not commend itself to good citizenship?

MR. POWERS. It is the un-American domination by the hierarchy of the
people of that faith, the constant teaching that they must obey counsel, the belief that the head of the church is inspired and speaks the

---

4. The previous five questions and answers were cited by Utah Senator George
Sutherland on the Senate floor in favor of Smoot's election, in opposition to the resolution that Smoot not be seated.

word of God when he is inspired, and the interference in our political affairs, and the power that the church has to control our commerce and our business, through the interests that are held by the trustees in trust in all of our large corporations—I will not say all of them, but—

SENATOR HOPKINS. That claim is made, in a limited way, at least, against other churches.

MR. POWERS. I know of no other church as to which the claim is made as I make it here now. I know of no other church which has annexed to it what is in one sense of the word a secret organization; that has its temple rites; that acts concerning public matters as this church acts.

You have asked me for instances of church interference. They are hard to give, because the church is a secret institution. We see the result; we can not tell always just how that result was attained ...

MR. VAN COTT. What have you to say, in your judgment, as to the honesty and sincerity of the Mormon men and women?

MR. POWERS. I believe the Mormon men and women are as honest and as sincere—I am speaking of the great mass of the people now—as any people upon the face of the earth; and it has seemed to me that from that very fact, their sincerity, their honesty, their firm belief in their church tenets, and their fidelity to their leaders, their leaders have the opportunity to do what has been done politically.

MR. VAN COTT. With a leader who himself was honest and conscientious in that particular would there be anything to fear whatever, in your opinion?

MR. POWERS. Oh, no. The Mormon people are largely, of course, controlled by their leaders, and with an honest leader firmly believing and preaching American principles, certainly there would be nothing to fear.

SENATOR BAILEY. That, however, Judge, would be the rule of one man rather than the rule of all the people, would it not?

MR. POWERS. That is true. That is one of the things concerning which we have trouble.

MR. VAN COTT. But you have given your opinion as to what will be the ultimate outcome, in your opinion, as to a class of people who are honest and conscientious and earnest, as you have stated.

MR. POWERS. Why, I have great faith in the people, not only of the country at large, but of Utah. I can not believe otherwise than that in this free Government, after a time—that is the trouble; I fear I will not live to see it—the Mormon Church will take its place, where it ought to take it like the rest of the churches, in the country. ...

MR. VAN COTT. In 1895, you were chairman of the party that year?

MR. POWERS. I was.

MR. WORTHINGTON. Chairman of what, the Democratic State committee?[5]

MR. POWERS. Yes.

MR. VAN COTT. And in that year did not the Democrats nominate Mr. Moses Thatcher, an apostle, and Mr. [B. H.] Roberts, one of the first presidents of seventies, on account of what was thought to be their popularity with the people in the State?

MR. POWERS. Yes; on account of their ability and their popularity.

MR. VAN COTT. Their ability had only been shown in an ecclesiastical way, had it not?

MR. POWERS. Mr. Roberts showed his ability in that constitutional convention and he showed his courage. In that constitutional convention it was the desire of—

MR. VAN COTT. I am going to ask you about that a little later.

MR. POWERS. I want to finish this now.

MR. VAN COTT. That is not an answer to my question.

MR. POWERS. Very well.

SENATOR BAILEY. You asked him if they were not nominated for a certain reason. I should like to hear the full explanation.

MR. VAN COTT. I withdraw the objection. I thought the Judge was going to speak of the woman's suffrage, and I had that for a special question. It was not in answer to my question at present; but I withdraw any objection.

MR. POWERS. In that constitutional convention it was the wish of the majority that suffrage should be given to women. Mr. Roberts did not think it was going to benefit the women or benefit the State, and notwithstanding the fact that he was upon the unpopular side and was running counter to the wishes, I think, of the great majority of his own people, he delivered a speech in that convention that would do credit to any man, in opposition to it, and the people who disagreed with him on that subject admired him for his ability and his courage.[6]

---

5. Joseph F. Smith wrote to Smoot on March 20, 1904: "I see by last nights papers that O[rlando]. W. Powers, W[illia]m. H. King and J[ames]. H. Moyle are to be subpoenaed as witness. Why do not the 'Czar,' Dubois, Tayl[e]r and Co[mpany] ... subpoena the whole Democratic Party of Utah to show cause why the said party was not more successful during the last political campaign."

6. Roberts took a hostile position against women at the state constitutional convention. "Let [suffrage] operate twenty years," he said, and "we will have a womanhood from whom we will [be] dispose[d] to flee" (in D. Craig Mikkelson, "The Politics of B. H. Roberts," *Dialogue: A Journal of Mormon Thought* 9 [Summer 1974]: 28-30). Another dele-

MR. VAN COTT. Were not the leaders of the church also opposed to Mr. Roberts's position on woman's suffrage?

MR. POWERS. They were.

MR. VAN COTT. Strongly opposed?

MR. POWERS. They were; and that is one thing that commended Mr. Roberts to the gentile people of that community.

MR. VAN COTT. Mr. Roberts held this high position ecclesiastically that he now holds?

MR. POWERS. Yes, sir.

MR. VAN COTT. Now, Mr. Thatcher was popular on account of his ecclesiastical position, was he not?

MR. POWERS. He was popular on account of his ecclesiastical position and he was popular because of his power as an orator. He was a scholarly man and he was a man of great oratorical ability and power. He could influence and sway those who were favored with an opportunity of listening to him, and was a strong man outside of his ecclesiastical position.

MR. VAN COTT. But this power you speak of of both these gentlemen was principally shown in their ecclesiastical duties, was it not?

MR. POWERS. Yes; that, I think, perhaps is true, although Mr. Thatcher delivered a great many public addresses on other subjects.

MR. VAN COTT. And these were the men whom the Democrats nominated in 1895?

MR. POWERS. They did. ...

MR. VAN COTT. The "Deseret News" is the church organ?

MR. POWERS. It is the church organ. It so announces itself at the head of the column.

MR. VAN COTT. And have not the Republicans always complained about that paper helping the Democrats?

MR. POWERS. I think they have, more or less, made complaint.

---

gate could see no harm in his mother accompanying him to the polls, to which Roberts responded that she should "not only accompany the gentleman to the polls, but I doubt not it would be a most excellent thing for him, if she were constantly present with him to guide his footsteps through the meandering pathway of life (laughter and applause)." Roberts believed in an inherent "difference in man's nature and woman's nature" and that "all change is not progress" (in Gary J. Bergera, ed., *The Autobiography of B. H. Roberts* [Salt Lake City: Signature Books, 1990], 186, 190). LDS President Wilford Woodruff thought Roberts "had done more harm in his Speaches in the Convention than all the liberal [Party] elements in the city," in that the church's objective was to widen the election margin between Mormons and non-Mormons in Utah (in Thomas G. Alexander, *Things in Heaven and Earth: The Life and Times of Wilford Woodruff, a Mormon Prophet* [Salt Lake City: Signature Books, 1991], 310-11).

MR. VAN COTT. Has not the "Salt Lake Tribune," the Republican organ, also charged that the "Deseret News" has favored the Democrats?

MR. POWERS. It has, at times. ...

MR. VAN COTT. In a general way, where did you get your information that the Republicans could go out on the stump and could talk and proselyte, and that the Democrats must keep quiet?

MR. POWERS. Well, from many different sources. That is a matter that has been discussed ever since the division upon party lines. There is a particular report of that in the "Salt Lake Tribune" of May 10, 1896, it being the report of a meeting where the manifesto was presented for confirmation at Logan [Utah] on the 3d day of May, 1896, and speeches were made there by Heber J. Grant, by Joseph F. Smith, and by John Henry Smith, and reference was made to the agreement that had been made in the Gardo House, to the effect that those believing in Democratic principles should remain quiet, while those who are Republicans should go abroad, in order that there might be more Republicans in the State. That was a complaint made at that meeting against Moses Thatcher that he had not obeyed that agreement made at the Gardo House.

MR. VAN COTT. And the other data that you have furnished to the committee has also been obtained from the "Tribune," has it not?

MR. POWERS. From the "Tribune," from the "Deseret News," from the "Salt Lake Herald,"[7] and from the knowledge that one gains by living among a people and hearing the people talk.

MR. VAN COTT. The "Tribune" has been, with the exception of a brief period, since statehood, distinctly anti-Mormon, has it not?

MR. POWERS. Yes; it was the Liberal organ up to the time of the division on party lines.

MR. VAN COTT. Has it not been your experience that several things, a good many of the things, that they have charged have been inaccurate?

MR. POWERS. Yes. I do not think any newspaper can be absolutely accurate. I think they all try to be.

MR. VAN COTT. Calling your attention to Mr. B. H. Roberts in particular,

7. A few weeks prior to this testimony, Joseph F. Smith expressed his frustration to Smoot regarding the Democratic *Herald*'s coverage of the hearings: "Why cannot the Herald be made a respectable organ of its party, and a good Newspaper, and treat all sects on equal and honorable terms. As a republican and a 'Mormon' I think the Herald is a good thing, as it is, to drive democratic 'mormons' out of the party ranks, to the camp of 'the enemy'—or to the ranks of the populists. I hope good may come out of the evil it does" (Apr. 9, 1904).

and to the year 1895, yesterday you spoke of him being in everyone's mind for nomination. Will you explain that a little more in detail?

MR. POWERS. I did not mean all over the State. I meant at the convention.

MR. VAN COTT. That is what I understood [of] you.

MR. POWERS. Why, it seemed as if he was the choice of the party. That is what I mean by that.

MR. VAN COTT. And that included Mormons and gentiles?

MR. POWERS. Yes.

MR. VAN COTT. Mr. Roberts was a polygamist then?

MR. POWERS. I understand he was.

MR. VAN COTT. And living in unlawful cohabitation?

MR. POWERS. I did not know that at the time.

MR. VAN COTT. It was a matter of general reputation?

MR. POWERS. Not so much so as it was in the next campaign.

MR. VAN COTT. The next campaign? Very well.

MR. POWERS. Yes; in that campaign I do not think it was discussed at all by anybody. I do not recall now of having seen anything in any of the papers nor having heard anything concerning it.

MR. VAN COTT. At that time you knew, I suppose, that George Q. Cannon[8] had been expelled from Congress for being a polygamist?

MR. POWERS. I did.

MR. VAN COTT. Coming to the campaign of 1898, at that time it was known that Mr. Roberts, in all human probability, had obtained the consent of the church to run for that office?

MR. POWERS. Yes, sir.

MR. VAN COTT. Were you chairman that year?

MR. POWERS. What year was that?

MR. VAN COTT. 1898.

MR. POWERS. No; I was not chairman.

MR. VAN COTT. You took an active part in the campaign?

MR. POWERS. I took an active part in the campaign.

MR. VAN COTT. And you and other gentiles spoke for Mr. Roberts on the stump?

MR. POWERS. I spoke for Mr. Roberts on the stump; I went upon the stump

---

8. George Q. Cannon (1827-1901) was ordained an apostle on August 26, 1860. He served as a counselor to four church presidents, and beginning in 1872 he simultaneously served as Utah's territorial delegate to Congress. In April 1882, a month after the Edmunds Act passed, the House of Representatives expelled him from office for polygamy (David Buice, "A Stench in the Nostrils of Honest Men: Southern Democrats and the Edmunds Act of 1882," *Dialogue: A Journal of Mormon Thought* 21 [Fall 1988], 104.

for him. I defended him as well as I knew how, and, unlike some other Democrats who sustained the ticket and yet never mentioned his name, I mentioned his name in the meetings and spoke for him.

MR. VAN COTT. And made special arguments for him?

MR. POWERS. I made as good an argument for him as I could.

MR. VAN COTT. Well, that would be a good one.

MR. POWERS. I do not think that I was any more culpable in naming him and advocating him than you would have been if you had gone upon the stump, which I understand you did, and supported him without mentioning his name by supporting the ticket.

MR. VAN COTT. You mean supporting the ticket without mentioning his name?

MR. POWERS. Yes; supporting the ticket without mentioning his name.

MR. VAN COTT. It was known at that time that Mr. Roberts was living in unlawful cohabitation?

MR. POWERS. It was charged in the newspapers.

MR. VAN COTT. Well, it was general reputation, was it not?

MR. POWERS. It was general reputation. I must say I did not believe all that was charged against him.

MR. VAN COTT. It was charged in the "Tribune?"

MR. POWERS. It was charged in the "Tribune," but the "Tribune" does not own me, nor—it is not my guide in political matters. I try to guide [the *Tribune*] in the courts as well all I know how.

MR. VAN COTT. You supported Moses Thatcher in his candidacy for United States Senator?

MR. POWERS. I did.

MR. VAN COTT. In the legislature of 1896?

MR. POWERS. I did. I withdrew in his favor.

SENATOR DUBOIS. Before you go on with that, who was running against Mr. Roberts?

MR. POWERS. Mr. [Alma] Eldridge, of Coalville [Utah].

SENATOR DUBOIS. Was he gentile or Mormon?

MR. VAN COTT. He was a Mormon.

SENATOR DUBOIS. Well, compare the two Mormons, then—Mr. Roberts and Mr. Eldridge. How would you diagnose them?

MR. POWERS. I am very glad of the opportunity to make answer to that. There were charges made against Mr. Roberts in the newspapers, as I say, many of which I did not believe. I thought seriously over the matter as to what my duty was with regard to sustaining him on the stump as well as I could, and I took counsel and advised with the best coun-

cilor that I have upon earth. We discussed it all over. There was
Eldridge, without the ability of Roberts; there was Roberts, who was
competent and qualified for the position. There was Roberts, who, if
he was living in polygamy, as they charged, was simply doing that
which Eldridge connived at, aided, abetted, and believed in. I could
not see any distinction between the men in that regard. Besides, I was
a strong bimetallist. Mr. Roberts represented my views; Mr. Eldridge
did not. In addition to that, I noticed upon the stump, teaching the
people, such men as Apostle John Henry Smith, who was as culpable
as Mr. Roberts could be, and my friends on the other side were willing
to accept the aid of men of that class. So I determined that I would
support the ticket, as I have always done, and I went out upon the
stump and I defended him as well as I knew how. I did all I could to
help elect him, and under the circumstances I would do the same
thing again. I have nothing to take back. ...

Mr. Van Cott. Very many Mormons in the Democratic party were opposed to Roberts's candidacy, were they not?

Mr. Powers. They were opposed to his nomination, and I may say that I
did not vote for Mr. Roberts in the convention.

Mr. Van Cott. And they were opposed because he was a polygamist and
supposed to be living in unlawful cohabitation?

Mr. Powers. That was the opposition that was made to him.

Mr. Van Cott. Now, calling your attention to Moses Thatcher—Moses
Thatcher was also a polygamist at the time of that candidacy, was he
not?

Mr. Powers. He was a polygamist; but, as I have always understood it, he
was living within the law. I have always so been informed, and I never
knew anything to the contrary.

Mr. Worthington. What do you mean by that?

Mr. Powers. I mean by that that he was not living in unlawful cohabitation; that while he had been married to plural wives prior, he was
obeying the law of Congress. That is as I understood it.

Mr. Van Cott. Judge, do you understand that when a man like Apostle
[Heber J.] Grant, for instance, wages a campaign against Moses
Thatcher, that it is really the church?

Mr. Powers. No, not unless he is set apart, as the saying is, for that work.
With us [in Utah] we have a church phrase that if a man is designated
to do some particular thing, he is set apart to do it, and it has seemed
to us that Heber J. Grant has been set apart as the Democratic apostle
to make us trouble a good many times. (Laughter.) ...

MR. VAN COTT. Do not the Mormons vary in their opinions, some liberal, some very liberal, and others not so much so?

MR. POWERS. Yes; and I want to say, as I apprehend you are concluding my examination, that I have not intended any criticism of the Mormon people as a whole. They are like other people, and there is much that can be said in their favor. They are kind people. There are no people on earth that are more hospitable. There are no people that are better to their poor. There are no people who are more reverent toward the aged. It is the system that I condemn.

MR. VAN COTT. But, Judge, do not very many of the Mormons, for instance, object to the stand that is taken by some of their leaders on extremes such as this and other points?

MR. POWERS. They have objected to me, personally and privately—many of them, and yet one of their conferences would come along, and just exactly as I have told you with regard to leaving the name of Moses Thatcher off that list in that April conference, 1896, and promulgating that political manifesto, not one of them seemed to dare to say that his soul was his own, or stand up in defense of that man or in defense of the political liberties of the people. ...

MR. VAN COTT. Judge, there are a few questions that I desire to put to you. What have you to say, in a general way, about the interest of the Mormon people in education, both in their own schools and in the schools of the State?

MR. POWERS. I think the Mormon people have as much interest in the advancement of education and in the training of their youth as any people. I know that there is an impression abroad that such is not the fact, but we have as good schools in Utah as they have in Boston.

The Mormon Church schools are splendid educational institutions. They have many educators who would do credit to any people, and the State need not be ashamed of its school facilities, nor need it be ashamed of the record that many of its children have made. I want to say that in art, upon the stage, in the sciences, and in practical life it has many representatives of note. ...

So I say that the suggestion that Utah takes no interest in educational affairs and that her people are not progressive people along educational lines is inaccurate. ...

MR. VAN COTT. ... I wish you would state the attitude of Mormon jurors in regard to criminal cases generally, in regard to their fairness, their integrity, and things of that kind when serving as jurors?

MR. POWERS. Their attitude, so far as I have observed it, has been as fair as you could expect of any people. I have in mind one case where I defended a man where the Mormons naturally would be interested against him, and I had a jury that was both gentile and Mormon. My client received fair treatment.

MR. TAYLER. He was acquitted, was he?

MR. POWERS. He was acquitted. (Laughter.)

MR. VAN COTT. There are Mormon judges also in the State, are there not?

MR. POWERS. Yes; there are a number of Mormon judges.

MR. VAN COTT. And what have you to say about their conduct in the administration of the law?

MR. POWERS. I never have observed any indication on the part of the Mormon judges to do other than to follow the law as they understand it. By that I do not mean that they would understand it in a way that was unfair. I mean that they have not known Mormon or gentile, so far as I have observed, in their decisions. ...

THE CHAIRMAN. Judge, do you know Apostle Grant?

MR. POWERS. Do I know him?

THE CHAIRMAN. Yes.

MR. POWERS. I do, indeed.

THE CHAIRMAN. Where is he?

MR. POWERS. He is reputed to be in England—not in England. The last information concerning Grant was that he was over attending some kindergarten school in Germany, a representative of the State of Utah.[9]

THE CHAIRMAN. That is an international convention, is it not?

MR. POWERS. Yes.

THE CHAIRMAN. Has he been designated as a delegate, as you understand, to represent Utah?

MR. POWERS. Yes; the governor designated him as a delegate from the State of Utah.

THE CHAIRMAN. He is a great educator, I believe.

MR. POWERS. In some lines.

THE CHAIRMAN. What lines?

MR. POWERS. Well, he made a speech up at the university this last winter. He had been in Japan looking after the Japan missions, and he came back—

---

9. In a letter to Heber J. Grant on September 12, 1904, Francis M. Lyman offered that Powers's "testimony at Washington" was "some of the worst given and will do us the most damage when it is summed up" (Archives, Church of Jesus Christ of Latter-day Saints, Salt Lake City).

THE CHAIRMAN. The University of Utah?

MR. POWERS. Yes; he came back to Utah, and I think he was there a couple or three weeks. During those two or three weeks he was quite active. He made a speech at the University of Utah to the young men and women there, a State institution supported by the taxes of Mormons and gentiles, and he made a contribution of $150. He told them it was $50 for himself and $50 for each wife, having two, and he said that he regretted that the laws prevented him from having more.

THE CHAIRMAN. That was before the pupils of that State institution?

MR. POWERS. It was.

MR. WORTHINGTON. Were you there?

MR. POWERS. No. I wish I had been; because that is a matter that I, as well as other gentiles, have resented and desire to resent, and many of the Mormons, too, I guess. We do not like it.

THE CHAIRMAN. Do you know how it was received by the students?

MR. POWERS. There was no hostile demonstration to it.

THE CHAIRMAN. And he is the gentleman who is designated by the governor to represent the State at this great international convention?

MR. POWERS. Yes. During the same period he was home he went down to Provo, and in a public meeting he took a Mormon lawyer to task because he had undertaken for a woman a case which Grant thought clashed with the doctrines, perhaps, of the church; but they afterwards settled their differences by a signed card in the paper. I think the Mormon lawyer held his own.

THE CHAIRMAN. Do you know of any special reason why he is absent from the country at this time?

MR. POWERS. I understand that a warrant was issued for him and placed in the hands of the sheriff, and he departed suddenly.

THE CHAIRMAN. Upon his mission?

MR. POWERS. Upon his mission.

THE CHAIRMAN. Has he returned to this country since?

MR. POWERS. No; that is, we do not understand that he has. If he has, I do not believe that any body knows of it.

MR. WORTHINGTON. Where was the warrant issued, Judge?

MR. POWERS. In Salt Lake City.

MR. VAN COTT. Judge, was it not well known and understood in the community that Apostle Grant was going over on that mission before ever this warrant was issued?

MR. POWERS. I think so. I do not mean to be understood as saying that he went on the mission on account of the warrant being issued, but I

think he got out of town the way he did on account of the warrant being issued. As I understand, he left in the night. ...

MR. VAN COTT. As to what took place at the university at the time that
Grant spoke there, there were different versions of it in the newspapers, were there not?

MR. POWERS. I thought they all concurred pretty well that the substance
of it was as I have stated.

MR. VAN COTT. But as to the manner?

MR. POWERS. Yes; there were different versions as to the manner. Some
said he said it in a joking way and some said he said it seriously.

MR. WORTHINGTON. How many people were present at the time?

MR. POWERS. I do not know how many pupils they have now.

MR. WORTHINGTON. Well, several hundred people?

MR. POWERS. As I understand, the pupils of the university.[10] ...

---

10. For James E. Talmage's version of the Grant story, see *Smoot Hearings*, 3:420-23.
On April 24, 1904, Carl Badger noted in his journal:

> Ost Powers is the arch-hypocrite. He first told Van [Cott] and F[ranklin]. S. [Rich-
> ards] that he would be fair, and then after making as shameful an argument against
> us, said after he came off the stand the first day ... that he only wanted an opportunity
> to 'square' himself with the Mormons. On cross examination, Van went as far as pos-
> sible, even to a noticeable extent to give him an opportunity, and everything he said
> he qualified until it recoiled unfavorably upon us, and then when he got off the stand
> he complained that he had not been given a chance to say something favorable, that
> Van had not asked him something that would admit of anything favorable. Van
> asked him what he could say and the only thing he could think of was the educational
> activity of the people which would never [do] when he told that the doctrines of the
> church are there taught" (in Badger, *Liahona and Iron Rod*, 219).

13.
Moses Thatcher
Monday & Tuesday, April 25-26

"Afternoon sessions of the committee have been discontinued on account of the stress of business in the senate. All the Utah witnesses and counsel in the case, Mormon and Gentile, attended the baseball game between Columbia and Virginia this afternoon."
—*Salt Lake Herald,* Apr. 25, 1904

Moses Thatcher,[1] having been duly sworn, was examined and testified as follows[2] ...

MR. TAYLER. Prior to 1895, Mr. Thatcher, what controversies had you had with your quorum of apostles personal to yourself?

MR. THATCHER. Now, do you refer to the quorum as such or to the individual members?

MR. TAYLER. I mean to the quorum of apostles as apostles.

MR. WORTHINGTON. As a quorum?

MR. TAYLER. As a quorum.

MR. THATCHER. I do not remember, sir, that that question ever came before the quorum of the apostles.

MR. TAYLER. Had you conceived yourself, prior to 1895, as being out of harmony with your quorum?

---

1. At the time of this testimony, Moses Thatcher (1842-1909) was sixty-two years old and lived in Logan, Utah. He had trekked west with the main body of the Latter-day Saints in 1847. He was ordained an apostle on April 7, 1879, but was removed from office on April 6, 1896.

2. A day prior to Thatcher's testimony, Carl Badger noted in his journal that the former apostle made a "pathetic" show of himself in conversation with Badger:

He said he was broken in health; that he knew the gospel was true; that he knew that many of the people were praying for him; that he did not care for himself, but would not hurt the Church for anything; that this investigation was being conducted by men not half as worthy as those whom they were investigating. He said he had not slept ten hours in the four nights while in Washington; that at one time he had gone fifteen nights without four hours sleep, but it had been just such experiences as these which had broken him down. Bro. Thatcher said: 'If I can only get the spirit of the Lord when I am on the witness stand. I will be all right.' I told him that I felt that he would be helped for certainly there was never a time which he was more in need of it; nor the Church" (in Rodney J. Badger, *Liahona and Iron Rod: The Biography of Carl A. and Rose J. Badger* [Bountiful, Utah: Family History Publishers, 1985], 219).

MR. THATCHER. Only so far as disagreement on any question subject to discussion before such a body of men, which was reconciled. No, sir.

SENATOR DUBOIS. Mr. Tayler, would it disturb you if I ask Mr. Thatcher a question right there?

MR. TAYLER. No, sir.

SENATOR DUBOIS. The apostles have individual differences among themselves the same as Senators have individual differences among themselves, have they not?

MR. THATCHER. I think, sir, that the quorum recognizes the right of discussion freely on any question that comes before them.

SENATOR DUBOIS. And you can differ with individual members of your quorum, and no doubt do?

MR. THATCHER. Why, certainly.

MR. TAYLER. But except as to natural differences of opinion that might be thrashed out in discussion among you, you were not out of harmony with your quorum?

MR. THATCHER. I have always held the position that the right of discussion being freely accorded, after the majority decides a question, then a man would be out of harmony if he undertook to advance his own individual ideas.[3]

MR. TAYLER. Precisely; and upon that philosophy your conduct as an apostle was based?

MR. THATCHER. So far as I know, it was.

MR. TAYLER. In other words, if prior to 1895 you differed with the other members of the quorum of apostles respecting any subject which was discussed and had to be acted upon by you, and the majority was against you, you freely acquiesced in the determination of the majority and submitted your will to their determination?

MR. THATCHER. I have always sought to do so.

MR. TAYLER. And, as a matter of fact, so far as you know you did so?

MR. THATCHER. Yes, sir.

MR. TAYLER. When did you first learn that your brother apostles, or any of them, took offense at any conduct of yours or any position that you had taken?

MR. THATCHER. Would that question relate to political matters?

MR. TAYLER. I am referring now to what occurred in the fall of 1895. If

---

3. In a meeting of the Quorum of the Twelve in 1889, Thatcher and Heber J. Grant had accused George Q. Cannon, then in the First Presidency, of what they considered to be unscrupulous business dealings. See Ronald W. Walker, *Qualities That Count: Heber J. Grant as Businessman, Missionary, and Apostle* (Provo: BYU Studies, 2004), 195-229.

there was anything before that I would like to have you refer to it—I mean anything that eventuated in important results.

MR. THATCHER. The first that I can remember that there was any friction at all that could be called such was immediately subsequent to a speech which I made in the Ogden [Utah] Opera House, early, I think, in 1892. Perhaps I had better refer to that date so as to get it right. It was May, 1892. Shall I go on, sir?

MR. TAYLER. Yes; I will be very glad to have you proceed with any statement you desire to make in that connection.

MR. THATCHER. I was called from the audience or by the audience and addressed them upon general political principles, trying to show from my standpoint the advancement in civilization and the growth of liberty for a thousand years; and doubtless in that speech, of which I have not a copy I am sorry to say, I may have made some caustic allusions to my Republican friends.[4] I can not say as to that, because my memory does not serve me wholly; but at all events that speech called out severe criticisms on the part of the "Ogden Standard," the right of which on the part of the "Standard" I readily conceded, but it also called out an open letter which was published in the "Ogden Standard" at the same time, I think, and in the same issue, as the "Standard's" criticisms of the speech. That was signed by Joseph F. Smith and John Henry Smith as Republicans, descendants of Whigs.[5] ...

MR. VAN COTT. Will you state, in brief language, what was the point of conflict in your mind between the political manifesto or rule, as it is called, and your position?

MR. THATCHER. From the "Times" interview,[6] authorized by the presi-

---

4. According to Church President Wilford Woodruff, Thatcher said that "Satan was the Author of the Republican Party" (in Susan Staker, ed., *Waiting for World's End: The Diaries of Wilford Woodruff* [Salt Lake City: Signature Books, 1993], 392).

5. The two church leaders objected to Thatcher's assertion that Jesus Christ would be a Democrat. See Edward Leo Lyman, "The Alienation of an Apostle from His Quorum: The Moses Thatcher Case," *Dialogue: A Journal of Mormon Thought* 18 (Summer 1985): 73-74.

6. The "Times Interview" Thatcher refers to was the June 23, 1891, *Salt Lake Times* article, wherein Wilford Woodruff and George Q. Cannon were questioned about the dissolution of the People's Party:

[Q.] Are we to understand that the church will not assert any right to control the political action of its members in the future?

[A.] This is what we wish to convey and have you understand. As officers of the church we *disclaim* the right to control the political action of the members of our body. ...

[Q.] Is there any reason why the members of the church should not act freely with the national parties at all times?

dent of the church and signed by him, as I understand it, and his first councilor, George Q. Cannon, the noninterference of the church with political matters and with the liberty of the individual in reference to such matters was clearly set forth. The manifesto, as presented to me, and the impressions which it made on my mind, on the 6th day of October, 1896, seemed to be in conflict with those declarations; and as there had been at that time no definition of its scope and meaning as to the officers of the church to whom it might be applied, for that reason I was unable to accept it.

MR. VAN COTT. And you refused to sign it for that reason?

MR. THATCHER. That was the idea I had in my mind—it was on that ground.

MR. VAN COTT. Then followed your controversy and difference with the church authorities from then on until the high-council decision?[7]

MR. THATCHER. Yes, sir. ...

MR. VAN COTT. At the time that high-council decision was rendered, did you write a letter that went in as a part of the decision?

MR. THATCHER. Yes, sir. ...

MR. VAN COTT. And the decision of the high council and your letter and the acceptance of the presidency of the Salt Lake Stake of Zion all go as one document, do they not?

MR. THATCHER. I never could have accepted the decision of that high council in reference to that matter had I not fully understood that that letter became a part of the decision, which was to the effect that there was absolutely no conflict between the political manifesto as issued and published and the former declarations of the authorities as embodied in the "Times;" and I specifically referred to that fact in this letter. I make my letter a part of their decision, because it left me just where I stood before, absolutely free as an American citizen to exercise my right as such. It left all the officers of the church absolutely free, and the members, as I understood it, and as I now understand it. It simply applied to the higher authorities of the church, to which I had no objection. Is that an answer?

[A.] We know of no reason why they should not. ...

[Q.] Is it your understanding that the Mormon people differ [in opinion] as to the Republican and Democratic parties, and that they will act in accordance with their convictions in uniting with those parties?

[A.] That is our understanding (in *Smoot Hearings,* 1:976-77; emphasis added).

7. The Salt Lake Stake High Council ruled on August 14, 1897, that to retain his membership, Thatcher would have to publicly deny the church was trying to influence politics in Utah (Lyman, "Alienation of an Apostle," 89).

Mr. Van Cott. And the decision of the high council and your letter and the acceptance all went together?

Mr. Thatcher. All went together. ...

Mr. Van Cott. Mr. Thatcher, if that political manifesto at the time it was presented to you had been interpreted as it was by the high-council decision in connection with your letter and the acceptance, would you have signed the political rule?

Mr. Thatcher. Why, certainly.

Mr. Van Cott. Do you think, Mr. Thatcher, that there would have been any deposition from the quorum of apostles if you had understood in the beginning the interpretation that was given to that political rule by the high council?[8]

Mr. Thatcher. I do not think so.[9] ...

The Chairman. One other question. The endowment house, I believe, has been taken down?

Mr. Thatcher. That is as I understand it. It has been taken down.[10]

The Chairman. Has the ceremony of the endowment house been wiped out also, or is that performed now?

Mr. Thatcher. I am just trying to think whether I have been through the temple in the light in which I went through the endowment house, to give you a correct answer on that, but my impressions are that the ceremony has not been changed.

The Chairman. You have seen the ceremony in the temple? You have witnessed it?

Mr. Thatcher. I think I have heard it?

The Chairman. And you think there is no change in it?

Mr. Thatcher. No, sir.

The Chairman. When did you go through the endowment house?

Mr. Thatcher. My impressions are when I married the wife of my youth, in 1861.

The Chairman. Will you state to the committee the ceremony in the endowment house? I do not mean the ceremony of marriage; but did you go through the endowment house when you became an apostle?

Mr. Thatcher. No, sir; it was not necessary.

---

8. For more on Thatcher, see ibid., 67-91; Kenneth W. Godfrey, "Moses Thatcher in the Dock: His Trials, the Aftermath, and His Last Days," *Journal of Mormon History* 24 (Spring 1988): 54-88.

9. The previous two questions and answers were included in Tayler's closing argument for the plaintiffs; see *Smoot Hearings*, 3:660-61.

10. The Endowment House was razed in 1889.

THE CHAIRMAN. You have been through the endowment house, then, but once?

MR. THATCHER. Yes, sir.

THE CHAIRMAN. Will you state to the committee the ceremony of the endowment house?

MR. THATCHER. I think, Mr. Chairman, that I might be excused on that.

THE CHAIRMAN. Why?

MR. THATCHER. For the reason that those were held to be sacred matters and only pertaining to religious vows.

THE CHAIRMAN. Are you obligated not to reveal them?

MR. THATCHER. Yes, I think I am.

THE CHAIRMAN. What would be the effect if you should disclose them? That is, is there any penalty attached?

MR. THATCHER. There would be no effect except upon my own conscience.

THE CHAIRMAN. That is all?

MR. THATCHER. That is all.

THE CHAIRMAN. But you are under obligation as a part of the ceremony not to reveal it?

MR. THATCHER. Yes, sir; I feel myself under such obligation.[11]

THE CHAIRMAN. I have nothing further.

MR. TAYLER. Such obligation as is taken is taken but once, in whatever particular ceremony it may have occurred? I understood you to say you thought you went through the endowment house at the time of your marriage.

MR. THATCHER. Yes, sir.

MR. TAYLER. And at that time, whatever obligation in formal words was ever taken by one who passed through the endowment house, you took at the time of your marriage?

MR. THATCHER. I have only passed through the endowments once; that is all.

MR. TAYLER. Others might pass through the endowment house—that is to say, might go through a ceremony in which an obligation occurs—and not be married?

MR. THATCHER. They might; yes.

MR. TAYLER. Then I assume that this obligation to which I have referred and which you feel you have no right to disclose, is imposed on every person who passes through the endowment house and may be done

---

11. This entire exchange, as abridged, was included in the minority's report submitted by Senator Foraker on June 11, 1906; see *Smoot Hearings*, 4:532.

in connection with the marriage ceremony or in the absence of the marriage ceremony?

MR. THATCHER. That is my understanding of it; yes, sir. ...

MR. VAN COTT. Mr. Thatcher, you stated that when you ceased to be a member of the quorum of apostles, you were simply a member of the church, not an officer, and a free American citizen?

MR. THATCHER. Yes, sir.

MR. VAN COTT. Did you or not consider yourself a free American citizen while you were a member of the quorum of apostles?

MR. THATCHER. I am glad you asked the question, as perhaps my former answer would be misleading. I have never experienced a moment in my life since I reached mature years when I did not feel that if I was not free I would go where I would be free; for, while my allegiance to God is very high, I hold that a man must give his allegiance as well to this country. That has been my position[12] ...

MR. TAYLER. Mr. Chairman, I would like to have placed in the record the letter which President Joseph F. Smith wrote to the chairman in response to an inquiry that I made of him and a promise that he made to assist, in so far as he might, in procuring the attendance here of Apostle [John W.] Taylor and two or three other witnesses.

THE CHAIRMAN. Have you gentlemen any objection to that?

MR. WORTHINGTON. Certainly there is no objection. ...

THE CHAIRMAN. The president of the church writes me, explanatory of this, as follows:

Office of the First Presidency of the
Church of Jesus Christ of Latter-Day Saints,
Salt Lake City, Utah, April 15, 1904

Hon. Julius C. Burrows, Chairman
Committee on Privileges and Elections,
United States Senate, Washington D.C.

Sir: It is with regret that I inform you of my inability to procure the attendance of Messrs. John Henry Smith, George Teasdale, Marriner W[ood]. Merrill, John W. Taylor, and Matthias F. Cowley before the Senate Committee on Privileges and Elections.

---

12. The day after Thatcher's testimony, Carl Badger wrote in his journal:

Yesterday Moses Thatcher completed the statement he made before the Committee on Privileges and Elections. Aside from a few remarks which were volunteered and were not necessary to the answering of the questions asked him I think he did well from his standpoint. The day before, when he went to the stand, he was very nervous; and I think the adjournment was fortunate. When he commenced yesterday morning, he felt more at home" (in Badger, *Liahona and Iron Rod*, 220).

Hon. John Henry Smith is still quite ill, but has signified his willingness to appear before the committee, if desired, as soon as his health will permit.

I am informed that Mr. Marriner W[ood]. Merrill is still in such poor health that he is unable to leave his home.

My latest reports from Mr. Teasdale are to the effect that his health is still poor, but improving.

In accordance with the suggestion of Mr. Robert W. Tayler, I communicated to Messrs. John W. Taylor[13] and M[atthias]. F. Cowley[14] my earnest desire that they should appear and testify before the committee, and am in receipt of letters from them stating, in substance, that they are unwilling, voluntarily, to testify in the Smoot investigation. As this is a political matter, and not a religious duty devolving upon them or me, I am powerless to exert more than moral suasion in the premises.[15]

---

13. In a letter to Joseph F. Smith from Canada dated March 16, 1904, Taylor explained his reasons for not attending the hearings:

I do not think for a moment there is anything in the Smoot case which would warr[a]nt me neglecting my personal interests in order to go to Washington [D.C.] ... [T]he whole stir concerning Senator Smoot was hatched by that meddlesome coterie of busy bodies known as the Ministerial Association of Salt Lake City ... Those religio-political meddlers would have me carry faggots to their fire; in other words, they would use me to help carry out their diabolical schemes. President Smith, this I cannot do and maintain my own self respect. ... I trust you will not misunderstand me in this matter, or construe my refusal to voluntarily go before the Senatorial Committee to be in any wise disrespectful to you, and least of all as affecting in any way our official relations to the Church. ... In my official labors as an apostle in the Church, I hold myself entirely subject to your direction; but in a matter so personal and purely political, concocted for the purpose of prying into the domestic relations of men who are in nowise amenable to this class of schemers, nor even to the department of the U.S. government represented by this honorable committee, I must ask to be excused from entering upon a task so humiliating.

14. Twelve days after John W. Taylor declined to appear before the Senate committee, Cowley begged off from attending as well, explaining to President Smith that:

... my case does not differ materially from those of the Brethren already examined and as my testimony would be merely cumulative, I draw the conclusion that the purpose of those contesting the seat of Senator Smoot is to keep his case as long as possible before the country and to intensify thereby the prejudice and agitation of the people of the United States against the Church of Latter-day Saints and which Church is not a party to such proceedings. If subpoenaed, I should of course consider it my duty to go. Under the circumstances, however, I have concluded to decline making a voluntary appearance before the Senate Committee in Washington. I ask ther[e]for[e] to be excused in my refusal to accede to your request (Mar. 28, 1904, in Harvard S. Heath, "Reed Smoot: First Modern Mormon," Ph.D. diss., Brigham Young University, 1990, 127).

15. Six days prior to this letter to Burrows, Smith had informed Smoot of the responses the two missing apostles had sent him:

With reference to the others named the facts are as above stated. Again expressing my sincere regret that I am unable to procure the attendance of these gentlemen, I am,

Very respectfully, Joseph F. Smith. ...

You will see that they both refuse to voluntarily go before the Committee. Elder Cowley says if he is subpoenaed he will go but will not put himself in the way. I regret that these brethren have decided to do as they have. I would very much rather that they had been willing to go, but it is taken by them as a matter of conscience and not a matter of religion or church duty, and they must judge for themselves in such matters. And you will pardon me if I say that after the scandalous treatment I have received from the public press on account of my testimony given before the Committee, I cannot blame these gentlemen for the conclusion they have reached half so much as I might have done under other circumstances and fairer treatment. Of course you know how I have been horribly caricatured and made hideous in cartoons, and slandered and lied about most outrageously, and all for what? Well, I will not take time to answer here" (Apr. 9, 1904).

Kathleen Flake suggests that Smith could have compelled both apostles to testify but decided instead to recommend they not respond to the subpoenas. See Kathleen Flake, *The Politics of American Religious Identity: The Seating of Senator Reed Smoot, Mormon Apostle* (Chapel Hill: University of North Carolina Press, 2004), 102-03.

Angus M. Cannon Jr.

Monday, May 2

"The testimony of Angus [Cannon Jr.] ... had about as much foundation and amounted to as much real evidence as the gossip hearsay and balderdash to which the committee listened from Critchlow, Powers, Cobb and Hiles, and miscalled 'history.' ... Prurient curiosity may not be satisfied with the result of the latest phase of this investigation, but just and thoughtful men and women will have no doubt left as to the falsehood of the story as it affects President Smith." —*Deseret News*, May 3, 1904

Angus M. Cannon, jr.,[1] having been duly sworn, was examined, and testified as follows ...

MR. TAYLER. What relation was Apostle Abraham H. Cannon to you?

MR. CANNON. He was my cousin.

MR. TAYLER. Whose son was he?

MR. CANNON. George Q. Cannon.

MR. TAYLER. He died, I believe, in 1896.

MR. CANNON. In 1896.

MR. WORTHINGTON. That is, Abraham H. Cannon died then?

MR. CANNON. Yes, sir.

MR. TAYLER. Abraham H. Cannon—what was his age? How old was he when he died?

MR. CANNON. I think he was about 39.

MR. TAYLER. He was not far from your age? He was but a little older than you?

MR. CANNON. Not far from my age; a little over 2 years.

MR. TAYLER. You were raised together there?

MR. CANNON. Yes, sir.

MR. TAYLER. Had you always been friends?

MR. CANNON. Yes, sir.

MR. TAYLER. Had you been particularly intimate?

---

1. The witness was a son of Angus M. Cannon, who had testified less than two weeks earlier. Angus Jr. (1861-1913) was a resident of Salt Lake City and had lived there forty-two years. He was LDS but, by his admission, "not ... in good standing."

MR. CANNON. I had been very closely associated with him in business affairs.

MR. TAYLER. And personally you were intimate?

MR. CANNON. Yes, sir; we were very intimate. We were cousins.

MR. TAYLER. You were always warm friends?

MR. CANNON. Yes, sir.

MR. TAYLER. You say you had had business relations with him?

MR. CANNON. I was in his employ when he was managing the "Deseret News" ...

MR. TAYLER. Had you known of his associating with Lillian Hamlin prior to his death?

MR. CANNON. I had known of him taking her out riding.

MR. TAYLER. When and where?

MR. CANNON. In the month of May, 1896. I met them out one night. He was driving my horse and buggy. I met them out driving one evening.

MR. TAYLER. How often did you see them out driving?

MR. CANNON. Two or three times. ...

MR. TAYLER. What talk did you have with him in the summer of 1896 about Lillian Hamlin?

MR. CANNON. I never had any talk with him about her particularly. I had spoken to him about her, he having told me that she was engaged to his brother David, who had died on a mission to Germany.

MR. TAYLER. When did David die on his mission to Germany?

MR. CANNON. I have forgotten what year it was, but I think it was eleven or twelve years ago.[2]

MR. TAYLER. Some three or four years before Abraham died?

MR. CANNON. Yes; more than that.

MR. TAYLER. More than that?

MR. CANNON. Yes.

MR. TAYLER. He told you that she had been engaged to his brother David?

MR. CANNON. Yes, sir; to his brother David.

MR. TAYLER. Did he say that he was going to marry her.

MR. CANNON. No, sir.

MR. TAYLER. Did he not have a talk with you to that effect?

MR. CANNON. No, sir; he never did.

MR. TAYLER. Were you present when he married Lillian Hamlin?

MR. CANNON. No, sir.

---

2. David Cannon died on October 17, 1892, in Silesia, a region of Poland (Prussian at the time).

Mr. Tayler. Did you not see Joseph F. Smith marry them?

Mr. Cannon. No, sir.

Mr. Tayler. Did you within the last two weeks tell Mr. E. W. Wilson,[3] of Salt Lake, that you were present and saw Joseph F. Smith perform the marriage ceremony between Abraham H. Cannon and Lillian Hamlin?

Mr. Cannon. Yes, sir; I did tell him that.

Mr. Tayler. E. W. Wilson is a banker there, is he not?

Mr. Cannon. Yes, sir.

Mr. Tayler. You have known him a long time?

Mr. Cannon. Yes, sir.

Mr. Tayler. You and he have been personal friends?

Mr. Cannon. Yes, sir.

Mr. Tayler. The kindest relations have existed between you?

Mr. Cannon. Very warm friends. ...

Mr. Tayler. Did you tell him within the last two weeks that you were aboard a vessel which had been chartered by somebody at Los Angeles and that aboard that vessel was a party of ten or twelve people, who went to Catalina Island on it?

Mr. Cannon. Yes, sir.

Mr. Tayler. Did you say that among the party were Joseph F. Smith and one of his wives, Abraham H. Cannon and his wife, Mary Croxall, is it—

Mr. Cannon. I think I said that. I would not be positive. ...

Mr. Tayler. And Abraham H. Cannon and Lillian Hamlin?

Mr. Cannon. Yes, sir.

Mr. Tayler. And that after you had gone out a ways, before reaching Catalina Island, the party, with one or two exceptions, retired to the cabin, and that there Joseph F. Smith married Abraham H. Cannon and Lillian Hamlin?

Mr. Cannon. Yes, sir.

Mr. Tayler. Did you say to him that the third wife, Mary Croxall Cannon, when she discovered what was going on, became very angry, and refused to stay to witness the ceremony and left the cabin?

Mr. Cannon. He asked me how she took it and I said she got angry and left. I believe I told him something to that effect.

Mr. Tayler. Then did you say that it was understood that nothing was to be said about it?

---

3. Wilson was one of the original plaintiffs against Smoot (*Smoot Hearings,* 1:591).

MR. CANNON. I do not know that I said that. I may have. I would not be positive.

MR. TAYLER. Then did you go on to say that you went on to Catalina Island, and you all went in bathing?

MR. CANNON. I do not remember whether I did say that or not.

MR. TAYLER. Anyhow, you told Mr. Wilson, with considerable detail and circumstance, this story, the central point of which was that you had seen Joseph F. Smith marry Abraham H. Cannon and Lillian Hamlin?

MR. CANNON. Yes, sir.

MR. TAYLER. Now later in the same day, Mr. Wilson having sent for Mr. E. B. Critchlow, did you tell Mr. Critchlow the same story?

MR. CANNON. I told Mr. Critchlow practically the same story; that is, the story that you have just spoken of was the one related to both of them together. When I mentioned it to Mr. Wilson, I just mentioned the fact that Joseph F. Smith did know of plural marriages that had taken place since the manifesto.

MR. TAYLER. And he asked you what marriages?

MR. CANNON. And I told him that I saw him marry Abraham H. Cannon to Lillian Hamlin.

MR. TAYLER. And where?

MR. CANNON. I did not tell him then where.

MR. TAYLER. You are sure you did not tell him where?

MR. CANNON. I do not think I did, then. I might have.

MR. TAYLER. You have a very distinct recollection of what you told him?

MR. CANNON. Yes, sir; I have, and he told me he wanted to see me again; then I told him this story when he and Mr. Critchlow were together.

MR. TAYLER. You went over these details—

THE CHAIRMAN. The story you have just related you told both to Mr. Wilson and Mr. Critchlow?

MR. CANNON. Yes, sir.

THE CHAIRMAN. Was anyone else present?

MR. CANNON. No, sir; no one else was present.

MR. TAYLER. Then it was asked whether you would be willing to come to Washington and testify?

MR. CANNON. Yes, sir; they asked me that. I told them no; that I did not want to come to Washington, but I would go before the committee when it came to Utah, and testify there.

MR. TAYLER. And testify to that story?

MR. CANNON. Yes, sir.

MR. TAYLER. Later than that, did you, of your own volition, seek out Mr. Perry Heath[4] and tell him the same story?

MR. CANNON. No; I told Perry Heath, I believe it was the same day. I would not be positive.

MR. TAYLER. Where was he when you told him?

MR. CANNON. In the "[Salt Lake] Tribune" office.

MR. TAYLER. You went up there to see him?

MR. CANNON. Yes, sir; I telephoned him first, and he asked me if I could not come over to his office, and I went over there.

MR. TAYLER. Did you go over the story in detail to him, as you had to Mr. Critchlow and Mr. Wilson?

MR. CANNON. No, sir; I do not think I told him the whole story.

MR. TAYLER. What did you tell him?

MR. CANNON. Speaking about Joseph F. Smith's testimony in Washington, I think I told him that Joseph F. Smith did know of plural marriages that had been performed since the [Wilford Woodruff] manifesto. I told him that I knew that he married Abraham H. Cannon to Lillian Hamlin on the high sea near Los Angeles; something to that effect. I was to see him again, but I did not see him.

MR. TAYLER. You did not see him?

MR. CANNON. No, sir.

MR. TAYLER. Then about that time you received a subpoena to appear here before the committee?

MR. CANNON. Yes, sir.

MR. TAYLER. You could not come at once because you were ill or something of that sort?

MR. CANNON. Yes, sir. I was ill and I was unable to leave my bed for several days.

MR. TAYLER. You did not see him or Mr. Critchlow or Mr. Wilson again—

MR. CANNON. No, sir.

MR. TAYLER. After this talk you had with them?

MR. CANNON. No, sir.

MR. TAYLER. And you have not seen them since?

MR. CANNON. No, sir. I saw Mr. Critchlow the day I received the subpoena and I was to see him the next day, but I was too ill to go up town.

MR. TAYLER. Where was Mr. Critchlow when you saw him—the day you received the subpoena?

MR. CANNON. In his office.

---

4. Heath was the non-Mormon publisher and general manager of the *Salt Lake Tribune* (1902-04) and was active in Utah politics.

MR. TAYLER. What talk did you have then?

MR. CANNON. I talked with him about the subpoena. I was drinking at the time, and I said if I had to come to Washington I wanted him to arrange it so that my brother-in-law could come with me.

MR. TAYLER. That is Mr. Lynch?[5]

MR. CANNON. Yes, sir.

MR. TAYLER. When did you first tell this story to Mr. Lynch that you told to Mr. Critchlow and Mr. Wilson?

MR. CANNON. I do not think I told it to him [at] all.

MR. TAYLER. Do you mean that he has never heard the story from you?

MR. CANNON. I think he heard it from Critchlow and Wilson; some of those parties. I never told him the story.

MR. TAYLER. Do you mean that you had never talked with him about the marriage of Abraham H. Cannon to Lillian Hamlin?

MR. CANNON. I had talked to him about the matter and the marriage, but I do not think I ever told him I saw it.

MR. TAYLER. You told him you knew who had married them?

MR. CANNON. Yes, sir. I told him I was satisfied that Joseph F. Smith had married them.

SENATOR DUBOIS. Are you still satisfied of that?

MR. CANNON. Well, of course I do not know it, but I am satisfied in my own mind that he did.

THE CHAIRMAN. Where?

MR. CANNON. In California.

THE CHAIRMAN. On the occasion that you speak of?

MR. CANNON. I think it was at the time they were down in southern California.

MR. TAYLER. Who was the next person, Mr. Cannon, to whom you told this story after you had told it to Mr. Critchlow and Mr. Wilson and Mr. Heath?

MR. CANNON. I do not think I told it to anybody else.

SENATOR DUBOIS. The Maltby Building [in Washington, D.C.].

MR. CANNON. It is right across the way.

THE CHAIRMAN. You were inquiring for the room where the committee met?

MR. CANNON. Yes.

MR. TAYLER. Did you inquire for Senator Smoot?

MR. CANNON. No, sir.

---

5. Cannon's brother-in-law clerked for the United States Mining Company.

MR. TAYLER. This was a little time after you came in on the train?

MR. CANNON. No. I had been to the cafe down here on the corner opposite the B[altimore]. and O[hio]. [Railroad] depot and had had breakfast.

MR. TAYLER. You had breakfast?

MR. CANNON. Yes, sir.

MR. TAYLER. Then you inquired of this officer, who told you that in vacation[,] committees generally met in the Maltby Building?

MR. CANNON. Yes, sir.

MR. TAYLER. And when you got up to the Maltby Building you met Senator Smoot?

MR. CANNON. I met him coming out on this side.

MR. TAYLER. You went up with him to his committee room?

MR. CANNON. I addressed him and went up to his room and explained to
him how it was that I was subpoenaed down here.

THE CHAIRMAN. You explained it to whom?

MR. CANNON. I did not explain it fully.

THE CHAIRMAN. But to whom did you explain it?

MR. CANNON. To Senator Smoot. ...

MR. CANNON. I met Mr. Smoot, and we went up to his room in that building, and he told me that the committee met at 11:30. I said, "I will
have plenty of time to go and get shaved." Carl Badger, who is a former acquaintance of mine in Salt Lake, was there, and Senator Smoot
asked him to show me the way to the barber shop. He came over with
me. He left me in the barber shop, and I got shaved and went back.

MR. TAYLER. You went back over to Senator Smoot's room?

MR. CANNON. Yes, sir.

MR. TAYLER. Was it during the first or the second visit that you told him
how it was that you came to be subpoenaed?

MR. CANNON. I told him partially at first, and I then told him and Mr.
Richards together there that I had been drinking and how it was that I
happened to get talking with Wilson and what statement I had made
to him—to Wilson—

MR. TAYLER. You told Mr. Smoot what story you had told Mr. Wilson?

MR. CANNON. Yes, sir; Mr. Wilson and Mr. Critchlow. I did not tell him in
full, I think; not as fully as I have here.

MR. TAYLER. Did anybody talk with you about it after you saw Mr.
Critchlow and Mr. Wilson and Mr. Heath in Salt Lake?

MR. CANNON. No, sir. ...

MR. TAYLER. How, if you were not present, did you get the information that Joseph F. Smith had married Abraham H. Cannon and Lillian Hamlin?

MR. CANNON. I got the impression from what I had heard my sister[6] say.

MR. TAYLER. Your sister.

MR. CANNON. I had heard her say—

MR. WORTHINGTON. Is this competent, Mr. Chairman?

THE CHAIRMAN. I think under the circumstances, Mr. Worthington, we will hear this witness.

MR. CANNON. I had heard her say that she was satisfied that President Smith had performed the ceremony.

MR. TAYLER. Your sister was Abraham Cannon's second wife, I believe?

MR. CANNON. Yes, sir.

SENATOR DUBOIS. Have you not heard Frank Cannon, who is a brother of Abraham H. Cannon, say that he was satisfied that they were married?

MR. CANNON. No: I never heard him say it. ...

SENATOR DUBOIS. Do they not recognize her as one of the family?

MR. CANNON. Yes, sir.

SENATOR McCOMAS. As the wife of Abraham H. Cannon?

MR. CANNON. As the wife of Abraham H. Cannon.

SENATOR McCOMAS. You were in California once with Abraham H. Cannon?

MR. CANNON. I never was down there with him.

SENATOR McCOMAS. Were you ever in California?

MR. CANNON. Yes, sir.

SENATOR McCOMAS. When?

MR. CANNON. I was there last in 1891.

SENATOR McCOMAS. What was the year he was there when he is supposed to have been married?

MR. CANNON. In 1896.

MR. WORTHINGTON. He died in 1896.

SENATOR McCOMAS. Did you tell Mr. Wilson that you had been in California with Abraham H. Cannon?

MR. CANNON. I think so. I told him I was there at the marriage of Abraham H. Cannon.

SENATOR McCOMAS. That you were on the vessel?

MR. CANNON. Yes, sir.

---

6. Wilhelmina Mousley Cannon (1859-1941) married Abraham Cannon on October 15, 1879.

SENATOR McCOMAS. And that you had seen these people when they went down into the cabin and were married.

MR. CANNON. Yes, sir.

SENATOR McCOMAS. And you gave the names of the people who were present?

MR. CANNON. Yes, sir.

SENATOR McCOMAS. And then when Mr. Critchlow and Mr. Wilson came you repeated with more detail the same statement about the matter?

MR. CANNON. I repeated the same thing.

SENATOR McCOMAS. Did you call up Mr. Heath, or did he call you up?

MR. CANNON. I called him up. I told him I was satisfied that Joseph F. Smith knew of plural marriages that had taken place since the manifesto.

SENATOR McCOMAS. You told him substantially the same story?

MR. CANNON. I told him part of it. I did not give him the details.

SENATOR McCOMAS. You told him about the marriage ceremony having been performed by Joseph F. Smith?

MR. CANNON. Yes, sir.

SENATOR McCOMAS. And the stateroom of the vessel where it was performed?

MR. CANNON. I did not tell him it was in a stateroom. I did not tell him it was on a vessel, I think, but I simply said in California.

SENATOR McCOMAS. You said to Mr. Critchlow and Mr. Wilson that it was on a vessel, and gave the details?

MR. CANNON. Yes, sir.

SENATOR McCOMAS. Then when you spoke to Mr. Lynch, your brother-in-law, did you tell him what you had told Wilson and Critchlow?

MR. CANNON. I told him what I had told them. I was sick at home and I told him to go to these fellows and see if they could not get the subpoena withdrawn; it was all hot air. ...

SENATOR McCOMAS. And now, in your judgment, it is not hot air. You believe that Joseph F. Smith performed the marriage ceremony between Abraham H. Cannon and Lillian Hamlin?

MR. CANNON. I believed I knew—

SENATOR McCOMAS. And now you do not believe it was hot air?

MR. CANNON. I do not think there was any hot air about the marriage, but it was hot air about my being present.[7]

---

7. The *Deseret News* picked up on the term "hot air" and reported that even the "examining attorney," Mr. Tayler, exhibited "disgust" at Angus's reversal in testimony, that "the committee has been kept here and attorneys brought from long distances just to

SENATOR McCOMAS. And about the ceremony having been performed by Joseph F. Smith?

MR. CANNON. Yes, sir.

THE CHAIRMAN. You have said that you were satisfied that plural marriages were being performed?

MR. CANNON. I think that marriage was performed.

THE CHAIRMAN. You say you were satisfied that plural marriages were being performed?

MR. CANNON. Yes, sir.

THE CHAIRMAN. Did you ever hear of any other plural marriages except this one?

MR. CANNON. I never heard of any other.

THE CHAIRMAN. You had in mind only this one marriage?

MR. CANNON. Yes, sir.

SENATOR McCOMAS. Is it hot air that ... the other people whom you have detailed to Mr. Tayler as being present at that marriage?

MR. CANNON. I was talking to Wilson and Critchlow. I done it more to make them feel good than anything else, when I was telling them that story.

SENATOR McCOMAS. How would it make them feel good?

MR. CANNON. Anything they thought would hurt the Mormon Church, or would go against it, would tickle them all over.

THE CHAIRMAN. And being a Mormon, you were trying to please them?

MR. CANNON. I was drinking at the time. I was doing it more as a joke than anything else. I had no idea that it would ever come to this, that I would be subpoenaed to Washington.

THE CHAIRMAN. After the subpoena was served on you, Mr. Heath and Mr. Critchlow and Mr. Wilson were all within reach. Why did you not call them up at once?

MR. CANNON. I was still drinking at the time. When I came to myself I was sick. I had an appointment with Mr. Critchlow uptown, but could not keep it, so I got my brother-in-law, James Lynch—

THE CHAIRMAN. That we understand. ...

SENATOR McCOMAS. You said a while ago that you told this thing as a joke.

---

hear him tell his [hearsay] beliefs ("Angus M. Cannon Jr.'s Testimony," May 2, 1904). The next day, the *News* continued this theme, offering that "Critchlow, lawyer, and 'Mormon' hater," and "Wilson, politician and banker, have been 'gold-bricked.' They admit that. Their friends have been laughing about it all day and the incident will be the subject of a vast amount of witticism and good natured joshing for a long time to come" ("Critchlow and Wilson Were 'Gold-Bricked,'" May 3, 1904).

Being kindly to Joseph F. Smith and having been a friend of Abraham H. Cannon, what was the joke when Abraham was dead to impute to him and to the head of the church a serious violation of the law? What was the joke, in your mind?

MR. CANNON. I was just talking to Wilson and Critchlow. I did not think it would result in anything.

SENATOR McCOMAS. You liked Cannon, and yet you imputed to this dead friend of yours a crime. Why did you do that and call it a joke?

MR. CANNON. I was speaking more about Joseph F. Smith having performed the ceremony, and I was not casting any reflection on Abraham.

SENATOR McCOMAS. But you did impute to Joseph F. Smith and Abraham Cannon a violation of the laws of the country. You knew your friend Abraham H. Cannon was dead. Why did you do that?

MR. CANNON. I was not thinking about that at the time. I was thinking more about Joseph F. Smith than anything else.

SENATOR McCOMAS. You felt kindly toward him?

MR. CANNON. Not particularly so.

SENATOR McCOMAS. Did you or did you not know that the statement had been made here by Joseph F. Smith that this marriage had not taken place?

MR. CANNON. I had read his testimony where he had said that he did not know of any plural marriages.

SENATOR McCOMAS. Yet you did impute to him this marriage after you had heard of his testimony here?

MR. CANNON. Yes, sir; after I had heard of his testimony here.

THE CHAIRMAN. Whom did you first tell that this story was untrue?

MR. CANNON. My wife and Mr. Lynch, my brother-in-law.

THE CHAIRMAN. Since you left Utah, whom have you told that it was untrue?

MR. CANNON. I told Mr. Tayler.

THE CHAIRMAN. Did you tell Mr. Smoot?

MR. CANNON. I told Mr. Smoot what I had told them. I did not tell him—

THE CHAIRMAN. You say you told your wife before you left that the story was untrue?

MR. CANNON. Yes, sir. She knew it was untrue because she knew I was not in California that year.

THE CHAIRMAN. If you told her it was untrue the day you left, could you not have told Wilson and Critchlow?

MR. CANNON. I did not see them.

THE CHAIRMAN. Why could you not see them? The marshal could have taken you to their offices.

MR. CANNON. The marshal was down to the house and I had to get ready. I was not ready.

THE CHAIRMAN. Why did you not tell them?

MR. CANNON. If I had made an effort I suppose I could have. I intended to try—

THE CHAIRMAN. Why did you not make the effort?

MR. CANNON. I told the marshal I would leave on Friday, and he came down on Thursday—

THE CHAIRMAN. Did you not know that you had been subpoenaed, because of the statement you had made to Mr. Wilson and Mr. Critchlow?

MR. CANNON. Yes, sir; and that is the reason I got my brother-in-law to go to them and try to have the subpoena withdrawn.[8] ...

---

8. A few days later, the *Deseret News* reported:

Senator Reed Smoot returned today from the national capital, and was warmly welcomed by a host of friends of different political and religious faiths and opinions. He looked well and hearty and has gained ten pounds in weight since he last left his city. He feels cheerful and confident over the outlook, and does not show any signs of that 'worry' which some people and papers have imagined he was suffering. The Senator has been an active worker, particularly as a member of the committee on pension and of the committee on claims. ... Smoot did not appear anxious to go into detail in relation to the good work he has performed for the benefit of this State, nor to claim what is due to him in that regard, and attributed to others ("Senator Smoot Home," May 6, 1904).

In another *News* article the same day, Smoot was quoted as saying: "I haven't the least doubt in the world but what I will be seated. ... I have never intentionally done a man, woman or child a wrong in my life. If I have, I am willing at this or any other time to make reparation. There is nothing to prevent my being a good American citizen. If the time ever comes when I can't be a good citizen of the United States I am going to leave it. I do not want to live in a country when I cannot be a good citizen." When asked if a Senate sub-committee was coming to Utah for further investigation, he responded: "Personally, I know nothing about my case. It does not interest me half as much as it does some other people. I am going ahead and doing my duty as a senator just as though nothing of the kind were in progress. I have read that a sub-committee is to come to Utah. It can do so as far as I am concerned. It can go where it pleases; do as it pleases. I court the fullest investigation possible. I have done nothing wrong; there is not reason why I should not be seated, consequently, the matter does not worry me in the least" ("Smoot Says He Is Confident").

Senator Julius Caesar
Burrows (R-Mich.), chair
of the Committee on
Privileges and Elections.
Courtesy Library of Con-
gress, Prints and Photo-
graphs Division, LC-DIG-
cwpbh-05225.

LDS President Joseph F. Smith at the witness table. *New
York Herald*, Mar. 10, 1904.

Salt Lake City attorney
Waldemar Van Cott assisted
D.C. attorney A. S. Worthington in Smoot's defense. Courtesy Utah State Historical Society.

SENATOR SMOOT HEARS PRESIDENT SMITH'S TESTIMONY.

The *Salt Lake Herald*,
Mar. 4, 1904, imagined
the shock to Senator
Smoot when President
Joseph F. Smith conced-
ed that he had fathered
eleven children by five
wives since the Mani-
festo. Courtesy Brigham
Young University Family
History Center.

SCENES AT THE SMOOT HEARING.

Some of the participants in the hearings acquired quasi-celebrity status as their words and likenesses were broadcast around the country. *Washington Post*, Mar. 11, 1904. Courtesy L. Tom Perry Special Collections, Brigham Young University

SCENES AT THE SMOOT SENATORIAL INQUIRY.

The lead defense attorney was Augustus S. Worthington (top, left), a prominent Washington, D.C., lawyer. Edward B. Critchlow (top, right), shown here
testifying, was a Utah legislator, Assistant U.S. Attorney in Utah, and one of
nineteen signers of the Salt Lake Ministerial Association's petition to unseat
Senator Smoot. *Washington Post*, Mar. 12, 1904. Courtesy L. Tom Perry Special
Collections, Brigham Young University.

Senator Fred Thomas Dubois (D-Idaho), Smoot's nemesis. Courtesy Library of Congress, Prints and Photographs Division, LC-USZ62-54438.

Senator Albert Jeremiah Beveridge (R-Ind.) supported Smoot until closing arguments when the Indiana Senator became "very unsettled in his mind." He ultimately voted in Smoot's favor. Courtesy Library of Congress, Prints and Photographs Division, LC-USZ62-61460.

Franklin S. Richards was the attorney representing the interests of the LDS Church at the hearings.

Carl Badger, secretary to Reed Smoot, was twenty-six years old when the hearings began. Photograph from Elwood Esshom, *Pioneers and Prominent Men of Utah*, 1913, p. 54.

Chairman (Executive Session)—Well! Now what shall be our next move against the Mormon Church?

The LDS *Elders' Journal,* Mar. 1, 1907, portrayed the hearings as an attack on the church, with committee chair Burrows as the devil. Courtesy L. Tom Perry Special Collections, Brigham Young University.

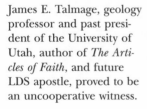

James E. Talmage, geology professor and past president of the University of Utah, author of *The Articles of Faith*, and future LDS apostle, proved to be an uncooperative witness.

Alpha May Smoot, wife of Senator Reed Smoot, attended the
hearings for the first time on
April 12, 1906, to hear the closing arguments. Courtesy Utah
State Historical Society.

LDS Apostle Moses
Thatcher was a confirmed
Democrat. He stated in
1892 that "Satan was the
author of the Republican
Party."

B. H. Roberts, a president of the LDS First Council of Seventy, was opposed to church interference in politics.

What's the Constitution Between Friends!

A witness in the Smoot case, Roberts was himself denied a seat in the U.S. House of Representatives in 1898 because he had three wives. *Salt Lake Tribune*, Feb. 22, 1905. Courtesy Brigham Young University Family History Center.

A ghoulish patriarch is depicted bringing an Easter gift to one of his incarcerated wives. *New York World*, Mar. 13, 1904.
Courtesy Perry-Casteñeda Library, University of Texas at Austin.

The *Salt Lake Herald*, Utah's major Democratic-leaning newspaper, once edited by B. H. Roberts, took soft jabs at Smoot, portraying him as a "featherweight," Jan. 7, 1904.

Editor of The News Revising Revelations and He Obeys As It Is "Revised."

Throughout the hearings, the newspaper wars in Utah were heated—the *Deseret News* supporting Smoot and the *Tribune* opposing him. *Salt Lake Tribune,* Dec. 18, 1904.

When the hearings resumed after a seven-month recess, Smoot was out of the frying pan into the fire again. *Pittsburg Post*, Dec. 14, 1904. Courtesy Perry-Casteñeda Library, University of Texas at Austin.

ON THE FIRE AGAIN.

LET PRESIDENT SMITH GET THIS REVELATION.

Mormon reverence for the U.S. Constitution apparently did not extend to its amendments, according to the *Salt Lake Tribune*, Mar. 16, 1905.

John G. Carlisle (D-Ky) was co-counsel for the prosecution. He had previously served in the U.S. Congress (Speaker of the House), the U.S. Senate, and in President Grover Cleveland's cabinet as Secretary of the Treasury.
Courtesy Library of Congress, Prints and Photographs Division, LC-BH826-30848.

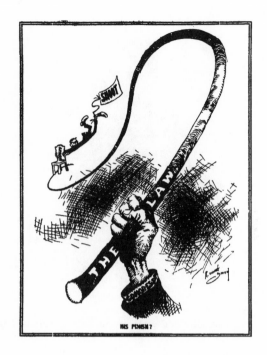

The general impression was that Smoot was holding onto his Senate seat by his fingernails. *Pittsburg Post*, Jan. 30, 1905. Courtesy Perry-Casteñeda Library, University of Texas at Austin.

NOT AFRAID OF BEARS

Teddy Roosevelt stood by his fellow Republican from Utah at considerable political cost. *Salt Lake Tribune*, Mar. 25, 1906.

But Wasps are More Than the President can Endure

As the hearings entered their third year, the prospects for Smoot's exoneration looked increasingly slim. *Washington Post*, Mar. 3, 1906.

On December 11, 1906, the U.S. Senate debate on whether to expel Smoot began with a scathing tirade by Burrows, followed two days later by an equally venemous attack by Dubois. *Salt Lake Tribune*, Dec. 14, 1906.

V.

DECEMBER

1904

15.

George Reynolds

Monday, December 12

"When the senate elections committee met at 20 minutes before 11 this morning to continue its hearing ... the scene in the committee room showed [only] slight changes from ... last May. There was about the same number of women gathered, ... little changed from last season. Scattered through the room were some 15 or 20 residents of Utah who are understood to have come to testify ... Owing to a heavy snow which covers the streets to the depth of more than a foot, very few curiosity seekers appeared among the audience."
—*Deseret News*, Dec. 12, 1904

George Reynolds,[1] being duly sworn, was examined and testified as follows ...

MR. TAYLER. As you have a certain method of joining in marriage, do you also have one for severing the marriage relation?

MR. REYNOLDS. Yes, sir; the church grants divorce of those who have been married for time and eternity. For the legal wives that is not done until the courts have acted and separated the parties. For plural wives—that is, marriages which are not recognized by the law, they are granted divorces on application, without any action of the courts, because the courts will take no action, as they do not recognize the marriage.

SENATOR FORAKER. Are these divorce proceedings confined to the living? You spoke of marriages after death.

MR. REYNOLDS. I have known very rarely of a woman seeking to be separated from her husband after he was dead, and the president of the church hearing her statement has directed that the marriage be canceled on the records.

SENATOR FORAKER. Do you say you have heard of that frequently or infrequently?

MR. REYNOLDS. No, sir; not frequently. Once in a long while.[2]

---

1. At the time of his testimony, Reynolds (1842-1909) lived in Salt Lake City and was a secretary to the LDS First Presidency, as well as a president of the Council of Seventy. His 1878-79 trial before the U.S. Supreme Court had been a test case for polygamy.

2. The previous two questions and answers were used by Tayler in his closing argument for the plaintiffs (*Smoot Hearings*, 3:579).

MR. TAYLER. Is it not also customary for those who have been married solely for eternity—that is to say, a living person married to a dead person—to have that marriage also dissolved?

MR. REYNOLDS. I have no recollection of ever having heard of such a thing or having to do with anything of that kind. I presume it is possible.

MR. TAYLER. It is possible.

MR. REYNOLDS. It is possible; but it has not come in my experience according to my present recollection.

MR. TAYLER. How often have you known of a divorce being granted by the church to a man or a woman whose husband or wife, as the case may be, had died?

MR. REYNOLDS. I can not answer that question.

MR. TAYLER. Many times?

MR. REYNOLDS. I should not call it many; a few I should say.

SENATOR FORAKER. You confined your statement, as I understood you, to cases where women had applied for divorces from husbands who were deceased?

MR. REYNOLDS. Yes, sir.

SENATOR FORAKER. Have there been any cases where the husband has applied for a divorce from the wife who was deceased?

MR. REYNOLDS. Never to my knowledge.

MR. TAYLER. Do you know whether the church grants a divorce, in so far as the church can do so, to what are called legally married persons prior to the order of the court in that respect?

MR. REYNOLDS. In the early history of the church in Utah they did so, but for very many years they have not done so.

MR. TAYLER. Ordinarily—

SENATOR FORAKER. Mr. Tayler, if I do not interrupt you—

MR. TAYLER. Not at all.

SENATOR FORAKER. I should like to ask another question before we get away from the matter. It is about these divorces that are granted to women from their husbands who are deceased. Is that divorce, in the few cases you have referred to, granted on account of something that the man did in lifetime or something he is supposed to have done after death?

MR. REYNOLDS. In lifetime. We do not know anything they do after death.

SENATOR FORAKER. The proceeding is taken against him without making him a party or giving him a chance to be heard?

MR. REYNOLDS. That is exactly it, and that is why so few have been granted, because it has been regarded as unjust to the person who could not appear. But when the wife produced evidence sufficient to cause it to be evident that he had done certain things, making him unworthy of being her husband, then the divorce has sometimes been granted.

SENATOR FORAKER. Is anyone appointed to defend the dead man in such cases?

MR. REYNOLDS. No, sir.

SENATOR FORAKER. The proceeding is purely ex parte?

MR. REYNOLDS. Purely.

MR. TAYLER. Then the man who dies, the fortunate possessor of a half a dozen wives, has no assurance that he will find them at the end; that is to say, the church on earth has the power to dissolve after a man's death the bonds of matrimony that have tied him to several wives?

MR. REYNOLDS. Yes, sir.

THE CHAIRMAN. I understand you to say that the power exists and is exercised through the president of the church?

MR. REYNOLDS. When exercised, it is exercised through the president of the church. He is the only man who has the right to seal and to loose.

THE CHAIRMAN. The president alone.

MR. TAYLER. So that, in so far as celestial marriage is concerned [with] the relation of husband and wife in the future world, the president of the church has absolute control of the fact of that relation and can dissolve it at will?

MR. REYNOLDS. That is the theory.

SENATOR OVERMAN. What notice do you receive that a person who is dead desires baptism?

MR. REYNOLDS. As a general thing it is done by the descendants of the dead—the son, the daughter, the grandson, the granddaughter, or other relative—who feel an interest in the salvation of their ancestors, and go and perform the work. Sometimes they will be notified in dreams or visions or by direct communication from the dead that they wish this done. But as a general thing it is done by reason of the love and regard they bear for their ancestors.

SENATOR OVERMAN. The communication generally comes by a dream?

MR. REYNOLDS. If any communication comes at all; but as a general thing there is no communication, only what they deem the inspiration of the spirit of the Lord to do the work.

MR. TAYLER. That applies generally to those who in their lifetime did not have the opportunity of learning of the Mormon Church and its belief?

MR. REYNOLDS. Those who have not had the opportunity to accept the Gospel in its fullness as now preached upon earth. ...

MR. TAYLER. You are familiar with the several volumes printed by the church called "Journal of Discourses?"

MR. REYNOLDS. I have read them sometimes, sir. I am not familiar with them. They ceased to be published a number of years ago.

MR. TAYLER. It is a well-known publication, is it not, among your people?

MR. REYNOLDS. It was when it was published.

MR. TAYLER. Is it not known now?

MR. REYNOLDS. It ceased to be published many years ago.

MR. TAYLER. Yes; it ceased to be published, but it has not gone out of the knowledge or memory of men, has it?

MR. REYNOLDS. Not of the older members, sir; but the copies preserved are very few. Very few of our people have ever seen it.

MR. TAYLER. You think very few of your people read the discourses of Brigham Young?

MR. REYNOLDS. Far fewer than there ought to be in my opinion.

MR. TAYLER. I only want to call attention to a statement of the doctrine you have just referred to, which seems to me to accord with what you have said, to ask you whether it is recognized by the church as correctly representing your view of the authority of the president of the church in this matter of severing the marital bond.

MR. WORTHINGTON. What is the date of that?

MR. TAYLER. This is a book in the Congressional Library. I did not want to have it put in the record. I will ask you to look at the book. ...

MR. TAYLER. This book, as you are aware, contains a large number of sermons and discourses by various officials of the Mormon Church, as recited in the title page, and among them Brigham Young. Now, on page 55 of this volume, in a sermon entitled "The people of God disciplined by trials—Atonement by the shedding of blood—Our Heavenly Father—A privilege given to all the married sisters in Utah. A discourse by President Brigham Young, delivered in the Bowery, Great Salt Lake City, September 21, 1856," I find the following: "Now, for my proposition. It is more particularly for my sisters, as it is frequently happening that Women say they are unhappy. Men will say, 'My wife, though a most excellent woman, has not seen a happy day since I took my second wife; no, not a happy day for a year,' says one. And another has not seen a happy day for five years. It is said that women are tied down and abused; that they are misused and have not the liberty they ought to have; that many of them are wading through a perfect flood of tears because of the conduct of some men, together with their own folly.

"I wish my own women to understand that what I am going to say is for them as well as others, and I want those who are here to tell their sisters, yes, all the women of this community, and then write it back to the States, and do as you please with it. I am going to give you from this time to the 6th day of October next for reflection, that you may determine whether you wish to stay with your husbands or not, and then I am going to set every woman at liberty and say to them: 'Now, go your way, my women with the rest, go your way.' And my wives have got to do one of two things—either round up their shoulders to endure the afflictions of this world and live their religion or they may leave, for I will not have them about me. I will go into heaven alone rather than have scratching and fighting around me. I will set all at liberty."

Do you understand that to be an expression by Brigham Young of the doctrine of authority to divorce?

MR. REYNOLDS. No, sir; he spoke as an individual with regard to his wives. I don't understand that he spoke as the president of the church.

MR. TAYLER. I did not put my question that way.

MR. REYNOLDS. Excuse me, then, sir; I so understood it.

MR. TAYLER. I will ask the stenographer to repeat the question.

The question was read, as follows: "Do you understand that to be an expression by Brigham Young of the doctrine of authority to divorce?"

MR. REYNOLDS. No; I don't think it related to his official authority as president of the church to divorce.

MR. TAYLER. Do you mean that Brigham Young did not intend by that language to say that if certain things did not happen he would divorce these women?

MR. REYNOLDS. He certainly did not do it.

MR. TAYLER. I am not asking if he did. I am asking you whether that was what he meant by that statement.

MR. REYNOLDS. I don't think he meant it at that time.

MR. TAYLER. Then what do you think he meant by it?

MR. REYNOLDS. I simply think that he was talking as a man does sometimes when he gets annoyed and did not mean what he said.

MR. TAYLER. Do you understand that that was habitual with Brigham Young?

MR. REYNOLDS. No, sir; but it was occasional.

MR. TAYLER. And when he made this proclamation to his people he did not intend ever to exercise it?

MR. REYNOLDS. That is my understanding.

MR. TAYLER. That may be true; but do you mean that he did not intend to be interpreted as assuming the power and ability to do it?

MR. REYNOLDS. It don't strike me at all in that light.

MR. TAYLER. It does not?

MR. REYNOLDS. I don't believe it; no, sir.

MR. TAYLER. What do you think he meant when he said this, immediately after what I have read: "I will set all at liberty. What, first wife, too? Yes; I will liberate you all." What did he mean by that?

MR. REYNOLDS. If he was serious, he meant ecclesiastically he would liberate them.

MR. TAYLER. What do you mean by "liberate them?"

MR. REYNOLDS. What I believe he intended to say was to free them from their marriage relations; but I don't believe he was serious for a moment.

MR. TAYLER. That is the same thing, is it not, as you have stated to us the President now has authority to do?

MR. REYNOLDS. Yes; but he doesn't do it, only when it is brought before him in a regular manner by the complainant.

MR. TAYLER. Exactly.

MR. REYNOLDS. Not on general principles.

MR. TAYLER. Is there any limitation on the method by which the president shall exercise that authority?

MR. REYNOLDS. It is either on the complaint of the party directly, either personally or in writing, by complaint made through their local officers—their bishops.

MR. TAYLER. Where did the president of the church get his authority to loose on earth?

MR. REYNOLDS. By that same authority and revelation that gave him the authority to bind on earth.

MR. TAYLER. Precisely. Was that authority given to him with any limitation?

MR. REYNOLDS. Only those limitations that righteousness and justice require.

MR. WORTHINGTON. That authority is in writing in the books, is it not, Mr. Tayler?

MR. TAYLER. I suspect it is. Who is the judge of what are righteous limitations?

MR. REYNOLDS. He must be.

MR. TAYLER. Proceeding with this sermon of Brigham Young's I quote: "I know what my women will say; they will say, 'You can have as many women as you please, Brigham.' But I want to go somewhere and do something to get rid of the whiners; I do not want them to receive a part of the truth and spurn the rest out of doors.

"I wish my women and Brother [Heber C.] Kimball's and Brother [Jedediah M.] Grant's to leave, and every woman in this Territory, or else say in their hearts that they will embrace the Gospel—the whole of it. Tell the Gentiles that I will free every woman in this Territory at our next conference. 'What the first wife, too?' Yes, there shall not be one held in bondage; all shall be set free. And then let the father be the head of the family the master of his own household; and let him treat them as an angel would treat them; and let the wives and the children say amen to what he says, and be subject to his dictates, instead of their dictating the man, instead of their trying to govern him."

Now, to what extent, Mr. Reynolds, is that doctrine declared by Brigham Young—whether he intended to exercise it or not upon those women—qualified by the teachings of the church to-day, that the president of the church might, as Brigham Young declared he would, dissolve the marriage relation?

MR. REYNOLDS. I have never read that discourse before, and I don't know what to say with regard to it. I don't think I fully understand your question.

MR. TAYLER. The stenographer will read it.

The question was read, as follows: "Now, to what extent, Mr. Reynolds, is that doctrine declared by Brigham Young—whether he intended to exercise it or not upon those women—qualified by the teachings of the church to-day, that the president of the church might, as Brigham Young declared he would, dissolve the marriage relation?"

MR. REYNOLDS. I don't believe that the president of the church claims to-day any right to dissolve the marriage relation of anyone but those who make application to him for that marriage to be dissolved and show causes why it should be dissolved.

MR. TAYLER. The president of the church, as you have stated, dissolves what we call the legal marriage as well as the plural marriage relation, does he not?

MR. REYNOLDS. After the parties who have been legally married have been divorced by the courts, and not without.

MR. TAYLER. Before you grant a divorce on that ground, do you always know that that is the fact?

MR. REYNOLDS. Always. If it is not so stated when the matter has been brought before me, I have invariably made the inquiry.[3] ...

MR. TAYLER. Have you any daughters married in polygamy?

MR. REYNOLDS. I believe I have one.

MR. TAYLER. To whom is she married?

MR. REYNOLDS. If married, she is married to Benjamin Cluff, jr.[4]

MR. TAYLER. When was she married to him?

MR. REYNOLDS. I have no idea.

MR. TAYLER. How old is she?

MR. REYNOLDS. Probably 31, or probably more.

MR. TAYLER. You do not mean that she is indefinitely 31 or more?

MR. REYNOLDS. No; I mean to say I don't remember at the present time her exact age. I couldn't tell you when her birthday was.

MR. TAYLER. You do not mean that she might be 40?

MR. REYNOLDS. Certainly not.

MR. TAYLER. I did not think you meant to be uncandid in the answer or to have any wide margin. But she is about 31?

MR. REYNOLDS. She is about 31.

MR. TAYLER. When did you first have the idea that she was married to Benjamin Cluff?

MR. REYNOLDS. A few years ago.

MR. TAYLER. What was he doing at that time?

MR. REYNOLDS. I think he was in South America; but as to that my memory won't serve me with accuracy.

---

3. A few months earlier, on October 6, 1904, Carl Badger wrote optimistically to Heber J. Grant in England that there was "every reason to believe that the Senator will retain his seat. He has a very strong legal position; the Senate is a very conservative body, and will be governed in large by the legal and constitutional phase of the question. However, if public sentiment should creep in and demand its victim, there is no telling what will happen" (in Rodney J. Badger, *Liahona and Iron Rod: The Biography of Carl A. and Rose J. Badger* [Bountiful, Utah: Family History Publishers, 1985], 224). Curiously, eight days later Badger wrote to his wife that he thought "the Senator's case is in a very serious condition. ... The Republican Party, and President Roosevelt, will not stand for any new polygamous marriages. ... And if Senator Smoot voted to sustain an active, new polygam[ist] at the last conference, or voted to sustain a man charged with having taken a new polygamous wife, without having investigated and disproved that charge, he will not, in my opinion, be allowed to retain his seat. I do not know what has been done in John W. Taylor's case, but his is a dangerous one" (October 14, 1904, in ibid., 225).

4. Cluff was third president of Brigham Young University (1892-1903). His post-Manifesto marriage to George Reynolds's daughter Florence Mary Reynolds (1874-1932) was revisited many times during the hearings.

MR. TAYLER. She was there then, was she?

MR. REYNOLDS. No, sir; she was in Mexico.

MR. TAYLER. When was it that he was in South America?

MR. REYNOLDS. He was in charge of an exploring expedition. It was a few years ago, but I don't remember when. I had no particular interest in it. ...

MR. TAYLER. Did she go to Mexico about the time that Mr. Cluff went?

MR. REYNOLDS. I think so.

MR. TAYLER. They went together, did they not?

MR. REYNOLDS. I don't know.

MR. TAYLER. Is that your understanding about it—that they went together?

MR. REYNOLDS. I don't know whether they went together, or nearly at the same time.

MR. TAYLER. I do not know that it is important that they went in immediate company, but I mean the party or two or three parties that went down there about the same time. She and he were in those parties?

MR. REYNOLDS. I don't know whether she went previously or later, sir.

MR. TAYLER. When did you first learn of her supposed marriage to Benjamin Cluff? That was his name—Benjamin Cluff, jr.?

MR. REYNOLDS. Yes; Benjamin Cluff, jr.

MR. TAYLER. When did you first learn of that?

MR. REYNOLDS. I couldn't tell you. It was some time after, I presume, the marriage had taken place. It is all presumption on my part.

MR. TAYLER. That was when, however? Not with reference to the time she was married, but absolutely, or with reference to the present time, when was it that you learned it?

MR. REYNOLDS. I learned it a few years ago.

MR. TAYLER. Was it three or four years ago?

MR. REYNOLDS. It may be three or four or five—somewhere about that. It is more than three, I am satisfied.

MR. TAYLER. Did you learn who married them?

MR. REYNOLDS. No, sir.

MR. TAYLER. Have you seen her since?

MR. REYNOLDS. She paid me a short visit once since.

MR. TAYLER. Has she children?

MR. REYNOLDS. She has two children, I believe.

MR. TAYLER. How old are they? Are they little children?

MR. REYNOLDS. One is an infant and the other is a little girl of a few years old.

MR. TAYLER. Did she tell you anything about when she was married?

MR. REYNOLDS. No, sir; not a word.

MR. TAYLER. You did not ask her anything about it?

MR. REYNOLDS. No, sir.

MR. TAYLER. Why did you not?

MR. REYNOLDS. Because I was satisfied in my mind that they had been married, and she never wrote to me or told me anything about it, and I made no inquiries.

MR. TAYLER. Why did you make no inquiries?

MR. REYNOLDS. Because she was away, you see, nearly all the time, and it would be difficult for me to say why, at the time, I didn't make inquiries.

MR. TAYLER. Of course you do not desire any inference to be drawn from the ignorance that you have of that fact that you have any less affection for your children than any other man would have for his children?

MR. REYNOLDS. No, sir; I claim to be a good father.[5]

MR. TAYLER. And if you failed to inquire as to that, was it not wholly on account of the fact that you believed that she was a plural wife and that you did not care to know about such a fact?

MR. REYNOLDS. It was largely that, sir. ...

SENATOR DUBOIS. I believe you said your legal wife is dead?[6]

MR. REYNOLDS. Yes, sir.

SENATOR DUBOIS. If you should marry to-morrow who would be your legal wife?

MR. REYNOLDS. My understanding is, if I were to marry to-morrow, the woman I married would be my legal wife.

SENATOR DUBOIS. And you would not be then violating the laws of the land, would you?

MR. REYNOLDS. By marrying to-morrow?

SENATOR DUBOIS. Yes.

MR. REYNOLDS. I understand not.

SENATOR DUBOIS. That is your understanding?

5. A few days prior to Reynolds's testimony, Carl Badger wrote in his diary: "Senator [Smoot] says that Geo[rge]. Reynolds was going to testify that he did not know that his daughter was married [to Benjamin Cluff in Mexico], though she came to his house with a baby; he did not ask her who was her husband, but he has been persuaded that it would be a shocking thing to the public conscience. Think of the infamy of such an attitude" (in ibid., 236).

6. Reynolds married his first wife, Mary Ann Tuddenham, on July 22, 1865. She passed away twenty years later on December 17, 1885.

MR. REYNOLDS. That is my understanding.

SENATOR DUBOIS. Having two wives now, if you married to-morrow you would not be violating the laws of the land?

MR. REYNOLDS. I should be violating the laws of the land if I continued to live with them as wives any longer. Then I should be subject to the laws pertaining to adultery—the State laws.

SENATOR DUBOIS. But having testified you have two wives, you could take a wife to-morrow and she would be your legal wife, and you would not be violating the laws of the land? You would not be in polygamy according to your understanding?

MR. REYNOLDS. I understand that I should not be violating the law of the land by marrying that woman, but if it was not one of my two plural wives I should have to entirely cease the relationship of wife and husband with the two women who are my present plural wives. That is my understanding. I may be wrong.

SENATOR DUBOIS. You are holding out to the world now these two women as your wives. It is understood they are your wives, is it not?

MR. REYNOLDS. It is understood that I have never repudiated them ...

SENATOR DUBOIS. What interpretation did you put upon the manifesto when it was issued in regard to your conduct toward your plural wives?

MR. REYNOLDS. My understanding was that it did not affect my relationships with my plural wives at the time it was issued. I considered, and so understood at the time, that it only related to the fact that the president of the church, who held the right to say so, declared that no more plural marriages should take place. At that time I understood that it in no wise affected those who had plural wives; that the old relationships would continue or might continue if the parties saw fit.

SENATOR DUBOIS. That is, you understood it to mean that you could continue your relation as husband to your two wives?

MR. REYNOLDS. Certainly.

SENATOR DUBOIS. That was your understanding of the manifesto when it was issued?

MR. REYNOLDS. Most certainly it was, sir.

SENATOR DUBOIS. Do you think that was the general understanding of your people?

MR. REYNOLDS. I believe it was. I feel confident it was.

SENATOR DUBOIS. I have not the reference here, but I think you disagree entirely with all the previous witnesses.

MR. WORTHINGTON. It was testified that afterwards, when President [Wilford] Woodruff gave his explanation of the manifesto, they accepted it as forbidding plural cohabitation as well as plural marriages.

SENATOR DUBOIS. I thought from his answer he was living up to the spirit of the manifesto.

MR. WORTHINGTON. You will notice that he says "when it was issued." He does not say that continued. It is in the record already that a year, I think it was, after the manifesto the president preached a certain sermon, in which he expounded the manifesto as applying to cohabitation as well as to plural marriages, and from that time on they so understood it.

THE CHAIRMAN. Mr. Reynolds, you have no children by these two wives?

MR. REYNOLDS. I have no children by the plural wives, did you say?

THE CHAIRMAN. Yes; I asked if you have.

MR. REYNOLDS. Oh, I have children by all three of my wives.[7]

THE CHAIRMAN. You have children by these two women you are living with now?

MR. REYNOLDS. I have children by my two plural wives, sir.

THE CHAIRMAN.[8] When was the last one born?

---

7. Reynolds's wives and children were: 1. Mary Ann Tuddenham (1846-85), married Reynolds 1865—children George Tuddenham (1866-67), Amelia Emily (1868-1943), Heber Tuddenham (1870-72), Alice Louise (1873-1938), Florence Mary (1874-1932), Amy Tautz (1876-1955), Eleanor Elizabeth (1878-1920), Julia Durrant (1879-80), John Leslie (1881-1933), Harold Godfrey (1883-1940), and Herbert (1885); 2. Amelia Jane Schofield (1853-1911), married Reynolds 1874—children Sidney Schofield (1875-1933), Marion Groves (1876-1952), Charles Hewitt (1877-79), Susanna Alberta (1880-1941), George Bruford (1881-1937), Edwin Don Carlos (1883-1937), Willard Hyrum (1885-1939), Nephi Windsor (1887-1940), Ethel Georgina (1889-1937), Josephine Edna (1891-1960), Bruford Alan (1895-1947), and Olive Gertrude (1898-1973); and 3. Mary Goold (1859-1936), married Reynolds 1885—children Georgia Ann (1886-1966), Polly Anatroth (1888-1959), Philip Caswallon (1890-1966), Gwendolyn (1891-95), Rosalie Temple (1893-1917), Julia Adelaide (1895-1983), George Gordon (1897-1983), Arthur Reed (1900-72), and Clifford Meredith (1903-76).

8. Nine days prior to this testimony, Smoot had described some of Burrows's tactics in a letter to Joseph F. Smith:

Mr. Worthington ... went up to Senator Burrow's office and found the Senator closeted with Attorney Tayler and C[harles]. M[ostyn]. Owen. ... Burrows informed him that he proposed to resume the hearings on December 8th, or at the latest December 12th. Attorney Worthington tried to argue with him that none of my attorneys had received notice of the proposed resumption of the hearings, and that it would be very unjust to Mr. Van Cott for him to be required to come to Washington upon such a short notice. Burrows in his usual haughty manner informed Mr. Worthington that the witnesses had been subpoenaed and that they would be here on the 12th of December and that the case would be proceeded whether Mr. Van Cott was here or not. ... The dirty old reprobate has not changed in the least, and I hardly think that he is going to do so, for [President] Roosevelt told me today that he had ...

MR. REYNOLDS. The last one born of the woman [who is] my third wife was born probably sixteen or eighteen months ago.

MR. VAN COTT. Months?

MR. REYNOLDS. Months; yes, sir.

THE CHAIRMAN. Have you children by both of these wives?

MR. REYNOLDS. I have children by both, but the youngest by the other wife is 5 or 6 years old now.

MR. WORTHINGTON. He said, Mr. Chairman, that for several years he had been living with only one of these women as her husband.

THE CHAIRMAN. I understood that; but you said one of these children is 5 or 6 years old?

MR. REYNOLDS. Yes.

THE CHAIRMAN. And the other is 18 months old?

MR. REYNOLDS. The other is 18 months old.

THE CHAIRMAN. And they have two mothers?

MR. REYNOLDS. Yes.

MR. TAYLER. They are both the plural wives?

MR. REYNOLDS. They are the children of my plural wives. My legal wife has been dead nearly twenty years.

THE CHAIRMAN. That we understand, but you have had children by both these wives since 1890?

MR. REYNOLDS. Yes, sir.

THE CHAIRMAN. The last by one of the wives about five years ago and the other about eighteen months ago?

MR. REYNOLDS. Yes, sir.

THE CHAIRMAN. How many children have you had by these two women all told?

MR. REYNOLDS. I have had thirty-two children by the three wives. ...

SENATOR MCCOMAS. Would you not have felt a little hampered about preaching against polygamy after the Woodruff manifesto, if you engaged in it yourself, because of the disparity between practice and preaching. ...

MR. REYNOLDS. I have never preached for or against polygamy.

SENATOR MCCOMAS. And you would not do that now?

MR. REYNOLDS. No; I would hold my tongue.

SENATOR MCCOMAS. Your situation, perhaps, would influence you to hold your tongue, would it not?

---

talked to him about my case over and over again, but reason did not seem to appeal to [Senator Burrows], and that it was apparently useless to say any thing further to him about the case (Dec. 3, 1904).

MR. REYNOLDS. I guess it would.

SENATOR McCOMAS. You understood that President Wilford Woodruff, in making that manifesto, did it in order to break up in the Mormon Church the practice of polygamy, did you not?

MR. REYNOLDS. He did it on purpose to stop all future plural marriages, and, as I believe now, it was also in his mind that the practice of living with a plural wife should cease; but I did not so regard it at the time.

SENATOR McCOMAS. But you do now regard the purpose of the manifesto on his part as being to stop the practice of polygamy?

MR. REYNOLDS. To prevent all future plural marriages, and also to stop the people living in plural marriage; that that was in his mind at the time.

SENATOR McCOMAS. Now, apart from your personal practice in polygamy—a great many of us preach some things and do not practice them—what have you done in your high place as one of the seven presidents of the seventies, preaching the gospel of Mormonism abroad throughout the world, to advance the purpose of that manifesto? Have you locally, in Salt Lake City, or in the United States, or elsewhere in the world been preaching at all in accordance with the injunction of Woodruff's manifesto?

MR. REYNOLDS. I have said just now that I have no recollection of ever, during the time I have been in the church, preaching on the subject of plural marriage at all.

SENATOR McCOMAS. Why did you not obey this revelation and why did you not begin to preach against polygamy; or if you could not because you were hampered by circumstances personal to yourself, have you ever urged others to preach against it among the seven presidents of seventies that you speak of?

MR. REYNOLDS. No, sir; I have not urged them. I never talked to them on the subject.

SENATOR McCOMAS. You never did?

MR. REYNOLDS. No; never.

SENATOR McCOMAS. Did they ever urge you to quit your practices and preach in accordance with the Wilford Woodruff manifesto?

MR. REYNOLDS. No, sir.

SENATOR McCOMAS. They never did?

MR. REYNOLDS. No, sir.

SENATOR McCOMAS. Did they or you, in your high place, ever make any endeavor to check the practice of polygamy and to impress upon people their obligation to obey the law of the land?

MR. REYNOLDS. I don't know what the others did, but I never have.

SENATOR McCOMAS. And, so far as you know, your associates never did either?

MR. REYNOLDS. As far as my knowledge is concerned, I have no recollection of having heard them.

SENATOR McCOMAS. Have you heard or do you know of any concerted effort on the part of those higher in authority than yourself, the first presidency and the apostles, to have people obey the law of the land and not continue to encourage plural marriages and not practice polygamy?

MR. REYNOLDS. No, sir; I know of no concerted effort.

SENATOR McCOMAS. So, from 1890 down to this time—and I do not want to misstate you—you have not had knowledge, in your important position in the church, of any concerted effort by the officials of the church, the president, the council, the apostles, or the seven first presidents of the seventies—by either of those bodies or all of them jointly—to stop polygamy in accordance with President Woodruff's manifesto?

MR. REYNOLDS. I consider that polygamy was stopped there and then.

SENATOR McCOMAS. I want an answer to my question. I did not ask what you consider. I ask you what either or all of these bodies have done, to your knowledge, to carry out this manifesto and to stop plural marriages, or to denounce and discourage the practice of polygamy? Just answer my question.

MR. REYNOLDS. I have not heard them denounce it.

SENATOR McCOMAS. You have heard of no general effort on the part of the authorities of the church to do that thing, have you?

MR. REYNOLDS. No, sir.

SENATOR McCOMAS. They have simply been keeping silent officially?

MR. REYNOLDS. Some of them have. Some of them have quite strongly talked on the subject, but not in my presence.

SENATOR McCOMAS. You do not know what you did not hear?

MR. REYNOLDS. No; I do not.

SENATOR McCOMAS. So your answer would stand that, so far as you know, there has been no effort made, either individually or as separate official bodies, or as a number of official bodies jointly acting together, to carry out the Woodruff manifesto?

MR. REYNOLDS. I only know of what I have been told they have done individually.

SENATOR McCOMAS. What you know is not what you have heard. That is all, sir. ...

SENATOR McCOMAS. Mr. Reynolds, are you the George Reynolds who was selected to make the test case?[9]

MR. REYNOLDS. I am the George Reynolds.

SENATOR McCOMAS. Mr. Worthington asked you in respect of the practice of polygamy by those who had been married prior to the manifesto, and the preaching against plural marriages thereafter. To make it quite clear, I want to now ask this question: Do you now say that your first presidents of the seventies ever took any action in pursuance of Woodruff's manifesto to discourage or forbid subsequent plural marriages? Did anybody take any action?

MR. REYNOLDS. Not officially, sir.

SENATOR McCOMAS. Not officially?

MR. REYNOLDS. No; we had nothing to do with it.

SENATOR McCOMAS. So far as you are advised in your church, did the higher official bodies take any other action to have Woodruff's manifesto enforced? Do you know of any subsequent acts, supplementing the manifesto, taken by the first presidency and the apostles, to prevent future violations of the law of the land by polygamous marriages after the manifesto?

MR. REYNOLDS. Yes, sir; on two occasions in the general conference the whole church has voted with regard to it, and the last time it was presented by unanimous vote the church decided that any man who performed such a ceremony in future should be excommunicated from the church.[10]

SENATOR McCOMAS. I asked you about the first presidency and the apostles. You are now telling me about the general conference. I want to know whether there was any general act of the first presidency and the apostles.

MR. REYNOLDS. They were the ones who presented the matter to the conference.

SENATOR McCOMAS. In the general conference?

MR. REYNOLDS. In the general conference, after having decided in their own councils so to do. ...

SENATOR McCOMAS. In your teaching and preaching as a body of presi-

---

9. Reynolds was selected by the First Presidency to become the U.S. Supreme Court "test case" regarding the constitutionality of the Morrill Act of 1862. The case was intended to delay, and ultimately to avoid, prosecution of such high-ranking church leaders as George Q. Cannon. For more on this episode, see Bruce A. Van Orden, *Prisoner for Conscience' Sake: The Life of George Reynolds* (Salt Lake City: Deseret Book, 1992).

10. Reynolds is referring to the so-called Second Manifesto issued by Joseph F. Smith in April 1904.

dents of the seventies what teaching and preaching have you arranged
to do all over the world—because you must have concert of action for
seven of you to preach all over the world—what have you resolved, or
done, or ordained to carry out that effort to stop polygamy?

MR. REYNOLDS. There is no polygamy in the outside missions of the
church.

SENATOR McCOMAS. There is none?

MR. REYNOLDS. No, sir.

SENATOR McCOMAS. Do you prohibit that or discourage it, or what do you
do?

MR. REYNOLDS. We [the Seventies] have never permitted it.

SENATOR McCOMAS. You have not permitted it outside of the United
States?

MR. REYNOLDS. Not in the foreign missions of the United States which we
have control over.

SENATOR McCOMAS. How about Mexico?

MR. REYNOLDS. Mexico is included in the stakes of Zion, over which we
have no jurisdiction.

SENATOR McCOMAS. You have no jurisdiction?

MR. REYNOLDS. Not as seventies; no, sir.

SENATOR McCOMAS. Have you known of any acts, any efforts, made by the
first presidency and the apostles to make effective in Mexico the prohibition of which I have just spoken?

MR. REYNOLDS. I know so little of what is done in Mexico that my opinion
is worthless. As far as my knowledge is concerned, I don't know anything about it.

SENATOR McCOMAS. I will confine it to Utah. Can you now recall any acts,
declarations, or publications made by the first presidency and the
apostles to carry out this prohibition of the Woodruff manifesto?

MR. REYNOLDS. I should think those were entirely sufficient—the two
things at the general conference, where the people all joined together and voted. I should think that was sufficient for everything.

SENATOR McCOMAS. Has it been sufficient? Has it in your judgment
stopped polygamy?

MR. REYNOLDS. What do you mean by polygamy—more plural marriages?

SENATOR McCOMAS. I mean a man who lives in the relation of marriage
with more than one woman.

MR. REYNOLDS. It is very rapidly decreasing sir.

SENATOR McCOMAS. It is rapidly decreasing?

MR. REYNOLDS. Yes; the number of those living in plural marriage is very rapidly decreasing.

SENATOR McCOMAS. Do you mean to say there have been since that manifesto no plural marriages at all?

MR. REYNOLDS. I mean to say there have been no plural marriages, to my knowledge, only the one to which I have referred.[11]

SENATOR McCOMAS. Only that one?

MR. REYNOLDS. Only that one. I know of no others. ...

MR. REYNOLDS. ... I have never preached either for or against it. It has not been within the scope of my special duties.

SENATOR McCOMAS. You said a while ago that you did not at the time, or for some time thereafter, understand the Woodruff manifesto to mean what you now understand it to mean, to wit, a prohibition of living in the polygamous relation by reason of past polygamous marriages. When did that light appear to you, from that language, which has not been changed since it was published by Woodruff?

MR. REYNOLDS. Oh, it was very gradual, sir. From the talk of the brethren with whom I associated, and other things, gradually I came to the conclusion that that was President Woodruff's intention.

SENATOR McCOMAS. Did you take the trouble to read the declaration yourself at the time? You were there, were you not?

MR. REYNOLDS. Yes, sir.

SENATOR McCOMAS. You heard it at the time?

MR. REYNOLDS. I heard it; yes, sir.

SENATOR McCOMAS. You read it thereafter, did you not?

MR. REYNOLDS. I assisted to write it.

SENATOR McCOMAS. You helped to write it?

MR. REYNOLDS. Yes, sir.

SENATOR McCOMAS. If you helped to write it, when was it that it came to you that the writing you helped to compose and to publish had ceased to have one meaning and had another?

MR. REYNOLDS. I can't tell you when it commenced.

SENATOR McCOMAS. It came gradually, did it?

MR. REYNOLDS. Very gradually.

SENATOR McCOMAS. It took three or four or five years—it was a gradual process?

MR. REYNOLDS. A gradual process.

---

11. Earlier in his testimony, Reynolds had acknowledged his daughter's marriage to Benjamin Cluff Jr. in Mexico.

SENATOR McCOMAS. Then, after you did come to the conviction that the president of your church had made a manifesto which positively prohibited all these marriages thereafter, can you tell me why you and the council to which you belonged, the seven presidents of the seventies did not take some effective means to carry out the official declaration of the president of your church? If you thought he was sincere, and you were all sincere, and it meant that, and you intended to carry it out, why did you not begin to do it?[12]

MR. REYNOLDS. Because we would have been interfering with the judicial courts of the church, which is none of our business. We are not a judicial body.

SENATOR McCOMAS. And neither you nor the members of your body, even unofficially, expressed or sanctioned a heartfelt purpose to carry out the purpose of the manifesto?

MR. REYNOLDS. I consider we showed extreme sincerity in accepting the manifesto, and we did our utmost. We did all you could expect of people. We gave up our religious convictions to the decree of the nation to which we belong, and I think you little understand, sir, how much it cost us to do so.

SENATOR McCOMAS. I can understand how much it cost you; but I understand you now also to say that you think you did your utmost, when the fact is, as you have said, that you did not say yea or nay, took no sides and said nothing about it.

MR. REYNOLDS. I think so.

SENATOR McCOMAS. You think that was the utmost you could do with the strain upon your conscience—to say nothing and do nothing, officially or personally, to carry out the purpose of the manifesto in the prohibition of plural marriages. Is that a fair statement?

MR. REYNOLDS. Is that fair to me?

SENATOR McCOMAS. Yes.

MR. REYNOLDS. No, sir.

SENATOR McCOMAS. Your purpose was to do nothing. Is that the idea?

MR. REYNOLDS. The difference, as I understand it, is that the duties of the first council of the seventies did not lie in those directions. They were the duties of other officers of the church. Probably if we had occupied the other positions we should have done differently.

SENATOR McCOMAS. I only ask you these questions because you said your

---

12. For more on the events leading up to the Manifesto, see Thomas G. Alexander, "The Odyssey of a Latter-day Prophet: Wilford Woodruff and the Manifesto of 1890," *Journal of Mormon History* 17 (1991): 169-206.

body were preachers and teachers of the faith and the practice of your religion. ...

MR. WORTHINGTON. You said something about helping to write the manifesto. Will you explain that?

MR. REYNOLDS. President Woodruff wrote it in his own hand—and he was a very poor writer, worse, I believe, than Horace Greeley[13]—and he gave it into the hands of three of the elders to prepare it for the press. I was one of those three.

MR. WORTHINGTON. Who were the three?

MR. REYNOLDS. C[harles]. W. Penrose, John R. Winder, and myself.

MR. WORTHINGTON. What did you do? You said you helped to write the manifesto, and I want to have an understanding of what you mean by that.

MR. REYNOLDS. The answer came from the fact of the question coming to me whether I had read it and understood it, and I answered that I had assisted in writing it.

MR. WORTHINGTON. Did you three, then, transcribe these notes of President Woodruff, or did you rewrite it, or what?

MR. REYNOLDS. We transcribed the notes and changed the language slightly to adapt it for publication.

MR. WORTHINGTON. It contained the substance?

MR. REYNOLDS. Yes; it contained the substance.

SENATOR McCOMAS. Did you, in transcribing the utterance of President Woodruff, make such change of phraseology as would make it ambiguous, so that it might apply to marriages subsequent and not to living with wives who had been married prior?

MR. REYNOLDS. No, sir.

SENATOR McCOMAS. It must have come to your mind when you were copying and changing the phraseology whether this is to apply to the future and whether the past is to be expected, did it not?

MR. REYNOLDS. No, sir; I have told you honestly what my feelings and opinions were.

SENATOR McCOMAS. It did not occur to you then?

MR. REYNOLDS. No, sir.

---

13. Greeley, founder of the *New York Tribune*, had "a notoriously illegible scrawl," according to a survey of famous people with bad handwriting ("Nowadays, Writing Is Off the Wall," *Time* magazine, Jan. 28, 1980). The story was told that he once "scribbled a note to a reporter telling him he was fired for incompetence; so indecipherable was the missive that for years afterward the man was able to pass it off as a letter of recommendation." In 1859 Greeley traveled to Utah to interview Brigham Young. The interview was published in the *Salt Lake Tribune* on August 20, 1859.

SENATOR McCOMAS. That required years?

MR. REYNOLDS. Yes, sir. We wrote it as we understood the president intended, with his manuscript before us.

THE CHAIRMAN. I do not know but I may have misunderstood. I understood this manifesto was inspired.

MR. REYNOLDS. Yes.

THE CHAIRMAN. That is your understanding of it?

MR. REYNOLDS. My understanding was that is was inspired.

THE CHAIRMAN. And when it was handed to you it was an inspiration, as you understand, from on high, was it not?

MR. REYNOLDS. Yes.

THE CHAIRMAN. What business had you changing it?

MR. REYNOLDS. We did not change the meaning.

THE CHAIRMAN. You have just stated you changed it.

MR. REYNOLDS. Not the sense, sir; I didn't state we changed the sense.

THE CHAIRMAN. But you changed the phraseology?

MR. REYNOLDS. We simply put it in shape for publication—corrected possibly the grammar and wrote it so that—

THE CHAIRMAN. You mean to say that in an inspired communication from the Almighty the grammar was bad, was it? You corrected the grammar of the Almighty, did you?[14]

MR. REYNOLDS. That was not a revelation—"Thus saith the Lord." It was simply that the inspiration of the Lord came to President Woodruff, and he gave it in his own language. It had nothing to do with correcting what the Lord said.

THE CHAIRMAN. Then was it inspired?

MR. REYNOLDS. I consider it so. There are various degrees of inspiration, in some of which the man simply has the ideas and he writes it in his own language. I regard the manifesto as one of those.

THE CHAIRMAN. Do you remember what it was before you changed it?

MR. REYNOLDS. No, sir. I haven't any idea whatever.

THE CHAIRMAN. You have no idea what it was?

MR. REYNOLDS. Do you mean to say I haven't any idea—

THE CHAIRMAN. Before you revised this revelation from the Almighty, can you state what it was?

MR. REYNOLDS. No, sir.

---

14. Of this testimony, the *Salt Lake Tribune* opined that "as a grammarian the Lord is not a success, according to Recorder George Reynolds. Revelations from the Almighty are not couched in language to suit the first presidency and the apostles" ("Mormon Doctrines Under Fire: Grammar Was Very Faulty," *Salt Lake Tribune*, Dec. 12, 1904).

THE CHAIRMAN. You do not remember?

MR. REYNOLDS. I believe the copy was destroyed right off.

THE CHAIRMAN. Who destroyed it?

MR. REYNOLDS. I don't know; I suppose one of us three. When we had done with it, we probably—

THE CHAIRMAN. After you had revised it, did you submit it to the president of the church?

MR. REYNOLDS. Yes, sir; and he accepted it as his ...

THE CHAIRMAN. ... You spoke of this manifesto as being a revelation that did not on its face appear to come from the Lord; that it did not say, "Thus saith the Lord," and that revelations which are prefaced with that declaration or that have that declaration connected with them, "Thus saith the Lord," are regarded as inspired?

MR. REYNOLDS. I regard that the servant of the Lord who receives the word of the Lord may have more or less inspiration in this respect; that sometimes the Lord only gives the general idea. Sometimes He gives the concrete idea without giving the exact words, and other times He will inspire the man with the exact words He wishes said.

THE CHAIRMAN. This manifesto did not say, "Thus saith the Lord?"

MR. REYNOLDS. No, sir; it did not.

THE CHAIRMAN. It did not purport to come from the Lord?

MR. REYNOLDS. It purported to be the instruction of the president of the church to the people.

THE CHAIRMAN. And nothing more?

MR. REYNOLDS. No.

THE CHAIRMAN. Which would you regard as higher authority, the book of Doctrine and Covenants or this manifesto?

MR. REYNOLDS. I should regard the book of Doctrine and Covenants as the higher authority.

THE CHAIRMAN. I find in the book of Doctrine and Covenants, prefaced with the statement, "Thus saith the Lord," the following at page 473: "If any man espouse a virgin, and desires to espouse another; and the first give her consent; and if he espouse the second and they are virgins, and have vowed to no other man, then is he justified; he can not commit adultery, for they are given unto him; for he can not commit adultery with that that belongeth to him and no one else;

"And if he have ten virgins given unto him by this law, he can not commit adultery, for they belong to him; and they are given unto him; therefore is he justified."[15]

---

15. D&C 132:1, 61-62.

This revelation is accompanied with this declaration: "Thus saith the Lord." Would you regard that of greater binding force than the manifesto?

MR. REYNOLDS. No, sir; because I understand that the Lord has full right, after giving a general revelation, and may make special provisions at certain times for the carrying out of a law; and he has, through the inspiration of his servant who held the keys, who stood at the head of the church, and was his mouthpiece, said that there should be no further plural marriages.

THE CHAIRMAN. I understood you to say that this manifesto did not appear to come from the Lord; that it was written by the president and then passed over to three gentlemen named and they fixed it up and revised it and had it published.

MR. REYNOLDS. I think you misunderstood me.

THE CHAIRMAN. That is not as great authority as the Book or Doctrine and Covenants, you say?

MR. REYNOLDS. I regard it for the time being as our rule of church practice, because it came from the head of the church, who has the right to direct in all such things.

THE CHAIRMAN. Very well; it is a rule of the church.

MR. REYNOLDS. Yes; the rule of the church is binding now since we have accepted it, and by our vote at conference declared we would accept it. Therefore we are bound to regard it in all respects. In my mind, there is no conflict. ...

16.

George H. Brimhall, Wilhelmina C. Ellis, J. H. Wallis Sr., and August W. Lundstrom

Tuesday-Thursday, December 13-15

"The [dimming] allure of witnesses ... caused an early adjournment of [this morning's] session ... Joseph Smith, president of the Reorganized church, has been in constant attendance since Monday and expects to testify, but it is not intended by Tayler to call him to the stand. Senators Burrows and Overman constituted the elections committee when the afternoon session began 20 minutes late. Senator Burrows left shortly after [Mr.] August Lundstrom was called to the stand, and remained absent a quarter of an hour. During that time Senator Overman was the sole member of the committee present." —*Deseret News,* Dec. 14, 1904

George H. Brimhall,[1] being duly sworn, was examined and testified as follows ...

SENATOR DUBOIS. Is this Brigham Young Academy[2] a church institution?

MR. BRIMHALL. Yes, sir.

SENATOR DUBOIS. Is it supported entirely by the church?

MR. BRIMHALL. No, sir; not by the church entirely; by the church and tuitions and contributions from both members and nonmembers of the church.

SENATOR DUBOIS. Do nonmembers of the church contribute money to the support of the institution?

MR. BRIMHALL. Yes, sir; they have done so.

---

1. Brimhall (1852-1932) was fifty-three years old at the time of his testimony. He lived in Provo, Utah, where he presided over Brigham Young University. He was a polygamist.

2. Brigham Young Academy changed its name to Brigham Young University in late October 1903, but there was some confusion in people's minds about the name, indicated a few lines later when Waldemar Van Cott refers to it as Brigham Young College. In 1903 a member of the LDS First Presidency commented on the new designation of "university": "I hope their head will grow big enough for the hat" (John P. Hatch, ed., *Danish Apostle: The Diaries of Anthon H. Lund, 1890-1921* [Salt Lake City: Signature Books and the Smith-Pettit Foundation, 2006], 247-48).

SENATOR DUBOIS. In about what proportion to the funds contributed by the church?

MR. BRIMHALL. I should say that perhaps 80 or 85 per cent of the funds and tuitions and all came from the church and church members.

SENATOR DUBOIS. There are no contributions from the State to support it?

MR. BRIMHALL. None whatever. ...

MR. VAN COTT. Does Mr. Smoot give active attention to the Brigham Young College at Provo?

MR. BRIMHALL. Yes, sir; he is interested especially in the financial support of it, and often comes and speaks to the students.

MR. VAN COTT. Is it at their general assembly?

MR. BRIMHALL. Yes, sir; at their chapel services in the morning.

MR. VAN COTT. That is the character of his remarks at those assemblies?

MR. BRIMHALL. The general burden of his remarks on those occasions is "character forming, basis of honesty;" and he is noted among the students there as "honesty, the foundation of religion." That is an expression.

MR. VAN COTT. Anything regarding obeying the laws?

MR. BRIMHALL. Yes, sir; he delivered several addresses there in which students have been urged to be true to their country and stand by its laws and the flag. That was especially so in an address he delivered to the general assembly under the auspices of the business college.

MR. WORTHINGTON. When?

MR. VAN COTT. When?

MR. BRIMHALL. That address was given two years ago.

MR. VAN COTT. Have you heard Senator Smoot speak on other occasions?

MR. BRIMHALL. Yes, sir; I have heard him speak at our conferences and our stake priesthood meetings.

MR. VAN COTT. Has he ever said anything there in regard to obeying the law?

MR. BRIMHALL. I have in mind one special occasion, at a priesthood meeting, when he spoke very earnestly on our being true to the laws of our country, and being earnest. At that meeting he read a letter that impressed me very strongly. ...

MR. VAN COTT. Tell us what was said by Mr. Smoot.

MR. BRIMHALL. Do you want me to tell the contents of the letter as I remember it?

MR. VAN COTT. Yes; as he read it.

MR. BRIMHALL. The letter contained a warning to Mr. Smoot and to all of-

ficers in the church, as I remember it against officiating in or foster-
ing polygamy among the members or officers of the church. The
name of Francis M. Lyman was signed to the letter, as president of the
twelve apostles. That is as I remember the circumstances.

MR. VAN COTT. Did Senator Smoot say anything in addition to the letter?

MR. BRIMHALL. If I remember, he said "we can not treat this matter
lightly." That is as I remember it.

MR. VAN COTT. And what was his manner in what he said?

MR. BRIMHALL. His manner was that of earnestness and positiveness in it,
associated with an element of pleading also.

MR. VAN COTT. What do you understand to be Mr. Smoot's attitude in regard to polygamy—that is, whether it is negative ...

MR. TAYLER. ... I do not think that anything witnesses might say as to what
they understand is Senator Smoot's attitude on a question is going to
help us. ...

Mrs. Wilhelmina C. Ellis,[3] being duly sworn, was examined and testified as follows ...

MR. TAYLER. How old were you when you married Abraham Cannon?

MRS. ELLIS. Nineteen.

MR. TAYLER. You were a plural wife?

MRS. ELLIS. Yes, sir.

MR. TAYLER. And, I believe, his first plural wife?

MRS. ELLIS. Yes, sir.

MR. TAYLER. He lived for twenty years or more after he married you. (A
pause.) When were you married to him?

MRS. ELLIS. October 15, 1879.

MR. TAYLER. 1879?

MRS. ELLIS. Yes, sir.

MR. TAYLER. And he died in July, 1896?

MRS. ELLIS. July 19, 1896.

MR. TAYLER. When did he marry Lillian Hamlin?

MRS. ELLIS. I do not know the date.

MR. TAYLER. I do not care about the exact date.

MRS. ELLIS. After June 12 and before July 2.

MR. TAYLER. Of what year.

MRS. ELLIS. 1896.

MR. TAYLER. He was at that time an apostle?

---

3. Wilhelmina Ellis (1859-1941) was the daughter of Angus M. Cannon Sr. and wid-
owed plural wife (as well as cousin) of Abraham H. Cannon. She lived in Salt Lake City.

Mrs. Ellis. Yes, sir.

Mr. Tayler. One of the twelve?

Mrs. Ellis. Yes, sir.

Mr. Tayler. About how long had he been an apostle?

Mrs. Ellis. I do not know exactly; four or five years.

Mr. Tayler. Did he, before he married Lillian Hamlin, talk to you about it?

Mrs. Ellis. Yes, sir.

Mr. Tayler. Did he tell you that he was going to marry her?

Mrs. Ellis. Yes, sir.

Mr. Tayler. How long before the 12th of June did he first talk with you about his marrying Lillian Hamlin?

Mrs. Ellis. Oh, several weeks.

Mr. Tayler. At that time he had how many wives?

Mrs. Ellis. Three.

Mr. Tayler. He married another after marrying you?

Mrs. Ellis. Yes, sir. ...

Mr. Tayler. Did he state with any more particularity where he could marry her, whether in Mexico or Canada or on the high seas?

Mrs. Ellis. I do not remember that he did. He said they were going—he was going to California on this trip.

Mr. Tayler. And that he was going to marry her while on that trip?

Mrs. Ellis. No; I do not think he said that then.

Mr. Tayler. Not then. Later? Did you see him before he went away?

Mrs. Ellis. Yes, sir; I saw him the evening he left.

Mr. Tayler. What conversation did you have with him then about his going away and about his getting married again? What did he say first about going?

Mrs. Ellis. He told me he was going to marry her for time, and that she would be David [Cannon]'s wife for eternity.

Mr. Tayler. What did you say?

Mrs. Ellis. I told him if he married her, there being a law against marriages at that time, that I could not, my conscience would not allow me to, live with him when her marriage would not be acknowledged by the church or the land.

Mr. Tayler. What did he say to that?

Mrs. Ellis. I do not remember that he made any reply.

Mr. Tayler. Have you given us, as nearly as you can, the conversation that took place at that time?

Mrs. Ellis. Yes, sir.

Mr. Tayler. Did he say he was going away that day, or that evening to California?

Mrs. Ellis. He told me to pack his grip or his satchel and told me he was going on this trip.

Mr. Tayler. What did he say about Miss Hamlin?

Mrs. Ellis. Of course I understood, in fact he said she was going with him and President [Joseph F.] Smith.

Mr. Tayler. And President Smith?

Mrs. Ellis. Yes, sir.

Mr. Tayler. And that they were going to be married?

Mrs. Ellis. Yes, sir.

Mr. Tayler. When did he come back?

Mrs. Ellis. As nearly as I can remember, on July 2.

Mr. Tayler. And when he returned he was very ill?

Mrs. Ellis. Yes, sir; very.

Mr. Tayler. And as a result of the illness, died within the next two or three weeks. Is that correct?

Mrs. Ellis. Yes, sir. ...

Mr. Tayler. When did you first learn, Mrs. Ellis, that he had in fact married Miss Hamlin? Was it immediately after he got back?

Mrs. Ellis. I think within two weeks.

Mr. Tayler. Was Miss Hamlin there during his sickness?

Mrs. Ellis. The last few days. She did not stay ... not in my home.

Mr. Tayler. Did she come with him to the house?

Mrs. Ellis. No, sir.

Mr. Tayler. He was brought to your house, and later she came and went, from time to time. ...

Mrs. Ellis. Yes, sir.

Mr. Tayler. Until he died? What did Mr. Cannon say to you shortly before his death about his having married Miss Hamlin?

Mrs. Ellis. He told me he had married her and asked my forgiveness.

Mr. Tayler. What else did he say about it?

Mrs. Ellis. He said he had never had a well day since he had married her. I think it killed him.

Mr. Tayler. You have stated, have you not, Mrs. Ellis, to several of your relatives and acquaintances in Salt Lake that he also told you that Joseph F. Smith married him?

Mrs. Ellis. No, sir; I have never said that.

Mr. Tayler. You have never said that?

Mrs. Ellis. No, sir; not that he told me.

MR. TAYLER. You have stated frequently that Joseph F. Smith did marry them?

MRS. ELLIS. Yes, sir. ...

MR. TAYLER. Have you any knowledge of the fact that Joseph F. Smith had married them?

MRS. ELLIS. No, sir.

MR. TAYLER. That was based solely upon the fact that your husband was an apostle; that he had gone to California for the purpose, among other things, perhaps, of marrying Miss Hamlin; that he was going to marry her on the high seas. ...

MR. WORTHINGTON. The witness has not said that Abraham Cannon was going to marry her on the high seas.

MR. TAYLER. And that Mr. Joseph F. Smith was with them. Is that the only basis of your conclusion?

MR. WORTHINGTON. I object to that question, because the witness has not said that her husband told her he was going to marry Miss Hamlin on the high seas. The question assumes that he told her so.

THE CHAIRMAN. I do not think the witness said that.

MR. WORTHINGTON. She has not stated that her husband told her that he was going to marry Miss Hamlin on the high seas.

MR. TAYLER (to the witness). Did your husband tell you where he was married?

MRS. ELLIS. No sir.

MR. TAYLER. Did you not know they were married on the high seas?

MRS. ELLIS. Only from reports.

MR. TAYLER. That is not an essential part of the inquiry. (To the witness.) It was an inference from the fact that your husband said he was going to marry her, and went away to California for that purpose, and that Joseph F. Smith went along with them. From that you inferred that Joseph F. Smith had married them?

MRS. ELLIS. Yes, sir.

MR. TAYLER. I was not seeking to put any unfair question.

THE CHAIRMAN. Did your husband tell you who did perform the ceremony?

MRS. ELLIS. No, sir.

SENATOR DUBOIS. Have you ever heard it rumored that anybody else than Joseph F. Smith married them?

MRS. ELLIS. I thought he had married them until he was here last year, or at the last term of Congress.

MR. TAYLER. Until he testified here in the committee?

MRS. ELLIS. Yes, sir.[4] ...

MR. VAN COTT. Did you make any inquiry as to whether the manifesto really prohibited that kind of a marriage?

MRS. ELLIS. Yes, sir; I went to President Smith.

MR. WORTHINGTON. To whom?

MRS. ELLIS. To President Smith and asked him, not naming the parties, if such a marriage could be, explaining the case, but withholding names.

MR. VAN COTT. What was his answer?

MRS. ELLIS. He said it could not be.

MR. VAN COTT. Now, when you say President Smith, whom do you mean?

MRS. ELLIS. He was at that time, I believe, Counselor Joseph F. Smith.

MR. VAN COTT. He was not president of the church at that time?

MRS. ELLIS. No, sir.

MR. VAN COTT. Now, Mr. Cannon went away, and you say that on his return he came home ill?

MRS. ELLIS. Yes, sir.

MR. VAN COTT. You stated also that you thought that it killed him. What did you mean by that?

MRS. ELLIS. Well, he said he never had a well day after that. The pain was in his head; in his brain. He was a very conscientious person, and I think it worried him. ...

MR. VAN COTT. Yes, one question please. (To the witness:) Did you ever know anything definite at all, more than mere rumor or gossip, to the effect that Joseph F. Smith performed that ceremony?

MRS. ELLIS. No, sir.

MR. VAN COTT. You answered Mr. Tayler that you believed up to "the time President Smith testified here that he had performed the ceremony." What is the state of your belief since he testified as to whether he performed it?

MRS. ELLIS. I do not believe he did. ...

Testimony of J. H. Wallis, SR.[5] —Recalled

---

4. This entire section was used by Tayler in his closing argument for the plaintiffs (*Smoot Hearings*, 3:540-46).

5. A lapsed Mormon, Wallis (ca. 1842-1913) was born in London, England. He joined the LDS Church in 1851 and later settled in Nephi, Utah. At the time of the hearings, he was living in Salt Lake City. The previous day, Tuesday, December 13, he had testified regarding the LDS temple ceremony, demonstrating four "obligations" and "vows," as well as "what we used to call the 'oath of vengeance.'" Tayler had cautioned Wallis that he was not interested in "a detailed account" of the ceremony, but Wallis

J. H. Wallis, Sr., having been previously sworn, was examined and testified as follows ...

MR. WORTHINGTON. Did you reduce to writing at any time the obligations which you have testified here you took on the numerous occasions when you say you went through the [LDS temple] endowment ceremony?

MR. WALLIS. Not the obligations, sir. I did amuse myself in coming here in writing part of the ceremony, but the obligations I did not.

MR. WORTHINGTON. That part of it you never reduced to writing at all?

MR. WALLIS. No, sir.

MR. WORTHINGTON. Did you communicate the substance of it to any person before you took the stand?

MR. WALLIS. Oh, yes, sir. I have frequently in conversation alluded to that.

MR. WORTHINGTON. To whom have you communicated it?

MR. WALLIS. Well, in general conversation; I could not say how many.

MR. WORTHINGTON. You have told it to lots of people, gentiles and Mormons?

MR. WALLIS. Yes, sir.

MR. WORTHINGTON. Out where you live?

MR. WALLIS. Yes, sir.

---

seemed more than eager to say all he knew. In total, the questions and answers regarding the obligations and vows occupied about two pages of the transcript, the prosecution's stated intent having been to determine whether anything was said or done in the temple that encouraged disloyalty to the United States—in other words, regarding the alleged oath of vengeance (*Smoot Hearings*, 2:73-85).

Some two weeks earlier, the *Salt Lake Tribune* had warned of individuals who were prepared to testify about the content of the temple ceremony:

On Saturday afternoon [Dec. 3] there will be an exhibition of the robes used by the Mormon ecclesiastics in their endowment ceremonies in the great Temple at Salt Lake City. All the robes used have been secured and the sample ceremony will be conducted by one familiar with the service, in the committee room of Senator Dubois. This will be a sort of dress rehearsal for the Senate Committee on Privileges and Elections, that is investigating the charges against Senator Smoot. The ceremony will also be performed publicly before the committee in session on December 12. It is said the ceremonies are an adaptation of a part of the Masonic ritual" ("Endowment Ceremony Will Be Exemplified," Dec. 1, 1904).

In point of fact, the promised enactment of the ceremony never took place, either in the Senator's chambers or in the committee room. Throughout the hearings, the prosecution's questions about the temple were limited to, and almost exclusively focused on, whether Mormons swore defiance to the government. The only exception was a short exchange between Senator Burrows and August W. Lundstrom, the witness who followed Wallis, regarding the meaning of temple garments. Lundstrom offered an opinion but admitted it was "an inference" and "was not explained" to him in the temple (*Smoot Hearings*, 2:182-83).

MR. WORTHINGTON. How long ago did you begin telling about this?

MR. WALLIS. Well, I could not say that, but almost any time the subject of Mormonism came up.

MR. WORTHINGTON. Have you been telling about this out there for several years?

MR. WALLIS. Well, no; not for several years.

MR. WORTHINGTON. Several months?

MR. WALLIS. Several months.

MR. WORTHINGTON. A year?

MR. WALLIS. I dare say; say about the time of the last meeting of this committee.[6]

MR. WORTHINGTON. You told about it generally to people around there to whom you talked?

MR. WALLIS. Yes, sir.

MR. WORTHINGTON. Mormons and gentiles?

MR. WALLIS. Yes, sir.

MR. WORTHINGTON. Just what you told here?

MR. WALLIS. Yes, sir; or words to that effect. I made one slight mistake yesterday.[7]

MR. WORTHINGTON. I suppose any witness has a right to correct mistakes.

THE CHAIRMAN. You can correct it if you desire.

MR. WALLIS. In repeating the obligation of vengeance I found that I was wrong.

THE CHAIRMAN. I can not hear what you say. Please stand up.

MR. WALLIS. In repeating the obligation of vengeance I find I made a mistake; I was wrong. It should have been "upon this nation." I had it "upon the inhabitants of the earth." It was a mistake on my part.[8]

MR. WORTHINGTON. When you told it to all of these other people in the last year did you always make that mistake or did you tell it as you have now told it here?

MR. WALLIS. As I have told it to-day.

MR. WORTHINGTON. To whom did you tell it out there in that way?

---

6. Newspaper reports of the April-May hearings, including questions about the supposed oath of vengeance, probably prompted Wallis to talk about the subject. B. H. Roberts had been asked on April 20 if "there is anything in that ceremony that ... abridges a man's freedom of political action" and if it "binds you to disobey the laws of the land, or to make any agreement against the Government, or its officers, or anything of the kind" (see chapter 10).

7. See *Smoot Hearings*, 2:73-85.

8. The previous three questions and answers were used by Tayler in his closing argument for the plaintiffs (*Smoot Hearings*, 3:580).

Mr. Wallis. I should not be so confused in private conversation as I might be here to-day.

Mr. Worthington. Let the reporter read the answer.

The reporter read the answer.

Mr. Worthington. My question is to whom did you tell it?

Mr. Wallis. Do you wish me to identify some one by name?

Mr. Worthington. Not some one, but everyone you can remember to whom you told it out there, Mormons or gentiles.

Mr. Wallis. I have spoken to Mr. [Charles Mostyn] Owen on the subject.

Mr. Worthington. Yes, I suppose so. Anybody else?

Mr. Wallis. I could not call another one by name at the present time. But of course it is rather recent in that case.

Mr. Worthington. Although you have been telling it for a year, you say, out there to a great many people, you can not give us the name of a single person to whom you told it except that of Mr. Owen?

Mr. Wallis. No, sir; I do not know that I could. I am not very good at remembering names. ...

Mr. Worthington. When did you find out you had made this mistake which you are now correcting?

Mr. Wallis. On thinking it over last night. I read the paper, and I saw what I had said, and I knew then I was wrong.

Mr. Worthington. Have you talked with anybody about it since you were on the stand?

Mr. Wallis. I mentioned it to Mr. Owen when I came in.

Mr. Worthington. To Mr. Owen. You have not mentioned it to anybody else?

Mr. Wallis. No, sir.

Mr. Worthington. That is all we can go on with now, Mr. Chairman.

The Chairman. I wish to ask a question. You mentioned to Mr. Owen this morning the fact that you had made a mistake?

Mr. Wallis. Yes, sir.

The Chairman. Will you repeat now the obligation as you remember it.

Mr. Wallis. "That you and each of you will never cease to importune High Heaven for vengeance upon this nation for the blood of the prophets who have been slain." That is as near as I can get at it; that is the substance of it.

The Chairman. Do you gentlemen want this witness any further?

Mr. Worthington. We may want him. I hope he will not be discharged. Let the stenographer read the obligation.

The reporter read the obligation.

MR. WORTHINGTON. Was there anything in that obligation about inhabitants?

MR. TAYLER. That was not all of the answer. Let the entire answer be read.

The reporter read as follows: "Mr. Wallis. 'That you and each of you will never cease to importune High Heaven for vengeance upon this nation for the blood of the prophets who have been slain.' That is as near as I can get at it; that is the substance or it."

MR. WORTHINGTON. Was there anything in that obligation about inhabitants?

MR. WALLIS. Nothing about inhabitants. I found I was wrong about that.[9]

...

August W. Lundstrom,[10] having been duly sworn, was examined and testified as follows:[11] ...

MR. TAYLER. How many times, in all, did you go through that temple, as that process is called?

9. For more on the oath of vengeance, see David John Buerger, *The Mysteries of Godliness: A History of Mormon Temple Worship* (San Francisco: Smith Research Associates, 1994), 133-72.

10. Lundstrom (ca. 1867-?) was born in Sweden, where he joined the LDS Church at age fifteen; he later immigrated to Ogden, Utah, and served in various church callings, including bishop's counselor, ward teacher, and Sunday school teacher. He left the church in 1901. At the time of this testimony, he lived in Salt Lake City.

11. Prior to this testimony, Smoot obtained a copy of a letter from Senator Burrows to Senator Dubois "in which the former tells the latter that he (Dubois) and Owen are making 'commendable progress in securing the evidence which we want.'" Smoot interpreted this to imply bias on Burrows's part and explained to Joseph F. Smith that he would release the letter to the committee and the press if he had permission from the person who had copied the letter, but "we have no permission as yet." Legal counsel Augustus Worthington thought it would do well to approach Burrows privately and demand an explanation, confident that if the letter were released to the press it would "absolutely kill Senator Burrows as far as any influence he may have in the future as a Senator." President Roosevelt had seen the letter and told Smoot he found it "damnable" (Smoot to Smith, Dec. 3, 1904).

Apparently the letter had reached Utah already. A month earlier, LDS apostle Anthon Lund reported that "Senator Burrows is pretending to be friendly to Smoot, but we have read a letter of his to Senator Dubois in which he begs him to get up all the evidence he can in Idaho and Wyoming in regard to new marriages and unlawful cohabitation. He also wants Charles Mostyn Owen to do his utmost to rake up cases in Utah. Just think of Burrows as chairman of a committee sitting as judges on a fellow senator acting the role of a prosecuting attorney or rather inquisitor! I wish we had the original of that letter, it would disqualify him from sitting on that committee" (Lund to Heber J. Grant, Sept. 12, 1904, Archives, Church of Jesus Christ of Latter-day Saints, Salt Lake City). Because of the political risk involved in disclosing the source of the leak, Smoot was never able to blow the whistle on Burrows.

MR. LUNDSTROM. Six days, except the one day each time used for baptism. That would be eight days altogether.

MR. TAYLER. Where did you first go through the temple, at Salt Lake City or at Logan?

MR. LUNDSTROM. At Salt Lake City.

MR. TAYLER. How many times in those six days did you go through the separate ceremony called the ceremony of the endowment house, or the endowment ceremony?

MR. LUNDSTROM. I didn't understand your question.

MR. TAYLER. Let me direct your attention, say, to the obligations. There are certain obligations taken in these ceremonies, are there not?

MR. LUNDSTROM. Yes.

MR. TAYLER. Oaths or obligations?

MR. LUNDSTROM. Yes.

MR. TAYLER. There is an obligation of sacrifice, is there?

MR. WORTHINGTON. I suggest, Mr. Chairman, that the witness should be asked what the ceremony is and should not be told.

MR. TAYLER. I am not leading the witness at all.

MR. WORTHINGTON. I think that is very leading, Mr. Tayler.

MR. TAYLER. I am not trying to do that. I am only desiring to get along as rapidly as possible.

MR. WORTHINGTON. I object to getting along rapidly by telling the witness the answer that is desired.

THE CHAIRMAN. I did not understand Mr. Tayler to state what the answer was.

MR. TAYLER. I did not, Mr. Chairman, but I would not offend anybody's sensibilities in this respect.

THE CHAIRMAN. I understood him to be calling the witness's attention to one obligation if there were any such obligation.

MR. WORTHINGTON. He did not ask him if there was any such obligation, but said there was.

MR. TAYLER. Nobody denies that there was such an obligation.

MR. WORTHINGTON. This witness has not said so.

THE CHAIRMAN. You may proceed, Mr. Tayler.

MR. TAYLER. Do you take an obligation in this ceremony?

MR. LUNDSTROM. Yes, sir.

MR. TAYLER. How many times in your presence were these obligations taken?

MR. LUNDSTROM. Six times.

MR. TAYLER. Is there any obligation called the obligation of sacrifice?

MR. LUNDSTROM. Yes, sir.

MR. TAYLER. Is there an obligation called the obligation of vengeance?

MR. LUNDSTROM. It is called retribution.

MR. TAYLER. How many times did you take or hear taken the obligation of sacrifice and the obligation of retribution?

MR. LUNDSTROM. Six times.

MR. TAYLER. How long is required for the entire ceremony?

MR. LUNDSTROM. From six to seven hours, generally. It all depends on the crowd.

MR. TAYLER. It depends on the number who take it at once?

MR. LUNDSTROM. Yes. ...

MR. TAYLER. When did you go through this ceremony?

MR. LUNDSTROM. The first time in 1894, in August, and the second time I believe it was in 1898, in Logan.

MR. TAYLER. And you stated that you went through the ceremony altogether six times. How many times did you go through in Salt Lake in 1894?

MR. LUNDSTROM. I went through four days, but one day was baptizing.

MR. TAYLER. But the other ceremony?

MR. LUNDSTROM. Three days; that is all.

MR. TAYLER. And at Logan?

MR. LUNDSTROM. The same.

MR. TAYLER. At that time did you consider yourself a devout Mormon?

MR. LUNDSTROM. Yes, sir.

MR. TAYLER. And this ceremony, to you, was solemn?

MR. LUNDSTROM. Yes, sir.

MR. TAYLER. It was so felt by you to be during the entire time that it was carried on?

MR. LUNDSTROM. Yes, sir.

MR. TAYLER. At what stage of the ceremony—as to time, I mean—how near an approach to the end of the ceremony did you reach the obligation? When was the first obligation taken?

MR. LUNDSTROM. The whole proceeding is a series of obligations.

MR. TAYLER. How many different obligations are taken during the ceremony?

MR. LUNDSTROM. I can't give you the number now.

MR. TAYLER. Can you recall what other obligations are taken—I mean by some descriptive word—besides the obligation of sacrifice and of retribution?

MR. LUNDSTROM. Yes; the law of chastity, and others which I could not recollect just now. I can't remember them all.

MR. TAYLER. Which came first, the obligation of sacrifice or of retribution; do you remember?

MR. LUNDSTROM. The law of sacrifice came first.

MR. TAYLER. Was the obligation of retribution the last of the obligations that you took?

MR. LUNDSTROM. It was one among the last. ...

MR. TAYLER. Can you give us the obligation of retribution?

MR. LUNDSTROM. I can.

MR. TAYLER. You may give that.

MR. LUNDSTROM. "We and each of us solemnly covenant and promise that we shall ask God to avenge the blood of Joseph Smith upon this nation."[12] There is something more added, but that is all I can remember verbatim. That is the essential part.

MR. TAYLER. What was there left of it? What else?

MR. LUNDSTROM. It was in regard to teaching our children and children's children to the last generation to the same effect.

MR. TAYLER. Teach that obligation?

MR. LUNDSTROM. Teach that obligation.

MR. TAYLER. Was the obligation taken in both temples in the same words and on all of these days?

MR. LUNDSTROM. Yes, sir [13] ...

MR. TAYLER. Did you have any trouble with the church authorities?

MR. LUNDSTROM. Not exactly any trouble.

MR. TAYLER. Well, any difference?

MR. LUNDSTROM. The difference, of course, was because of myself.

MR. TAYLER. Describe that and tell us all about it.

MR. LUNDSTROM. I found inconsistencies in the doctrine—changes being made. I had become a Mormon because I thought it was the only true religion. I was sincere as long as I believed it to be the true church and being revealed from God; but when I found changes creeping

---

12. Ten days after this testimony, on December 24, Carl Badger wrote to his wife:

You pick out a vital point when you say that the witnesses have lied in saying that the temple ceremony includes an oath to "avenge the blood of the prophets on this nation," but I do not know that the Senator will be allowed to introduce testimony to disprove this, because in doing that he would have to prove the exact nature of the ceremony and, of course, that he will not do. It is a very bad thing to be misrepresented, but that does not worry me like that which is true in the testimony. It is entirely unworthy of us that we should pray for vengeance ... but the wrong part is the nature of the penalties ... the day will come when they will be no more and when we will be ashamed of them (in Rodney J. Badger, *Liahona and Iron Rod: The Biography of Carl A. and Rose J. Badger* [Bountiful, Utah: Family History Publishers, 1985], 242).

13. The previous five questions and answers would be used by Tayler in closing arguments for the plaintiffs (*Smoot Hearings*, 3:579-80).

in—later revelations, as they were called, being open contradictions to former revelations—I began to study a little closer, and in fact I found a weak point in the wall, and when I touched it it became a large enough hole so that I could crawl through. The foundation was not solid, so I left it. My conviction that I had before fell through. Believing sincerely that it was the truth previously, I became just as well convinced after that it was not the truth.

Mr. TAYLER. Did you have any discussion of this subject with any of the authorities of the church?

Mr. LUNDSTROM. Yes.

Mr. TAYLER. With whom?

Mr. LUNDSTROM. Matthias Cowley. ...

Mr. TAYLER. Matthias Cowley is an apostle, is he?

Mr. LUNDSTROM. He is one of the apostles.

Mr. TAYLER. Will you state what occurred between you and Cowley in this relation?

Mr. WORTHINGTON. One moment. Are we to go into the discussion between a member of the church who is about to leave it and one of the apostles, as affecting Mr. Smoot?

THE ACTING CHAIRMAN (SENATOR OVERMAN). We have been rather liberal here in going into everything.

Mr. WORTHINGTON. It is the rule of the committee, then, that everything may go in?

Mr. TAYLER. I do not want to proceed upon that theory.

Mr. WORTHINGTON. I asked the question in order to know what may be done when our time comes.

Mr. TAYLER. That is all right. We propose to prove by this man the controversy with Apostle Cowley, who for the time being is not discoverable and the importance of whose position is minimized as a mere Apostle; but the discussion which this witness had with Apostle Cowley went to the very heart of this whole business of subordination, absolute control of the church over the mind and the deeds of its members. That was the subject.

Mr. WORTHINGTON. Is it intended to bring the conversation to the knowledge of Senator Smoot?

Mr. TAYLER. No, no. We are proving what it is this church stands for and what it actually does, and if Senator Smoot does not know it let him go on the witness stand and say so.

THE ACTING CHAIRMAN. I think it is competent on that line.

Mr. TAYLER. Tell us what occurred between you and Apostle Cowley.

What was the nature of the discussion? What was the point of difference? What did he claim was your duty as a Mormon respecting especially the subject of obedience, if he claimed anything or talked anything in that connection?

MR. LUNDSTROM. Well, at the time the controversy occurred, if a controversy it should be called, it was in regard to certain changes in regard to baptizing—rebaptizing—and at the time we could not agree on the argument. So Cowley, he asked me if I did not believe in the living oracles, and I said "I used to." He says, "Well, that is the word of God. That is inspiration. That is revelation." Of course I could not be satisfied with that unless it corresponded with things previously taught. That is the substance of the conversation.

MR. TAYLER. What did he describe to you by the term "living oracles?"

MR. LUNDSTROM. Why, he meant the leaders of the church, the president and the apostles.

MR. TAYLER. What did he say respecting their authority over you?

MR. LUNDSTROM. How is that?

MR. TAYLER. What did he say respecting the authority of these living oracles upon you?

MR. WORTHINGTON. What, if anything.

MR. TAYLER. I will let you amend the question to that effect. What, if anything, did Apostle Cowley say?

MR. LUNDSTROM. He said, as I stated, that their word is revelation.[14] ...

MR. VAN COTT. Just what was your point with Apostle Cowley about that ordinance of rebaptism?

MR. LUNDSTROM. It was in regard to the discontinuance of rebaptizing, which previously had been customary, when cases came up and rebaptizing was requested by parties; and at that time we received instructions not to rebaptize any more. Hence, that was the first cause for my investigation in the direction which I followed after that.

MR. VAN COTT. Was that the hole in the wall that you referred to yesterday?[15]

MR. LUNDSTROM. Yes; the changes taking place in the church, that being one of the changes, and I considered it a weak place in the wall.

MR. VAN COTT. What was the later revelation that you referred to that was creeping in and was contradictory to former revelations?

14. The day's testimony "wore me out," Carl Badger confided to his wife. The topics covered were "simply terrible," and he added: "It made me weak to listen to the temple ceremony as told by the witnesses" (in Badger, *Liahona and Iron Rod,* 237).

15. Lundstrom's testimony was carried over from Wednesday to Thursday.

MR. LUNDSTROM. First of all was the manifesto. I considered that a revelation or a word spoken by the living oracle which was in contradiction to the first revelation supposed to have been given to Joseph Smith commanding polygamy.

MR. VAN COTT. And these differences continued from 1898 until 1899?

MR. LUNDSTROM. Yes, sir. And it was about two years after I began my investigation, after the doubt had crept into my mind—it took about two years before I left the church.

MR. VAN COTT. When did you leave it?

MR. LUNDSTROM. In 1901.

MR. VAN COTT. Did you then go to Salt Lake?

MR. LUNDSTROM. Yes, sir.

MR. VAN COTT. Did you formally leave the church?

MR. LUNDSTROM. I did.

MR. VAN COTT. In 1904?

MR. LUNDSTROM. Yes, sir. ...

THE CHAIRMAN. ... (To the witness.) Have you stated all the reasons why you withdrew from this organization in 1901?

MR. LUNDSTROM. I have not; but the main reason, of course, was that I became in doubt of the truthfulness of the doctrine, and I considered that a sufficient reason. Of course, I had many foundations for my doubts.

THE CHAIRMAN. But that was the controlling reason? You spoke of the tokens. What do you mean by that—revealing tokens?

MR. LUNDSTROM. Well, those are certain signs which are customary among secret societies.

THE CHAIRMAN. Was this ceremony of such a character as to impress you with the solemnity of it, or was it a joke, as it has been characterized?[16]

MR. LUNDSTROM. For my part, I took it seriously. I considered it sacred as long as I believed the doctrine to be true.

THE CHAIRMAN. That is all.

MR. VAN COTT. Did you tell anyone in Utah about these penalties?

MR. LUNDSTROM. No, except to refer to them in my lectures occasionally; that is, to refer to some of them in order to illustrate my views on the subject.

MR. VAN COTT. Lectures against the Mormon Church?

---

16. Far from "a joke," LDS people took their vows so seriously, President Smith told Franklin S. Richards "that in the event of the divulgence of the temple ceremony, 'if there was anything in the church which the Lord desired removed, he hoped he would remove it,'" as related by Badger (ibid.).

MR. LUNDSTROM. Yes, sir.

MR. VAN COTT. And about how many of those lectures did you deliver?

MR. LUNDSTROM. I delivered four different lectures in Salt Lake, giving the reasons why I left the church. I considered it my duty.

MR. VAN COTT. Where were they delivered?

MR. LUNDSTROM. In the Swedish Lutheran Church.

MR. VAN COTT. In Salt Lake City?

MR. LUNDSTROM. In Salt Lake City.

MR. VAN COTT. Those lectures were public, I suppose?

MR. LUNDSTROM. Yes, sir.

MR. VAN COTT. Did you refer to these penalties in those lectures?

MR. LUNDSTROM. I referred to them some.

MR. VAN COTT. So that people generally who attended the meeting would know about them?

MR. LUNDSTROM. Yes, sir.

MR. VAN COTT. About when were those lectures delivered?

MR. LUNDSTROM. It was in the winter of 1901 and 1902. The first meeting was the 6th of October, 1901.

MR. VAN COTT. That is all.

MR. TAYLER. Did you publish in the Swedish tongue an account of these observances and ceremonies?

MR. LUNDSTROM. Yes.

MR. TAYLER. About the same time—about 1901 or 1902?

MR. LUNDSTROM. No; later; a couple of years later.

SENATOR DUBOIS. Did any Mormon ever protest to you with respect to the accuracy of your description?

MR. LUNDSTROM. Not the officials, but individuals not knowing the exact condition of the church, not being familiar with them. They used to call me a liar. That was true in regard to the revelation proposition.[17]

SENATOR DUBOIS. Did they point out to you any inaccuracy in your statement? Did any Mormon ever tell you where you were inaccurate?

MR. LUNDSTROM. They have endeavored to.

SENATOR DUBOIS. And correct you?

MR. LUNDSTROM. They have endeavored to.

SENATOR DUBOIS. In writing or in conversation?

MR. LUNDSTROM. Both in writing and in lectures and in conversation. ...

THE CHAIRMAN. You said something about lack of faith in the manifesto.

---

17. A month later, one of Smoot's witnesses, a Mr. Fernstrom, would testify that Lundstrom's reputation in the community was that he "misrepresents or lies" about nearly every transaction he had ever undertaken (*Smoot Hearings,* 2:1011-12).

What do you mean by that? You gave that as one of the reasons for severing your connection with the church?

MR. LUNDSTROM. The reason was this. In the first revelation commanding polygamy, it was stated that anyone to whom it is revealed must obey it or be damned, and now the manifesto doing away with it. I held that God had either changed His mind or else Wilford Woodruff had made a mistake or else the mistake was in the first place, and it made it just as bad one way as the other.

THE CHAIRMAN. So that the two revelations got you mixed up somewhat?

MR. LUNDSTROM. Yes, sir.

MR. VAN COTT. Did you go into polygamy?

MR. LUNDSTROM. Yes.

MR. VAN COTT. Did you?

MR. LUNDSTROM. Only to a certain extent. I had another wife sealed to me in the temple for eternity; but I only had one wife in this life, [the other] ... was dead when I [was sealed to] her. ...

MR. VAN COTT. So that as a matter of fact you were never a practical polygamist?

MR. LUNDSTROM. No, sir.

MR. VAN COTT. You did not obey the first revelation?

MR. LUNDSTROM. I did not.

MR. VAN COTT. And you objected to the second?

MR. LUNDSTROM. Yes, sir.[18] ...

---

18. In 1914, Lundstrom asked for forgiveness and was allowed to rejoin the LDS Church.

17.

Charles H. Jackson,
Charles W. Penrose, and William Budge

Friday & Saturday, December 16-17

"Four senators sat for two hours today as the committee on elections to listen to reasons for the attack on Senator Smoot's right to
occupy his seat. The day's session came to an end at 12 o'clock,
when the chairman announced that owing to desire of senators to
hear the debate on the Philippine bill this afternoon, there will not
be [a] meeting of the committee." —*Deseret News,* Dec. 16, 1904

Charles H. Jackson,[1] having been duly sworn, was examined and testified as follows ...

MR. TAYLER. How long, Mr. Jackson, have you given attention to political
conditions in Idaho?

MR. JACKSON. I have engaged in every campaign since 1894.

MR. TAYLER. As a matter of public and political history, what subjects
have agitated the minds of the people of Idaho particularly in the last
few years?

MR. JACKSON. The great question with us in Idaho has been the growing
power of the Mormon Church in its interference in State affairs.

MR. TAYLER. And has that been generally or only locally interesting and
discussed?

MR. JACKSON. It was made the paramount issue in the last campaign. It
was the one subject which the Democratic party and independents
discussed.

MR. TAYLER. In what particular forms has this question of so-called Mormon interference in State affairs expressed itself?

MR. JACKSON. By the visits of the apostles of the church, residents of Salt
Lake City, coming into Idaho and directing the people of their faith
how to vote, both by saying that it was the revelation that they should
vote such and such a ticket and the desire of the church authorities to
have them do so.

---

1. At the time of the hearings, Jackson (ca. 1863-?) lived in Boise, Idaho. He had
moved to the state from New York twelve years earlier. He worked in insurance and
ranching and chaired Idaho's Democratic Party. He was not LDS.

MR. TAYLER. And what public legislation has been effected or sought or threatened by this so-called Mormon invasion?

MR. JACKSON. The matter became one of vital interest two years ago when the apostle, John Henry Smith, came to Boise while the Idaho legislature was in session, and there procured the passage of a resolution through the Idaho legislature providing for submitting to the people at the next election the question whether a constitutional convention should be held for the purpose of taking out of our State constitution that clause which prohibits polygamy in the State. During that same session of the Idaho legislature, John Henry Smith promoted or secured the passage of an act which provided a bounty on all sugar raised in the State during the years 1903 and 1904.[2] These two measures were and are to-day, by public opinion, attributed to the active interference of John Henry Smith.

MR. TAYLER. What interest had John Henry Smith or the Mormon Church, if you know, in the subject of a bounty on sugar, so far as the State of Idaho was concerned?

MR. JACKSON. The Mormon Church, as I understand it, with Joseph F. Smith, owns the sugar factories, with one exception. President Joseph F. Smith of the Mormon Church is president of—I believe it is called the Idaho Sugar Company, recognized as a Mormon institution. ...

THE CHAIRMAN. ... I want to ask about Mr. Smith. His name is John Henry Smith, I think you said?

MR. JACKSON. Yes.

THE CHAIRMAN. What position does he hold in the Mormon Church, if you know.

MR. JACKSON. He is an apostle.

SENATOR FORAKER. What did the defeat of Governor [John T.] Morrison have to do with Mormonism?[3] How is it connected?

MR. JACKSON. It is understood in Idaho that the Mormon Church defeated Governor Morrison for renomination.

SENATOR FORAKER. Under the leadership of [Frank R.] Gooding?[4]

MR. JACKSON. Yes, sir.

SENATOR FORAKER. Is Gooding a Mormon?

MR. JACKSON. I do not think so.

MR. TAYLER. You may briefly state what is the ground of the belief that

2. A bounty in this context was a subsidy for local farmers to promote the sugar industry.

3. John T. Morrison served one term as governor, 1903-05.

4. Frank R. Gooding served two terms as governor, 1905-09.

the Mormon Church defeated Governor Morrison for the renomination.

MR. JACKSON. In Idaho we have 21 counties, of which 6 are absolutely controlled by the Mormons; that is, the large percentage of the voters of those 6 counties are Mormons. The Mormon counties voted entirely for Mr. Gooding; and whatever the Mormon Church desires in Idaho is carried out. It is impossible for any man or any party to go against the Mormon Church in Idaho, whether he is a Republican or a Democrat.

THE CHAIRMAN. You mean it is impossible to go against them?

MR. JACKSON. I mean that unless the Mormon Church supports the individual, you might as well give up. There is no hope for you.

MR. TAYLER. You say there are 6 out of 21 counties that are controlled absolutely by the Mormons?

MR. JACKSON. They are called Mormon counties. Then there are other counties along the southern tier of counties of Idaho in which the Mormons have large colonies and where they practically hold in the counties the balance of power, as in the State they hold the balance of power.

MR. TAYLER. The result is that in the legislature how many members of the senate and how many of the members of the house are necessarily, if the Mormon Church desires it, elected by it?

MR. JACKSON. Well, practically, the six Mormon counties return about a third of the Idaho legislature. We have one senator from each county, therefore there would be six senators from the Mormon counties. Then, in addition, in some of the other southern counties the Mormons have, as I stated, the control and are able to secure the nomination, whereby the party usually controls in the legislature. ...

SENATOR DUBOIS. You say all the delegates from the Mormon counties are not necessarily Mormons in religion, but they are Mormons in politics. Will you explain that to the committee?

MR. JACKSON. Those are what we call the jack-Mormons, Senator.[5] They are worse than the original article. They are willing to go to greater lengths than any Mormon is willing to go. They are put up by the Mormons, really, to do the heavy work for them, and while they are nominally known as gentile, and not affiliated with the church, everyone knows that they are Mormons for political purposes. ...

5. The term "jack-Mormon" has changed over the years to mean a non-practicing Mormon. At the time, it meant a non-Mormon who was friendly or sympathetic toward Mormons.

MR. VAN COTT. Which apostles of the Mormon Church went to Idaho and stated that it was a revelation that they should vote such and such a ticket, and likewise that it was the desire of the church that they should do so?

MR. JACKSON. In 1902 it was charged that Apostle Mat[t]hias Cowley went through Oneida County directing the people there to vote the Republican ticket as being the will of the church.

MR. VAN COTT. Did you see him?

MR. JACKSON. No, sir.

MR. VAN COTT. Did you hear him?

MR. JACKSON. No, sir.

MR. VAN COTT. How did this word come to you?

MR. JACKSON. It came to me through the protests of Mormon Democrats of Oneida County. They had nominated a county ticket there, and Apostle Mat[t]hias Cowley went through saying, especially to the women, that the church desired the election of the Republican ticket; and the Mormon leaders themselves, the Democrats who were on our county ticket there, proposed to withdraw their county ticket as a rebuke to the church and to Apostle Mat[t]hias Cowley for his interference.

MR. VAN COTT. What year was that?

MR. JACKSON. 1902.

MR. VAN COTT. Was there any other apostle?

MR. JACKSON. I have known of Apostle John Henry Smith being in the State making political speeches.

MR. VAN COTT. Stating it was a revelation to vote such and such a ticket?

MR. JACKSON. It is always a revelation when an apostle of the Mormon Church addresses the Mormon people.[6]

MR. VAN COTT. Was that my question?

MR. JACKSON. That is the answer to it.

---

6. John Henry Smith later testified:

MR. WORTHINGTON. Mr. Jackson told us something about members or officers of your church going to Idaho with revelations to the members of your church how to vote; that what you said to them was a revelation. Tell us, as far as your experience and knowledge go, if anything of that kind obtains in your church.

MR. SMITH. ... As far as the question of revelation is concerned, no such words have ever been used by me as affecting any man in seeking to influence him in his political views by an application of my church authority and dignity. Upon the contrary, I have stood upon the platform a hundred times and announced that I was there as a citizen of the United States, exercising my rights; that I asked no quarter and expected to give none so far as the question[s] of politics were concerned.

MR. WORTHINGTON. So far as you know, has any other member of your church—

MR. VAN COTT. Did John Henry Smith say it was a revelation to vote such and such a ticket?

MR. JACKSON. His personal presence there was the revelation. He did not actually state it in words.

MR. VAN COTT. Is that true of M[atthias]. F. Cowley?

MR. JACKSON. It is true regarding every leading official of the Mormon Church.

MR. VAN COTT. And the same answer holds true?

MR. JACKSON. That their presence in a political campaign is a direct revelation to Mormon voters how to vote. ...

MR. VAN COTT. Will you explain, Mr. Jackson, what justified you in making the statement you did yesterday [Friday, Dec. 16] that the Mormons controlled in the nomination of the governor, for instance, Frank R. Gooding, if they hold only a third of the representation?

MR. JACKSON. The politicians of Idaho know, regardless of their politics, that whichever way the Mormons vote so goes the State. No man can be elected governor in our State without the Mormon support, and no party can be successful without it. Therefore, when the Mormons come up in a bunch and indicate a preference for any man, the politicians are usually too glad to put that man on the ticket.

MR. VAN COTT. That is, the one-third of the convention wags the two thirds and makes it go the way it desires. Is that correct?

MR. JACKSON. That is apparently so.

MR. VAN COTT. Apparently so?

MR. JACKSON. But you must remember that in the balance of our State, especially in the southern counties, there are strong Mormon settlements, which go to control part of what are called the Gentile counties. The Mormon Church absolutely controls six counties, and it holds practically the balance of power in six other counties. So, while ostensibly the number of Mormons in our conventions or in our legislature is apparently only one-third, yet as a matter of fact the control is always in the hands of the Mormon Church, because they hold the balance of power in the other counties and they use the Gentiles there as well as the Mormons to represent them.

MR. VAN COTT. That is, the Gentiles are willing to subserve the will of the Mormon Church, in your opinion?

MR. SMITH. Never to my knowledge.

MR. WORTHINGTON. Endeavored or in any way sought to convey to the minds of members of the church that they were speaking by authority or by revelation?

MR. SMITH. Never to my knowledge (*Smoot Hearings,* 2:297).

MR. JACKSON. I think when an election is offered to a man if he will do certain things that nine times out of ten they will do it. That has been my experience.

MR. VAN COTT. That is your opinion of the Gentiles in Idaho?

MR. JACKSON. Not of the Gentiles, but of the politicians.

MR. VAN COTT. The politicians can not carry the conventions and the elections?

MR. JACKSON. I have usually found that the politicians have a great deal to say about it.[7] ...

MR. VAN COTT. I call your attention to what appear to be the returns of the Idaho election for 1904. The copy I hand you is not certified, but I assume that it is correct. It appears to be. Would you think so, Mr. Jackson?

MR. JACKSON (after examining). Yes, sir; I should say from some of these returns that I recognize that this is official.

MR. VAN COTT. Calling your attention, for instance, to the vote for governor, do you mean to say that Mr. Gooding would not have been elected if the Mormons had not voted for him?

MR. JACKSON. No, sir.

MR. VAN COTT. He would have been elected if every vote in every Mormon county had never been counted?

MR. JACKSON. No, sir; he would have been defeated.

MR. VAN COTT. I will ask you, then, to look at the returns before you, and state what was the vote for Mr. Gooding?

MR. JACKSON. The total vote?

MR. VAN COTT. Yes, sir.

MR. JACKSON. Forty-one thousand eight hundred and seventy-seven (41,877).

MR. VAN COTT. What was Mr. Heitfeld's vote?

MR. JACKSON. Twenty-four thousand one hundred and ninety-two (24,192).

MR. VAN COTT. His plurality was 17,685?

MR. JACKSON. Yes, sir.

MR. VAN COTT. I will ask you if the total vote of the six Mormon counties in Idaho, for the republican candidate for governor, was not only 14,668, about three thousand less than Mr. Gooding's majority in the Gentile counties?

MR. JACKSON. What was the total vote in the six Mormon counties?

MR. VAN COTT. Fourteen thousand six hundred and sixty-eight (14,668).

---

7. This entire section was used by Tayler in his closing argument for the plaintiffs (*Smoot Hearings*, 3:505-06).

MR. JACKSON. Assuming that to be correct, that would have been less, apparently, than Mr. Gooding's plurality. But such is not the case. It is only an apparent situation.

MR. VAN COTT. If you take all the Mormon counties and throw their votes out, eliminate them, Mr. Gooding would still have a plurality of over 3,000 votes over Mr. Heitfeld.

MR. JACKSON. But when you have thrown out the votes of the six Mormon counties you have not by any means thrown out the Mormon vote of the State.

MR. VAN COTT. That is, these gentiles who are influenced by the Mormons to vote?

MR. JACKSON. No, sir; it is the Mormons themselves. There are settlements in practically all of the southern tier of what are called "gentile counties"—strong Mormon settlements.

MR. VAN COTT. Take these six Mormon counties, as they are called. Are there not gentiles in all of those counties?

MR. JACKSON. Oh, yes sir.

MR. VAN COTT. And in the question I put to you, I told you to eliminate the whole vote in those six counties.

MR. JACKSON. Yes, sir.

MR. VAN COTT. And still Mr. Gooding is elected?

MR. JACKSON. If you eliminate the whole vote of those counties Mr. Gooding would have had a very much better chance, because, as I understand it, almost all the gentiles, whether they were Democrats or Republicans, in those Mormon counties voted to support our ticket.

MR. VAN COTT. Notwithstanding that, the Republican ticket was overwhelmingly elected?

MR. JACKSON. Yes. sir. ...

Charles W. Penrose,[8] having been duly affirmed,[9] was examined and testified as follows ...

---

8. Penrose (1832-1925) joined the LDS Church in England in 1850, immigrated to Utah in 1861, and was ordained to the Quorum of the Twelve on July 7, 1904. He lived in Salt Lake City, where he edited the *Deseret News*. A few days prior to his testimony, the *Salt Lake Tribune* editorialized:

Without attempting an analysis of the Penrose character, which is sui generis—even among a peculiar people—The Tribune extends congratulations to such Senators as are members of the Committee of Privileges and Elections, and to Apostle Penrose, upon the wonderful opportunity which will be afforded by the meeting—the Senators will hear the most skillful expounder of the Mormon faith and doctrine tell all about the Smoot case—unless the Hon. Charles shall choose to talk about the weather, in which case he will probably be able to make it appear to himself that the

MR. TAYLER. What official position do you occupy in the church?

MR. PENROSE. I am at present one of the twelve apostles since last July.

MR. TAYLER. You are editor of the "Deseret News?"

MR. PENROSE. Yes, sir.

MR. TAYLER. How long have you been editor of that paper.

MR. PENROSE. I was connected with the editorial department in 1877, and have been most of the time since; but on two occasions, two years, I was on the "Salt Lake Herald," and a couple of years in the church historian's office, and during that time I was not connected with the paper. But with those exceptions I have been connected with the paper right along.[10]

MR. TAYLER. You are not now church historian?

MR. PENROSE. I say I was for a couple of years one of the assistant church historians.

MR. TAYLER. How long have you been a member of the Mormon Church?

MR. PENROSE. Ever since 1850.

MR. TAYLER. You were not born a member of the church?

MR. PENROSE. No.

MR. TAYLER. That is to say, your parents were not, at the time of your birth, members of it?

MR. PENROSE. No; they were not.

MR. TAYLER. Did you become a member of the church in Utah?

weather is the sole subject under discussion. And so we may well believe that the Hon. Chas. will scoot around the important points with the facile and yet aggravating ability which has made him at once the envy and the admiration of all the other apostles ("Charlie at Washington," Dec. 11, 1904).

9. Penrose was one of three witnesses who elected to "affirm" rather than "swear" an oath that they would tell the truth. The other two were Joseph F. Smith and his son Hyrum F. Smith.

10. Penrose was a Democrat, and his politics surfaced on the editorial pages of the *Deseret News* in its coverage of Smoot, a Republican. Carl Badger, in a letter to his wife on November 26, 1905, discussed this:

The difficulties between the Senator and Editor Penrose have gone quite far. I do not see how they can be settled without charges and a [church] trial. The Senator says he will not forgive Penrose, and in cases where such bitter feelings are involved as in politics, and when one hates so royally as does the Senator, I do not see how a settlement can be peacefully reached, without the intervention of third parties and a finding of facts by a trial. This is a strange condition of affairs between apostles of him who said that the first commandment was to love God. ... I sit here and enjoy the humor of the thought that these two representatives of Christ stand for the very essence of the things that he did not stand for. They are poor human children that arrogate to themselves superior virtues and powers that they do not possess, and they are so lacking in 'the saving grace of humor' that they do not see how ridiculous they make themselves" (in Rodney J. Badger, *Liahona and Iron Rod: The Biography of Carl A. and Rose J. Badger* [Bountiful, Utah: Family History Publishers, 1985], 286).

MR. PENROSE. No; in London, England.

MR. TAYLER. When did you come to this country?

MR. PENROSE. In 1861.

MR. TAYLER. Have you lived in Utah ever since?

MR. PENROSE. Yes; my home has been there since. I have been absent in Europe two or three times.

MR. TAYLER. Your home has been in Salt Lake since that time?

MR. PENROSE. Yes, sir.

MR. TAYLER. Are you a polygamist?

MR. PENROSE. Yes, sir.

MR. TAYLER. How man wives have you?

MR. PENROSE. My legal wife is dead, and I have two wives whom I recognize as my plural wives.[11] ...

MR. TAYLER. You became an apostle last July?

MR. PENROSE. Yes.

MR. TAYLER. In place of Apostle [Abraham Owen] Woodruff, I believe, who died?

MR. PENROSE. Yes.

MR. TAYLER. Was that Apostle Woodruff a son of Wilford Woodruff?

MR. PENROSE. A son of Wilford Woodruff.

MR. TAYLER. Will you tell us how, in so far as you have knowledge of it, you came to be elected apostle?

MR. PENROSE. I was selected by the presidency of the church and the other apostles—

MR. TAYLER. Yes; go ahead.

MR. PENROSE. Who were present in the meeting in the temple. I was chosen to be one of the twelve by them.

MR. TAYLER. Were you present at the meeting?

MR. PENROSE. No; I was not there until after the decision had been made.

MR. TAYLER. Until after they had made their choice?

MR. PENROSE. Yes.

---

11. Penrose's wives and children were: 1. Lucetta Stratford (1834-1903), married Penrose in 1855—children Charles Kimball (1856), Ernest Stratford (1857-1932), Jessie Lucetta (1858-1944), Kate (1860-1931), Bertha (1861), Alice Cecilia (1862-1918), Clara Matilda (1864), Cora Eliza (1864), Lucetta (1865-66), Emma Louise (1869), Lettie (1870), George William (1871-1913), Ella Maude (1872-73), Frederick Edgar (1873), Lou Bell (1874), Edwin C. Centennius (1876-1935), Wallace Harold (1877), and Lucile (1880-1971); 2. Louise Elizabeth Lusty (1843-1925), married Penrose 1863—children Amy Blanche (1863-1952), Herbert Lusty (1869-1937), Ettie May (1871-1963), Nellie (1875-1963), Frank William (1876-1949), Flora (1878), Lulu (1880-1965), Arthur James (1881-82), Bertrand August (1883-1918), and Leo Eugene (1886-1974); and 3. Esther Romania Salina Bunnell (1839-1932), married Penrose 1886—no children.

MR. TAYLER. Did you then meet with them?

MR. PENROSE. Yes; I was sent for and informed that they had unanimously chosen me to fill the place made vacant by the death of Mr. Woodruff.

MR. TAYLER. Where was it you met them when you were called for?

MR. PENROSE. I met them in a room in the temple.

MR. TAYLER. Was it the regular meeting place of the apostles?

MR. PENROSE. Yes, sir.

MR. TAYLER. Or was it on a ceremonial occasion?

MR. PENROSE. It was the regular meeting place where they usually assemble when they have a meeting.

MR. TAYLER. Who were there?

MR. PENROSE. President Joseph F. Smith, President John R. Winder, President Anthon H. Lund, Francis M. Lyman, John Henry Smith, Rudger Clawson. I do not know whether Reed Smoot was present or not; I could not remember about that; but there were Hiram M. Smith and George A. Smith. They were all who were present.

MR. TAYLER. Was George Teasdale there?

MR. PENROSE. No, sir.

MR. TAYLER. Why not, if you know?

MR. PENROSE. I do not know. I did not inquire.

MR. TAYLER. Was he in the country, if you know?

MR. PENROSE. Not that I know of.

MR. TAYLER. Was John W. Taylor there?

MR. PENROSE. He was not.

MR. TAYLER. Do you understand that he is out of the country?

MR. PENROSE. That is my understanding of it, but I do not know of my own knowledge where he is.

MR. TAYLER. Heber J. Grant was on a foreign mission?

MR. PENROSE. He was in Europe, as I understand.

MR. TAYLER. Was Apostle [Marriner Wood] Merrill there?

MR. PENROSE. No. I understood he was too sick to be present. He has not been in Salt Lake for a long time. He makes his home in Richmond.

MR. TAYLER. You know those men were not there?

MR. PENROSE. Oh, yes; I know they were not there.

MR. TAYLER. You know that all the others were there except Mr. Smoot?

MR. PENROSE. All that I mentioned. I will not be certain whether Mr. Smoot was there or not. I do not remember.

MR. TAYLER. Mr. Smoot is the only member of the presidency and the twelve apostles concerning whom you are unable to speak definitely one way or the other. Is that right?

MR. PENROSE. Yes; in regard to his presence.

MR. TAYLER. In regard to his presence there?

MR. PENROSE. Yes; I think he was there, but I am not sure.

SENATOR DUBOIS. Was Apostle [Matthias F.] Cowley there?

MR. PENROSE. No, sir.

SENATOR DUBOIS. Where was he?

MR. PENROSE. I do not know.

MR. TAYLER. Is that all, Senator?

SENATOR DUBOIS. Yes.

MR. TAYLER. You were elected, you say, in July, and your election came up to be sustained, or you were sustained, when, after that?

MR. PENROSE. At the general conference in October.

MR. TAYLER. And at that time you and all of the first presidency and the twelve apostles were unanimously sustained?

MR. PENROSE. Yes; I believe so. I saw no contrary vote.[12] ...

MR. TAYLER. The "Deseret News" is the organ of the Church of Jesus Christ of Latter-Day Saints?

MR. PENROSE. It is in this sense, as we have published repeatedly, that whenever the authorities of the church have anything to say publicly they will say it through the "Deseret News" over their signatures. And any church news or intelligence, information for the general public, is published in the columns of the "News."[13]

---

12. This entire section was used by Tayler in his closing argument for the plaintiffs (*Smoot Hearings,* 3:561-63).

13. Smoot was, in fact, annoyed by the lukewarm coverage of his case by the *Deseret News.* He complained to Joseph F. Smith on January 9, 1904: "Think of such things as this being used: 'The Church has deserted Smoot since the last city election in Salt Lake City.' As proof, the articles in the *Deseret News* are submitted, with the cuts of Senator Sutherland and Representative Howell" (in Kathryn Smoot, "The Role of the Newspaper in the Reed Smoot Investigation: 1903-1907," M.A. thesis, University of Utah, 1964, 47). Harvard Heath found that the *Deseret News* "was not anti-Smoot, but it did not take hard stands or promote his cause with the same fervor that the *Tribune* exerted to destroy him. ... At a time when Smoot needed all the support he could get, Penrose appeared more intent on supporting Democratic positions than Republican ones. In Smoot's eyes, it was not a matter of partisan politics but a matter of Church survival. Since his case was now the Church's cause, the Church paper should give unqualified support in every way possible to aid in his bid to retain his seat" (Heath, "Reed Smoot: First Modern Mormon," Ph.D. diss., Brigham Young University, 1990, 154-58). Joseph F. Smith's view was "the least said by us [in the newspaper] the better," and that the church was "not ... afraid of the truth, or to discuss the facts." Smith did "regret very much indeed that anything should have appeared in the *Deseret News* calculated to dis-turb the poise of mind of your friends" but in the long run it was best not to offer new material that would "afford [Smoot's enemies] the opportunity to twist and turn things" (Smith to Smoot, May 18, 1906).

Mr. Tayler. The paper belongs to the church, does it not?

Mr. Penrose. Yes, sir.

Mr. Tayler. And the building?

Mr. Penrose. The building and the plant.

Mr. Tayler. And the paper itself?

Mr. Penrose. Yes; I understand so.

Mr. Tayler. And it is edited by one of the twelve?

Mr. Penrose. It is now.

Mr. Tayler. What office did you hold before you became an apostle?

Mr. Penrose. For some time I was one of the presidents of the Salt Lake stake of Zion, as it is called, second counselor to Angus M. Cannon.

Mr. Tayler. The Salt Lake stake of Zion is the largest of all the stakes?

Mr. Penrose. It was then. There have been four made out of it since, and one of them is the Salt Lake stake, which is not the largest now.

Mr. Tayler. Do you know, Mr. Penrose, whether one of your wives has recently changed her name, her public name, so as to indicate that she is your wife?[14]

Mr. Penrose. I believe while I was in Mexico, that, having moved her place of business—she is a doctor, a graduated doctor—she added the name of Penrose to her sign or to her advertisement in some way.

Mr. Tayler. She had previously gone as a doctor by her name, the name which she had before she married you?

Mr. Penrose. Yes. ...

The Chairman. Do you remember, Mr. Penrose, whether the apostles are required to go through the endowment house or take the endowments before they are eligible to the office of apostleship?

Mr. Penrose. I never heard that mentioned as a necessary qualification.

The Chairman. So far as you know, is that the fact?

Mr. Penrose. No; I do not know. I should explain, Senator, that what we call the endowment house is not the temple. There was a building called the endowment house, in which endowments were celebrated, but that building was pulled down, and all the same or similar ceremonies are performed in the temple. So we always use the term "temple," and not endowment house. Do you mean go through the endowment ceremony?

The Chairman. Yes.

Mr. Penrose. No, sir. I have never heard that mentioned as a necessary qualification to be an apostle.

---

14. The wife Penrose referred to here was Romania Bunnell Pratt Penrose. Her sealing to Parley P. Pratt was dissolved in 1881, prior to marrying Penrose five years later.

THE CHAIRMAN. Have you taken the endowment?

MR. PENROSE. Yes, sir.

THE CHAIRMAN. In the old endowment house?

MR. PENROSE. Yes, sir.

THE CHAIRMAN. The same ceremony, in substance, is performed in the temple?

MR. PENROSE. Yes, sir.

THE CHAIRMAN. It is already in evidence that that building had been destroyed. Before 1890, before the manifesto, was the practice of taking plural wives quite prevalent?

MR. PENROSE. Yes; to some extent. Of course it had to be to a limited extent, because the number of males in the Territory was in excess of the females, according to the census.[15]

THE CHAIRMAN. Then it was limited by the difference between the male and the female population?

MR. PENROSE. That would have some effect, undoubtedly. ...

SENATOR McCOMAS. Only a question, Mr. Penrose. You are editor of the "Deseret News?"

MR. PENROSE. Yes, sir.

SENATOR McCOMAS. You control its policy; you are the editor in chief?

MR. PENROSE. The editor in chief.

SENATOR McCOMAS. You control its policy?

MR. PENROSE. As far as I possibly can. I do so when I am there.

SENATOR McCOMAS. Your personal politics is what?

MR. PENROSE. I am a Democrat myself, but the paper is independent.

SENATOR McCOMAS. Sometimes supporting the Republican party and sometimes the Democratic party.

MR. PENROSE. We have not supported either party, but we have supported measures. We have sustained the Administration in its Philippine policy[16] and on questions of that character, but not with reference to any party—only in regard to measures that we thought were for the good of the country.[17]

---

15. The 1890 census showed 110,463 males and 97,442 females in Utah Territory.

16. Roosevelt's policy was an extension of U.S. President McKinley's (assassinated 1901) occupation of the Philippines. Following the Spanish-American War in 1899, the United States purchased the Philippines from Spain for $20 million. However, the people of the Philippines announced independence and fought a fourteen-year insurgency against the United States.

17. Soon Republicans began discussing lower tariffs for the Philippines—something the "sugar beet Republicans" in the West opposed. Smoot wrote to Joseph F. Smith on January 26, 1906:

SENATOR McCOMAS. You have never supported in your paper the Democratic or the Republican party?

MR. PENROSE. No, sir; not as parties. The paper has been accused sometimes of being Democratic and sometimes of being Republican, but when the matter has been investigated the people had to "read between the lines," as they call it, to gain that impression either way. We have endeavored to keep it wholly independent, politically—that is, in a partisan sense.

SENATOR McCOMAS. With leanings to one side or the other, according to the independent policy?

MR. PENROSE. As it might be so interpreted by either party.

SENATOR McCOMAS. The "Deseret News," for instance, leaned to the Democratic party about the time President [Grover] Cleveland favored the admission of the State, did it not?

MR. PENROSE. We leaned to the admission of the State into the Union.

SENATOR McCOMAS. And to his Administration at that time?

MR. PENROSE. I do not think there was anything supporting his Administration particularly as being Democratic.

SENATOR McCOMAS. At that time?

MR. PENROSE. We supported his aim to bring the State into the Union, of course.

SENATOR McCOMAS. And only that?

MR. PENROSE. I do not now remember anything else.

SENATOR McCOMAS. Recently your paper has leaned toward the support of President Roosevelt's Administration generally or only on the Philippine policy?

MR. PENROSE. I do not think we have taken up any other question. I do not remember now taking up any other national question except in regard to the Philippines. We may, perhaps, however, have supported the position of the Administration in regard to the Panama Canal.[18]

SENATOR McCOMAS. And only to the extent you have mentioned?

MR. PENROSE. Yes, sir; that is all.

The Washington Post, of Jan. 22, 1906, had a nasty article on its front page, in which it was claimed that the Mormon Church is at the bottom of the fight against the Philippine Tariff Bill, and that its power is being made manifest among Western Senators. It said that you are president of seven sugar companies in the State of Utah; and of all the sugar companies in the State of Idaho; that the Church has millions invested in these companies; and that through the influence of the Church Western Senators are opposing the Philippine Tariff and the Statehood Bills.

18. In 1903 Roosevelt instigated Panamanian independence from Columbia so the United States could obtain a ten-mile wide strip of land for a canal. The U.S. paid $10 million, plus an annual fee, for this real estate.

MR. TAYLER. Mr. Penrose, you have been a rather conspicuous figure in the church in Salt Lake City for many years, have you not?

MR. PENROSE. In some respects.

MR. TAYLER. I am not asking you to say anything that would make you blush to say it.

MR. PENROSE. Thank you.

MR. TAYLER. I mean as respects self-praise. But you have been for so long a time at the head of the chief newspaper, as you would call it, of that region that the public generally has been very familiar with you personally.

MR. PENROSE. Yes, sir.

MR. TAYLER. You have not, as you say, flaunted or advertised the fact that you were a polygamist?

MR. PENROSE. No.

MR. TAYLER. I know of no one who has charged that against you. Nor, on the other hand, has there been any studious concealment of that fact?

MR. PENROSE. No; I think not.

MR. TAYLER. Do you not understand that the fact that you are a polygamist is one that is known of all men—

MR. PENROSE. I think it is.

MR. TAYLER. Who know you?

MR. PENROSE. Pretty generally understood.

MR. TAYLER. Have you the slightest doubt at all that Mr. Smoot knew that, as the rest of the world knew it?

MR. PENROSE. I should think that he would know it on general principles. That is all. He had no special reason. He is not acquainted, I think, with my family affairs.

MR. TAYLER. Did you read the testimony that was taken before this committee generally last spring?

MR. PENROSE. Yes.

MR. TAYLER. Was there a reference to you in that testimony as being a polygamist, do you remember?

MR. PENROSE. I believe that President [Joseph F.] Smith, on being asked the question, said I was a polygamist.[19]

MR. TAYLER. That is what I thought. So if Mr. Smoot heard that[,] he would have pretty fair testimony of the fact that you were reputed to be a polygamist?

MR. PENROSE. Yes; from general reputation, anyway.

---

19. On having been asked whether Penrose was "a polygamist," President Smith had answered: "I understand that he is" (*Smoot Hearings*, 1:158-59).

MR. TAYLER. Now, let me understand what I fear is grossly misunderstood if the interpretation put upon your remark is the natural one. Do you mean to say that any person can or does become a member of the twelve apostles without taking what are called "the ordinary endowments?"

MR. PENROSE. I said I thought it was possible. I do think it is entirely possible. But I think as a matter of fact they would all very probably have been through the endowments. But I would not know as a matter of fact.

MR. TAYLER. Now, suppose that one is ordained, if that is the word—never mind the word—to the Melchisedec priesthood. He would have to take some kind of an endowment ceremony or pass through one?[20]

MR. PENROSE. Oh, no.

MR. TAYLER. He would not?

MR. PENROSE. No; not necessarily.

MR. TAYLER. Not necessarily?

MR. PENROSE. No.

MR. TAYLER. If he were a priest, would he have any authority in respect of conferring or conducting the endowment ceremonies?

MR. PENROSE. No; not because he was a priest.

MR. TAYLER. Not because he was a priest?

MR. PENROSE. Oh, no.

MR. TAYLER. Who may conduct those ceremonies?

MR. PENROSE. Only persons who are specially called and set apart for the work, and they need not be apostles. An apostle might do so if so set apart.

MR. TAYLER. I understand that. Then this endowment ceremony is one that may be taken by any person who is a member of the church, provided the proper authority says that he is suitable, and it need not be taken by any member of the church?

MR. PENROSE. That is correct. He has to be properly recommended in order to receive the ceremony.

MR. TAYLER. Precisely.

MR. PENROSE. But he can be a member of the church in full fellowship and standing without going through the ceremonies.

MR. TAYLER. President Joseph F. Smith perhaps never passed through the temple in the sense of going through the endowment ceremony?

20. The requirement that men hold the Melchizedek Priesthood before entering the temple seems to have first appeared in print in a *Circular of Instructions* issued in 1913.

MR. PENROSE. I should not like to say that he never did, because it is pretty well known that he did.

MR. TAYLER. That he did?

MR. PENROSE. That he passed through the endowment ceremony.

MR. TAYLER. Would it surprise you if it was understood that Joseph F. Smith had never taken the endowment ceremony?

MR. PENROSE. It would, because he has officiated there himself in the house in years gone by. It would surprise me very much.

MR. TAYLER. Would it surprise you to learn that Apostle Smoot had not taken it?

MR. PENROSE. I think I should be surprised if I heard that stated.

MR. TAYLER. Have you the remotest suspicion that he has not? I am not referring to Mr. Smoot himself, but to any person high in the church.

MR. PENROSE. I should think as a rule they had all gone through the endowment ceremony. I should think so, but I do not know it as a matter of fact.[21] ...

William Budge,[22] being duly sworn, was examined and testified as follows ...

MR. WORTHINGTON. It appears, then, that in your case all your marriages were before the manifesto.[23] Can you tell us what has been going on in

21. Two months earlier, Penrose was called by the LDS First Presidency to "a committee of three" with B. H. Roberts and James E. Talmage to "thoroughly examine all the evidence and references to Church doctrines and publications ... as accumulated during the investigation by the Senate Committee relative to the protest against the confirmation of Senator Reed Smoot's place in the U.S. Senate," as Talmage recorded in his journal on October 14, 1904. "The so-called investigation has developed into an arraignment of the Church," Talmage wrote. He continued: "The brethren regard the work of examination as so important that the committee this day appointed, or rather each member of the committee, [is] advised to lay aside all other work possible." However, if a formal response was anticipated, it never materialized (L. Tom Perry Special Collections, Harold B. Lee Library, Brigham Young University).

22. At the time of the hearings, Budge (1828-1919) had been a resident of Paris, Idaho, for thirty-five years and president of the church's Bear Lake Stake since 1877. He converted to Mormonism in 1848 in Scotland and immigrated to Utah in 1860. He was a polygamist, a Republican, and a former member of the Idaho State Senate.

23. Budge's wives and children were: 1. Julia Stratford (1839-1912), married Budge 1856—children William (1857), William Scott (1859-60), Emily (1860), Julia (1861-1938), Zilpah (1863), Annie (1864-1949), Marion (1867), Andrew Scott (1868), Louis Scott (1869-71), Charles Penrose (1872-73), Mary Scott (1875-1968), and Jesse Robert Stratford (1878-1967); 2. Elizabeth (Lizzie) Pritchard (Jones) (1834-1908), married Budge 1861—children Arthur (1862-1937), Nina (1863-64), Helen (1865), Rose (1866-1948), (Judge) Alfred (1868-1951), Lizzie (1870-1945), Catherine (1872-80), Franklin (1874-

Idaho, where you have personal knowledge of the matter, as to any plural marriages since the manifesto?

MR. BUDGE. There have been no plural marriages in Idaho that I know of since the manifesto.

MR. WORTHINGTON. It has been brought out that you have been there a long time, and are perhaps the most prominent man there. Do you think any question of that kind, grave or small, could have occurred that you would not know about?

MR. BUDGE. Possibly I might not know what was done in some other county, but in a general way I think I would.

MR. WORTHINGTON. Has it come to your knowledge or information that there has been a plural marriage celebrated in Idaho since the manifesto?

MR. BUDGE. There never was a plural marriage celebrated in Idaho at all; but there was a time when those who were married in that way were married elsewhere.

MR. WORTHINGTON. Has it come to your knowledge or information, then, that since 1890 any of your men living in Idaho have been married to a plural wife anywhere?

MR. BUDGE. No, sir; I do not know of any such circumstance. ...

MR. WORTHINGTON. You have said ... that you vote as you think best. Is that true?

MR. BUDGE. Yes, sir.

MR. WORTHINGTON. Have you always exercised and had the privilege of voting for a Democrat or a republican or otherwise, just as you pleased?

MR. BUDGE. Always.

MR. WORTHINGTON. Have you in any way endeavored to or have you used any force or compulsion, on account of your position in the church, against any man to vote otherwise than he pleased?

MR. BUDGE. No, sir.

MR. WORTHINGTON. So far as you know, has the Mormon Church or any Mormon official done so in Idaho at any time?

MR. BUDGE. Not that I know of. ...

1933), and Frances Jane (1876-1972); and 3. Ann Hyer (1853-1931), married Budge 1868—children Isabella (1869-1959), Ezra Taft (1870-1928), Oliver Hyer (1872-1965), David Clare (1873-1947), Edwin Stratford (1876-1954), Thomas "B" (1878-1945), Clara (1881-1973), Lillian (1883-1943), Effie (1884-1952), Luella (1886-1952), Seth (1887-1978), Hugh Wallace (1889-1960), Alta May (1892-1963), Scott Merrill (1895-1972), and Jean Elsie (1898-1948).

SENATOR DUBOIS. Do you recall whether there was an Idaho test oath? Was there ever any such thing as an Idaho test oath?[24]

MR. BUDGE. Yes; I understand it.

SENATOR DUBOIS. Did you ever take that test oath?

MR. BUDGE. No; I never did.

SENATOR DUBOIS. Did you ever vote while that oath was in force?

MR. BUDGE. Possibly.

SENATOR DUBOIS. Then you took the test oath?

MR. BUDGE. I say possibly.

SENATOR DUBOIS. Do you not know whether you took the test oath? You could not vote unless you took the test oath, could you, up to the time that the laws putting it into effect were repealed, which was in 1892?

MR. BUDGE. There were a great many who did not take the test oath, I presume.

SENATOR DUBOIS. As a matter of fact, did any Mormon who was in good standing in the church take the test oath and vote?

MR. BUDGE. I couldn't say what the good Mormons did do. I don't remember.

SENATOR DUBOIS. That test oath was in force until after statehood, was it not?

MR. BUDGE. There were a number of years, I know, that we did not vote in consequence of the test oath; but as to what years we did not vote I couldn't tell.

SENATOR DUBOIS. It seems to have been a matter of some indifference to you. Now, as a matter of fact, were not a number of Mormons cut off from the church immediately prior to the election of 1888, in order that they might vote?

MR. BUDGE. No, sir; no such thing ever occurred where I am or as far as I know.

SENATOR DUBOIS. Is it not a matter of fact that some 150 or 200 of them were arrested on account of this?

MR. BUDGE. Yes, sir; it is true that a good many were arrested. I don't know the number; but I say that no man was cut off the church to vote.

---

24. The test oath was instituted in 1884 to disfranchise Mormon voters. It read in part: "You do solemnly swear (or affirm) ... that you are not a bigamist or polygamist; that you are not a member of any order, organization or association which teaches, advises, counsels or encourages its members, devotees or any other persons to commit the crime of bigamy or polygamy or any other crime defined by law, as a duty arising or resulting from membership in such order" (in Merle W. Wells, "The Idaho Anti-Mormon Test Oath, 1884-1892," *Pacific Historical Review* 24 [Aug. 1955]: 235-52).

SENATOR DUBOIS. You say you do not know whether they were cut off for that purpose?

MR. BUDGE. That may be your statement; but I say it was not so, to my knowledge.

SENATOR DUBOIS. Were not a number of them arrested, and was it not proven?

MR. BUDGE. No, sir.

SENATOR DUBOIS. By their own testimony?

MR. BUDGE. No, sir; not where I live, I say.

SENATOR DUBOIS. Did you give the orders to the bishops to give these men a certificate that they should withdraw from the church?

MR. BUDGE. Oh, that is a different thing. One of the judges that we had in the district where I live stated to the people that if they did not belong to the Mormon Church they could vote; so they withdrew from the church—from any connection with the organized church—to vote, but they were still Mormons, or claimed to be, just as a Mormon would be a member who came from England with a certificate of standing as a Mormon—came to this country and held it in his pocket. He is a Mormon, but he does not belong to the church organization.

SENATOR DUBOIS. Then they could take the test oath and could swear that they did not belong to or contribute to the support of an organization which permitted polygamy, etc.?

MR. BUDGE. Such was the advice given by one of the district judges.

SENATOR DUBOIS. Was it not your advice to these Mormons and bishops to give them this certificate that they had withdrawn?

MR. BUDGE. Not mine in particular that I know of.

SENATOR DUBOIS. Did you not approve of it?

MR. BUDGE. Well, I approved of it this far, that if it would give the people what we considered to be their rights, I had no objection; but I don't interfere with people, you know, in such things as that if they wish to do it.

MR. TAYLER. I understand he issued the certificates. Is that it?

SENATOR DUBOIS. He directed the bishop to issue the certificates.

MR. WORTHINGTON. Certificates of withdrawal.

SENATOR DUBOIS. Certificates of withdrawal from the church, and they resumed their active membership in the church immediately after election, did they not; immediately after they voted?

MR. BUDGE. Some of them did, I believe.

SENATOR DUBOIS. And on account of this, what was considered a transparent subterfuge, a great many of them were arrested, and as a matter of history is it not true that one was in jail and taken out on a writ of habeas corpus, and on that account the test oath came before the Supreme Court of the United States?

MR. BUDGE. The Senator is making an explanation. If there is any question for me to answer I will do so.

THE CHAIRMAN. I was about to ask the Senator to name the individual in the case.

MR. BUDGE. I don't recollect of any persons that withdrew from the church to exercise their political privileges that were imprisoned. I don't remember it—not in our county; but I can remember of people being arrested for unlawful cohabitation and polygamy ...

MR. BUDGE. Do you remember, Senator, you and I having a conversation at Salt Lake City?

SENATOR DUBOIS. Yes, sir.

MR. BUDGE. Do you remember promising me, as you thought it right and proper, to use your influence at the following election to remove that test oath?

SENATOR DUBOIS. I have no doubt about it; because I openly took that stand, and I was the first man to take it.

MR. BUDGE. You at that time, like a good, considerate, just man, regretted that the Mormon people were embarrassed and oppressed as they had been, and you promised that you would help, at the next favorable opportunity, which would be two years or about two years from that time, to remove that law that was read here from the statutes.

SENATOR DUBOIS. Previous to that, however, I had written a letter advocating that course. I was the very first one to advocate that course. There is no discrepancy between us. That was based on the manifesto.

MR. BUDGE. So, if some of the people did vote, thinking they were safe enough in doing it, they were simply carrying out practically what you, in your good feeling and sympathy, thought ought to be allowed them.

SENATOR DUBOIS. As a matter of fact, President Budge, did not the legislature of 1892 remove the restrictions?

MR. BUDGE. If the Senator will be good enough to state the circumstances, I would be able to give the committee more satisfaction; but as I have stated already, my business is not politics. I don't pass much time in keeping track of political affairs and I don't remember dates. That is, I have not tried to remember them.

SENATOR DUBOIS. When the manifesto was issued in 1890, then for the first time the question arose about restoring the franchise. The State was admitted in 1890. You did not vote at the first election, but after the manifesto was issued all parties and all individuals united in restoring your franchise. Is not that a fact?

MR. BUDGE. Yes, sir; I believe that is right.

SENATOR DUBOIS. So that you voted in 1894 for the first time?

MR. BUDGE. Yes, sir.

SENATOR DUBOIS. Up to that vote in 1894 your votes had all been cast for the Democratic party. Then they divided about equally, as they did in Utah?

MR. BUDGE. I think you and I agree on that, Senator. ...

18.

John Henry Smith

Saturday, Monday & Tuesday,
December 17, 19-20

If the prince of liars were living today, Ananias[1] would gladly [hand] over the palm to some Utahans who have testified in the Smoot inquiry before the Senate committee. This is the consensus of opinion of all those who have listened to the evidence thus far, save the witnesses themselves." —*Salt Lake Tribune,* Dec. 17, 1904

John Henry Smith,[2] having been duly sworn, was examined, and testified as follows[3] ...

MR. TAYLER. We have heard a great deal about you, Mr. Smith, and your capacity as a public speaker; so be sure and speak so the Chairman can hear you.

MR. SMITH. You flatter me, sir.

THE CHAIRMAN. The voices of most of the witnesses seem to be very feeble.

MR. SMITH. Well, we are mild-mannered men, Mr. Chairman.

MR. TAYLER. You did not need to say that, Mr. Smith; we could see that [ourselves]. ... You were one of those also who testified [in Utah] respecting your interpretation of the [Wilford Woodruff] manifesto?

MR. SMITH. No, sir; I have never made any interpretation that I remember of.

MR. TAYLER. Do you remember the interpretation put upon it by Wilford Woodruff and the other leaders of the church?

MR. SMITH. Yes, sir.

MR. TAYLER. And the testimony of Joseph F. Smith respecting the meaning of the manifesto?[4]

---

1. In the New Testament, Ananias lies about a real estate transaction and is struck dead (Acts 5:1-5).

2. At the time of the hearings, Smith (1848-1911) lived in Salt Lake City. He was a son of George A. Smith and a second cousin to Joseph F. Smith. He was ordained an apostle on October 27, 1880.

3. Smith had been subpoenaed during the first round of hearings but was unable to attend because of poor health.

4. For interpretations of the Manifesto, see the *Smoot Hearings,* 1:106-09.

MR. SMITH. Yes, sir.

MR. TAYLER. Its application as well to polygamous cohabitation as to entering into new polygamous relations?

MR. SMITH. Yes, sir.

MR. TAYLER. You subscribe to their view of it, do you?

MR. SMITH. Yes, sir.

MR. TAYLER. But deny it in the practice?

MR. SMITH. My position in regard to that matter, Mr. Tayler, is simply this, that nobody could take from me my family; that I was responsible to God myself, and that I must take the consequences of my countrymen punishing me if they saw fit to do so. That has been my position in regard to that matter.

MR. TAYLER. Of course, you know now that your plural wife was taken after there was a law forbidding it?[5]

MR. SMITH. I knew it full well at the time, but with this fixed idea in my own heart, that the first amendment to the [U.S.] Constitution having never been passed upon in regard to that question, it was a question in abeyance, and that I expected, when the courts of this country decided it, that I could not be interfered with in the practice of that principle or in the maintenance of that wife.

MR. TAYLER. So that you denied and still deny the validity of that law as applied to you?

MR. SMITH. No, sir; I do not deny it. The law has been passed upon. The court has decided that.

MR. TAYLER. But you say you propose to—

MR. SMITH. I held that when I married that woman.

MR. TAYLER. You propose to continue the practice that you then started, upon the theory that there is a higher obligation upon you than the obligation to obey the law?

MR. SMITH. Yes; I must suffer the consequences, if my countrymen see fit to punish me.[6] ...

---

5. John Henry Smith married his second wife, Josephine Groesbeck, in 1877. The Supreme Court ruled on the Constitutionality of the Morrill Act in 1879. However, John Henry's and Josephine's last of eight children was born in 1898. He also had eleven children by his first wife, Sarah Farr, the last of whom was born in 1891, and was sealed to three additional women after their deaths (Jean Bickmore White, ed., *Church, State and Politics: The Diaries of John Henry Smith* [Salt Lake City: Signature Books and Smith Research Associates, 1991], xi).

6. The previous nine questions and answers were used by Tayler in his closing argument for the plaintiffs (*Smoot Hearings*, 3:534-35).

MR. TAYLER. Did you ever hear the charge made that Apostle [John W.] Tayler had taken two additional wives?

MR. SMITH. Not until I read it in the testimony taken before this committee.

MR. TAYLER. Have you taken any steps to find out if there is any truth in that?

MR. SMITH. No, sir; I have not.

MR. TAYLER. Have you made any suggestion that it would be a good thing for Apostle Taylor to come before the committee and testify to the truth?

MR. SMITH. I have not seen Apostle Taylor for years myself.

MR. TAYLER. Where is he?

MR. SMITH. I presume he is in Canada. I don't know. Mr. Tayler will remember that I was subpoenaed before this body of men some months ago. I was then confined to my room. A second subpoena was sent and I was there still. I am still laboring under the effects of that sickness and wholly unfitted, really, for any hard work. For seven months I was unable to dress myself. I just make that explanation. I haven't looked after anybody or paid any attention to anybody's interests except my own.

MR. TAYLER. So that so far as you are concerned, you have not been so situated, even if you had the disposition, as to take up any of these inquiries?

MR. SMITH. No.

MR. TAYLER. You used to take an interest in politics?

MR. SMITH. Yes, sir; I have been a very intense man in politics all my life.

MR. TAYLER. You have always been a Republican, have you?

MR. SMITH. My race [ancestors] were Federalists and Whigs, and I inherit every element of that stock, on both sides, as intense as ever was put in man. ...

MR. WORTHINGTON. You said, Mr. Smith, that of the apostles you were next to President [Francis M.] Lyman.[7] What did you mean by that?

MR. SMITH. I was ordained after he was ordained an apostle; next to him.

MR. WORTHINGTON. Is there any rule about the line of succession of the apostles to the president?

MR. SMITH. They go forward—they have so far—by seniority.

MR. WORTHINGTON. Has that been an invariable rule since the organization of the church, so far as you know from the history of it?

---

7. The reference is to comments John Henry Smith made on the first day of his testimony, Saturday, December 17 (*Smoot Hearings*, 2:284).

MR. SMITH. Yes, sir; so far as I remember.

MR. WORTHINGTON. Then the fact that President Lyman is now the president is due to the fact that he came to that place by seniority?

MR. SMITH. Yes, sir.

MR. WORTHINGTON. And you come second?

MR. SMITH. Yes, sir.

MR. WORTHINGTON. And, so far as you can recollect there has been no break in that law—unwritten law—or custom of the church?

MR. SMITH. Not so far as I can tell.

MR. WORTHINGTON. Are you acquainted with a member of your church named A[lexander]. F. McDonald?[8]

MR. SMITH. Yes, sir; I know him. I will say that he is now dead.

MR. WORTHINGTON. How long is it since he died?

MR. SMITH. I think within the present year, but I am not certain.

MR. WORTHINGTON. There is some testimony here tending to show that he performed a plural marriage ceremony after the manifesto. Have you at any time had anything to do with giving him instructions or directions in regard to that matter?[9]

MR. SMITH. Yes, sir.

MR. WORTHINGTON. State the whole matter, please.

MR. SMITH. After Lorenzo Snow became president of the Mormon Church [in September 1898] I was instructed by him upon a certain occasion, in going to visit Mexico that there had been an intimation made to him that Mr. McDonald had been exercising some powers that the president did not regard as belonging to him. He instructed me, upon my visit to Mexico to say to Mr. McDonald that should [I] be informed of his marrying anybody during his administration, or sealing anybody, I was instructed to have him dealt with by the authorities of the church in that section.

MR. WORTHINGTON. Did that apply to any sort of marriage ceremony, or simply to plural marriages?

---

8. Alexander F. McDonald (1825-1903) fled the United States to avoid prosecution for polygamy in the mid-1880s, thereafter serving as a counselor to the president of the Mexican Mission.

9. Carl Badger confided to his journal on December 18, 1904:

I just told the Senator that I was discouraged with the Church leaders, and that unless something was done, I did not know what the effect would be upon the young people—that is, something must be done with those who have violated the pledge against the taking of new wives. The Senator answered, "Nothing will be done; I believe they were authorized to take the wives" (in Rodney J. Badger, *Liahona and Iron Rod: The Biography of Carl A. and Rose J. Badger* [Bountiful, Utah: Family History Publishers, 1985], 238).

MR. SMITH. Wholly to plural marriages.

MR. WORTHINGTON. When was this that you received these instructions—about when?

MR. SMITH. I can not say. It was shortly after the coming of President Snow to be the president of the church, after the death of Wilford Woodruff; but I can not say just when it was.

MR. WORTHINGTON. That is immaterial. It is in the record. Did you do anything in pursuance of that instruction?

MR. SMITH. I visited Mexico. I called upon Mr. McDonald and informed him that information had reached President Snow that he had been exercising some authority in that matter, and I notified him that if the information did come to me that he had done so, or attempted to do so in the future, I would insist upon the authorities in that section dealing with him for his fellowship in the church.[10]

MR. WORTHINGTON. So far as your information or knowledge goes—that is up to the time that the testimony was given here the other day—what do you know with respect to his complying with your instructions?

MR. SMITH. I have no knowledge of his violation of them, so far as I am concerned.[11]

MR. WORTHINGTON. You have neither knowledge nor information to that effect?

MR. SMITH. No, sir.

MR. WORTHINGTON. Testimony has been given here to the effect that there must be special authority from the president of the church to authorize any subordinate officer to perform the ceremony of plural marriage. What is that?

MR. SMITH. Under the established rule of the church no person could secure a plural wife, except by the consent of the president of the church. But it is said that during the latter days of [President] John Taylor, some time previous to his [July 1887] death, in Mexico and Southern Arizona, some men were authorized to solemnize single

---

10. According to Smith's account of this trip to Mexico: "I had a talk with A. F. McDonald about Sealings and I told him if he was sealing Plural Wives to men his standing in the church was in danger" (in White, ed., *Church, State and Politics*, 485).

11. Plural marriages had been performed in the LDS Mexican colonies on a regular but discreet basis until November 1900 when President McDonald began granting the favor to anyone who requested it, without consulting with church headquarters (D. Michael Quinn, "LDS Church Authority and New Plural Marriages, 1890-1904," *Dialogue: A Journal of Mormon Thought* 18 (Spring 1985): 88.

marriages—that is, one marriage, but in no sense, that I know of, to
solemnize plural marriage.[12]

MR. WORTHINGTON. Is this authority which the president gives to some
subordinate officers of the church to perform plural marriages the
authority to perform some particular marriage or generally to perform plural marriages? I am speaking of the time when that privilege
was given.

MR. SMITH. Never having been given the authority, I really do not know.

MR. WORTHINGTON. You say you have understood that in President Taylor's time, which was prior to 1890, he had given Mr. McDonald some
authority in this regard, and perhaps had given it to others.

MR. SMITH. I presume there were others. It is simply a presumption.

MR. WORTHINGTON. Was it to perform a particular plural marriage ceremony, or to perform plural marriages in general?

MR. SMITH. To perform single marriages, but parties may have assumed
otherwise.

MR. WORTHINGTON. While I am on this subject, have you any knowledge or
information that President Smith has at any time since the manifesto,
or any other president of the church, authorized any plural marriage,
in violation of the manifesto?

MR. SMITH. I know of none myself. I know only of my own. Brigham
Young authorized—

MR. WORTHINGTON. I say, since the manifesto, do you know of any?

MR. SMITH. No, sir.

SENATOR DUBOIS. Did you ever know the president of the church at any
time to authorize a plural marriage?

---

12. In a letter to George Teasdale five months prior to this testimony, Francis M.
Lyman wrote:

We have just held our very interesting quarterly council meeting. ... We laid down
the rule that no Apostle can be sustained in uttering sentiments among the Saints
counter to the public pledges of the President and the Church before the Saints and
the world. No man can be allowed to enter into or perform plural marriage but by direct sanction of the only one man who holds the keys of that sacred order. Every
member of our council must sustain the stand taken by President [Joseph F.] Smith
and must not talk nor act at cross purposes with the Prophet. What has already been
done is shaking the confidence of Latter-day Saints. We are considered two-faced
and insincere. We must not stand in that light before the Saints of the world. ... It has
come to this juncture, that the Presidency hold me responsible to see to it that the
members of our Council be thoroughly advised that we will not be tolerated in anything out of harmony with the stand taken by President Joseph F. Smith before the
Senate Committee on the subject of plural marriage. We must uphold his hands and
vindicate the Church. ... If any one of us go contrary to this it will be at his peril before the Church and the nation. Neither the Presidency nor the Church will carry
the responsibility (July 9, 1904).

MR. SMITH. Senator, Brigham Young authorized Daniel H. Wells to marry me to a second wife.

MR. WORTHINGTON. You did not understand the question.

SENATOR DUBOIS. Yes, that is right. Do you know of any other case except yours?

MR. SMITH. No, sir; I do not call to mind a single instance.

SENATOR DUBOIS. At any time within the history of the church?

MR. SMITH. Not a single instance. There may have been an instance, but I do not call it to mind. ...

SENATOR DUBOIS. So you made political speeches in Idaho in 1902. Did any other apostle make political speeches in Idaho in 1902?

MR. SMITH. I never knew any other apostle, to my remembrance, to make political speeches in Idaho.

SENATOR DUBOIS. Did Apostle [Matthias F.] Cowley make speeches in Idaho?

MR. SMITH. I know nothing about Cowley's work in Idaho.

SENATOR DUBOIS. Did any Democratic apostle ever make speeches in Idaho?

MR. SMITH. I do not know about that, sir; I am not sponsor for the Democrats.

SENATOR DUBOIS. Where did you make political speeches in Idaho?

MR. SMITH. I made them in so many places that I could not say now.

SENATOR DUBOIS. Did you make them outside of the Mormon settlements and the Mormon country? Did you make them in Boise?

MR. SMITH. No, sir; I was never asked.

SENATOR DUBOIS. Did you make them in any of the so-called gentile counties?

MR. SMITH. I think not, Senator.

SENATOR DUBOIS. Your speeches were confined not only to the Mormon counties, but to the Mormon settlements, were they not?

MR. SMITH. I went where the chairman sent me.

SENATOR DUBOIS. I understand; and he sent you to Mormon settlements?

MR. SMITH. I presume that is the case. He did it.

SENATOR DUBOIS. If you should decide in your own mind to take a polygamous wife to-morrow, would you feel justified in doing so without consulting your associates?

MR. SMITH. Senator, such a thing is not probable as my deciding to do that sort of thing.

SENATOR DUBOIS. Well, if any apostle has entered into polygamy since 1890, has he done so without the knowledge or consent of his associates?

MR. SMITH. I do not know, but I absolutely believe he has.

SENATOR DUBOIS. Even if he were an apostle?

MR. SMITH. Yes, sir; even if he was an apostle.

SENATOR DUBOIS. An apostle then could retain his standing as an apostle, although he has entered into polygamy since 1890; new polygamy?

MR. SMITH. The answer, Senator, to that is, unless, perchance, he were handled by the laws of his country.

SENATOR DUBOIS. He would not lose standing in the church or among his apostolic associates, he being an apostle, if he has married into new polygamy since 1890?

MR. SMITH. I think if you demonstrated to his council that he had married since that time they would deal with him.

SENATOR DUBOIS. You mean that some gentile would have to present it to the apostolic quorum?

MR. SMITH. No, sir; any citizen.[13]

SENATOR DUBOIS. You think they would deal with him?

MR. SMITH. Yes, sir; I can say for myself that I would.

SENATOR DUBOIS. Would he lose standing?

MR. SMITH. Would he lose standing?

SENATOR DUBOIS. Yes; in the church.

MR. SMITH. He would lose standing if he was dismembered from the church.

SENATOR DUBOIS. Oh, well; would he lose standing if he entered into a polygamous marriage since 1890?

MR. SMITH. Should it be absolutely demonstrated in the courts, yes.

SENATOR DUBOIS. Do you imagine, or is it your opinion, that an apostle could enter into a new polygamous marriage now without the knowledge or consent of his associates?

MR. SMITH. I could not say. I should think not, but what men may do is beyond my ken.[14]

---

13. A few minutes later, John Henry Smith clarified:

The impression I left, one of my friends suggests, is that the church took no cognizance of moral derelictions or violations of polygamy, so far as they were concerned, without the law first took cognizance of them. Now, I did not mean to make that impression. The bishop of every ward is a competent tribunal to consider any case, and those cases come by appeal, as you have seen here, from the bishop to the high council, and from the high council to the presiding authority of the church. The apostles themselves are not engaged in the business of trying these cases (*Smoot Hearings*, 2:348).

14. Unknown to Smith, Rudger Clawson had been secretly sealed to a plural wife by Matthias Cowley in Arizona on August 3, 1904. The sealing was later annulled by Heber J. Grant.

SENATOR DUBOIS. Was there not some objection to your speaking, before you spoke at Oxford [Idaho], in the 1902 campaign, by the Democratic party of Idaho?

MR. SMITH. Not to my knowledge. They never made any objection to me, that I know of.

SENATOR DUBOIS. Did they not make objection in person to Joseph F. Smith, president of the church?

MR. SMITH. I know nothing about that.

SENATOR DUBOIS. Was it not published in the papers?

MR. SMITH. Now, as to whether or not—

SENATOR DUBOIS. Was it not in fact notorious throughout that country, before you spoke at Oxford, that the Democratic party objected to Mr. Cowley and yourself speaking in these Mormon settlements and advising the people how to vote?

MR. SMITH. I have no knowledge of it. I have never consulted Mr. Joseph F. Smith or anybody else in regard to my—

SENATOR DUBOIS. You never saw it in the newspapers at the time?

MR. SMITH. I do not remember it.

SENATOR DUBOIS. You do not recollect that a representative of the Democratic State committee went to Salt Lake City and had a conference—

MR. SMITH. Since you call it up, I believe I do recollect that there was something of that sort. But I was not by. I know nothing about it.

SENATOR DUBOIS. Do you not recollect that it created a very considerable stir and was published in all the newspapers, and that you and Mr. Cowley were mentioned by name?

MR. SMITH. Sometimes, Senator, a man is far removed from centers of information, and he may not see the papers for some time. Many a one has been missed by me.

SENATOR DUBOIS. You do not recollect that this was before the meeting at Oxford and at Teton?

MR. SMITH. I know nothing about it as an occurrence, only as I may have read it in the newspapers or hear you tell it now.

SENATOR DUBOIS. That is all. ...

MR. TAYLER. I asked you yesterday a question or two about the suggested or claimed marriage of Apostle Abram Cannon.[15]

MR. SMITH. Yes, sir.

---

15. Tayler means the previous Saturday when he asked Smith several questions about Cannon (*Smoot Hearings*, 2:287-89).

MR. TAYLER. I think you said that you heard some rumors about it at the time.

MR. SMITH. I stated that Mr. [Patrick] Lannon, the owner and editor of the "Salt Lake Tribune," the organ of Senator Kearns,[16] told me that he had heard of such a matter.

MR. TAYLER. When was it?

MR. SMITH. I could not tell you as to the time.

MR. TAYLER. That was some time ago?

MR. SMITH. Yes, sir.

MR. TAYLER. Before this testimony?

MR. SMITH. Way back in the past. It would be after Mr. Cannon was dead, too.

MR. TAYLER. You have heard the charge made that President [Joseph F.] Smith had performed that ceremony?

MR. SMITH. Yes, sir; I heard that charge made.

MR. TAYLER. That has been charged—not proved—for some years, has it not?

MR. SMITH. I could not say. I remember going to him myself and asking him the question whether he did that marrying, and he simply said "No, sir."

MR. TAYLER. Why did you go to him and ask him that question?

MR. SMITH. I did that because Mr. Lannon had told me that such a thing had occurred, and the story was that Mr. Smith had done it.

MR. TAYLER. So that you were in a state of doubt until you could consult President Smith about it?

MR. SMITH. Necessarily.

MR. TAYLER. If the president of the church wanted to perform such a ceremony he could do it?

MR. SMITH. Yes, sir. Any man might take the liberty to do things that he ought not to do, even the president of the church.

---

16. Thomas Kearns (1862-1918) served a short term of four years as U.S. Senator, 1901-05. With the support of LDS President Lorenzo Snow, this Park City mining magnate broke the deadlock in the Utah legislature that had existed since 1899 when the state had failed to elect a Senator—going two years with only one Senatorial seat filled. However, in 1903 Smoot's political machine took over the state Republican Party and squeezed out Kearns. Kearns reciprocated by purchasing the *Salt Lake Tribune* and launching a crusade against Smoot and the LDS Church. For instance, he worked behind the scenes for the plaintiffs during the Smoot hearings. In his final speech on the Senate floor, he repeated many of the criticisms that had been raised during the Smoot hearings. See Kent S. Larsen, *The Life of Thomas Kearns* (New York: Latter-day Renaissance, 2005), 141-65.

MR. TAYLER. When President Smith said he had not, did you make any further inquiry?

MR. SMITH. I believed him absolutely.[17]

MR. TAYLER. Oh, yes. I am not making any inquiry further about that. Did you make any inquiry as to who did perform it?

MR. SMITH. I have made inquiries; yes, sir

MR. TAYLER. Do you know who did perform it?

MR. SMITH. I never gained any information on that subject which was tangible.

MR. TAYLER. You, as an apostle of the church, have never had the slightest doubt that Abram Cannon did marry Lillian Hamlin in 1896?

MR. SMITH. I have had the most serious doubts.

MR. TAYLER. You have had the most serious doubts?

MR. SMITH. I have had.

MR. TAYLER. Then, as an apostle of the church, what was the explanation that you gave to yourself for the status in which he appeared to be upon his return from California?

MR. SMITH. I have never made any explanation to myself that was at all satisfactory.

MR. TAYLER. You knew, did you not, as well as most men know anything, that he returned from California with Lillian Hamlin and proclaimed her as his wife?

MR. SMITH. Never, sir; not to my knowledge. I never knew of his proclaiming her as his wife.

MR. TAYLER. Did not President Smith tell you?

MR. SMITH. No, sir.

MR. TAYLER. That Abram Cannon—

MR. SMITH. He made no explanation to me in regard to the matter; only that he did not do it.

MR. TAYLER. You therefore are still in doubt—

MR. SMITH. Absolutely.

MR. TAYLER. Wait until I ask you the question. You are therefore still in doubt as to whether Apostle Abram Cannon did believe or did present Lillian Hamlin as his wife?

MR. SMITH. I know nothing absolutely about it, so far as the explanation—

---

17. Although the committee realized it was being stonewalled, it was not sure whether the church had officially authorized new marriages or had simply looked the other way when violations had occurred. Senator Dillingham for one "believed [President Smith] to be perfectly honest," so it was an open question about who had performed the marriage in question (Smoot to Joseph F. Smith, May 24, 1906).

Mr. TAYLER. Mr. Smith, I am not asking you for things you know absolutely. I am talking about things as men know them in this world. If
you do not want to discuss the subject, and will so express yourself,
then I will know how to proceed about it.

Mr. WORTHINGTON. I suggest that there is nothing in what the witness has
said to justify any reflection of that kind.

Mr. TAYLER. I do not intend to reflect upon the witness.

THE CHAIRMAN. Mr. Smith will answer the question.

Mr. SMITH. I am here to answer anything I know. ...

Mr. TAYLER. You stated that you had doubt as to whether she was his
wife.

Mr. SMITH. I have had doubt and have doubt now.

Mr. TAYLER. Has it interested you at all—the consideration of the question whether—

Mr. SMITH. No, sir.

Mr. TAYLER. Not at all?

Mr. SMITH. Not at all.

Mr. TAYLER. Although a brother apostle, and you knew him well?

Mr. SMITH. I knew him as a child. I was his bishop.

Mr. TAYLER. You knew him as a man better than as a child?

Mr. SMITH. Very limited as a man. I was largely away from home and so
was he.

Mr. TAYLER. He was a member—

Mr. SMITH. Mr. Tayler, there may be this explanation made in regard to
us. The world is our home. Take us men. We are everywhere. I know
little of conditions in Utah or in any other section.

Mr. TAYLER. That does not change the aspect of this particular inquiry I
am pursuing. You had no interest, then, in the question as to whether
Abram Cannon had taken a plural wife or not?

Mr. SMITH. He was dead.

Mr. TAYLER. He was dead?

Mr. SMITH. Yes.

Mr. TAYLER. And all the interest that you ever could have had in the question as to whether Abram Cannon had taken a plural wife was as to its
effect upon him personally in life?

Mr. SMITH. Yes, sir.

Mr. TAYLER. The fact that it might reflect upon the good faith of your
church was wholly without interest to you?

Mr. SMITH. I may say, yes.

Mr. TAYLER. It did not make any difference to you whether it was thought that the church had broken faith through the plural marriage of one of its apostles?

MR. SMITH. I can simply say in regard to that proposition that I have never interested myself in looking up criminals. I have never taken any part in it. It has never been my business, whether as to polygamists, thieves, or murderers, or any other class of criminals. I have never taken any part in that work.

MR. TAYLER. I suppose your answer is intended to be responsive to the spirit of my question?

MR. SMITH. Yes, sir; I intended it should be.

MR. TAYLER. I think you meant it to be.

MR. SMITH. Yes.

MR. TAYLER. And so I see that you do not apprehend the spirit of my question. If it was learned to-day that yesterday Joseph F. Smith, in the city of Salt Lake, had taken a plural wife—which I do not conceive to be possible, but let us assume the strong case—I gather from the way in which you have answered my questions that your interest in that subject would be confined to its personal aspect as applied to Joseph F. Smith and what penalties might be laid upon him for it?

MR. SMITH. If I knew that Joseph F. Smith had married a wife yesterday, and there was a grand jury assembled in Salt Lake City, I would go before that grand jury and give my testimony.

MR. TAYLER. And that is all you would care about it—to see that he was personally prosecuted for it?

MR. SMITH. Yes, sir.

MR. TAYLER. Its effect upon the church—

MR. SMITH. The church has to take care of itself.

MR. TAYLER. The discredit that might follow in consequence of that act of the president of the church, you would consider as apart from the consideration of it, and of no consequence?

MR. SMITH. Yes, sir. ...

MR. TAYLER. Why would you go before the grand jury and prosecute him?

MR. SMITH. I would go before the grand jury just as I would give information of any other crime of extreme moment where the public was interested.

MR. TAYLER. Do you not understand that President Smith is daily violating the law?

MR. SMITH. Yes, sir. I would say, no, sir; I do not. (To the stenographer:) Change that, please. My answer is "No, sir."

MR. TAYLER. Why do you say "no, sir."

MR. SMITH. Because I do not know that he is daily violating the law.

MR. TAYLER. You do not?

MR. SMITH. No, sir.

MR. TAYLER. In order for you to speak with any positiveness, you must have such a degree of knowledge—

MR. SMITH. I must know.

MR. TAYLER. As you do not possess in the case of Joseph F. Smith, in his relations to his present wives?

MR. SMITH. Yes, sir.

MR. TAYLER. What kind of knowledge would you want to have of his having married another wife if you do not know enough about his present status?

MR. SMITH. I should want to have seen it.

MR. TAYLER. So that if Joseph F. Smith yesterday in Salt Lake was married, it would not be possible for you ever to take steps to prosecute him, would it, because you did not see it?

MR. SMITH. No, sir. ...

THE CHAIRMAN. Mr. Smith, I want to ask you one or two questions about which I am not entirely clear. Have you ever been engaged in foreign missions at all?

MR. SMITH. Yes, sir.

THE CHAIRMAN. In your missionary work you make use of the Book of Doctrine and Covenants?

MR. SMITH. Yes, sir.

THE CHAIRMAN. Is that the main book?

MR. SMITH. No, sir; the Bible is the main book we use. ...

THE CHAIRMAN. You use the Book of Mormon?

MR. SMITH. We use the Book of Mormon; yes, sir.

THE CHAIRMAN. And that does not contain the doctrine of polygamy?

MR. SMITH. No, sir.

THE CHAIRMAN. The teaching of polygamy?

MR. SMITH. No, sir.

THE CHAIRMAN. And the Book of Doctrine and Covenants does?[18]

MR. SMITH. Yes, sir.

---

18. The First Presidency resented the criticism of the Doctrine and Covenants, given the support for polygamy in the Bible. They asked Smoot: "Is it not strange that we are not charged with this also? [F]or in this book we read much more about polygamy being practiced by holy men of God than we do in the book of Covenants" (First Presidency to Smoot, Jan. 20, 1904).

THE CHAIRMAN. And you make use of that in your foreign missionary work?

MR. SMITH. We make use of them all.[19] ...

MR. TAYLER. Mr. Smith, I should like to ask you a question as an authority of the church. Is the taking of the endowments, so called, a necessary prerequisite to marriage in the temple, or in a temple of the church?

MR. SMITH. Well, really, no; not absolutely; and yet, in the main, yes. It is both "yes" and "no" to that question.

MR. TAYLER. Did I ask you the question whether Mr. Smoot could be an apostle without having taken the endowments?

MR. SMITH. He could have been; yes, sir.

MR. TAYLER. Putting the question in this form: Could he have been married to his wife for time and eternity without taking the endowments?

MR. SMITH. There have been cases of that kind; yes, sir.

MR. TAYLER. It could occur now?

MR. SMITH. It could possibly occur now.

MR. TAYLER. And does occur?

MR. SMITH. I can not say as to that. I presume not, however.

MR. TAYLER. You presume not?

MR. SMITH. Yes.

MR. TAYLER. The inference, then, that we are to draw from your testimony in the case, is that you have no knowledge at all on the subject as to whether Senator Smoot took the endowments?

MR. SMITH. No, sir; I have no knowledge myself, but I have my belief in regard to that matter.

MR. TAYLER. Your belief is that he did take them?

MR. SMITH. Yes, sir.

MR. TAYLER. Would you as readily have voted to make him one of the apostles if you had known that he had not taken the endowments—

MR. SMITH. Yes, sir.

MR. TAYLER. As if you knew that he had?

MR. SMITH. Yes, sir; from my acquaintance with him.

MR. TAYLER. That is all I want to ask.

---

19. On December 19, 1904, Carl Badger told his wife how frustrated he was with Smoot: "He has not the tact to take me into his confidence. And this is a fundamental weakness; I find it in other things. The Senator is not frank; he is not accurate. That is a bad indictment from his secretary, but it is a true one, and I think there is no danger in the path of the Senator's retaining his seat that looms up so portentous as the Senator himself. ... [T]he Senator will be drug all to pieces on the witness stand" (in Badger, *Liahona and Iron Rod*, 238).

THE CHAIRMAN. Previous to your becoming one of the apostles you took the endowments?

MR. SMITH. Yes, sir; I took the endowments.

THE CHAIRMAN. Do you know of anyone of the apostles who has not?

MR. SMITH. I do not, and I do not know as to their taking them. ...

19.

Benjamin B. Heywood, Charles Mostyn Owen, and Charles W. Penrose

Tuesday, December 20

"The star witness of the day was C. M. Owen. He was also the most willing witness who has appeared. He fairly beamed with delight at the opportunity to make public in the official records of the senate a mass of information with which he has stored his dome of thought during five years." —*Deseret News,* Dec. 20, 1904

"Today Chairman Burrows and Senator Dubois were the only members of the committee present. [The official record included Senator Pettus.] At the same time the interest of the newspapers has been growing and the number of reporters has been increased daily. Today a change in the committee room arrangements was made by which the reporters were given seats of absentee senators at the committee table, and there were enough of them to occupy all the places." —*Salt Lake Herald,* Dec. 20, 1904

Benjamin B. Heywood,[1] being duly sworn, was examined and testified as follows ...

MR. TAYLER. Are you a Mormon?

MR. HEYWOOD. I am not.

MR. TAYLER. Were you ever?

MR. HEYWOOD. I was baptized when I was 8 years old.

MR. TAYLER. Except as to that baptism, have you been an adherent of the church?

MR. HEYWOOD. Never.

MR. TAYLER. You are not, then, an apostate of the church?

MR. HEYWOOD. I do not so consider myself.

MR. TAYLER. Under the direction of the Sergeant-at-Arms of the Senate you were called upon to subpoena witnesses.

MR. HEYWOOD. I was.

---

1. Heywood (1854-1909) was a life-long resident of Utah. He was appointed U.S. Marshal on January 28, 1902.

MR. TAYLER. To appear before this committee?

MR. HEYWOOD. Yes, sir.

MR. TAYLER. Some of them you succeeded in finding and summoning?

MR. HEYWOOD. I did.

MR. TAYLER. And others you did not. Will you tell us which of the witnesses whom you were called upon to subpoena were not found, or
were found by you and are not here? First give us those whom you did
not find at all.

MR. HEYWOOD. Mr. Heber J. Grant.

MR. TAYLER. Why did you not find him?

MR. HEYWOOD. I learned that he was in England, supposed to be in Liverpool. That was the information furnished me by his wife.

MR. TAYLER. England?

MR. HEYWOOD. Yes, sir.

MR. TAYLER. Who else?

MR. HEYWOOD. John W. Taylor. I could get no information as to his whereabouts at all. Called at his home. There was no one there. The blinds
were drawn, and I made two calls. I did not find anyone there.

MR. TAYLER. Where was his home?

MR. HEYWOOD. In Salt Lake City.

MR. TAYLER. What other effort did you make to find him?

MR. HEYWOOD. I made some inquiries of prominent people there who, I
thought, might possibly know. It was generally reported that he had
not been in the State for practically a year—general repute.

MR. TAYLER. And that is why you did not find him?

MR. HEYWOOD. Yes, sir.

MR. TAYLER. Now the next?

MR. HEYWOOD. Mr. [Matthias F.] Cowley.

MR. TAYLER. Apostle Cowley?

MR. HEYWOOD. Apostle Cowley.

SENATOR DUBOIS. What was Mr. Grant in the church?

MR. HEYWOOD. Mr. Grant is a member of the quorum of the twelve apostles, as I understand it.

SENATOR DUBOIS. And Mr. Taylor?

MR. HEYWOOD. The same.

MR. TAYLER. What about Mr. Cowley?

MR. HEYWOOD. I called at his home twice; could get no information in regard to him. Mrs. Cowley was not at home. The maid came to the
door and said Mrs. Cowley had gone. She did not know when she
would return. Mr. Cowley was not at home, and she did not know

where he was. I made some inquiries from people who, I thought, might possibly have knowledge as to his whereabouts without getting any information that would assist me in serving the subpoena.

THE CHAIRMAN. Did you get any information as to where he was, whether in this country or abroad?

MR. HEYWOOD. I did not. Only a general rumor that the gentleman was in Canada.

MR. VAN COTT. Who was that, Mr. Taylor?

MR. HEYWOOD. Mr. Cowley. I made an effort to get Miss [Lillian] Hamlin, without any results. Well, it was convincing, as soon as you started on that case, that she was not in the district—could not be found. I could get no clue.

MR. TAYLER. How generally did you inquire—how earnestly and industriously did you endeavor to learn where she might be found?

MR. HEYWOOD. I was busy all the time—from the time I received those subpoenas until the time I started here, devoting most of my attention personally to it. I had a very busy term of court, and I had to pay some attention to that, but I was personally engaged all the time and had others at work in different parts of the State. I was as diligent as I knew how to be.

MR. TAYLER. You were so diligent that you satisfied yourself, for instance, as to Lillian Hamlin, that she was not in the State?

MR. HEYWOOD. Absolutely.

MR. TAYLER. And where did your inquiries lead you to believe she was?

MR. HEYWOOD. That she might be in New York or she might be in Mexico —old Mexico. ...

Charles Mostyn Owen,[2] being duly sworn, was examined and testified as follows ...

MR. TAYLER. Have you for some years had familiarity with conditions in Utah respecting the practice of polygamy?

MR. OWEN. I have.

MR. TAYLER. Can you state how it came about that you informed yourself in respect to that subject?

MR. OWEN. In January, 1899, I received an offer from the New York Journal to act as its correspondent in the anti-[B. H.] Roberts campaign. The New York Journal was then opening or had determined to open

---

2. Owen (ca. 1859-?) arrived in Utah in 1899 and worked—or posed—as an engineer while reporting on polygamy for the *New York Evening Journal,* a William Randolph Hearst newspaper.

a campaign having for its purpose the unseating, if possible, of Brigham H. Roberts, then elected to Congress, in the House of Representatives. I accepted the offer under the provision that it should not interfere with my engineering work. Later it became such a burden that it was impossible to carry on the two, both my engineering work and my newspaper work, and by September of that year—

Mr. Worthington. What year was that?

Mr. Owen. 1889. I gave up my engineering practice entirely, to devote myself to the carrying on of the antipolygamy or anti-Roberts campaign.

I remained in connection with the Journal until 1900. I was subsequently retained by the Woman's Interdenominational Council, of New York, for the special purpose of making further investigation in regard to the State of Idaho, which I did.

That completed I returned to my engineering practice and stayed with it until January, 1903—the 1st of January, 1903—when I was again retained on behalf of the protestants in the Smoot investigation and my duties laid along the former lines of investigation as to the practice of polygamy, and also of preparing the whole evidence to be laid before the Senate Committee on Privileges and Elections in the matter of Mr. Smoot's right to a seat in the Senate of the United States. I am still so employed.

Mr. Tayler. Had you, prior to 1899, made any study of the situation?

Mr. Owen. Only as any other citizen possibly would have done, except that possibly in connection with my engineering practice, which would take me and did take me all over the State, or over a great portion of the State of Utah, and also in Idaho and Wyoming, I came more or less in contact with the polygamous element.

Mr. Tayler. During the time that you have given attention to this subject, have you devoted practically all of your time to it?

Mr. Owen. Yes, sir.

Mr. Tayler. To what extent have you traveled over Utah and the surrounding country gathering information?

Mr. Owen. Over almost the whole of Utah. There is a small section in the south, in St. George, and the southeast corner of Moab and Monticello that I have not been into at all. With that exception, however, I think I can say that I have been all over the whole of Utah, almost settlement by settlement, at different times; over a large portion of southeastern Idaho and southern Idaho and western Wyoming completely.

Mr. Tayler. And in making these journeys what effort have you made to learn what the facts were? How would you prosecute your inquiries?

MR. OWEN. There is hardly a settlement throughout Utah, Idaho, or Wyoming, a purely Mormon settlement, where there is not either an apostate or a member of the church in good standing who is opposed quietly to the practices; there is hardly a settlement where I do not know somebody whom I can trust and whose information I can rely upon. They do not dare to express themselves openly, but under the seal of confidence and protection as to their identity I have undoubtedly the closest information possible, and I have never accepted any one man's statement about any one person's polygamy. I have checked and checked and checked, and not until I have satisfied myself of the truth of the condition have I ever made any statement about it. ...

THE CHAIRMAN. Where did you say [Heber J.] Grant was?

MR. OWEN. Grant is in England.

THE CHAIRMAN. When did he go to England?

MR. OWEN. He left suddenly on the night of the 10th of November last year—1903.

THE CHAIRMAN. November, last year?

MR. OWEN. Yes.

THE CHAIRMAN. Do you know anything of the circumstances?

MR. OWEN. Yes, sir.

THE CHAIRMAN. Will you state them?

MR. OWEN. About the 5th or 6th of November he made a statement before the students of the State university at Salt Lake City, in which he held out in a very objectionable manner his association with two women as his wives. I was absent from the city on that day, but on my return I immediately went to work to find if I could get evidence of these statements as printed in the paper. I got the evidence in a shape which was satisfactory to me, and I went before the county attorney and swore to an information for him, and a warrant was issued on that information. Before Mr. Grant was served, however, he left the country.

THE CHAIRMAN. When did he leave as to the time of the issuing of the warrant?

MR. OWEN. When I next heard of him he was in Salt Lake—that afternoon, I understood—but he got on the train at Provo that night about midnight.

THE CHAIRMAN. Where were those statements made to the students of the university?

MR. OWEN. In an assembly organized or called together for the purpose of organizing or helping an alumni association.

THE CHAIRMAN. What were the statements?

MR. OWEN. That he regretted that the rules of the association were such that no single subscription of greater than $50 could be received, but to show his interest in the association he would give them $50 for himself and $50 for "each of my wives; and I have got two wives, and I would have a third, if it were not for the law."

THE CHAIRMAN. How many were present when he made that statement?

MR. OWEN. I understand there were nearly a thousand students present.

MR. VAN COTT. How many?

MR. OWEN. Nearly a thousand at the time. It was the university in general assembly, I understood.

MR. VAN COTT. Not quite a thousand?

MR. OWEN. I understood it was about that.

THE CHAIRMAN. Has he returned since that time?

MR. OWEN. No, sir.

SENATOR PETTUS. Is he still an apostle?

MR. OWEN. Yes, sir.[3]

THE CHAIRMAN. He is doing missionary work in the field?

MR. OWEN. He is in charge of the European mission. In that connection I may state that last March I took some further action in regard to Mr. Grant. He received the credentials of the State from the governor authorizing him to appear as the representative of the State of Utah, or one of the representatives of the State of Utah, at the first international congress for school hygiene to be held at Nuremberg. I did not hear of it—I was in Washington [D.C.] at the time, and I did not hear of it immediately—but as soon as I heard of it I obtained certified copies of the complaint, the warrant, and the credentials given him by the governor of Utah, and I then filed them first with the German ambassador, who regretted that his position was such that he could not officially take any cognizance of it; that it was not within the scope of his duties. I was then referred to [U.S.] Assistant Secretary of State Loomis, to whom I presented the same matter the next day, and who expressed himself as being very much upset at the idea of a man who was living in such notorious relations being chosen by the governor of the State of Utah to represent the State in a foreign country.

THE CHAIRMAN. And he was accredited as a delegate to what congress?

---

3. For another view, see James E. Talmage's testimony, *Smoot Hearings*, 3:420-23.

MR. OWEN. The first international congress for school hygiene, held in Nuremberg last April, I think, on the 9th. It lasted a week.

MR. TAYLER. What steps, Mr. Owen, beginning with 1899, have you taken in the way of instituting prosecutions against persons violating the law?

MR. OWEN. When I was first connected with the Roberts fight it was not my intention, nor was it considered possible within the scope of my duties as a newspaper correspondent, to institute arrests and legal proceedings against these men, but when, in February of that year, I went into Cache County [Utah]–

MR. WORTHINGTON. What year?

MR. OWEN. 1899; and subsequently published in the "New York Journal" columns a schedule of polygamists then living in the active practice of their profession in Cache County, giving the names of the men, the names of their wives, and the names of their children born since the manifesto, the editorial column of the "Deseret News" was pleased to denominate me or to specify me, the correspondent, whoever he might be, of the "New York Journal," as a liar.

It was rather objectionable, seeing I was holding to the facts, but they further came with a challenge, if my recollection serves me, that if these conditions were true the laws of Utah were ample, the courts of Utah were open, and that it was the duty of any person calling himself a good citizen to institute proceedings in a legal manner for the conviction of such persons.

At that time there was a lady named Mattie Hughes Cannon, the fourth wife of Angus M. Cannon, then stake president of Salt Lake stake, who was sitting in the legislature of the State as a State senator, who was evidently in a very interesting condition [pregnant].[4]

I kept more or less watch of her, and shortly after the adjournment of the legislature heard of the birth of the child, and I then determined that after a reasonable time–I did not desire to force what might be called persecution on the woman so as to injure her physically; I thought a month would be ample time for her to recover–I would institute proceedings against Angus M. Cannon, as he was an exceedingly prominent man in the church and she a prominent woman in the State, and to make a test of the question whether the courts were open or not.

However, two weeks after the birth of the child Mrs. Cannon left

---

4. For Angus M. Cannon's testimony, see *Smoot Hearings,* 1:775-94.

the city and the State, and did not return, to my knowledge at any rate, until the 4th day of July, when I happened to see them driving on the street—Mr. Cannon and Mrs. Mattie Hughes Cannon and the baby. On the following day I went before the county attorney, Mr. Putnam, and laid a verbal information before him.

MR. WORTHINGTON. Of what county?

MR. OWEN. Salt Lake County; stating the facts as I knew them or understood them to be, and declaring myself as being prepared to swear upon information and belief to a criminal information. He refused me, declined to issue such an information. I think it was on the evening of the 7th or 8th of July, although I am not quite sure which; I think it was on the 7th—

MR. TAYLER. Are you still on the Cannon matter?

MR. OWEN. Yes. ...

MR. OWEN. ... During September of 1903 was my next attempt to have the law enforced, and I thereafter called upon the county attorney in Salt Lake County and offered an information against Joseph F. Smith—

THE CHAIRMAN. The president of the church?

MR. OWEN. The president of the church, alleging him to have been guilty of unlawful cohabitation, upon the testimony which he himself admitted was correct in this room, namely, that he had gone to St. Louis with one wife, and later had attended, within some thirty days, I think, a lunch party at Senator [Thomas] Kearns's residence with another wife; and I was refused that information [complaint]. That county attorney, however, was a Gentile; but I have found that the Gentiles are even more difficult, in some respects, than the Mormons to induce to enforce these questions, for the reason that their election, their renomination, depends wholly on the good will they have from these people, and he was afraid really to lose it. ...

MR. WORTHINGTON. ... Did you see, in the "Washington Times" within the last week, a picture purporting to represent the garments which the Mormons wear in the endowment ceremony?[5]

_____

5. See "Mormons Taking Oaths of Endowment House," *Washington Times,* Dec. 14, 1904 (front page). A year later, Carl Badger explained:

I met the sneak [Owen] in the Stationery Room the other day, and did not speak to him. I do not like to do a mean thing, but I have often thought that he was one fellow I would like an introduction to just for the opportunity to refuse my hand. The trouble is that we cannot be consistent. Last spring I had to meet him frequently, and was on speaking terms, so that my ignoring him the other day was not consistent. I think, too, that if we are going to make a mistake it had best be on the side of agreeableness, and if a disagreeable thing is to be done, it should be in a good cause,—never

MR. OWEN. Yes, sir.

MR. WORTHINGTON. Did you have anything to do with having that picture published in the paper?

MR. OWEN. I had nothing to do with it to the effect of getting the paper to publish it. I stood for the pictures.

MR. WORTHINGTON. Where did you go and stand for those pictures?

MR. OWEN. In Clinedinst's gallery.

MR. WORTHINGTON. Who inspired that proceeding?

MR. OWEN. I did.

MR. WORTHINGTON. Why did you inspire it?

MR. OWEN. I thought it was a good thing to get out.

MR. WORTHINGTON. Had you endeavored to have it presented to this committee, or do you not think that was the way to present it, if it was a good thing to get out?

MR. OWEN. No; it seemed to be hardly germane to the proceedings of this committee.

MR. WORTHINGTON. You think nothing is germane to the proceedings of this committee which is good to get out against the Mormons?

MR. OWEN. There are some things it is possibly difficult to get into testimony that would be effective testimony. That is a matter, to my mind, of great public interest, but yet hardly within the scope, as I understand it.

MR. WORTHINGTON. How were you led to understand that it was not within the scope of this inquiry?

MR. OWEN. I talked the matter over with other people.

MR. WORTHINGTON. With whom?

MR. OWEN. Other counsel.

MR. WORTHINGTON. Other counsel?

MR. OWEN. I think I have talked the matter over with Mr. Tayler. I forget whether I have or not. I certainly have with my Salt Lake counsel.

MR. TAYLER. There are some things, Mr. Worthington, you must admit that even I thought were not right.

MR. WORTHINGTON. I wish to give you the credit, Mr. Tayler, of bringing this out.[6] You know that I knew you had advised that you would not have anything to do with bringing that thing in here; and Mr. Owen

unnecessarily" (Dec. 14, 1905, in Rodney J. Badger, *Liahona and Iron Rod: The Biography of Carl A. and Rose J. Badger* [Bountiful, Utah: Family History Publishers, 1985], 290-91).

6. By "bringing this out," Worthington means Tayler's renunciation of Owen's actions.

takes it and puts it in the papers. That is all I wish to ask on that subject.[7] ...

Documentary Evidence[8]

THE CHAIRMAN. What further, Mr. Tayler.

MR. TAYLER. Mr. Chairman, in the first place, I may say that except as to
some documentary evidence, to which I will allude in a moment, all
of the testimony that the protestants have intended and are able to
present to the committee has been offered.

The committee will understand that a large amount of valuable
testimony, which seemed to us to be available under such conditions
as would meet our desires, was unavailable on account of the inability
of the committee to go, or to send a subcommittee, to Utah.[9] There
we felt, and still feel, sure a very large amount of testimony cumulative
to and emphasizing all that has been presented would have been produced before the committee. Then, as the evidence discloses, a large
number of witnesses whose testimony seemed to us to be very important and, indeed, striking and conclusive on the points concerning
which they were expected to testify are not found. They have disappeared. Without undertaking to attach any sinister purpose or meaning to the word "disappeared," whether it is thin air or thick air or
dark air, where or how they have gone, we can not find them, and the
reason why we wanted them has appeared in the testimony of Mr.
Owen and has developed in the other testimony in the case.

While, as I say, we propose to close our case here, and while it is in
the province of this committee to take testimony whenever it is inclined to do so, regardless of what may be the conduct of counsel or
their desire, I do not mean, in so far as I might do so or could be
charged with doing so, to foreclose myself from putting in before the
committee at some future time testimony of any of these witnesses
whom we have been unable to obtain; or, if there was anything that

---

7. Ten days earlier, Carl Badger had written that Owen was "going to assert that we
teach in the religion classes that Mary and Martha were the wives of the Savior. Tell me
candidly, is there the least suggestion of a truth in this? I know that the belief is quite general among our people that such was the case, but is there any truth that such is being
taught in the religious classes?" (Badger, *Liahona and Iron Rod*, 235). Owen neglected to
mention this, perhaps because he was not asked a relevant question.

8. The Documentary Evidence section includes documentary extracts and debate
between committee members and counsel for both sides (*Smoot Hearings*, 2:428-38).

9. The plaintiffs, encouraged by Senators Burrows and Dubois, had planned to send
a fact-finding subcommittee to Utah in May 1904.

was so striking that upon presentation to the committee the committee would feel we ought to present it, to have that new testimony offered. But I do not apprehend any such occasion will arise, and I advert to it now only that my words at this moment may not be quoted
for the purpose of confounding me later on. ...

Mr. Worthington. Mr. Chairman, this is a very embarrassing situation to
us. We have been told, or rather we have expected from what has been
said, that the testimony on behalf of the protestants would close this
week, and I understand the chairman to say that he would require
them to close this week. We wish to proceed as diligently as we can
with our testimony, and we have arranged to go to work in the preparation of it and to give a number of the names to the chairman very
soon, perhaps to-day; but we do not feel that we ought to be called
upon to go on with our evidence until the prosecution in this case has
closed and has announced it has closed.

The Chairman. The chair understands it is closed.

Mr. Worthington. Yes; it is closed; but counsel say it is closed with the reservation that if they find any more testimony they will ask leave to
produce it.

The Chairman. I understand there is a reservation that if Apostle Grant,
or any of these parties who have not been reached by subpoena,
should appear he would claim the right to have them examined. That
is as I understand the scope of the statement.

Mr. Tayler. Surely; and, Mr. Chairman, more than all that—

Mr. Worthington. They have not been subpoenaed.

Mr. Tayler. We want to get them. I close it without reservation, as far as
that is concerned, but I give notice to the counsel on the other side,
what must appeal to his sense of propriety, that if at any time in the future, in an investigation of this character, we should desire to present
some testimony that was so significant and so important that the
committee itself would say that it ought to be heard, surely, however
much it might embarrass the other side, it would be heard. We have
no expectation that any of these witnesses will be found, or that they
will be here, but if they are, we are not going to be modest and say that
the case is ended and that we must not again open our mouths, or endeavor, in other words, to inform the Senate. That is all. ...

Mr. Worthington. Who does that book purport to be by?

Mr. Tayler. Parley P. Pratt. It is entitled "Key to Theology."

Mr. Worthington. Is that offered here as representing his views, or the
views of the church, or what?

Mr. Tayler. It is offered here in support of the proposition I have just read: "The Mormon priesthood, according to the doctrines of that church, is vested with supreme authority in all things temporal and spiritual."

MR. WORTHINGTON. I object, then, to the introduction of that article, on the ground that there is nothing yet to show that the church had anything to do with its publication. The charge says "The Mormon priesthood, according to the doctrines of that church." Is everything that every Mormon happens to take it into his head to publish to be taken as representing the church?

MR. TAYLER. Possibly not, but I want to know if Mr. Worthington, representing Senator Smoot, disputes this work as being one of the authoritative works of the church—not that everything in it is deemed to be of divine origin, and controlling, but—

MR. WORTHINGTON. I have just been informed by those who are supposed to know that it is not a promulgation of the church and does not purport to be. It is simply the private views of Mr. Pratt.

MR. TAYLER. Undoubtedly the private views of Mr. Pratt; that is what we put it in for.

MR. WORTHINGTON. Then I object to it, Mr. Chairman. Under a charge that the Mormon priesthood, according to the doctrines of that church, do something, instead of giving us the official books of the church, which show what it proclaims, or the official pronouncements of its heads, here is a book published by one of its members purporting to state what he thinks and acknowledges.

MR. TAYLER. I will ask one of these apostles, Mr. Chairman, a question about Parley Pratt. If he is going to discredit that leading man in the church, why let us know it.

MR. WORTHINGTON. I do not discredit the fact that he was a leading man in the church; but I do say that no man, whether he is a leading man in the church or a mere layman, can speak for the church unless he has some authority to do it.

MR. TAYLER. If the statement of a leading man of the church was the binding and controlling dogma and doctrine of the church, we would have the whole church convicted of treason to-day.

MR. WORTHINGTON. You would have what?

MR. TAYLER. If what some prominent leading and supposed-to-be controlling authority in the church said was supposed to fully represent all that the members of that church stood for, there would not be anything left of this case or of the church as an organization. We do not make any such claim as that. That very written work, by high authority—

Mr. Worthington. I think, Mr. Chairman, what everybody must have observed is that although the resolution under which this committee is acting directs it to inquire as to the qualifications of Senator Smoot to a seat in the Senate, this inquiry has been directed against the Mormon Church almost entirely and exclusively. I am not the representative of the Mormon Church, and of course I am not a Mormon and in sympathy with its peculiar doctrines, about which we have heard so much here; but I do say, in common fairness to any person, or party, or church, or body accused before such a high tribunal as this of such serious offenses, that the committee ought not to allow to go into its records, as representing the theories, doctrines, or practices of that church, anything except what is proclaimed by the authority of the church. ...

The Mormon Church has published plenty of official documents. Its heads have made plenty of official promulgations; and I do submit that those and those only should be accepted as tending to show what the Mormon Church holds to be its doctrines and its tenets.

The Chairman. Let me ask, Mr. Worthington, would the declaration of the head of the church, President Joseph F. Smith, be, in your judgment, admissible upon the question of the doctrines of the church?

Mr. Worthington. If he was undertaking at the time to speak for the church, of course it would be evidence on the subject. If it happens to be in a casual conversation on the street or in a speech or something of that kind, it would not; because, let me remind you, Mr. Chairman, of what you and we all know, that Joseph F. Smith, although he is the president of the church, can not change the doctrines of that church or make any revelation, as they term it, until it has been submitted to and approved by the body of the church in conference assembled, and Joseph F. Smith has no more power to declare a certain thing to be the doctrine of the Mormon Church than I have. He can submit it to the people, and the people can say it is the doctrine of their church.

Mr. Tayler. Would it give any information to the committee as to the doctrines of the church when the head of the church, in a sermon, should declare—

Mr. Worthington. I should say not the slightest.

Mr. Tayler. That is what I supposed our friends would say.

Mr. Worthington. Not the slightest. If he says it in the form of a special proclamation, in order to bind the church he must submit it to the conference. If he says it anywhere else, any Mormon has the same right to repudiate it that I have, and that has been proved here twenty times, and not disputed by anybody. ...

I have a recollection that President Smith was asked about Orson Pratt, and said ... he had some things which had been published by the authority of the church, and it so appeared; and many other things he had published, for which the church was not in the slightest degree responsible.[10] If a thing of this kind is to be brought here to be accepted as what is done by the Mormon Church, there should certainly be some evidence tending to show that it was issued by authority of the church, or that the church, if it has been published, has accepted it as an official promulgation. As a matter of fact, it has appeared by witness after witness, and is now an established fact, that there are certain books which have been named here which do contain the doctrines of the Mormon Church, and that nothing else does. It has been shown here that the Bible, the Old and the New Testaments, the Book of Mormon, the Doctrine and Covenants, the Pearl of Great Price, and the Manifesto contain those doctrines; that every revelation which has been made has to be submitted to the church and submitted to the people. Those have all been published and are all in the books which are here except the Manifesto. There is no other authority on the face of the earth, and no other publication which can speak for the Mormon Church as to its doctrines except those.

THE CHAIRMAN. Perhaps, Mr. Tayler, this matter can be expedited by conference with counsel in looking this over and coming to an agreement as to what may be admitted, and concerning which there will be a controversy.

MR. TAYLER. No; we never can agree, Mr. Chairman, upon any such basis as that. The exclusion of Parley Pratt is monstrous—that is, the idea of it would be to the true Mormon. I do not care anything especially about Parley Pratt, but Parley Pratt was a member of the church. The church does not admit that Parley Pratt had a revelation from Almighty God, and that the church has accepted this as binding upon them. ... [However,] we have almost all the apostles in the last forty years [on record,] quoted in this document as giving their view of what the church stands for, what they stand for, what their power is; and we are not going, because of this miserable little book of Parley Pratt's, to say that we shall not notice the statements of all this long line of saints and apostles who have been making the church what it is.

So that it goes to the entire question of the informing value, to the

---

10. Smith had testified that Orson Pratt was "an authoritative writer" in some areas but that in other areas "he was not" (*Smoot Hearings*, 1:88).

committee and the Senate and the country, of the declarations by its leading minds and leading authorities. Of course, on the theory that Joseph F. Smith and others here have stated, their declarations have not the force of the Word of God. They say they have not, although the Book of Doctrine and Covenants says they have. But they say they have not, because they must be submitted to the people. The people have to pass on the question as to whether God has to be obeyed or not; but we propose to undertake to put in all of the statements of these important Mormon officials.

MR. WORTHINGTON. All of those whom somebody has selected for you.

MR. TAYLER. I have no way of giving everything they have ever said. I certainly am not going to put in colorless matter, a thing that has no meaning at all; and I am surprised that counsel oppose this. This is historical matter, and it would appear as if the respondent in this case was afraid to face the facts of history. We do not want anything else.

MR. WORTHINGTON. I have been too long a practitioner in contested matters, Mr. Chairman, to be affected by the remark of the gentleman that we are afraid to do this or that. I have come here to represent Senator Smoot, with the idea that, wide as is the range of inquiry here, there are some limitations which would be placed upon it, and that common gossip and talk in the community or Utah or other States or this Union as to what the Mormon Church teaches as its doctrines would not be received as evidence or what those doctrines are, when the doctrines themselves have been formally promulgated for many years in books and documents. ...

Here are the books which show the doctrines of the Mormon Church are thus and so. Every doctrine which binds the members of that church is here before this committee. Every sentence of it has either been introduced in evidence already or is in the books which the committee has in its possession. Why should we go around and hear what some member of that church said in Utah, or what some member or the church concocted in his closet and put in his book, as undertaking to state the doctrines or that church, when the doctrines are here? I say let us have them and not what somebody else has said as affecting other members of it, or perchance affecting Senator Smoot as a member of it, which he and every member of the Mormon Church would have the right to repudiate.

THE CHAIRMAN. Mr. Tayler, it is evident that it will be impossible to conclude this matter this afternoon, and the Chair will adopt the suggestion of counsel that you prepare a statement of what you propose to put in under these various articles, and the committee will pass upon the question later.

MR. WORTHINGTON. Let us know where the book or document is from which you quote, so that we can in the first place verify the quotation and then see whether there is anything further that we desire to have go in.

THE CHAIRMAN. It will be impossible to conclude this afternoon.

MR. TAYLER. I think so. It would seem to me that is the better way.

THE CHAIRMAN. We may as well adopt the suggestion, and you can prepare a statement of what you propose to offer under each one of these charges and let counsel on the other side be advised of it, and then the committee will pass upon it. Is there anything further this afternoon? Under the statement, then, of counsel for the protestants, the committee will adjourn. And what is the wish of counsel for Senator Smoot as to the time of meeting again?

MR. WORTHINGTON. Mr. Chairman this is an exceedingly important matter, because you will see at once that if extracts from what a certain member or priest of the Mormon Church has said here and there is to go in evidence then we want time to collect evidence of what other members and officers of the Mormon Church have said all over the world, and put it in to show.[11] ...

Charles W. Penrose, having been previously sworn,[12] was examined and testified as follows ...

---

11. On December 21, 1904, Carl Badger recorded in his journal a conversation with church attorney Franklin S. Richards:

> Last night I had a talk with F. S. Richards and asked him to give me a reason why I should not go outside of the Church if I doubted, disbelieved in things that all orthodox Mormons consider essential. He said he would illustrate his reasons. In 1877 he went on a mission to the Sandwich Islands with Jos. F. Smith. Up to that time no one had thought that polygamy was not mandatory upon all the Church; and would have lost his standing if he had voiced other sentiments. [Ten years later] in 1887, [Richards] was here in Washington with Jos. F. who was on the underground. [Richards] thought he must argue before the Senate Committee that polygamy was not mandatory upon the Church. Jerry Wilson agreed with him; Jos. F. opposed it strongly; he believed it was mandatory, but Richards got him to consent that the argument be made; it would not hurt the Church anyway. When Richards got home he came near to losing his fellowship. On the witness stand before the Committee in 1904, Pres. J. F. Smith testified that the doctrine never had been mandatory. Now why not stay with the Church, there is good here, and truth, and noble men and women. 'I have done more for those whom I love by staying with them than I could have done by fighting what I considered their faults'" (Badger, *Liahona and Iron Rod,* 240).

12. Penrose had previously testified on December 17 (see chapter 17 in this volume).

MR. TAYLER. And you are also a kind of an ecclesiastical expert in your church, are you not?

MR. PENROSE. I don't know that I have that reputation.

MR. TAYLER. I do not intend the word offensively at all. I mean you were called?

MR. PENROSE. I am very familiar with the doctrines of the church. ...

MR. TAYLER. You are familiar with the history of your church and of its prominent men?

MR. PENROSE. Yes, sir.

MR. TAYLER. You know, of course, who Parley P. Pratt was?

MR. PENROSE. Yes.

MR. TAYLER. He was one of your most eminent writers?

MR. PENROSE. That is correct.

MR. TAYLER. And his work entitled "Key to Theology" is not what you call an inspired work at all?

MR. PENROSE. No.

MR. TAYLER. I mean it is not inspired in the sense that the four great books are inspired?

MR. PENROSE. No.

MR. TAYLER. But apart from that element of it, he is considered one of your greatest writers on the theology of the Mormon Church?

MR. PENROSE. Yes; he is figured in that light.

MR. TAYLER. And his books have not been published by the church?

MR. PENROSE. I think not. They are the property of Parley P. Pratt and his heirs. They lay claim to them. They were his own property.

MR. TAYLER. Has the church never published the Key to Theology?

MR. PENROSE. Not as a church. I think probably the Liverpool office, which was conducted under the direction of the church, has published it, like they publish a great many other works, but not as an authority of the church.

MR. TAYLER. Has it been published in Salt Lake City?

MR. PENROSE. I am not aware of that. It may have been.

MR. TAYLER. Has the "Deseret News" ever printed—

MR. PENROSE. I could not tell you that. I think it was published by the "Juvenile Instructor" office, but I am not sure of it.

MR. TAYLER. The "Juvenile Instructor" office is a branch of the Mormon Church?

MR. PENROSE. No.

MR. TAYLER. Is it not? Who is the president of it?

MR. PENROSE. The "Juvenile Instructor" office?

MR. TAYLER. Yes; the "Juvenile Instructor."

MR. PENROSE. The "Juvenile Instructor" is the property of the company called the Juvenile Instructor Company. The "Juvenile Instructor" is a religious publication.

(Mr. Penrose subsequently requested the stenographer to record his answer to the foregoing question as follows: "The 'Juvenile Instructor' is published by the Sunday School Union.")

MR. TAYLER. It is a Mormon religious publication?

MR. PENROSE. Yes.

MR. TAYLER. And the property of the Juvenile Instructor Company is the property of the Mormon Church, is it not?

MR. PENROSE. No.

MR. TAYLER. Whose is it?

MR. PENROSE. Why, the company itself. It was originally George Q. Cannon & Sons. Who owns it now I do not know.

MR. TAYLER. It is owned by the church, the way the "Deseret News" is owned by the church?

MR. PENROSE. No.

MR. TAYLER. The "Key to Theology" is referred to, is it not, in every book written by a Mormon on ecclesiastical subjects?

MR. PENROSE. Oh, no.

MR. TAYLER. Is it not?

MR. PENROSE. Oh, no; it is referred to by some.

MR. TAYLER. Do you know this work of Dr. [James E.] Talmage?

MR. PENROSE. Yes; the "Articles of Faith," you mean.

MR. TAYLER. Yes; the "Articles of Faith." Was that published by authority of the church?

MR. PENROSE. I believe it was.

MR. TAYLER. By appointment? He was appointed by the church to do so, and the book was published by the church, was it not?

MR. PENROSE. Yes; I believe so.

MR. TAYLER. You remember the book of Brigham H. Roberts, the last that he wrote, I think, entitled "Mormonism?"

MR. PENROSE. It was a little pamphlet.

MR. TAYLER. Yes. That was published by the church, was it not?

MR. PENROSE. No; I think it was published by Roberts, and I think the church bought it. They bought the copyright.

MR. TAYLER. Was Parley P. Pratt the first of your great theological writers?

MR. PENROSE. No.

MR. TAYLER. Who was?

MR. PENROSE. I don't know that there was any particular first. Orson Pratt ranked high as a writer, as well as Parley.

MR. TAYLER. I did not mean first in authority or ability, but I meant first in time. Orson Pratt was before him, was he?

MR. PENROSE. I couldn't tell that. Parley P. Pratt wrote a work in the early days of the church called "The Voice of Warning," which is one of the first that was published. The "Key to Theology" was later.[13]

MR. TAYLER. Apostle George Q. Cannon was a highly respected and capable apostle of the church in his lifetime, was he not?

MR. PENROSE. He was.

MR. TAYLER. Was his orthodoxy ever questioned in the church?

MR. PENROSE. I don't think it was ever questioned by the church, but it may have been in the church. There may have been people who took different views from his.

MR. TAYLER. I understand there were different apostles who had varying views on different subjects.[14]

MR. PENROSE. Yes.

MR. TAYLER. Apostle John Tayler, who was afterwards president of the church, was recognized as an orthodox Mormon?

MR. PENROSE. Yes; and a prominent writer and speaker.

MR. TAYLER. There were publications known as the "Journal of Discourses?"

MR. PENROSE. Yes.

MR. TAYLER. They were published by the church?

MR. PENROSE. I think they were published by George D. Watt and J. D. Long, originally, in Liverpool, England.

MR. TAYLER. In the interest of the church?

MR. PENROSE. Of course they were all supposed to be in the interest of the church, but I don't think the church published them. I am not sure about that.

MR. TAYLER. Have you ever heard the authority of that publication questioned?

---

13. These two Parley P. Pratt works remain in print, most recently published together as one volume (Parley P. Pratt, *Key to the Science of Theology/Voice of Warning* [Salt Lake City: Deseret Book, 2002]).

14. For two studies of differing views among LDS general authorities, see Gary James Bergera, *Conflict in the Quorum: Orson Pratt, Brigham Young, Joseph Smith* (Salt Lake City: Signature Books, 2002); and Ronald W. Walker, *Qualities that Count: Heber J. Grant as Businessman, Missionary, and Apostle* (Provo: Brigham Young University Press, 2004), 195-229.

MR. WORTHINGTON. What do you mean by the authority of it?

MR. PENROSE. In what way do you mean? That is what I want to get at.

MR. TAYLER. Can you answer the question—the correctness of the publication?

MR. PENROSE. Do you mean the correctness of its contents?

MR. TAYLER. Yes.

MR. PENROSE. Oh, yes; there are some things in there that have been disputed.

MR. TAYLER. That is, disputed by the persons who spoke them?

MR. PENROSE. Oh, no; disputed by others.

MR. TAYLER. By others.

MR. PENROSE. Yes, sir.

MR. TAYLER. I understand.

MR. PENROSE. You were asking me about the authority of the publication.

MR. TAYLER. I mean whether or not the fact that an address by Brigham Young, printed in the "Journal of Discourses," was—

MR. PENROSE. Actually delivered?

MR. TAYLER. Actually delivered.

MR. PENROSE. Yes; I think that is considered to be correct.

MR. TAYLER. That is what I meant.

MR. PENROSE. As far as that is concerned, but—

MR. TAYLER. As to how authoritative or binding it was upon the church—

MR. WORTHINGTON. Let him finish his answer, please.

MR. TAYLER. Oh, no; I am going along all right.

MR. WORTHINGTON. I submit a witness has a right to finish his answer without your going along all right.

MR. TAYLER. The witness and I will have no trouble if you will only keep quiet.

MR. WORTHINGTON. I shall not keep quiet when you interrupt the witness when you have the part of the answer you want, and are trying to keep out, it would seem, the part you do not want.

MR. TAYLER. There is nothing Mr. Penrose could say that I do not want.

MR. WORTHINGTON. He was in the middle of an answer, and I ask that he be allowed to finish it.

MR. TAYLER. If you would only keep quiet about it we would get through.

MR. WORTHINGTON. I will not keep quiet about it until I get a ruling of the chairman. Mr. Chairman, this witness was interrupted in the midst of an answer, and I am insisting that he should be allowed to finish an answer to one question before another is asked.

MR. TAYLER. While all this storm is going on, the witness says he does not know where he was, and can not answer it any further. ...

MR. PENROSE. ... We did not regard these books as authorities, only as works of reference, sometimes, to give the ideas that these men maintained on these subjects.

MR. TAYLER. That is what I understood you to say, Mr. Penrose, and I want you to understand I am not seeking to have you say that those books, or what Brigham Young said, or what any other apostle said, is authoritative upon the members of the church.

You have stated that, so far as you understand, a sermon printed in the "Journal of Discourses" purporting to be a sermon of Brigham Young was in fact a sermon of Brigham Young, but its authority and effect upon the Mormons is an entirely different question.

MR. PENROSE. I may add to that, Mr. Tayler, if you will allow me, that there are some sermons published in the "Journal of Discourses" the authenticity of which has been disputed—for instance, some of the sermons attributed to Joseph Smith, the prophet. They were taken down at the time in longhand and have been published in the "Journal of Discourses" and there have been disputes as to their correctness.

MR. TAYLER. Those are the only ones, are they, that have been disputed?

MR. PENROSE. They are the only ones I am reminded of now.

MR. TAYLER. I am glad you said that. I believe there is no reference here to any such sermon of [Joseph Smith]. Roberts's "Outlines of Ecclesiastical History" is a work written by Brigham H. Roberts?

MR. PENROSE. Yes.

MR. TAYLER. Is it endorsed by the church officials?

MR. PENROSE. I think perhaps it is, in the main, although there have been a great many disputes in regard to some portions of it that have arisen in the societies where it has been discussed—in the Mutual Improvement Associations, for instance, where it has been read—and some disputes have arisen in regard to its correctness.[15] ...

---

15. With Elder Penrose's testimony, the plaintiffs closed their case. In a letter of December 29, 1904, Carl Badger told his wife that she "need not fear for the result of the investigation, as far as its touching the Senator. It appears to me that he is safe. ... Richards and Van Cott and the Senator are talking about a Constitutional amendment [regarding polygamy], but I think it out of the question. I would not be opposed to an amendment if I thought it the only way to stop these new polygamous marriages, but I think they will pass away with time. President Smith has said that they will" (in Badger, *Liahona and Iron Rod*, 243).

20.

William J. McConnell, Burton Lee French, James H. Brady, J. W. N. Whitecotton, Hiram E. Booth, and Arthur Pratt

Wednesday-Friday, January 11-13

"Senator Smoot's side of the case against him opened today with more members of the committee present than at any time this session. ... [Senator] Knox ... succeeds Senator Hoar [deceased] on the committee, and today made his first appearance. In the audience were the usual number of women, and the same faces which have appeared so often were noticed." —*Deseret News,* Jan. 11, 1905[1]

William J. McConnell,[2] being duly sworn, was examined, and testified as follows ...

MR. VAN COTT. Do you belong to any church?

MR. McCONNELL. I do.

MR. VAN COTT. What church?

MR. McCONNELL. The Presbyterian Church.

MR. VAN COTT. In your long residence in Idaho have you had opportunity to become acquainted with the Mormon people there?[3]

---

1. Committee members had originally agreed to reconvene on Smoot's birthday, January 10, but because the defense was not ready they delayed a day. In preparation for his defense, the LDS First Presidency had advised Smoot:

> The witnesses who are to testify in your behalf, and in behalf of the church as well, ... will have to depend almost entirely on the nature of the questions put to them by your counsel in order to afford them opportunity of correcting, bringing out and developing such things in a way in which they ought to appear in the record. ... [I]t will not be necessary for us to remind you that the stronger and more complete the evidence for the Church is made, the stronger must be your prospects for retaining your seat. This phase of your case ought, in justice to the Church, to receive your own personal attention as much as possible, seeing that only one of your counsel is acquainted, even in a general way with our doctrines. We do not wish you to understand by this that we expect you yourself to go through the record, and note its defects and prepare the way ... as that will be done here; what we do desire is that you will do all you can yourself by way of seeing that this is done, and impressing your counsel with the importance of it" (Dec. 9, 1904).

2. McConnell (1839-1925) served as governor of Idaho from 1893 to 1897. He was born in Michigan, relocated to California in 1860, and moved to Idaho in 1863. At the time of the hearings, he was living in Moscow, Idaho.

3. Some newspapers wondered why Smoot's team called witnesses to testify about

MR. McConnell. Yes, sir.

MR. Van Cott. Will you indicate how thoroughly?

MR. McConnell. My first acquaintance with the Mormon people in Idaho was in 1882. At that time Nez Perces County embraced what is now Nez Perces and Latah counties. While I was not then residing in Idaho, being a resident at that time of Oregon, I was largely interested in business in Idaho, and the people of the town of Moscow were ambitious to be detached from Nez Perces and set off in a separate county, known as Latah. ...

I found that the Mormon members who were there were a different type of men from the average Gentile. A great many of the Gentiles were practicing the science of what we call "poker" out in that country during the night and sometimes day time. I found the Mormons clannish. They seemed to stay by themselves, and my business as a lobbyist took me around wherever I could find the members. I never found any of the Mormons either drunk or gambling. I will admit that I had a prejudice against the Mormons at that time, owing to their peculiar institution of polygamy, and I was rather surprised to find that they were really more moral in their behavior than the other members.

At that time I believe the first efforts to disfranchise the Mormons was made in the legislature. A bill was introduced by the president of the council—Mr. Wall, I think he was; I forget what county he was from, but if it is necessary to know I have it. He was president of the council.

At the time I visited there they voted me the privileges of the council, and when I was in that body I was given a seat. The only vacant seat in the council happened to be by the side of a Mormon bishop from Bear Lake County, by the name of Robinson. I did my writing at the desk. It was a double desk. Some days after we had got acquainted he submitted to me this bill, which was looking to the disfranchisement of the Mormons, and asked me what I thought of it. "Well," I said, "Bishop, you realize, I suppose, that I am a Gentile, and we Gentiles hold that plurality or plural marriages constitute bigamy—adultery. I am not prepared to say whether it would be a proper

---

Idaho politics. In response, the *Deseret News* wrote that "the Idaho matter was introduced by the 'prosecution' ... and so [defense] witnesses from Idaho have occupied the attention of the committee ... in rebuttal of the [prosecution's] statements." The paper criticized the prosecution's "inquisition on the private lives of men over whom [Smoot] has no control, and hot air stories about the Church of which he is a member" ("Hear the Other Side," Jan. 13, 1905).

thing to disfranchise all adulterers or not. But this occurs to me as class legislation. If you will permit me to suggest an amendment to this bill I think you will see the propriety of supporting it." He asked me to do so, and I drafted as an amendment—"And provided further, That you have not cohabited with any other than your legal wife."

He looked at it and said that if the council would adopt the amendment he would support the bill. But the council would not adopt the amendment, and he did not support it. There was a motion made to table it, and it carried the bill with it. The bill was defeated.

That was my first acquaintance with the Mormons.

MR. VAN COTT. Now, in a general way, have you had opportunities to become acquainted with them since then?

MR. MCCONNELL. Yes, I think so.

MR. VAN COTT. Have you traveled among them?

MR. MCCONNELL. I have. Next, my attention was called to the manifesto that was issued by the Mormon Church in 1890, I think. At that time no Mormons voted or held office.[4]

THE CHAIRMAN. In Idaho, you mean?

MR. MCCONNELL. Yes, sir; in Idaho. I am speaking only of Idaho now, because I do not know anything about the conditions in these other Territories.

In 1892 the Republican State convention met, which nominated me for governor. There were no Mormons in that convention. The Mormons in Idaho were understood to be Democratic. A resolution was introduced into that Republican convention looking to the restoration of the right of suffrage. It was adopted by the convention and made a plank in the Republican platform on which I ran for governor. The Republicans carried the State, and I was elected, together with the other nominees.

When the legislature convened the following year, they proceeded to carry out that plank in the platform. My understanding of it was that it was for a double purpose—that it was un-American to disfranchise a large portion of the home builders and the wealth producers of the State, the taxpayers. The great proportion of the taxpayers and wealth producers and home builders in southeastern Idaho, what is known as the Mormon counties, were taxed, but had no representation.

Furthermore, we were looking to the adoption of female suf-

4. Mormons could not vote because of Idaho's anti-Mormon test oath. Idaho was admitted to the Union as the 43rd state on July 3, 1890.

frage, which we could not adopt if the test oath had remained on our statute book. No self-respecting woman would qualify as an elector or an officeholder if she had to be subjected to the questions or take the oath which citizenship required.

The gist of what was termed the "test oath" was embodied in our State constitution, and is still in that instrument, and it was self-enacting. There seems to be a difference of opinion as to that, but I was present and participated in the arguments at the time that article was adopted, and it was the understanding of the members of the constitutional convention that with the exception of section I the article was self-enacting, and it carries with it all the provisions necessary to prevent the practice of polygamy or plural marriage. It prohibits a man or woman from holding office and from voting, from taking part in elections, if they are polygamists or if they belong to any church or organization which teaches polygamy or encourages it.

MR. VAN COTT. In other ways have you become acquainted with the Mormon people by traveling among them?

MR. McCONNELL. I have. After encouraging and assisting in repealing the test oath, I felt it my duty to go among these people, many of whom were colonists from foreign nations, the States of Europe, and who never had voted, who know nothing about our Government, its responsibilities and duties—I felt it my duty, I say, to go among these people, which I did, and delivered a lecture in all the prominent towns and wards in Idaho on the duties and responsibilities of American citizenship.

I was their guest in the towns and at their homes. I had an opportunity to observe their manners and methods. It was, of course, quite a revelation to me. I was, like everybody else would be, I presume, curious as to the people and their methods. I found one peculiarity, which was that in every family the father at the head of the table might ask a blessing himself in the morning, or he might ask his wife or one of the children. There was no hesitancy on the part of any member of the family who was asked to say grace. They would immediately proceed to do it.

All my meetings were opened with prayer, the same as though they were religious meetings[5] ...

---

5. The *Salt Lake Tribune* expressed disappointment with McConnell's friendly testimony, noting that he seemed to be "willing to have the whole membership of the Legislature Mormon" ("Slanderous and Contemptible," Jan. 13, 1905). Four days later, the paper heaped ridicule on Governor McConnell, predicting that Idahoans "who have not

Burton Lee French,[6] being first duly sworn, was examined, and testified as follows ...

MR. WORTHINGTON. What is your observation and knowledge as to the extent to which polygamy exists—I mean polygamous cohabitation—in your State [Idaho] now as compared to what it was when you became a man and observed these things, or came to know them, say, ten years ago?

MR. FRENCH. Well, I have inquired very carefully, because I have wanted to be right upon this question, in the trips that I have made through those counties, and I have been told everywhere that the polygamous relations, or the cases of living in polygamy, are rapidly on the decrease. I have been told by Mormons that there are only about half as many now who have plural wives as lived in the State in 1890.

MR. WORTHINGTON. What do you hear as to the common understanding there as to whether there are any new polygamous marriages in the State?

MR. FRENCH. I have failed to find any. I have inquired, I presume, in every county, and probably many times, whether or not there are such cases, and I have failed to find anyone who could point out a single case. I would say that I remember a talk I had with Doctor Hoover, a Gentile living in Montpelier. I drove from Paris to Montpelier to speak at night. I had spoken at Paris in the daytime during this last campaign. I asked him about this and he said to me: "I am a doctor and practice my profession throughout this county. I am satisfied I would know of any polygamous marriages if they exist, and I do not know of a single instance of polygamous marriage since the manifesto." I have asked others and have obtained similar answers.

MR. WORTHINGTON. It was testified by Mr. [Charles H.] Jackson that he was in doubt whether [Idaho] Governor [Frank R.] Gooding is a Mormon, because as many people say he is a Mormon as say that he is not. What do you know about that?

MR. FRENCH. No; Governor Gooding is a Gentile.

MR. WORTHINGTON. Is there any doubt about it in the State?

---

spoken to him for years will feel like talking to him with a club; and some women who would not have touched him in the past, even with a forty-foot pole, will feel like touching him with a rawhide." He had allegedly infected "the decent people of Idaho with an itching ... desire to take his scalp, to tweak his nose, 'to yank his whiskers,' and to duck him in a horse-pond. And the foregoing is a very mild synopsis of Idaho opinions, transmitted to the Tribune" ("One 'Hill' M'Connell," Jan. 17, 1905).

6. A life-long Republican, French (1875-1954) represented Idaho in the U.S. House of Representatives for three non-consecutive terms, 1903-33. He lived in Moscow, Idaho.

MR. FRENCH. I never heard any serious doubt raised. I remember that during the campaign it seemed that in Nampa somebody started the question, and we joked him some about it, but nobody took it seriously, and I never heard the question mentioned seriously in the campaign. No; I never heard of such a thing seriously.

MR. WORTHINGTON. You were not here when Mr. Jackson told us seriously about it?[7]

MR. FRENCH. I heard the statement.

MR. WORTHINGTON. In your travels in the Mormon counties and in your talks with the Mormons, have you got any impression or knowledge as to what the feeling of the younger Mormon people is—the Mormons themselves, the younger element—about this matter of polygamy?

MR. FRENCH. There is no question about their feeling. It is very pronounced against it. I have among my friends a great many of the younger Mormons. I have asked them frankly that question, and talked with them about it, and they feel just the same as other people do in regard to it, so far as I have been able to learn. They respect their parents, those of them that have polygamous parents in it. They respect the older members of the church who have lived in polygamy, but, so far as continuing it for a custom or doctrine or belief, they do not approve of it at all.

MR. WORTHINGTON. What is your impression as to what would be the result if the manifesto had not been issued or if the law was not against it, as to what would be the result of polygamy in Idaho?

MR. FRENCH. If the manifesto had not been issued and if no laws had been made against it, of course I do not know. It might be that as long as it was a question of religion they might approve of it, but I think that without any further legislation polygamy would end just as soon as it will under any other way. ...

THE CHAIRMAN. I want to ask one or two questions, Mr. French. You are a Member of Congress from Idaho?

MR. FRENCH. Yes, sir.

THE CHAIRMAN. You have just been reelected?

MR. FRENCH. Yes, sir.

THE CHAIRMAN. So you have made a canvass of the State twice?

MR. FRENCH. Yes, sir.

---

7. Jackson gave conflicting testimony on whether Gooding was Mormon, saying "I do not think so" and "Well, I have heard as many people say he is a Mormon as I have heard say that he is a Gentile, so I am in doubt" (*Smoot Hearings*, 2:198, 215).

THE CHAIRMAN. In that canvass you took no thought of the support of the Mormon Church one way or the other?

MR. FRENCH. I never did. I never in any campaign or any convention took any thought of the Mormon Church as a church. There are people who belong to churches. There are Methodists who belong to the Methodist Church, and so on.

THE CHAIRMAN. I understand.

MR. FRENCH. We think of them as individuals. I have.

THE CHAIRMAN. Your answer is that you take no thought of the organization.

MR. FRENCH. No, sir; I have not, nor have I conferred with any leader of the organization relative to politics.

THE CHAIRMAN. Very well. You have conferred with none of the leaders?

MR. FRENCH. No, sir.

THE CHAIRMAN. No bishop?

MR. FRENCH. No; not relative to church support. Of course I know them as individuals, and talk politics to them as I talk politics to other individuals, but never what the church could do—

THE CHAIRMAN. But not with the thought that they could have any influence any more than anybody else?

MR. FRENCH. Only as an individual.

THE CHAIRMAN. That is all?

MR. FRENCH. That is all; yes, sir.

THE CHAIRMAN. You never visited, I suppose, in either of these campaigns, Salt Lake City?

MR. FRENCH. I never did.

THE CHAIRMAN. I wanted simply to find out the fact about it.

MR. FRENCH. I passed through Salt Lake once as a very small boy, and I passed through a year or so ago during a trip West from the East—not during a campaign.[8] ...

James H. Brady,[9] being duly sworn, was examined and testified as follows ...

---

8. The *Salt Lake Tribune* thought French confirmed that speaking against polygamy would be "fatal to his political prospects. He might well have admitted," the *Tribune* continued, "that any other attitude toward the Mormons than the one he assumed in his testimony, would be equally fatal. He was testifying for his political life, and, under all the circumstances, what a position of humiliation and shame the giving by him of that testimony involved!" ("Slanderous and Contemptible").

9. Brady (1862-1918) was governor of Idaho, 1909-11, and represented Idaho as a U.S. Senator, 1913-18. Born in Pennsylvania, he moved to Idaho in 1901, where he oper-

Mr. VAN COTT. Have you had any occasion to observe whether any members high in the Mormon Church have come into Idaho and talked politics?

Mr. BRADY. I have.

Mr. VAN COTT. And who were the men?

Mr. BRADY. John Henry Smith and Mr. [Matthias F.] Cowley.

Mr. VAN COTT. Both Republicans?

Mr. BRADY. Both Republicans.

Mr. VAN COTT. Did you also observe the effect that their work had in Mormon counties, cities, and precincts where they spoke?

Mr. BRADY. Well, I was satisfied that I could do better without them than with them, and for that reason I had no occasion to use them, and I did not use them. I did not want them to come into the State for any political purpose whatever; and my honest judgment is that there never has been a time that their coming to Idaho and making speeches made any particular difference in the vote cast.

Mr. VAN COTT. It has been mentioned that [LDS Stake] President [William] Budge went over to some part of Idaho and did work there in this last campaign for the Republican party. Did you have occasion to observe the result of that work?

Mr. BRADY. We lost Blaine County.

Mr. VAN COTT. Is that where he worked?

Mr. BRADY. Yes, sir.

Mr. VAN COTT. What became of the precinct where he worked?

Mr. BRADY. We lost that.

Mr. VAN COTT. What is your opinion as to the sentiment among the young Mormon people as to polygamy?

Mr. BRADY. I think they are unalterably opposed to polygamy and unlawful cohabitation, just as much so as your daughters and your sons in this country. ...

Mr. VAN COTT. I will go on with another question until we find it. What is the sentiment in Idaho regarding disturbing or leaving undisturbed those men who went into polygamy prior to the manifesto of 1890?

Mr. BRADY. To be absolutely frank in the matter, my judgment is that a majority of the men in Idaho would favor leaving those old men to live out their lives just as they have started in.

Mr. VAN COTT. While you were chairman, did you go to Salt Lake to consult the Mormon Church?

---

ated irrigation canals, owned a power plant, and chaired the state Republican committee. He lived in Pocatello.

MR. BRADY. I did not.

MR. VAN COTT. Does the Mormon Church get whatever it wants in Idaho?

MR. BRADY. It never has, or else they wanted very little. They have never had but one elective State officer in the fourteen years ...

MR. VAN COTT. Can or do the minority Mormon people in Idaho get whatever they want in the State and control and dictate affairs?

MR. BRADY. They can not. That is simply all bosh in Idaho—that kind of talk. They can not do it. There are no conditions that exist that would permit them to do it. It is just the same as down in Kansas and Nebraska—when a fellow gets beat, he attributes it to the railroads. When they get beat out there, they attribute it to the Mormons; but outside of the fear in the minds of some people of what is going to happen, I do not think it is possible to cite an instance where anything has happened that would be injurious or detrimental to our State. ...

J. W. N. Whitecotton,[10] being duly sworn, was examined, and testified as follows ...

MR. VAN COTT. When, to your knowledge, did Reed Smoot first take an active part in politics in Utah?

MR. WHITECOTTON. He was in it when I got to the Territory.

MR. VAN COTT. For the Republican party?

MR. WHITECOTTON. No; not for the Republican party, because there was not any Republican party there.[11]

---

10. At the time of the hearings, Whitecotton (1859-?) lived in Provo, where he was active in the Democratic Party. Born in Kentucky, not himself a Mormon, he nevertheless moved to Provo in 1889 to practice law. The day previous to Whitecotton's testimony, the *Tribune* editorialized about him and other witnesses for the defense after Smoot called them the "flowers of Utah and Idaho":

Think of McConnell drooping as a pale lily in the presence of the rude men who compose the Committee. ... Why, if McConnell knew anything bad about Smoot or anybody else, his lips would be too chastely delicate to utter it. Ah! There before the Committee stands, 'A most unspotted lily'. ... And Whitecotton ... He is a violet—he is 'a violet by a mossy stone, half hidden from the eye; fair as a star, when only one is shining in the sky.' Again alas! He is 'a violet in the youth of primy nature; forward, not permanent, sweet, not lasting.' ... Is there a Senator so dense as ... not [to] yield all harshness in the presence of this empurpled bloom. ... The others are merely roses—white and red and yellow; full-blown roses, with thorns. And having them, there is no reason why Smoot should not claim that his present position is a bed of roses" ("The Flowers of Utah and Idaho," Jan. 12, 1905).

11. During the territorial period (1850-96), the LDS Church organized itself into the People's Party (1870-91) in response to the anti-Mormon Liberal Party (1870-93). Prior to this time, political candidates ran without party affiliation. Both parties were subsumed into the national parties a few years before statehood in 1896.

MR. VAN COTT. But for the People's Party?

MR. WHITECOTTON. For the People's Party.

MR. VAN COTT. Now, when the division came, was he active in politics?

MR. WHITECOTTON. Yes, sir; he was one of the very first men. He was known to be for protection.[12] He had some Republican heresies in his head when I went there. He was the manager of a woolen mill, and he was always talking protection for that woolen mill.[13]

MR. VAN COTT. He was a Republican then; I assume, if he was talking protection?

MR. WHITECOTTON. Oh, yes; he was a Republican:

MR. VAN COTT. Was he active in the Republican party?

MR. WHITECOTTON. He was, as soon as there was a party to be active in.

SENATOR FORAKER. What are some of the other heresies he had?

MR. WHITECOTTON. That is the chief one; and he always voted the Republican ticket. It is a kind of an unpleasant thing for us Democrats to have too many fellows do that. But they do it.

MR. VAN COTT. Speaking of the other heresies that Mr. Smoot had, what was the general understanding in the community in Provo about any heresy that Mr. Smoot had as being opposed to the practice of polygamy in those early days?

MR. WHITECOTTON. He was a heretic on that, too.

MR. VAN COTT. He was opposed to polygamy?

MR. WHITECOTTON. He was opposed to polygamy; he was understood so to be. He was looked upon as one of the young men in Utah who were to redeem Israel.

MR. VAN COTT. Going along with the politics, did Mr. Smoot gain prominence in the Republican party in Utah?

MR. WHITECOTTON. Yes; he was always prominent in the party.

---

12. "Protection" here refers to tariffs on imports to check foreign competition. During his career in the Senate, Smoot favored protectionism even as the country's mood during the Progressive Era turned toward reciprocal trade agreements. Later Smoot would co-sponsor the famous Harley-Smoot Tariff Act, which is thought to have exacerbated the Great Depression.

13. From its inception, the Republican Party was opposed to polygamy, so Mormons sympathized with the Democratic Party; Mormons also tended to accept the Democrats' other positions on issues. Therefore, it was in fact "heretical" during the territorial period, in the eyes of fellow Democrats, for a well-known Mormon to defend anything Republican. For more on this, see Edward Leo Lyman, *Political Deliverance: The Mormon Quest for Utah Statehood* (Urbana: University of Illinois Press, 1986), 2-4; Thomas G. Alexander, *Mormonism in Transition: A History of the Latter-day Saints, 1890-1930* (Urbana: University of Illinois Press, 1986), 7.

MR. VAN COTT. Was he at that time talked of for governor of the State of Utah?

MR. WHITECOTTON. Yes. That, I think, was four years ago last fall.

MR. VAN COTT. Was he also talked of for Senator?

MR. WHITECOTTON. He was talked of for Senator from that time on. The general understanding was that when he dropped out of the gubernatorial race it was with his eye on the other office.

MR. VAN COTT. Before Mr. Smoot became an apostle in the Mormon Church, I will ask you who was the logical and most prominent candidate in the State of Utah in the Republican party for United States Senator?

MR. TAYLER. Is Mr. Whitecotton an expert on that subject?

MR. VAN COTT. I think he is.

MR. WORTHINGTON. I think he is as much of an expert as Judge [Ogden] Hiles, who testified that Mr. Smoot never would have been thought of for United States Senator if the church had not backed him.[14]

MR. TAYLER. That is the truth. I was only referring to party politics. I gathered from what Mr. Whitecotton said that he is a Democrat.

MR. WORTHINGTON. Judge Hiles is a Democrat.

MR. VAN COTT. We want to show whether it is the truth or not.

THE CHAIRMAN. Let the witness answer. Do you understand the question?

MR. WHITECOTTON. I think I understand the question. It is easier to understand the question than it is to answer it. When you come to talk about who was the logical candidate, there were so many people who thought they were the logical candidates that we differ.

MR. VAN COTT. Answer it the best you can.

THE CHAIRMAN. In your judgment.

MR. WHITECOTTON. In my judgment he was the inevitable candidate. I can scarcely say the logical, but from the discussion that was had about this matter Governor [Heber M.] Wells, who was one—

THE CHAIRMAN. Do you want him to go into that?

MR. VAN COTT. I am satisfied for the present with the result. That is the result, in your opinion?

MR. WHITECOTTON. Yes; it was understood among the Republicans.

MR. VAN COTT. Is it correct, in your judgment, to say that before Mr.

---

14. Hiles had testified that "Mr. Smoot would never have been elected United States Senator unless he had been an apostle ... When Smoot's candidacy was announced and it was known that he had the consent of the church, it was then known that he would become Senator of the United States. ... I mean he had no standing as a candidate ... [and] then everybody said, 'Why, that is the end of it. That settles it'" (*Smoot Hearings*, 1:692).

Smoot became an apostle he had never been heard of or mentioned in the State of Utah for the position of United States Senator?

MR. WHITECOTTON. Oh, no; that is not true.

MR. VAN COTT. When Mr. Smoot became an apostle there was a campaign waged.

MR. WHITECOTTON. On the apostleship?

MR. VAN COTT. Oh, no. After he became an apostle and the campaign came up to elect a United States Senator and other officials, there was a campaign waged in the State of Utah on that issue.

MR. WHITECOTTON. That was in 1902.

MR. VAN COTT. What was the most prominent part of that issue?

MR. WHITECOTTON. The issue really before the people, aside from being a Republican or Democrat, was, Smoot or not Smoot for Senator.

MR. VAN COTT. In your judgment, did the fact that Reed Smoot was then an apostle in the Mormon Church assist him or hurt him in the election in Utah as a candidate for United States Senator?

MR. WHITECOTTON. Really, I do not know as to that. There were a great many people who opposed Smoot for the Senate—

MR. VAN COTT. In your opinion—

MR. WHITECOTTON. Because he was an apostle, but there were probably others—there seemed to have been many—who did not care anything about it; and there may have been some who supported him because he was an apostle. I do not know anything about that. I know there were very many bitterly opposed to him because he was an apostle—Mormons.

MR. WORTHINGTON. Mormons, you say?

MR. WHITECOTTON. Yes.

MR. VAN COTT. Were legislators nominated in Gentile counties and conventions who were pledged to support Reed Smoot for United States Senator?

MR. WHITECOTTON. Yes; that was done in Salt Lake County.

MR. VAN COTT. In a Gentile convention and in a Gentile county?

MR. WHITECOTTON. Gentile. They were not divided on Gentile and Mormon, but the Gentiles have controlled Salt Lake City ever since 1890 when there has been any division on such lines as that.

MR. VAN COTT. For instance, did Gentiles go out on the stump when it was known that Reed Smoot would be the Senator if the Republican party won?

MR. WHITECOTTON. Everybody knew it but them. I suppose they must have known it.

MR. VAN COTT. Did some of those same men move, for instance, to make unanimous the nomination of legislators who were pledged to support Mr. Smoot?

MR. WHITECOTTON. It was reported in the newspapers that Mr. Critchlow moved to make the nomination of the Salt Lake County delegation unanimous after the convention had closed. Of course the fight was made before the convention. It was Smoot or not Smoot, and the Smoot people won, and when they won, Mr. Critchlow, being of the opposite faction, it was reported, moved to make the nomination of those candidates for the legislature unanimous.

MR. VAN COTT. Do you know whether Mr. Critchlow went out on the stump, too?

MR. WHITECOTTON. I do not know personally, but I know that a big meeting was appointed at Springville, which is 6 miles south of Provo, for the night before the election. Mr. Critchlow was billed to be there, and the newspapers reported he was there, but I do not know anything further than that. ...

SENATOR OVERMAN. Was any other Mormon a candidate for the Senate except Senator Smoot?

MR. WHITECOTTON. For Senator?

SENATOR OVERMAN. Yes.

MR. WHITECOTTON. I think not, to any considerable extent. Governor Wells was reckoned as a candidate, but he was laboring under the disability that our constitution provides that no person can become a candidate for the United States Senate during the term for which he was elected governor. Governor Wells, I believe, had a few votes. He was considered a candidate.[15]

SENATOR OVERMAN. Was it understood that Senator Smoot was the candidate of the church?

MR. WHITECOTTON. Of the church?

SENATOR OVERMAN. Yes.

MR. WHITECOTTON. No; I never heard tell of that until I heard it from down here.

SENATOR OVERMAN. Was it understood that he had the permission of the church to run; that he had obtained the permission of the church to run before he made the fight?

MR. WHITECOTTON. I think it was understood from the affairs of 1895 and

---

15. Wells received two votes in the Utah Senate and four in the House ("Smoot Is Now a Real Senator," *Deseret News,* Jan. 20, 1903).

1896 that he must have the consent or he might get into trouble with the church, because he was an apostle.

SENATOR OVERMAN. It was understood that he did have the consent?

MR. WHITECOTTON. I do not know anything about that, and I never heard that discussed until I saw it discussed in some of the testimony here.

MR. WORTHINGTON. The president testified that he gave him consent.

MR. VAN COTT. In Utah is this consent understood as a leave of absence or understood as an endorsement?

MR. WHITECOTTON. It is leave of absence from duty, as I understand it.

MR. VAN COTT. Is that the general opinion there among the people of the State?

MR. WHITECOTTON. It is the opinion of a great many people, and there are other people who have sought to construe that as an endorsement. But that is chiefly from the American party,[16] as I understand it they construe it in that way.

SENATOR OVERMAN. I did not understand that. How does the American party construe it?

MR. WHITECOTTON. The American party construes it, or says it does, as an endorsement—that is, as I understand it. They claim for an apostle to have consent is simply to put upon him the seal of approbation; that it goes beyond leave of absence. The people do not so understand it, however, I think. ...

MR. VAN COTT. What is your opinion as to the independence of the younger Mormons in Utah in regard to politics?

MR. WHITECOTTON. I do not think there is any doubt in the world about the independence of the young Mormons in respect of politics.

MR. VAN COTT. State their sentiment whenever it is said or rumored that the leaders of the Mormon Church are interfering in politics—that is, whether they approve of it or resent it.

MR. WHITECOTTON. I have never heard one of them approve of it. I have heard many young men speak in terms of the very strongest condemnation of anybody seeking to interfere, and I never have heard one admit that he was interfered with. They all say that if anybody has been

16. The American Party was a reincarnation of the Utah-based Liberal Party. It received support from former Senator Thomas Kearns, who left the Republican Party in 1904. Kearns blamed Smoot and the LDS hierarchy for his defeat and used his newspaper, the *Salt Lake Tribune*, to undermine Smoot. He also hired former U.S. Senator Frank J. Cannon as an editor. Cannon had left the Republican Party in 1900; he had also left the LDS Church (Richard S. Van Wagoner and Steven C. Walker, *A Book of Mormons* [Salt Lake City: Signature Books, 1982], 47-48).

interfered with it was somebody else—that they have never felt that pressure.

MR. VAN COTT. Outside of a few men who may be in the American party, I will ask you what is the general opinion among Gentiles as to [whether] Senator Reed Smoot or men like Reed Smoot, who are prominent in the Mormon Church, prominent in politics, who are opposed to polygamy and in favor of the enforcement of the law, should be encouraged or not?

MR. WHITECOTTON. I do not know that I can answer the question. (To the reporter.) I wish you would read it.

The reporter read as follows: "Mr. Van Cott. Outside of a few men who may be in the American party, I will ask you what is the general opinion among Gentiles as to whether Senator Reed Smoot or men like Reed Smoot, who are prominent in the Mormon Church, prominent in politics, who are opposed to polygamy and in favor of the enforcement of the law, should be encouraged or not?"

MR. WHITECOTTON. I should say the best answer I could give to that question would be Mr. Smoot's election. I do not know how better to express it.

SENATOR OVERMAN. What political positions had Senator Smoot occupied before he was elected Senator, if any?

MR. WHITECOTTON. What political positions?

SENATOR OVERMAN. Yes; in the State.

MR. WHITECOTTON. He never had held any that I know of.

SENATOR OVERMAN. He had held no State office at all?

MR. WHITECOTTON. No; he had never held a State office.

SENATOR OVERMAN. Had he ever canvassed the State?

MR. WHITECOTTON. Yes.

SENATOR OVERMAN. Had he made a thorough canvass of the whole State?

MR. WHITECOTTON. I would not say that he had, and yet he may have done so.

SENATOR OVERMAN. He had never been in the legislature?

MR. WHITECOTTON. No, sir; he had never held an office that I know of, and I think I should know it if he had.

SENATOR OVERMAN. Was he known generally by the people of the State?

MR. WHITECOTTON. Oh, yes; there was no man, or scarcely a man in the State better known generally than he was. That State is a wool-growing State. Mr. Smoot had been superintendent of the Provo Woolen Mills, and he goes into every holder in that State, buying wool and looking after those interests. He has done that for many years.

Scarcely a man is better known in the State than Mr. Smoot. ...

MR. TAYLER. You understand that the husband of a plural wife, who continues to live with that wife and to have children borne by her, does so
upon the theory that he took upon himself that obligation of a husband to a plural wife with the approval of God?

MR. WHITECOTTON. Before the manifesto; yes.

MR. TAYLER. And that no law of the land has any right to dissolve or interfere with that relation?

MR. WHITECOTTON. Well, I think that is his point of view, but I do not concur in it.[17]

MR. TAYLER. Oh, I am not saying that you take that view. Of course not.
You can not. You are not a Mormon.

MR. WHITECOTTON. I understand that is his point of view.

MR. TAYLER. That the law then does not speak to him?

MR. WHITECOTTON. No.

MR. TAYLER. That a higher law controls that situation?

MR. WHITECOTTON. No; I am not quite able to say that, Mr. Tayler. I believe
that the Mormons who are now living in polygamy admit that they are
doing it in violation of the law of God and of man ...

MR. TAYLER. And do you not know that President Joseph F. Smith proclaimed to the 10,000 of his people since he testified here that if he
recognized the customs of the world in respect to the matter of living
with more than one wife he would be eternally damned?

MR. WHITECOTTON. I did not know he had made such a statement as that.

MR. TAYLER. Would it surprise you? ...

MR. WHITECOTTON. No; because I think Joseph F. Smith is a thorough fanatic.[18] ...

Hiram E. Booth,[19] being duly sworn, was examined, and testified as
follows ...

---

17. By "his point of view," Whitecotton means the point of view of the husband of
plural wives.

18. The *Salt Lake Triune* scoffed at Whitecotton's testimony: "We must all treat him
as he treats the situation—with smiling jocularity. There was nothing to it but drollery.
He simply went down to have a little fun at the expense of the United States, and he had
it. If the rest of the United Stated did not appreciate that he was in a mood of buffoon-
ery, and that he did not take any serious view of the situation, it is simply because the
country lacked all sense of humor. It is no fault of Whitecotton ... if other men do not enjoy his harlequinade" ("Whitecotton's Joke," Jan. 21, 1905).

19. Booth (1860-1940) moved to Salt Lake City from Iowa in 1888. He was a non-
Mormon attorney who was active in politics.

MR. WORTHINGTON. Now I want to ask you, Mr. Booth, from your long acquaintance with political affairs there, whether or not it is your judgment, from what you have observed and the general reputation there, that the Mormon Church does or does not interfere and govern in political results there?

MR. BOOTH. The Mormon Church, as a church, in my opinion, does not interfere in political affairs.

MR. WORTHINGTON. Do you mean by that to qualify it? You say "as a church."

MR. BOOTH. I mean as a church action. There are individual members, of course, of the church that take active part in politics—from elders to apostles.

MR. WORTHINGTON. They exercise their rights as American citizens, the same as non-Mormons do, do you mean?

MR. BOOTH. Yes.

MR. WORTHINGTON. Do you mean anything more than that?

MR. BOOTH. I mean nothing more than that. I mean to say, further than that, that the church is divided. The apostles, the bishops, the councilors and presidents of stakes, and elders are divided like other people as to who shall be nominated for office, where they belong to the same political party, and do not act as a unit or as a church.

MR. WORTHINGTON. What would you say as to the constancy with which the Mormons adhere to their political parties and convictions as compared with the non-Mormons in your State?

MR. BOOTH. It is my opinion that the Mormon people are as true to their political convictions as any people in any State. ...

MR. WORTHINGTON. Can you give us any information on the subject of alleged failure to arrest Heber J. Grant when he was about to leave the country?

MR. BOOTH. Yes; I have investigated that subject. Last fall it was charged against the sheriff, Mr. C. Frank Emory, who is a Mormon, that after the warrant was issued he permitted Heber J. Grant to leave the State without any attempt whatever to arrest him. That was charged by the American party to secure Mr. Emory's defeat. I was a supporter of Mr. Emory, so I investigated the truth of that assertion. I found the facts to be about as follows ...

Mr. Steel was a deputy in the criminal department of the sheriffs office and is a Gentile, a non-Mormon. The warrant was issued and delivered to Mr. Steel, as chief deputy, about 5 o'clock in the afternoon. Mr. Steel at once made an investigation, and made an affidavit to the effect that he learned that at the time this warrant was delivered to him, Heber J. Grant had departed from the State of Utah. In other words, the warrant was delivered to him at 5 o'clock in the afternoon, and Heber J. Grant had left on the train at 3 o'clock in the afternoon, and was at that time in the State of Wyoming or near the line, so he could not be apprehended. That is, as I understand the fact to be in reference to that.[20]

MR. WORTHINGTON. Do you know Senator Smoot?

MR. BOOTH. I know Senator Smoot; yes, sir.

MR. WORTHINGTON. How long have you known him?

MR. BOOTH. For ten years, I should say—longer than that by reputation, but ten years personally.

MR. WORTHINGTON. I was about to ask you if you have been familiar with his reputation and standing in that community of Utah for ten or twelve years?

MR. BOOTH. I have, since 1890. That is about fourteen years, more or less.

MR. WORTHINGTON. I will ask you to tell us what information you can give us, if any, in reply to what Judge Hiles testified here [regarding Smoot's candidacy]. ...

MR. BOOTH. I should say that statement is incorrect, and does Senator Smoot a grave injustice.

MR. WORTHINGTON. What are the facts, as you understand them?

MR. BOOTH. The facts, as I understand them to be, are that he has been a prominent Republican ever since the Mormons and Gentiles divided on party lines, I think before the Liberal party disbanded, from 1891 down to the present time. He made speeches throughout the southern counties of Utah, and traveled more or less throughout the entire State of Utah. As testified to by Mr. Whitecotton, he was a prominent manufacturer and a buyer of wool and had spread the Republican gospel generally throughout Utah for many years prior to that time.

MR. WORTHINGTON. As a stump speaker?

---

20. The First Presidency explained Grant's exodus this way:

Brother Grant's family left here yesterday afternoon. He had intended leaving here at the same time but having learned as we suppose that a warrant was to be issued for his arrest on account of certain utterances said to have been made by him before the student body of the University of Utah, he left us quite unexpectedly without affording us the pleasure of bidding good-bye. We are glad however that he did so, as his arrest might have produced perplexing complications seeing that the scheme was concocted by the Ministers Association of this city for the purpose of prejudging Senator Smoot's case in Washington" (in Harvard S. Heath, "Reed Smoot: First Modern Mormon," Ph.D. diss., Brigham Young University, 1990, 107).

MR. BOOTH. As a stump speaker in the southern part of the State, in the southern counties, and generally as a talker for the Republican party throughout other portions of the State. He was so prominent that in my judgment he could have been nominated for an office from 1896 down to the time he was elected United States Senator. I do not know that he ever aspired to hold any State office, but he was generally regarded as a man high in the councils of the Republican party.

MR. WORTHINGTON. Did it cause you any surprise when you heard he was talked of for Senator?

MR. BOOTH. No; I was opposed to him. I favored George Sutherland,[21] and went into the convention in Salt Lake County and did all I could to defeat his candidates for the legislature, with Mr. Critchlow and George Sutherland and others. I was a candidate myself, an anti-Smoot candidate, for nomination for the legislature at that time, but through the votes of a number of prominent Gentiles Senator Smoot's candidates for the legislature received the nomination.

MR. WORTHINGTON. It was the Gentiles who threw the balance to him, then?

MR. BOOTH. The Gentiles threw the balance. Mr. Joseph Lipman, now the manager of the "[Salt Lake] Tribune," turned all of his forces in favor of Senator Smoot's candidates.

SENATOR OVERMAN. Were the candidates Mormons? Were those who were nominated Mormons or Gentiles?

MR. BOOTH. Both Mormons and Gentiles.

MR. WORTHINGTON. As a man who was right in that fight, what evidence did you see of church interference in that election?

MR. BOOTH. There was no church interference at all. We would have defeated Senator Smoot's candidates if it had not been for Mr. Lipman, who was then the political manager of the senior Senator from Utah. If it had not been for his influence and the influence of the senior Senator from Utah we could have defeated Senator Smoot's candidates in Salt Lake County.

---

21. George Herbert Sutherland (1874-1931) lived in Salt Lake City. His parents joined the LDS Church in England and immigrated to Utah. Shortly after arrival, his parents renounced Mormonism and raised George outside the church—although he attended school at Brigham Young Academy. After studying law at the University of Michigan and practicing in Utah, Sutherland was elected to U.S. House of Representatives (1901-03), followed by election to the U.S. Senate (1905-17), then an appointment by U.S. President Warren G. Harding to the U.S. Supreme Court, where he served 1922-38. He married Laura Jane Jones in 1902; they had ten children. A Smoot ally, Sutherland delivered a Senate speech in his favor on January 22, 1907.

MR. WORTHINGTON. Were there Mormons in that legislature that elected Senator Smoot?

MR. BOOTH. Oh, I think so; yes; many Mormons.

MR. WORTHINGTON. Did they go solidly one way or the other, or did they divide?

MR. BOOTH. I do not remember the exact vote as it was taken in the legislature.

MR. WORTHINGTON. It is in evidence here.

MR. BOOTH. But it was generally understood, after his candidates had been nominated during the campaign, that he would be the candidate for United States Senator, and was so accepted. After we were defeated we accepted that. We accepted our defeat as such, and went in and helped elect these men, knowing they would vote for Senator Smoot.

MR. WORTHINGTON. It was known that he had obtained the consent, under this rule you have spoken of, to run?

MR. BOOTH. It was known he had obtained that consent.

MR. WORTHINGTON. Was it accepted, as soon as that was known, that that was the end of it, or did you fight him?

MR. BOOTH. We did not fight him at all. We supported our ticket.

MR. WORTHINGTON. You mean after he was nominated.

MR. BOOTH. After his candidates were nominated for the legislature we supported all of those candidates.

MR. WORTHINGTON. You were speaking before of the primaries?

MR. BOOTH. No; I am speaking of the election, after the nomination.

SENATOR DUBOIS. When was it known that he had received the consent [of] the authorities to become a candidate for the Senate? Before your primaries?

MR. BOOTH. It was known that he could not run unless he had obtained that consent. The [Moses] Thatcher rule and the [B. H.] Roberts rule was well known at that time, that it was necessary for him to obtain that consent before he could be a candidate. Everybody understood that.

THE CHAIRMAN. Let me ask you, right there, what effect it would have had if he had not obtained the consent of the church and had attempted to be a candidate?

MR. BOOTH. I can not undertake to say, what the church would have done to him.

THE CHAIRMAN. What is your best judgment?

MR. BOOTH. My judgment is he would have been nominated, whether the church consented to it or not.

THE CHAIRMAN. How about the election?

MR. BOOTH. And would have been elected whether the church consented to it or not, for this reason: Senator Smoot had a political influence separate and apart from his apostolic influence. His political influence was such that it would have obtained for him the nomination whether the church consented to it or not. He had that power, and I think the church recognized that as the reason they gave their consent. ...

MR. TAYLER. Undoubtedly. You live in a part of the city where you are well buttressed ecclesiastically?

MR. BOOTH. Yes.

MR. TAYLER. The hierarchy is all about you?

MR. BOOTH. What do you mean by the hierarchy?

MR. TAYLER. I mean apostles and the first presidents. They are in your neighborhood, many of them?

MR. BOOTH. In my neighborhood; yes, sir.

MR. TAYLER. Joseph F. Smith lives a block or so from you?

MR. BOOTH. His wives do. He lives in the official residence now, at the Bee Hive House, which is three blocks from where I live.

MR. TAYLER. And Anthon H. Lund lives across the street from you?

MR. BOOTH. Apostle Lund lives just across the street.

MR. WORTHINGTON. He is not an apostle now. He is a councilor.

MR. BOOTH. He is councilor to the president—one of the first presidents, as they call them there.

MR. TAYLER. M[atthias]. F. Cowley, you say, lives where?

MR. BOOTH. Right across the street—right beside Apostle Lund.

MR. TAYLER. And what other apostle?

MR. BOOTH. John Henry Smith lives just a block toward town.

MR. TAYLER. Does he not also live just a block from town, too?

MR. BOOTH. Yes; I live two blocks from the town, and he lives between me and the city.

MR. TAYLER. Has he not a house on each side of you?

MR. BOOTH. Yes; the house where one of his wives lives, at the end of West Temple street, on the north end there, on First North street; but his wife that he lives with—his residence—is known as across from the temple grounds, beside his son, George A[lbert]. Smith.[22]

---

22. Carl Badger exchanged letters with his friend and future LDS president, George Albert Smith, who had recently been ordained an apostle. George Albert Smith was a monogamist. Badger expressed frustration with the testimony given by some church officials. Smith responded on March 31, 1905:

MR. TAYLER. Apart from the varying views that people might take of this plural marriage entered into and followed by polygamous cohabitation, these are all reputable, respected people?

MR. BOOTH. They are. ...

SENATOR DUBOIS. Mr. Booth, do you not understand that these children who are now being born into the world in this polygamous relation come into the world contrary to the laws of God and man?

MR. BOOTH. Well, they do contrary to the laws of man. The other law is not so well defined and definitely settled as to enable me to testify concerning it.

SENATOR DUBOIS. Would you take the authority of Joseph [F.] Smith, the president of the church, on that point, as to whether it is contrary to the law of God?[23]

MR. BOOTH. I do know this. Senator—

SENATOR DUBOIS. Would you take his authority? If you are not clear on that yourself, would Joseph F. Smith's authority be good?

MR. BOOTH. I do know this—that the women who have gone into polygamy have done so from pure motives, believing it to be the law of God, and these children are born under those conditions.

SENATOR DUBOIS. If you are not clear as to whether they come into the

---

The air is heavy with misrepresentation, [and] falsehoods of the most diabolical kind are daily published by the Tribune. The air seems tainted with a spirit of hatefulness, causing the people to wonder what will happen next. ... Don't be misled into believing that the Church or its President has gone wrong: This is only a trick of the Devil to lead some of our young people astray. The lie is always a weapon for the unrighteous. The class of people who are furnishing the slanders against us is sufficient evidence of the master they serve. Frank J. Cannon is as near crazy as he can be and will not last long if he does not repent of the evil he is seeking to bring upon the people. I am informed that he is using the strongest of stimulants to nerve him for the work he has sold himself to do. Poor Frank; what a splendid opportunity he had to make a record in the world for ability and for the blessing of the people amongst whom he was reared. He chose to be unclean and the result is evident in his ruined life. Reproached by those of his own blood, despised by those who pay him for his services, pitied by those who tried to make him useful and who did all they could to reform him when he had disgraced himself and the name he bore, he rushes along to sure destruction, not heeding the pleading of his own family and loved ones" (in Rodney J. Badger, *Liahona and Iron Rod: The Biography of Carl A. and Rose J. Badger* [Bountiful, Utah: Family History Publishers, 1985], 264-65).

Cannon had just been excommunicated on March 14. Over the course of a decade, the Senator had gained a bad reputation for frequenting Salt Lake City brothels, fathering an illegitimate child, drunkenness, and slander against Joseph F. Smith (Van Wagoner and Walker, *Book of Mormons*, 45, 48).

23. Joseph F. Smith had testified that it was "contrary to the rule of the church and contrary as well to the law of the land for a man to cohabit with his wives" (*Smoot Hearings*, 1:129).

world contrary to the law of God, would you take Joseph F. Smith's testimony, and Francis M. Lyman's testimony,[24] the present president, and the next president, if he outlives Smith, of the church?

MR. WORTHINGTON. Mr. Booth is not a Mormon.

MR. BOOTH. I am not a Mormon. I am not subject to their control in any way.

SENATOR DUBOIS. I ask that question. Have you any sympathy for these children, who are now being born into the world in this relation?

MR. BOOTH. I certainly have.

SENATOR DUBOIS. You have for the children?

MR. BOOTH. I have for the children and I have for the women.

MR. TAYLER. Is your sympathy for the children, who are in nowise responsible, equal to your sympathy for the plural wives?

MR. BOOTH. Well, that would be a matter of separation that I could not make.

MR. TAYLER. You could not make that?

MR. BOOTH. I do not think so. My sympathies are for both.

MR. TAYLER. You would not undertake to stop it at all? Your sympathy for the children is not so great that you would undertake to stop their being brought into the world contrary to the laws of God and man?

MR. BOOTH. Yes; I would if I knew any way to do it without visiting the penalties and hardships upon these women. I have thought of that for years; and if you can point out a way to do that I would be glad to accept it and carry it out as far as I can.

MR. TAYLER. Do you think that the Gentiles of Utah generally have more sympathy with these plural wives than they have for these poor children?

MR. BOOTH. I could not say as to that. The Gentile population are somewhat divided, as you know, concerning these matters. I am speaking from my point of view, from a long study of this question, embracing years, and I want to do the right thing when I act. A vigorous prosecution of unlawful cohabitation would mean the isolation of these Mormon women.

MR. TAYLER. It would stop, however, the bringing into the world of these children, would it not?

MR. BOOTH. Yes; it would do that, but that would cease anyway in a short time. It is only a matter of a few years when that will pass by. ...

24. Lyman's statement was: "Mr. Chairman, I fully intend to be true to my obligations and covenants with the Lord and with my wives and children," adding that he had not intentionally harmed his country (*Smoot Hearings,* 1:430).

MR. TAYLER. Would you think John Henry Smith's chief work is spiritual, ecclesiastical work?

MR. BOOTH. It is spiritual, ecclesiastical work.

MR. TAYLER. Is that the reason why John Henry Smith is such a politician?

MR. BOOTH. I do not understand that John Henry Smith is any great politician.

MR. TAYLER. Do you not?

MR. BOOTH. I would not give a farthing for his support politically in any matter.

MR. TAYLER. That may be your view of his value, but do you not know that he is a very active politician, that he stumps?

MR. BOOTH. He has been in a way.

MR. TAYLER. Do you not know that perhaps his field of political endeavor is not so much Salt Lake as it is Idaho and Wyoming?

MR. BOOTH. I do not know what his political influence in Idaho and Wyoming is, but—

MR. TAYLER. I am not talking about his influence at all. I know you do not know anything about that. You say he has none, but he is an active politician, is he not?

MR. BOOTH. I say so far as his political influence is concerned in Salt Lake County, or in Utah, it is not great. It does not amount to much.

MR. WORTHINGTON. The testimony is that wherever he spoke in Idaho his party got licked.[25]

MR. BOOTH. I pride myself upon the fact that I have more political influence in my precinct among the Mormons than he has. I think I could defeat him on any political matter if we were opposed.

MR. TAYLER. Well, you are like John Henry. Each of you has a good opinion of himself.

MR. BOOTH. That is my opinion. There are a great many Mormons in that precinct who are not high church officials who have a great deal more political influence than John Henry Smith has.

MR. TAYLER. I do not doubt that. I know fellows in my ward at home who can beat me to a frazzle any day.

MR. BOOTH. I am afraid of those fellows, but I am not afraid of John Henry's influence.

MR. TAYLER. I do not take any discredit to myself because they can do that, either. That is all, Mr. Booth.

THE CHAIRMAN. Mr. Booth I should judge from your statement that you

---

25. Senator Worthington is referring to James Brady's testimony in this chapter.

rather approve and justify the continuous polygamous cohabitation and the rearing of new children.

MR. BOOTH. I do not say that, Senator.

THE CHAIRMAN. Well, what do you say?

MR. BOOTH. I simply say that we have been unable to find a way to stop it.

THE CHAIRMAN. Stop what?

MR. BOOTH. The unlawful cohabitation.

THE CHAIRMAN. Would an amendment to the Constitution of the United States prohibiting unlawful cohabitation accomplish it?[26]

MR. BOOTH. Mr. Chairman, I believe it would have a good effect. However, I am not prepared at this time to give a settled opinion upon that question. I have thought about it a great deal.

THE CHAIRMAN. That would be your judgment?

MR. BOOTH. The only objection to it would be that it would not be necessary. This condition is passing away so rapidly that it would not be necessary to have a constitutional amendment.

THE CHAIRMAN. How rapidly is it passing away with the president of the church?

MR. BOOTH. It certainly can not continue much longer. Age puts a limit on nearly everyone.

THE CHAIRMAN. It will pass away with his death probably.

MR. BOOTH. Well, probably before that.[27] ...

------

26. Both Smoot and the LDS hierarchy opposed such an amendment to the Constitution. Smoot explained:

I have taken the position that I am opposed to any more constitutional amendments, and as a citizen of Utah, I am particularly opposed to an amendment that is directed against my people and my State ... I have suggested that the best way to reach this question is to pass a national marriage law, and I have assured the Senators that I will support any measure, no matter how strict or what penalties it imposes,—provisions for the punishment of fornication, adultery, incest, unlawful cohabitation, and kindred offences ... I hardly think that we need worry much about this constitutional amendment proposition" (Smoot to Joseph F. Smith, Apr. 9, 1904).

President Smith voiced the same sentiment, although laced with irony, in a letter he sent to Smoot the very same day: "I say let the National Solons amend the constitution, to punish and insult and degrade this little handful of men who are rapidly passing away, and when they shall see the magnitude of their acts compared with the insignificance of the cause, they and their historians will laugh at their folly, and write them down as asses in the broadest sense."

27. Frank J. Cannon warned readers of the *Salt Lake Tribune* in an editorial that non-Mormons were "being used at Washington as defenders and supporters of the hierarchy, and of polygamy" and recommended:

prompt repudiation of them ... public meetings in which you shall denounce the Judas Iscariots, who have claimed to be Gentiles and yet have fawned, as no ignorant Mormon convert from the South Sea islands would fawn, at the feet of the Mormon

Arthur Pratt,[28] being duly sworn, was examined and testified as follows ...

MR. VAN COTT. What is the name of your father, please.

MR. PRATT. Orson Pratt.

MR. VAN COTT. Is that the Orson Pratt who has been mentioned in the course of the proceedings here?

MR. PRATT. He is.

MR. VAN COTT. He was a member of the Mormon Church?

MR. PRATT. He was.

MR. VAN COTT. Were you ever a member of the Mormon church?

MR. PRATT. I was not.

MR. VAN COTT. Have you ever been?

MR. PRATT. I never have been.

MR. VAN COTT. Commencing in your early manhood, were you ever connected in any way with the prosecution of polygamists or of persons engaged in unlawful cohabitation?

MR. PRATT. Yes, sir.

MR. VAN COTT. In what way?

MR. PRATT. As deputy United States marshal. ...

MR. VAN COTT. Have you occupied similar positions since then?

MR. PRATT. I have. ...

MR. VAN COTT. And from what year to what year?

MR. PRATT. From the fall of 1874 to about 1882, and commencing again in either 1885 or 1886, up to 1890.

---

priesthood. If you want to be servile, insensate tools of priestcraft, tell the church leaders that you are its creatures forever more. And if you want to be men, stand up in the splendor of your citizenship and say that the women and children of your race will be protected against outrage, even if you have to do as your forefathers did to maintain their sacred rights ("It Is Time," Jan. 15, 1905).

The next week, another Utah newspaper, *Goodwin's Weekly*, responded to Cannon:

Surely the emotional editor needs some soothing lotion to quiet his pulsating nerves. In the full swing of his present mental distemper, he apparently thinks it possible to make his newly developed paroxysms contagious among the peaceful citizens who refused to be whipped into political subservience to the man [Kearns] for whom the editor is now fulminating. And apparently he expects people to forget whose pen is fashioning this lurid doctrine, and to forget the tremendous change that has come over his spirit since the days when this same influence made him a Senator and when, in consequence, he was ostensibly a good Mormon himself and on terms of the most conspicuous amity with church authorities" ("Signs of the Times," Jan. 21, 1905).

28. At the time of the hearings, Pratt (1853-1919) lived in Salt Lake City. Though born in Utah to LDS Apostle Orson Pratt and Sarah Barnes Pratt, he was not raised Mormon and opposed polygamy.

MR. VAN COTT. In what way has the discharge of your duties called you to different parts of Utah?

MR. PRATT. ... I was the chief deputy in charge of the criminal business of the State, and I had to visit every district, and did so.

MR. VAN COTT. Are you generally acquainted with the Mormon people?

MR. PRATT. I am.

MR. VAN COTT. Without too much detail, give the committee a general idea of the number of polygamists, the number of men you have arrested for unlawful cohabitation, to show your familiarity with the practice in the different parts of the State?

MR. PRATT. Well, that would be impossible, to tell the number. I have for years followed that business and arrested, I should say, more than any other one officer in the State of Utah; but how many I could not say, commencing as early as 1875, when I arrested George Reynolds.

MR. VAN COTT. And continuing down to a late date?

MR. PRATT. Continuing down to 1890.

MR. VAN COTT. Did you arrest Brigham H. Roberts?

MR. PRATT. I did.

MR. VAN COTT. In a general way, just before the manifesto, what was the feeling between Gentiles and Mormons?

MR. PRATT. Do you mean just before or doing the prosecutions?

MR. VAN COTT. During the prosecutions.

MR. PRATT. During the prosecutions the feeling was very intense and very bitter as between Mormons and Gentiles, the Mormon people, of course, claiming that they were being persecuted, and the Gentile people insisting on the enforcement of the law.

MR. VAN COTT. And at that time did you have general knowledge as to whether polygamists were living openly with their wives in Utah or whether they were in the penitentiary or in hiding?

MR. PRATT. I did.

MR. VAN COTT. What is the fact of it?

MR. PRATT. The fact of it is that they were not living during those days openly with their wives. They were living with them. A great many hundreds of them were sent to the Utah penitentiary, which then was a Government prison, and a great many were what we termed on the underground—that is, they were in hiding.

MR. VAN COTT. As a preface to other questions, I wish you would state what was the practical result of your prosecutions on polygamous families—that is, polygamous wives and their children, young and old.

MR. PRATT. It entailed a great deal of suffering throughout the State of

Utah. It did not cause so much suffering, or any particularly among the better class or wealthy ones, but among the people as a whole it caused a great deal of suffering and anxiety and poverty among the Mormon people. The women and the children were the ones who got the worst of that prosecution. They suffered from it.

MR. VAN COTT. What is the sentiment in Utah among Gentiles regarding the prosecution of men who are living in polygamy who were married before the manifesto, and why, in your opinion, does that sentiment exist?

MR. PRATT. The sentiment, to be brief, is just the same as has been expressed here by two or three former witnesses in regard to the Gentile people. They have explained it very fully.

MR. VAN COTT. And the reason is the same?

MR. PRATT. And the reason is the same.

MR. VAN COTT. Is it out of any pity or sympathy for the men?

MR. PRATT. It is not. It is simply out of sympathy and out of the suffering that would be entailed on the women and the children.

MR. VAN COTT. Do you, as a Gentile out there, concur in that sentiment?

MR. PRATT. I have; yes.

MR. VAN COTT. What would you say about the decrease of polygamy in Utah since 1890?

MR. PRATT. Why, there is no doubt about it. Since 1890?

MR. VAN COTT. Yes.

MR. PRATT. There is no question about it, as far as we can have any knowledge, and I guess there is no one who can swear to it as knowing it personally. It is only from repute, what we hear, and information we can gain as officers. There is no question about the decrease. It has been all that could be expected, I think, since 1890. ...

MR. VAN COTT. What position do you hold now?

MR. PRATT. I am warden of the State prison of Utah.

MR. VAN COTT. How long have you held that position?

MR. PRATT. Only about ten months—that is, at this time.

MR. VAN COTT. Have you held any other political office in Utah?

MR. PRATT. I have.

MR. VAN COTT. What?

MR. PRATT. I was chief of police of Salt Lake City for six years.

MR. VAN COTT. During what years were you chief of police?

MR. PRATT. I was chief of police of Salt Lake City—elected in the fall of 1893.

MR. WORTHINGTON. From 1893 to 1899, then.

MR. PRATT. Yes, sir.

MR. VAN COTT. Have you held any other political office?

MR. PRATT. I have.

MR. VAN COTT. What?

MR. PRATT. I was auditor of public accounts.

MR. VAN COTT. I mean since the manifesto.

MR. PRATT. Oh, since the manifesto? I was elected about 1891 as a member of the school board of Salt Lake City.

MR. VAN COTT. Now, taking that into consideration, and also your activity, if any, in politics, what is your opinion as to the constancy of the Mormon people in adhering to party lines and voting their tickets?

MR. PRATT. My experience has been—I speak from having been a member of the State committee for a great many elections in Utah that they are more constant, if anything, than what we call the Gentile population. I base it on somewhat different figures from what some of the former witnesses have used.

MR. VAN COTT. But that is the result?

MR. PRATT. That was the result.

MR. VAN COTT. Take the great body of the Mormon people. What is your opinion as to their independence in politics and in political action?

MR. PRATT. I think they are just as independent, and have been, as any other.

MR. VAN COTT. Do you know Reed Smoot?

MR. PRATT. I do.

MR. VAN COTT. How long have you known him?

MR. PRATT. For a good many years, fourteen or fifteen, maybe twenty. I don't know exactly.

MR. VAN COTT. Did you know him in politics in Utah?

MR. PRATT. I did.

MR. VAN COTT. As what?

MR. PRATT. As a Republican.

MR. VAN COTT. Before he became an apostle, was he prominent in Republican politics?

MR. PRATT. He was.

MR. VAN COTT. And was it anything surprising, from what existed out there, that he should be a candidate for the United States Senate, even although not an apostle?

MR. PRATT. Not at all.

MR. VAN COTT. In your opinion, was he unknown and unthought of before he became an apostle and a candidate for the position of United States Senator?

MR. PRATT. He was very well known and very well thought of for some high office.[29] ...

---

29. At the end of testimony on January 13, 1905, Carl Badger wrote that "the hardest test will come when [Smoot] goes on the stand himself":

I was a little surprised to-day when the subject was mentioned to have the Senator express some doubt as to the wisdom of his taking the stand. He finally said that he guessed he would have to testify. The trouble is right here; if the Senator does not go on the stand it will look as though he were afraid of something; either that he would have to disclose something that would be damaging to his case, or to the Church, or something that would bind him and the Church for the future in a manner that is not desired by himself or the Church to be bound. ... I pity him for the ordeal that he must go through" (in Badger, *Liahona and Iron Rod*, 245).

21.

Hugh M. Dougall, Alonzo Arthur Noon, John P. Meakin, Robert T. Burton Jr., James A. Miner, and William M. McCarty

Saturday & Monday, January 14, 16

"The bright sky and clear atmosphere outside brought the Capitol a great many ladies and the seats reserved for them were filled as well as any day in the past. Among them were a dozen new faces ... Senator Smoot was absent at the opening of the afternoon session for the first time and only one member of the committee, Burrows, conducted the investigation." —*Deseret News,* Jan. 16, 1905

Hugh M. Dougall,[1] being duly sworn, was examined, and testified as follows ...

MR. WORTHINGTON. When you were a Mormon did you go through the ceremony which is called "taking the endowments?"

MR. DOUGALL. Yes, sir.

MR. WORTHINGTON. And when did you do that?

MR. DOUGALL. In 1862.

MR. WORTHINGTON. How old were you then?

MR. DOUGALL. About 25 years old.

MR. WORTHINGTON. Twenty-five?

MR. DOUGALL. Yes, sir.

MR. WORTHINGTON. Was that before or after you were married?

MR. DOUGALL. I went there to be married.

MR. WORTHINGTON. Did you take your endowments at any other time than on this occasion when you were 25 years old?

MR. DOUGALL. No, sir.

MR. WORTHINGTON. Where did you take them?

MR. DOUGALL. In the old Endowment House in Salt Lake.

MR. WORTHINGTON. In the Endowment House in Salt Lake?

MR. DOUGALL. Yes, sir.

---

1. Dougall (1838-1906) owned a flour and grist mill in Sanpete County, Utah, although he lived in Springville, near Provo. He left the LDS Church in the mid-1870s. He was a Republican.

MR. WORTHINGTON. Have you a recollection of what transpired when you took your endowments?

MR. DOUGALL. I have a general recollection. I could not give—

THE CHAIRMAN. We can not hear the answer.

MR. DOUGALL. I could not give, even if I tried, the whole detail.

MR. WORTHINGTON. I want to ask you whether on that occasion this or anything like it happened. First let me ask you, did others go through with you?

MR. DOUGALL. Oh, yes; there were 150 went through that same day, I should judge.

MR. WORTHINGTON. I want to ask you whether you, or any of those who went through with you, to your knowledge, were called upon to agree to what I now read, or to it in substance: "That you, and each of you, do promise and vow that you will never cease to importune High Heaven to avenge the blood of the prophets upon this nation."

MR. DOUGALL. No, sir.

MR. WORTHINGTON. Did anything like that occur?

MR. DOUGALL. Well, as I remember, there is something that might possibly have resembled that.

THE CHAIRMAN. We can not hear the witness.

MR. DOUGALL. There was something, as I remember, that might have led one to believe that such a thing was being done. As I remember it, they importuned Heaven to avenge the blood of the prophets and the martyrs on this generation, I think.

MR. WORTHINGTON. "On this generation?"

MR. DOUGALL. I think so; that is as near as I can remember. I would not vouch for that being correct; nothing in regard to this nation.[2]

MR. TAYLER. This generation?

MR. DOUGALL. As I remember it.[3]

MR. WORTHINGTON. Did anything draw your attention particularly to that part of the ceremony?

MR. DOUGALL. Yes, sir.

MR. WORTHINGTON. What was it?

MR. DOUGALL. Previous to going there I had read a book that purported to give an exposé of the Mormon endowment ceremony, and among them was an obligation that you took, some obligation of disloyalty

2. The previous four questions and answers were included in Carlisle's closing argument (*Smoot Hearings,* 4:425).

3. The previous five questions and answers were used by Tayler in his closing argument (*Smoot Hearings,* 3:581).

or enmity to this Government. I was looking out particularly for that particular point.

Mr. Worthington. You were looking for it?

Mr. Dougall. Yes, sir.

Mr. Worthington. Did it come?

Mr. Dougall. No. sir.

Mr. Worthington. Was there anything of that nature in the ceremony?

Mr. Dougall. No, sir.

Mr. Worthington. Do you remember whether there was anything about Joseph Smith?

Mr. Dougall. There was not a thing I remember. I do not remember his name being mentioned at all. ...

Mr. Tayler. You say that as you remember this obligation, it was that the blood of the prophets should be avenged on this generation.

Mr. Dougall. Well, to ask God to avenge the blood—

The Chairman. We can not hear you at all.

Mr. Dougall. To ask God to avenge the blood of the prophets and martyrs on this generation. That is the way I remember it. It may not be correct.

Mr. Tayler. What did you understand was meant by the "prophets?"

Mr. Dougall. I do not know.

Mr. Tayler. Had the oath no meaning to you?

Mr. Dougall. No; it had no meaning in that connection. I was looking for something else.

Mr. Tayler. You did not know whether it meant Joseph Smith or not?

Mr. Dougall. No. I do not know who it meant.

Mr. Tayler. Who are the martyrs in the Mormon Church?

Mr. Dougall. In the Mormon Church?

Mr. Tayler. Yes.

Mr. Dougall. I suppose Joseph Smith and Hyrum Smith.

Mr. Tayler. And who are the prophets in the Mormon Church?

Mr. Dougall. Joseph Smith and Hyrum Smith, who have been martyred, I presume. I do not know anything more.

Mr. Tayler. What did you understand "this generation" to mean?

Mr. Dougall. I do not know that I understood it to mean much.

Mr. Tayler. Much?

Mr. Dougall. No. I was there that day to be married. That was my principal business.

Mr. Tayler. And you were more interested in that than in the other?

Mr. Dougall. Yes, sir.

MR. TAYLER. I understood you to say you were watching out very carefully for this obligation.

MR. DOUGALL. I was; for the obligation of disloyalty to the Government.

MR. TAYLER. Exactly.

MR. DOUGALL. Yes, sir.

MR. TAYLER. But you did not inquire of anybody what was meant by the expression "this generation?"

MR. DOUGALL. I have inquired since—since this discussion came up—and I am told that it was in the lecture that this was inculcated, and that it was from some chapter in Revelation—copied from that. I do not remember. I have told what I remember.[4]

MR. TAYLER. When you prayed God to avenge on this generation, you did not interpret it to mean that it was to avenge on the Mormon Church, did you, or on the Mormon people?

MR. DOUGALL. No, sir; certainly not.

MR. TAYLER. Or upon the inhabitants of China?

MR. DOUGALL. No.

MR. TAYLER. You did not stop to think about it at all?

MR. DOUGALL. Very little, Mr. Tayler.

MR. TAYLER. Was this a plural marriage that you were entering into?

MR. DOUGALL. No, sir.

MR. TAYLER. Were you ever a polygamist?

MR. DOUGALL. No, sir.

MR. TAYLER. That is all.

THE CHAIRMAN. You say there were several who took this at the same time?

MR. DOUGALL. Yes, sir. The rooms were crowded—filled full.

THE CHAIRMAN. How long did it take to perform the ceremony?

MR. DOUGALL. It took from probably early in the morning till about 4 o'clock—from, say, 8 or 9 o'clock in the morning until 4 o'clock in the afternoon.

THE CHAIRMAN. A very lengthy ceremony?

MR. DOUGALL. Yes, sir.

THE CHAIRMAN. Can you tell the committee what it was?

MR. DOUGALL. No, sir.

---

4. Dougall's reference is to the "lecture at the veil," an instructional part of the temple ceremony for first-time initiates until it was discontinued in 1905. The lecture did not include the so-called "oath of vengeance" (David John Buerger, "The Adam-God Doctrine," *Dialogue: a Journal of Mormon Thought* 15 [Spring 1982]: 32, 34; cf. Fred C. Collier, *Unpublished Revelations* [Salt Lake City: Collier's Publishing, 1979], 1:113-18). The scripture Dougall refers to is Rev. 6:9-10.

THE CHAIRMAN. Why not?

MR. DOUGALL. Conscientious scruples. I have promised secrecy. I have kept it for forty years or more, and feel under moral obligation to keep it.

THE CHAIRMAN. Were you sworn to secrecy?

MR. DOUGALL. I think so. As I remember it, I was. I think so.

THE CHAIRMAN. You were obligated to secrecy?

MR. DOUGALL. Yes, sir.

THE CHAIRMAN. Never to reveal what occurred in the Endowment House while you were there?

MR. DOUGALL. That is right.

THE CHAIRMAN. Was there any penalty attached if you did reveal it?

MR. DOUGALL. I think there was.

THE CHAIRMAN. What was it?

MR. DOUGALL. I do not care about saying what it was, Mr. Burrows.

THE CHAIRMAN. You decline to state what the penalty was?

MR. DOUGALL. Yes, sir.

THE CHAIRMAN. Was it a severe penalty?

MR. DOUGALL. As my memory goes, I think it was.

THE CHAIRMAN. Was it a penalty of death?

MR. DOUGALL. I do not think that I care about answering any more questions on that point, Senator.

THE CHAIRMAN. All who were present that day, going through that ceremony, were obligated to secrecy the same as you were?

MR. DOUGALL. Yes, sir.

THE CHAIRMAN. You have stated your recollection as to a portion of the ceremony, and you decline to state the whole of the ceremony?

MR. DOUGALL. Yes, sir.

THE CHAIRMAN. You were married at that time?

MR. DOUGALL. I was married that day. ...

THE CHAIRMAN. Were you and your wife dressed in your ordinary wearing apparel?

MR. DOUGALL. Well, Senator, I think that is coming down to that part as to which I decline to answer.

THE CHAIRMAN. You feel that under your oath of secrecy you can not disclose it?

MR. DOUGALL. Yes, sir.

THE CHAIRMAN. You would not want to state whether you wore garments with certain symbols on them, indicating the punishment to be inflicted on you in the event of disclosure?

MR. DOUGALL. No, sir; I would not.

THE CHAIRMAN. Do you know whether that ceremony is continued up to the present time?

MR. DOUGALL. I do not. I presume it is, but I do not know. It is forty years since I was there, Senator.

THE CHAIRMAN. Is this a public ceremony?

MR. DOUGALL. No, sir.

THE CHAIRMAN. No one is permitted to be present except those who take the obligations?

MR. DOUGALL. And the officers.

THE CHAIRMAN. And the officers?

MR. DOUGALL. Yes, sir.

THE CHAIRMAN. Who officiated at the time you took the endowments?

MR. DOUGALL (after a pause). I think it was Heber C. Kimball. There were a great many more. There were a great many.

THE CHAIRMAN. Name the others who officiated.

MR. DOUGALL. I could not do it, even if I was willing. ...

THE CHAIRMAN. What position did he [Kimball] hold in the church at that time?

MR. DOUGALL. He was the next man to Brigham Young.[5]

THE CHAIRMAN. Let me ask you another question. I understand you to state that where the marriage was consummated in the Endowment House by the officials of the church it was necessary to take the endowments?

MR. DOUGALL. Yes, sir. ...

THE CHAIRMAN. What time did you say you left the church; the year? ...

MR. DOUGALL. It was in 1874 or 1875 or 1873; 1874 or 1875.

THE CHAIRMAN. 1875?

MR. DOUGALL. Yes, sir.

THE CHAIRMAN. Thirty years ago?

MR. DOUGALL. Yes, sir.

THE CHAIRMAN. And this obligation you took at that time, although you have severed your connection with the church, is of such a character that you can not reveal what occurred?

MR. DOUGALL. I never revealed a thing of it; kept it secret from the time I took it, and have conscientious scruples about divulging it now or ever.

---

5. Kimball (1801-68) served as first counselor to Brigham Young from 1847 until his death.

THE CHAIRMAN. That is all.[6] ...

MR. WORTHINGTON. Was the obligation of secrecy which you took when you went through the endowment ceremony in the nature of an oath? It has been referred to as an oath in questions which have been propounded to you.

MR. DOUGALL. I do not remember. I know there was an obligation of secrecy, but whether directly an oath or not, I do not remember.

MR. WORTHINGTON. Do any of the other secret societies which you have testified you are connected with have an obligation of secrecy?

MR. DOUGALL. Yes, sir.

MR. WORTHINGTON. Would you be willing to reveal here what transpires in those ceremonies?

MR. DOUGALL. No, sir.

MR. WORTHINGTON. Is the obligation which you took when you took your endowments any different, in your mind, in its nature or binding effect upon you, than when you went through the ceremony with respect to the other secret societies?

MR. DOUGALL. It would not have any more effect upon me, but the ceremony was different.

MR. WORTHINGTON. Of course. But I mean, is the conscientious obligation of secrecy which you say you feel any different in relation to what transpired in the Mormon Church ceremony from what transpired in a secret society?

MR. DOUGALL. Not a bit, so far as the secrecy is concerned.

MR. WORTHINGTON. Would you mind answering whether in the other secret societies there is any penalty imposed for a violation of the obligation of secrecy?

MR. DOUGALL. I do not remember any?

MR. WORTHINGTON. You do not remember any?

MR. DOUGALL. No.

MR. WORTHINGTON. That is all.

---

6. James E. Talmage wrote in his journal a few days later on January 26:

Certain members of the Committee (Burrows who is the Chairman, and Dubois) have tried persistently to obtain from witnesses a description of the temple or endowment ceremonies. One J. H. Wallis ... and a few other apostates from the Church have professed to give details as to these sacred ceremonies, but have presented their evidence in so garbled and false a form as to disprove itself. Particular attention has been given to alleged 'oaths' and prescribed penalties for divulging the same. Reed Smoot has been virtually lost sight of in the case, it is the Church that is assailed. The opinion of the attorneys for Smoot is that their "case" is in good condition. I am not so confident as to the outcome (L. Tom Perry Special Collections, Harold B. Lee Library, Brigham Young University, Provo).

THE CHAIRMAN. But you do remember that there is a penalty for this obligation?

MR. DOUGALL. In the Mormon Church?

THE CHAIRMAN. Yes.

MR. DOUGALL. Yes, sir. ...

THE CHAIRMAN. In answer to a Question of Senator Knox you have said there was nothing in this obligation that would in any way interfere with your allegiance to the State or nation.[7] Why, then, do you refuse to disclose what it was?

MR. DOUGALL. What the ceremonies were?

THE CHAIRMAN. Yes.

MR. DOUGALL. Because I took an obligation that I would keep it secret. I consider myself morally bound to do it.

THE CHAIRMAN. You have already stated, have you not, Mr. Dougall, what the ceremony was, in part?

MR. DOUGALL. Yes; in part—in reference to this martyr and prophet business.

THE CHAIRMAN. You have stated some portion of the ceremony?

MR. DOUGALL. Well, I presume so.

THE CHAIRMAN. Now, in respect to this portion of the ceremony in relation to the obligation, you have denied in a negative way that it was an obligation hostile to the Government?

MR. DOUGALL. Put that just as positive as you please, Senator.

THE CHAIRMAN. Now, we want you to state to the committee what the obligation was, so that the committee may judge.

MR. DOUGALL. What the obligation was?

THE CHAIRMAN. Yes, sir. You have given your version of the obligation. Will you please state to the committee what the obligation was?

MR. DOUGALL. Excuse me; I scarcely savvy you.

THE CHAIRMAN. I beg pardon?

MR. DOUGALL. I scarcely understand what you want to know.

THE CHAIRMAN. You have told the character of this obligation and your version of it, and I am now asking you to state what the obligation was, so that the committee may judge as to its obligation.

MR. DOUGALL. The obligation of secrecy?

THE CHAIRMAN. No, sir; the obligation. You took some obligation, did you not?

---

7. Dougall had testified earlier in the day. In his initial testimony, Senator Knox had asked whether there was anything in the temple vow in conflict with "giving full and supreme allegiance to the United States" or with one's "duty as a citizen of the United States," to which Dougall had answered "Not one thing" (*Smoot Hearings*, 2:782).

MR. DOUGALL. Yes, sir; I suppose so.

THE CHAIRMAN. A vow?

MR. DOUGALL. Yes, sir.

THE CHAIRMAN. We ask you now to state what those obligations were?

MR. DOUGALL. I refuse to do it. I do not remember it. I could not do it.

THE CHAIRMAN. Why do you refuse?

MR. DOUGALL. Simply on the ground that it is like any other secret order, I presume, that you pledge yourself to secrecy in regard to the ritual.

THE CHAIRMAN. But you have already stated a part of it?

MR. DOUGALL. The part that is unimportant.

THE CHAIRMAN. You regard the obligation with respect to fidelity to the Government as important?

MR. DOUGALL. Yes, sir.

THE CHAIRMAN. And that you will not disclose?

MR. DOUGALL. Well.

THE CHAIRMAN. You will not disclose what that obligation was?

MR. DOUGALL. An obligation of fidelity to the Government?

THE CHAIRMAN. I say you have disclosed some things in relation to the ceremony in the Endowment House, and the committee now want you to state what the obligation was which was taken by you in relation to avenging the blood of the prophets, or if there was any such thing, of Joseph Smith. Did you hear any such obligation?

MR. DOUGALL. Simply the prayer to God to avenge the blood of his saints and martyrs; something like that.

THE CHAIRMAN. You remember that now?

MR. WORTHINGTON. He said that before—"on this generation."

MR. DOUGALL. I said that before.

SENATOR KNOX. The point is if he is willing to state that much of it at your instance, Mr. Worthington, why is he anxious to hold back the remainder of it?

MR. WORTHINGTON. That is what I can not understand.

THE CHAIRMAN. The whole ceremony was under the obligation of secrecy?

MR. DOUGALL. Yes, sir. ...

Alonzo Arthur Noon,[8] being duly sworn, was examined, and testified as follows ...

8. Noon (1837-1911) lived in Provo, where he was a justice of the peace. He was a Republican. He left the LDS Church in 1870.

MR. WORTHINGTON. You are a townsman of Senator Smoot, and have been for a long time?

MR. NOON. I have, sir.

MR. WORTHINGTON. Have you known him since you have been there?

MR. NOON. I have known him since he was a boy.

MR. WORTHINGTON. You know him well?

MR. NOON. Yes, sir.

MR. WORTHINGTON. Are you a Mormon?

MR. NOON. I am not now a Mormon.

MR. WORTHINGTON. When were you a Mormon?

MR. NOON. I was a Mormon up to about 1870.

THE CHAIRMAN. 1870?

MR. NOON. Yes, sir.

MR. WORTHINGTON. Was your separation from the church voluntary or involuntary?

MR. NOON. Decidedly voluntary.

MR. WORTHINGTON. Was there a formal leave-taking of the church, or did you simply drift away?

MR. NOON. I just left the church.

MR. WORTHINGTON. Did you give notice to your bishop?

MR. NOON. In talking over the matter I did.

MR. WORTHINGTON. You told him you had left?

MR. NOON. I disbelieved in modern revelations. I began to disbelieve it, and finally it impressed me so thoroughly that I entirely disbelieved it.

MR. WORTHINGTON. Did you tell him to consider you no longer a member of the Mormon Church?

MR. NOON. He did so.

MR. WORTHINGTON. Since that time have you been affiliated with any religious organization?

MR. NOON. Yes.

MR. WORTHINGTON. What?

MR. NOON. I have not been a member of any organization, but my family—of course, I have quite a large family—have been associated with the Christian church in Provo—first the Methodist Church, and finally they took their choice, the Congregational.

MR. WORTHINGTON. In view of your remarks that you have a large family, I must ask you whether you have more than one wife?

MR. NOON. No, sir; one wife is all I wanted, and I had family enough by the one. ...

MR. WORTHINGTON. Did you take your endowments, as they are called, when you were a Mormon?

MR. NOON. Yes, sir.

MR. WORTHINGTON. Are you a Mason?

MR. NOON. I am, sir. I have been one since 1863.

MR. WORTHINGTON. Since 1863?

MR. NOON. Yes, sir; I was made a Mason in Southern Africa.

MR. WORTHINGTON. Have you been a member of that organization since?

MR. NOON. I have been a charter member of a lodge in Provo.

MR. WORTHINGTON. When did you take your endowments?

MR. NOON. I took the endowments in 1865 or 1866; maybe 1866.

MR. WORTHINGTON. Was that preliminary to your marriage or a part of the marriage ceremony?

MR. NOON. I was married.

MR. WORTHINGTON. How old were you when you took the endowments?

MR. NOON. I must have been about 28—between that and 30.

MR. WORTHINGTON. How long was it before you left the church because you did not believe in revelations?

MR. NOON. I left about 1870.

MR. WORTHINGTON. Have you a recollection of the endowment ceremony?

MR. NOON. Well, partially, yes; I think I have.

MR. WORTHINGTON. I want to ask you whether, in going through that ceremony, anything like this occurred. I want you to understand I am not asking you about these precise words, but anything like this, or in substance: "That you and each of you do promise and vow that you will never cease to importune high heaven to avenge the blood of the prophets upon this nation?"

MR. NOON. No, sir; it was not said.

MR. WORTHINGTON. Was anything like that said?

MR. NOON. No; not in those words.

MR. WORTHINGTON. Was there anything that imported hostility to the country?

MR. NOON. No, sir.

MR. WORTHINGTON. To the United States?

MR. NOON. No, sir.

MR. WORTHINGTON. To the Government of the United States?

MR. NOON. No, sir.

MR. WORTHINGTON. Are you clear about that?

MR. NOON. Yes, sir; I am perfectly clear about that. ...

THE CHAIRMAN. You say that you took the endowments?

Mr. Noon. Yes, sir.

The Chairman. Were others with you at the same time?

Mr. Noon. Yes, sir; quite a few.

The Chairman. How many?

Mr. Noon. I could not begin to tell.

The Chairman. Were there ten thousand, five thousand, or a hundred?

Mr. Noon. Oh, I do not know. There may have been perhaps fifty or sixty; maybe more or less.

The Chairman. How long did the ceremony take?

Mr. Noon. It took, if I remember aright, from the morning about 10 or 11 o'clock, before we went out in the afternoon some time possibly.

The Chairman. Was there any change in your apparel in taking the ceremony?

Mr. Noon. I think that when a man enters into any organization, there are some matters associated with all organizations that are not public.

The Chairman. I am asking you about the ceremony you went through.

Mr. Noon. I should refuse to answer the question, Senator.

The Chairman. Why?

Mr. Noon. Because I think it would be improper to answer the question.

The Chairman. Why improper?

Mr. Noon. Because it would be endeavoring to reach, like any other secret organization, the form of the organization.

The Chairman. Then you regarded the organization at that time as a secret organization, of course?

Mr. Noon. I did.

The Chairman. Was there any penalty attached to the disclosure of the ceremony?

Mr. Noon. Yes; there was a penalty.

The Chairman. What?

Mr. Noon. There was a penalty attached.

The Chairman. What was it?

Mr. Noon. That is like any other question; it would be the same question, and I would not desire to answer it—as to what the penalty was.

The Chairman. You decline to state what the penalty was?

Mr. Noon. Yes; I think it is proper not to answer it.

The Chairman. Was it a severe penalty?

Mr. Noon. Fairly severe. I presume it would be like any other organization.

The Chairman. I am not talking about other organizations. I am asking you about this. Was the penalty a severe penalty? Was it a penalty of expulsion?

MR. NOON. I believe that is a question I would refuse to answer.

THE CHAIRMAN. What do you say as to the penalty being the tearing out of the tongue or the tearing open of the breasts and taking out the vitals? What do you say about that?

MR. NOON. I answer the same as the other—that is, I would refuse to answer it.

THE CHAIRMAN. You decline to answer it?

MR. NOON. I decline to answer. ...

John P. Meakin,[9] having been duly sworn, was examined, and testified as follows ...

MR. WORTHINGTON. Do you belong to any of the organizations that are called secret societies in this country?

MR. MEAKIN. Nearly all of them.

MR. WORTHINGTON. You do?

MR. MEAKIN. Yes, sir; I am a "joiner."

MR. WORTHINGTON. Just give the names of two or three of the leading ones you belong to?

MR. MEAKIN. I belong to the Knights of Pythias, and am the Past Grand Chancellor of our State. I belong to the Benevolent Protective Order of Elks, and I served as chaplain for six months. I belong to the Fraternal Order of Eagles, to the Woodmen of the World, to the Maccabees, and I still have a standing in the Odd Fellows, but not active.

MR. WORTHINGTON. You are a member of the Odd Fellows?

MR. MEAKIN. Yes, sir; I am a fraternalist.

MR. WORTHINGTON. Previous to your leaving the church on account of your opposition to the doctrine of polygamy, did you take the endowments?

MR. MEAKIN. Yes, sir.

MR. WORTHINGTON. When and where?

MR. MEAKIN. I went through the Endowment House—that is our phrase in Utah—in the winter of 1869 or 1870; I am not positive as to the month or the year.

MR. WORTHINGTON. How old were you then?

MR. MEAKIN. I was just turned 18; I was 18 in July, 1869.

MR. WORTHINGTON. Do you recall the ceremony?

---

9. Meakin (1852-1916) was a traveling correspondent for the *Salt Lake Tribune*. He left the LDS Church in the early 1870s.

MR. MEAKIN. Not definitely.

MR. WORTHINGTON. Do you recall whether there was any obligation, which has been referred to here as the obligation of vengeance or retribution?

MR. MEAKIN. No, sir; I have no recollection of it at all.

MR. WORTHINGTON. I will ask you whether this, or anything like it, took place? Did others go through with you?

MR. MEAKIN. To the best of my recollection there were others that went through with me.

MR. WORTHINGTON. I will ask you to state whether this took place, as to you or any of the others, in your hearing: "That you and each of you do promise and vow that you will never cease to importune High Heaven to avenge the blood of the prophets upon this nation?"

MR. MEAKIN. No, sir.

MR. WORTHINGTON. Or anything about avenging the blood of Joseph Smith on anybody?

MR. MEAKIN. No, sir.[10] ...

Robert T. Burton, jr.,[11] being duly sworn, was examined and testified as follows ...

MR. VAN COTT. Have you ever been a member of the Mormon Church?

---

10. Dillingham later asked Smoot "why the Church did not appoint some one ... to come and give the endowment ceremony, and thus do away with the mystery and misgivings in relation to this matter." He could not understand "why the Church should object to stating its exact nature" since it had raised a question of national allegiance—"the loyalty of the Church and its members," whose "liberties [might be] endangered." Smoot "called [Dillingham's] attention to the Masonic ceremony ... and stated that the Mormon people felt themselves under even stronger obligations not to reveal the endowment ceremony." According to Smoot, Dillingham

> was very nice about what he said, and did not want me to think that he was trying to dictate, and his only reason for making the suggestion was to help the people, if possible. I suppose it is out of the question to consider this suggestion, but I thought proper to let you know just how one of my friends looks at this matter. W. W. Riter, Bishop Taylor, or A. W. Smith could come down here with a written statement of the order of the ceremony, or even testify as to the ceremony; but the danger I see in this is being compelled to give the signs. They could not profess to give the full ceremony without giving all, for enough is known to the public now to make the omission of the signs noticeable, and this would discredit all that they might give. Perhaps they could give the ceremony all but the signs, naming the signs and refusing to divulge them because they refer to the hereafter only. If we cannot discredit the witnesses they bring here to testify this time it is going to be hard with us" (Smoot to Joseph F. Smith, Jan. 9, 1906).

11. Burton (1853-1926) lived in Salt Lake City, and although his father was a high-ranking LDS official, Robert Jr. was not himself Mormon.

MR. BURTON. No, sir.

MR. VAN COTT. You have been engaged in business in Salt Lake City?

MR. BURTON. Yes, sir.

MR. VAN COTT. Do you know Angus M. Cannon, jr.?[12]

MR. BURTON. Yes, sir.

MR. VAN COTT. How long have you known him?

MR. BURTON. I have known him for a number of years. I could not say just the number—a long time.

MR. VAN COTT. Do you know E. B. Critchlow?[13]

MR. BURTON. Yes, sir.

MR. VAN COTT. How long have you known him?

MR. BURTON. Fifteen or twenty years.

MR. VAN COTT. Calling your attention to last year, did you have any conversation with Mr. Critchlow regarding the testimony that Angus M. Cannon, jr., had given here?

MR. BURTON. I had a conversation with Mr. Critchlow on his return from Washington last spring. ...

MR. VAN COTT. What did he say to you?

THE CHAIRMAN. After Cannon had testified here?

MR. VAN COTT. Yes, sir. What did Mr. Critchlow say to you?

MR. BURTON. Mr. Critchlow asked me what I knew about Angus M. Cannon. I said, "Mr. Critchlow, you know Angus M. Cannon just as well as I do."

THE CHAIRMAN. You know what?

MR. BURTON. "You know Angus M. Cannon, jr., just as well as I do." He said, "Well, Mr. Burton, what do you know about him?" I said, "Mr. Critchlow, you know just as much about him as I do, and have known him just as long as I have." He said, "Mr. Burton, I wouldn't believe him on oath."

MR. VAN COTT. Angus M. Cannon, jr., has lived in Salt Lake a good many years?

MR. BURTON. Yes, sir.

MR. VAN COTT. And so has Mr. Critchlow?

MR. BURTON. Yes, sir.

MR. VAN COTT. That is all.

MR. TAYLER. Do you mean it would be impossible, therefore, for Angus M. Cannon ever to be a witness to anything?

---

12. For Cannon Jr.'s testimony, see *Smoot Hearings*, 1:1059-1086.

13. For Critchlow's testimony, see *Smoot Hearings*, 1:542-76, 577-89, 590-629, 629-87.

MR. BURTON. The statement that—

MR. TAYLER. Do you mean Angus M. Cannon can not tell the truth?

MR. BURTON. I mean that I would not believe it.

MR. TAYLER. You mean you would not believe him at all?

MR. BURTON. No, sir. ...

James A. Miner,[14] being duly sworn, was examined, and testified as follows ...

MR. WORTHINGTON. For four years did you have anything to do with the prosecution of persons who were charged with polygamous cohabitation?

MR. MINER. Well, a great many of those cases were tried before me, as associate justice. I was assigned to the first district.

MR. WORTHINGTON. I was going to ask. Your headquarters were at Ogden [Utah]?

MR. MINER. During that four years, yes.

MR. WORTHINGTON. What was your jurisdiction, or district?

MR. MINER. It included the first district, which included the Provo District.

MR. WORTHINGTON. Did it include Salt Lake City?

MR. MINER. No.

MR. WORTHINGTON. It was on both sides of Salt Lake City?

MR. MINER. On both sides of Salt Lake City. The district had been divided, and there was another justice assigned to the Provo district—that is, in my district—but I had a clerk in that court and also in the Ogden court.

MR. WORTHINGTON. Could you give us some idea of the nature of those prosecutions, and the result of them—how the people acted who were prosecuted?

MR. MINER. Yes. When I went there in July, 1890, there were a great many criminal prosecutions for polygamy and unlawful cohabitation pending, and a great many more were brought during that year. Of course they were tried before myself, as the judge of that court.

MR. WORTHINGTON. Did they plead guilty, or were they convicted, or what?

MR. MINER. Many of them would plead guilty, and many of them con-

14. Miner (1842-1907) had resided in Salt Lake City since he was appointed in 1890 by U.S. President Benjamin Harrison as Associate Justice of the Utah Territorial Supreme Court. He was elected to the Utah State Supreme Court in 1894. He was not Mormon.

tested it. Of course the purpose of the court—and I think of all the courts at that time—was to get the people charged with polygamous practices [or] with unlawful cohabitation to promise to obey the law. It was understood at that time that they were advised by their authorities above them not to obey the law; that is, they were not to be guilty of it. I remember one instance that might illustrate the others, if you wish it.

MR. WORTHINGTON. Just state it, Judge.

MR. MINER. One young man about 30 years old, perhaps a little over, was brought before me and pleaded guilty to polygamy at one time during my first experience there on the bench. I asked him if he could not promise to obey the law in the future. He said no, sir; he could not. I asked Judge Rolapp—I think Judge Rolapp was a Mormon lawyer—if he would not take the young man out privately and talk with him, and see if he would not promise to obey the law in the future, because the purpose was to get them to obey the law, or promise to obey it, and as a rule they would keep their promise. Mr. Rolapp took the young man out, and after a time returned with the statement that he could not make him promise. I then asked him why he could not make the promise. I said we all had to obey the law, and I asked him why he could not.

Well, he was very respectful in his reply. He said that he was brought up in the Mormon Church; he had been taught from his infancy that polygamy was right; that some three or four years prior he had married his first wife and had a couple of children by her; that a year or two later he took his second wife, and he had a child by her; that a year or two prior to the trial he had taken his third wife, and had a child by her. "Now," he said to me, "I have promised those wives to live with them and provide for them." He said: "I love those children. Those wives and children love me." He said: "Would I not be a hypocrite to desert those wives and children now?" It was somewhat new to me at the time. I sentenced him, I think, for four or five years in the penitentiary, but subsequently, after the manifesto was issued, I learned he was disposed to make the promise, and I made every effort to get him out of the penitentiary. I felt sorry for him, and I got him out.

MR. WORTHINGTON. You say after the manifesto he was disposed to make a promise. What promise?

MR. MINER. To obey the law.

MR. WORTHINGTON. I want to ask you whether, at about the time the manifesto was issued, any change came over the Mormons in reference to whether they would or would not make the promise?

MR. MINER. Yes, sir.

MR. WORTHINGTON. Did the prosecutions then stop?

MR. MINER. The prosecutions largely stopped.

MR. WORTHINGTON. After the manifesto, and during the continuance of your term there, which took you down to 1894, the prosecutions were very few, were they?

MR. MINER. Very few.

MR. WORTHINGTON. Could you give us an idea of the number?

MR. MINER. No; I could not. I presume I sent up a hundred or more to the penitentiary—perhaps 200 of them—during the time I had there. I know they came very rapidly. It became sickening and tiresome to me to send those people to the penitentiary, and I therefore used every effort I could to get them to promise to obey the law, and when I got the promise from them as a rule they would keep the promise.

MR. WORTHINGTON. After the manifesto, which was in the fall of 1890, the prosecutions were very few?

MR. MINER. Yes, sir.

MR. WORTHINGTON. We know, then, that from that time down to the time the State was admitted into the Union, which was in January, 1896, the officers of the United States were in charge there.

MR. MINER. They were.

MR. WORTHINGTON. The prosecuting officers, the governor of the Territory, the judges, and everything.

MR. MINER. Yes, they were; right along. We had quite a good many United States marshals at Ogden, where I resided at that time.

MR. WORTHINGTON. Can you tell us anything about what was done in prosecuting Mormons during that period, between the time of the manifesto and the time the State was admitted into the Union, as to whether they overlooked the fact, or continued to prosecute men who lived in polygamy, who had taken plural wives before the manifesto?

MR. MINER. Yes; they were brought right along continuously, but not as numerous. They dropped off largely after that.

MR. WORTHINGTON. There were very few of them?

MR. MINER. Very few. The officers were, of course, vigilant—I think they were—watching these people all the time.

MR. WORTHINGTON. Naturally, from your being in that relation to the State when you went there, and living there ever since, you must have observed the history and progress of the State in reference to this matter of polygamy?

MR. MINER. I have.

MR. WORTHINGTON. What can you tell us, as to whether it is increasing or decreasing?

MR. MINER. It is very much decreasing; it has decreased nearly 100 per cent since I went there. I should say there was 90 per cent at least decrease in the number of polygamous families from that time to this out of 100. ...

MR. VAN COTT. Do you know Mr. Smoot?

MR. MINER. I do.

MR. VAN COTT. Have you known him personally several years?

MR. MINER. Yes; since 1891.

MR. VAN COTT. Do you know of his being prominent in Utah politics?

MR. MINER. I do.

MR. VAN COTT. How early?

MR. MINER. My personal acquaintance with Senator Smoot did not begin until 1891 or 1892; somewhere along there. I can not tell definitely the exact date. But I knew him by reputation from the time I first went there in July, 1890.

MR. VAN COTT. How active, in your opinion, has he been in Republican politics in the State?

MR. MINER. I think he has been quite active since I have known him.

MR. VAN COTT. When he became a Senatorial candidate was he prominent or not for that position?

MR. MINER. He was.

MR. VAN COTT. He was prominent?

MR. MINER. Yes; he was so.

MR. VAN COTT. Do you know anything about the reputation he bore in those early days in regard to the practice of polygamy?

MR. MINER. Yes, sir.

MR. VAN COTT. What was it?

MR. MINER. My deputies were deputies for that district, which included Mr. Smoot's residence—that is, Utah County, and those deputies, during the year 1890, from July on, were over the entire district, and before I personally became acquainted with Mr. Smoot—during the time of these prosecutions or about the time of the manifesto—they reported to me, and I obtained from that reputation and from others, in speaking of him, that he was an active, bright young man from Provo, and his leanings were strongly in favor of the enforcement that is, the people should obey the law. He was against the practice of polygamy. They regarded him as the coming young man of the State. He was so regarded, I think, from that time on as a bright, active, law-abiding man, of excellent character and habits.

MR. VAN COTT. What is the sentiment in Utah among the Gentiles in regard to the prosecution of unlawful cohabitation cases where the marriages were contracted prior to the manifesto; and what reasons, if any, are given?

MR. MINER. Of course the disposition from July, 1890, when I went there, was to prosecute them, and a great many of those cases were brought before my court, as other courts, and they were tried and convicted, and many of them sent to the penitentiary. But since the manifesto the disposition to prosecute these older men has not prevailed so generally, I do not think. But if any new marriages had occurred, I think the disposition would be to prosecute them, and that disposition, I do not think, is confined entirely to the Gentile population, because I have heard Mormons talk about it, and they were adverse to these plural marriages since that time—since the manifesto.

I have noticed another thing. Since the manifesto we have had Mormon jurors. Before that we had no Mormon jurors. The marshals would select Gentiles to the exclusion of Mormons. But after the manifesto we commenced having Mormon jurors instead of all Gentiles, and I found that in many cases a Mormon jury would convict anyone for adultery or unlawful cohabitation quite as well as a Gentile—that is, the feeling kept growing in that direction. And so far as the violation of the marital obligation is concerned, the Mormon people would convict a man who broke it as readily as a Gentile, and I think more so. They seem to have a feeling against Mormons who would violate that obligation, and I think among that class of young people there is more virtue than among almost any other class. ...

MR. TAYLER. You are a lawyer, I suppose? I did not mean any reflection, in view of the fact that you have been a judge, but there are prosecuting officers who are not lawyers. You classify the crime of polygamous cohabitation in Utah with lewd or immoral cohabitation as it exists elsewhere, do you?

MR. MINER. I speak of it in that sense.

MR. TAYLER. You compare that State with the District of Columbia and other places where similar crimes are committed. You do not, therefore, attach any importance to that phase of the crime of polygamous cohabitation which is based upon the defiant declaration that it is done in accordance with the will of God, do you?

MR. MINER. I speak of it as a violation of law.

MR. TAYLER. I know; of course you do; but do you make any point of that phase of it?

MR. MINER. Well, I do not know that I have associated—

MR. TAYLER. You do not know?

MR. MINER. That directly with it.

MR. TAYLER. The fact that a man says he is violating the law, but that he does it with the approval of God; that he will be damned—using the word in its strict sense—if he obeys the law of man, is, in your judgment, the same kind of offense against society, against government, and against morals as if a man committed the ordinary offense of unlawfully cohabiting with a woman? Is that your view?

MR. MINER. I do not know that I quite catch your meaning.

MR. TAYLER. Read the question.

THE CHAIRMAN (to the reporter). Read the question.

The reporter read as follows: "Mr. Tayler. The fact that a man says he is violating the law, but that he does it with the approval of God, that he will be damned—using the word in its strict sense—if he obeys the law of man, is, in your judgment, the same kind of offense against society, against government, and against morals, as if a man committed the ordinary offense of unlawfully cohabiting with a woman? Is that your view?"

MR. MINER. Of course I do not like the proposition.

MR. TAYLER. I have not made it. It is made here in the case.

MR. MINER. I do not myself believe in the practice of polygamy, nor in the violation of the seventh commandment.

MR. TAYLER. Nobody assumes that you do, but I think my question is susceptible of a categorical answer. (A pause.)

THE CHAIRMAN. Let the reporter read the question again.

The reporter again read the question.

MR. MINER. That is the moral, but it is not the legal view of it.

MR. TAYLER. What is the moral view of it?

MR. MINER. The fact that a man, as you put the question, is obeying, or thinks he is obeying, the law of God when he commits an offense that is considered immoral in the sight of the law of man.

MR. TAYLER. The law—you ought to know—does not necessarily involve morality or immorality in the acts which it prohibits. Do you not understand that the Government is founded on law?

MR. MINER. Oh, certainly.

MR. TAYLER. And when law is proclaimed by proper authority, government can only follow upon obedience to that law?

MR. MINER. That is true.

MR. TAYLER. Now, if one violates the law, as men ordinarily violate it, and we undertake to punish them, there is no undermining of society by that fact, unless it is universally prevalent, is there?

MR. MINER. No, probably not.

MR. TAYLER. But if that law, upon which government is based, is violated upon the proclaimed reason that the law, as to that party, is invalid, or rather that God permits that violation, that God will damn him if he obeys that law, if he conforms to the customs of society in respect to such matter, do you not understand that that is infinitely deeper seated in its menace to the Government and society than the mere violation of law as we see it every day everywhere?

MR. MINER. I do not see much difference.

MR. TAYLER. You do not see any difference?

MR. MINER. They are both wrong.

MR. TAYLER. Do you not think your association with those people and in that atmosphere has brought you to that sort of a distorted view of what society and government are?

MR. MINER. The atmosphere of Salt Lake and the society of Salt Lake are quite as good as those that surround any other well-governed community.[15] ...

William M. McCarty,[16] being duly sworn, was examined, and testified as follows ...

MR. WORTHINGTON. Did anything special come to your notice with relation to this question of polygamy while you were district judge from 1895 to 1900?

MR. MCCARTY. In 1898—I think that was the year—there was some agitation there in regard to men living in polygamous relations—men who had contracted the marriage relation prior to the manifesto—and I called a grand jury to investigate those charges and rumors, and specifically invited their attention to that class of offenses.

---

15. The *Salt Lake Tribune* was unimpressed with Miner's testimony, writing that he "is a poor witness for himself and for the defense ... If he did not know that polygamous cohabitation was prevalent here, until the church leaders told him so, how can he tell anything about the extent of new polygamy or the number of years necessary to eradicate the practice until these same leaders advise him?" ("A Learned Judge," Jan. 17, 1905).

16. McCarty (1859-1918) was born in Alpine, Utah. He was appointed a U.S. District Attorney in 1889, elected as a Republican district judge in 1895, and elected to the Utah State Supreme Court in 1902. He was not Mormon.

MR. WORTHINGTON. Polygamous cohabitation or polygamous marriages, or both?

MR. McCARTY. No; polygamous cohabitation. At that time I was not aware that there were any new marriages being contracted—polygamous marriages.

MR. WORTHINGTON. That is a question I am going to ask you about after a while. What was the result of the grand jury's investigation in 1898?

MR. McCARTY. Well, they were in session several days, but they failed to find any bills against men who were alleged to be living in those relations.

MR. WORTHINGTON. To go back a moment, Judge, when you ran for district judge in 1895—you have told us about the vote in Sevier County—how did you run in the Mormon precincts generally, in the precincts where the Mormon voters were who passed on your candidacy?

MR. McCARTY. I generally ran with my ticket. They were all Mormon precincts. I don't think there was a Gentile precinct except Marysvale in the district at that time.

MR. WORTHINGTON. Have you any knowledge as to why it was you ran behind in Sevier County?

MR. McCARTY. Yes, sir; the non-Mormons.

MR. WORTHINGTON. The non-Mormons?

MR. McCARTY. The non-Mormons were the people who worked against me—the saloon element and the non-Mormons generally. That was particularly in Richfield. That is where the cut was made. I resided at Monroe at that time.

MR. WORTHINGTON. You had been an antisaloon man, then, as well as antipolygamist, in your prosecutions?

MR. McCARTY. Yes; I had paid special attention to that class of offenses—selling on Sunday, gambling, and the illicit selling of liquor.

MR. WORTHINGTON. Did any cases of polygamous cohabitation come before you while you were district judge from 1895 to 1900?

MR. McCARTY. Yes, sir. I wish to correct my first statement. I think it was in about the year 1897 that the grand jury was called. You have the record there, I believe. I may have gotten those dates confused.

Mr. Van Cott (handing paper to witness). I do not think that is the grand jury matter.

MR. McCARTY. In 1898, I think it was, when the grand jury was called. In 1899 this record is certified to by the officer or by the reporter. Will you read the last question?

The reporter read as follows: "Mr. Worthington. Did any cases of polygamous cohabitation come before you while you were district judge from 1895 to 1900? Mr. McCarty. Yes, sir. I wish to correct my first statement. I think it was in about the year 1897 that the grand jury was called. You have the record there, I believe. I may have gotten those dates confused."

MR. McCarty. In 1899 some informations were filed in the district court over which I presided.

MR. Worthington. For polygamous cohabitation?

MR. McCarty. Yes; unlawful cohabitation is usually the term.

MR. Worthington. Did the cases come up before you?

MR. McCarty. They did.

MR. Worthington. What was the result?

MR. McCarty. The result was, my recollection is, that the defendants claimed that they understood they would be permitted to live in those relations, and I read them a lecture and defined the law as I understood it and imposed fines, after getting a promise from them that they would observe the law in the future. ...

MR. Worthington. You say these men claimed they understood that they were not to be interfered with. Were they men who had been married before the manifesto?

MR. McCarty. Yes.

MR. Worthington. In every case?

MR. McCarty. In every case.

MR. Worthington. How many of them were there?

MR. McCarty. My recollection is there were four of them. I have the record here. ...

MR. Van Cott. Now, passing along to the time of your candidacy for the supreme court bench, who was your opponent in that fight?

MR. McCarty. Maj[or]. Richard W. Young.[17]

MR. Van Cott. You know him personally, do you?

MR. McCarty. Yes, sir; I am well acquainted with him.

MR. Van Cott. Just briefly, I wish you would state as to his efficiency and popularity in the State.

MR. McCarty. Well, he was the war hero of our State at that time. He had just returned from the Philippine Islands.

MR. Van Cott. Was he a graduate of West Point?

MR. McCarty. He was a graduate of West Point.

MR. Van Cott. A grandson of Brigham Young?

---

17. Young testified the next day (*Smoot Hearings,* 2:950-89; 3:129-43).

Mr. McCarty. A grandson of Brigham Young and, I believe, a graduate of a law school. That is my understanding.

Mr. Van Cott. He had practiced law in Utah?

Mr. McCarty. Yes; he had an office there for several years.

Mr. Van Cott. He had been in the Philippine Islands during the war?

Mr. McCarty. He had.

Mr. Van Cott. Had he been on the supreme bench in the Philippine Islands?

Mr. McCarty. I so understand; yes.

Mr. Van Cott. He came back to Utah and ran on the Democratic ticket?

Mr. McCarty. On the Democratic ticket.

Mr. Van Cott. You understand that Major Young was a Mormon?

Mr. McCarty. I do.

Mr. Van Cott. Was he popular in the State?

Mr. McCarty. I regarded him as the most popular man in the Democratic party.

Mr. Van Cott. Tell us what you noticed, under those circumstances, as to the way you ran in the Mormon precincts, counties, and cities in Utah?

Mr. McCarty. I have here the report of the secretary of state, which gives the vote in each voting precinct of the State. I will say, as a preliminary, that I expected the Major would run away ahead of me in the Mormon communities, and I expected to even up in the mining district. I thought among those Irish my name would be a drawing card, but on looking over the returns here I find that the Democratic Gentiles voted for Major Young, and the Republican Mormons voted for me throughout the State.

Mr. Tayler. Was this last year?

Mr. McCarty. Two years ago. In Park City I beat him by 5 votes. In the Gentile mining camp of Eureka I ran 10 votes ahead of him—in the camp I used to work in as a miner, and where I was acquainted with a great many of the people. In the Mormon districts and precincts there was only a difference occasionally of half a dozen and probably up to 40 or 50 votes in some of the most populous districts. I believe there was one where he ran ahead of me about 50 votes. ...

22.

Richard W. Young and
E. D. R. Thompson

Tuesday & Thursday, January 17, 19

"Members of the committee have grown thoroughly tired of the long drawn out hearing, which is regarded as having gone just as far as necessary. Senator Burrows believes still that the last witness will have been heard before Saturday night and that next week will see the end of this, the most extraordinary case ever heard before a committee of the senate." —*Deseret News,* Jan. 17, 1905

Richard W. Young,[1] being duly sworn, was examined, and testified as follows ...

MR. VAN COTT. Are you a member of the Mormon Church?

MR. YOUNG. I am.

MR. VAN COTT. Have you always been?

MR. YOUNG. I have.

MR. VAN COTT. Have you ever been a polygamist?

MR. YOUNG. I never have.

MR. VAN COTT. Are you any relation to Brigham Young?

MR. YOUNG. I am a grandson. ...

MR. VAN COTT. Do you hold any official position now in the Mormon Church?

MR. YOUNG. I do.

MR. VAN COTT. What?

MR. YOUNG. I am president of one of the four stakes into which the city of Salt Lake is divided. ...

MR. VAN COTT. Calling attention, now, to the polygamy question, have you, in your residence in Salt Lake City, traveled over the State considerably?

MR. YOUNG. Yes, sir; considerably.

MR. VAN COTT. In politics or otherwise?

---

1. At the time of his testimony, Young (1858-1919) lived in Salt Lake City and was an LDS stake president. He was a graduate of the U.S. Military Academy at West Point and the Columbia University College of Law.

MR. YOUNG. Politics and otherwise.

MR. VAN COTT. Have you been in most of the settlements in Utah?

MR. YOUNG. Yes; one time or another in my life.

MR. VAN COTT. What is the sentiment of the Mormon people regarding the entering into polygamy since the manifesto?

MR. YOUNG. It is decidedly hostile.

MR. VAN COTT. What would you say as to whether the mere issuance of the manifesto created a sentiment against polygamy, or whether the manifesto was the mere expression of a sentiment already existing in Utah?

MR. YOUNG. I should say that it was the result both of a sentiment and the creation of a sentiment—an additional sentiment.

MR. VAN COTT. What are your own views as to whether it is right to practice polygamy, since the manifesto?

MR. YOUNG. I believe it is not right.

MR. VAN COTT. Do you know whether there is any teaching or promulgation of polygamy, or whether it is discountenanced in the councils and quorums of the Mormon Church?

MR. YOUNG. There has been, so far as my knowledge extends, and I have had, I suppose, good opportunities of observation, absolutely no teaching of the principle of polygamy since the manifesto. ...

MR. VAN COTT. Do you know of its being discouraged or not in the quorums and councils of the Mormon Church?

MR. YOUNG. Certainly. There has been no other view of the subject taken than that of discouragement.

MR. VAN COTT. Since the manifesto?

MR. YOUNG. Yes, sir; since the manifesto. ...

MR. VAN COTT. Calling your attention, now, to politics, there has been mentioned this matter of whisperings. I wish you would explain your views about it, and who it is that does that, and whether or not it is resented by members of the Mormon Church?

MR. YOUNG. We have heard whisperings in various political campaigns—that which seems to be denominated whisperings here. But I know of no instance where whisperings have been traced back to the authorities of the church, either generally or in the stake. What little experience I have had on that subject has been that those whisperings have originated with underlings in the church organization having political axes to grind.

MR. VAN COTT. And when you undertake to run down to earth any of those underlings who claim that the church desires people to vote in a certain way, have you ever been able to find an instance where they would admit finally, when brought face to face with the charge, that they were so authorized?

MR. YOUNG. I do not recall, Mr. Van Cott, any instance in which I have ever run one of them down.

MR. VAN COTT. Or of anyone else?

MR. YOUNG. I can only speak of the general understanding. My belief has been that the authorities of the church have been sincere in their declarations to the effect that they desired to exert no influence over the political actions of church members.

I might, perhaps, in this connection, refer to my own experiences in that regard.

MR. VAN COTT. Yes.

MR. YOUNG. No person has ever suggested or indicated what my politics should be. No person has ever suggested or indicated how I should vote. No person has ever endeavored to interfere in any way with my running for any office.

And, answering a question which you asked, the second or third question before this, the people do resent any attempt at interference with their political liberty.

MR. WORTHINGTON. The Mormon people?

MR. YOUNG. The Mormon people; and that for many reasons, one of which is this: The authorities of the church have declared time and again, they declared when this movement was first inaugurated, in the "Salt Lake Times;" President Woodruff declared later in an official document, which was published at the head of the editorial columns of the "[Deseret] News," and repeatedly on other occasions, that they had no desire in any way to control the politics of the members of the church; and I think the Mormon people have accepted that in absolute good faith. I know that, personally, when I have heard the whisperings which have been referred to, I have taken very great pleasure in reading before political meetings these official declarations of the officers of the church as an answer, an authoritative answer, to anything of that sort.

MR. VAN COTT. Do you know what the politics is in Washington County, Utah?

MR. YOUNG. Washington County, Utah?

MR. VAN COTT. Yes; whether Democratic or Republican?

MR. YOUNG. That is the stronghold of the Democratic party in the State of Utah.

MR. VAN COTT. About what per cent of the voters there would you say are Mormons?

MR. YOUNG. I could only speak from general impression. I should think 95 per cent of the voters there are Mormons.

MR. VAN COTT. Was Senator Smoot, when he was a candidate, able to carry that county for the Republican ticket?

MR. YOUNG. I think the legislative ticket was quite badly defeated in that county.

MR. VAN COTT. Has the Republican party ever been able to carry that county?

MR. YOUNG. Never.

MR. VAN COTT. I should like a little more fully on record here the intensity of the feeling of the Mormon people in regard to carrying out his manifesto and in abstaining from polygamy, and their feelings in regard to rumors and charges; as to how they feel against certain members of the Mormon Church who are reputed to have done that thing?

MR. YOUNG. I may state that as I understand the figures—and in looking over the proceedings of this committee I saw estimates made, I believe, by Senator Dubois, which are presumed to be substantially correct, giving at least a large enough percentage of polygamists—I understand that not more than 20 to 25 per cent of the marriageable Mormons ever did go into polygamy, even in the days when polygamy was preached, and you may say enforced, so far as advice and counsel could enforce it upon the people, which I take it, if I may be allowed to offer the suggestion, was an indication that the people, the majority of the people, were never truly converted to the principle of polygamy, or at least to the living of it. ...

I may say that personally—and I fancy I have had some rather good opportunities of information—I never suspected, until within a year or so, that there had been any violation of the manifesto with reference to new marriages. The idea had not crossed my mind. I would have sworn, at least to my belief, that polygamous marriages had absolutely terminated, ... except in the one case, I will state, of Apostle Abraham Cannon, concerning whom there were some rumors. As to the facts I knew nothing. I had no real impression upon that subject.[2]

2. The *Salt Lake Tribune* cried foul on such feigned ignorance of plural marriage. The *Tribune* argued that the "facts [were] so common as to be within the knowledge of any Mormon child twelve years old" ("An Officer and a Gentleman," Jan. 20, 1905). In an interesting sidebar the next year, the *Tribune* speculated that Young would fill a va-

I believe I may state that the people—the great majority, practically all of the people—believe in the doing away of plural marriages, and that is not confined to the young Mormons. It includes the middle-aged and it includes those even who are polygamists. I have talked with polygamists—old time polygamists—on this subject. ...

MR. TAYLER. Were you here when any of the witnesses testified respecting the obligation in the endowment ceremonies?

MR. YOUNG. That was inquired into yesterday.

MR. TAYLER. And the declination or refusal of the witnesses to state what was contained in the ceremony or in any part of it?

MR. YOUNG. Yes, sir; I heard that.

MR. TAYLER. That is fairly representative, I suppose, of the posture that all good Mormons take respecting the disclosure of what occurred in the case of that ceremony?

MR. YOUNG. I think so, inevitably, from the obligation they feel themselves to be under.

MR. TAYLER. Let me ask you if this is representative of the sentiment of any considerable number of the Mormon people? It was stated that at a meeting of the Young Men's or the Young Women's Mutual Improvement Society, I think it is called, or as one of the societies of the church is called, I believe—

MR. YOUNG. There are two societies. There is the Young Men's Mutual Improvement Association and the Young Ladies' Mutual Improvement Association.

MR. TAYLER. That is the organization of which President [Joseph F.] Smith testified he is the head?

MR. YOUNG. Of the Young Men's Association.

MR. TAYLER. It has been stated—and I want to know if this is possible or if it is what would be in the minds of many good Mormons—that Sunday night last, before a large number of members of the Young Men's Mutual Improvement Association—and Young Women's—at Eureka—where is Eureka?

MR. YOUNG. It is about 90 miles southwest of Salt Lake City, in Juab County.

---

cancy in the Quorum of the Twelve ("Richard W. Young to Succeed Apostle Merrill," *Salt Lake Tribune*, Apr. 8, 1906). Rather than admit they were wrong, they quoted an unnamed source later that day confirming that their scoop had killed Young's appointment: "The announcement in headlines in The Tribune on Sunday morning that Young was selected for this place caused a reversal of the conclusion of the hierarchy, and he was left out of the list" ("R. W. Young Must Wait For Next," Apr. 8, 1906).

Mr. Tayler. Bishop Daniel Connelly—do you know him?

Mr. Young. I do not.

Mr. Tayler. Denounced at much length persons who had betrayed temple and endowment oaths at Washington. That would not be an unnatural frame of mind, I suppose, for any good Mormon to be in to whom information had come, whether true or not, that temple and endowment oaths had been given out?

Mr. Young. I presume that would be a natural frame of mind, particularly if the persons who made the disclosure were adherents of the church. It would depend very largely upon that.

Mr. Tayler. And that he continued then and said: "They are traitors, and I shall treat them as traitors. I have known men to be shot for betraying oaths. I advise you to not betray your oaths, but to be true to them and not fall into the error of the traitors." You do not think that fairly represents the state of mind of Mormons generally, do you?

Mr. Young. There are several divisions of the subject, Mr. Tayler. I would agree with his advice that people should not be traitors. The proposition that he has known traitors to be shot—if he made any such statement—certainly could not have any reference to the affairs of the Mormon Church. He never has heard, I undertake to say, of traitors to the Mormon Church being shot.[3]

Mr. Tayler. I would not dispute that at all, but I am speaking now wholly of the state of mind in which you would find—

Mr. Young. I think, unquestionably, Mr. Tayler, speaking generally, that would indicate the frame of mind of the Mormon people toward peo-

---

3. Connelly's quote appeared in the *Salt Lake Tribune* on January 15, 1905. When the *Deseret News* interviewed him five days later, he complained that he had been "greatly misrepresented" by the *Tribune*. "I did not say by word or intimation that I had known men to be taken out and shot for disclosing such matters as had been disclosed during the Smoot hearing at Washington," he explained, "or because they had revealed a church secret of any kind. Any intimation to that effect is wholly and maliciously false." He then gave his version of the disputed remarks: "I have known of men who were traitors to their country and the Constitution in times of danger being taken out and shot. I have no respect or sympathy for men of this character, nor have I any sympathy for persons who are traitors to their church or people" ("Country Traitors and Not Church," Jan. 20, 1905). In addition to being an LDS bishop, Connelly was also a Socialist Party leader in Eureka, a Utah mining town where 40 percent of his fellow-Socialists were Mormon (John R. Sillito and John S. McCormick, "Socialist Saints: Mormons and the Socialist Party in Utah, 1900-20," *Dialogue: A Journal of Mormon Thought* 18 [Spring 1985]: 123). Connelly was installed as a bishop in June 1900 by Reed Smoot (Stan Larson, ed., *A Ministry of Meetings: The Apostolic Diaries of Rudger Clawson* [Salt Lake City: Signature Books and Smith Research Associates, 1993], 178).

ple who would betray those oaths; that having betrayed them they were traitors to that extent, if you may use that expression.

MR. TAYLER. And that when taken to task for the violence of his language he replied that he was indignant at the witnesses; did not know that a reporter was present or he would have been more careful; but said the United States shoots men for breaking their vows, but that to break the covenants with God, as witnesses had done, is much more sacred than to violate oaths to the Government. Is that a just expression of the state of mind of the Mormon people respecting that kind of a disclosure?

MR. YOUNG. I scarcely think so. My own view is that an oath is an oath. An oath is always made to the Almighty, and the obligation of it rests upon a person, wherever it may be made, with equal force.

MR. TAYLER. Do you not think that that is rather an intellectual view that you take of it, Colonel, than otherwise? I mean do you not arrive, with your educated intelligence, at that conclusion by an intellectual process—that an oath is an oath, but that each is equally entitled to your obedience?

MR. YOUNG. I think not.

MR. TAYLER. Let me go on, so that you may answer it.

MR. YOUNG. Yes.

MR. TAYLER. And that that would not be true of the majority of the people of the Mormon Church, as of any other set of people anywhere?

MR. YOUNG. No; I do not think that it requires an educated intelligence nor any unusual understanding at all to conclude that the obligation of an oath is equal wherever the oath may be taken. That would be my judgment, and I believe that the Mormon community would take that view. ...

THE CHAIRMAN. Something has been said about the reorganized church.[4] That is a church holding to belief in the Mormon Bible or doctrine. Wherein does that organization differ from yours? I call your attention directly to the point of polygamy.

MR. YOUNG. I understand. The reorganized church entertains the view that Joseph Smith never taught polygamy and never practiced it. Our own church combats both of those propositions.

THE CHAIRMAN. What do you say as to the reorganized church teaching and practicing polygamy now?

---

4. That is, the Reorganized Church of Jesus Christ of Latter Day Saints—later renamed the Community of Christ—headquartered in Independence, Missouri, and presided over at the time by Joseph Smith III.

MR. YOUNG. I have no idea that they do either.

THE CHAIRMAN. Do you know whether they have any ceremony by which the adherents are oath-bound to anything?

MR. YOUNG. I can only speak from general impression. I understand they have no temples, no ceremonies corresponding to the temple ceremonies. Whether they have any other ceremonies or not, I am unable to state.

THE CHAIRMAN. But they have nothing corresponding to that?

MR. YOUNG. I believe not.

THE CHAIRMAN. Do you know whether any of the membership of the reorganized church is in Utah?

MR. YOUNG. They have some branches there, some chapels, and are doing some missionary work among the people of Utah.

THE CHAIRMAN. Do you attend their services?

MR. YOUNG. It is possible that I have been there once, yes, sir; just out of curiosity, however.

THE CHAIRMAN. They have no temples and no ceremonies?

MR. YOUNG. Not in Utah.

THE CHAIRMAN. I mean of the character you have?

MR. YOUNG. No, sir; I understand not.

SENATOR McCOMAS. How numerous are they in Utah?

MR. YOUNG. The reorganized?

SENATOR McCOMAS. Yes.

MR. YOUNG. Speaking from general impression, there can not be more than a few hundred of them.

SENATOR McCOMAS. Does your church extend a friendly hand to them? Do the people of your church manifest any friendship for those people who oppose polygamy and have reorganized the Mormon Church to oppose polygamy?

MR. YOUNG. No. The attitude of the two churches is one of considerable antagonism from a doctrinal point of view.[5]

---

5. An editorial in the *Deseret News* the next year illustrated this point with transparent hypocrisy:

Among the most persistent and most unscrupulous of the maligners of the "Mormons" are the active apologists of the so-called "Reorganization." Its missionaries and many of its chief preachers devote most of their time and public discourses, to misrepresentation and stirring up strife against the Utah Elders in the different States of the Union, and seem to take extreme delight in holding them up to public reprobation. ... The venom and malignity with which those Reorganites assail the Church ... are indicative of the spirit by which their system of contention and tricky disputation is animated. The claims of its builders are so utterly devoid of reason

SENATOR McCOMAS. Is it because the one favors polygamy and the other opposes it?

MR. YOUNG. No. I think that is merely one phase of the situation.

SENATOR McCOMAS. Is there any distinctive doctrinal difference?

MR. YOUNG. I believe there is. The main point of distinction between the two churches, I understand, revolves upon the question of the presidency of the church, our own church taking the view that upon the death of Joseph Smith, who was the president, the original founder of the church, the succession devolved upon the quorum of the twelve apostles, at the head of which was Brigham Young, and that, I understand, is disputed by the reorganized church.

SENATOR McCOMAS. What do they say?

MR. YOUNG. They dispute that proposition.

SENATOR McCOMAS. About that point, I mean.

MR. YOUNG. And Joseph Smith, jr. [III], the son of the founder of the church, subsequently became—I think some ten or twelve years after the death of Joseph Smith—the head of the reorganized church.

SENATOR McCOMAS. That was my impression. ...

MR. TAYLER. One other question. Is it a fact that, in theory at least, the title of the first presidency and the twelve apostles to their several places in the hierarchy is as much dependent upon their being semi-annually sustained by a conference of the church as that their original nomination should be approved by a conference of the church people?

MR. YOUNG. I do not recall ever having seen that point discussed, but my impression would be that that would not be the case. That is, that having been originally put in the position, if for any reason there might be no conference, for instance—

MR. TAYLER. Yes.

MR. YOUNG. That they would continue until such time as there might be.

MR. TAYLER. But suppose there was a conference; they must be sustained—

MR. YOUNG. That is the rule.

MR. TAYLER. By the conference, as certainly as originally their nomination was sustained?

MR. YOUNG. I think that is correct; yes, sir.

---

and right that they ought to receive no recognition from people who are posted. But we have no quarrel with them or their followers. We do not attack them, and most of the time we do not say anything in reply to their assaults" ("'Reorganite' Duplicity," Apr. 17, 1906).

MR. TAYLER. So that if there is any criticism of the original election of a polygamist as an apostle, that act of election is not to be differentiated, in its importance and validity, from the semiannual sustaining of others, who, prior to that time, may have been chosen apostles and were polygamists?

MR. YOUNG. Well, there is a rule of the church, as I understand, that a person having been elected, appointed, upheld for a position in the church, shall not lose that position until he shall have had his day in court, until charges shall have been preferred against him, and he shall have been tried. That, perhaps, is somewhat aside from the question of sustaining a man by conference. I do not think that an apostle would necessarily lose his position by reason of not having been sustained. I think there would be, in addition to that, a trial, and that upon that trial he might be dropped from his position. The effect of not sustaining him would simply be that the exercise of his office would be held in abeyance for the time being.

MR. TAYLER. I am glad to get this information. That is what I want. So that if at any of the semiannual conferences, at the temple or the tabernacle, wherever they are held, each one of the apostles' names being read out to be sustained, the people should by uplifted hand dissent and refuse to sustain any particular apostle, that refusal thus expressed would not operate to vacate his seat?

MR. YOUNG. You are discussing questions that I do not feel quite competent to settle, because I have never examined them to any extent. I may express my impression, and that would be that should the conference absolutely vote against a man, that would vacate the position. But, following the order of the church, as I understand it, the conference would refuse to do so, unless he had been previously tried and condemned by some tribunal having authority of the church for the offense that led to his suspension.

MR. TAYLER. So that in truth and in fact, as a practicality in your church organization, the people in conference are powerless to depose an apostle?

MR. YOUNG. I would not say that. My last answer stated that I feel satisfied—at least I meant to say, that I feel satisfied that a conference would not do it without the previous trial. However, if the conference should do it, taking that method, I am under the impression that office would be vacated. ...

MR. WORTHINGTON. Let me suppose this case, to see whether I understand what you have said in answer to Mr. Tayler's questions. Suppose that when you should go back to your home, you should find that while you were away some young girl who had mingled with you and your family, had become the plural wife of a member of the church, and was living with him in that relation. Would you allow her to be introduced to your family and treat her the same as you would if she were married to the man as his first and legal wife?

MR. YOUNG. Oh, I could not just say. It would depend upon what her previous relationship may have been. It would also depend upon the extent and state of my knowledge of her. I believe that the world everywhere exercises a good deal of charity in those things. I would not like to say, Mr. Worthington, just what I might do. We wink at a great many things—speaking now of mankind generally—that we know to be wrong. We pass by ulcers—

MR. WORTHINGTON. I know that, but I did not suppose that in our community, or in any part of the United States, anyone who is an open, acknowledged adulteress, is brought into respectable families and admitted as such, and I wondered if it was different in your neighborhood.

MR. YOUNG. No; it is not different there. Possibly my hesitation and uncertainty in answering that and Mr. Tayler's question depends upon the fact that I might think there were extenuating circumstances.

MR. WORTHINGTON. That is what I supposed. Now, if the case were one in which the young woman had been led to believe, and did really believe that she could be legally married according to the law of the church, then you would take a different view of it, would you?

MR. YOUNG. Entirely, and I think everybody else would, too.

MR. WORTHINGTON. Then if she knew what you say you know and understand, that the ceremony performed by a priest of your church would be of no legal efficacy, and notwithstanding that fact she had entered into that relation with the man, knowing that she was not married to him either by the law of the land or the law of the church, would you have her associate with your household?

MR. YOUNG. I would not. I will state this, Mr. Worthington, to state my mind on the subject: If a woman and a man, construing the manifesto as I construe it—namely, that it prohibits new polygamous marriages—had, to my conviction, entered into that relationship, I would consider them as living in an adulterous relation.

MR. WORTHINGTON. And you would ostracize them, so far as you were concerned, would you not?

MR. YOUNG. Yes, sir; that is correct.

MR. WORTHINGTON. Do you not believe that your neighbors in the church would do the same, under the same circumstances?

MR. YOUNG. I believe so. ...

E. D. R. Thompson,[6] being duly sworn, was examined, and testified as follows ...

MR. VAN COTT. And of course you have known, in a general way, about the rumors of unlawful cohabitation and polygamy, and such things as that?

MR. THOMPSON. Yes, sir.

MR. VAN COTT. What is the sentiment among the Gentiles in regard to violations of the law against unlawful cohabitation where the marriages were performed prior to the manifesto?

MR. THOMPSON. Well, they have always been treated by the Gentiles in a spirit of toleration.

MR. VAN COTT. Does that express your full idea on the subject? If it does, I will proceed. Were you in Salt Lake City when Joseph F. Smith testified for the protestants in this case?

MR. THOMPSON. Yes. sir.

MR. VAN COTT. Were you connected in any way at that time with finding out what the sentiment was on that particular subject?

MR. THOMPSON. Yes, sir; in this way: There was a meeting called in Salt Lake City by some of the non-Mormon citizens to take some steps with reference to sending a protest here against the view taken by Joseph F. Smith in his testimony, in which he stated, I believe, that the non-Mormon community had condoned these offenses. I signed that protest, and at that meeting I was appointed chairman of a committee to investigate the advisability of forming an opposition, politically, to the Mormons there in Salt Lake County. In that capacity, and at the suggestion of the meeting that this committee should be increased to twenty-five, I submitted the proposition to certain prominent Gentiles as to whether they would become members of the committee. I approached several prominent Gentiles on the subject and they refused to have anything to do with it. They refused to become members of the committee and stated that they thought it was ill advised and injudicious, and that it would be a great deal better to leave matters as they were; that they would finally adjust themselves. ...

MR. VAN COTT. As I understand, you do draw a distinction between what

6. At the time of his testimony, Thompson (1857-?) lived in Salt Lake City. Born in Wisconsin, he was active in Utah politics as a Republican, was a lawyer, and was non-Mormon.

is termed "condonation" and what is termed "toleration," and, you use the word advisedly?

MR. THOMPSON. Yes, sir. ...

MR. VAN COTT. Now, Mr. Thompson, what is the sentiment of the Gentiles in Utah, why they do not inform and report on these cases? I wish you would give it as fully as you can, so that we will have a correct appreciation.

MR. THOMPSON. Well, the general idea has been that this condition of things would gradually die away by the lapse of time. It has been generally repugnant to most people to take any position as against the Mormons in this matter which would imply either prosecution or persecution. In other words, they did not care to be informers.

MR. VAN COTT. Now, in regard to other offenses. Salt Lake City is just like other cities, in a way, is it, in that there are violations of the law?

MR. THOMPSON. Yes, sir.

MR. VAN COTT. And do Gentiles, or do Mormons, whenever they know of a violation of law, go and report it?

MR. THOMPSON. No, sir; they would not report, and have not reported, these cases of unlawful cohabitation any more than they have reported offenses against public morals in the way of gambling or of liquor selling on Sunday, which is carried on there all the time to the knowledge of everyone.

SENATOR McCOMAS. They do not tell on each other?

MR. THOMPSON. They do not tell; no.

MR. VAN COTT. Do you mean that they do not tell on each other, Mr. Thompson?

MR. THOMPSON. No; I do not mean that.

MR. VAN COTT. You do not mean that all the men there indulge in these practices?

MR. THOMPSON. Oh, no. ...

MR. VAN COTT. How long have you known Reed Smoot?

MR. THOMPSON. I have known Senator Smoot intimately for four years.

MR. VAN COTT. Has he been prominent in the politics of the Republican party in Utah?

MR. THOMPSON. He has been very prominent for the last four years to my certain knowledge.

MR. VAN COTT. Do you know whether he was before that?

MR. THOMPSON. I think he was.

MR. VAN COTT. What is your opinion as to whether the fact that he was an apostle helped or handicapped him in the race for United States Senator?

MR. THOMPSON. I do not think it helped him any.

MR. VAN COTT. What would you say, taking the political conditions as they existed at the time of his candidacy, as to whether he was a logical candidate for the position?

MR. THOMPSON. He was the logical candidate for many reasons.

MR. VAN COTT. For many reasons?

MR. THOMPSON. Or, I will say for a number of reasons.

SENATOR OVERMAN. What were the reasons? State the reasons.

MR. THOMPSON. Well, in the first place, geographically, as we term it in politics, he was the logical candidate, because he lived in Utah County, and it was not desirable that both Senators should come from Salt Lake County. He was the logical candidate in that respect. He was a logical candidate because at the time of the State convention, four years ago, he was talked of prominently as a candidate for governor and was considered the Republican leader in what we call the southern section of the State. ...

23.

James E. Talmage

Wednesday, Thursday & Tuesday,
January 18, 19, 24

"Prof' Talmage of this city has been selected by the church hierarchy to appear as an authoritative witness in behalf of Senator
Smoot ... What he says, unless the hierarchy shall conclude to repudiate all or part of it, is supposed to be the binding declaration."
—*Salt Lake Tribune,* Jan. 22, 1905

James E. Talmage,[1] being duly sworn, was examined and testified as
follows: ...

MR. WORTHINGTON. Are you a Mormon?

MR. TALMAGE. Yes, sir; I am, sir.

MR. WORTHINGTON. And have been since when?

MR. TALMAGE. Since my birth.

MR. WORTHINGTON. Are you a polygamist?

MR. TALMAGE. No, sir.

MR. WORTHINGTON. Have you ever been?

MR. TALMAGE. Never.

MR. WORTHINGTON. Have you any position in the church, or are you a lay
member?

MR. TALMAGE. I am a lay member in the sense of holding no position of
authority or local control. I am, however, a member of the Sunday
school board, having general supervision over Sunday-school matters throughout the church.

---

1. Talmage (1862-1933) taught geology at the University of Utah, but would become
a member of the LDS Quorum of the Twelve on December 8, 1911. Fourteen days prior
to his testimony, he noted in his journal: "Shortly before midnight I was served with a
subpoena by the United States Marshall for Utah,—a subpoena issued by the United
States Senate ... Committee on Privileges and Elections, citing me to appear in Washington on the 10th inst." He arrived in Washington mid-day on January 16 and "was called
to a consultation at the home of the senior counsel for Senator Smoot—Mr. Augustus S.
Worthington. It was midnight when I returned to the hotel." The following day, he had
"another night session in consultation with Colonel Worthington" (in James E. Talmage
Diary, L. Tom Perry Special Collections, Harold B. Lee Library, Brigham Young University, Provo).

MR. WORTHINGTON. How long have you had that position?

MR. TALMAGE. Three or four years past.

MR. WORTHINGTON. Are you the author of the book called "The Articles of Faith," which has been referred to here?[2]

MR. TALMAGE. Yes, sir.

MR. WORTHINGTON. In what way did you prepare that book; by what authority; and what was done in the way of giving it authenticity?

MR. TALMAGE. I had been requested by the presidency of the church to prepare a work or works dealing with the doctrines of the church, and, after consultation, had agreed to undertake the work, and thereupon received a written appointment to that effect.

Before the work was really begun, before it had passed beyond the stages of making plans and drawing outlines of the ground to be covered, I was asked to give a course of lectures on the doctrines of the church before a large class of students; and then it was decided by myself, primarily, with the consent of those who had appointed me to do the other work, to combine the two purposes and to deliver the lectures in such a way as to make the lectures take the place of the chapters in the proposed book.

MR. WORTHINGTON. After the book was prepared, was anything done in the way of submitting it to the church or anybody representing the authorities of the church?

MR. TALMAGE. The lectures were submitted at my own instance, and in accordance with my own request a committee was appointed to examine the same. This committee was appointed by the first presidency, and it passed upon the substance of the lectures or of the book in this way: The committee undertook to decide whether the views there presented were my own alone, or whether they were in accord with the generally accepted doctrines of the church. The book was then published by the church; not by myself.

MR. WORTHINGTON. And that committee was composed of Elders Francis M. Lyman, Abraham H. Cannon, and Anthon H. Lund, Elder George Reynolds, Elder John Nicholson,[3] and Dr. Karl G. Maeser?[4]

---

2. Chapter 23, "Submission to Secular Authority" (*The Articles of Faith* [Salt Lake City: Deseret News, 1899]) was entered into the committee's official record (*Smoot Hearings*, 1:294-304).

3. John Nicholson (1839-1909), chief recorder of the Salt Lake temple and a polygamist, testified on December 15, 17, 1904 (*Smoot Hearings*, 2:165-75, 230-52).

4. Karl G. Maeser (1828-1901) joined the LDS Church in Europe, immigrated to Salt Lake City in 1860, and served as principal of Brigham Young Academy in Provo from 1876 to 1892. He was a polygamist.

MR. TALMAGE. Yes.

MR. WORTHINGTON. The preface to the work as published shows the facts about that?

MR. TALMAGE. Yes, sir.

MR. WORTHINGTON. Are you the author or compiler of any other of the church books? Let me ask you particularly about the Pearl of Great Price.[5] Have you had anything to do with the revised edition of that work?

MR. TALMAGE. I made the revision. The last edition of the Pearl of Great Price, one of the standard works, as it now appears, has been revised by me in this way: The matter has been compared with the original manuscripts, and the division into chapters and verses, and the references given are my own.

THE CHAIRMAN. Doctor, right at this point, before you pass from this work on "The Articles of Faith," the title page, I suppose, expresses the fact when it says "Written by appointment and published by the church?"

MR. TALMAGE. Yes, Mr. Chairman; the title page is not my composition.

THE CHAIRMAN. But that is correct, as a matter of fact?

MR. TALMAGE. That expresses the truth.

THE CHAIRMAN. Excuse me, Mr. Worthington.

MR. WORTHINGTON. Certainly. (To the witness.) Have you otherwise than in the preparation of these books made a special study of the matter of the faith and doctrines of the church to which you belong?

MR. TALMAGE. Yes, sir; I may say that I have been a student of the doctrines of the church and a teacher of the same in the schools of the church for many years. ...

MR. WORTHINGTON. Now as to the apostles. What authority, if any, have the apostles to direct the president or the presidency in their work?

MR. TALMAGE. Absolutely none.

MR. WORTHINGTON. Suppose the president should call in the apostles for consultation about some church matter, and the apostles were all to advise a certain course to be pursued, would that be binding upon him?

MR. TALMAGE. In no sense.

MR. WORTHINGTON. He could act just as he pleased, without regard to that?

MR. TALMAGE. Very true, and he does so act.

---

5. The Pearl of Great Price is one of four books of canon in the LDS Church, along with the Bible, Book of Mormon, and Doctrine and Covenants.

SENATOR OVERMAN. Have the apostles any authority over things temporal as well as spiritual?

MR. TALMAGE. The apostles have no authority at all in the organized stakes and wards of the church, unless they are appointed especially for some particular inquiry, work, or investigation by the first presidency.

SENATOR OVERMAN. Has the first presidency any authority in things temporal?

MR. WORTHINGTON. I was going to ask him as to that point.

SENATOR OVERMAN. Excuse me.

MR. WORTHINGTON. I am going to ask him all about that. Of course, if the apostles would have no authority as a body, a single apostle would much the less have any.

MR. TALMAGE. Certainly. If an individual apostle be appointed to a special mission, that is his mission.

MR. WORTHINGTON. I understand. But neither a single apostle nor the whole body of the apostles would have any control over the president in regard to anything within the scope of the powers of the president, except to advise him.

MR. TALMAGE. That is true. The apostles as a body have no authority whatever while the first presidency is in an organized and acting condition.

MR. WORTHINGTON. Now, I should like to ask you something next about the courts of your organization. What are those courts?

MR. TALMAGE. In every ward, as stated, there is a presiding body known as the bishopric. The bishop and his two counselors are charged with the care of the members of that ward in church matters, and by and with the assistance of their teachers they try to keep in close touch with the people of the ward individually and as expressed in the terms of the revelation, which is regarded as the law of the church on that matter, they try to see that there shall be no iniquity in the church. If there be such iniquity, any hard feeling manifested between members of the church, or any charge made by one against another, they try conciliatory methods of adjusting those matters. If they fail, a bishop's court is convened, consisting of the bishop and his two counselors, then sitting as a church court—an ecclesiastical court.

The accused is served with a notice of the charge against him and is asked to appear, and a thorough investigation is held and a decision rendered.

This bishop's court may be regarded, and in fact is, the first or lowest of the courts commonly called the church courts.

MR. WORTHINGTON. Before you leave that subject, let me ask you a question. Do the counselors, when they sit with the bishop as a court, have equal power with him, and can the two counselors outvote the bishop when sitting as a court?

MR. TALMAGE. In no organization of the church are there two officers with equal power. The bishop, if he wishes, may consult his counselors, but the decision must be rendered by the bishop, and not by his counselors. He may, as I say, consult them and ask an expression of their opinion, and doubtless would do so, but the decision is his, and not the decision of the bishopric in such a trial.

MR. WORTHINGTON. Proceed with the next tribunal in order.

MR. TALMAGE. The next higher of the church courts is that known as the high council, consisting of 12 properly called and ordained high priests, constituting that council in each stake, presided over by the three presidents of the stake, or the presidency of the stake. The high council in each stake has powers of original as well as appellate jurisdiction. It may begin an action from the first, if the complaint be properly filed, but usually the council acts only as an appellate court.

If after a decision has been rendered by the bishop's court in any ward either of the parties is dissatisfied, he may take an appeal by giving written notice to the clerk of the high council, said appeal being to the high council. And the high council will then examine the transcript of the record which the bishop's court has been required to furnish, and will decide whether a new trial shall be held or whether a review of the evidence simply will suffice.

MR. WORTHINGTON. Do they ordinarily hear the case anew, have the witnesses brought before them, or do they decide the case on the transcript of the record as made below?

MR. TALMAGE. In the majority of cases they try the case anew; in by far the majority of cases. The decision, after the trial has been held, is rendered by the president of the stake.

MR. WORTHINGTON. Let me ask you a question right here. Besides his two counselors he has the twelve, composing the high council?

MR. TALMAGE. Yes, sir.

MR. WORTHINGTON. Is he bound by the action of the majority of those councilors and assistants, or may he go against the decision of all of them?

MR. TALMAGE. He is bound to this extent. After each member of the council has been given every necessary and proper opportunity for expressing his views, and after the parties in the case have expressed their views and the president has consulted with his counselors, a decision is announced as the decision of the president. If a majority of the council of 12 men refuse to sustain that, it falls.

MR. WORTHINGTON. After the decision by the high council, what is next, or what may be next?

MR. TALMAGE. The case may then be carried directly to the first presidency of the church.

MR. WORTHINGTON. Before you proceed, in any case does an appeal lie, or any sort of action, to or by the apostles?

MR. TALMAGE. To the apostles?

MR. WORTHINGTON. Yes.

MR. TALMAGE. Oh, in no sense. The apostles are not in the line of local officers or of organizations having any local jurisdiction at all.

MR. WORTHINGTON. And neither are the seventies?

MR. TALMAGE. No, sir.

MR. WORTHINGTON. Proceed, then.

MR. TALMAGE. If an appeal be taken from a decision of the high council, as I say, it is taken to the first presidency. The transcript of the proceedings is then furnished, and a careful examination made. The first presidency, sitting as the highest court of the church, certainly would have powers of original jurisdiction, but I have never known them to be so exercised.

MR. WORTHINGTON. Does the court, composed of the first presidency, when hearing cases on appeal from the high council of the stake, ever hear the witnesses, or hear the case anew; or does it decide it on the transcript of the case in the lower court?

MR. TALMAGE. Generally they decide it on the transcript, though witnesses may be called; that is to say, if witnesses are called, both parties are notified to be there at the time. If there be any part of the evidence that is possibly in an unsatisfactory or obscure condition, witnesses having given testimony upon that point may be called in the presence of the parties.

MR. WORTHINGTON. Is that a usual course, or is it infrequent?

MR. TALMAGE. From experience I am not able to say, as there are very few appeals of that kind pressed to an actual trial and decision by the first presidency.

SENATOR OVERMAN. Are the plaintiffs and defendants allowed to be represented by counsel in any of those courts?

MR. TALMAGE. Not in the usual way, Mr. Senator. They are there themselves, and may have their witnesses present, and if any request is made for counsel—not necessarily legal counsel in the usual acceptation of the term—it would be allowed. I have witnessed many instances of that kind in my own experience.

SENATOR OVERMAN. Who generally represents them? Do lawyers generally represent the parties?

MR. TALMAGE. No. One purpose of the church courts is to steer clear of lawyers.

SENATOR OVERMAN. They are allowed to have some representative of the church?

MR. TALMAGE. Yes, sir. If there be any member or officer of the church whom they would like to have represent them, they would certainly be given that opportunity. They would have a right to demand it, in fact.

MR. WORTHINGTON. Is it not the usual thing, when the case is before the high council of a stake, to have some member of the high council specially delegated to represent one of the parties?

MR. TALMAGE. Oh, indeed, sir. I have not given the details of the trial in any sense; but since you refer to it, I will say that when a high council is organized as a court to attend to the details of a trial, six of the twelve, determined by lot, become the counsel of the accused, and six become the counsel of the plaintiff; and from among those six one is selected on each side as a speaker, a spokesman for the others, who, while having no greater authority than the rest, is the one who would speak, unless there would be good reason for others speaking.

MR. WORTHINGTON. I presume a man is not excluded from being a high councillor, or holding any other office in the church, because of the fact that he is a lawyer?

MR. TALMAGE. No. We have some lawyers as members of high councils in the different stakes, and with care we find they do pretty well.

MR. WORTHINGTON. What can legally be done, according to the doctrines of the church, by those courts?

MR. TALMAGE. They have power to investigate any charge of unChristianlike conduct against any member of the church, or of heresy—that is to say, the teaching of false doctrines that would be detrimental to the church; and the limit of their power to inflict penalties is removal from the church—excommunication from the church. ...

MR. WORTHINGTON. There is one thing to which I should like to go back for a moment now, because something has been said here about it in the record; that is, whether in any case there is an appeal [to a First Presidency verdict], and if so, in what way [can one dissent] from a decision of the first presidency, when the matter has been taken up before it?

MR. TALMAGE. Yes, sir.

MR. WORTHINGTON. What is that?

MR. TALMAGE. An appeal would lie from the first presidency to the assembled quorums of the priesthood; that is to say, the church as a body is the supreme court before which the cases [are brought] involving [the] church.

The assembled quorums or organizations of the priesthood may be said to be in session at every general conference of the church. But, of course, in the same assembly with the quorums of the priesthood, standing and church rights may be tried.

Under those conditions are the lay members of the church, and questions are submitted to this general assembly of the church at every recurring semi-annual conference.

MR. WORTHINGTON. As a matter of fact, I believe there has been no case in which there has been an appeal taken from the decision of the first presidency and submitted to the presiding quorums only?

MR. TALMAGE. I call to mind no instance of record in which there has been an appeal formally taken from the decision of the first presidency, but I call to mind instances of record in which the announced decision of the first presidency in the matter of nominations has been entirely set aside by the assembled quorums of the priesthood.

MR. WORTHINGTON. What are those instances?

MR. TALMAGE. There is a case in which three nominees for the apostleship were presented by Joseph Smith, the first president of the church, and were voted down by the assembled people, the quorums of the priesthood. I think I can give you the reference.

MR. WORTHINGTON. I was going to ask you to give a reference to any authentic work where that matter is described.

MR. TALMAGE. The cases to which I refer are those of Lyman E. Johnson, Luke S. Johnson, and John Boynton, who were rejected by the people assembled in conference at Kirtland.

MR. WORTHINGTON. Ohio?

MR. TALMAGE. Ohio, in 1837. The record will be found in volume 16 of "Millennial Star;" on page 56. I would add, however, that in that particular volume you will find a typographical error, that book giving the date 1827, which was long before the church was organized. ... [T]he date of the publication shows that 1837 is intended.

That, however, will be found republished by authority in volume

2, of the "History of the Church," page 509, which book is at your disposal.[6] ...

MR. WORTHINGTON. What are the accepted standard works of the church which bind all of its members?

MR. TALMAGE. The standard works are four in number—the Bible, King James version or translation; the Book or Mormon; the Doctrine and Covenants; and the Pearl or Great Price.

MR. WORTHINGTON. We have been treated to extracts from a number of books by Orson Pratt and Brigham H. Roberts and others. Will you tell me what is the effect or binding operation of those works, or what is said in them, upon the church or any member thereof?

MR. TALMAGE. Nothing that is said in any of those works, or works of that kind, has any binding effect upon the people as a whole or upon any individual. They are to be regarded as the expressions of the authors.

MR. WORTHINGTON. Is it not true that, in order to have such binding effect, any work or instrument that purports to set forth the doctrines of the church must be submitted to a general conference and accepted by it?

MR. TALMAGE. That is true, sir. And the four works designated by me as standard works have been so submitted and so adopted by the vote of the people as their guide in faith and practice.

MR. WORTHINGTON. Now, as an illustration of that, what happened when you revised and divided into chapters, and so on, the Pearl of Great Price, one of the four standard works?

MR. TALMAGE. The changes made in that work, while not in any sense a change in the matter, except as to the correction of typographical errors and the omission of certain parts now appearing in the Doctrine or Covenants, made it necessary that that book should be readopted by the vote of the assembled quorums in conference, and the book was presented to the people at one conference, with an account of the alterations in arrangement, and they were told that at the next conference, six months later, they would be asked to vote upon it.

They were invited to examine it in the meantime and to compare it with the earlier editions; and at the succeeding conference, six months later, the people voted to readopt the Pearl of Great Price, or to adopt the Pearl or Great Price in its revised form, as their guide in faith and doctrines, and to give it place, as before, among the standard works of the church.

MR. WORTHINGTON. Now, in further illustration, let me ask you about this

<hr />

6. See Joseph Smith et al., *History of the Church of Jesus Christ of Latter-day Saints* (Salt Lake City: Deseret Book, 1948), 2:509-10.

work [of] which you are the author—the "Articles of Faith." You say you were authorized by the high church officials to prepare such work. You did give these lectures and you incorporated them into this volume, and it was approved by a committee of high officers of the church, appointed by the presidency. Is that work, or anything in it, binding upon any member of your church?

MR. TALMAGE. Oh, in no sense.

MR. WORTHINGTON. It would have to be submitted to the church conference and adopted by them before it would bind any Mormon?

MR. TALMAGE. Most assuredly.

MR. WORTHINGTON. Is it not true that a charge of apostasy was made against you for something in that work?

MR. TALMAGE. No charge was actually made, though I was notified I would be so charged. But as one of the church officials had already expressed himself as holding the views set forth by myself in that work, and he being very much larger game, he was singled out first, and as the proceedings against him ended in a disappointing way, I was never brought to trial.[7]

MR. WORTHINGTON. As another illustration, we have heard something about Orson Pratt and his works. Has there been any action taken in reference to these works in the way of submitting them to the people, or in any other way?

MR. TALMAGE. No, sir; not in the way of adoption, but I find instances of record in early church history of the people being warned repeatedly against Orson Pratt's publications, or certain of them[8]—

SENATOR OVERMAN. Do not the missionaries take them around with them through the country?

MR. TALMAGE. Excuse me, Senator, until I finish my answer.

SENATOR OVERMAN. Certainly.

MR. TALMAGE. Because they were not in accord with the doctrines of the church, set forth in the standard works.

---

7. From the January 13, 1899, passage in Talmage's journal, James P. Harris has surmised the unidentified "larger game" was probably George Q. Cannon. At issue was Cannon's view that the Holy Ghost was a distinct personality and not simply a manifestation of the godhead (James P. Harris, ed., *The Essential James E. Talmage* [Salt Lake City: Signature Books, 1997], xxv, xxxix).

8. For instance, Brigham Young denounced Pratt's views on the "Holy Spirit" (published as a tract in *A Series of Pamphlets* [Liverpool: Franklin D. Richards, 1856]), offering that the author "drowns himself in his own philosophy every time he undertakes to treat upon principles that he does not understand" (Gary James Bergera, "The Orson Pratt-Brigham Young Controversies: Conflict within the Quorums, 1853-1868," *Dialogue: A Journal of Mormon Thought* 13 [Summer 1980], 16).

SENATOR OVERMAN. I ask you—Did not the missionaries carry Orson Pratt's works with them and have them on sale throughout the country?

MR. TALMAGE. I do not know what the practice of missionaries may be as to putting books on sale. They carry many books with them.

SENATOR OVERMAN. Do they not carry these books?

MR. TALMAGE. I do not know, sir. I would infer that in all probability they do, because some of the smaller church publishing houses—called church publishing houses because connected with church organizations in a way, but not under the immediate control of the general authorities of the church—have continued to publish some of these books. Many of Orson Pratt's works are of great value, I take it; that is to say, they present the views of a man who was a careful student, and one whose utterances are worthy of consideration.

SENATOR OVERMAN. He understood the doctrines of the church pretty well, did he not?

MR. TALMAGE. Yes, indeed; but in several of his works he has allowed his imagination to play rather than to work; and, personally, I have taken issue with some of his published statements.

MR. WORTHINGTON. Are you through, Senator Overman?

SENATOR OVERMAN. Yes.

MR. WORTHINGTON. The fact that Orson Pratt publishes a certain work, and certain of your missionaries happen to have it with them and distribute it, does not make it binding on the church?

MR. TALMAGE. In no sense.

SENATOR HOPKINS. Any more than the "Life of St. Paul," by Lyman Abbott, is binding on his church?[9]

MR. TALMAGE. The analogy is an excellent one.

MR. WORTHINGTON. Is there any publishing house authorized to publish works and send them out, which works bind the church as an organization?

---

9. Lyman Abbott (1835-1922) was a respected contemporary theologian, author of *Life and Letters of Paul the Apostle* (Boston: Houghton Mifflin, 1898). Later this same year, Abbott's name would be evoked twice in LDS general conference, although both times for condemnation. In April, Joseph F. Smith said he heard the Reverend Abbott preach in Brooklyn and it was "one of the most eloquent discourses I ever listened to" and entirely devoted to "false religion, if you can call it religion at all" (*Conference Reports,* Apr. 1905, 84). Picking up the same theme at the October general conference, Rulon S. Wells said: "To my mind, it is just such doctrines as those put forth by Joseph Hamilton and Lyman Abbott that are responsible for much of the infidelity in the world today," in particular because of their acceptance of evolution (ibid., Oct. 1905, 59).

MR. TALMAGE. No such publishing house could be named. But I may say, by way of explanation, that the only supervision exercised by the church over the publications put out by these several publishing houses is in regard to reissuing standard works—three of the standard works. The church, of course, does not undertake to print the Bible, as Bibles can be obtained through the usual channels.

MR. WORTHINGTON. The "Deseret News" has been spoken of here frequently as the organ of the church. Has anybody in your church the power to put in the "Deseret News" anything which is not in the standard works, that shall bind the people of your church, if it has not first been approved by the people?

MR. TALMAGE. No one, not even the president of the church; that is, in matters of rules of religious practice. Of course, if this be carried to an unwarranted extreme, the statement may appear not to be strictly true. For example, every six months the first presidency of the church publishes, through the columns of the "Deseret News," an announcement that a general conference of the church will be held such and such a place. That is binding on the people. If they want to exercise their rights as voters they must be there.

MR. WORTHINGTON. I restricted my question to something not covered by your standard works.

MR. TALMAGE. No one could make anything binding by simply publishing it in the "Deseret News," or any other medium, or any other form.

MR. WORTHINGTON. While I am on this subject I wish to ask you about something that appears in the early part of the record. Some questions were asked which seem to indicate that there was in the mind of the questioner the impression that the people of the church have a veto power on the Almighty. You remember that passage in the record?[10]

MR. TALMAGE. Yes, sir.

MR. WORTHINGTON. Would you like to express your views on that subject?

MR. TALMAGE. I judge from the context, although I have not in mind the name or names of those who used the expression, that it was spoken with some attempted humor and with some ironical coloring. But in one sense there is more truth in it than might appear.

The Lord himself has given the people the right to veto, in one sense; that is, to reject. He has given them free agency, and has re-

---

10. Joseph F. Smith had said he was unaware of "any revelation made by God to the first president of the church" that had been rejected by the church (*Smoot Hearings*, 1:97).

spected it much more fully than they respect one another's free agency. I have in mind the human family in general. The command, written amidst the thunders of Sinai, was "Thou shalt not kill," but every murderer vetoes that commandment, so far as it has application to himself, and sets it at defiance.

In that sense the people of the church, which bears the name of Him from whom the revelation of free agency came, have the right to reject any commandment or any instruction that the Lord may give, and then take the consequences. Free agency necessarily entails individual responsibility. But never since the organization of the church in this dispensation has there been an instance of divine revelation given to the church and made binding upon the people in the sense of robbing them of their right and freedom to choose or reject. ....

Mr. Worthington. Let me suppose, to make this matter clear here, that you were a Senator from the State of Utah and that a measure should be pending before the Senate, and the head of the church should instruct you how to vote on that pending measure. What would be the extent of his authority or of your obligation to obey him?

Mr. Talmage. To me it is an unsupposable case.

Mr. Worthington. Well, I, perhaps, ought to ask your pardon and his for supposing it, but I will suppose it, inasmuch as it seems to have been supposed by others in this case, and the charge is flatly made that Mr. Smoot, as a Senator, is bound to obey the orders of the church.

Mr. Talmage. Well, adopting what I have called an unsupposable case, for the purpose of illustration, and answering your question as to my own probable attitude in the matter, I think if the president of the church, or any other officer of the church, were to presume to instruct me in my position as a Senator, I should remind him that I was the Senator and he was not.

Mr. Worthington. Well, that is very well as expressing your personal attitude; but what do you say as to whether you would have a right to take that position under the doctrines of your church?

Mr. Talmage. Most assuredly. I think any man would take that position.
...

Mr. Worthington. Now, I want to go to another subject which is of some interest here—the subject of polygamy. First, it has been contended here, as I understand, that under the original dispensation of your church, when that doctrine was first proclaimed through a revelation coming through Joseph Smith, jr., it was mandatory on the members of the church. What do you say to that?

MR. TALMAGE. I have never so understood it, and I would have to interpret plain English in a very different way from what I do to so interpret it, even from the revelation as it is now published and has been published from the first. The revelation referred to appears in the Doctrine and Covenants as section 132. It is headed "Revelation on the Eternity of the Marriage Covenant, Including Plurality of Wives."

MR. WORTHINGTON. I may say to you, Doctor, that the whole of that chapter is already in evidence and in the record in this case.[11]

THE CHAIRMAN. It is all in.

MR. WORTHINGTON. So it is not necessary to read it; but if there is any particular part of it which bears upon the matter about which I am asking you I would like you to refer to it and state why you have reached the conclusion you have stated.

MR. TALMAGE. I thank counsel for his explanation; I was not intending to read it, but desired to emphasize the significance of the title.

MR. WORTHINGTON. Yes.

MR. TALMAGE. It is primarily a revelation on the eternity of the marriage covenant, and if analyzed with care it will be seen that that is the fundamental thought pervading the whole revelation appearing as this section. The meaning, I think, could be made clear by a very few short paragraphs.

MR. WORTHINGTON. Very well.

MR. TALMAGE. The revelation purports to be a declaration of the Lord through Joseph Smith—perhaps I should say to Joseph Smith—as to what is here called "the new and everlasting covenant." ...

Paragraph 7 sets forth in an explicit manner just what the nature of that new and everlasting covenant is. Paragraph 7 reads: "And verily I say unto you, that the conditions of this law are these: All covenants, contracts, bonds, obligations, oaths, vows, performances, connections, associations, or expectations that are not made and entered into and sealed by the Holy Spirit of promise of Him who is anointed, both as well for time and for all eternity, and that, too, most holy, by revelation and commandment through the medium of mine anointed, whom I have appointed on the earth to hold this power (and I have appointed unto my servant Joseph to hold this power in the last days, and there is never but one on the earth at a time on whom this power and the keys of this priesthood are conferred), are of no efficacy, virtue, or force, in and after the resurrection from the

---

11. See *Smoot Hearings*, 1:202-208.

dead; for all contracts that are not made unto this end have an end when men are dead."

I emphasize this phase of it because the new and everlasting covenant here referred to is a covenant that can be entered into under proper authority, to be of effect after death and not simply in this world.

I make this explanation, because it will be seen, if you read the entire revelation with care, that the feature of marriage is incidental in a way, to that general statement of this new law or new and everlasting covenant. The revelation then goes on to explain that if a man marry a wife under the laws of this earth in any nation, that marriage is valid as long as life shall last. The words of the English marriage service are not here incorporated, but the spirit is the same—"until death do you part." But, according to this new and everlasting covenant it was made clear that there is an authority by which covenants may be made that shall not be annulled with death. Then, in a manner—that is, relatively speaking or incidentally speaking—the Lord answers the question put by the Prophet Joseph Smith as to how he could justify Abraham and Isaac and Jacob and Moses and David and Solomon in living in polygamy, by explaining that they had received their wives under this eternal covenant, and he says that in no instance did they sin except in the case of David's grave crime; and the punishment that was visited upon that great man on account of his sin is set forth in strong terms.

Now, returning to the question and apologizing for this long introduction, I will take occasion to say there is no paragraph in that revelation which, to my mind, confirms the inference that it was ever intended to be mandatory except upon one man. It is declared here that Joseph Smith was the man unto whom the keys of that authority were transmitted, that any such marriage would have to be solemnized by that authority then delegated to him (either solemnized by him in person or by one whom he would appoint for the purpose), the keys of the authority, to use the term employed in the revelation, resting with him.

Now I take it, it would have been inconsistent, at least to my feeble mind, the delegating or giving of that power to a man and then not requiring him first to obey that law himself. He was the man, to whom that command was given. In other cases it was permissive only. By way of illustration of that—

THE CHAIRMAN. Mr. Worthington, do you care for all this?

MR. WORTHINGTON. I do; yes, Mr. Chairman.

THE CHAIRMAN. All right.

MR. WORTHINGTON. I do not see, when so much time has been spent here in trying to show that it was mandatory, why the church may not properly present somebody here to show that it is not.

THE CHAIRMAN. I will only suggest to the witness, without leaving out anything, to be as brief and as rapid as possible.

MR. TALMAGE. I say, by way of illustration of that natural interpretation—the interpretation that has always been in my mind the only one that I can give—we read here that if a man shall marry a wife or shall marry wives, under the new and everlasting covenant, "he shall be justified." I have not usually found in these revelations that the Lord commands a man to do a thing and then tells him he will excuse him for doing it.

MR. WORTHINGTON. Where is the word "justify" used? In what section and paragraph? Well, you need not spend any time in looking for that, but you can give it to the reporter later on and he will insert it.

MR. TALMAGE. I can give it in a minute. I can give you the exact paragraph. It is in section 132, paragraph 62. To make it plain, I must read first paragraph 61: "61. And again, as pertaining to the law of the priesthood: If any man espouse a virgin and desire to espouse another, and the first give her consent; and if he espouse the second and they are virgins and have vowed to no other man, then is he justified; he can not commit adultery, for they are given unto him; for he can not commit adultery with that that belongeth unto him and to no one else. 62. And if he had ten virgins given unto him by this law, he can not commit adultery, for they belong to him, and they are given unto him, therefore is he justified."

Now, I ask you to contrast that with the remarks addressed directly to the man to whom this revelation was given, beginning at paragraph 1: "1. Verily, thus saith the Lord unto you, my servant Joseph, that inasmuch as you have inquired of my hand, to know and understand wherein I, the Lord, justified my servants Abraham, Isaac, and Jacob, as also Moses, David, and Solomon, my servants, as touching the principle and doctrine of their having many wives and concubines: 2. Behold! and lo, I am the Lord thy God, and will answer thee as touching this matter: 3. Therefore, prepare thy heart to receive and obey the instructions which I am about to give unto you; for all those who have this law revealed unto them must obey the same."

I say again the mandatory feature has application to one man and to one man only.

THE CHAIRMAN. As I understand you, this law was revealed to only one individual.

MR. TALMAGE. The revelation was given to one man, Mr. Chairman.

THE CHAIRMAN. And he, alone, was bound to obey it?

MR. TALMAGE. At that time, he alone.

MR. WORTHINGTON. There has been no similar revelation to anybody else?

MR. TALMAGE. No; of course, with his death, that same power descended to his successor.

I would ask the privilege of saying, if you are through with that subject, that another feature of that revelation, upon which some comment has been made, is the threatened destruction of the woman who would oppose obedience to that law on the part of her husband. I think it is, if possible, even more plain that that threatened destruction applied to but one woman. It was absolutely required that the man to whom that revelation was given and unto whom the keys of that power were transmitted should obey that law, and he is told here that if his wife opposed that, the Lord would deal with her. The paragraph reads: "And again, verily, verily, I say unto you, if any man have a wife, who holds the key of this power, and he teaches unto her the law of my priesthood, as pertaining to these things, then shall she believe, and administer unto him, or she shall be destroyed, saith the Lord your God, for I will destroy her; for I will magnify my name upon those who receive and abide in my law."

MR. WORTHINGTON. Now, you have practically answered, in reading that chapter and in what you have said about it, my next question as to what is meant by celestial marriage, a phrase which has been often used in this record.

MR. TALMAGE. Celestial marriage is the order of marriage sanctioned by this authority of the priesthood described as the authority existing and operating under "the new and everlasting covenant," and being a marriage for eternity as well as for this mortal probation called time, by a covenant between the parties, authorized and sanctioned by the authority transmitted as described.

MR. WORTHINGTON. Then the phrase "celestial marriage" is not at all synonymous with "polygamous marriage?"

MR. TALMAGE. In no sense.[12]

---

12. The term "celestial" marriage originally meant "plural" marriage, but toward the end of the nineteenth century it was redefined to mean "eternal" marriage, and D&C 132 was edited to reflect this new understanding (B. Carmon Hardy, *Solemn Covenant: The Mormon Polygamous Passage* [Urbana: University of Illinois Press, 1992], 54, 297-98, 342).

MR. WORTHINGTON. The first marriage may be a celestial one as well as a subsequent one?

MR. TALMAGE. Yes, sir; and most of the celestial marriages solemnized in the Church of Jesus Christ of Latter-Day Saints have been monogamous marriages—always have been.

MR. WORTHINGTON. Then we have the expression frequently used here of a man being sealed to a woman. Is there any difference between the true meaning of that expression and the phrase "celestial marriage?"

MR. TALMAGE. No, sir. The term "sealed" is sometimes used synonymously with the "marriage for time and eternity," or "marriage for eternity," if that were meant.

MR. WORTHINGTON. Now, the next matter in order in this connection is the manifesto of President Woodruff, which was submitted to a conference on the 6th of October, 1890. I believe you were present when that manifesto or revelation was submitted?

MR. TALMAGE. I was present when the manifesto was submitted to the conference.

MR. WORTHINGTON. And of course you voted to sustain it?

MR. TALMAGE. I did, sir. ...

MR. WORTHINGTON. Doctor, you have used the expression here "holding the keys" in connection with that revelation involving polygamy, when it was given to Joseph Smith, jr., that he was the only man who held the keys to that power. He only, at that time, or some person delegated by him, could make a plural marriage that would be valid according to the laws of the church. Am I right in that?

MR. TALMAGE. Yes, sir.

MR. WORTHINGTON. From that time on down to the time that President Woodruff issued this manifesto, which the church approved in conference assembled, the same principle obtained?

MR. TALMAGE. Yes, sir.

MR. WORTHINGTON. That a plural marriage could not be valid, according to the law of the church, only when celebrated by the president, or by somebody authorized by him to celebrate it. Is that right?

MR. TALMAGE. That is strictly true.

MR. WORTHINGTON. Then when this revelation which is called the manifesto came and it was submitted to the people and accepted by them, that power was taken away from the president, was it not?

MR. TALMAGE. Yes, sir.

MR. WORTHINGTON. So that since the 6th of October, 1890, the president of the church has had no power to solemnize a plural marriage according to the law of the church, even?

MR. TALMAGE. That is true.

MR. WORTHINGTON. And no power to authorize anybody else to celebrate one?

MR. TALMAGE. That is true.

MR. WORTHINGTON. So that if any person has undertaken to enter into plural marriage, if any woman has become the plural wife of a husband since the 6th day of October, 1890, she is no more a wife by the law of the church than she is by the law of the land?

MR. TALMAGE. That is true.

MR. WORTHINGTON. And it is not in the power of the president to revive the old system so that he can make a valid plural marriage or authorize one, unless he does it through the general conference of the church?

MR. TALMAGE. Certainly. It is now a rule of the church that that power shall not be exercised. The power is there, but the exercise of it is entirely stopped; and a rule of the church thus made and sanctioned is equally binding with the law founded upon revelation, and the president therefore has in one sense half voluntarily, inasmuch as he was the chief individual to bring it before the conference, but by the action of the conference, properly speaking, has surrendered that power as far as its exercise is concerned.

MR. WORTHINGTON. It takes the action of the people to restore it, does it not?

MR. TALMAGE. Most assuredly.[13] ...

MR. WORTHINGTON. Have you taken your endowments in the church?

MR. TALMAGE. Yes, sir.

MR. WORTHINGTON. When.

MR. TALMAGE. I think in the year 1882. Yes; I am fairly certain as to the date.

MR. WORTHINGTON. Have you passed through that ceremony at any time since?

MR. TALMAGE. I have witnessed the ceremony since, and have taken part in it, not for myself, but, according to the rules and procedure of the church, in a vicarious position.

MR. WORTHINGTON. And down to what time?

---

13. This entire exchange, as abridged here, was included in the "View of the Minority" submitted by Senator Foraker on June 11, 1906 (*Smoot Hearings*, 4:511).

MR. TALMAGE. Oh, I have not witnessed the ceremony for many years.

MR. WORTHINGTON. On about how many occasions would you say, all told, including the occasion when you went through yours?

MR. TALMAGE. Oh, I have passed through and witnessed the ceremonies or taken part therein between one and two score times.

MR. WORTHINGTON. I want to ask you whether in the course of that ceremony anything occurs like this, that the persons who are taking their endowments agree to what I read or to that in substance: "You and each of you do promise and vow that you will never cease to importune high heaven to avenge the blood of the prophets upon this nation?"

MR. TALMAGE. No.

MR. WORTHINGTON. Anything like that?

MR. TALMAGE. No, sir.

MR. WORTHINGTON. Or anything which in any wise relates to a man's obligations or duty to his country or to his State?

MR. TALMAGE. Absolutely nothing, according to my remembrance.

MR. WORTHINGTON. Is there anything about avenging the blood of Joseph Smith, jr., the prophet?

MR. TALMAGE. No, sir.

SENATOR McCOMAS. Do you remember the terms of that oath?

MR. TALMAGE. I know not which oath is referred to, and, moreover, I know of no oath that is administered or taken in any part of the endowment ceremony. I know I have never taken an oath there.

SENATOR McCOMAS. Do I understand you now to say you do not know to which oath Mr. Worthington is referring?

MR. WORTHINGTON. I did not use the word "oath," I think, Senator.

SENATOR McCOMAS. What word did you use?

MR. WORTHINGTON. The word "obligation."

SENATOR McCOMAS. You do not know now to which obligation or oath counsel referred when he was asking the question?

MR. TALMAGE. I understood counsel to read to me something and ask me if I recognized that as forming a part of the endowment ceremony in any phase.

SENATOR McCOMAS. In any part?

MR. TALMAGE. Yes; and I answer no.

SENATOR McCOMAS. Can you remember all of that ceremonial which you say does not include this or anything like it?

MR. TALMAGE. No; I do not remember details. It is many years since I have witnessed the ceremony; but I know that what has been read is not a part of the ceremony.

SENATOR McComas. That is, from the impression of years ago made upon your mind?

MR. TALMAGE. Yes, sir.

SENATOR McComas. You only have an impression as to what is included in that ceremonial, but you have a very decided opinion that this is not anywhere near it.

MR. TALMAGE. Yes; I am willing to accept that as a fair statement of my position in the matter. ...

MR. TAYLER. Doctor, what are the inspired authorities of the church?

MR. TALMAGE. You mean the written authorities?

MR. TAYLER. No; I do not.

MR. TALMAGE. Then you mean, who are the inspired authorities?

MR. TAYLER. No; I mean what are the inspired authorities of the church? Is there anything besides the Bible, the Book of Mormon, the Doctrine and Covenants, the Pearl of Great Price, and the Manifesto of 1890?

MR. TALMAGE. Those are the only standard works of the church which are adopted and made binding upon the church. As to inspiration, I think there are many books used by members of the church that are inspired, published by members of the church, and published by many who are not members of the church. Any book that sets forth truths, I take it, is in a manner an inspired work. I do not wish to evade the question. Those are the only works that are accepted by the church, or that can be authoritatively referred to and quoted as representing or presenting the law of the church.

MR. TAYLER. How do the revelations contained in the Doctrine and Covenants differ in the divinity of their origin or their authoritative character from other revelations, if there are or were any, not contained within the covers of that book?

MR. TALMAGE. Other revelations received by or given to the church?

MR. TAYLER. Yes.

MR. TALMAGE. There are none. I do not mean to be understood as saying that other revelations, specific and definite, may not have been received; but if so, it is not known. They are not promulgated. They are not given out to the people. They are not binding on the people. The people never heard of them, and have never had a chance to accept or reject them; and I know of none that are thus held in abeyance.

MR. TAYLER. So that until they are accepted or rejected, what do they amount to?

MR. TALMAGE. They amount to nothing; and as far as my knowledge goes, they are not.

MR. TAYLER. When was the polygamy revelation accepted by the people?

MR. TALMAGE. Do you refer to the revelation now embodied in the Doctrine and Covenants?

MR. TAYLER. Yes.

MR. TALMAGE. When the Doctrine and Covenants was accepted as a work. I do not know whether that revelation was ever voted upon separately or not.

MR. TAYLER. Was there ever a doctrine of the church more ardently believed in by those who believed in it at all than the revelation pertaining to celestial marriage?

MR. TALMAGE. I do not know. The celestial marriage part of that revelation, I take it, is practically universally believed.

MR. TAYLER. That is to say, the plural marriage part of it?

MR. TALMAGE. That has been believed in, according to my observation and judgment, by a very small part of the membership of the Mormon Church at any time, and has been practiced by a very much smaller portion.

MR. TAYLER. Exactly. So that you deny the proposition that the revelation as to plural marriage, whatever might have been a man's view as to his own personal practice of it, was right? You deny that?

MR. TALMAGE. Will the reporter read the question? I did not catch the first part of it.

The reporter read as follows: "Mr. Tayler. Exactly. So that you deny the proposition that the revelation as to plural marriage, whatever might have been a man's view as to his own personal practice of it, was right? You deny that?"

MR. TALMAGE. I deny that the question was explicit.

MR. TAYLER. You deny that the question is explicit?

MR. TALMAGE. Yes, sir.

MR. TAYLER. I did not ask you to deny that. You might have asserted it.

MR. TALMAGE. I will assert it, if that will suit better, but I can not answer it in that form.

MR. TAYLER. Then you do not agree with Joseph F. Smith when he says that you might just as well deny any other principle of the church as to deny that?

MR. TALMAGE. Counsel appears to be proceeding upon the supposition that I have denied. I have denied nothing in regard to that revelation. ...

MR. TAYLER. I asked you whether the revelation respecting plural marriage had ever been submitted to a conference of the Mormon people?

MR. TALMAGE. Yes, it has been submitted as part of the volume known as the Doctrine and Covenants, but I repeat, as to whether it was ever voted upon separately or not, I do not know. It has always been a part of the standard work known as the Doctrine and Covenants since I began to read such.[14]

MR. TAYLER. Yes, but I have understood you to say—and I fear I have done you an injustice—that no revelation amounted to anything unless it was accepted by the people.

MR. TALMAGE. I would be sorry to make the statement in that way. A revelation certainly amounts to something. If it is a revelation it is a revelation, and amounts to just so much; but as to being a binding law upon the church—a law of practice and action—it would have to be first adopted by the church to become such.

MR. TAYLER. Now, when was this revelation respecting plural marriage adopted?

MR. TALMAGE. I say again, as to whether it was ever adopted separately or not I do not know. The Doctrine and Covenants, the compilation, order, and arrangement of which has not been changed for many years, has been adopted.

MR. TAYLER. All right. Let us dismiss this blanket business.

MR. TALMAGE. Dismiss what, sir?

MR. WORTHINGTON. What do you mean by that, Mr. Tayler? The witness says the whole book was adopted.

MR. TAYLER. Exactly. That is what I am coming at.

MR. WORTHINGTON. Very well.

MR. TAYLER. Do you mean to say that that revelation respecting plural marriage never was presented to the Mormon people except in some edition of the Doctrine and Covenants?

MR. TALMAGE. I repeat my words, hoping that counsel will this time understand me. I do not know.

MR. TAYLER. You do not know?

MR. TALMAGE. I have so stated several times.

MR. TAYLER. Very well. Then do you want us to understand that no other treatment was given to that revelation than that which is described in your last answer?

---

14. Section 132 was published for the first time in the *Deseret News* on September 14, 1852, then added to the Doctrine and Covenants in 1876. Simultaneously, a previous section on marriage (D&C 101, 1835 edition) was dropped because of its stipulation that "one man should have one wife; and one woman but one husband, except in the case of death, when either is at liberty to marry again" (Richard S. Van Wagoner, "Mormon Polyandry in Nauvoo," *Dialogue: A Journal of Mormon Thought* 18 [Fall 1985]: 70).

Mr. Talmage. My last answer was that I do not know, and I do not see how that could be construed as a description of the kind of treatment given to that revelation.

Mr. Tayler. Then the plural marriage revelation, as such, and separated from other revelations, was never laid before the Mormon Church for its adoption?

Mr. Talmage. For counsel's benefit, I repeat my former answer. I do not know. I have never found any record of such.

Mr. Tayler. And that is the only answer you can make to that?

Mr. Talmage. It is.

Mr. Tayler. When the revelation suspending it was received, that was submitted to the people?

Mr. Talmage. The document known as the manifesto was submitted to the people, yes, sir.

Mr. Tayler. Not the revelation?

Mr. Talmage. According to my interpretation, not the revelation.

Mr. Tayler. So far as the records of the church go, therefore, a revelation suspending the plural marriage revelation was adopted, although there was no record of the adoption of the original revelation?

Mr. Talmage. I would not like to think that counsel is intentionally twisting the words of a witness. I have endeavored to state that that revelation to which counsel is referring most assuredly has been adopted by the people. The whole book has been adopted.

Mr. Tayler. When?

Mr. Talmage. The Doctrine and Covenants, as one of the standard works, was adopted at the time of its first compilation, the date of which I am not able to give you just now; but after it had been rearranged as to chapters and verses it was adopted again during the semiannual conference of the church, on October 10, 1880. On that date the Doctrine and Covenants, having then undergone some rearrangement in the matter of versification, was adopted by the people.

Mr. Tayler. When did section 132, which is the plural marriage revelation, first become incorporated in the Book of Doctrine and Covenants?

Mr. Talmage. I do not know. It has been a part of every edition of the Doctrine and Covenants I have ever been able to see or get possession of.

Mr. Tayler. When was the first edition of the Doctrine and Covenants?

Mr. Talmage. I do not know.[15]

---

15. The Doctrine and Covenants was first published in 1835. As Karl F. Best has

MR. TAYLER. You have known so much, Doctor, about the history of your church that I hoped you might refresh your recollection on that.

MR. TALMAGE. I would be very pleased to give the information—very pleased to have it; but I do not know offhand when the Doctrine and Covenants was first adopted.

MR. TAYLER. I did not say adopted. When was it first published?

MR. TALMAGE. That I do not know.

MR. TAYLER. When was the plural marriage revelation received?

MR. TALMAGE. According to the superscription of the revelation as it appears in section 132—

MR. TAYLER. I can read the superscription, Doctor, myself. When was it, as a matter of fact, in the church history received?

MR. TALMAGE. I will continue my answer. According to this superscription it was given July 12, 1843. As to any other date I have absolutely no knowledge.

MR. TAYLER. What is the name of your work?

MR. TALMAGE. Of what, sir?

MR. TAYLER. Of your work—your theological work?

MR. TALMAGE. There is a book here, for which I am responsible, called the "Articles of Faith."

MR. TAYLER. Now, as the author of that work and as a student generally of the tenets of the Mormon Church, have you obtained no information respecting the giving of the revelation respecting plural marriage except that which is contained in the heading of section 132?

MR. TALMAGE. None whatever. The work to which counsel is kind enough to refer does not treat the subject of plural marriage.

MR. TAYLER. What is it?

MR. TALMAGE. The work to which counsel has referred does not treat the subject of plural marriage except in a purely incidental way, as illustrative of continuous revelation, and the necessity of bringing in the details as to the date of this particular revelation, etc., did not appear. I will simply say that I have never questioned the correctness of the date given in the Doctrine and Covenants, and never have felt it incumbent upon me or necessary from my point of view to investigate that.

MR. TAYLER. Have you never heard that the revelation, or part of it, at least, came earlier?

---

observed: "When the 1835 conference voted to accept the book as scripture, church members hadn't even seen it yet: it was still on the press. Few had seen the updated revelations in any form" ("Changes in the Revelations, 1833-1835," *Dialogue: A Journal of Mormon Thought* 25 [Spring 1992], 110.

MR. TALMAGE. No, sir; not definitely or authoritatively.[16] ...

MR. TAYLER. How do you know that polygamy was practiced prior to the date [July 12, 1843] of that revelation?

MR. TALMAGE. I have not said that I knew anything of that.

MR. TAYLER. What is the state of your mind on that subject?

MR. TALMAGE. I have no definite views at all. I understood counsel to ask me if I had heard that it had been. I answer yes; I have heard that, but I do not know of any way of proving it or disproving it. I find nothing of record in regard to it.

MR. TAYLER. Is it not a matter recognized by the Mormons as having occurred prior to 1843?

MR. TALMAGE. I do not know that there is any general recognition or repudiation of any claim of that kind.

MR. TAYLER. Is it not, in your church history, recognized as a fact that Joseph Smith had received a revelation respecting plural marriage prior to that time, and that in consequence, indeed in obedience to that revelation, he had taken a plural wife, or, more, that he had conveyed that revelation to others?

MR. TALMAGE. I could not refer you to and could not produce any reference in church history that would definitely meet your question.[17]

MR. TAYLER. Then you are unable to say whether it is recognized among the church people that, as a historical fact, not proven by you as an eyewitness, or others, that polygamy was to some extent practiced among the Mormons prior to the date of the revelation given in the Book of Doctrine and Covenants?

MR. TALMAGE. I can answer that, yes. I do not know what the general state of the mind of the members of the church is on that matter, and I have in mind no historical record or reference that I would consider

---

16. After Talmage's testimony on Wednesday, he recapped in his journal that when the "cross-examination" began about mid-afternoon, he was "under fire until adjournment" from Tayler, whom he characterized as "tricky, and practically unprincipled in his methods rather than strong." Talmage complained that he "had to demand repeatedly that [Tayler] frame his questions so as to make them definite and unambiguous before I would attempt to answer." Talmage found it "a questionable compliment" to have his book, *The Articles of Faith,* referenced and then have to explain the meaning of various passages.

17. William W. Phelps, Orson Pratt, and Joseph F. Smith all asserted that Joseph Smith "seriously considered plural marriage as a part of the restitution of all things as early as 1831. In fact, there is some evidence to support the contention that he might have taken his first plural wife later that same year," according to Kenneth W. Godfrey in "The Coming of the Manifesto," *Dialogue: A Journal of Mormon Thought* 5 (Fall 1970), 11-12.

sufficiently definite to warrant me in saying yes or no to a question of that kind.

Mr. Tayler. Do you know that polygamy was ever practiced at all in the church?

Mr. Talmage. Yes, sir.

Mr. Tayler. Do you know how soon they commenced to practice it?

Mr. Talmage. After the organization of the church, do you mean?

Mr. Tayler. I do not suppose they practiced it before the organization, Doctor; but how early?

Mr. Talmage. Since counsel takes exception to that question, I will ask him to be explicit. Do you mean in my experience or from my reading of what took place in the early days of the church?

Mr. Tayler. Yes.

Mr. Talmage. Which?

Mr. Tayler. The latter.

Mr. Talmage. Then I do not know.

Mr. Tayler. Have you any idea?

Mr. Talmage. No other than to say it was toward the end of the lifetime of Joseph Smith, I assume.

Mr. Tayler. Then you are ready to say that it was practiced prior to the death of Joseph Smith?

Mr. Talmage. According to my understanding, it was. I have met women who have told me that they were the wives of Joseph Smith.

Mr. Tayler. You have met women who have told you that?

Mr. Talmage. Yes, sir.

Mr. Tayler. Did you learn how long before his death they had married him?

Mr. Talmage. No, sir.

Mr. Tayler. How many such women have you seen, Doctor?

Mr. Talmage. I think I can definitely say I have met two.

Mr. Tayler. That is, who were plural wives?

Mr. Talmage. Yes, sir.

Mr. Tayler. Have you ever seen the published statement of Joseph and Hyrum Smith denying the practice of polygamy in the church?

Mr. Talmage. I do not know to which statement you refer. I do not recognize any by that description.

Mr. Tayler. Do you know whether he made more than one?

Mr. Talmage. I do not know that he made one. A gentleman in this room called my attention yesterday, in a hurried manner—that is, I was in a state of hurry—to some publication in which there was a short article with the names of Joseph and Hyrum Smith appended. I did not read it with sufficient care to be able to express any opinion upon it, and I answer your question in this guarded way because you asked me if I had ever seen such an article.

MR. TAYLER. I will read what I had in mind: "NOTICE. As we have been lately credibly informed that an elder of the Church of Jesus Christ of Latter-day Saints by the name of Hiram Brown has been preaching polygamy and other false and corrupt doctrines in the county of Lapeer, State of Michigan, this is to notify him and the church in general that he has been cut off from the church for his iniquity; and he is further notified to appear at the special conference on the 6th of April next to make answer to these charges." That is found in "Times and Seasons," Volume V, page 423 (Dated February 1, 1844). Had you heard of that?

MR. TALMAGE. No.

MR. TAYLER. Has not that letter been the subject of frequent discussion?

MR. TALMAGE. I do not remember ever having seen that in print before yesterday. I recognize it now as the one to which my attention was called, and I am not prepared to deny its authenticity or to question or affirm that it is not authentic.

MR. TAYLER. It is referred to in this communication of Joseph F. Smith as a "seeming" denial.

MR. TALMAGE. When was that communication of Joseph F. Smith's published, if you please, and where? You kindly read the communication but you did not give me the date, if I remember correctly. I was listening for it.

MR. TAYLER. It was published on the 20th of May, 1886, in the "Deseret News." Do you understand that that is a denial of the revelation respecting plural marriage, which, in fact, Joseph Smith did receive?

MR. TALMAGE. No, sir.

MR. TAYLER. What do you interpret it to mean?

MR. TALMAGE. I would interpret that to mean that some man had been teaching, as a doctrine of the church, what had not been adopted by the church as one of its doctrines, and he was therefore worthy of excommunication for such an act—for teaching a doctrine he was not authorized to teach and preach.

MR. TAYLER. It was therefore a false doctrine and a corrupt doctrine, was it?

MR. TALMAGE. I do not know how he preached it at all.

MR. TAYLER. I am only quoting from the notice.

MR. TALMAGE. From that I could not be definite. If he was preaching as a doctrine of the church what had not been adopted by the church as a doctrine it was false in its claim to be a doctrine of the church. If he was teaching anything, whether correctly or incorrectly named by title, corrupt, it was a corrupt doctrine.

MR. TAYLER. That is to say, if Joseph Smith had received this revelation in the terms in which it is now contained in the Book of Doctrine and Covenants, if that revelation came to another Mormon through the channels that Joseph Smith had made, would not that be a revelation to him?

MR. TALMAGE. I am not quite able to follow you. You say if that revelation had come to another member of the church?

MR. TAYLER. Yes.

MR. TALMAGE. Through what kind of channels?

MR. TAYLER. We will assume—it is easier for us to ask another question than to discuss the old one. If Joseph Smith conveyed this revelation to one of his associates, and one of his associates conveyed it to Hiram Brown—named in this notice—then would you say that Hiram Brown had no authority to preach it or teach it or live it?

MR. TALMAGE. Most assuredly.

MR. TAYLER. What?

MR. TALMAGE. I would answer yes; he had no authority to preach that unless he was so commissioned to do.

MR. TAYLER. And doing so would be to preach false and corrupt doctrines?

MR. TALMAGE. In the sense in which I have answered that question before; yes.

MR. TAYLER. Now, this appears over the signature of Hyrum Smith:

Nauvoo, March 15, 1844.

To the Brethren of the Church of Jesus Christ of Latter-Day Saints living on China Creek, in Hancock County, greeting:

Whereas Brother Richard Hewitt has called on me to-day to know my views concerning some doctrines that are preached in your place, and stated to me that some of your elders say that a man having a certain priesthood may have as many wives as he pleases, and that that doctrine is taught here, I say unto you that that man teaches false doctrine, for there is no such doctrine taught here; neither is there any such thing practiced here. And any man that is found teaching privately or publicly any such doctrine is culpable and will stand a chance to be brought before the high council and lose his license and membership also; therefore he had better be aware of what he is about. Hyrum Smith.

Do you understand that to be a denial of the doctrine of polygamy?

MR. TALMAGE. Not if I understand English.

MR. TAYLER. Not if you understand English?

MR. TALMAGE. Yes.

MR. TAYLER. But it is a denial that a man having a certain priesthood may have as many wives as he pleases. That is what it denies, is it?

MR. TALMAGE. Plainly so.

MR. TAYLER. And it was not intended to convey the impression that polygamy was not permitted at all, was it?

MR. TALMAGE. I have not so stated and can not so state, from counsel's reading. I should want to consider the context and the conditions and circumstances under which that was given, but, interpreting it from the single reading, I should say no, it was not so intended, as I gather from the reading.

MR. TAYLER. I will read it over, because I do not want to—

MR. TALMAGE. Would counsel permit me to read it, if you please?

MR. TAYLER. Surely; and I ask you the question whether, upon reading it—and I will be obliged if you will read it aloud before you answer the question—whether that was intended to leave the impression that polygamy was not practiced?

Mr. Talmage (after examining the letter). Did I understand counsel to request me to read this?

MR. TAYLER. Yes, and answer it.

MR. WORTHINGTON. Yes; I would like to have you read aloud the part you are going to refer to, so that we will all know what is the subject of discussion.

MR. TALMAGE (reading). ... I would answer counsel's question by saying that I see there no denial that polygamy had been practiced before that time. I see nothing that would justify the inference that it had been, but I see a positive denial of what is there designated as false doctrine, in the matter of the alleged preaching of this man, to the effect that a man having a certain grade of priesthood was at liberty to wed as many wives as he liked, and that that was not practiced at the place from which the letter was sent.

MR. TAYLER. So that if you had been called upon, under the circumstances that existed at that time, to meet the charge that a man holding a certain priesthood could have as many wives as he wanted, you would have felt that this answer, if you had given it so, would have been candid and not intended to be misleading?

MR. TALMAGE. Yes, sir. The charge, as I understand it there, is not that men in the church were practicing polygamy—

MR. TAYLER. No.

MR. TALMAGE. But that men having a certain grade of priesthood were claiming certain rights, as privileges attached to that grade of priesthood which they held, and among them to take as many wives as they liked; and by implication and inference those who had not reached that grade of priesthood were to be limited in the number of their wives, and I think that would be a very bad condition.

MR. TAYLER. I see. So that the important thing, and the outrageous thing, in that, was not that a man might not have as many wives as he wanted, but that one grade of priesthood could have more than another grade?

MR. TALMAGE. The latter point appears to be the one that is there denounced, and the other is not touched upon; and I take it that question is not before me unless counsel presents it in a specific way.

MR. TAYLER. The president of the church—

THE CHAIRMAN. Mr. Tayler, before you go to another subject, I would like to ask this question for my information: I understood you to say that you knew that President Smith had two plural wives?

MR. TALMAGE. Joseph Smith?

THE CHAIRMAN. Yes.

MR. TALMAGE. I made the statement that according to my remembrance I have met at least two women who have said that they were plural wives of Joseph Smith; yes, sir.

THE CHAIRMAN. Are those women now living?

MR. TALMAGE. One of them died recently. The other, I think, is still living. Yes, she is still living.

THE CHAIRMAN. Do you know where?

MR. TALMAGE. Yes; in Salt Lake City.

THE CHAIRMAN. What is her name?

MR. TALMAGE. Bathsheba Smith.[18] ...

---

18. The next day, Talmage modified his testimony:

Yesterday, counsel for the protestants, I think, asked me in regard to my statement that there were women known to me who had stated that they were wives of Joseph Smith; and I named one whom I should not have named, who was present at the time I was talking with others. That was Mrs. Bathsheba Smith. ... The names I intended to

Mr. Tayler. How did Joseph F. Smith get into the twelve apostles after he was a first counselor?

Mr. Talmage. As I say, the custom has been that after a man has been ordained to the office of an apostle, and has been made one of the quorum of the twelve, and then has been removed from that by being elevated to the presidency, on the death of the president he is still considered to be one of the apostles. Of course, if there were twelve members in that quorum before the death of the president, and his two counselors had been previously ordained apostles, there would be fourteen apostles at that time.

Mr. Tayler. Then, as a matter of fact, have there ever been, actively, in what you call the quorum of twelve, thirteen men.

Mr. Talmage. Of course, thirteen men would not be supposed to compose the quorum of twelve, but there have been, and are to-day, I suppose, more than thirteen apostles.

Mr. Tayler. But can there be more than fifteen apostles?

Mr. Talmage. Yes, sir.

Mr. Tayler. There can be?

Mr. Talmage. There are to-day more.

Mr. Tayler. Who are they?

Mr. Talmage. I do not know. There are men who have been ordained to the apostleship and are not members of the quorum of the twelve.

Mr. Tayler. I am not talking about men who are deposed. Is Moses Thatcher an apostle?

Mr. Talmage. No, sir. I do not mean that either. There have been men who have been ordained to the apostleship and who have never been members of the quorum of the twelve.

Mr. Tayler. There are?

Mr. Talmage. Yes, sir.

Mr. Tayler. Who?

Mr. Talmage. I do not know the names of living men, to be definite and sure.

Mr. Tayler. This is an interesting subject that we had not known about. Who has been?

Mr. Talmage. The man's given name I forget. May I be permitted to ask a question openly, just to get an initial or a name?

Mr. Tayler. It is only a matter of getting it later. You may get it and give it to us to-morrow.

give [were] ... Lucy W. Kimball, a personal acquaintance of mine, and the other, now dead, Mrs. Zina D. H. Young (*Smoot Hearings,* 3:115).

Mr. Talmage. There is a man named Young, but his first name I can not tell you.[19]

Mr. Tayler. Do you mean to say that now there are fifteen apostles?

Mr. Talmage. I say there may be. There are more apostles than twelve. ...

Mr. Tayler. In your opinion the Mormon people are chaste both in their life and in their opinions, are they not?

Mr. Talmage. Yes, sir.

Mr. Tayler. That is one of the chief glories of your people?

Mr. Talmage. It is one of their virtues.

Mr. Tayler. I mean, not one of their special virtues, but one of their virtues that is claimed to be their distinguishing virtue as compared with other peoples in the world?

Mr. Talmage. Well, they are not in the habit of making invidious comparisons. They simply attach, I think, a greater degree of gravity to offenses that are opposed to chastity and virtue.

Mr. Tayler. That is what I mean. Then any person who has entered into plural marriage since the manifesto has committed an unchaste act?

Mr. Talmage. Is that a statement or a question?

Mr. Tayler. It is a question.

Mr. Talmage. In my judgment, yes.

Mr. Tayler. Do you understand that persons, if there are any, who have entered into such relations since that time have been so considered by the community?

Mr. Talmage. I do not know of any who have entered into such relations since that time.

Mr. Tayler. You do not?

Mr. Talmage. No, sir.

Mr. Tayler. Have you heard of Apostle Abram Cannon?

Mr. Talmage. If counsel desires to bring up rumors, I have heard of many. I have heard that I have entered into plural marriage since the manifesto, but I knew it to be untrue.

Mr. Tayler. We have got you on the stand now and you deny it—not that I ever heard the rumor or thought of asking any such question. But you attach to the Abram Cannon case no more importance than that of a mere rumor?

Mr. Talmage. I have never investigated it.

Mr. Tayler. Have you read the testimony in this case?

19. Talmage meant John Willard Young, a son of Brigham Young, who at age eleven was ordained an apostle by his father but never became a member of the Quorum of the Twelve.

MR. TALMAGE. Yes, sir.

MR. TAYLER. All of it respecting that episode?

MR. TALMAGE. Well, that episode recurs again and again. I have read a great part of the testimony presented in volume 1. I have not had access to the whole of volume 2.

MR. TAYLER. And, reading the testimony in the case, do you believe that Abram Cannon took a plural wife about 1896?

MR. TALMAGE. I have no belief on the subject. Abram Cannon is dead.

MR. TAYLER. That would not affect your belief, would it? Or is it that you do not want to do injustice to a man who is not here to defend himself?

MR. TALMAGE. That is in part the case. I would like to ask him. I have not seen yet any proof—

MR. TAYLER. You have not?

MR. TALMAGE. That is to me conclusive, but I have not given the subject thorough study, realizing—

MR. TAYLER. You have no—

MR. VAN COTT. Finish your answer, Doctor.

MR. TALMAGE. Realizing that there are the proper means of investigation into that, or would be if he were still living.

MR. TAYLER. So that you had no opinion about it that he had a plural wife?

MR. TALMAGE. Oh, he had a plural wife. I understand he had plural wives.

MR. TAYLER. Married to him in 1896?

MR. TALMAGE. No; I have no definite opinion.

MR. TAYLER. You have no knowledge that Lillian Hamlin was his plural wife?

MR. TALMAGE. Only what I have heard or read here.

MR. TAYLER. That would make no impression upon you mind, in the way of forming an opinion one way or the other?

MR. TALMAGE. In the way of forming an opinion upon which I would rely; no, sir. I do not consider, in other words, that there is proof.

MR. TAYLER. You know that Lillian Hamlin's name is associated with him in that relation, do you not?

MR. TALMAGE. Yes sir; I have heard it associated frequently.

MR. TAYLER. And you have heard also that she had a child that was called Cannon, have you not?

MR. TALMAGE. I read that in the testimony,[20] but I had never heard of it otherwise.

---

20. Abraham's cousin, Angus M. Cannon Jr., testified earlier that Lillian Hamlin

MR. TAYLER. Have you any opinion upon the question, upon the one hand, that Lillian Hamlin was an unchaste woman, or that Abram Cannon did not marry her?

MR. TALMAGE. I do not think I am brought to the alternative of forming one or the other of those opinions. From what little I know of the lady named, she has always appeared to me to be a lady of refinement and of high virtues in all respects.

MR. TAYLER. If she did marry Abram Cannon in 1896, then she was not a chaste woman, according to your standard?

MR. TALMAGE. I say again, is that a statement or a question? If a statement, I pronounce it untrue. If a question, I answer no; that is not my opinion. ...

MR. TAYLER. Do you imagine that if Abram Cannon took a plural wife in 1896 he suspected that he was taking her otherwise than in violation of the law of the church and of the land?

MR. TALMAGE. I am not Abram Cannon's judge. I do not know how he interpreted that manifesto. I do not know by what authority, if any, he took a wife in 1896 or any other time subsequent to the manifesto.

MR. TAYLER. Was there difficulty in interpreting the manifesto in respect to the matter of new marriages?

MR. TALMAGE. There ought not to have been, I take it. ...

MR. TAYLER. ... The book which is now called the Doctrine and Covenants, under whatever name it may have appeared, was first published seventy years or more ago, was it not?

MR. TALMAGE. I do not know anything about the date of its first publication.

MR. TAYLER. I am not asking as to the exact date.

MR. TALMAGE. Then I answer, I do not know even approximately the date of its first publication.

MR. TAYLER. I do not want to press you on these matters, nor to do you the slightest injustice about them. I want you to correct me if I have erroneously apprehended your posture before this committee. I have assumed that you were here as an expert on the subject of the theological history and polity of the Mormon Church, and that as such you would know quite as definitely as anybody else about these matters with respect to which I am inquiring.

MR. TALMAGE. I must beg to decline the honor that counsel would attribute to me of appearing here as an expert on church doctrine. I am

---

had a child named Marba Cannon. The name "Marba" is "Abram" spelled backwards. See chapter 14 in this volume; *Smoot Hearings,* 1:1067.

here as one who has given some little time to the study of the church doctrines and am perfectly willing to give any information I may have without reservation.

MR. TAYLER. I understand.

MR. TALMAGE. The date of the adoption of the Doctrine and Covenants by the church and the date of its first publication I can not give for the best and most sincere of reasons—I do not know.

MR. TAYLER. I do not doubt that at all. You have no doubt that the Doctrine and Covenants, whether by that name or some other, containing nearly all of what is now embodied in the book called the Doctrine and Covenants, was published in the early days of the church?

MR. TALMAGE. Comparatively speaking, early days, yes. I can not give the date, however.

MR. TAYLER. There was a revelation respecting marriage prior to the revelation respecting celestial and plural marriage, was there not?

MR. TALMAGE. I know of no revelation bearing specifically on that subject.

MR. TAYLER. In the original publication of the Covenants and Commandments was there a section on the subject of marriage?

MR. TALMAGE. I do not know. I do not think I have ever seen the book itself ... but have seen references to such. ...

THE CHAIRMAN. Do you know whether or not the services at Kirtland [Ohio], in the temple, are now open; are public services?

MR. TALMAGE. Are now open?

THE CHAIRMAN. I do not mean this minute, but whether they are open services or secret services?

MR. TALMAGE. At the present time?

THE CHAIRMAN. Yes.

MR. TALMAGE. I know nothing about it. The Church of Jesus Christ of Latter-Day Saints has nothing to do with the Kirtland temple. It is in the hands of the reorganized church. I say I know nothing about it, though I do know this—

THE CHAIRMAN. I am speaking of the reorganized church occupying that building. Do you know whether their services are secret or public?

MR. TALMAGE. I know nothing. I have had the privilege of visiting that building once—

THE CHAIRMAN. Have you any information on the subject?

MR. TALMAGE. No, sir; nothing except a general impression.

THE CHAIRMAN. Is it your impression that they are secret?

MR. TALMAGE. No, sir; my impression is they are public, but I know nothing definite on the subject.

MR. TAYLER. Do you understand that the reorganized church has departed from the methods that were prevalent prior to the death of Joseph Smith?

MR. TALMAGE. I confess my ignorance as to the tenets and practices of
the reorganized church. I am thoroughly convinced of the departure
of the reorganized church, so called, from the possession and exercise of and control by the authorized priesthood, and I have taken no
interest in investigating them further.

MR. TAYLER. Is it your understanding that the reorganized church has
repudiated, repealed, or modified a single revelation that the church
was known to be in possession of prior to the death of Joseph Smith?

MR. TALMAGE. I know of no specific instances of such, and therefore
could not answer.

MR. TAYLER. Your understanding is, whatever different interpretations
may have been put upon revelations, that the reorganized church
assumes and claims to stand upon every word and line that the other
branch of the church stood upon prior to Joseph Smith's death?

MR. TALMAGE. I have heard that that is the assumption by them.

MR. TAYLER. And that in their books they publish every word and line
that was known to the people prior to that time?

MR. TALMAGE. I have heard that they so claim.

MR. TAYLER. Now, as to the date when secrecy in these ceremonies first
appeared, you can give me no information?

MR. TALMAGE. No, sir.

MR. TAYLER. You stated, if I remember correctly, that there was no vow or
obligation taken during the ceremony?

MR. TALMAGE. I am not aware of having said anything of the kind.

MR. TAYLER. What was it you said in that connection?

MR. TALMAGE. I stated that there was no oath taken. Most assuredly an
obligation is taken when one enters into any kind of an ordinance, sacred or otherwise. There must be some obligation. There is an obligation connected with the ordinance of baptism. There is an obligation connected with the ordinance of marriage, within or outside the
church. But, in the matter of oaths, I have stated that I have taken no
oath in any part of the temple ceremony or in any other ceremony
connected with the church.

MR. TAYLER. But that you had taken certain obligations?

MR. TALMAGE. I had considered myself under certain obligations. As to
whether I took them in formal manner or not, I am not impressed
that I did, except in the marriage vows, which are of a kind, common

in nature to those made elsewhere, with the modification implied in the revelation of celestial marriage.

MR. TAYLER. I understand. Then, if I use the term, it will be in the sense in which you are using it—that it was an obligation that you assumed, whether it was in formal terms, as you put it, or whether it came from the method in which the duty was enjoined upon you. Was an obligation of chastity taken?

MR. TALMAGE. I consider myself under an obligation of chastity.

MR. TAYLER (to the reporter). Will you read the question?

THE CHAIRMAN. That is not answering the question.

MR. TALMAGE. I do not remember any definite obligation there taken in a formal manner—I am not trying to evade the question at all—but, as already stated, in answer to counsel, there are certain obligations under which I consider myself placed, whether taken formally or not, and in connection with my membership in the church, I consider myself under that obligation, and it is just as binding on me as if I had taken it in the form of an oath.

THE CHAIRMAN. Now the question was a very simple one—whether you took an obligation of chastity?

MR. TALMAGE. In the sense in which I have used the term "obligation," in considering myself under it, whether taken in due form or not, I answer "yes."

THE CHAIRMAN. The question is whether such an obligation was taken?

MR. WORTHINGTON. In that ceremony?

MR. TALMAGE. And in the sense in which I have used the term; yes.

THE CHAIRMAN. In the sense that you feel yourself under that obligation all the time, without regard to that—

MR. TALMAGE. Whether administered in formal manner or not I can not say—

THE CHAIRMAN. But can you not tell the committee whether in that ceremony there was an obligation of chastity?

MR. TALMAGE. I answer yes. I have already explained what I mean by obligation.

THE CHAIRMAN. We understand. What next, Mr. Tayler.

MR. TAYLER. Was there an obligation of sacrifice?

MR. TALMAGE. No; not as I understand your term.

MR. TAYLER. Was there anything in this ceremony that led you to promise, either in terms or by implication, to devote yourself for life, and your best efforts, to the cause of your church?

MR. TALMAGE. To the question presented in that form I will have to answer "no." I am quite willing to make an explanation if desired.

MR. TAYLER. Yes.

MR. TALMAGE. I can not say that any specific obligation was administered or taken to that effect, but by implication I consider myself under obligation to devote my energies and weak talents to the advancement of truth, but not to the advancement of the church specifically. I know of no obligation to that effect.

MR. TAYLER. Then there is nothing at all specific in the ceremonies which refers to any personal duty on your part to the church?

MR. TALMAGE. Is that a question?

MR. TAYLER. Yes.

MR. TALMAGE. I call to mind nothing of the kind.

MR. TAYLER. Is there any obligation respecting the prophets?

MR. TALMAGE. Is that the whole of your question?

MR. TAYLER. Yes.

MR. TALMAGE. I do not understand it.

THE CHAIRMAN. Read the question.

The reporter read as follows: "Mr. Tayler. Is there any obligation respecting the prophets?"

MR. TALMAGE. I can not tell what you mean by an obligation respecting the prophets. Will you kindly be specific?

MR. TAYLER. If you think I must be.

MR. TALMAGE. Certainly, sir, if I am to answer it, because I can not answer what I do not understand.

MR. TAYLER. You have no idea what I mean?

MR. TALMAGE. No, sir.

MR. TAYLER. None at all?

MR. TALMAGE. No, sir. Your question suggests to me absolutely nothing connected with any ceremony I have passed through.

MR. TAYLER. Then there is not anything about it. Why could you not answer it that way?

MR. TALMAGE. Because the question is so indefinite and I do not wish to give definite answers to indefinite questions. You asked me if there be any obligation with respect to the prophets?

MR. TAYLER. Exactly. Is there or is there not? Can you not tell, or have you forgotten, or do you not know?

MR. TALMAGE. If that question is to be considered definite, I simply have to answer I know nothing about it.

MR. TAYLER. Is there any reference to the prophets in the ceremonies?

MR. TALMAGE. I remember none.

MR. TAYLER. Is there any reference by name, or description, or implication to Joseph Smith?

MR. TALMAGE. I remember none.

MR. WORTHINGTON. You mean Joseph Smith, jr., the prophet?

MR. TAYLER. Of course.

MR. TALMAGE. I remember none.

MR. TAYLER. And your attention is nowhere in the ceremony called to any of the early leaders of the church?

MR. TALMAGE. I remember none; that is, I remember no instance of my attention being called to such as you ask.

MR. TAYLER. There was a witness here the other day, put on the stand by Senator Smoot, who testified that there was an obligation to the effect that they were to pray God to avenge—

MR. WORTHINGTON. The blood of the prophets on this generation.

MR. TAYLER. The blood of the prophets on this generation. Do you recall anything in substance of that kind?

MR. TALMAGE. Not as I have read it.

MR. TAYLER. Not as you have what?

MR. TALMAGE. And nothing in the way of any covenants respecting, or prayer for vengeance on anybody in any sense that is other than spiritual; and the details I do not remember.

MR. TAYLER. So, if you felt free to state what the language was upon which this statement of Mr. [Hugh M.] Dougall seems to be based, you would say that it contained no such words?

MR. TALMAGE. I should like to see the statement of Mr. Dougall to which you refer. I have not read that part. I have not had those sheets in my hands.

MR. TAYLER. Mr. Worthington quoted it for me. I want to be careful not to make a mistake about it. But it seems that the copy containing that expression is in the printing office.

MR. WORTHINGTON. I am perfectly clear in my recollection of the exact substance. He said it was an obligation to avenge the blood of the prophets on this generation.

MR. TAYLER. I am sure that is right, also.

MR. WORTHINGTON. He said something about its being said in a lecture, but that was the language.

THE CHAIRMAN. Used in the course of the ceremony.

MR. TAYLER. Yes. If you felt free to repeat this whole ceremony, you would not be able to tell us what was said in respect to the subject that Mr. Dougall had in mind when he testified. Is that correct?

MR. TALMAGE. That is correct. I do not remember the details. It is many years since I have thought of these matters.[21]

MR. TAYLER. That is all.

THE CHAIRMAN. Right here, when did you say you took the endowments?

MR. TALMAGE. In 1882, Mr. Chairman. ...

THE CHAIRMAN. And when were you last present at such a ceremony?

MR. TALMAGE. I stated yesterday, and can be no more definite to-day, several years ago; five anyway, possibly more.

THE CHAIRMAN. Five years ago?

MR. WORTHINGTON. At least five.

MR. TALMAGE. At least five. (A pause.) Oh, it is more than that. It is at least eight, as I call to mind the years. It is at least eight, and more than that, most likely. ...

MR. WORTHINGTON. Doctor, there is some testimony in this case about the repute as to what Heber J. Grant said on a certain occasion with reference to his having two wives, and if I remember correctly, that he wished he had another, or something to that effect. You have read the evidence on that subject, have you?

MR. TALMAGE. Yes, sir.

MR. WORTHINGTON. Can you give us any information as to the repute in the institution where that is said to have occurred about that transaction?

SENATOR MCCOMAS. Is this a young ladies' seminary?

MR. VAN COTT. No; it was at chapel exercises at the University of Utah.

THE CHAIRMAN. In some exercises in the University of Utah he made a speech in which be said that he contributed so much, I think $150, $50 for each of his wives.

MR. WORTHINGTON. He is reputed to have said that, but we have had no testimony from anybody who heard it. It was also stated that he was reputed to have said he only regretted that he had not another wife, so that he could give another $50. I am asking the Doctor if he knows anything about the repute in the institution where that is said to have occurred in regard to it.

MR. TALMAGE. Yes, sir.

MR. WORTHINGTON. How did you get your information as to the reputation?

MR. TALMAGE. I was not present at the chapel exercises referred to. The exercises are somewhat misnamed. They are known among the students as their assembly gathering or assembly exercises. They are not

---

21. See chapter 21 in this volume; *Smoot Hearings*, 2:758-59, 762-65.

intended to be religious exercises wholly, and sometimes not at all religious. On the occasion referred to, though, I was in the building. I was not in the room, not knowing that Mr. Grant was going to speak. I am informed he was there by invitation, as many men have appeared in turn by invitation, and was referring to the action taken by the alumni association of the university in establishing an alumni scholarship fund, and expressed his regret that there had not been a more prompt and more liberal response, and that the remarks referred to by counsel were then made. I made inquiry, having heard casually of what had been said, and I know the impression made upon the president of the university, who at the time was presiding over the assembly, and upon several of the professors and upon a great many of the students, but I was not present myself.

MR. WORTHINGTON. Nobody has testified about who was present, so I will ask you what the reputation is in the institution where the thing is said to have happened?

MR. TALMAGE. The president of the university[22] informed me, soon after the occurrence, that the event, in his judgment, was insignificant in a way, and that most assuredly Mr. Grant had not intended to there announce or affirm his belief in polygamy in the sense of trying to induce others to adopt that belief.

THE CHAIRMAN. This is what the president told you? You did not hear it?

MR. TALMAGE. I repeat. sir, I was not present, and this is the statement made to me by the president very soon after the occurrence, and repeated to me a few days before I left on my journey hither.

SENATOR MCCOMAS. You were not present and did not hear it, and you are now undertaking to give, from hearsay, a statement of the president as to what his impression was of what Mr. Grant thought or intended?

MR. TALMAGE. Precisely so, as that is what counsel asked for.

MR. WORTHINGTON. This was stated by persons who were not present, Senator.

SENATOR MCCOMAS. What the president stated as to what this man intended to say, it seems to me, is not of any value to us.

MR. WORTHINGTON. What I am trying to get is the effect it made upon those who heard this statement, as to whether it was a serious statement or simply a jest.

SENATOR MCCOMAS. A jocular remark?

---

22. The president of the University of Utah was Joseph T. Kingsbury, who served from 1892 to 1894 and again from 1897 to 1916. Talmage had been president between Kingsbury's two terms (*Smoot Hearings*, 3:112-13).

MR. WORTHINGTON. A jocular remark. The Doctor has talked with the faculty and a great many of the students who heard this, I understand.

MR. TALMAGE. Yes, sir.

MR. WORTHINGTON. I do not care about your going into the details of conversations you had with any particular person, but from information obtained in this way, what do you say as to what the understanding there was, that it was said in jest or seriously?

MR. TALMAGE. I have found no one, either a member of the faculty or a student, who was present and who regarded the incident in any other way than as a jest. Many of them made the remark that it was ill-timed humor, and I have not found any of them who commends the remark; but they are all unanimous—those with whom I have spoken, and I have spoken with many—in saying that the remark appeared to be called forth and suggested by the occasion. Mr. Grant had made the remarks to which I refer and expressed regret that more members of the association had not responded liberally. He said that he had paid $50 in for each of three—"Myself"—

THE CHAIRMAN. Three what?

MR. TALMAGE. Three members of the alumni association.

MR. WORTHINGTON. He is going on to state it, Mr. Chairman.

MR. TALMAGE. "Myself," said he, "and each of my two wives." Thereupon there was an incipient cheer on the part of some, a slight clapping, and some little laughter, as the president and others have described to me, and the speaker appeared to be embarrassed, and added, "Yes, I have two wives," and then made some remark that he regretted he had not another—the precise words I know not—perhaps to serve as an excuse, as the chairman has very properly suggested, for giving another $50.

SENATOR MCCOMAS. It was not a joke that he had two wives?

MR. TALMAGE. That is no joke; that is a fact. And, having admitted that, or said so much, he very frankly followed it by the remark that seems to have caused some misunderstanding. Anyone who knows Mr. Grant will know very well that he is very frank in his remarks and that he intended nothing more than what was said.

MR. WORTHINGTON. Was there not a limitation there, that each person was limited to $50 for each individual?

MR. TALMAGE. I so understand; and many had paid much less than that, and he paid the full $50 for himself and the two ladies who were members of the association before they were his wives, and he regretted that he had not an excuse for paying more in the same way.

MR. WORTHINGTON. Which meant that he regretted he could not contribute more to the institution. That is what he meant?

MR. TALMAGE. Perhaps so. He said he regretted he had not another wife, and I believe it.

SENATOR OVERMAN. That he had not married another member of the alumni association? (Laughter.)

MR. TALMAGE. Yes. I would desire to add, since I have been permitted to give the results of my inquiry, that I asked the president, who is ex officio a member of the board of regents, and other members, how they regarded it, and was told—

THE CHAIRMAN. Mr. Worthington, do you want the witness to give the conversation he had with all the people he talked to?

MR. WORTHINGTON. My idea about it is that all the testimony on this subject ought not to have been received, and that it is utterly unworthy of any consideration whatever; but if it is competent for witnesses to take the stand and tell what they hear about a general sort of rumor about what took place there, why is it not competent to have what was said stated by those who were there? It is much better evidence to have what those who were present said than what people on the street say, it seems to me.

THE CHAIRMAN. If we let the witness go on and detail all the conversations he has had with every person at the school it will take us the balance of the week.

MR. WORTHINGTON. No; I do not ask that. I would like the witness to be allowed to finish this particular statement that he was about to make.

THE CHAIRMAN. Very well; witness, proceed and make it as brief as you can and as rapidly as you can.

MR. TALMAGE. I had already stated, I believe, that I had spoken with members of the board of regents and made inquiry as to whether the matter had been considered by them, and I am told that the members of the board of regents, who were in no way connected with the Mormon Church, regarded it in the light I have described, and were quite willing to accept the money. The feeling was openly expressed that if there was anything improper about it, that money ought not to be accepted. It has not only been accepted, but students are very eager to get the benefit from it.

MR. WORTHINGTON. This is not a Mormon institution, then, solely?

MR. TALMAGE. Not at all, sir. It is the State University.

MR. WORTHINGTON. The president, to whom you spoke, was a Gentile?

MR. TALMAGE. Yes, sir.

MR. WORTHINGTON. And some of the members of the faculty?

MR. TALMAGE. Yes, sir; many of them.

MR. WORTHINGTON. And many of the professors and students?

MR. TALMAGE. Yes, sir.

MR. WORTHINGTON. That is all.

SENATOR MCCOMAS. What use did you propose to make of all this inquiry from so many people about a remark which you thought was merely a jocular remark?

MR. TALMAGE. For the simple reason that an inflammatory sheet published in Salt Lake City did not so regard it and tried to make out there was something serious about it. I inquired of a number of the faculty who are members of the Mormon Church and they had little to say, any more than that they were sorry that the remark had been made, because so much was being made out of it, and that it was not worthy of the attention given it. Then I inquired of a number of the non-Mormon members of the faculty and of very many of the students, and of members of the board of regents, some of whom were present.

SENATOR MCCOMAS. How many members of the faculty were there?

MR. TALMAGE. Present?

SENATOR MCCOMAS. No; altogether, in the faculty.

MR. TALMAGE. Of professors and instructors, above 30.

SENATOR MCCOMAS. About how many of them were Mormons?

MR. TALMAGE. I could not tell you without reckoning up, but—

SENATOR MCCOMAS. Half?

MR. TALMAGE. No; less than half.

SENATOR MCCOMAS. Two-thirds?

MR. TALMAGE. Less than half, Senator.[23]

SENATOR MCCOMAS.[24] That is all.[25] ...

---

23. For another view on the episode, see Charles Mostyn Owen's testimony in chapter 19 of this volume; *Smoot Hearings*, 2:401-02.

24. McComas left the Senate at the end of his term in 1905. On the selection of his replacement, Smoot wrote, "A member of the committee ... came to me and asked me whom I wanted on the Committee on Privileges and Elections to fill the vacancy caused by Sen. McComas going out. I told him I would prefer Dolliver [R-Iowa] as first choice and Dick [R-Ohio] as second. My friends on the committee will work to that end" (Smoot to Joseph F Smith, Dec. 12, 1905). Smoot got his wish: Dolliver was named as McComas's replacement.

25. Carl Badger wrote to his wife on January 19: "Dr. Talmage has been on the stand for two days; he has made the star witness. The papers do not do him justice; he has simply floored Tayl[e]r. ... The [Salt Lake] Tribune is making a cur of itself; Frank Cannon

---

[editor] is a fool. The trouble with a man when he begins to fight something that he thinks is wrong is that he is likely to go to the extreme. This is especially true when it comes to religion, which arouses us to the greatest love and hate." To his wife again on January 22, Badger related a conversation with Talmage wherein the professor spoke of someone who had said that "anyone who wanted to get a new wife could do so" and Talmage's reprimand of the church member who had expressed the sentiment. This was music to Badger's ears:

> There is no denying that such a doctrine has been preached by some of the leading men and women of the Church, and that some of our best young women have fallen victims of the deception. Well. I feel better: I can stand with the authorities in a clean up, but I cannot, and will not, in shielding the wrong doers, and will denounce and fight any campaign of fraud and dishonor in which it is attempted to deceive the government and people of the United States. Such a plan of deception has been attempted in the past few years by a few leaders, and it [is] the foundation of all our shame and ill repute at the present time, and is damnable, and must stop" (in Rodney J. Badger, *Liahona and Iron Rod: The Biography of Carl A. and Rose J. Badger* [Bountiful, Utah: Family History Publishers, 1985], 246).

24.

Glen Miller and John W. Hughes

Thursday, January 19

"Chairman Burrows is still unable to induce senators to attend the sessions of the committee, Senators Overman and Dubois being the only ones in any way constant in presenting themselves. But when the attorneys proceed with their arguments, which will be some day next week, it is probable that nearly all will be on hand, in fact, promises have been made by every one to listen to the summing up." —*Deseret News,* Jan. 19, 1905

Glen Miller,[1] being duly sworn, was examined and testified as follows ...

MR. VAN COTT. Did you have anything to do with the convention in Salt Lake County that nominated legislators who would sit in the legislature that elected Mr. Smoot as United States Senator?

MR. MILLER. Yes, sir.

MR. VAN COTT. What did you have to do with them?

MR. MILLER. I was a delegate in that convention, and I was chairman of our delegation.

MR. VAN COTT. Were you what is called a Smoot man?

MR. MILLER. No, sir.

MR. VAN COTT. Were you anti-Smoot?

MR. MILLER. I was opposed to Senator Smoot, or rather to the candidates for the legislature who were in his favor. I was opposed to them.

MR. VAN COTT. My question is in that sense.

MR. MILLER. Yes, sir.

MR. VAN COTT. Was it understood in the convention which legislators would be Smoot and which anti-Smoot?

MR. MILLER. Yes, distinctly.

MR. VAN COTT. You have spoken of some districts being strongly Mormon

---

1. Miller (1863-1936) was forty-one years old at the time of his testimony. He was born in Ohio and moved to Utah in 1889. A non-Mormon, formerly of the Liberal Party, he had worked in the banking industry and on the *Salt Lake Tribune* editorial staff. He had also been a state senator and U.S. marshall.

or strongly Gentile. Do you know of any districts in that convention that were Mormon and at the same time opposed to the legislators who were supposed to support Mr. Smoot?

MR. MILLER. Yes, sir.

MR. VAN COTT. What is the fact?

MR. MILLER. The western portion of the fourth precinct, of which I am chairman, is almost distinctly a Mormon district. I suppose 85 per cent of the population there are Mormons. Those three districts (the thirty-seventh, thirty-eighth, and thirty-ninth districts) cast their votes solidly against the Smoot candidates for the legislature. The Gentile districts in that precinct, being in the eastern end, are probably 75 per cent Gentiles. They cast their votes for the Smoot candidates. It was a case in which the Gentile delegates voted for the Smoot candidates and the Mormon delegates voted against them.

MR. VAN COTT. And Mr. Smoot was at that time an apostle?

MR. MILLER. Yes, sir.

MR. VAN COTT. And that was known?

MR. MILLER. Yes, sir; absolutely.

MR. VAN COTT. Did any of the Gentiles who supported Mr. Smoot in the convention—and by that I mean these legislators—afterwards oppose him?

MR. MILLER. Yes, sir.

MR. VAN COTT. Did these same Gentiles also work in the campaign?

MR. MILLER. Yes, sir.

MR. VAN COTT. For the election of these same legislators?

MR. MILLER. Yes, sir.

MR. VAN COTT. Do you know Mr. Smoot personally?

MR. MILLER. Yes, sir.

MR. VAN COTT. How long have you known him?

MR. MILLER. I presume about twelve years—certainly over ten years.

MR. VAN COTT. What can you say as to his prominence in respect to politics before his election as a United States Senator?

MR. MILLER. He was one of the most prominent, one of the foremost men in his party; I think probably he was the most prominent Republican in the section of the State from which he came.[2] ...

2. When James Talmage traveled to Washington, D.C., he wrote in his journal on January 12 that "Mr. Glen Miller of Salt Lake City, who was US Marshall for Utah," was among the passengers, along with "Mrs. Coulter of Ogden" (in L. Tom Perry Special Collections, Harold B. Lee Library, Brigham Young University, Provo, Utah).

John W. Hughes,[3] having duly sworn, was examined and testified as follows ...

MR. VAN COTT. Do you belong to the Mormon Church?

MR. HUGHES. No.

MR. VAN COTT. Have you ever?

MR. HUGHES. No.

MR. VAN COTT. Do you belong to the Presbyterian Church?

MR. HUGHES. Yes.

MR. VAN COTT. Are you connected in any way with the newspaper business.

MR. HUGHES. Yes; I have been in the newspaper business for about twenty years.

MR. VAN COTT. What paper do you conduct, if any, at the present time?

MR. HUGHES. "Truth," of Salt Lake City, a weekly paper.

MR. VAN COTT. Have you been a reporter on any daily papers in Salt Lake City.

MR. HUGHES. Yes, sir; I was a reporter on either the "Tribune" or the "Herald" from 1891, the time I went there first, until three years and a half ago, when I started my own paper.

MR. VAN COTT. Have you had occasion to travel over the State any?

MR. HUGHES. Not a great deal. I have traveled some.

MR. VAN COTT. You are interested, I suppose, in getting the news?

MR. HUGHES. Yes.

MR. VAN COTT. Calling attention first to the political conditions, were you a member of the Liberal party?

MR. HUGHES. No; the Liberal party was just on the eve of disbanding, and the Democratic and Republican parties were just about being formed, when I went to Salt Lake, and I did not belong to the Liberal party.

MR. VAN COTT. In politics what are you?

MR. HUGHES. I am a Republican.

MR. VAN COTT. Have you taken any interest in watching the Mormon vote; that is, whether it shifted back and forth, or whether it was constant?

MR. HUGHES. Yes. In the course of my duties as reporter on the papers, I was obliged to watch it closely and take a good deal of interest in it.

MR. VAN COTT. What is you opinion as to the constancy of the Mormon voters in adhering to their party lines?

---

3. Hughes (ca. 1857-1908) was born in Great Britain and relocated to Utah in 1891. He had been a reporter for the *Salt Lake Tribune* and *Salt Lake Herald* for some eleven years.

MR. HUGHES. As far as I have observed, and by comparison of figures at election times in Mormon precincts and Gentile precincts, I think the Mormon people have been more faithful to their party lines than the Gentiles.

MR. VAN COTT. Have you noticed when Mormon candidates, for instance, are opposed to Gentiles, as to whether Mormons in those cases adhere to their party lines?

MR. HUGHES. They do.

MR. VAN COTT. Do you know Joseph F. Smith or do you know of him?

MR. HUGHES. I know him by sight, and have known him for years. I never spoke to Mr. Smith.

MR. VAN COTT. What is the sentiment among Gentiles as to whether he is sincere in keeping the church out of politics?

MR. HUGHES. The sentiment is that he is exceedingly sincere and very honest in that regard, and in all regards, in fact. They think he is a fanatic in religion, but very honest, and that he is determined to keep the church out of politics, and has done so since he has been president. That is a strong feeling among the Gentiles. ...

MR. VAN COTT. Have you had any occasion to investigate and find out the number of polygamists, for instance, in Salt Lake City?

MR. HUGHES. Yes.

MR. VAN COTT. What is the population of Salt Lake City?

MR. HUGHES. It is approximately 70,000 to 75,000.

MR. VAN COTT. Has this investigation been recent?

MR. HUGHES. About two weeks ago.

MR. VAN COTT. How many polygamists did you find in Salt Lake City?

MR. HUGHES. Seventy-four.

MR. VAN COTT. And how many over, say, 60 years of age and under 70?

MR. HUGHES. I think more than 50 of them were over 60.

THE CHAIRMAN. Witness, when you say 74, do you mean 74 heads of families—males?

MR. HUGHES. Yes; I mean 74 men who have more than one wife.

MR. VAN COTT. Can you give their ages? I mean to group them. I do not mean in detail.

MR. HUGHES. I think about fifty of them were over 60 years of age. I have not the figures right with me.

MR. VAN COTT. And the others were over what age?

MR. HUGHES. Oh, some of them were over 70, and one or two were over 80. I think there were only two under 50. ...

MR. VAN COTT. What progress, I probably should have said. What has been the progress, in your opinion, in Utah, toward the settlement of the difficulties there during the fourteen years that have elapsed since the issuance of the manifesto?

MR. HUGHES. I think we have made very great progress. There have been a few lapses, but take it altogether it has been marvelous, the progress that has been made and the difference in sentiment, to what it was when I went to Salt Lake first. The Mormons were clannish to a great extent and stuck by themselves. The Gentiles did the same thing. They were at dagger's points. The Mormons persisted in their polygamy. The Gentiles insisted in their fighting; and the Mormon people now are as much against polygamy as the Gentiles. They are intermingled together in business and socially. They intermarry much more than they used to do; and, taking the last ten or twelve years—ten years especially—we have made wonderful progress.

MR. VAN COTT. Do you know whether a great many young Mormon men go away from Utah to be educated in the universities and colleges?

MR. HUGHES. They do. A great many go to Ann Arbor and some go to Harvard.[4]

MR. VAN COTT. Some of the young girls, too?

MR. HUGHES. Yes. ...

---

4. Two future apostles illustrate this trend: Richard R. Lyman, who had recently received a degree in civil engineering from the University of Michigan, and John A. Widtsoe, who had recently graduated in chemistry from Harvard University.

25.

Reed Smoot

Friday, January 20

"When adjournment was taken this evening it was half an hour earlier than usual, and was taken at the request of counsel for the apostolic Senator, who stated that his client was ill and needed rest; and he showed it. Pale, hollow-eyed and nervous to a high degree, he took the stand at 11 o'clock this morning. When he stepped down this evening he showed more than ever the terrible strain under which he was laboring." —*Salt Lake Tribune*, Jan. 20, 1905

MR. WORTHINGTON. Mr. Chairman and gentlemen, I wish to make an apology and explanation as to my being so late this morning. The witnesses whom we have been expecting have not yet arrived, and Mr. Van Cott and I thought we would ask the committee to adjourn today on that account. But in order to save a day we concluded that we would put Senator Smoot upon the stand at once. That necessitated my going over some matters with him, as to which I have had no opportunity to talk with him. We are now ready to go on, and I shall put him on the stand. I would suggest, Mr. Chairman, that while we have proceeded, by general consent, with much less than a quorum of the committee, it may be that if the members of the committee who are not here now knew that Senator Smoot was about to go upon the stand they might wish to be present to hear his examination. I suggest that word be sent to them that he will be upon the stand, so that, if they desire, they may be here.

THE CHAIRMAN. The Chair has been authorized by the absent members of the committee to count them for the purpose of making a quorum, which the Chair has done; but the Chair will take very great pleasure in sending for all the members of the committee who are not present.

After a little delay Mr. Dillingham, Mr. Hopkins, Mr. Foraker, Mr. Pettus, and Mr. Bailey entered the committee room.

THE CHAIRMAN. A quorum of the committee is present. ...

Reed Smoot, being duly sworn, was examined, and testified as follows ...

MR. WORTHINGTON. Give us the names of your parents, please?

SENATOR SMOOT. My father's name was Abraham O. Smoot. My mother's name was Anne K. Smoot.[1]

MR. WORTHINGTON. Both of your parents were Mormons, I believe?

SENATOR SMOOT. They were.

MR. WORTHINGTON. And I believe that your mother was a plural wife of your father?

SENATOR SMOOT. She was.

MR. WORTHINGTON. Is your father living?

SENATOR SMOOT. He is dead.

MR. WORTHINGTON. About when did he die?

SENATOR SMOOT. In 1895.

MR. WORTHINGTON. Is your mother living?

SENATOR SMOOT. She is also dead.

MR. WORTHINGTON. And she died when?

SENATOR SMOOT. She died in 1896.

MR. WORTHINGTON. Are you yourself a member of the Mormon Church?

SENATOR SMOOT. I am.

MR. WORTHINGTON. And have you been since you attained years of discretion?

SENATOR SMOOT. I have.

MR. WORTHINGTON. Are you a married man?

SENATOR SMOOT. I am.

MR. WORTHINGTON. When were you married?

SENATOR SMOOT. On September 17, 1884.[2] ...

MR. WORTHINGTON. Have you lived with her in the relation of husband and wife since that time?

SENATOR SMOOT. I have.

MR. WORTHINGTON. Have you children by her?

SENATOR SMOOT. I have.

MR. WORTHINGTON. How many?

SENATOR SMOOT. I have six children by her—three girls and three boys.[3]

MR. WORTHINGTON. Have you at any other time married any other woman?

---

1. For more, see Loretta D. Nixon and L. Douglas Smoot, *Abraham Owen Smoot: A Testament of His Life* (Provo: Brigham Young University Press, 1994).

2. Smoot's wife, Alpha May Eldredge (1863-1928), would die in Washington, D.C., at age sixty-five, during her husband's last term as U.S. Senator.

3. Reed and Alpha Smoot's six children were Chloe (1888-1977), Seth Eldredge (1891-?), Harlow Eldredge (1891-1956), Anne Kristine (1893-1938), Zella Esther (1900-85), and Ernest Winder (1902-69).

SENATOR SMOOT. I have not.[4]

MR. WORTHINGTON. Have you at any other time cohabited with any other woman in the relation of husband and wife—

SENATOR SMOOT. I have not.

MR. WORTHINGTON. Or in any other way?

SENATOR SMOOT. I have not.

MR. WORTHINGTON. When you were married to your wife, were you married according to what is known here as the celestial ceremony?

SENATOR SMOOT. I was.

MR. WORTHINGTON. Not in the temple?

SENATOR SMOOT. In the temple at Logan [Utah].

MR. WORTHINGTON. Did you at that time pass through the ceremony which is called taking the endowments?

SENATOR SMOOT. No, sir; I did not. I will state, however, that I took the endowments before.

MR. WORTHINGTON. I was just about to ask you that question. When?

SENATOR SMOOT. In the early spring of 1880.

MR. WORTHINGTON. You were then 18 years old?

SENATOR SMOOT. I was then 18 years old.

MR. WORTHINGTON. Perhaps, as that is a matter to which some importance is attributed here, you might tell us how it came that you took your endowments at that early age?

SENATOR SMOOT. My father was going to visit the Sandwich [Hawaiian] Islands for his health, and he asked me to go with him. I of course was very pleased, indeed, to accept the invitation, and before going my father asked me if I would go to the endowment house and take my endowments. I told him I did not particularly care about it. He stated to me that it certainly would not hurt me if it did not do me any good, and that, as my father, he would like very much to have me take the endowments before I crossed the water or went away from the United States. ...

MR. WORTHINGTON. Have you ever been through that ceremony except on the one occasion when you were about 18 years of age?

SENATOR SMOOT. I have not. ...

MR. WORTHINGTON. Did you take any oath or obligation when you became an apostle?

---

4. Smoot later spoke in defense of his Senate seat and emphatically declared that he was not a polygamist (Michael Harold Paulos, "'I am not and never have been a polygamist': Reed Smoot's Speech before the United States Senate, February 19, 1907," *Utah Historical Quarterly* 75 [Spring 2007], 100-115).

SENATOR SMOOT. I did not.

MR. WORTHINGTON. Do you recall the ceremony or parts of the ceremony through which you went when you took your endowments?

SENATOR SMOOT. I could not remember it if I wanted to.

MR. WORTHINGTON. Do you mean that you do not remember anything about it or that your recollection is vague?

SENATOR SMOOT. I have not enough of the details to give the committee any information.

MR. WORTHINGTON. Tell me whether or not at that time anything of this kind took place—that somebody said this which I am about to read, in substance, and that you assented to it: "That you and each of you do promise and vow that you will never cease to importune high heaven to avenge the blood of the prophets upon this nation."

SENATOR SMOOT. I did not.

MR. WORTHINGTON. Was there anything said about avenging the blood of the prophets or anything else on this nation or on this Government?

SENATOR SMOOT. No, sir.

MR. WORTHINGTON. Was there anything said about avenging the blood of Joseph Smith, jr., the prophet?

SENATOR SMOOT. No, sir. And it seems very strange that such a thing should be spoken of, because the endowments have never changed, as I understand it; it has been so testified, and that Joseph Smith, jr., himself was the founder of the endowments. It would be very strange, indeed, to have such an oath to avenge his death when he was alive.

MR. WORTHINGTON. Now let me ask you whether when you took your oath as a Senator of the United States[5] you took it with any mental reservation?

SENATOR SMOOT. None whatever.

MR. WORTHINGTON. And whether there is anything in your past life, either in connection with the church or anything else, which, in the slightest degree, affects your loyalty to your country, as recognized by that oath?

SENATOR SMOOT. No, sir.

---

5. The oath of office for a U.S. Senator reads: "I do solemnly swear (or affirm) that I will support and defend the Constitution of the United States against all enemies, foreign and domestic; that I will bear true faith and allegiance to the same; that I take this obligation freely, without any mental reservation or purpose of evasion; and that I will well and faithfully discharge the duties of the office on which I am about to enter: So help me God" (5 USC 3331).

MR. WORTHINGTON. How did you come to be a candidate for the office of Senator, Mr. Smoot?

SENATOR SMOOT. I have been rather active in politics—

MR. WORTHINGTON. Without being too modest on that subject, I wish you would give the committee a general idea of your activities in that direction prior to the time you were an open candidate for the place of Senator.

SENATOR SMOOT. I may say that before ever there was a division on party lines in the State of Utah I became interested in the principles of the two great national parties. I remember at the time of taking one of the leading Democratic papers and one of the leading Republican papers. It was about 1884, when I became manager of the Provo Woolen Mills.

I thought, of course, at the time that I was a Democrat. My father came from Kentucky. He was a staunch Democrat, and of course I thought I was a Democrat. He believed in protection, and of course it had been taught to me all my life and I believed in it.

But after studying the papers very carefully, indeed, with all the interest that I could, my mind gradually drifted toward the principles of the Republican party.

I think it was in 1888 that there were a few men in Provo, Republicans, and we organized a Republican party. That was before the division on party lines in our State. We used to meet quite often for the purpose of discussing the principles of the party, and I became deeply interested in them and in politics. I was prepared, or felt myself so, when the division on party lines came, to align myself with the Republican party, and I have been a Republican from that time on. ...

MR. WORTHINGTON. ... When did you yourself first consider the question of being a candidate for the position of Senator of the United States from Utah?

SENATOR SMOOT. Oh, I was spoken to by my political friends back as far as 1898, and especially my home town friends, to run for governor or for the Senate.

MR. WORTHINGTON. Let me interrupt you to ask whether these friends you speak of were Mormons or non-Mormons, or both.

SENATOR SMOOT. I think they were mostly non-Mormons.[6]

---

6. In a letter to Joseph F. Smith a month before Smith's testimony, Smoot had discussed the friendships he was forming: "I have made thousands of friends, and I have received hundreds of letters from different parts of the United States expressing sympathy for me and denouncing this unwarranted, religious and political fight being made

MR. WORTHINGTON. Just go along, please.

SENATOR SMOOT. I told them that I did not care about trying to run for an office until we could at least get our county into the proper column, and that is what we had been working for a long time, ever since the division on party lines, and that if the time came and it was proper I should like very much to go to the Senate of the United States. ...

MR. WORTHINGTON. That was in what year?

SENATOR SMOOT. In 1898.

MR. WORTHINGTON. I believe there was a Senator elected from your State in January, 1901?

SENATOR SMOOT. Yes; he was elected in January, 1901.

MR. WORTHINGTON. But the legislature which elected the Senator was elected in 1900?

SENATOR SMOOT. Yes.

MR. WORTHINGTON. The second McKinley campaign.

SENATOR SMOOT. It was the 1900 election.

MR. WORTHINGTON. Did you run for the Senatorship then, or make an effort?

SENATOR SMOOT. No; I was not an avowed candidate. ...

MR. WORTHINGTON. Now, come down to the year 1902, and let us know what you did then in the way of allowing your name to be used, and what, if anything, you did to further the successful issue of your candidacy?

SENATOR SMOOT. Early in the year I concluded that if all things were satisfactory I would be a candidate for the Senate of the United States, and I think it was on May 14, 1902, that I made an announcement that I would be a candidate.

MR. WORTHINGTON. In what way?

SENATOR SMOOT. I made it in a meeting. Before I made that announcement, of course, I realized that the rule which had been adopted by the church required me to ask the presidency of the church if they had any objections to my making that run, and if I was elected, whether I could have whatever time was necessary to fill my duties as a Senator of the United States. Or, in other words, I should require a leave of absence, and I wanted it understood that that leave of absence would be such that whatever requirement was made of me as a Senator they would have no objections whatever.

---

against me. There is scarcely a day passes but what some Senator introduces me to some friend or constituent, with a remark that the person had desired to meet me" (Feb. 5, 1904).

MR. WORTHINGTON. Right there, to avoid any misapprehension, when you speak of the rule adopted by the church do you refer to the rule which is printed on page 168 of the record in this case?[7]

SENATOR SMOOT. I do.

MR. WORTHINGTON. Go on.

SENATOR SMOOT. That consent was given, I think, sometime in the beginning of May. I could not tell the day, but I know that the announcement was made on the 14th of May, 1902.

Immediately I had my political friends form an organization, and we went into every precinct in our State, and we formed a regular organization of all of those precincts, and they worked from the primaries to the convention.

THE CHAIRMAN. Senator, pardon me. You said consent was given. I did not understand you to say by whom.

SENATOR SMOOT. The presidency. I asked the president of the church and his counselors at the time.

THE CHAIRMAN. The two counselors?

SENATOR SMOOT. Yes.

MR. WORTHINGTON. Since that interruption has occurred, I will ask you whether it was a formal application in writing or an informal one verbally.

SENATOR SMOOT. I went into the office. They were in the office there, at a table where they sit nearly every day, and I presented the proposition to them there.

MR. WORTHINGTON. Just state the substance of what occurred on that subject as nearly as you can now recall it.

SENATOR SMOOT. I think the answer already given covers the whole of what was said, with the exception that there may be some details which I do not remember. But the substance is there.

MR. WORTHINGTON. Did you talk at all to your brother apostles about that matter?

SENATOR SMOOT. Not at that time.

MR. WORTHINGTON. Go on. You were telling us that after having this conversation with the presidency you organized your forces.

SENATOR SMOOT. And we went to work, as I stated before, and the primaries were held, the county conventions were held, and our State convention was held. We saw wherever we could that candidates for the legislature were nominated at those conventions who were favorable

---

7. The full text of the so-called "Political Manifesto" is in *Smoot Hearings,* 1:168-71.

to me as Senator, and the organization was just as complete as I could make it. The work was done in that way.

MR. WORTHINGTON. What was it an organization of? Was it the organization of your party or the organization of your church?

SENATOR SMOOT. The organization of the Republican party.

MR. WORTHINGTON. The campaign having opened, I should like to go back and ask you what, if anything, from the time you took part in politics, the church has ever done as a factor in any of the movements to which you were a party?

SENATOR SMOOT. Not in the least.

MR. WORTHINGTON. I will ask you whether, at any time, either in your own matter or in reference to other candidates for other offices, so far as you know, the church had anything to do about it, any more than the Presbyterian or the Methodist Church in the State, excepting always what you have told us about asking for leave of absence under the rule?

SENATOR SMOOT. No man or woman that lives can come and say that I ever asked them to vote the Republican ticket on account of my being an apostle or a Mormon or anything connected with the church. Whatever argument I have made, I have based upon the question of Republican principles and as a Republican.

MR. WORTHINGTON. Have you yourself in what you have done in that regard from the beginning been dictated to in any wise by the church or any representative of the church?

SENATOR SMOOT. Not in the least; and I would not be. ...

MR. WORTHINGTON. Let me now in conclusion ask you the same question that I asked Doctor [James E.] Talmage the other day.[8] Suppose that some measure were pending before the Senate here upon which you are called upon to vote, and the church through its president or in some other way should direct you to vote in a certain way; what would you do?

SENATOR SMOOT. I would vote just the way that I thought was best for the interests of this country.

MR. WORTHINGTON. Would any dictation from the church or anybody representing it in the slightest degree guide you in casting your vote?

SENATOR SMOOT. None whatever; because it is not their business.

---

8. Talmage at first objected to this "unsupportable" assumption, then answered that if Joseph F. Smith or another church leader "presume[d] to instruct me in my position as a Senator, I should remind him that I was the Senator and he was not" (see chapter 23 in this volume; *Smoot Hearings*, 3:32-33).

MR. WORTHINGTON. As a matter of fact, has the church or anybody representing the church or purporting to represent the church undertaken in any way to dictate to you or direct you in the performance of your duties as a Senator?

SENATOR SMOOT. No, sir.

MR. WORTHINGTON. Would you submit for a moment to any dictation of that kind?

SENATOR SMOOT. I would not.

MR. WORTHINGTON. You have spoken of your own case. Let me ask you whether, so far as your knowledge goes, in respect of others, there has been any attempt to use the influence of the church as a church in political matters in your State?

SENATOR SMOOT. I never heard of it.

MR. WORTHINGTON. When you became an apostle, which was in April, 1900, I think you said—

SENATOR SMOOT. Yes, sir.

MR. WORTHINGTON. What was the state of your knowledge as to whether Joseph F. Smith was living in polygamous relations with several wives?

SENATOR SMOOT. I knew Joseph Smith had more than one wife, but I did not know anything about his relations with them; that is, as to his living with more than one wife.

MR. WORTHINGTON. Mr. Tayler read from a paper here the other day that certain persons who live in Salt Lake City were greatly surprised when they learned what Mr. Smith had testified to on that subject here. Were you also surprised?

SENATOR SMOOT. I was surprised as to the number of children he had had born since the manifesto, but I was not surprised at all that he had those wives. ...

MR. WORTHINGTON. Do the apostles have a separate room where they meet when they meet as a body?

SENATOR SMOOT. Yes; they have a separate room.

MR. WORTHINGTON. And that room, I believe, is in the [Salt Lake] temple?

SENATOR SMOOT. In the temple.

MR. WORTHINGTON. The first presidency have a room where they meet when they meet officially?

SENATOR SMOOT. Yes, sir; they have a room.

MR. WORTHINGTON. Does it adjoin or communicate with the room where the apostles meet?

SENATOR SMOOT. No; it does not adjoin or communicate.

MR. WORTHINGTON. It is in a separate part of the building?

SENATOR SMOOT. A separate part of the building.

MR. WORTHINGTON. You have attended, I presume, meetings of the apostles since you became an apostle?

SENATOR SMOOT. Oh, many times.

MR. WORTHINGTON. And even since you have been a Senator, when you were not here?

SENATOR SMOOT. When I am home, if I am in Salt Lake, I attend those meetings.

MR. WORTHINGTON. In reference to the charge here, in the first place, that the apostles are in a criminal conspiracy to further polygamy,[9] I want to ask you whether at any meeting of the apostles at which you have been present the question of polygamy or polygamous cohabitation has been considered or discussed or referred to in any way?

SENATOR SMOOT. No, sir; it has not.[10]

MR. WORTHINGTON. It appears here that sometimes the presidency call in the apostles, and the fifteen meet together.

SENATOR SMOOT. Yes, sir.

MR. WORTHINGTON. Are those meetings held in the room of the presidency?

SENATOR SMOOT. In the room of the apostles.

MR. WORTHINGTON. The presidency come to you?

SENATOR SMOOT. They come there.

MR. WORTHINGTON. Have you attended meetings of that kind?

SENATOR SMOOT. Yes; I have been there very often.

----

9. Worthington is addressing charge number six from the Salt Lake Ministerial Association: "The supreme authorities in the church, of whom Senator-elect Reed Smoot is one, to wit, the first presidency and twelve apostles, not only connive at violations of, but protect and honor the violators of the laws against polygamy and polygamous cohabitation."

10. At a meeting of the Twelve attended by Smoot on January 7, 1902, fellow apostle John Henry Smith offered his unqualified praise for "the principle of plural marriage," to which Smoot gave his own endorsement, saying that "if universally practiced, [it] would save the world much sorrow and distress," and that he himself "looked for its restoration" (in Stan Larson, ed., *A Ministry of Meetings: The Apostolic Diaries of Rudger Clawson* [Salt Lake City: Signature Books and Smith Research Associates, 1993], 378). It should be noted that the tone of this meeting was in contrast to quorum discussions of an earlier era, such as the meeting of January 9-10, 1900, three months before Smoot was ordained, in which the apostles expressed contempt for the law forbidding plural marriage and voiced their intent to violate the law, even referring with sarcasm to "President [Lorenzo] Snow's little love-letter to the gentiles" reassuring outsiders that polygamy had been discontinued (in John P. Hatch, ed., *Danish Apostle: The Diaries of Anthon H. Lund, 1890-1921* [Salt Lake City: Signature Books and the Smith-Pettit Foundation, 2006], 69-71).

MR. WORTHINGTON. Since you became an apostle, of course?

SENATOR SMOOT. Yes,

MR. WORTHINGTON. Not to take too long time as to things about which there is no dispute, perhaps, have you observed or is it your understanding that when the apostles are called in in that way they are called in simply as advisers?

SENATOR SMOOT. We are advisers to the president.

MR. WORTHINGTON. And that the president may do what he pleases in regard to the matter under consideration, although all the apostles advise him another way?

SENATOR SMOOT. Oh, yes; he has the ultimate decision.

MR. WORTHINGTON. Now, at any joint meeting of the presidency and the apostles has the matter of polygamy or polygamous cohabitation ever been raised, discussed, or mentioned in any way when you were present?

SENATOR SMOOT. Not while I have been there.

MR. WORTHINGTON. What do you say to the charge that the fifteen or the twelve have been and are in a conspiracy to further polygamy or polygamous cohabitation in Utah?

SENATOR SMOOT. I say it is not true.

MR. WORTHINGTON. Is there a particle of foundation for it, so far as concerns anything that has ever come under your observation?

SENATOR SMOOT. Not that I know of.

MR. WORTHINGTON. You learned by the testimony of Joseph F. Smith here last March that he was living with his five wives?

SENATOR SMOOT. Yes.

MR. WORTHINGTON. You have no knowledge except what everybody else may have from his statement as to the manner in which he has lived with them after the birth of the last child?

SENATOR SMOOT. No more than any other person.

MR. WORTHINGTON. It appears that at the general conference of your people held in the tabernacle on the 6th day of April last, after President Smith so testified here, he was sustained as president. Were you present at the conference which was held and before which he was sustained, or where you not there at the time?

SENATOR SMOOT. I was not there in April.

MR. WORTHINGTON. You were here?

SENATOR SMOOT. Yes; I was in Washington.

MR. WORTHINGTON. The hearings of this committee ran after that time, and you were here, and were present?

SENATOR SMOOT. Yes, sir.

MR. WORTHINGTON. Were you present at the general conference of your people which was held in the tabernacle on the 6th day of October, 1904?

SENATOR SMOOT. I was.

MR. WORTHINGTON. Before I take up that subject I must ask you about another matter. What knowledge, if any, have you as to Apostle [John W.] Taylor having taken a plural wife since the manifesto, except the evidence which has been given in this case?

SENATOR SMOOT. That is all I know about it—what I have heard here. I never heard of it before I heard of it in this room.

MR. WORTHINGTON. What evidence have you as to whether Matthias Cowley has been guilty of that offense, except the evidence or the alleged evidence in this case?

SENATOR SMOOT. None whatever; the same.

MR. WORTHINGTON. What evidence have you, except as it appears in this case, or what knowledge or information, except as it appears in the evidence in this case, that any apostle or any member of the presidency since the manifesto has taken a plural wife or has married anybody else to a plural wife?

SENATOR SMOOT. I have no evidence, only what I have heard since the beginning of this investigation.

MR. WORTHINGTON. Were you present at any meeting that was held of the apostles or of the fifteen last October prior to the nomination of the officers and their being sustained by the assembled conference?

SENATOR SMOOT. Was I present?

MR. WORTHINGTON. Were you present at any meeting of the fifteen or the twelve?

SENATOR SMOOT. I was present.

MR. WORTHINGTON. I believe that sufficiently appears here.

SENATOR SMOOT. I should like to state, however, that there were not fifteen present.

MR. WORTHINGTON. No.

SENATOR SMOOT. Of course.

MR. WORTHINGTON. We all know that.

SENATOR SMOOT. From your question it looked as if you thought they were present.

MR. WORTHINGTON. Mr. Taylor was not there?

SENATOR SMOOT. No.

MR. WORTHINGTON. Nor Mr. Cowley?

SENATOR SMOOT. No.

MR. WORTHINGTON. Nor Mr. [Heber J.] Grant?

SENATOR SMOOT. Nor Mr. Grant.

MR. WORTHINGTON. Nor Mr. [George] Teasdale?

SENATOR SMOOT. Nor Mr. Teasdale.

MR. WORTHINGTON. Mr. [Marriner Wood] Merrill is ill, I believe.

SENATOR SMOOT. He was sick; he was not there.

THE CHAIRMAN. What meeting was that?

MR. WORTHINGTON. A meeting of the presidency and the apostles held just before the conference of October 6, 1904. Now, while those matters are perhaps in your church considered private, I think the committee has a right to know what took place at that meeting, so far as you are concerned, in reference to the charges that have been made here against Apostle Taylor and Apostle Cowley, for instance.[11]

SENATOR SMOOT. Maybe I had better tell you about Mr. [Charles W.] Penrose, as that was the first business that came up.

MR. WORTHINGTON. Very well. Let me, then, ask you another question. At that conference Mr. Penrose was—

SENATOR SMOOT. At that meeting.

MR. WORTHINGTON. At that meeting he was proposed and at the conference he was sustained—

SENATOR SMOOT. Yes, sir.

MR. WORTHINGTON. As an apostle to take the place of Mr. [Abraham Owen] Woodruff, who had died after the April conference?

SENATOR SMOOT. Yes, sir.

MR. WORTHINGTON. And what was the state of your knowledge at the time of this assemblage in October last as to Mr. Penrose's matrimonial relations?

SENATOR SMOOT. At the meeting referred to I had no intimation whatever that there would be a nomination made that day, and I doubt very much whether there was one of the apostles who did. But at that

---

11. The day after this testimony, the *Salt Lake Tribune* questioned whether the church was ernest in its investigation:

Some weeks ago The Tribune stated that the whisper had gone out from church headquarters to the effect that Apostles [John W.] Taylor and [Matthias F.] Cowley were being investigated and were being held in a state of suspension. Not one public utterance has been made on this subject; but it was intended by the hierarchy that the whisper should march forth throughout the land, so that the hierarchy could make use of the common knowledge, if circumstances should show advantage therein. The time has come; and the use is being made of it. It was a fraud in its entirety, and fraudulent use is being made of it" ("Apostle Against Apostle," Jan. 21, 1905).

meeting President Joseph F. Smith, whose right it was, nominated
Charles W. Penrose as an apostle to fill the vacancy caused by the
death of Abraham O. Woodruff, and in nominating him, or stating
that it was his opinion that he was the proper person, he spoke of his
labors and what he had done, and also of his fitness for the calling of
an apostle and for the work that was more than likely to devolve upon
the different members of the quorum; and he was sustained[12]—

MR. WORTHINGTON. This matter may be of some importance, and if you recall the details of those remarks I should like to have you state them.
What did he say about the work that might devolve upon the members of the quorum of apostles?

SENATOR SMOOT. I have not thought of it since then, and I would not, perhaps, be able to give it in detail. But the substance, of course, was that
a good many of the older apostles were unable to go out and do very
much preaching; that George Teasdale was very poorly, indeed—liable to drop off at any time;[13] and Apostle Merrill could not get out, nor
had he been out to a conference, as I remember, for years; and that the
last appointments that had been made to the apostleship, from
Clawson down, were young men; and that he thought that Charles W.
Penrose, a man who was capable of writing, a good speaker, one that
could help along that line, would be a proper man for the place.[14]

---

12. In a letter to George Teasdale, Francis M. Lyman discussed Penrose's calling as
an apostle:

Yesterday we closed our council and met with the Presidency at 10 a.m. and trans-
acted much business. I was mouth at the altar and asked the Lord to manifest to President [Joseph F.] Smith who should be called to fill the vacancy in our Council
caused by the death of Brother [Abraham O.] Woodruff. When we came to the sac-
ramental table and the emblems were blessed by President [Anthon H.] Lund, President Smith arose and announced the name of Charles W. Penrose as the man presented to his mind for the position. We each expressed our views as in harmony with
the President's. I then moved "that we accept of the nomination of Charles W.
Penrose to the office of an Apostle by President Joseph F. Smith as the mind and will
of the Lord." This was seconded by John Henry Smith and carried unanimously.
Brother Penrose was sent for and answered President Smith that he would accept of
the office and responsibilities and do all in his power to build up the Kingdom of
God. We all then laid our hands upon him and President Smith ordained him an
Apostle and one of the Twelve Apostles. ... [There is] no man with stronger testimony or greater devotion to the doctrines of the Lord than Charles W. Penrose. He
has never quailed or faltered. He has been true as steel when men of his day have
gone by the board. ... He has always been sound in doctrine (July 9, 1904).

13. During this portion of the hearings, Teasdale, who was residing in Mexico, "read
aloud the Smoot investigation until we were tire[d] of it and glad to go to bed" (in
Kathleen Flake, *The Politics of American Religious Identity: The Seating of Senator Reed
Smoot, Mormon Apostle* [Chapel Hill: University of North Carolina Press, 2004], 200.

14. In his closing argument, Tayler stated that Charles Penrose "had been for years

I did not object at all to Mr. Penrose's nomination, and at the time I thought that he only had one wife. But I do not want the committee to understand that I want to hide behind that at all, because I do not want to. I take this position: I think it proper and right, where a man was married before the manifesto, or in other words, before there was any church law against it, that that man, when it comes to a church position, purely a church position, can accept any position in the church, for he did not violate any law of the church, and therefore is, or should be, qualified to fill the position in the church. I would qualify that by saying this, that I do not think that a man who was violating the law should hold a Government position, or an appointment from the Government; and I do not believe there is a single soul in our State who does.[15] ...

MR. WORTHINGTON. Of course, as a Senator you are frequently called upon to make recommendations as to Federal offices in your State, and to confer with the President and perhaps with your brother Senators in that regard. Let me know in what instance, if at all, you have, since you have been a Senator, recommended the appointment to office of any man who was a polygamist?

[SENATOR] SMOOT. I have made no such recommendation, nor do I ever intend to.

MR. WORTHINGTON. Now, to go back to that conference of last October, you have not told us what, if anything, took place in reference to Apostles Taylor and Cowley.

SENATOR SMOOT. At that meeting the question came up of sustaining—I brought it up myself—John W. Taylor and Mathias F. Cowley as apostles in the church after listening to or hearing the testimony that was given before this committee. By the way, I ought to state that it was at the meeting before this that this question came up. It was some time before that, Mr. Worthington; a month or two before that. We held quarterly meetings there of the apostles—

MR. WORTHINGTON. Let me understand you before you go further. Was

a polygamist, and had himself been pardoned by the president for polygamous cohabitation; yet Senator Smoot says that not a word was said in that discussion about it. John Henry Smith tells us the same thing. It illustrates the state or mind, gentlemen of the committee, in which the true Mormon gets. It is but another phase of the spirit or disregard and defiance of law, because their concerns are higher than the law. This election was unanimous, and Senator Smoot participated in it" (*Smoot Hearings,* 3:564).

15. This entire section above was used by Tayler in his closing argument for the prosecution; see *Smoot Hearings,* 3:564-65).

this a meeting of the apostles only or of the presidency and the apostles?

SENATOR SMOOT. No; the presidency and the apostles.

MR. WORTHINGTON. All right.

SENATOR SMOOT. I brought up the question whether they should be sustained at the coming conference, and spoke of their being sustained at the April conference.

MR. TAYLER. That is, you spoke of their having been sustained at the April conference?

MR. WORTHINGTON. He said he spoke of their having been sustained at the April conference.

SENATOR SMOOT. I asked the question. I was not at the April conference. So I do not know. But the April conference came up, too.

MR. TAYLER. All right.

SENATOR SMOOT. I asked President Smith if it was a proper thing to sustain those men, or to ask the people to sustain them, under the circumstances, and he stated to me that as a member of the church I must know that no man could be dropped without a hearing, and that—

THE CHAIRMAN. Who said this?

SENATOR SMOOT. President Smith. And that it was a rule of the church that a man could not be dropped, excommunicated, or disfellowshipped from the church without first having a chance to defend himself.

I recognized that as a rule of the church, and it was on that only that I consented that he should be presented and that I voted for him. But it was with the distinct understanding that there should be an investigation made; and I have every reason to believe that that investigation is under way, or has been for some time; and I believe also that they will have that hearing, and I believe that it will be probed to the bottom. That is my belief in the matter.

MR. WORTHINGTON. Suppose, as a result of that investigation, or otherwise, it should turn out that either of those apostles has taken a plural wife since the manifesto, or has married somebody else to a plural wife since then, and the question comes up about their being sustained after that result is reached, may I ask what you would do about it?

SENATOR SMOOT. If it is proven that they are guilty of violating that law of the church, I shall not sustain them ...

MR. TAYLER. What kind of a Mormon were you, Senator? You say you were not—

SENATOR SMOOT. At what time, Mr. Tayler?

MR. TAYLER. Well, I am now referring to your own characterization of yourself, and I want it made a little more explicit.

SENATOR SMOOT. No; I said "active."

MR. TAYLER. Yes; active. When I said "What kind of a Mormon were you?" I meant as to activity.

SENATOR SMOOT. I held no special office in the church, as I said, Mr. Tayler, until 1895, and then of course it was only in our Utah stake.

MR. TAYLER. That is, at Provo?

SENATOR SMOOT. At Provo.

MR. TAYLER. You were, however, a firm believer in the faith?

SENATOR SMOOT. I had faith in my mother, and I had faith in my father. I always had faith. My faith in Mormonism was stronger than any other faith I ever—

MR. TAYLER. What is that?

SENATOR SMOOT. I say my faith in Mormonism up to that time was stronger than any faith I could have for any other religion.

MR. TAYLER. Well, your faith in your religion and the religion of your parents has not abated since you became an apostle, has it?

SENATOR SMOOT. Oh, no; not at all. In fact, it has increased, Mr. Tayler.

MR. TAYLER. Increased because of the responsibility, duty, and relations of the apostles?

SENATOR SMOOT. No. I have become older; I have seen a great many things; my experience is much wider, and it is through that that my faith has increased.

MR. TAYLER. And your convictions have deepened?

SENATOR SMOOT. I think so, Mr. Tayler.

MR. TAYLER. Of course you had all of the respect for your father and your mother that a son could have for his parents?

SENATOR SMOOT. No man ever had a better mother in the world than my mother was.

MR. TAYLER. And what they did and what they believed you respected on that account, as much as a good son would ever respect?

SENATOR SMOOT. Oh, when I was younger; yes.

MR. TAYLER. When did you begin to take an interest in public affairs?

SENATOR SMOOT. You mean in a business way?

MR. TAYLER. No; generally. I mean in your church and in the history of your State and your community?

SENATOR SMOOT. Well, in my church, it was some time after I returned from a mission to England. I returned in the fall of 1891.

MR. TAYLER. The fall of 1891?

SENATOR SMOOT. After that; yes.

MR. TAYLER. How long had you been there?

SENATOR SMOOT. I was gone ten months. I went over in December, I think, of 1890, and returned in October of 1891. As far as my business is concerned, of course I have been in business there for a number of years.

MR. TAYLER. During the period from your marriage down to this period of ten months, during which you were abroad on a mission, you were, of course, in daily contact with and had knowledge of what was going on in Utah?

SENATOR SMOOT. Oh, yes.

MR. TAYLER. You were familiar with the prosecutions of the Mormons?

SENATOR SMOOT. I was.

MR. TAYLER. Of those charged with polygamy and polygamous cohabitation?

SENATOR SMOOT. I was. ...

MR. TAYLER. Do you remember when the Edmunds Act was passed?

SENATOR SMOOT. Yes.

MR. TAYLER. You were familiar with its general details?

SENATOR SMOOT. Well, partially so, I should say.

MR. TAYLER. You knew when the Edmunds-Tucker Act passed?

SENATOR SMOOT. Yes.

MR. TAYLER. Five years later [1887]?

SENATOR SMOOT. Five years later.

MR. TAYLER. Was your father ever prosecuted?

SENATOR SMOOT. He was arrested, and stood trial, and was acquitted.

MR. TAYLER. Did he leave the country at any time?

SENATOR SMOOT. He did not.

MR. TAYLER. You knew of many who did, did you?

SENATOR SMOOT. Well, I knew there were a great many in the State who did from report. Of course I did not know many people who had done it.

MR. TAYLER. You were, of course, familiar with the manifesto. Were you present when that was adopted?

SENATOR SMOOT. No; I was not.

MR. TAYLER. You knew about it?

SENATOR SMOOT. I knew about it.

MR. TAYLER. Was it a matter of deep interest to you?

SENATOR SMOOT. I approved of it. ...

MR. TAYLER. You yourself have no doubt about the divinity of its origin?

SENATOR SMOOT. The doctrine of polygamy?

MR. TAYLER. Yes.

SENATOR SMOOT. I think the doctrine and covenants—the revelation that was given to Joseph Smith—

MR. TAYLER. That is, it came from God?

SENATOR SMOOT. That he received it from the Lord.

MR. TAYLER. And that it was righteous to practice polygamy until the manifesto suspended it?

SENATOR SMOOT. Well, I could not say as to that, Mr. Tayler. I had better give you my view as to that, and then you can see how I feel. As an abstract principle, approved by the Bible and permitted by the doctrine and covenants, I believe it; but as a practice against the law of my country, I do not.

MR. TAYLER. You do not? When did you reach that conviction?

SENATOR SMOOT. All my life; ever since I have been a man.

MR. TAYLER. All your life. That is to say—you have always said that it was unlawful?

SENATOR SMOOT. I have always said since the final decision by the [U.S.] Supreme Court that it was unlawful.

MR. TAYLER. When was that final decision?

SENATOR SMOOT. There was a decision given in 1878 in the Reynolds case.

MR. TAYLER. Yes.

SENATOR SMOOT. By the Supreme Court.

MR. TAYLER. Yes.

SENATOR SMOOT. Of course I was but a mere boy then; but I do know from what I have heard from the leaders of the church, and from men in general and members of the church, that they felt that the decision and the law were against bigamy. While the decision takes in the whole question of polygamy and bigamy, they felt that it was not fairly tried, and they thought they would have it tested in the Supreme Court of the United States again. I think the final decision of that matter, which was perfectly satisfactory to all of the people, was in 1890. That is as I understand it, Mr. Tayler.

MR. TAYLER. You have read the opinion, have you not?

SENATOR SMOOT. Yes; I have read the opinion lately, of course.

MR. TAYLER. And to your intelligence, now, do you have any doubt about its destroying the principle that one man may take two wives because his religion says he may?

SENATOR SMOOT. That is, speaking of the—

MR. TAYLER. Of the Reynolds case.

SENATOR SMOOT. Speaking of the Reynolds case, my opinion would be that it was a decision that would prevent that.

MR. TAYLER. That would prevent that?

SENATOR SMOOT. Yes.

MR. TAYLER. Then there has been, according to your view of it, no justifiable marriage since that time?

SENATOR SMOOT. Well—

MR. TAYLER. I mean plural marriage.

SENATOR SMOOT. I would not want to go that far, Mr. Tayler. Technically, if the people had believed that to be a decision of the Supreme Court against polygamy and final, that is true; but they did not.

MR. TAYLER. I see.

SENATOR SMOOT. And it was for that they were fighting—for a religious conviction.

MR. TAYLER. Yes; exactly.

SENATOR SMOOT. And they thought they were doing right, and they took it to the Supreme Court of the United States, and when it was finally decided there they accepted it.

MR. TAYLER. So that it was proper for a man who said that that decision was wrong, or did not reach the case of a plural wife, to continue to take plural wives?

SENATOR SMOOT. Well, you must take into consideration, Mr. Tayler, this fact: that that was in 1878, and nothing was done at all, you know, for four years or so after that.

MR. TAYLER. Nothing was done?

SENATOR SMOOT. That is, in the way of prosecutions.

MR. TAYLER. What remained to be done, Senator? The law was there.

SENATOR SMOOT. The law was there, but I mean the enforcement of it.

MR. TAYLER. George Reynolds had been prosecuted.

SENATOR SMOOT. Well, George Reynolds came and gave himself up.

MR. TAYLER. Yes.

SENATOR SMOOT. And furnished all the testimony.

MR. TAYLER. Yes

SENATOR SMOOT. And he himself claimed that it was not presented in the right light, and that if it had been the decision would have been otherwise. I have heard him say so over and over again.

MR. TAYLER. Yes, exactly. But nevertheless the court did decide it in a certain way, and he did suffer the penalty.

SENATOR SMOOT. There is not a doubt about it in the world.

MR. TAYLER. And the court has never indicated any other doctrine since, has it?

SENATOR SMOOT. No; it has not.

MR. TAYLER. And that case was never reheard by the court, was it?

SENATOR SMOOT. I do not think it was.

MR. TAYLER. So that they undertook to excuse themselves after 1878 until what time?

SENATOR SMOOT. Until 1890. I think the decision was given then. ...

MR. TAYLER. Do you understand that Joseph [F.] Smith is obeying the law?

SENATOR SMOOT. I do not know. I heard his testimony here that he was living with his wives. I do not know that he is cohabiting with them. If he is, he is not living the law; and he did say that in the past he had broken the law of the land. But I rather think that is brought about in this way, that, as I stated here this morning, from the date, or shortly after the date, of the manifesto the cases that were then in court—at least many or them—were dismissed, and when the docket was clear there were very, very few prosecutions. The officers having in hand the prosecution of this class of cases were appointed by the Government, and I think that being the case, and on account of the discussion that came up at the constitutional convention (and the habit that has been growing there has instilled it in the hearts of the people there, or the minds of those that are in that condition), that the people would tolerate it, at least, and they were in a position where they did not know what to do.

THE CHAIRMAN. Pardon me, Senator. I do not think you understand the question. I wish the reporter would read the question to the Senator, in fairness to him.

The reporter read as follows: "Mr. Tayler. Do you understand that Joseph [F.] Smith is obeying the law?"

THE CHAIRMAN. That is the question.

SENATOR SMOOT. Do you mean to-day?

MR. TAYLER. I know nothing more about it than that he testified on that subject here.

MR. WORTHINGTON. I think he did answer the question, Mr. Chairman.

MR. VAN COTT. I ask to have the answer read, if there is any discussion as to whether he answered it.

SENATOR BEVERIDGE. The part of the answer that was not responsive to the question was the latter part. He went on to say that if such and such were true, then he was disobeying the law. Then he proceeded to say, "It comes about in this way;" and for the life of me I, for one, could not connect his explanation as to how it did come about.

THE CHAIRMAN. Mr. Reporter, will you read the question again?

SENATOR BEVERIDGE. His explanation did not explain.

THE CHAIRMAN. Repeat the question.

SENATOR SMOOT. Mr. Chairman, just take that same question and leave the explanation off.

THE CHAIRMAN. That is entirely satisfactory, only I thought that perhaps you did not understand the question exactly; and I would like to have it answered.

The reporter again read the question, as follows: "Mr. Tayler. Do you understand that Joseph [F.] Smith is obeying the law?"

THE CHAIRMAN. That is a simple question.

MR. VAN COTT. Yes; and it has been answered.

SENATOR SMOOT. I understand that Joseph F. Smith said that he had not obeyed the law in the past, but I can not say what he is doing now.

THE CHAIRMAN. The question is, Do you understand he is disobeying the law?

SENATOR SMOOT. No; I do not, Mr. Chairman.

THE CHAIRMAN. You do not so understand?

SENATOR SMOOT. No.

MR. TAYLER. Of course I am not asking you for knowledge, but for your understanding.

SENATOR SMOOT. And I say that, Mr. Tayler.

MR. TAYLER. You do not understand anything about it?

SENATOR SMOOT. I understand that he has broken the law. There is no doubt in my mind.

MR. TAYLER. Did you not understand that he did disobey the law; that he had, by plural wives, some ten or twelve or more children after the manifesto?

SENATOR SMOOT. I heard it in his testimony.

MR. TAYLER. You heard him say that?

SENATOR SMOOT. He testified to it.

MR. TAYLER. You heard his testimony throughout, did you?

SENATOR SMOOT. Most of it. I was here.

MR. TAYLER. Did he not leave on your mind the impression that he proposed to continue to disobey the law, and did he not so frankly say in effect?

SENATOR SMOOT. I rather think he said that he did not know but what he would continue to live with his wives. I do not know whether he intends to cohabit with them or not.

SENATOR DILLINGHAM. Does not the evidence show what he said?

SENATOR BEVERIDGE. There is no necessity for stating what the evidence shows. It is a matter of record.

THE CHAIRMAN. There is no doubt about that. But, Senator, let me call this to your attention. The committee want to know about that. Mr. Smith himself testified before the committee, if you remember, that he had had eleven children since the manifesto.

SENATOR SMOOT. I remember that, Mr. Chairman.

THE CHAIRMAN. You remember that?

SENATOR SMOOT. Yes.

THE CHAIRMAN. By his five several wives?

SENATOR SMOOT. Yes.

MR. WORTHINGTON. But that he had not had one for four years.

THE CHAIRMAN. That does not matter. It was since the manifesto.

SENATOR SMOOT. I remember that.

THE CHAIRMAN. Now, remembering that, what is your answer to that question?

SENATOR SMOOT. Why, Mr. Chairman, I could not say that he has lived with those wives since—

THE CHAIRMAN. But he has said himself he has, and has had children.

SENATOR SMOOT. Oh, he has since the manifesto.

SENATOR BEVERIDGE. Is not that a violation of the law?

SENATOR SMOOT. It is a violation of the law.

THE CHAIRMAN. I thought you did not want to put yourself in the position—

SENATOR SMOOT. I did not know that was the direct question.

MR. WORTHINGTON. I think you misunderstood him, Mr. Chairman. He said quite clearly that he was violating the law in cohabiting with those wives, but that he did not know whether he was violating the law now.

THE CHAIRMAN. I understood the witness to say that he did not know whether Mr. Smith was cohabiting with them now, to-day, this minute.

SENATOR SMOOT. I do not want to go into technicalities, Mr. Chairman.

THE CHAIRMAN. I knew you did not want to leave it that way. I wanted to have it made plain.[16] Go ahead, Mr. Tayler.

---

16. Exchanges like these rankled President Theodore Roosevelt, who sided with Smoot, according to Senator Dolliver. At a social event when the topic was raised, "for nearly an hour the President told Burrows just what he thought of him and everybody else engaged in this unwarranted fight against [Smoot]." Dolliver told Smoot he

MR. TAYLER. The question I have asked, the Senator has answered, without disrespect to him at all, as I supposed he would answer it; that is, whether he understood that Joseph F. Smith was living today in violation of the law, and, notwithstanding what President Smith said at the hearing here last spring, he says he does not know anything about it or have any understanding about it. You know Apostle John Henry Smith, of course?

SENATOR SMOOT. I do.

MR. TAYLER. You understand he is violating the law?

SENATOR SMOOT. He has violated the law since the manifesto.

MR. TAYLER. And do you understand that he is now?

SENATOR SMOOT. If I was going to express an opinion, I would say yes; but I would not like to do that.

MR. TAYLER. I will put it back eight or ten weeks, Senator, because I have not heard from Mr. Smith since he testified.[17]

SENATOR SMOOT. I think so, up to the time he testified here.

MR. TAYLER. Do you remember the ground—the reason—that he gave for violating the law?

SENATOR SMOOT. As I remember it, it was that those wives were his; that he owed an obligation to them; that he would have felt that it was his duty to act as a husband to them; and that he would take his chances with the law in violating it.

MR. TAYLER. And did he not say that he took those obligations with the plural wife with the approval of God?

SENATOR BEVERIDGE. Mr. Tayler, may I ask whether you are not examining the present witness as to what some other witness said here?

MR. WORTHINGTON. That is just what he is doing.

MR. TAYLER. I am cross-examining the witness.

MR. WORTHINGTON. I submit that all he has a right to ask this witness is what impression is on his mind from that testimony. We have the testi-

---

"thought it strange that the President should speak so earnestly in [his] behalf in public," to which Smoot replied that he had been "perfectly frank with the President and had kept nothing from him" (in Kathryn Smoot, "The Role of the Newspaper in the Reed Smoot Investigation: 1903-1907," M.A. thesis, University of Utah, 1964, 19). Roosevelt was equally frank with Smoot, telling him, for instance, "to have the temple ceremonies abolished, they were foolishness" (in Gary Bergera, "Secretary to the Senator: Carl A. Badger and the Smoot Hearings," *Sunstone* 8 [Jan. 1983], 39).

17. John Henry Smith's testimony regarding the Manifesto was that "nobody could take from me my family; that I was responsible to God myself, and that I must take the consequences of my countrymen punishing me if they saw fit to do so" (see chapter 18 in this volume; *Smoot Hearings,* 2:286).

mony here and can read it for ourselves, and although he may misunderstand it it does not affect the question of his position here.

THE CHAIRMAN. Do you take exception to the statement of what it was?

MR. WORTHINGTON. I object to his being asked about what the testimony is, as a useless consumption of time.

MR. TAYLER. Not at all.

SENATOR HOPKINS. I suppose that is preliminary to the other questions Mr. Tayler will put. First he wants to know whether this witness understands what the other witness said, and then, after he understands that, to put the question as to the interpretation that he puts upon it.

MR. TAYLER. Precisely. That is it exactly.

THE CHAIRMAN. I suppose it is the same idea as the Chair had in mind when he called the attention of the witness to the fact that Mr. Smith had testified he had 11 children by his five different wives since the manifesto, so that he could answer the question whether in his judgment he committed the crime.

SENATOR KNOX. On Senator Hopkins's suggestion, the proper form of question would be "assuming that he testified so and so."

MR. TAYLER. I think it would be very much better to have the impression that comes to the witness from a positive knowledge of what his ears did hear than a mere assumption that somebody might have said something, because this witness has had time to have impressions made upon him, and he heard [Mr. Smith's] testimony. But if he misunderstood it or does not understand it as I understand it, then he is entitled to the benefit of that situation in which he finds himself. You heard John Henry Smith testify?

SENATOR SMOOT. I was out some little, Mr. Tayler, but I think I heard him testify the greater part of the time.

MR. TAYLER. Now, what was it I was saying when I was interrupted? I want to continue that.

The reporter read as follows: "Mr. Tayler. And did he not say that he took those obligations with the plural wife with the approval of God?"

SENATOR SMOOT. I can not just remember whether those were the words or not, Mr. Tayler.

MR. TAYLER. Do you understand that is the view that all good polygamist Mormons take of their relations to their plural wives today, that they take upon them the obligations of husband to a plural wife with the approval of God?

SENATOR SMOOT. I should think that would be what they thought.

MR. TAYLER. And that John Henry Smith said that no law of the land could interfere with or dissolve that relation?

SENATOR SMOOT. No; I do not remember him saying that.

MR. TAYLER. Do you not understand that that is the view that good polygamist Mormons take?

SENATOR SMOOT. No; I do not understand that, Mr. Tayler. ...

MR. TAYLER. You became an apostle early in 1900, shortly after the [B. H.] Roberts [Congressional] case was disposed of?

SENATOR SMOOT. A year and a half after, or something like that.

MR. TAYLER. The Roberts case was disposed of in January, 1900.

SENATOR SMOOT. Well, it was right after it was disposed of, then. His election was in 1898, and then, of course, he would come here in 1899. That is about right, I suppose.

MR. TAYLER. You were naturally interested in the Roberts case? You followed that situation?

SENATOR SMOOT. Yes; I did. I want to say that as far as Mr. Roberts's election is concerned, he would not have been elected if I could have helped it.

MR. TAYLER. He was the Democratic candidate for Congress that year?

SENATOR SMOOT. Yes.

MR. TAYLER. You were not supporting the Democratic ticket, were you?

SENATOR SMOOT. No; I was not.

MR. TAYLER. You recall that in the debate in the Roberts case there were charges made against various prominent Mormons as being polygamists?

SENATOR SMOOT. No; I do not recall that, Mr. Tayler. There may have been, though.

MR. TAYLER. Do you mean there may have been charges?

SENATOR SMOOT. Yes; that is what I mean.

MR. TAYLER. Do you mean that you know you did not know it?

SENATOR SMOOT. That there were polygamists?

MR. TAYLER. That there were charges made against various prominent Mormons that they were polygamists and living in polygamy.

SENATOR SMOOT. There may have been charges that they were polygamists.

MR. TAYLER. I know; but you do not catch the thought. Do you mean to say that you did not know that any such charges were made?

SENATOR SMOOT. I understand the charge was made against Brigham H. Roberts, and it may have been against others.

MR. WORTHINGTON. Senator, please do not answer about what may have

been. It is only what you recollect. We can all guess what may have
been.

MR. TAYLER. I want to know whether you say—

SENATOR SMOOT. I recollect that B. H. Roberts was charged with living
with more than one woman, and I believed it.

MR. TAYLER. Do you recollect that charges were made against other
prominent Mormons that they were living with plural wives?

SENATOR SMOOT. No; I do not remember that that came in the discussion
at all.

MR. TAYLER. Do you read the "Deseret News" occasionally?

SENATOR SMOOT. Yes.

MR. TAYLER. At that time were you reading the "Tribune?"

SENATOR SMOOT. I have always done so. It made no impression upon me,
though, Mr. Tayler; I can say that.

MR. TAYLER. That is, the charges of polygamous living made no impression upon you?

SENATOR SMOOT. No; any more than the whole case. I did not follow it any
more than simply, as a matter of fact, as to how it came out.

MR. TAYLER. You had no special interest in what developed there about
the Mormon people or the Mormon Church?

SENATOR SMOOT. That was Mr. Roberts; it was not the Mormon Church.

MR. TAYLER. But do you not know that the Mormon Church was attacked
there on the floor, and that the speech in which the attack was made
was printed in Salt Lake City?

SENATOR SMOOT. It may have been.

MR. TAYLER. And that the "Deseret News" attacked the maker of that
speech with great vigor—said he was slandering the church and the
State? Do you recall anything about that?[18]

SENATOR SMOOT. Not definitely enough to say. ...

THE CHAIRMAN. Where do you stand in the line of succession to the presidency?

SENATOR SMOOT. Three apostles have been appointed since I was appointed.

THE CHAIRMAN. Do you mean you are about the sixth or the fifth?

SENATOR SMOOT. That would be the twelfth.

Senator Dubois. You are the ninth.

18. Tayler is probably talking about himself. He spoke for approximately one hour
on December 5, 1899, on the House floor against Roberts's right to take his seat as a
Congressman. The vote against Roberts was 302-30 (see "Statement of Mr. Roberts,"
Deseret News, Dec. 5, 1899).

SENATOR SMOOT. Oh, no, Senator. There is the presidency, and the two counselors take their place.

THE CHAIRMAN. In order that the committee may understand the matter, I will ask you a question. Suppose, when you contemplated becoming a candidate for the Senate, the first presidency had refused their consent and you had run for the office in the face of that refusal, what action, if any, would the church have taken?

SENATOR SMOOT. I do not know that they would have taken any action. ...

MR. TAYLER. Do you know whether any effort was made to have John W. Taylor come and report for himself?[19]

SENATOR SMOOT. I think there has been. I know there was, when President Smith left here and went home, a telegram [was] sent; and how I know this telegram was sent is that it was sent back to Chicago to a Mr. Gibbs, and from Mr. Gibbs it went back to Mr. [George F.] Gibbs of Salt Lake City, and then it was sent here to me. It was not delivered in Canada.

MR. WORTHINGTON. Mr. Gibbs is the secretary of the presidency?

SENATOR SMOOT. And not only that, but I know it because from letters written from John W. Taylor, and I read them to the chairman of this committee—from him and Cowley, I know that the president of the church did that much.

MR. TAYLER. Where was Taylor's letter from?[20]

---

19. In a letter to his wife, February 13, 1905, Carl Badger discussed the behind-the-scenes dynamics of testimony regarding Apostles Cowley and Taylor, writing that the Senator "could not prevent" his attorney from participating in the discussion:

The whole matter had been talked over, and it had been specifically decided that the attorneys should not say anything, but when it came to the heat and excitement of the speech, Mr. Worthington told of the incident ... Mr. Richards was very severe on Worthington for having said what he did, and so was Van Cott, and Mr. Worthington's statement will be changed, or will be left out completely in the printed brief. The way Worthington said it before the Committee left the impression that President Smith was unwilling to do any thing in the case of the absentee Apostles, (which is the truth, according to the best I can learn), but that is a very dangerous attitude, as the committee is afraid that the Church is not honest in its declaration that it will punish those who have taken new wives. Worthington's brief has been changed, as I understand it, to leave the impression that something will be done; that though there has been delay, there is no bad faith. But this only puts off the day of reckoning; it comes inevitably (in Rodney J. Badger, *Liahona and Iron Rod: The Biography of Carl A. and Rose J. Badger* [Bountiful, Utah: Family History Publishers, 1985], 253).

20. On October 28, 1905, Taylor tendered his resignation from the Quorum of the Twelve. Smoot was notified but was asked not to broadcast it. Taylor admitted that he was "out of harmony" with the church leadership "as to the scope and meaning of the Manifesto issued by President Wilford Woodruff and adopted by the General Conference on Oct 6 1890 and also as to the meaning of the last clause of the petition for am-

SENATOR SMOOT. I think it was from Canada, was it not, Mr. Chairman?

THE CHAIRMAN. I do not remember.

MR. WORTHINGTON. It was from some place in Canada. That is right.

MR. TAYLER. Where was Cowley's letter from?

SENATOR SMOOT. From some place in Iowa, was it not, Mr. Chairman?

THE CHAIRMAN. I have no recollection of the place.

SENATOR SMOOT. I think it was. I read it to you, and I think he was in Iowa somewhere.

MR. TAYLER. In Iowa, did you say?

SENATOR SMOOT. Yes, in Iowa, when he wrote that letter.

MR. TAYLER. Did he say he would not come?

SENATOR SMOOT. I would rather have the letters themselves produced.

MR. TAYLER. I am only trying to get the tone of them. Of course I would rather have the letters.

SENATOR SMOOT. I do not want to put a construction upon them.

MR. TAYLER. No.

SENATOR SMOOT. But in substance they were, that they did not think this was a question of religion at all, and was a mere matter of investigating something that they had no concern in, and that they did not feel that it was proper to come. Now, I do not know that that is the substance of them, but I know of those letters, and I read them to the chairman, and perhaps I did wrong in doing so. They were sent to me, and I did not want anything concealed, and I read them to the chairman of this committee.

------

nesty to President Benjamin Harrison in Dec. 1891." Clarifying his difference of interpretation, he continued:

> I have always believed that the government of the United States had jurisdiction only within its own boundaries and that the term "laws of the land" in the manifesto meant merely the laws of the United States. I find now that this opinion is different to that expressed by the church authorities who have declared that the prohibition against plural marriages extended to every place and to every part of the Church. It is doubtless true that this view of the matter has been given by President Woodruff and others, but I have never taken that as binding upon me or the Church, because it was never presented for adoption by "Common Consent" as was the Manifesto itself and I have disputed its authority as a law or rule of the Church. I acknowledge that I received a request from President Joseph F. Smith by letter, to appear as a witness in the Reed Smoot case before the Senate Committee on Privileges and Elections, but I declined to do so because, while I recognized his right to direct me in church affairs, I did not think his authority extended to civil affairs to the extent that I should expose my family concerns and be questioned and held up to public ignominy as some of my brethren were before that body, and I still hold the same views upon that matter. In as much as I have not been in harmony with my brethren in these subjects and I have been called in question concerning them, I now submit myself to their discipline and to save further controversy tender this my resignation and hope for such clemency in my case as they may deem right and just and merciful.

MR. TAYLER. That is the substance of what President Smith said in his letter, is it not?

SENATOR SMOOT. Perhaps it is.

MR. TAYLER. Was not President Smith's letter based upon the letters to which you refer?

SENATOR SMOOT. I forget about Mr. Smith's letter.

MR. WORTHINGTON. We ought to have those letters, instead of having the witness's vague recollection of them.

THE CHAIRMAN. You do not know what was in President Smith's letter?

SENATOR SMOOT. No; I know there is a letter in the record.

MR. TAYLER. It is printed.

SENATOR SMOOT. I believe it was written to you, Mr. Chairman, and I believe you had it printed in the record. That is as I understand it.

THE CHAIRMAN. You do not know the contents of the letter that he wrote to these apostles?

SENATOR SMOOT. No; but I would judge from the answer that he received that he had asked them to come.

THE CHAIRMAN. I did not know but that you had seen that letter.

SENATOR SMOOT. No, sir; I have not. In fact, I think it was a telegram, and not only a telegram but a letter. I believe President Smith telegraphed from Washington City when he was here.

MR. TAYLER. Telegraphed to whom?

SENATOR SMOOT. I think he telegraphed to Salt Lake City, to Secretary George F. Gibbs—now, this is as I remember it, but I do not know that it is true—to locate, if possible, Cowley and Taylor.

THE CHAIRMAN. Then the president did not know at that time where two of his apostles were?

SENATOR SMOOT. I do not think he did. I think his testimony here shows that Matthias F. Cowley was taking a trip through the missions.[21]

THE CHAIRMAN. Is there anything else, Mr. Tayler?

MR. WORTHINGTON. Mr. Tayler, will your cross-examination be much longer?

MR. TAYLER. I will not be able to get through to-day.

MR. WORTHINGTON. Mr. Chairman, I suggest an adjournment at this hour. The Senator has been on the stand a long time, and you know he is not in good condition.

---

21. Smith testified regarding Cowley's whereabouts that "the last I heard of him he was making a tour of the northern missions of the church in Idaho and Montana and Oregon; that he started out some weeks ago on that line. I do not know where he is to-day" (*Smoot Hearings*, 1:142).

SENATOR SMOOT. I have had a very bad case of indigestion ever since Christmas. However, I am perfectly willing to go until 5 o'clock if you insist upon it.

THE CHAIRMAN. The Chair will not insist upon it if you are not well.[22]

SENATOR SMOOT. I can stand it all right.

THE CHAIRMAN. It is not a question of standing it.

SENATOR OVERMAN. I think we had better adjourn. The Senator has been on the stand a long time.

THE CHAIRMAN. We do not want you to remain on the stand any longer if it inconveniences you.

SENATOR SMOOT. Whatever you decide will be satisfactory to me.

MR. WORTHINGTON. What would you prefer if it was left to you—to take an adjournment now or to run along?

THE CHAIRMAN. The committee generally sits until 5 o'clock. Perhaps we might run along for five or ten minutes more.

MR. WORTHINGTON. Senator, what is your preference about the matter?

SENATOR SMOOT. Of course I am a little tired, but whatever the chairman says will be satisfactory to me.[23]

MR. TAYLER. I think we might as well adjourn, Mr. Chairman.[24] ...

---

22. On February 7, 1905, Smoot related to Joseph F. Smith the strain he was under: "You will remember that I was suffering a little from indigestion while home during the holidays. On my return to Washington I was so crowded and so worried that it was impossible for me to eat my food and I lost flesh very rapidly. My indigestion increased till it was so bad and so painful that I could not sleep at night. Especially was this the case the last week of the hearings, and the day I went on the witness stand, I could hardly hold my head up" (in Joseph Heinerman, "Reed Smoot's 'Secret Code,'" *Utah Historical Quarterly* 57 [Summer 1989]: 259).

23. James Talmage wrote in his diary that "Bro. Smoot did his case much good by his own testimony." The only criticism Talmage had was over Smoot's "uncertainty ... in connection with questions on the doctrin[e] and theology of the church." Talmage noted the "early adjournment ... owing to Bro. Smoot's indisposition" (Jan. 20, 1905; L. Tom Perry Special Collections, Harold B. Lee Library, Brigham Young University, Provo).

24. On February 7, 1905, Smoot informed Joseph F. Smith:

The feeling against the church, I suppose, has never been so strong and bitter as at the present time. Franklin S. Richards thinks that he can never remember the time when the feeling was so strong and so universally opposed to the church as at the present time. Whenever the question comes up, and it comes up very often, the first thing that they say is that the Church has not been true to its covenants. ... It was intimated to me to-day by a friend of ours, that the opposition has secured a number of detectives and that they have left for Utah for the purpose of visiting all parts of the State, to secure evidence, if possible, of other new polygamous marriages.

26.

Reed Smoot

Saturday & Monday, January 21, 23

"Apostle Reed Smoot has taken the witness stand ... The principal sensation created by his testimony is one of supreme regret that the hearing could not have been held in the Tabernacle in Salt Lake City, before a congregation of ten thousand Mormons, that they might know how their religious faith is kicked about like a football by the men whom they uphold as prophets, seers and revelators of God." —*Salt Lake Tribune,* Jan. 21, 1905

"Probably nine out of ten readers ... picture a ... large, spacious chamber [for the hearings] ... [rather than a small] room about the size of the Salt Lake Theater lobby. ... The hearings open at 10 each morning, [but the spectator section is] promptly pre-empted by half-past nine [by] ... Mrs. Charles Mostyn Owen [and a group of] ... austere looking women [including] ... a venerable old lady [in a] ... deep black bonnet of Salvation Army style [and] ... a score of equally severe ... women, who betoken a New England type of the old-day school. Few ever emit a smile, move a facial muscle or stir ... These ladies ... are said to be the representatives of various religious, reform, and denominational societies; doubtless on hand to see that the interests of the land are not subverted by the wicked influx from Utah" —*Deseret News,* Jan. 28, 1905

Reed Smoot, having been previously duly sworn, was examined, and testified as follows ...

SENATOR OVERMAN. Senator Smoot, do you believe that the Church of Jesus Christ of Latter-Day Saints has received and does receive revelations from God?

SENATOR SMOOT. I believe they can receive revelations from God. I think that if God gave revelations in the early days, God certainly can give revelations to-day.

SENATOR OVERMAN. And you believe he did in the early days?

SENATOR SMOOT. I do.

SENATOR OVERMAN. And that he will or can do it now?

SENATOR SMOOT. He can do it now.

SENATOR OVERMAN. To whom would those revelations come?

SENATOR SMOOT. I think any good man could receive a revelation, but nobody but the president of the church could receive a revelation that would bind the church, nor would the church be bound by any revelation until it had been presented to the church and accepted and adopted by the conference.

SENATOR OVERMAN. You believe, then, that if God should make a revelation to Joseph Smith, and that was submitted to the church in conference and accepted by the church, it would be the law of the church?

SENATOR SMOOT. It would be a rule and law of the church.

SENATOR OVERMAN. You think the laws of God are superior to the laws of man?

SENATOR SMOOT. I think the laws of God, upon the conscience of man, are superior. I do, Mr. Senator.

SENATOR OVERMAN. You think the laws of God, as revealed to Joseph Smith and accepted by the church, would be binding upon the members of the church superior to the laws of the land?

SENATOR SMOOT. I think it would be binding upon Joseph Smith.

SENATOR OVERMAN. Well?

SENATOR SMOOT. And I think if a revelation were given to me, and I knew it was from God, that that law of God would be more binding upon me, possibly, than a law of the land, and I would have to do what God told me, if I was a Christian.

SENATOR OVERMAN. I speak of a law—

SENATOR SMOOT. But I want to say this, Mr. Senator. I would want to know, and to know positively, that it was a revelation from God.

SENATOR OVERMAN. I was not speaking—

SENATOR SMOOT. And then I would further state this, that if it conflicted with the law of my country in which I lived, I would go to some other country where it would not conflict.[1]

SENATOR OVERMAN. I was not speaking of a revelation to you. I was speaking of a revelation that comes to the president of the church, is submitted by the president to the conference, and accepted by the conference. Is that binding upon the members of the church generally, and is it superior to the law of the land?

SENATOR SMOOT. As a rule of the church, but not binding upon any member of the church who does not want to follow it. Free agency in our church is a heritage God has given, and not only in our church, but

---

1. The previous four questions and answers were included in Carlisle's closing argument (*Smoot Hearings*, 4:416).

given to everybody. That God can not take that free agency away from me. If He could, He could not judge me when I died and went to the bar of justice, because—

SENATOR OVERMAN. Then if there was a commandment given by God to the church and accepted by the church, any member of the church has a right to violate that command?

SENATOR SMOOT. They have.

SENATOR BEVERIDGE. I direct your attention, Senator, to the last portion of Senator Overman's question prior to the last one, which was whether or not any revelation that might be given through any of the processes you mention could, under any circumstances, be superior to the law of the land? That is the question I should like to have you direct your answer to.

SENATOR SMOOT. I should like—

SENATOR BEVERIDGE. I suggest that you have the last part of Senator Overman's question read.

SENATOR SMOOT. I will ask the reporter to read it.

The reporter read as follows: "Senator Overman. I was not speaking of a revelation to you. I was speaking of a revelation that comes to the president of the church, is submitted by the president to the conference, and accepted by the conference. Is that binding upon the members of the church generally, and is it superior to the law of the land?"

SENATOR BEVERIDGE. I should be glad to have you direct your answer to the last part of the question.

SENATOR SMOOT. I do not believe it is superior to the law of the land.

SENATOR OVERMAN. Then if you yourself got a revelation from heaven, I understand you would regard that as superior to the law of the land, and would have to submit to it or leave the country?

SENATOR SMOOT. That would be a revelation from God to me direct, and if I believed that it was from God I would consider it compulsory on me to obey it; and, as I stated, Senator, if I lived in this country and that command of God was against the laws of my country I would move to some other country where I could obey that law.

SENATOR OVERMAN. Do you believe those revelations are ever given by God to individuals?

SENATOR SMOOT. Well, I have heard men so testify, but I could not say positively.

SENATOR OVERMAN. What is your belief about it, Senator?

SENATOR SMOOT. I believe that God could do such a thing.

SENATOR OVERMAN. Do you believe He has done it and that He will do it again in time?

SENATOR SMOOT. I rather think that God did it in former days, and I feel that He can do it now.

SENATOR OVERMAN. That is all.

SENATOR DUBOIS. If the president of the church received a revelation from God and submitted it to the conference, and they sustained it, and you, for instance, did not see fit to obey it, how would that affect you as regards your relation to the church?

SENATOR SMOOT. I hardly think it would affect me. I remember now an instance in our church of a revelation being received for the establishment of the United Order.[2] I know that Brigham Young went from one end of the State to the other and preached the new order, and instructed the people to organize and follow out that revelation. He went from St. George [Utah] to the north, and I know that it was never adhered to or followed out by the people, and is virtually a dead letter to-day.

SENATOR DUBOIS. Do you mean to have me infer from that that if the Lord gave a revelation to the president, which was submitted to the church and they sustained it, a member of the Mormon Church could disregard that and maintain his fellowship and standing in the church?

SENATOR SMOOT. Oh, yes; I understand so. Take the law of tithing. It is a law of the church, and I know there are many, many people who belong to the church to-day who do not obey it, and they are in fellowship, Senator. We try to teach the principles as revealed, and we try to have men live lives of honor and uprightness and honesty, and that is our duty and that is required of us.

SENATOR DUBOIS. Let us be clear about this. Under those circumstances you could refuse to obey such revelation which had been sustained by the church?

SENATOR SMOOT. I could.

SENATOR DUBOIS. And as an apostle you could go out among your people and take that position; and the people could refuse to obey it also and retain their standing?

SENATOR SMOOT. I would not want to go as far as I infer your question would lead—that is, I would not want to say that a man could go from

---

2. The United Order, in LDS doctrine, refers to an egalitarian, cooperative society. Goals of the United Order included income equality, group self-sufficiency, spiritual unification, and elimination of poverty (in *Encyclopedia of Mormonism*, ed. Daniel H. Ludlow [New York: Macmillan Publishing, 1992], 4:1493-95).

one end of the church to the other and make a special point of preaching against a certain doctrine of the church and be in full fellowship. I would not want you to understand, Senator, that I mean that, because I think that would be not only nonbelief in it, but it would be open rebellion, and through that you would be out of harmony. ...

SENATOR OVERMAN. The [Wilford Woodruff] manifesto is a revelation from God, which was submitted to the church and accepted by the church. Then any member of the church as a free agent has a right to disobey it?

SENATOR SMOOT. They have. They have the free agency.

SENATOR DUBOIS. Senator Smoot, if you refused as an apostle to accept a revelation received by Joseph Smith and sustained by the church, could you retain your position as an apostle in the church?

SENATOR SMOOT. If I did not understand that revelation, I think so.

SENATOR DUBOIS. My question is if you refused to accept it?

SENATOR SMOOT. I rather think so; the same as a member of the church would in not living up to any of our principles that they may not live up to. I would be derelict.

SENATOR DUBOIS. Could you answer directly whether or not you would retain your position as an apostle of the church?

SENATOR SMOOT. I could not answer that direct, yes or no, because I do not know what the church would do.

SENATOR DUBOIS. You would be out of harmony, would you not?

SENATOR SMOOT. I say I would be derelict, I think.

SENATOR DUBOIS. You do not know what the consequences would be as regards your apostleship?

SENATOR SMOOT. I could not say, Mr. Senator. ...

SENATOR FORAKER. I understood you to say that rather than to undertake to obey such a revelation you would leave the country and go where the law of the land would permit obedience to the revelation?

SENATOR SMOOT. Yes; if God had given it to me himself, then I would, because I would feel then that I was under direct obligation to my Maker to carry out what He revealed directly to me, and if I could not do it in this country I would go to some other country where I could.

MR. TAYLER. So that you would, of course, obey the revelation coming from God?

SENATOR SMOOT. If I knew that God had spoken to me I would obey it.

MR. TAYLER. Suppose the revelation commanded of God was that you should do a certain thing and also stay in the country?

SENATOR SMOOT. Well, I do not think the God I worship is such a God.

MR. TAYLER. That is your answer to the question?

SENATOR FORAKER. You think that is hardly a fair suppositions case?

SENATOR SMOOT. I do not think it is probable or possible.

SENATOR OVERMAN. If you have a right to disobey the law of God given to the church, why would you not have a right as a free agent to disobey a revelation given to you as an individual?

SENATOR SMOOT. I would have that, Senator. God could not take it away from me.

SENATOR OVERMAN. Then you would not have to leave the country? You could disobey it?

SENATOR SMOOT. I would not obey it. I say it is not necessary for me to obey it, even though God spoke to me.

SENATOR OVERMAN. You would not be condemned by God, then, if you disobeyed it?

SENATOR SMOOT. Certainly I would.

SENATOR OVERMAN. Then, if you disobeyed a revelation given to the church and accepted by the church, you would also be subject to be condemned by God?

SENATOR SMOOT. Whatever wrong there may be in it, I would have to answer for that wrong.

MR. TAYLER. You say that the law of the land would prevail, because that is a fundamental doctrine of the church?

SENATOR SMOOT. I say so.

MR. TAYLER. That is the reason?

SENATOR SMOOT. I say that that—

MR. TAYLER. Is that the reason?

SENATOR SMOOT. I think you could infer that.

MR. TAYLER. Was the law commanding polygamy a revelation from God?

SENATOR SMOOT. I understand so. ...

MR. TAYLER. When God commands, as you interpret it, it is equally a command whether it is to do one thing or another, is it?

SENATOR SMOOT. I think so; but He did not command a man to go into polygamy or to practice it.

MR. TAYLER. I understand.

SENATOR SMOOT. It was permissive and not mandatory.

THE CHAIRMAN. It is a command only on the man who receives the revelation?

SENATOR SMOOT. I think if He commanded me, Mr. Chairman, to go into it, then it would be a command to me, and I would have to obey it; but otherwise I would not.

SENATOR FORAKER. But you do not understand that He ever did make any such command?

SENATOR SMOOT. Not on the church. He said it was permissive. I understand from the revelation that He did make a command on Joseph Smith, and he is the only one.[3] ...

MR. TAYLER. I read from the "Journal of Discourses," by Brigham Young.

MR. WORTHINGTON. What page?

MR. TAYLER. Page 457, where, amongst other things, he said: "No man need judge me. You know nothing about it, whether I am sent or not; furthermore, it is none of your business, only to listen with open ears to what is taught you, and serve God with an undivided heart."[4]

SENATOR SMOOT. That would never do to-day. I do not think that Brigham Young ever said that under any inspiration of the Lord, if he did say it.

MR. TAYLER. You have no doubt of his saying it? It is published in the "Journal of Discourses."

SENATOR SMOOT. There are quite a number of things in the "Journal of Discourses" which are not accepted by the church.

MR. TAYLER. I understand that, but you believe it to have been said?

SENATOR SMOOT. As I said before, our people are called up from the audience to speak. Nobody knows when he is going to be called on. There is no special preparation for any sermon. A man gets up and speaks, and sometimes I think he says things that perhaps he would not say under calmer consideration. I know men sometimes speak under the spirit of inspiration, as it were. At other times it is a labored effort on their part, and they can hardly express themselves.

MR. TAYLER. Now, what do you think about the spirit that moved Joseph F. Smith, December 5, 1900, when—

MR. WORTHINGTON. What page?

MR. TAYLER. Page 458. When he said this: "I believe in union. I believe that except we are one in those things which pertain to the building up of Zion we are not God's children. But I want to say to you that we are not one. There is not that union amongst us that should exist.

3. The next day Carl Badger wrote to his wife: "The Senator has been on the stand for two days and has done well, remarkably well the first day. He was worn out the second day, and this was shown in his testimony. He was asked a great many hypothetical questions,—silly ones, I think" (in Rodney J. Badger, *Liahona and Iron Rod: The Biography of Carl A. and Rose J. Badger* [Bountiful, Utah: Family History Publishers, 1985], 246).

4. This excerpt was taken from a sermon by President Brigham Young, "Comprehensiveness of True Religion—The Saints But Stewards," delivered in Salt Lake City on December 5, 1853 (F. D. & S. W. Richards, comps., *Journal of Discourses* [London: Latter-day Saints Book Depot, 1854], 1: 341; *Smoot Hearings*, 2:457).

Sometimes when President [Lorenzo] Snow tells a brother what he would like him to do, he at once turns on his heel and says that comes in contact with his manhood and his independence, and he prefers to follow the bent of his own mind rather than to take such counsel."[5]

SENATOR SMOOT. That man has that perfect right.

MR. TAYLER. Who, Joseph [F.] Smith or the other man?

SENATOR SMOOT. No; the man to complain. He has a perfect right to complain.

MR. TAYLER. Then Joseph [F.] Smith was not speaking the will of the church?

SENATOR SMOOT. Oh, he was speaking thus: That it was the wish of the authorities of the church, and the church itself, more than likely, that there should be unity among the members of the church, and which I believe would be a very good thing, not only in the Mormon Church, but in any other church upon the earth.

MR. TAYLER. And that a man ought not to turn on his heel, when President Snow speaks to him, and say that conflicts with his manhood and independence?

SENATOR SMOOT. I do not say that. If he felt like that, that is what he has a right to do. ...

MR. TAYLER. In the "Journal of Discourses," volume 5, page 83, are some remarks by President [Wilford] Woodruff. You knew President Woodruff in his lifetime?

SENATOR SMOOT. I did.

MR. TAYLER. He there said: "Now, whatever I might have obtained in the shape of learning by searching and study respecting the arts and sciences of men, whatever principles I may have imbibed during my scientific researches, yet if the prophet of God should tell me that a certain principle or theory which I might have learned was not true, I do not care what my ideas might have been, I should consider it my duty, at the suggestion of my file leader, to abandon that principle or theory. Suppose he were to say the principles by which you are governed are not right, that they were incorrect, what would be my duty? I answer that it would be my duty to lay those principles aside, and to take up those that might be laid down by the servants of God."[6] Have you any doubt about his having said that?

---

5. The Joseph F. Smith quote was taken from a sermon, "Temple Work and the Law of Tithing," delivered in Salt Lake City on October 7, 1900 (*Deseret News*, Dec. 1, 1900; *Smoot Hearings*, 2:458-59).

6. This Wilford Woodruff excerpt was taken from a sermon, "Necessity of Adher-

SENATOR SMOOT. I do not know that he said it. I could not say whether he did or did not.

MR. TAYLER. The "Journal of Discourses" is published by the church?

SENATOR SMOOT. My opinion is if it is in the "Journal of Discourses," more than likely he said it.

MR. TAYLER. At least until 1890 the people of the church did live up to that principle, did they not?

SENATOR SMOOT. I could not say that they did—as broad as that.

MR. TAYLER. That is, the latter part of it?

SENATOR SMOOT. I never heard it preached in that way in my life.

MR. TAYLER. Senator, you testified respecting the endowment ceremony. Did you ever go through it more than once?

SENATOR SMOOT. But once. ...

MR. TAYLER. You heard the testimony of Mr. [Hugh M.] Dougall here?

SENATOR SMOOT. I did.

MR. TAYLER. A witness who was put on the stand by you.

SENATOR SMOOT. I did.

MR. TAYLER. You heard his statement that they were importuned to avenge the blood of the martyrs upon this generation?[7]

SENATOR SMOOT. I heard him say so.

MR. TAYLER. You say there is nothing at all like that in the ceremony?

SENATOR SMOOT. I do not recall it, nor do I believe that there is.

MR. TAYLER. I understood you to say a few moments ago that there was nothing in the ceremony anywhere like that. You said that positively—that there was nothing in the ceremony about avenging the blood of the martyrs or avenging the martyrs.

SENATOR SMOOT. You never asked me that, Mr. Tayler.

MR. TAYLER. I ask it now. Is there anything in the ceremony about avenging the blood of the martyrs or the martyrs?

SENATOR SMOOT. No; there is not. ...

THE CHAIRMAN. Let me ask a question, because I am sure, Senator, you want to be understood. How long did it take to perform this ceremony?

SENATOR SMOOT. My judgment would be from the beginning to the end about three or four hours.

THE CHAIRMAN. Were others present?

---

ing to the Priesthood in Preference to Science and Art," delivered in Salt Lake City on April 9, 1857 (*Journal of Discourses*, 5:83).

7. For Hugh M. Dougall's testimony, see chapter 21 in this volume; *Smoot Hearings*, 2:758-59, 762-65).

SENATOR SMOOT. When I went through?

THE CHAIRMAN. Yes.

SENATOR SMOOT. Yes.

THE CHAIRMAN. How many?

SENATOR SMOOT. Thirty or forty I should think; maybe not so many.

THE CHAIRMAN. Will you state that ceremony?

SENATOR SMOOT. I could not do it.

THE CHAIRMAN. State what you are able to recall?

SENATOR SMOOT. I would very much prefer not to, Mr. Chairman.

THE CHAIRMAN. Why not?

SENATOR SMOOT. For conscientious reasons. I want to say this, Mr. Chairman—

THE CHAIRMAN. Let me inquire—

SENATOR FORAKER. Let the witness answer.

THE CHAIRMAN. Certainly; the Senator shall have ample opportunity.

SENATOR FORAKER. He is answering now, and I should like to have the benefit of his answer at this point.

SENATOR SMOOT. I have conscientious reasons for it. I made a vow, not an oath, with my God, not with any man, not with the president of the church or with a living soul; but I did make a vow that I would keep those endowment ceremonies sacred and not reveal them to anybody, and I have kept that all my life, and if I went out of the church to-morrow and remained out of the church until I was gray-headed I would never feel that it was my duty, nor would I divulge what little even I remember of them.

THE CHAIRMAN. Is that the whole of your answer? You can, then, at this time recall some portions of the ceremony?

SENATOR SMOOT. Very little of it.

THE CHAIRMAN. I say you can recall some portion of it.

SENATOR SMOOT. I could not recall it so as to be accurate, Mr. Chairman.

THE CHAIRMAN. But I understand you to say that you decline to state that portion of it which you can recall?

SENATOR SMOOT. With all due deference and respect to the committee, I would prefer not to.

THE CHAIRMAN. That you entered into an obligation, I understand you to say, not an oath, but a promise, with the Lord, not to reveal these things?

SENATOR SMOOT. I did.

THE CHAIRMAN. Was there any penalty attached in the obligation for its violation?

SENATOR SMOOT. I prefer not to say anything further, Mr. Chairman.

THE CHAIRMAN. Do you remember whether there was or not?

SENATOR SMOOT. I prefer not to say anything further.

THE CHAIRMAN. Do you know why the oath of secrecy or the obligation of secrecy was imposed? What was there in the ceremony that makes secrecy a necessity?

SENATOR SMOOT. It is a purely religious ordinance, and refers absolutely to man's hereafter, and it has nothing whatever to do with anything other than man to his God; and I suppose that it is an ordinance in our church, and the rule is that it be not revealed.

THE CHAIRMAN. Were there any signs, passwords, or grips?

SENATOR SMOOT. I prefer, Mr. Chairman, to say nothing about it.

THE CHAIRMAN. I will not press it, of course. You decline to state any of the ceremony?

SENATOR SMOOT. Yes, sir. ...

SENATOR OVERMAN. How much money is collected each year by the church in the way of tithes; what is the total sum?

SENATOR SMOOT. I could not say. I do not know.

SENATOR OVERMAN. Have you any idea?

SENATOR SMOOT. I would not want to give a guess at it, and it would be a mere guess.

SENATOR OVERMAN. Do you collect as much as a million dollars?

SENATOR SMOOT. I have understood that some years it was about that and some years under.

SENATOR OVERMAN. Say it is a million. How is it invested?

SENATOR SMOOT. Of course I know little about that. There is about a hundred and forty thousand dollars of it that goes to the educational institutions. I am only telling you just what I have heard indirectly. There is about a hundred thousand dollars of it that goes for the feeding of the poor, other than what they collect as fast offerings in the wards. Then there is a great deal of it that goes for the payment of missionaries' fares returning home. They pay their own fare and expenses while upon a mission, but if they serve a mission two years, a faithful mission, and receive honorable release, their fare is paid home.

SENATOR OVERMAN. What I wish to get at is this: Is any of it invested in industrial and commercial institutions?

SENATOR SMOOT. The church has some of those, but the church is in debt, Mr. Senator. They issued bonds, you know, and I think they have outstanding bonds to the extent of about a million dollars, with some two hundred thousand or something, as I remember it ...

SENATOR OVERMAN. The investigation has gone very far into what the church is doing in Utah. I wanted it for my own information, in order that I might know what power the church has in the way of owning commercial industries, and as to the independence of the people.

SENATOR SMOOT. I assure you there are many Senators of the United States who own a great many times more money than the church does.[8] ...

THE CHAIRMAN. You heard the testimony here, I believe, of Joseph F. Smith?

SENATOR SMOOT. I did.

THE CHAIRMAN. In which he testified that he was living in defiance of the law of the land?

SENATOR SMOOT. I did.

THE CHAIRMAN. Did you also hear him state that he was living contrary to the divine law?

SENATOR SMOOT. I heard him testify, and make his qualifications.

THE CHAIRMAN. That he is living in defiance of the divine command. Has the church proceeded against him for the violation of these laws?

SENATOR SMOOT. They have not.

THE CHAIRMAN. No steps have been taken to try him for the offense of polygamous cohabitation?

SENATOR SMOOT. No, sir.

THE CHAIRMAN. I understood you to say this morning that it is the province of the apostles to counsel and advise the president?

SENATOR SMOOT. When asked by him.

THE CHAIRMAN. Only when requested?

SENATOR SMOOT. Yes.

---

8. Senator Bailey took offense at this possible insult and responded a few minutes later:

SENATOR BAILEY. ... The charge here, in its widest scope, is that the Mormon Church control the politics and industries of Utah. The ownership of the Mormon Church in these various industries might be entirely pertinent to an inquiry of that kind. But there is no charge that any Senator is controlling either the politics or the industries or the religion of a State. I hardly think that was a very apt reply.

SENATOR SMOOT. Mr. Chairman, I wish it distinctly understood that I had no intention whatever of casting a shadow of a doubt on a single Senator.

SENATOR BAILEY. I am not one of the Senators who would take any offense at that, and I think some of them are a little richer than is necessary.

SENATOR SMOOT. I shall ask then that that part of the answer be stricken out" (*Smoot Hearings*, 3:285).

THE CHAIRMAN. You are not, then, at liberty to advise him unless requested?

SENATOR SMOOT. I do not think he would object to it at all if I did.

THE CHAIRMAN. Are you at liberty to advise him unless requested?

SENATOR SMOOT. I do not think President Smith would object if I did. I do not know that I have any special right to do it, but I do not think he would object to it.

THE CHAIRMAN. I think my question was very plain. You have the right to advise him, even if he does not request it?

SENATOR SMOOT. That is a question which it is hard to answer yes or no, and I do not want to—

THE CHAIRMAN. After you heard President Smith testify here that he was living in violation of the laws of the State and of the law of God did you see him in the committee room and elsewhere?

SENATOR SMOOT. I did.

THE CHAIRMAN. How long was he here?

SENATOR SMOOT. Here in Washington, do you mean?

THE CHAIRMAN. Yes. I am not particular about it—two or three days?

SENATOR SMOOT. Two or three days.

THE CHAIRMAN. You saw him frequently?

SENATOR SMOOT. Not frequently. I saw him, though.

THE CHAIRMAN. Did you make any protest to him about his manner of living?

SENATOR SMOOT. I did not.

THE CHAIRMAN. You have visited Utah since?

SENATOR SMOOT. I have.

THE CHAIRMAN. You have seen him at Salt Lake since?

SENATOR SMOOT. I have.

THE CHAIRMAN. Have you protested against his living in polygamous cohabitation?

SENATOR SMOOT. I have not.

THE CHAIRMAN. Have you in any way sought to bring him to trial for those offenses?

SENATOR SMOOT. I have not.

THE CHAIRMAN. Do you intend to?

SENATOR SMOOT. I do not.

THE CHAIRMAN. Do you remember how many children he said had been born to him since 1890?

SENATOR SMOOT. I think he said eleven.

THE CHAIRMAN. And by all of his five wives?

SENATOR SMOOT. That I am not positive of.

THE CHAIRMAN. Now, with the full knowledge of these facts, testified to by him, you sustained him in October last?

SENATOR SMOOT. I did. If that is all you desire to ask, Mr. Chairman, I should like to say this: The manifesto as it was voted upon by the people had no reference to unlawful cohabitation. Two years after that there was an interpretation put upon it by President Woodruff, and it was his advice and counsel to the people to adhere to that interpretation, stating that he was going to do it, and he advised all of the other people to do it.

The question of unlawful cohabitation has never been presented and sustained by the people and voted upon at a general conference, and I take it for granted that perhaps some of the members of the church have felt that it was not binding upon them for that reason. ...

THE CHAIRMAN. You not only did not reprimand President Smith for his conduct, but you sustained him in October last in a public assembly?

SENATOR SMOOT. When he was presented to be voted upon as president of the church I voted for him as such.

THE CHAIRMAN. Have you indicated to him directly or indirectly that his conduct is displeasing to you?

SENATOR SMOOT. I have not.

THE CHAIRMAN. Have you resigned your position as an apostle?

SENATOR SMOOT. I have not.

THE CHAIRMAN. Have you severed your connection with the Mormon Church?

SENATOR SMOOT. I have not.

THE CHAIRMAN. And you intend to retain your relationship and your apostolic position and sustain the president in his crimes?

MR. WORTHINGTON. I object to that—that he intends to sustain the president in his crimes.

THE CHAIRMAN. I will modify the question. I will ask the witness whether he intended to sustain Mr. Smith in the commission of this crime?

SENATOR SMOOT. I do not sustain any man in the commission of crime.

THE CHAIRMAN. You sustained him in living in polygamous cohabitation?

SENATOR SMOOT. I have not said that.

THE CHAIRMAN. Did you not sustain him in October last?

SENATOR SMOOT. I sustained him as president of the church.

THE CHAIRMAN. And you have made no protest to him personally?

SENATOR SMOOT. It is not my place as an officer of the law nor within my place as a citizen of Provo. That is where I live. It is not my place to make any complaint to the officers of the law against President Joseph F. Smith.

THE CHAIRMAN. Against the head of the church?

SENATOR SMOOT. Against Joseph F. Smith, or John Henry Smith; I do not care whether he is the head of the church or a man living there.

THE CHAIRMAN. Then you think that your relation as an apostle does not impose upon you any duty to make complaint against the head of the church for any offense?

SENATOR SMOOT. I do not think it would be my duty.[9] ...

THE CHAIRMAN. Senator, I want to ask one or two questions, that I may be more thoroughly informed. Are you at liberty to resign your apostolate?

SENATOR SMOOT. I am.

THE CHAIRMAN. At any time?

SENATOR SMOOT. At any time.

THE CHAIRMAN. You are not under any restraint from any authority by which you are not, at any time? You can at any time resign?

SENATOR SMOOT. At any time.

THE CHAIRMAN. And is there anything in the rules or practice of your church which would debar you from severing your connection with the organization?

SENATOR SMOOT. None whatever.

THE CHAIRMAN. With the church itself?

SENATOR SMOOT. None whatever.

THE CHAIRMAN. You speak of the time when you took the endowments. I am not clear whether you stated if you were present at other times.

SENATOR SMOOT. I never have been, Mr. Chairman.

THE CHAIRMAN. You have never been present at any time since?

SENATOR SMOOT. Never.

THE CHAIRMAN. And you have not officiated in any way in conferring the endowments at any time?

SENATOR SMOOT. I never officiated in any way.

THE CHAIRMAN. I think you said to the Committee that you were surprised when you heard the president of the church testify as he testified before this committee?

SENATOR SMOOT. As to the number of children that he had.

THE CHAIRMAN. Yes. You were surprised?

---

9. The entire excerpt was used in the Senate debate on February 20, 1907. The previous six questions were used by Tayler in his closing argument for the prosecution (*Smoot Hearings*, 3:581-82).

SENATOR SMOOT. I was surprised as to the number of children that he had since the manifesto.

THE CHAIRMAN. Then you were, of course, surprised to learn that he was living in polygamous cohabitation?

SENATOR SMOOT. Well, I did not know that he was, and I had no reason to believe that he was.

THE CHAIRMAN. Of course. Then you were surprised when he testified that he had had 11 children since the manifesto?

SENATOR SMOOT. Yes, sir.

THE CHAIRMAN. And that surprise still continues, I suppose?

SENATOR SMOOT. No, sir; I know it now; or I think I know it, from what he—

THE CHAIRMAN. From what he testified?

SENATOR SMOOT. From what he testified to.

THE CHAIRMAN. You regard him, I suppose, a truthful man?

SENATOR SMOOT. I do.

THE CHAIRMAN. Did you make known your surprise to him?

SENATOR SMOOT. I did not.

THE CHAIRMAN. Neither then nor at any time since, have you?

SENATOR SMOOT. Neither then nor at any time since.[10] ...

THE CHAIRMAN. I wanted to inquire about it. I think you said before the October conference there was a meeting of the officials of the church. Did I understand you correctly—that the president and apostles had a meeting and that there was some discussion about some matters?

MR. WORTHINGTON. Prior to the 1904 conference, you mean.

THE CHAIRMAN. Yes; some preliminary meeting of the officials.

SENATOR SMOOT. Why, we had meetings right along, Mr. Chairman. I can not call to mind what you have reference to.

THE CHAIRMAN. I had reference to your testimony in chief in which you said there was a meeting of the president and the apostles a few days before the conference.

SENATOR SMOOT. At the time Mr. [Charles W.] Penrose was nominated?

THE CHAIRMAN. Possibly.

SENATOR SMOOT. Yes; I remember it.

THE CHAIRMAN. What I want to inquire about, is whether at that time you made known to Mr. Smith and those present your surprise to learn that the president was living in polygamous cohabitation.

SENATOR SMOOT. I did not.

---

10. Tayler used this excerpt in his closing argument (*Smoot Hearings*, 4:582-83).

THE CHAIRMAN. You did not say anything to him about it? Was anything said about it by anyone?

SENATOR SMOOT. Not that I remember.

THE CHAIRMAN. Mr. Penrose was proposed, as I understood you to say, at that meeting—

SENATOR SMOOT. By the president of the church.

THE CHAIRMAN. To fill the vacancy in the apostolate?

SENATOR SMOOT. Yes.

THE CHAIRMAN. Was Mr. Penrose a polygamist at that time?

SENATOR SMOOT. He was a polygamist. He had been married before the manifesto.

THE CHAIRMAN. Yes; I understand.[11]

SENATOR SMOOT. But of course, as I said, you know, Senator, at the time I did not know it. But it would have made no difference to me, as I said before.

THE CHAIRMAN. That is as I understand; but at the time you did not know he was a polygamist?

SENATOR SMOOT. I knew he had been a polygamist, and I knew that one of his wives died. I never knew anything about his family, and I thought he had had two wives and, one dying, he only had the one; but it proved that he had, before the manifesto, three wives instead of two. ...

THE CHAIRMAN. Have you made any inquiry to ascertain whether Mr. [Matthias F.] Cowley is now being investigated and what steps are being taken?[12]

---

11. This entire excerpt was used in the Senate debate before its vote on February 20, 1907.

12. Cowley tendered his resignation from the Quorum of the Twelve on October 29, 1905, one day after John W. Taylor submitted his. Cowley's was briefer:

I regret very much that I had done anything that has caused a lack of confidence in me, or that has occasioned the suspicion that the authorities of the Church have been untrue to their declarations concerning plural marriages since the Manifesto of 1890. I assert emphatically that the Presidency of the Church have not counseled or advised me to enter into plural marriages since that date. Also that I have not done so in violation of the laws of the United States of the State of Utah. There are some views in relation to these matters in which I have been out of harmony with the quorum and First Presidency but I have not intentionally violated any rule of the church as I understood the matter. I did not go to Washington as a witness in the Smoot case as requested by President Smith, as I considered the investigation rather as to the affairs of the Church than an inquiry into the qualifications of the Senator, and further I looked upon any private affairs as my own and not for the public. For my acts I am responsible and not the Church nor its President. But finding that I have been seriously out of harmony with my Quorum and wishing to bear my own

SENATOR SMOOT. Not since I left home.

THE CHAIRMAN. I understand you, Senator, to state that you do not teach polygamy?

SENATOR SMOOT. I do not.

THE CHAIRMAN. Or advise it? You teach and preach sometimes?

SENATOR SMOOT. I do.

THE CHAIRMAN. Do you preach against polygamy?

SENATOR SMOOT. I never have in a public gathering of people.

THE CHAIRMAN. Why do you not?

SENATOR SMOOT. Well, Mr. Chairman, I do not know why I should.

THE CHAIRMAN. You do not know why you should?

SENATOR SMOOT. Or why I should not. It is not a tenet now of the faith and—that is, what I mean to say is, it has been suspended, and I think it would not be proper for me to bring it up, because it is not preached, for or against.

THE CHAIRMAN. So, while it is literally true that you do not teach or preach polygamy, you have not taught or preached against it?

---

burden I hereby tender my resignation as a member of the Council of Twelve Apostles, and cast myself upon the forbearance and mercy of my brethren.

Nearly a year later, Smoot told the First Presidency he thought a "public announcement of resignations made at this late day would have an unfavorable effect upon the country and Senators. The time to have made the announcement was immediately after action was decided on by the Quorum." Smoot had promised to consult with President Roosevelt and Senate colleagues before advising whether the resignations were necessary. Now Smoot was reporting back:

In conversation with one of my [Senatorial] friends on this subject I said: Now Senator, you as an attorney would not convict Taylor and especially Cowley on the evidence in the record would you? He fairly went wild at once and said, "yes indeed I would, and you know they are guilty and I am surprised you would even intimate they were not. Why did they not come as witnesses the same as the others? Why are they in hiding now? Why does the church vote to sustain them and by so doing encourage and approve of their unlawful acts? Why do they show contempt for the Government of the U.S. ... by evading subpoenas? I am going to vote for you because I like you but I want you to know that this double dealing of the Church authorities with the Government I will never stand for" (Dec. 8, 1905).

Smoot wrote that he would "rather be expelled from the Senate, go home and resign from the Quorum than have it said now, or hereafter, that Taylor and Cowley was sacrificed or resigned to save me." In fact, "if Taylor and Cowley have done no wrong and their acts meet with the approval of the Brethren, for Heavens sake don't handle them but let us take the consequences." Yet Smoot could not believe the two apostles had acted under direction of the First Presidency in continuing to perform plural marriages. That would mean Church President Lorenzo Snow had intended to "deceive the Quorum" and that Joseph F. Smith was "untruthful." Smoot "would about as soon lose my life as to become convinced of it." So the two apostles deserved expulsion, but Smoot didn't want to be the one who would take the blame for it.

SENATOR SMOOT. No; I have not in a general—

THE CHAIRMAN. Senator, in your teaching and preaching have you at any time denounced polygamous cohabitation?

SENATOR SMOOT. I have not.

THE CHAIRMAN. And do I understand you to say you do not reprobate that practice and preach against it publicly?

SENATOR SMOOT. I have not.[13]

THE CHAIRMAN. There is some uncertainty about the manifesto, as to its meaning, I believe; that is, whether it prohibits polygamous cohabitation or simply the taking of plural wives.

SENATOR SMOOT. Well, the wording of the manifesto prohibits plural marriages.

THE CHAIRMAN. There is some doubt among the authorities as to the point whether it prohibits polygamous cohabitation.

SENATOR SMOOT. I can not speak for the authorities. I have heard it spoken of among the people. ...

THE CHAIRMAN. I will ask you this: Was Mr. Woodruff, at the time this revelation was received, reputed to be a polygamist?

SENATOR SMOOT. I think he was.

THE CHAIRMAN. These revelations from God—take, for instance, the manifesto—are they made to the head of the church usually?

SENATOR SMOOT. I think the manifesto was an inspiration from the Lord to Wilford Woodruff, the head of the church.

THE CHAIRMAN. Are these revelations made as the result of an invocation or an appeal from the mortal to be advised in relation to a certain course of conduct, or do they come as a surprise?

SENATOR SMOOT. I understand that this inspiration as to the manifesto came to President Woodruff by his pleading to the Lord for light. That is what his statement says, I think.

THE CHAIRMAN. Do you know whether the president of the church has appealed to the Lord for another manifesto to interpret that, so that there would be no doubt about it?

SENATOR SMOOT. I do not.

THE CHAIRMAN. The Lord might be appealed to, I suppose, to clear that question up, could he not, Senator, from a proper source?

SENATOR SMOOT. Oh, I guess anybody could appeal to the Lord.

THE CHAIRMAN. No such appeal has been made that you know of. I think that is all.

---

13. The previous eight questions and answers were used in the plenary debate before the full Senate on February 20, 1907.

MR. WORTHINGTON. Mr. Tayler, have you anything further to ask Senator Smoot?

MR. TAYLER. Yes; just a question. Senator, you said that you declined to reveal what occurred in the endowment proceedings because you had taken an obligation or made a vow or given a promise to God not to do so?

SENATOR SMOOT. I did.

MR. TAYLER. How do you know that you made it to God?

SENATOR SMOOT. Because that is the impression I had at the time, that I made that vow with my Heavenly Father.

MR. TAYLER. I am not dealing with this in any even suggestively sacrilegious way, Senator, but I want to get the process, mental or moral, by which this thing occurred. You do not understand, do you, that God revealed himself to you at the time that you took this obligation?

SENATOR SMOOT. No; I do not.

MR. TAYLER. You do not know that God required that obligation, do you?

SENATOR SMOOT. I do not.

MR. TAYLER. Or that He called for it in any way, either upon you or anybody else?

SENATOR SMOOT. He may have by instituting the endowment through His prophet, Joseph Smith, jr.

MR. TAYLER. When did God institute these endowments, Senator?

SENATOR SMOOT. I understood it was through the prophet, Joseph Smith, jr. ...

MR. TAYLER. Well, what do you say about this endowment ceremony? Do you understand that that proceeded from God?

SENATOR SMOOT. I have heard it so taught.

MR. TAYLER. So taught?

SENATOR SMOOT. Yes.

MR. TAYLER. Has it been approved by the church in conference?

SENATOR SMOOT. That I can not say.

MR. TAYLER. Do you understand that it ever was?

SENATOR SMOOT. Well, they were started in the early days of the church. I do not know, Mr. Tayler.

MR. TAYLER. Is it not your understanding, Senator, that the obligation of secrecy, by whatever name you describe it, is a mere voluntary offer made by the person who takes it?

SENATOR SMOOT. I did not so understand it. I understood, as I stated, that it was an obligation that I made to my Heavenly Father to keep the endowment secret.

MR. TAYLER. Exactly. Now, what I want to be certain about, Senator, is whether or how the duty was laid upon anybody to make any such obligation to God.

SENATOR SMOOT. I think the person takes the obligation upon himself.

MR. TAYLER. Yes; exactly. But whether God demanded that or not is quite important.

SENATOR SMOOT. He never demanded it of me.

MR. TAYLER. He had not demanded it of you. If the endowment ceremony proceeded from God, did it proceed from a direct revelation from Him or because one of his mouthpieces ordered that method?

SENATOR SMOOT. I can not say whether it was a direct revelation or not.

MR. TAYLER. So that when you say you made that obligation with God it is, after all, only that it was in your mind that you were promising God you would not reveal it?

SENATOR SMOOT. It was in my mind and I believed that that was proper to do, and I promised.[14] ...

SENATOR McCOMAS. Senator Smoot, you say you obtained leave of absence from the Mormon Church—

SENATOR SMOOT. From the presidency of the Mormon Church.

SENATOR McCOMAS. From the presidency of the church, when you came to attend the first session of the Senate?

SENATOR SMOOT. I obtained it, Mr. Senator, before I even announced my candidacy—

---

14. Four days following Smoot's testimony, on January 27, 1905, Carl Badger gave his wife another candid assessment of things:

I do not think the Senator consciously had in mind any effort to retain his seat while giving his testimony. I think he wanted his religion to appear reasonable and common-sensed to his fellow associates on the Committee. I do not know specifically to what you refer when you say that his words will have a bad effect on some of our people. The Senator is a very practical man, he is not spiritually minded. He is not well educated, has done comparatively little reading; his ideas are not exact, and his way of expressing them is vague and uncertain so that his testimony in some ways was unsatisfactory, but taken as a whole, and considering what I had expected from him I was well pleased with what he said. ... I like the Senator's definition of a prophet—one who speaks by the spirit of prophecy, and I feel as shy as he does about admitting that any particular man, at any particular time, is a prophet. ... The Senator is not a brave man in a moral sense, but we all shrink when it comes to the test. You must not allow anyone else to read my letters. Be very careful about quoting me. The Senator is an anomaly as an apostle, and the situation can only be explained by a recourse to the thought that the ways of the Lord are inscrutable to man. I do not say this in a light mood. I am thoroughly convinced that this investigation answers some divine purpose—that we need it and therefore it has come. I do not see how it could have come without Senator Smoot, therefore Senator Smoot. The Senator has been under a very severe strain, and deserves our sympathy" (in Badger, *Liahona and Iron Rod*, 247).

SENATOR McCOMAS. Yes, I understand that.

SENATOR SMOOT. For the Senate.

SENATOR McCOMAS. But in order to know if I am right, did you also obtain the assent of the presidency of the church when you came to attend the first session of the Senate?

SENATOR SMOOT. No; I told him when I first spoke to him that if I succeeded in my canvass and was elected Senator, my first duty would be here and whatever time it required of me to attend to that duty, that I should expect it as long as I held the position.

SENATOR McCOMAS. So you have asked no other consent to go to the Senate of the United States from the presidency of the Mormon Church?

SENATOR SMOOT. Not since that date. I can leave any day I want, when it is a duty that calls me as a Senator.

SENATOR McCOMAS. And that occurred when you were a candidate for the Senate—when you were on your canvass?

SENATOR SMOOT. Yes; before I announced—before my canvass; yes.

SENATOR McCOMAS. You have had no communication on that subject since with the presidency?

SENATOR SMOOT. I have not.

SENATOR McCOMAS. Nor deemed it necessary to have it?

SENATOR SMOOT. It will not be.

SENATOR McCOMAS. I wanted to understand how that was.

SENATOR SMOOT. I had that distinct understanding with them to start with.

SENATOR McCOMAS. That is all, Mr. Chairman.[15] ...

THE CHAIRMAN. May I interrupt you, Mr. Worthington?

MR. WORTHINGTON. Certainly.

THE CHAIRMAN. You have several papers you desire to present, and there is only a small number of the members of the committee here. If you have other witnesses, can you not proceed with them tonight, and then in the morning we will consider the other matters?

MR. WORTHINGTON. I would like to say now, however, in order that the committee may have this matter under consideration, and in order that counsel for the protestants may also, that we have here an affida-

---

15. Earlier in the hearings, Smoot was told he could bribe his way to victory: "The other day I was approached by a prominent Southern man who asked me if I wished to be assured of winning my case, and if I did he was in a position to give me that assurance, provided a certain amount of money could be furnished him. ... After I had got out of him all that I could, and he told me with whom he was working, I informed him that I did not expect to win my case in that way" (Smoot to Joseph F. Smith, April 9, 1904).

vit of Bathsheba Smith, who has been referred to here, that she is cognizant of the fact that she took her endowments during the lifetime of
the Prophet Joseph Smith, jr., and that they have remained unchanged.[16] We have also a certificate of her physician that she is over
80 years old, and that it is utterly impossible for her to come here; and
we are going to suggest that these affidavits be filed and that upon
them this committee shall have a commission issued to some person—if the committee decide that shall be done, counsel will have no
trouble about agreeing upon the commissioner, I suppose—and that
the commissioner there may take her deposition, all the parties here
having the right to be present for the purpose of cross-examination
and examination. We want to take the deposition of this old lady and
the deposition of Apostle [Marriner Wood] Merrill at his bedside.

The committee will perceive that these are matters of some consequence, because if it be true that these endowment ceremonies were
introduced by the Prophet Joseph Smith and that they have remained
unchanged, as many witnesses have testified, then it is impossible
that those ceremonies could have contained any allusion to the supposed vengeance for the taking of the life of Joseph Smith, because it
could never have referred to vengeance for his murder when he was
alive. ...

THE CHAIRMAN. In the morning we will be able to dispose of that matter. ...

THE CHAIRMAN. Who is your next witness, Mr. Worthington?

MR. WORTHINGTON. We are not prepared with any other witness at present, Mr. Chairman. I can say, almost certainly, that we will conclude
this matter to-morrow so far as we are concerned.

MR. TAYLER. As far as we are concerned, if that is your view, I think we
will probably save time by waiting until to-morrow. ...

THE CHAIRMAN. I call the attention of counsel to the fact that Mr. Tayler,
who represents the protestants, must assume his duties as a Federal
judge next Tuesday [Jan. 31], and it is important that this matter
should be brought to a conclusion this week. If counsel desire to be
heard on either side, it will be well to move along as rapidly as you
can. ...

---

16. For Bathsheba Smith's affidavit, see *Smoot Hearings,* 3:442.

27.

Frank B. Stephens

Tuesday & Wednesday, January 24-25

"Investigation of the Smoot case came to an abrupt termination this morning. Shortly after the Committee ... was called to order Counsel Worthington ... stated that the defense rested its case. ... Two witnesses summoned and present were George Sutherland, [Utah's] Senator-elect, and Arthur L. Thomas. These were not called to the stand. It has all along been held that Postmaster Thomas was to be the star witness. He was to furnish the testimony which would settle the question in favor of Smoot, but he was not permitted to talk" —*Salt Lake Tribune,* Jan. 25, 1905

"[Senator Depew] appeared today for the first time since the 'defense' was begun. Senator Knox of Pennsylvania has been severely criticized by the ... women['s] [organizations] because of his failure to attend the early sessions of the committee after his appointment. There is perhaps no member of the committee who has followed the case more carefully ... He has read and carefully considered every word of testimony thus far printed, and devotes an hour or more every evening to a perusal of the reports written out by the stenographers. The senator says he proposes reaching a conclusion ... exactly as ... if on the bench and the case argued before him. This is certainly true of other senators, notably Pettus, Overman, Foraker and Dillingham" —*Deseret News,* Jan. 24, 1905

Frank B. Stephens,[1] being duly sworn, was examined, and testified as follows ...

MR. VAN COTT. Calling attention to politics again for a few moments, did you have anything to do with the dissolution of what has been called the "Liberal" or "Gentile" party, so as to form the people into two political parties on national lines?

MR. STEPHENS. I do not know that I had anything to do with the dissolution of the Liberal party, but I had something to do with the forming of [new alliances for] the old [territorial] parties—that is, dividing on

---

1. Stephens (1855-1940) was born in Maine and had lived in Illinois and Nebraska before moving to Utah in 1888. A non-Mormon, he was appointed a U.S. Attorney in 1891, thereafter practicing law in Salt Lake City.

579

[national] party [rather than local religious] lines. I was one of the first five, as I remember it, who met to divide, to join on [national] party lines in one party.[2]

MR. VAN COTT. You favored that?

MR. STEPHENS. I did, sir.

MR. VAN COTT. What year was that?

MR. STEPHENS. It has been a long time since I gave that consideration. I think it was in 1891. I know it was when I was assistant United States attorney, and we met in the Federal court room shortly after the court adjourned.

MR. VAN COTT. Had you taken an active interest in the Liberal party before that time?

MR. STEPHENS. I had.

MR. VAN COTT. And you had been a member of it?

MR. STEPHENS. I had; yes, sir. I carried a banner with the rest of them.

MR. VAN COTT. Why did you favor the dissolution of the old parties and the formation of new political parties on national lines?

MR. STEPHENS. I did not favor the dissolution of the Liberal party until I became convinced that the [Wilford Woodruff] manifesto was issued in sincerity and that it was approved by the members of the Mormon Church generally; but when I felt convinced that that was sincere I was glad to divide on party lines, for this reason: That a continual hammering of a sect or people unites them, and when a man's religion is being attacked he defends it and is strengthened in it; that so long as we Gentiles on one side, in a minority, were hammering away at the Mormons, who were in the majority, we were, I felt, intensifying the old conditions, and I felt if we could divide upon party lines and have a Mormon bishop arguing Democracy and another Mormon bishop arguing Republicanism, and have it understood that they were expected to unite with their various political parties and be free

---

2. Stephens's meaning is difficult to grasp without the benefit of his subsequent testimony. What he seems to be saying is that the old political environment divided along Mormons and Gentile lines, as the People's Party and Liberal Party, but with the embrace of national political parties, the religious distinction became blurred. Most Liberals joined the Republicans and most Mormons joined the Democrats, but some Gentiles, including Stephens, sympathized with the Democratic Party on national issues and therefore cooperated with Mormons locally. In addition, some Mormons aligned themselves with the Republicans. For more on the politics of the times, see Thomas G. Alexander, "To Maintain Harmony: Adjusting to External and Internal Stress, 1890-1930," in *The New Mormon History: Revisionist Essays on the Past,* ed. D. Michael Quinn (Salt Lake City: Signature Books, 1992), 251-52.

to act in them, that this very arguing against each other in politics, instead of arguing against us and we against them, would go a long way toward solving the conditions.

There are some, I think, who have regretted that we ever did it, but they are in a very small minority. The great and vast majority of the people, I think, have approved the division on party lines.

SENATOR DUBOIS. You mean the vast majority of the Gentiles?

MR. STEPHENS. Yes, sir; of the Gentiles.

MR. VAN COTT. When was it that you became convinced that the manifesto was issued in sincerity?

MR. STEPHENS. Oh, that was a growing feeling. I could not locate any time when I was convinced. It was a matter of conditions, and I could not state any time. I felt I was willing to put them on trial. ...

SENATOR FORAKER. Have you stated why there are no prosecutions instituted by Gentiles of the men who are still living in polygamous cohabitation with plural wives taken before the manifesto?

MR. STEPHENS. I have stated in a general way.

SENATOR FORAKER. I did not hear all of your testimony.

MR. STEPHENS. I said that I agreed with Mr. [Edward B.] Critchlow that there is no general sentiment, which has got to be behind a prosecution. But I think the feeling is something like this, if I might illustrate.

SENATOR FORAKER. Certainly.

MR. STEPHENS. When I was on the board of police and fire commissioners I advocated the unrelenting extermination of gambling houses, because a gambler can take a shovel and go to work. I opposed the promiscuous raiding of houses of ill fame, driving the inmates from pillar to post and out of the city, because when once in that position they can never live in any other way. And I opposed doing it as a matter of humanity until there was some way provided for them to live. In other words, it was a condition that confronted us.

Now, in the matter of the offenses of polygamy and unlawful cohabitation, I would prosecute, I would give information to the officers, I would use every means to convict a man of taking a plural wife since the manifesto. But on the other hand, with reference to the families that are there and that are living in these relations, I do not feel that it is best, on the whole, to ferret them out and bring them to the public attention, for the reason that it will be a thing of the past, if there are no more marriages, when they die. My children, I think, would have grown up to maturity and heard little or nothing about these old conditions, as I prefer they should not, if it had not been for the recent investigations.

SENATOR FORAKER. I think I understand you. Do you think your feeling in that respect is pretty general among the citizens of Utah?

MR. STEPHENS. It is so general that there are no prosecutions.

SENATOR FORAKER. There is no public sentiment demanding, or that would support, prosecutions?

MR. STEPHENS. I would not say there is no public sentiment, but there is not sufficient to compel prosecutions.[3]

SENATOR FORAKER. There is no sufficient public sentiment?

MR. STEPHENS. I would say, however, where there are flagrant instances the feeling would be that they ought to be prosecuted. I have that feeling myself. I had the same feeling with reference to that that I would have toward a neighbor who had been guilty of adultery. I would say that if it was not known, I would not want it to be known, because I would not want my children to hear of it; but if it became a public disgrace and stench in the community, I would be willing that it should be prosecuted.

THE CHAIRMAN. Would you call the case of the president of the church a flagrant case, when he himself testifies that he has had 11 children by his plural wives since the manifesto?

MR. STEPHENS. I would, sir; and my personal feeling is that he ought to be prosecuted for not setting a better example; that he ought not to set such an example.

SENATOR FORAKER. That is what we want to get at—why he is not prosecuted.

MR. STEPHENS. I can not say why he is not prosecuted, except that I think Mr. Critchlow expressed it in his cross-examination when he said there did not seem to be a general sentiment to do it. I do not know why he is not prosecuted.

SENATOR FORAKER. And you explain the lack of prosecution in that case in the same way that you do in the other instances—

MR. STEPHENS. Yes.

SENATOR FORAKER. That there is not sufficient public sentiment?

MR. STEPHENS. That is to say, we have hardly got over the shock of reading about that. I have not. I have never seen a polygamous child born since the manifesto, and while I had heard rumors of those matters and of that kind I knew nothing about it personally. As a matter of fact, I know only one house where a polygamous wife lives, and her husband is nearly 80 years of age.

---

3. This entire section above, as abridged here, was included in Worthington's closing argument (*Smoot Hearings,* 3:719-20).

THE CHAIRMAN. With this flagrant case existing of the president of the church, what is your opinion as to the probability of his being prosecuted, judging from the sentiment existing in that community?

MR. STEPHENS. I would be unable to say whether he would be prosecuted or not. I could not answer that question one way or the other, whether he would be or not.[4] ...

MR. TAYLER. You talked to us a while ago quite freely about fanatics in the church—

MR. STEPHENS. Yes, sir.

MR. TAYLER. Who might take wives?

---

4. Eventually Joseph F. Smith would plead guilty to unlawful cohabitation, expressing himself as follows:

> May it please the court: I desire respectfully to present a brief statement in my behalf. My first [plural] marriage was contracted in 1866, and my last in 1884, more than 22 years ago. These marriages were all entered into with the sanction of the Church of Jesus Christ of Latter-day Saints, and, as we believe, with the approval of the Lord. According to our faith and the law of the Church they were eternal in duration. In the tacit general understanding that was had in 1890 and the years subsequent thereto regarding what were classed as the old cases of cohabitation, I have appreciated the magnanimity of the American people in not enforcing a policy that in their minds was unnecessarily harsh, but which assigned the settlement of this difficult problem to the onward progress of time. Since the year 1890, a very large percentage of the polygamous families have ceased to exist, until now the number within the jurisdiction of this court is very small and marriages in violation of the law have been and now are prohibited. In view of this situation, which has fixed with certainty a result that can be easily measured up, the family relations in the old cases of that time have been generally left undisturbed. So far as my own case is concerned, I, like others who had entered into solemn religious obligations, sought to the best of my ability to comply with all requirements pertaining to the trying position in which we were placed. I have felt secure in the protection of that magnanimous sentiment which was extended as an olive branch in 1890 and subsequent years to those old cases of plural family relationships which came within its p[u]rview, as did mine. When I accepted the manifesto, issued by President Wilford Woodruff, I did not understand that I would be expected to abandon and discard my wives. Knowing the sacred covenants and obligations which I had assumed, by reason of these marriages, I have conscientiously tried to discharge the responsibilities attending them, without being offensive to any one. I have never flaunted my family relations before the public, nor have I felt a spirit of defiance against the law, but, on the contrary, I have always desired to be a law abiding citizen. In considering the trying position in which I have been placed, I trust that your honor will exercise such leniency, in your sentence, as law and justice will permit" ("Prest. Smith in Court Room," *Deseret News,* Nov. 23, 1906).

According to the *Salt Lake Tribune,* President Smith "was fined $300 ... which he paid by depositing his personal check with the Clerk of the Court. The fine is the largest permitted by the law ... Judge Ritchie ... declining to impose the jail sentence ... [but taking] occasion to warn the offender at the bar that the next time he was before him for sentence on such a charge a much more severe penalty would be inflicted. He did not ask the culprit to make any promises for the future" ("Joseph F. Smith Pleaded Guilty before Judge Ritchie," Nov. 23, 1906). Appreciation to Will Bagley for pointing out this source.

MR. STEPHENS. Yes, sir.

MR. TAYLER. Did you mean that they might take wives believing it was right to take wives or that it was a mere lewd arrangement that those fanatics, as you would call them, would enter into?

MR. STEPHENS. I can not conceive how a member of the Mormon Church, and much less an apostle, could take a plural wife since the manifesto believing it was right. He would be a religious fanatic on the question of what is right and wrong to a greater extent than I can comprehend.

SENATOR DEPEW. A religious fanatic is one who believes so thoroughly and completely in the doctrines of his church that it overrides all other human commands or objections. The greater the fanatic, it strikes me, the less liable he would be, simply as a churchman, to go into a plural marriage after 1890. If I understand this question, Senator, President Woodruff received a revelation direct from God in 1890 prohibiting plural marriages and reversing the revelation which had been previously received. So from that time on, the prohibition of plural marriages was a revelation from God. Therefore an apostle, much more than a layman, who entered into a plural marriage after that, would not only violate the law of the land, but he would violate directly a revelation delivered to the head of his church. So he could not be a fanatic. He must be a lewd person.

MR. STEPHENS. That is true. He would be violating the law of the land and the law of God. I am willing that anyone may draw any inference they please from his act. I have no sympathy with his act.

SENATOR DEPEW. But he could not be a fanatic.

MR. STEPHENS. That is a metaphysical or psychological question which I do not feel competent to discuss.

SENATOR DEPEW. And if he attempted to escape, he would give a human reason to himself to escape from what otherwise would be a sin.

MR. STEPHENS. He might do so, but I want to say, Senator Depew, that so far as concerns the revelation and President Woodruff and the manifesto, I think there was a lot of pressure within the church. I think it came about as much from the people in the church as it did from God.

SENATOR DEPEW. But we have had direct testimony on many occasions from President [Joseph F.] Smith and several apostles that the manifesto was given in obedience to a direct revelation which had been received from God.

MR. STEPHENS. I think they believe that.

SENATOR OVERMAN. Do you think there is any considerable number of

Mormons who believe that the manifesto was the work of man and not the work of God?

MR. STEPHENS. I think, Senator, there is a growing feeling among the younger Mormons that revelation is a right conception of an eternal truth, and that any man, whether it is [Thomas] Edison, or Lyman Abbott, or Joseph F. Smith, who comprehends a truth not formerly known—I will say known to him—has to that extent had a revelation. I think the matter of getting a direct revelation from God is growing out of the Mormon people. I know, too, that a great mass of them still believe it. But I think the leaven is working in the lump.

SENATOR OVERMAN. What do they think about the manifesto? Do they think it is a revelation from God?

MR. STEPHENS. Oh, I think a great majority of them do, and I think they think and know that there was a lot of pressure within the church, too.

SENATOR OVERMAN. A considerable number do not believe it was a revelation from God?

MR. STEPHENS. I would not say a considerable number do not believe it was a revelation from God. I believe it is a mixed proposition. ...

THE CHAIRMAN. What would be your judgment as to the effect of an amendment to the Constitution of the United States prohibiting polygamy in all the States and Territories?[5]

---

5. The possibility of a Constitutional amendment banning polygamy was raised repeatedly in the hearings. On January 31, 1903, the *Deseret News* had reported:

Congressman Jenkins of Wisconsin today introduces the following amendment to the Constitution of the United States. ... No person shall willfully and knowingly contract a second marriage while the first marriage, to the knowledge of the offender, is still subsisting and undissolved. Any person who shall willfully and knowingly contract a second marriage while the first marriage, to the knowledge of the offender, is still subsisting and undissolved shall never hereafter hold, occupy or enjoy any office of honor or profit under the United States. Congress shall make all laws necessary and proper to carry the foregoing power into execution.

A year later, the *Deseret News* reported that "Senator Burrows has prepared for introduction this afternoon or tomorrow a joint resolution providing for an amendment to the Constitution absolutely prohibiting polygamy. He will ask that it lay on the table and will call it up early in December and make a speech on it" ("Burrows Introduces Resolution for Anti-Polygamy Amendment," Apr. 27, 1904). Ultimately Burrows elected not to introduce the resolution.

The idea was again floated in late 1904. "At today's session of the Senate," the *Salt Lake Herald* reported on December 8, "petitions were filed from several eastern states praying for the adoption of an amendment to the constitution to prevent polygamy. The petitions were on printed forms, and recited: 'In view of the facts presented before the committee on privileges and elections in the Smoot case we ask the adoption of a constitutional amendment taking all questions relating to polygamy or polygamous cohabita-

MR. STEPHENS. I think there would be no objection raised to an amendment to the Constitution of the United States prohibiting polygamy. I do not think it is necessary to pass such an amendment in order to stamp out future plural marriages, because I believe they will be discontinued anyhow. It can not exist in this day and age of the world in a civilized nation for any length of time. As to the question of passing a constitutional amendment with regard to the practice of unlawful cohabitation, my judgment is it would not be wise to do it.

THE CHAIRMAN. Why not?

MR. STEPHENS. Because the enforcement of such a law, under existing conditions, when it is fast dying out, would cause a feeling of bitterness. The children who are now the children of polygamous marriages, whether born before the manifesto or since, would have a stigma put upon them. They would not be reared to be as good and self-respecting citizens, in my own judgment, as they would to let it go on naturally.

THE CHAIRMAN. But, Mr. Stephens, let me suggest to you that a constitutional amendment would prevent those now living in polygamy from having further children by that relationship. Is that to be deplored?

MR. STEPHENS. That is not to be deplored. It is to be sought.

THE CHAIRMAN. Would that visit any disgrace on the children that would not be born?

MR. STEPHENS. You can not segregate the two.

THE CHAIRMAN. They have to be together?

MR. STEPHENS. That is the difficulty. Where one has married a wife many years ago and gone into it, as a great many and I think the majority did, from a religious motive and not from a lustful motive, and they have sustained the relation of husband and wife and are men and women of middle age, the going to the family and the sustaining of the relation of a father in other respects would, in too many instances, bring the other.

THE CHAIRMAN. The committee, of course, understand what you mean. Then the result of it is there is no end to that business, in your judgment, except death?

MR. STEPHENS. That is my judgment. ...

MR. WORTHINGTON. There is a matter here, Mr. Chairman, in respect to which the record should be in somewhat better shape than it is.

You will remember that after evidence had been introduced here

tion out of control of state courts and placing them in control of federal courts.'" Despite such efforts, an amendment banning polygamy never passed Congressional muster.

last spring to the effect that Apostle [George] Teasdale, having a legal wife living, had taken another wife, we had an executive session, and that was supposed to be, and it was, so far as we know, a private session, but it was telegraphed all over the country that it was developed in that session that things had happened in Apostle Teasdale's case which it had been shown were unfit for publication, or unprintable.[6] Now, while the members of the committee, or those who were present at that executive session, know what took place, there is nothing in this record, and there will be nothing when the matter goes before the Senate, which will show what the situation really was.

You will remember that we had before the committee in that executive session the transcript of the proceedings in the case in which Apostle Teasdale obtained a divorce, or a decree of nullification rather, as to his first marriage, and also the testimony upon which that decree was based. So far as I am concerned I see no reason why the transcript of the record, the ordinary showing which is made when a judicial proceeding is called into inquiry somewhere else, should not be put in here in open session, and I see no reason why the testimony should be put in [again], in open session or in closed session, and unless there is some objection of that kind I now offer in evidence the record. I do not care to read any part of it.

SENATOR MCCOMAS. Do you desire to put in the whole record or just parts of it?

MR. WORTHINGTON. It may be that we can agree with counsel on the other side in respect to parts of it. If not, we would like to have the whole record go in. I think it is due to Apostle Teasdale to say that there is nothing in the record that reflects unfavorably upon him.

THE CHAIRMAN. I will ask counsel to defer those matters for the present, and they can be attended to later. If there are other witnesses here, the committee would prefer to have you call them this afternoon and go on with the case.[7] ...

MR. TAYLER. I am going to make my [closing] argument right before the committee, and I am not going to say anything more, unless it should be a little condensed account of the testimony ...

THE CHAIRMAN. The Chair will personally see every member of the committee and ask him to be present. Some members of the committee have not attended with regularity because they were overwhelmed

---

6. This executive session discussing the Teasdale divorce occurred on March 10, 1904 (*Smoot Hearings*, 1:540).

7. For the Teasdale divorce transcript, see *Smoot Hearings*, 3:456-57.

with other business. The Senator from Pennsylvania (Mr. Knox) was not a member of the committee until recently, and all will desire, so far as I know, to hear the arguments. Every effort will be made to accommodate Senators, so that they can be here ...

SENATOR KNOX. I think it would be of very great benefit to the committee that the gentlemen have pretty full time to present not only the questions of law and fact which they propose to rely upon, but to recapitulate pretty fully the testimony in support of those propositions. I know it would be of great advantage to me, not having had the benefit of hearing the early part of the case.

THE CHAIRMAN. It would be of very great advantage to every member of the committee. ...

28.

Closing Statements
Robert W. Tayler, Waldemar Van Cott, and A. S. Worthington

Thursday & Friday, January 26-27

"The evidence is about all in. The arguments will follow. For the protestants it is believed that Judge [Robert W.] Tayler will make the effort of his life. He has handled the case in an admirable manner. It could not have been better handled. His examination of witnesses has been superb. He threw his whole soul into the case, and from the beginning he has never wavered. He has been confident that he would win, and he will." —*Salt Lake Tribune,* Jan. 22, 1905

"[The closing] argument[s] in the Smoot case [are] attracting large crowds, greater crowds, in fact, than have been in evidence at any time since the investigation began. There was exceptionally heavy attendance today while Attorney Van Cott presented his argument for the defense. But there was another renewal of interest in the Smoot case today [as] ... every senator received a letter this morning from the National Congress of Mothers urging him to vote to expel Reed Smoot from the senate." —*Salt Lake Herald,* Jan. 27, 1905

Mr. TAYLER. Mr. Chairman and gentlemen of the committee, I am reminded that it is more than a year since the hearing of this case commenced, when the committee was called upon to decide upon the scope and nature of the inquiry, and that since that time probably six weeks have been taken up by the committee in hearing testimony supposed to be pertinent to the inquiry that was being made.

I have no thought of indulging in any rhetorical flight or of traveling outside of the argument immediately applicable to the issues which are made in this inquiry. I have not the time and it would not be worth while. What I have to say I want to say to this committee. I have no other constituency that I am seeking to reach, I have no client who may suffer if you decide against my contention, and I ought to say here that it will be not only entirely agreeable to me, but I think it will minister to lucidity, and perhaps in the end to brevity, if I am interrupted by members of the committee by questions at any stage of my

589

argument. It will not at all disturb the continuity of my argument, and if perchance it should touch upon a point that later on I intend to develop, of course I will so indicate when the question is asked.

Now, a very large amount of testimony has been taken in the case, and only those who have sat through it can appreciate how much there has been of it and how generally it has been absolutely pertinent to the questions that are involved. I, of course, in no argument that I might be physically able to make could undertake to devote much time to quotation from this testimony. I think it is practically all so pertinent that such an effort would involve the reading of a large part of these 3,000 pages.

I have no need to emphasize the importance of this inquiry. It is one of the highest importance. It involves the dignity, the powers, and the prerogatives of the Senate and of Senators. No question in the nature of things could more intimately interest Senators than an inquiry of that sort, one affecting their body and one affecting them as individuals.

Now, I want to say here that according to my view of this case, which may not accord with the view of the multitude, this is purely a question of law and of government, whose foundation is law. It is not a question of morals in anything or in any other respect than incidentally. Of course there is a question of personal morals in certain of the acts which have formed the basis of this demand or remonstrance, but only some of the acts have that quality. But that is only incidental. In the large view which we must take of it, it is immaterial. It is a question of government. It is a question of that upon which government is based ...

Nor am I referring merely to the matter of obedience to law. A Senator may disobey a law with perhaps more injury to the public sense of respect for law than if one who is not a legislator disobeyed it. But, for one who is a member of a legislative body, especially for one who is a member of our highest legislative body, in form, in substance, to be above the law, to encourage defiance of law as law when his word might stop it, because there is a higher law respecting the subject, reaches right down to the very roots of government.

Another observation of this preliminary character. If I felt that the facts of history justified me in so doing I would not say a word against the personal character nor even against the law-abiding spirit, as such things are ordinarily defined, of any member of the Mormon hierarchy or of Senator Smoot. I do not want to intimate, for it is purposeless, considering the view I take of these facts and of this case, that they are lawless, that they are mere breakers of the law. If that were all their case would be trivial. It would not make a ripple on the surface of government, because the land is full of law-breakers. Our jails are filled with them. It is because we may assume that these men are men of the highest character, with respect for law, as they define and interpret law, that this situation is serious and full of menace.

Why is it that these men do what they profess to do, what they admit they do, what they confess they do? They do it because they are not lawless, but because the law which they obey is not in those respects the law of the land, but a higher law. Senator Smoot in his heart of hearts believes that he is less lawless than any of us, because he does obey the law—that which he calls the law; and when the man-made law comes in conflict with that which he knows is higher, as Senator Smoot puts it, he will remove to another country where that revelation will not conflict with the laws made by man. That strikes to the very heart of this whole controversy.

So I am ready to admit, and not at all for the mere purposes of argument, but because it is in the main a fact, that these strong men are not violating the law from any spirit of lawlessness, for with that you could deal easily, quickly, but because they are, in their view, law-abiding citizens, putting their own definition upon the source of law. ...

I do not need to say to this committee that the power of the Senate on any subject within its general scope is exceedingly broad. There is no limitation upon its power except that which the Constitution imposes, and the Constitution imposes very few limitations. It imposes absolutely no conditions upon the power of the Senate respecting the matter of the elections, returns, and the qualifications of its members. It is the sole judge of all questions which, within the Senatorial mind, may be encompassed within that inquiry. It does limit the power of expulsion by requiring that two-thirds of the members shall concur in such a motion. The constitutional provision giving the power to expel is very peculiar, and has given rise to much discussion since the institution of the Government. I myself have very decided convictions upon the meaning of that provision, and I do not think there ought to be any great difficulty in construing it. The language is: "Each House may determine the rules of its proceedings, punish its members for disorderly behavior, and, with the concurrence of two-thirds, expel a member." ...

In the present case the power of expulsion could be invoked, because the claim is made that the status of Senator Smoot, his relation
to this law-defying hierarchy, his own attitude toward law, the view
that he takes of his capacity to receive revelations from Almighty
God, all indicate a present status that if necessary brings it within the
power of the Senate to expel. ...

Now, gentlemen, this is the broad claim we make: That the [Mor-
mon] church is in fact higher tha[n] the law; that the hierarchy and its
members are in fact higher than the law. I do not mean that they consciously realize that in every act that they perform they are above the
law, or that they do not quite unconsciously generally obey the law, as
most men obey it, but that after all when we get to the inner consciousness that controls them they are obedient to a higher law, and
they are so because, as I indicated incidentally earlier in my argument, they or it receive revelations, because its membership, especially the hierarchy, are in immediate contact with God. I shall have
more to say about that as we go along. This is basic. I should like that
every word I say from now on should be considered in view of the fact
and with constant apprehension of the fact that revelation runs
through the Mormon mind and is the basis of the Mormon religion
and of its hold on the Mormon people to-day—revelation by actual
contact with the Almighty. ...

Senator Smoot declared that he believes that God reveals His will
to the head of the church and to individuals in the church; that he
himself may at any time receive such revelations from God; that if
God should, as He might, command him to do something in conflict
with the laws of his country, he would leave this country and go to another country where it would not violate the law; and in reply to a
question as to what he would do, if in addition to the command from
God he should be commanded to remain in the country, his only answer was that his God was not that kind of a God.

Let us examine this subject of revelation, as applied to Senator
Smoot as a legislator, as explained by him and made lucid by its manifest meaning when interpreted by the admitted facts of his church's
history and doctrines.

According to his own view he is capable of holding immediate intercourse with God. If not, then he has consciously perjured himself,
and I dismiss that suggestion as wholly untenable and unjust to him.
If that were the only alternative, then his case would be disposed of
for another and simpler reason; the Senate could not, for a moment,

tolerate the presence of a man who was known to have perjured himself before one of its committees. So I would have no implication arise from this reference to that alternative that I am desirous of even suggesting the possibility of such depravity.

We are therefore driven to the conclusion that his views on the subject of revelation as applied to himself personally are all that he has said they are and all that in the essential philosophy of it must be implied.

We are not now speaking either of a mere private citizen or of a mere lay member of a church holding certain beliefs. We are speaking of a Senator of the United States, of an apostle of the Mormon Church, of a man who has testified before us as to the nature of his relation to God, of one who is regularly "sustained" as prophet, seer, and revelator.

We are speaking of a man reared in the environment and atmosphere of the Mormon Church, born of a polygamous mother, and imbued with the spirit of his people, modified though it be by the fact that when he came to years of maturity murmurings against the practice of polygamy had swelled to something of a tumult.

But aside from that we know well that he is a true Mormon, bred in the bone and impregnated with all that it ever stood for in the matter of the fundamental principle of revelation. Now, what does revelation mean to him and what has it to do with him as a legislator?

He may receive, directly receive, commands from the Almighty, from a God of infinite goodness, power, and knowledge.

The edicts of that God, received by an intelligence conscious of the fact of their reception, must in the inevitable nature of things import not only absolute wisdom and power but absolute goodness as well. To deny that is to deny everything. It is to confess one's self a fool or a liar. Now, if God so certainly reveals His will how is it possible for the conscious recipient to deny any of its essential attributes?

If I know that God speaks to me, I know it. If He does speak, I know He speaks absolute wisdom; therefore I know it is right. If He speaks, I know He speaks as one omnipotent; therefore must I do His will or lose fellowship with Him. I deny Him if I do not do His will. If He speaks to me I know He does it with infinite goodness and tenderness, therefore I must be absolutely blameless, I must be absolutely exalted, I must rejoice if I obey Him. If I believed, as Senator Smoot believes, that this God might so speak to me; if in truth and in fact I felt, as Senator Smoot could, that He did speak to me, if I knew this, as

Senator Smoot thinks he knows it, and God, thus speaking, gave me His command and His will, I would obey it though the earth rocked and the Government fell.

What revelation has the all-powerful God given to some other man that can weigh for an instant or with a feather's weight against the revelation that I know He gives unto me, unto me?

Now, it is no answer to say that Senator Smoot deceives himself. Whether he deceives himself or actually speaks the truth is one and the same so far as this question is concerned. If he deceives him-self—that is, if he is honest, but mistaken—then the worse calamity happens, for he may receive what he thinks is revelation, but is in fact the fruit of his own vagaries or the product of his own caprice. It will not do to make light of his contention, of his asserted belief.

Several hundred thousand sincere men and women have believed and now believe, as they believe in their own existence, that Joseph Smith, jr., received revelations direct from God, and if anyone ever believed that, we must assume that Senator Smoot believes it.

Now, a Senator of the United States might believe anything else in the world but that and not be ineligible to a seat in the body to which he belongs. He might believe in polygamy; he might believe that mur-der was commendable; he might deny the propriety as a rule of life of all the ten commandments; he might believe in the sacrifice of hu-man life; he might believe in no God or in a thousand gods; he might be Jew or Gentile, Mohammedan or Buddhist, atheist or pantheist; he might believe that the world began last year and would end next year, but to believe with the kind of conviction that Reed Smoot pos-sesses that God speaks to him or may speak to him is to admit by the inevitable logic of his conviction that there is a superior authority with whom here and now he may converse, and whose command he can no more refuse to obey than he can will himself not to think.

Suppose he were a lawyer and you were considering as Senators the propriety of confirming his nomination as Chief Justice of the Su-preme Court of the United States?

As lawyers you would probably not be seriously concerned by the apprehension that God would interfere and advise him how he might wisely decide your case. If your case was good that prospect would doubtless be pleasing. But he might certainly think that God was speaking to him and advising him, and if he were honestly mistaken in that regard, what a monstrous thing would such a decision be. And would we not find established among us a new brand of lawyers whose trained specialty would be a hypnotic suggestiveness to the Chief Justice that God might reveal his will with infinite wisdom and justice? ...

We are all familiar, I doubt not, with the inception of this church. Joseph Smith, jr., when a very young man, as his account and the account of the church goes, found certain plates in the hill Cumorah, I believe is its name, in New York, written in some unknown tongue or hieroglyphics, and which he undertook to translate. No one knew what the language was, but he was provided in some divine way with the urim and thummin, a pair of spectacles which, being put before the eyes, transposed the characters from unknown and unintelligible hieroglyphics into a tongue which he could interpret; and which he thus translated by this physical thing interposed; and that book thus translated was the Book of Mormon.

He organized his sect, which grew slowly, and the Book of Mormon being insufficient for the purposes of this religion which he thus established, he had revelations. That is to say, God spoke directly to him, and from time to time his revelations came. They are published in the Book of Doctrine and Covenants. They are the basis, with the Book of Mormon, of the religion of Jesus Christ of Latter-Day Saints, believed in by that church as profoundly as the most devout Christian can possibly believe in the Bible.

I have interpreted what I felt, from the testimony, to be the meaning of the Book of Doctrine and Covenants, and I find no better expression of my view of the Mormon view of this than this paragraph which I happened to run across yesterday. It is fully expressive of the thought that is in my mind. I find it in the book called "Scientific Aspects of Mormonism," written by Nels L. Nelson, a Mormon of course and professor of English in the Brigham Young University, Provo, Utah. It seems to be a very scholarly book, and this is what he says: "If the Bible is more perfectly a revelation of God than is the Koran, it is not because God was partial to the Jews; it was doubtless owing to the fact that Israel was fitted for purer life, no less also than that its prophets were purer mediums. But the Bible, in its turn, is less perfectly a revelation of the divine word than are the Book of Mormon and the Doctrine and Covenants; representing, as these later scriptures do, the revelations of God to a dispensation capable of more exacting truth ideals."[1]

---

1. See Nels L. Nelson, *Scientific Aspects of Mormonism* (New York: G. P. Putnam's Sons, 1904), 209.

I think that fairly interprets the Mormon mind as we have had it disclosed in this case—that the Book of Doctrine and Covenants is a better work than the Bible, not because its origin is any more sacred or of any more certain divinity, but because it was revealed unto "a dispensation capable of more exacting truth ideals." ...

I think I have disclosed to the mind of the committee what the Mormon mind was relating to this subject [polygamous cohabitation], and all subjects wherein their revelations conflicted with the law of the land. How were they treated? Did they obey the law because either they evolved from their own consciousness a respect for law or because the Almighty, by any revelation or otherwise, put into their hearts the spirit of respect for law as law? Or for some other reason did they obey the law? ...

I am not attacking, I must not attack—the philosophy of my argument does not permit me to attack—the manhood of these men. From one point of view there are those who would applaud it because they stand by that which they believe to be true; but governments are instituted, unfortunately for the world in this early period of its development toward perfection, by men. Man alone makes these laws, so far as we know, except in the Mormon Church, and by man alone they must be administered; and he who applies any other rule or seeks any other power, save as he understands the Christian may get inspiration by prayer, has no part or place, and can have none, in that kind of government. His government is theocracy. It may be better than ours. It may have more hope for this country in it than ours; but it has no more part or parcel with it than the actual Kingdom of God, if it exists anywhere on earth.

But, gentlemen, I weary you, and must hurry along.

I have said so much about revelation that I think I need say no more. Frequent references to it are found in the testimony, and the general facts of it are thoroughly well known. We understand what is the origin of the priesthood; that these priests are the successors of Christ, that they are endowed with all the powers with which the priest ever was endowed since the dawn of time; that they have authority, and the spirit of obedience is taught. It is that which flows from revelation, and by their constant teaching.[2] ...

---

2. Tayler's arguments were not welcomed by LDS Church authorities. The *Salt Lake Tribune* explained:

Apostle Rudger Clawson at Logan [Utah] is said to have set the ears of his auditors tingling by his allusion to the treatment the revelation idea received at the hands of

So we gather the state of the Mormon mind. From the history of the church, from the concrete proof that is presented, we discover that it is the same church, the same people, moved by the same controlling and impelling causes, qualified, it is true, by the powerful influence of modern civilization and the strong arm of government and the sense of mankind operating upon them, improved, but with the spirit still there, that will be there so long as the head of the church is the mouthpiece of God. So long as the apostles are mouthpieces of God, prophets, seers, and revelators, so long will the church in its essence, and everywhere and always, whenever it can, be superior to the law of the land.

Gentlemen, I have come to the last word I shall have to say in this case. My part of this work is done. To me it has been most interesting. To you it must be most important. Judgment must come from the highest legislative body of what we have a right to say is the freest and greatest representative Government on earth. Your work is to make laws, and, being such, you must set an example of respect for law, and especially for that kind of law which, while formulated in statutes, is bottomed on a fundamental principle of society and demanded by the all but universal sense of civilized mankind.

If it be said, and truthfully said, of a member of the highest legislative body of the land that such a law so originating in the decent and sober sense of mankind, except of his own associates, is not worth obeying, or that it need not be obeyed, then is your legislative body but a mere sham and pretense which, while claiming and exercising the high prerogative of legislation, would defy its own laws. If our contention here be not sound, then it could not be said to be wrong if ninety Reed Smoots sat in this great body and each in his own way tes-

---

Judge Tayler. ... Clawson was justified in any animadversions [criticisms] which he may have made within the bounds of parliamentary language upon Judge Tayler's treatment of 'revelation' as 'revealed' by the 'revelators' of the Mormon church. Judge Tayler showed as complete a contempt for this sort of revelation as it was possible for a gentleman to exhibit in the presence of gentlemen. Naturally Apostle Clawson, who looks at this subject as one of sanctity, resents ... Tayler's attitude and utterances; all the apostles would not deserve c[e]nsure if he passed upon Judge Tayler the final condemnation to eternal perdition as an unbeliever. And if such shall be Judge Tayler's fate he has no reason to exhibit surprise nor has he any rightful claim upon apostolic mercy. His position has been one of a very thinly-disguised sneer at the revelators. He has even put into words some of the most cutting sarcasms which have ever been uttered against any real or pretended faith before any tribunal. And now, when the inevitable apostolic scourge falls upon him he may cry aloud for compassion, but his cry will be in vain. He deserves none; he will get none ("Respect for Revelations," Jan. 31, 1905).

tified that he was here to enact laws, but not to respect or obey them; that it was neither necessary nor reasonable that the legislative power should be exercised by those who were themselves respectful of their own enactments.

How can 80,000,000 citizens be expected to obey the law if they do not respect either the law or the makers of law?

How can government exist if the law be not supreme? How can the law of the land be supreme if a God, known to the subjects of that law to be of infinite goodness, power, and wisdom, directly speaks to that subject of the law? Whatever the respect we accord to one who sustains to the Almighty such a relation, how can such a one participate in a man-made government?

Among those who believe in present revelations from God, but one government can by right exist—a government by God; a theocracy.

A grave question is yours to answer. Reed Smoot himself is but a trivial incident in the mighty problem. It is the problem of government; the institutional question whether law or caprice shall govern people who know no ruler but the law, and no safe rule but respect for law.

A Senator from the State of Utah is a Senator of the United States.

He legislates for 80,000,000 people, who hold as their most cherished possession such a respect for law because it is law, as Reed Smoot, unhappily for him, has never felt nor understood from the moment of his first conscious thought down to the present hour. ...

SENATOR KNOX. Mr. Tayler, taking advantage of the request that you made of the committee to ask you such questions as would tend to clarify your position and to clear it up in your own minds, I desire to put three questions to you, which you may answer now or at any other time during the hearing, as you see fit. I do this for the purpose of getting an accurate conception of the views that you set forth in your argument yesterday.

First: Do you concede that your argument, intended to establish Senator Smoot's disqualification, applies with equal force to all members of the Mormon Church who entertain the beliefs confessed by Senator Smoot before this committee?

Second. Do you concede that your argument for disqualification, so far as it is based upon Senator Smoot's belief in a duty to obey Divine revelation, applies with equal force to all who believe in the duty to obey the Divine will, however ascertained?

Third. Would Senator Smoot be disqualified, in your opinion, by reason of being a Mormon, if Mormonism had never been tainted with polygamy?

MR. TAYLER. I would rather answer the questions now. To the first question I answer, no; emphatically, no.

"Do you concede that your argument, intended to establish Senator Smoot's disqualification, applies with equal force to all members of the Mormon Church who entertain the beliefs Senator Smoot has confessed?"

Most emphatically, no. The chief charge against Senator Smoot is that he encourages, countenances, and connives at the defiant violation of law. He is an integral part of a hierarchy; he is an integral part of a quorum of twelve, who constitute the backbone of the church. It is all there is to the church. The president is its creature. It may depose him; it may destroy him; it may annihilate him any day it pleases. We have the high authority of President Joseph F. Smith for that. He says they would not do it, but they could do it. They themselves determine who shall fill any vacancy that may occur in their number. Of course there is a formal nomination to the people, but the people themselves universally sustain that nomination. So the quorum of twelve, of which Senator Smoot is one, is the church in so far as authority—real basic authority—is concerned.

Now, then, I say that he, as one of that quorum of twelve apostles, encourages, connives at, and countenances defiance of law, and he can not separate himself from that fact, and in that respect, which is radical, which is to the last degree important, he is, of course, to be distinguished from every other member of the Mormon Church.

Now I will answer that question and the remainder of that which is involved in that question still, and the next question, by saying Yes—that is to say, any man who believes himself to be in personal relation to Almighty God, so that he is capable of receiving through it conscious fellowship and intercourse face to face with God, either by hearing his voice or by seeing his presence—the will and wish and command of a God of infinite goodness, wisdom, and power is constitutionally incapable of being a part of a man-made government.

He may be a citizen, because unless he commits some overt act he is doing no wrong, for his thoughts are his own. His belief he is entitled to possess; but when he comes to constituting himself a part of the fabric of the Government, which is based upon laws that are made by men and men alone, he is absolutely incapable of being a natural and proper part of it.

I do not know but that the spirit of the third question is answered, met by what I have already said.

"Would Senator Smoot be disqualified, in your opinion, by reason of being a Mormon, if Mormonism had never been tainted with polygamy?"

I will say this as to that: Practically nobody would ever have dreamed of disqualifying him, because men's beliefs become important to us, their lives as based upon those beliefs become important to us, only when they exhibit facts that are important, and polygamy, being essentially, in principle, being abstractly but a mere incident of the Mormon Church and its religion, is yet concretely so offensive to the sense of mankind, so at war with civilization, it so undermines the corner stone upon which our society is built, and we believe, as our laws have declared, as our Supreme Court has solemnly announced, that the attention of the public has been directed to it on account of its offensiveness and to the church on account of its adherence to that policy and the practice of it.

Now, if polygamy had not been associated with Mormonism, I say, as a practical circumstance, we never probably would have heard of this. But otherwise I would answer the question just as I did the second question: That, assuming the possession by Senator Smoot of the power of personal intercourse with Almighty God, with the certainty upon his part that that will may be revealed to him, not as an inspiration, not as a general and elusive and pervasive effulgence of truth, whereby he apprehends, as it were, by some inner mental operation that the truth is with him, but that by coming face to face with God and receiving his word, hearing his voice, he knows what our Mormon friends would describe, that it is a thing that comes "thus saith the Lord," with the same kind of certainty that you now have of my addressing you, then I do not care whether a man is a Mormon or what he is; he may be a good citizen, but he should have no part in legislation. ...

MR. VAN COTT. ... This alleged power to receive revelation is declared by the protestants' counsel to be the basis of the attack, it is the alleged basic element running through his argument; after all the testimony is introduced, after all the hue and cry, we are brought to one issue—should a United States Senator retain his seat if he believes man has the capacity to receive revelation from God? This is the offense not cognizable by law which the United States Senate is asked to punish. The record shows Senator Smoot has never in his forty-three years of life received a revelation. He may never receive one. He has never been asked to obey any revelation contrary to law. His only alleged offense is that he entertains the abstract opinion that man has been, and is, capable of receiving revelation and inspiration from God. As the protestants' counsel has made the above alleged principle the pivotal one, it is our duty to examine it with care to ascertain whether the contention is sound, and it must be borne in mind that we can not discuss any alleged basic principle other than revelation, because no other is charged or discussed by the protestants' counsel; the protestants in their judgment have taken the strongest point that exists against Senator Smoot.[3] ...

Senator Knox asked counsel for the protestants three questions, and we refer to them and the answers given. They immediately precede this argument.

As it is an integral part of the Mormon religion and of the reorganized Church of Jesus Christ of Latter-day Saints and of many other persons in the Christian religious denominations that man have the capacity to receive revelation, it follows that, if Senator Smoot may be expelled for such belief on his part, any lay member of any church, or any person not belonging to a church, so believing, may be expelled; if the United States Senate may expel a Senator because of so believing then it may do directly what it thus does indirectly, and in that

---

3. A few weeks later, Smoot updated Joseph F. Smith on the impact of the closing arguments on other senators:

> Senator Proctor [R-Vt.] spent considerable time yesterday in finding out how some of the leading Republicans felt about my retaining my seat and states that most all of them are going to support me even if Burrows and McComas of the Committee report against me. Senator Gallinger [R-N.H.] is very friendly and expressed himself so on many occasions. Senator Proctor congratulated me on my testimony and on my course from the time I entered the Senate until to-day. Stated I had commanded the respect of men who had bitterly opposed everything Mormon. Yesterday McComas had a talk with me in the cloak room. ... I shall always count him our enemy although he claimed to admire the thrift and industry of the Mormon people. ... He remarked as he was leaving that it was a lucky thing for the church that I was sent here as Senator for I was liked by both Democrats and Republicans and for that reason he did not expect I would be unseated (Feb. 10, 1905).

Responding, the First Presidency opined: "While we are pleased to learn of the kind personal feelings manifested towards you by Senator McComas, we feel quite disappointed in his lack of ability to see us in our true light, and must express the hope that the Senator, as well as others who are now blindly prejudiced, may yet know us better and appreciate conditions here, and the struggle we have had and are still having to maintain our political existence" (Feb. 15, 1905).

event could pass a Federal statute prohibiting any person from holding any Federal office or position who entertains any such belief; and thus there would be excluded from Federal office not only persons in the Mormon Church but all other persons who so believe, whether in the reorganized Church of Jesus Christ of Latter-day Saints or any other churches, together with those persons who so believe but do not belong to any church.

Why is a person of high position in a church less eligible to hold office than a person of low position, both believing the same and holding similar opinions? If Senator Smoot is ineligible to hold his position because of his belief in revelation, then, logically, how can any person holding the same belief be eligible? ...

Mr. Tayler, in his closing argument, stated that he was sorely misunderstood if the distinction was not clear between the revelation a Gentile receives by communing with God and the revelation a Mormon receives by communing with God. It is not clear to us by any means why God should treat a Gentile differently from a Mormon when each offers an earnest prayer for help. The counsel for the protestants has not elucidated this point, unless it is in the statement that God personally appears to a Mormon while He does not to a Gentile. If it be assumed (as Mr. Tayler argues) that God personally appears to Mormons and not to Gentiles, then we should all believe what the Mormon says in regard to revelation, as it comes from personal communion. If it be assumed that Mormons and Gentiles receive revelations from God in the mode religious people generally believe, then they are on an equality as to opinion and belief; that is, the revelation is more of a conception or conviction than an actual communion. It is impossible to tell just how men are persuaded and finally convinced as to a certain result or conclusion; this may be by inspiration; it may be by revelation; it may be mere persuasion; it may be reason; it may be fear of social ostracism; it may be fear of financial loss; it may be that mere politics produce the result; but in any event, the analytical mind of Senator Hoar was struck with the proposition whether this mere belief or conviction can properly be reached, and Senator Hoar's opinion seems to us to be to the effect that it can not. ...

There is a legal distinction between the active and passive participation in crime. If one actively encourages crime he is an accessory, and is usually punishable by the law. If he is merely passive, he is not an accessory, and is not punishable by law, but it is merely a moral question, and we here discuss both phases of this question.

"A" may see two men fighting in the street. He does not wish to mix in the brawl himself, and so passes by. A has violated no law, no legal obligation, by not mixing in the brawl and separating the combatants. He may commit a moral breach of good citizenship by so doing. This is a question that we will not discuss at this point. [Suppose] A, on the other hand, encourages two men to fight. This is wrong, legally and morally, and he should be punished for it.

A knows of his neighbor attending houses of ill fame, and therefore has good reason to believe that he is committing adultery, but he does not make complaint to the family of the violator, nor to the violator. Is A, under such circumstances, guilty of any violation of law or legal duty? A, on the other hand, encourages this same person to commit adultery. In that case he is a violator not only of morals but of law. ...

This, then, brings us to the question of the moral duty of Smoot in the premises. We shall not argue the question theoretically as to whether, morally, Smoot should have complained of the members of his quorum or of the members of his church who he knew violated the law of unlawful cohabitation, or who he had good reason to believe violated the law of unlawful cohabitation. This is a theoretical question and we believe its discussion throws no light upon the decision to be reached in this case. But we shall discuss the practical question of what men do generally, naturally, and reasonably under such circumstances.

Spying and informing, in all ages, have been detested. An officer can spy and inform, because it is his duty, and he is not held in general contempt for so doing; but when private citizens undertake to discharge any such function they are generally and publicly detested and held up to ridicule and contumely. We say practically it was not Smoot's duty to go to the members of his quorum or to the members of his church and complain of them when he had good reason to believe they were violating the law as to unlawful cohabitation. ...

MR. WORTHINGTON. Mr. Chairman, I wish at the outset of my argument to express my profound appreciation of the fact that it is impossible for me to present such an argument at this time and in this case as the committee is entitled to have at the hands of counsel. The long time that has been taken in the preparation of the evidence, and the fact that during the last few weeks my associate and I have been constantly engaged in arranging the evidence to be offered, has prevented us, until the testimony had actually closed, from so much as considering even the question of the points of the argument and how they were to be presented.

I would like to say, as preliminary to the argument in this case, that I have been greatly impressed with the contrast between the proceedings in the case when an officer of the Government is to be impeached by the Senate, or before the Senate, even though he may be an officer so comparatively unimportant as a district judge of the United States, and the proceedings which are provided in case one who is a member of the highest legislative body of this great nation is called to an account. When a district judge is impeached there is a carefully prepared indictment, setting forth exactly what he is to meet, and that he is called to respond in the Senate of the United States, with his counsel, and there the witnesses are heard before the assembled Senate, the presiding officer, as he did the other day, carefully reminding Senators that it is very important that they should all be present and hear the testimony and see the witnesses. And I see that you have carefully provided rules for the conduct of such an investigation as that, and have provided that counsel may be there to make objections, and that if any Senator wishes to ask a question he shall reduce it to writing and it shall be handed to the presiding officer and asked by him; and that if any objection is made to testimony, while the presiding officer shall rule upon it in the first place, it may, upon his motion, or upon the request of any Senator, be submitted to the entire Senate.

Yet, in the case in which a Senator is to be visited, if he be found guilty, with punishment like that which shall be inflicted upon the judge, of being turned out of his office, we find that we are here, as we found, and as Senators have found during the progress of this case, compelled to scramble through a record of nearly three thousand printed pages to find out what the issues are which we are trying, and that, in all probability, if every member of the committee should be asked the question, no two of them would agree as to precisely what the issues are. And we find that, while the testimony has been taken and reduced to print, the great mass of it has been heard by very few Senators, and that even on one occasion there was but one Senator present, the distinguished chairman of this committee, and when he was called out of the room for a moment, he intimated that we might go on in his absence; which we did not do.[4]

---

4. The sparse attendance by committee members must have signaled to Burrows that his case was losing momentum. A few days following the closing arguments, the

I make this suggestion in no spirit of complaint or faultfinding, but as bringing to the attention of the committee, and I might hope of the Senate, a question of importance, not only in the determination of this case, but of all like cases, hereafter, because Senator Smoot is to be tried and his case decided by a tribunal not one-tenth of which has seen any of his witnesses or heard any of them testify. We all know how exceedingly important it is, in determining what weight shall be attributed to the testimony of a witness, to see him and to hear him. I have in mind some witnesses in this case whose testimony reads as though it might be credible, when I do not believe any Senator who heard the witnesses would believe them for a single moment.

The slightest examination of the record will also show that unlike, I should suppose, the proceedings in the impeachment of a judge or other officer of the United States, we are practically without rules of evidence, because, as was stated several times in the progress of the case, this is not a trial at all, but an investigation, and the committee has the right to inquire for hearsay evidence, because A may tell that

---

Senate debated statehood bills for New Mexico and Arizona. The Michigan senator used the occasion to grandstand against Smoot and the LDS Church. The *Salt Lake Tribune* reported:

> The Mormon question was injected into the statehood debate shortly after 5 o'clock today, when ... Burrows went after it roughshod. ... When Senator Burrows arose, the Senate, which had been in an uproar, quieted down ... Senator Smoot, with his head resting in his hand, listened intently as Senator Burrows thundered out his charges. ... Many thought Senator Smoot would answer ... but he made no move to do so. Senator Burrows said: "I cannot vote for the admission of New Mexico and my reasons for voting against it is that I think it would be a dangerous thing to do. ... I shall vote against the admission of Arizona as a separate State. The condition with reference to polygamy is much worse in Arizona than it is in New Mexico. ... Polygamy exists in New Mexico. It has been declared that it is the breeding ground of polygamy and I happen to be in possession of information which I cannot make public for reasons which the Senate will readily understand, that the condition of things in New Mexico in this regard is startling. Of course, I am not going to discuss the question of polygamy, a crime that is so monstrous" ("Burrows Talks to Country," Feb. 7, 1905).

Responding to Burrows's allegations, the First Presidency bristled to Smoot:

> It is very apparent to us that Senator Burrows must feel somewhat chagrined at his failure so far to establish his case against you, and that he is now resorting to bluff tactics as a means of keeping up the fight. The telegram of Colonel George S. Pritchard, solicitor general of New Mexico, to Senator Burrows, challenging the truth of his statement on the floor of the Senate on the 7th inst. to the effect that polygamy exists in New Mexico, and that that territory is the breeding ground for polygamy ... was timely and good, and very refreshing to us. ... The fact that Senator Burrows is insincere in his warfare against you will, no doubt, lead him to resort to the most extreme measures as a means of win[n]ing his case, and this apparently is an evidence of it. But we feel that all such tactics will not only result in failure, but will prove helpful to you (Feb. 15, 1905).

B told him something, and B may say that he got it from C, and so we may lead to the original evidence. When my associate undertook to argue that in that way the record would be filled with matter which might come before members of the Senate who are not lawyers and who would not be able to distinguish between legal and illegal evidence, we were told that that was a matter which had become so well settled in the practice of the Senate that we would not be allowed to further argue it.

So that we are here before a great tribunal in which a defendant is called upon to respond to charges so serious that they may evict him from the Senate of the United States—and no greater punishment could be inflicted upon an honorable man, a man with any sense of the proprieties or honors of life—and his counsel are called upon to argue the case for him, upon a record which contains evidence nine-tenths of which we believe is not competent and may not be considered, and yet we do not know what may be in the minds of even members of the committee on that subject, much less in the minds of other members of the Senate who probably have not yet considered it.

Under all these difficulties I proceed to consider the questions which seem to arise in the case, guessing as to some of them, and having probable ground as to the others. ...

I proceed now to consider the obligation which Senator Smoot is charged with having taken, which is said to be inconsistent with his Senatorial oath.

I had supposed, until Mr. Tayler took his seat at the close of his argument, that he would discuss this question of the alleged obligation, but whether by oversight or by design he has so stated his position that we must suppose he stands now where he stood when this investigation was begun. Over and over again, when we were making our preliminary statements here, and afterwards in the early stages of the taking of testimony, Mr. Tayler stated in the most explicit terms not merely that he withdrew the charge that Senator Smoot was under such an obligation, but that he never had made it; and one of the honorable members of this committee, Senator Dubois, in the course of a colloquy between counsel and the committee which took place then, said: "Such a charge has never been made, and counsel for the respondent are trying to put the counsel for the protestants in a position which they never took." ... How then does it come that without a charge, without an issue, witnesses are brought here to testify to a thing which we were not to be called upon to meet?

Why, it happened in this way: After counsel had finished examining Apostle Lyman, the chairman of the committee asked him whether he had ever taken the endowment ceremony, and when he stated that he had, called upon him to tell what it was, which he declined to do. ... Several other witnesses who were brought here on behalf of the protestants were asked the same question, always, as I recollect it, by the chairman, and they all refused to disclose the endowment ceremony. After that had all been done, then three witnesses were brought here (Wallis, Lundstrom, and Mrs. Elliott), all of whom testified to having taken these covenants, and to a certain obligation which involved hostility to the United States. I am not going to go over that testimony. I have it all here, every reference to it in the testimony, including the discussions as to whether it was an issue or not. Every word that fell from the lips of those three witnesses on the subject is referred to, and the testimony of ten witnesses, five of them called by the protestants and the others by us, all of whom had taken the covenants, and everyone of whom denied that there was anything of the kind in the ceremony. ...

The committee will see, from the notes I shall give of what took place in reference to this matter, that after a number of witnesses had been asked the question as to whether there was anything of this kind in the ceremony, and had most positively and emphatically denied it, Colonel Young, a Mormon and an ex-officer of the Army, was upon the stand. I asked him the question whether there was any such obligation as these three witnesses had testified to, and he said that before answering that question he wanted to know whether, if he entered into the subject at all, he would be required to disclose the whole ceremony.

After a long argument, which is referred to in the notes, it was decided that if he undertook to say what was not in that ceremony; if he said there was nothing in it that referred to the nation, nothing in it that referred to or affected the question of his loyalty to his Government, then he would be called upon to testify as to the whole ceremony.[5]

Now, in the presence of the full committee I most respectfully protest against that ruling and against the effect that it had in stopping the inquiry being made by us of any further witnesses upon that question, because I maintain that the law is, and that the law ought to be, that if a man states that in a certain ceremony, in a certain conver-

---

5. The argument over this is in *Smoot Hearings,* 3:980-86.

sation, or in any place where he was, and where anything has taken place, there was nothing whatever said on a certain subject, it is not in the power of any tribunal investigating a case where only that thing is under consideration to require him to disclose everything that took place down to the most solemn covenants that a man can make with his Creator. ...

But suppose that the respondent did take such an obligation. Suppose that when Senator Smoot was a boy, as he testified—and there is no other evidence on the subject—his father, who was a religious man and who was going to the Sandwich Islands, said: "My lad, I want you to go with me, but before going I would like you to take your endowments," and the boy said, "I don't care anything about it, father." His father said, "Well, it can't do you any harm; you had better do it;" and he did it on the theory that it could not do any harm even if it did no good.

He testified he went through the ceremony when he was only 18 years of age, and he could not tell the ceremony, or much about it, if he wanted to. He was sure there was nothing in it that in any wise referred to hostility to his country, or he would never have gone through it. But suppose that in going through that ceremony he had taken an oath, in the language of these three witnesses—in regard to whom, in view of the testimony, I have hard work to speak with respect.

Suppose he had taken the obligation to invoke high Heaven to visit the blood of the prophets upon this nation, and suppose when he was elected Senator he was confronted with the proposition that "If you would come into this Senate you must first, without any mental reservations, take an oath which binds you to defend your country, the United States, against all enemies; will you take it?" And suppose he says, "Yes, I will take it, and without any mental reservation." I should say that if there was anybody to complain about that situation it was the Mormon Church and not the United States, because, having taken an obligation to the church he had renounced it, just as a man comes here from some foreign country and wants to become a citizen of the United States, and all he has to do after showing that he has the necessary qualifications is to say that he renounces his allegiance to that foreign country and will defend the Constitution of the United States. ...

Let us next consider whether, as Mr. Tayler seems to contend, a member of the Senate shall be expelled even if it be true that a considerable number of his constituents are violating the law of his State and he is doing nothing to put an end to such violations and perhaps sympathizes with the offenders.

My friend says that is the higher law. He invokes you to put Senator Smoot out of the Senate because he appeals to a higher law. Senator Smoot has not said anything of the kind. He has always obeyed the law. There is nothing here to show that he stands on anything of that kind. But suppose he did. It would not be the first time in the history of this country that men in high places, and whole communities, have said that there is a law higher than that which is in the written statutes. It is not the first time even that it has been heard that even the Constitution of the United States should not bind whole communities.

Why, let us remember the days before the civil war, when attempts were made to enforce the fugitive slave law throughout the North—a law which had been passed in pursuance of a provision of the Constitution. Do we not all know that hundreds and thousands of people in the North—and perhaps I might be permitted to say some of the best men in those States—said they would not obey that law, and they would do everything they could to prevent a slave being taken back to his slavery; and men of the highest standing in those communities, when referred to the Constitution of the United States, denounced it as a covenant with hell.

Do we not all know that after the war was over and the Union had been again restored there was a provision put into the Constitution that no man should be deprived of his vote by reason of his race, color, or previous condition of servitude? And do we not know that, although that is still a part of the Constitution of the United States, whole communities of people affected by it—the poor man, the rich man, the workman, and the laborer, and the men in the highest offices in the State—have proclaimed and have carried into effect their proposition that whatever the Constitution or the laws may say, white men will not submit to be governed by negroes?

And I would like to know what would be thought of the proposition, if it should be presented here, that if a member of this body should say that he sympathizes with that feeling for that reason he should be ejected from the Senate of the United States? ...

In reference to these matters of difference between church law and State law, let me remind the committee also that even the religious organizations, some of which participated in the preparation of this protest, put themselves in precisely the same condition. The Congress of the United States passed a law many years ago that in the

District of Columbia divorce might be obtained for cruelty, or deser-
tion, or drunkenness for a certain term or for adultery.

A great many divorces were obtained here, and great complaint
was made about the law, and ministers of churches here in council assembled openly proclaimed that whatever the law might do, the
church, except where the divorce was for adultery, would not recognize those people as being divorced; and women who by the law
which this Congress enacted had been declared entitled to remarry
and live an honorable life in the face of the community with a second
husband, were held by some ministers and churches—and it may be
very properly, for it is a part of their duty, if they think so—to be adul-
teresses. In the Roman Catholic Church a woman who has obtained a
divorce from her husband because of his adultery may not remarry
during his lifetime, on pain [of] excommunication. ...

The next objection personal to Senator Smoot to which I shall refer is one which was discussed by Mr. Van Cott—the fact that he obtained the "consent" of the president of his church before allowing
his name to be used as a candidate for the Senate. It seems to me that
when you take that political manifesto about which so much has been
said here and look to its substance, it is impossible to reach any conclusion in reference to it except that its purpose, and the only object
which it could accomplish, is to prevent high officers of the church
from retaining their offices under certain circumstances except with
the consent of the church, and not to say that such an officer shall not
run for any office he pleases without the consent of the church. Everybody admits the manifesto itself in effect says ... that if a high officer in the church wishes to run for an office and applies for leave of
absence and the church does not think it can spare him all he has to
do is to say: "I am going to run for the office whether you consent or
not. I tender my resignation of the church office."

If Congress shall say to the church you can not enforce such a rule,
then Congress would be interfering with the church by requiring it to
keep men in office when the church itself has held that they shall resign. Instead of the church attempting to regulate affairs of state, the
State would be regulating the affairs of the church.

I want now to recur to the last objection made to Senator Smoot.
When I listened to it yesterday it struck me with amazement. I read it
over again this morning in the stenographer's report to make sure
there was no mistake; and I do see that so eminent a counselor, so able
a man, one so experienced in public life as Mr. Tayler, has seriously

and solemnly asked the Senate of the United States to rule that, if a citizen of the United States believes that when he goes into his closet and prays to God for guidance [and] his God can hear him and may answer him, that man ought to be excluded from a seat in Congress, because he will be here to carry out the decrees of the Almighty.

Now, I had supposed until I heard that that nobody would deny that a man, to use the words of my Brother Tayler, who believes in a good, all-wise, and all-powerful Creator, can not do better in all the affairs of life than to seek the counsel of that Being and to abide by His judgment. I had supposed that it was the universal understanding of all Christian churches that the very foundation of their religion is that a man who believes in that great and good God ought to go to Him for advice and counsel. ...

And yet we are told that if Reed Smoot, when some question of grave State concern is before the Senate, should retire to his closet and commune with the Almighty for advice as to what he should do for the best interests of the country, and should think that the Lord gave him counsel in answer to his prayer, and should undertake to let his wandering feet go in the way in which the Lord had directed, he ought to be expelled from the Senate. I should [in] like word to be carried back to the ministerial association which had something to do with the origin of this case and for aught I know may have something to do with its prosecution, that for the purpose of carrying out the effort which it started, to have a member of the Mormon Church evicted from the Senate of the United States, it has been found necessary for their representative to come here and say to the people of all the churches all over the United States: "If you go and pray to the Almighty for guidance, and believe you get it, and act upon it, you can not sit in the Senate of the United States. ...

I do not know whether I may or may not be permitted, as one of the counsel of Senator Smoot, to say it, but unless I am stopped by the committee, I will say that I know from being actually present when it occurred in Salt Lake City a few weeks ago, that Senator Smoot urged the presidency to have Mr. [John W.] Taylor brought where the subpoena of this committee could be served on him. In view of the remarkably candid way in which President Smith testified before this committee and the evidence as to his honest and straightforward character it is fair to suppose that there are reasons which appear good and sufficient to him why no such action has been taken. The evidence before the committee shows that the president

last spring urged Taylor to come here and testify and that Taylor declined to do so[6] ...

And in this connection it should be borne in mind that whenever
either the president of the Mormon Church or Senator Smoot, pending this investigation, says or does anything indicating a disposition
to have the manifesto of 1890 carried out the intimation at once follows that they are influenced by a desire to pacify this committee and
are not acting in good faith. But whatever may be the reason that Mr.
Taylor is not here, Senator Smoot is in no degree responsible for his
absence. ...

Now, on the question of teaching—and I see my time is flying, and
I wish to address myself to another very important question in this
case for a little while—publications have been put in here, all of them,
except one, so far as I remember, antedating the time when Reed
Smoot became an apostle, in which certain members of the church
have undertaken to present the argument in favor of polygamy as a
thing in itself recognized by the Scriptures and as right.

I should say they are in precisely the same position in that regard
that our Southern brethren were after the war, in reference to the
question of slavery and the right of secession. They had upheld first
by their arguments and afterwards by arms the proposition that slavery was right. The vice-president of their confederacy announced at
the beginning of the war that they were going to erect a government,
the cornerstone of which would be human slavery. They contended,
as the people from that region of our country had contended for
many years, that under the terms of the Constitution of the United
States and the compact by which it was framed, any State had the right
to withdraw from the Union. When what Mr. Tayler would call the policeman's club was held up and by force of arms they were prevented
from carrying their intentions into effect, they accepted the situation
as the Mormons have accepted the situation since the manifesto.

But does anybody suppose that the opinion of a single man in all
the South was changed from what it had been before the war, as to
whether, as a matter of fact, the States had not the right to secede and

---

6. Carl Badger heard "from three different sources," according to his journal entry
for September 8, 1905, that Francis M. Lyman, president of the Quorum of the Twelve,
instructed John W. Taylor not to go to Washington because of a dream Lyman had in
which the spirit of Wilford Woodruff told him to so advise the younger apostle (in
Rodney J. Badger, *Liahona and Iron Rod: The Biography of Carl A. and Rose J. Badger*
[Bountiful, Utah: Family History Publishers, 1985], 273-74).

as to whether or not as a matter of fact slavery was right? Could not any man who believed slavery was a Divine institution and right, present an argument to the public in favor of it? Can not any man who thinks that the right of secession really existed write a book supporting his contention, giving the history of the transactions which led up to the framing of the Constitution? When he oversteps that line and urges the State to secede, he becomes an inciter to treason. When he undertakes to carry out measures which will have the effect of putting the negroes back into slavery, he commits an offense.

All that Mormon officials have done by any of the recent publications which I have seen has been, when the question was raised as to whether, as a matter of fact, they were right when they said polygamy was a Divine institution, to maintain their side of the argument. In one of those publications which was introduced the other day, containing an article by Brigham H. Roberts, which was published in the "Improvement Era" in [May] 1898, it is shown that the "Era" was challenged to debate on that subject. Thereupon Mr. Roberts published the argument, and the challenge and the reply to the challenge are published together. I respectfully submit that that is the right of any man in this country, as to the question of slavery or polygamy, or as to the right of secession as an abstract question.

SENATOR BEVERIDGE. My question went to the point whether there was a propaganda for the teaching of the breaking of the law. Then, to use your own analogy, very imperfectly, suppose there was an organized body, having a legal existence, which actually taught as a doctrine, not a religious doctrine, but a civil principle, and propagated the right and duty of secession. That is the question.

MR. WORTHINGTON. I should say doubtless, if it was advocating the duty of secession, it would be an incitement to a man—

SENATOR BEVERIDGE. Very well. My question is divisible into two branches. First, were they as a hierarchy practicing the breaking of law, and, second, were they teaching it. My question did not go to the freedom of opinion. I doubt very much whether anybody has a right to ask what somebody else believes. What we believe is our own affair.

MR. WORTHINGTON. So far as I can recall, in addition to what I have shown here, so far from their teaching it, the heads of the church have three times publicly proclaimed and submitted to the conference the opposite view, and there is not a word of testimony in this case tending to show that the heads of the church have in any way incited or encouraged people to enter into plural marriage since 1890, nor have they, except by the fact that some of them have practiced it themselves, in anywise encouraged others in the practice of polygamous cohabitation; and each of those who has practiced it has said as to that, "I take my risk with the law and I take my risk with my God."

SENATOR BEVERIDGE. You do not understand that there is a propaganda teaching that as a doctrine of the church?

MR. WORTHINGTON. Absolutely none. On the contrary, beyond peradventure, as a matter of fact, there has been no plural marriage in the church since the manifesto, and there can not be any.[7]

There can not be any plural marriage even in the church because the manifesto, which was the act of the Mormon people, took away the power of the president of the church to perform or to authorize anyone else to perform such a ceremony. A Mormon woman who becomes a plural wife now is an adulteress by the law of the church as she is an adulteress by the law of the land.

SENATOR OVERMAN. Do you claim that their missionaries and ministers do not teach polygamy?

MR. WORTHINGTON. I do.

SENATOR BEVERIDGE. That is my point.

SENATOR OVERMAN. Then, why do they not put the manifesto in some of their standard works, and publish it to the country and to the world?

MR. WORTHINGTON. That has been fully explained in the testimony of several of the witnesses, and it seems to me it is perfectly obvious. They use the Christian Bible. They send it out. So do all Christian people. In that there is set forth the example of Abraham, who took Hagar to wife, notwithstanding he had Sarah already as his legal wife. There is the example of Solomon, who had his wives and concubines by the hundreds, and there are many other illustrations which are known, showing that polygamy was practiced in those days by those people.

But nobody sends out with the Bible a statement that that is not lawful in these days. So as to the books which the Mormon missionaries use. They use the Book of Mormon. They are provided with it. It

---

7. Undoubtedly Worthington was not privy to the real complexities of post-Manifesto polygamy and how difficult the transition was to monogamy. In fact, eight members of the Quorum of the Twelve had taken new plural wives after the Manifesto: Abraham H. Cannon in 1896, Rudger Clawson in 1904, Matthias F. Cowley in 1899 and 1905, Marriner W. Merrill in 1901, John W. Taylor in 1890 and 1901, George Teasdale in 1897 and 1900, Abraham O. Woodruff in 1901, and Brigham Young Jr. in 1901. In addition, Apostles Anthon H. Lund and Francis M. Lyman had both performed post-Manifesto plural marriages (B. Carmon Hardy, *Solemn Covenant: The Mormon Polygamous Passage* [Urbana: University of Illinois Press, 1992], 206-32).

declares that polygamy shall not be allowed.[8] They have with them also the Doctrine and Covenants, in which there is the revelation as to polygamy, and in which book also there is a revelation saying it is the duty of every member of the church to obey the law of the land where he may be. They have both in the same book.

SENATOR BEVERIDGE. In other words, you claim that they take with them their sacred books just the same as our missionaries take with them our sacred books?

MR. WORTHINGTON. Certainly. The testimony of Joseph F. Smith is clear on this point. ...

SENATOR OVERMAN. But the church does not regard the manifesto as of sufficient importance to print it in the Doctrine and Covenants?

MR. WORTHINGTON. I say it ought to be printed; and President Smith, when he was here, said that as a matter of fact his attention had never been called to that question before, and that if any more editions of the Doctrine and Covenants were published, he would see that it was put in the volume. But it appears here that the manifesto is published in a separate pamphlet, and every missionary has it, as well as the other books. ...

It has been testified over and over again that their missionaries are carefully instructed not to mention the doctrine of polygamy, and so far as the testimony goes they never refer to it at all, except, if somebody comes along and says that Joseph Smith was an imposter and that the revelation of polygamy never came to him, they will assert that the doctrine called in question was a true revelation, and controvert the argument of the reorganized church that it was something imposed upon them by Brigham Young, or some of the successors of the prophet, and dated back.

THE CHAIRMAN. As you have been interrupted, pardon me if I ask a question for my own information. You stated in your opening: "We do not for a moment contend that if evidence to that effect could be brought here, and if it could be shown that Senator Smoot has a plural wife or has had at any time since he was elected a Senator, or since he was admitted to this body, he ought not to be expelled." Is it your contention that a different rule obtains in the case of polygamous cohabitation?

MR. WORTHINGTON. I do not understand your question. I understand the two propositions to be the same. I will certainly admit that if Senator Smoot were now living in polygamous cohabitation he ought not to be allowed to keep his seat.

---

8. Worthington is referring to Jacob 2:24-28 in the Book of Mormon.

THE CHAIRMAN. Then, the same rule that you stated in the one case would apply?

MR. WORTHINGTON. That is what I understood by the question.

THE CHAIRMAN. Then, to follow it a moment further, in the light of the testimony in the case, you would think if Joseph Smith was elected a Senator he ought not to take his seat?

MR. WORTHINGTON. I would vote against him if I had the opportunity.

THE CHAIRMAN. That is all.

MR. WORTHINGTON. These are questions that are addressed to me personally.

THE CHAIRMAN. I wanted your opinion.

MR. WORTHINGTON. My personal opinion. Of course I do not know what Senator Smoot would say upon the subject. ...

Let me say, however, in passing, that in this particular case [regarding church influence in politics] it happens that there were two witnesses examined who would know something about the fact if that legislature had been induced by the church authorities to elect Senator Smoot.

One of them is Joseph F. Smith, who was the head of the church, and who naturally would be supposed to know something about it if anything of that kind had been done. He was brought here by the protestants and he testified, in the most emphatic terms, that he did not interfere and the church did not interfere. A cloud of other witnesses testified who would only know it by the general understanding, and they testified that Mr. Smoot was the natural and logical candidate. ...

But it is said that, without regard to the particular relation that existed between the votes that elected Senator Smoot and the church, it appears here as a general proposition that in the State of Utah there is such a union of religion and politics that any man who is elected by reason of the influence resulting from that union should not be allowed to keep his seat in the Senate. In other words, it is said that there shall be no union in political campaigns of religious matters and political matters. Now, I do most respectfully but most emphatically deny that any proposition of that kind ought to be listened to for one moment. I contend that if any religious organization in this country wishes to organize itself into a political party, or if any political party wishes to organize itself into a religious party, it has the right to do it.

If the word should go out from this committee to the preachers throughout the country that it is seriously contended here that a man should be excluded from the Senate who recognizes the existence of a God with whom he can commune and from whom he can receive advice and help, it might well be that some Peter the Hermit would urge the hosts of Christianity to organize a party in this land to put into the Constitution of the United States what is not there, a recognition of the fact that there is a God, and a provision that a man might commune with Him in prayer and might receive from Him guidance in his vote or anything else and still should not be excluded from holding public office.[9] Suppose such a wave of revolution should spread over this country, and there should come here at some time a number of Senators elected on that religious-political issue, and it should appear that they were elected by a combination of all the Christian churches in the country working through their church organizations. I wonder if they would be told by the Senate, "Go back and tell your people they have done a very foolish and ridiculous thing. Go back, and be elected upon some such really material issue as the tariff, or the trusts, or silver, or railroad rates, or something of that kind, and we will let you in. But we can not allow people to come here who have been elected through the action of church organizations, because they believe in a God who hears and answers prayers."

I submit, Mr. Chairman, that any portion of the people of this country may at any time rightfully unite themselves into a party which shall combine both religious and political principles. I submit that the Mormon Church in Utah, the Catholic Church in New York, the Episcopal Church in Maryland, or any other church in any other State, may organize itself into a political party and through its preachers in the pulpit, through its church officials anywhere, may solicit votes, and they may have a religious caucus if they please and say we will vote for the officers who will be nominated by the head of this church organization, just as they might for officers nominated by a caucus of politicians; and I submit that such men would be no more ineligible to seats in the Senate than men elected by legislators who

9. A few hours after the day's testimony, Carl Badger explained in a letter to his wife his role in Worthington's argument: "I have just come from the Congressional Library where I have been attempting to find something for Mr. Worthington on 'prayer'— He wants to prove that the universal Christian practice and teaching is that God will guide those who seek him, and that, therefore, because Reed Smoot believes in a God who will guide him, that such belief is no disqualification to his holding a seat in the Senate of the United States. I am very tired to-night. I have been in the Committee room all day, except the time I have spent in the library" (Badger, *Liahona and Iron Rod*, 247).

would say, "Instead of going to a religious organization, we will go to a political organization and be bound by what it may say."

It is common knowledge that it frequently occurs that a legislature elects a Senator who had been selected for that office by the leader of the dominant party in the State where the election is held before the legislature had even met. Are we to have inquiries by this committee in the future as to whether a Senator-elect represents his State or the political "boss" of that State?

SENATOR KNOX. Do you understand that there is anything in the Constitution of the United States which prohibits a State from establishing a religion?

MR. WORTHINGTON. That is just what I was coming to.

SENATOR BEVERIDGE. What other churches are there, if you know, that claim to receive, either as a church or through their officers or members, revelations from God?

MR. WORTHINGTON. I understand that the Catholic Church, for instance—

MR. VAN COTT. And the Reorganized Church.

MR. WORTHINGTON. The Reorganized Church of Jesus Christ of Latter-Day Saints is another. The Catholic Church does claim that in all things relating to faith or to morals the Pope is the infallible head of the church, and speaks by authority of God, and every member of the church must accept what he says as true.[10] ...

SENATOR BEVERIDGE. What churches claim that their members are or may be in communication with the Almighty?

MR. WORTHINGTON. I understand that all churches do that, so far as my knowledge goes in that regard. There is no church in the land the ministers of which do not teach their children in their Sunday schools

---

10. On February 12, Badger mailed his wife an additional update:

The Senator's case is not going to be decided at this session. You must not tell any one,—not because there is anything that I tell you that you might not get from the papers, but because I get some things from original sources, and I should not be talking too much about these things. I hear that detectives have been sent to Utah to find out something about new marriages, with a view to opening up the case again. The Senators who are pushing this fight against the Church think that they have not presented their case as strongly and as conclusively as they might, and they want information on which they can open the case again ... I think too that perhaps the Committee is waiting to see what foundation is there to the statement made by Mr. Worthington and the Senator that [Apostles] Cowley and Taylor are being investigated [by the church], and that they want to see what the Church will do in the matter. This is a contemptible attitude for us to be in (ibid., 252).

Badger's journal the same day reads "Senator Gallinger tells Senator Smoot that the investigation was 'a big washing but a mighty little hanging out.' ... From all that I can learn, if anything is done with Cowley and Taylor, by the leaders of the church, it will be because they are forced to do something" (ibid., 253).

to go to their Maker when they are in doubt or trouble and ask for guidance.

SENATOR FORAKER. It is the belief of the Methodist Church that their ministers are called by God.

SENATOR BEVERIDGE. Yes.

SENATOR FORAKER. That they are moved by the spirit; that they receive a message.

SENATOR HOPKINS. And that is a very good church in my country.

SENATOR BEVERIDGE. Yes; there are six members of this committee who are members of it, including myself.

MR. WORTHINGTON. Let me make this further suggestion in this connection. When I was a lad, we had a party in this country that called itself the American party, and because it was a secret organization, it was called by others the Know-Nothing party. It had secret rites and ceremonials which it refused to disclose to anybody. I do not know whether a member of the Know-Nothing party was ever elected to the Senate, but I take it for granted if he had been he would have been admitted.

The whole principle upon which that party was founded was hostility to the Roman Catholic Church, and precisely the same charges were made against that Church at that time that are now made against the Mormon Church, in respect both of the authority of the head of the church and of the disposition of the church to control the political affairs of the country.

I wonder whether if the Catholic Church, through its officials, had organized itself to resist that kind of a party, and had sent one of its high officers to the Senate to resist any attempt that might be made to legislate against it, he would have been turned out of the Senate or refused admission thereto because he had been elected through the efforts of a religious organization or because he believed in the infallibility of the Pope. I think not.

The Constitution of the United States provides by almost its concluding clause that no religious test shall ever be required as a qualification to any office or public trust under the United States. The first amendment to the Constitution provides that "Congress shall make no law respecting an establishment of religion, or prohibiting the free exercise thereof." This prohibition applies to the United States only ... not to the States, as Mr. Van Cott has shown in his argument. In the early history of this country some of the States did have an established church.

MR. VAN COTT. Connecticut and Vermont.

MR. WORTHINGTON. And I believe it is perfectly competent now for any
State in this Union by an amendment to its constitution, if the people
please, to have an established church and to have an absolute and perfect union between the church and state, if they desire to have it. ...

MR. WORTHINGTON. Now, Senators, in conclusion, let me say a word on behalf of the Mormon people. They have been held up to odium and
have been execrated because it is said they defy the law. It is very true,
on this one matter of polygamy, they did for a long time insist that
marriage is one of those matters which is in the nature of a religious
institution, and a sacrament, peculiarly so under their doctrine, and
could not be interfered with by the State. But in all other regards they
have conformed to the law. They have shown their patriotism in so
many instances and in such a manner that nobody can doubt that
they are true American citizens.

As early as 1846, when the war with Mexico was flagrant, when
the Mormons during their migration from Nauvoo to Salt Lake City
were resting on the banks of the Mississippi River, the Government of
the United States sent to their camp and called upon them for volun-
teers to help form a regiment of a thousand men to march across the
desert to the State of California, there to aid in the operations in
which our Army was then engaged. In that Mormon camp, though it
was but two years after the murder of their prophet, they organized a
battalion of five hundred men, who with five hundred from other
sources made that historic march across the Great American Desert,
suffering great privations and enduring to the end.

Another significant illustration of their inherent patriotism is
the fact—not heretofore mentioned, I believe, in this hearing,—that
they believe the Constitution of the United States is an inspired document. And when in July, 1847, the advance guard of the Mormon
people reached Salt Lake City, which was then Mexican territory—
because it was months before the treaty of Guadalupe Hidalgo,
which transferred that territory to the United States—when they had
planted themselves on Mexican territory, to which they might be
supposed to have been glad to remove from the United States, the
first thing they did was to ascend the peak, which stands behind
their temple, and there unfurl the stars and stripes! Ever since that
day that eminence has been known as Ensign Peak,[11] and from the

11. In actuality, it wasn't an American flag that was unfurled on Ensign Peak but
rather Heber Kimball's "yellow bandana decorated with black spots," attached to Wil-

staff at its summit on the Fourth of July and on other gala days the flag still waves as an evidence that the Mormon people are not disloyal. And so far were they from seeking to escape from the jurisdiction of the United States that almost immediately after they reached Utah they applied for the admission of the Territory to the Union as the State of Deseret. ...

It is said here that this proceeding has been begun for the protection of the home. I have seen that expression used in this protest, and I have heard it used here from time to time—that the great object of this proceeding is to protect that necessary unit of American civilization, the home, where one man lives with one wife, and they bring up a family of children around them. Yet it is sought, in the attainment of such a result as that, to cast down and to cast out a man who was born in a polygamous household; a man who looks with the greatest reverence upon his sainted mother, and knows she was one of those against whom are aimed all these shafts which intimate that people who entered into those relations entered into them from other than the most sacred principles.

It is sought to cast out a man who was reared in such a way, who was surrounded by all the temptations which he had to enter into polygamous relations, who has been faithful when many were faithless, and who has in far-off Utah that single wife whom he married so many years ago, with his six children around her. It is proposed to strike that man down and that home, that sacred home, with one wife, and that family of children, and to do it because it is said you want to protect the home.

I say, Mr. Chairman and gentlemen of the committee, if it is your desire to protect the home, a home of that kind, let it be known that when a man who, under such temptations and trials stands up for the home, by his own example, and who never in his whole life has ever uttered one word in support of the practice of polygamy, comes to the Senate of the United States, you will not cast him out and say he shall suffer for the offenses of others. You will not punish young Utah for old Utah's sins.[12] ...

---

lard Richards's walking cane (Ronald W. Walker, "'A Banner is Unfurled:' Mormonism's Ensign Peak" *Dialogue: A Journal of Mormon Thought* 26 [Winter 1993]: 81-82; cf. B. H. Roberts, ed., *A Comprehensive History of the Church of Jesus Christ of Latter-day Saints* [Salt Lake City: LDS Church, 1930], 3:270-72, where the American flag legend is similarly contradicted).

12. Badger wrote in his journal on February 24: "Last Saturday Burrows tried to get the Committee to go to Utah, and intimated that he thought he could find Smoot's

MR. TAYLER. Mr. Chairman and gentlemen, I want first to make a reference to the observations and animadversions [criticisms] of Mr.
Worthington upon my statement respecting revelation.

I must have been sorely misunderstood if I was thought to confuse
or to identify as the same thing that kind of inspiration or instruction
or direction that Christian men and women are supposed to receive
through prayer from God with the kind of revelation concerning
which Reed Smoot testified, and which is the basis of the Mormon
Church; and I looked at what I said yesterday in reply to Senator
Knox's question—which was not said, as Mr. Worthington insisted,
with carefully weighed words, as the committee well knew—but as I
now look at them, I find I did state it accurately, though not as scien-
tifically as if I had undertaken to write it down; and this is what I said:
"That is to say, any man who believes himself to be in personal relation to Almighty God, so that he is capable of receiving, through a
conscious fellowship and intercourse, face to face with God, either by
hearing his voice or by seeing his presence," the will, and wish, and
command of God.

That is the kind of revelation to which I had reference, the kind
of revelation which I apprehend, as actually delivered, we are under
not the slightest danger of suffering in this country in this day and
generation.

The accuracy of what I said is to be further defined by what I have
said in my argument, taken from the work of a high authority in the
Mormon Church who defined inspiration and revelation.

So I was referring to that sort of thing. Then, as a practical question, I went on to show that it never could be raised, it never would be
raised, where it was a mere abstraction; where one merely possessed
that belief, in the very nature of things it would not be raised; and so
stated in reply to Senator Knox's question; but with Senator Smoot
and the officials of the Mormon Church, with the practices which
were approved in reference to them, the association of Senator
Smoot with his brother apostles, their power, their authority, the ease
with which they could make their people obedient to the law—that attitude and conduct were interpreted. They were clear. They were
given a certain character in consequence of the capacity of the leaders of this church to receive revelation. ...

second wife. ... Beveridge says that Burrows is 'a damn liar'" (Badger, *Liahona and Iron
Rod*, 257).

Senator Smoot says—I am illustrating this matter of want of knowledge—that he did not know that Apostle Penrose was a polygamist. Now, Charles W. Penrose has been one of the best-known men in his church. He was a polygamist, and had been for years, and, surely in the presence of Senator Smoot, for he was here constantly, Joseph F. Smith, the president of the church, on the second day he testified here, told us that Charles W. Penrose was a polygamist. Senator Smoot, we are told, did not know it—did not know it the following July when he united with all the rest of his colleagues to make this polygamist a member of this high body. True, he goes on to say it would not have made any difference if he had known it.

The fact is that the certainty that a high Mormon official is [likely to be] a polygamist makes the statement that any particular one is a polygamist of no sort of significance. It makes no impression upon the apostolic mind to have one of the high members of the church spoken of as a polygamist. That is why I assume that Senator Smoot, having heard with his own ears here the statement of Joseph S. Smith, as I doubt not he did, that Charles W. Penrose was a polygamist, forgot that he had heard any such thing and testified that he had never heard it.

Now, one other word. I hardly believed what I heard Mr. Worthington say on this subject of the propriety of unlawful cohabitation. No citizen of Utah, no Mormon, jack Mormon, or Gentile, has equaled Mr. Worthington in his eulogy of the propriety, necessity, legality, of unlawful cohabitation; and the logic of that position sent him to a proposition which surprised me.

If I understand his proposition, it is in effect that it is now the rule of the church that polygamous cohabitation may be practiced. A thing is either one or the other when it relates to such a subject as polygamy.

That is to say, it is either proper or it is improper. It is either according to the rule of the church, or it is against the rule of the church, that one should enter into plural marriage. It is either according to the rule of the church or against the rule of the church that one should continue polygamous cohabitation. I think there is no flaw in that position.

Mr. Worthington insists that the church has no authority to deal with any man who is engaged in the business of polygamous cohabitation. He insists that the president of the church is without authority to criticise, and that it is plain that Senator Smoot would be without authority to do it. Why? Because the manifesto of 1890 related alone to the contracting of new plural marriages, and that when anybody is charged with violating the law of the land or the rule of the church respecting polygamous cohabitation, he would answer: "The manifesto does not mean that. I was there. I held up my hand to sustain it, and I heard what was in it. It did not prohibit me from continuing to live with my wives. It prohibited me only from taking more wives."

THE CHAIRMAN. Who are you reading from?

MR. TAYLER. I am reading from Mr. Worthington, in his argument made here yesterday.

MR. WORTHINGTON. It does not mean that I was there, Mr. Chairman. I am quoting.

MR. TAYLER. I understand you were quoting the person whom the president of the church charges with being guilty of polygamous cohabitation.

SENATOR BEVERIDGE. His interpretation of the manifesto?

MR. TAYLER. Exactly. That is to say, that he had a right to violate the manifesto, and the church had no right to deal with him for it.

SENATOR BEVERIDGE. His interpretation of what he voted for?

MR. TAYLER. And that he had a right to interpret that manifesto as he pleased, and that therefore there was no rule of the church against polygamous cohabitation. There is no rule of the church against it, according to Mr. Worthington, and if there is no rule of the church against it then there is no objection to it. Therefore the church does encourage it, the church does connive at it, the church does countenance it. The president of the church and seven of his associate apostles do practice polygamous cohabitation. The president of the church has proclaimed more than once to the thousands of his people that the man who does not thus remain true to his wives will be eternally damned.

SENATOR BEVERIDGE. Mr. Tayler, do you not think that is rather daring reasoning, that because a church or any other organization does not specifically have something against a thing, therefore it is the rule of that church organization that it approves of that thing? Take many crimes that are not to be mentioned upon which there is absolutely nothing in any church to which any of us belong or to which you belong. The mere fact that we say nothing about it, you would not contend, would mean that we actually, as a rule of our bodies, approve of it as a matter of abstract reasoning?

MR. TAYLER. That is right, as a matter of abstract reasoning; but if the church to which you or I belong had established polygamy, and we had entered into polygamous marriage in consequence of the divine law, and proceeded to polygamously cohabit with all of our wives, and then the law commanding plural marriage had been suspended, and we continued to polygamously cohabit with the wives we took when the Lord permitted it, and the law, as we claimed, permitted it, and the church proclaimed that its law then was that no more plural wives could be received, but said nothing about continuing to live in polygamous cohabitation, and its high officials continued to live in polygamous cohabitation, then I say yes, that is the rule of the church in respect to polygamous cohabitation.

SENATOR BEVERIDGE. It is not important. I was merely testing, as I think you will appreciate, the accuracy of your abstract reasoning.

MR. TAYLER. I understand that.

SENATOR BEVERIDGE. I will take this case out of the question; but applying it to any possible case, I was testing the accuracy of your abstract reasoning by which you arrive at the conclusion that because any organization says nothing upon a certain subject, therefore it approves that subject.

MR. TAYLER. Undoubtedly. The Senator's view is right. I was not reasoning about the Mormon Church and a concrete situation. ...

Gentlemen, I am glad that I have been permitted to address you to this extent in reply to Mr. Worthington. I had not myself expected to do so, but that Mr. Carlisle, who was originally associated with me, would conclude the argument. I do not mean that as apologizing for any infirmity in any reply that I have made, because I have known ever since Mr. Van Cott commenced that I would make whatever reply was to be made. ...

I have tried to preserve during the hearing in this case as nearly a judicial attitude as would be possible for one who was engaged as counsel in the case. I think I have fairly well succeeded in that effort. I am not without the personal interest that an advocate has in the controversy in which he is participating, but I believe the committee will think, I believe the committee have apprehended, that I have tried only to inform it respecting the situation that exists in the State of Utah; that I have sought not to mislead them in any respect; that I have not endeavored to prejudice them in any way against the Senator who is their associate, but that, as nearly as it is possible for man with human qualities to do so, I have sought to discover and uncover the truth. ...

THE CHAIRMAN. I wish to say to counsel upon both sides that the commit-

tee is greatly obligated to the counsel for the assistance they have rendered in this investigation. That assistance can be further rendered
by counsel in making their briefs as full as possible, and referring to
testimony, as suggested by Senator Dillingham, and to everything
that they regard as material.

I would therefore be glad to know of counsel about how much
time they would like in order to make such elaborate briefs as the
committee would desire.

MR. WORTHINGTON. I think something was said the other day at the beginning of Mr. Van Cott's address to the effect that we would have until next Wednesday for that purpose. Of course between now and
Wednesday we can not prepare anything like a satisfactory digest.

THE CHAIRMAN. I think the committee, Mr. Worthington, would be glad
to have counsel take such time as they would like.

MR. WORTHINGTON. Then let us have until Saturday of next week.

SENATOR BEVERIDGE. Make your work perfect, and that will save time for
us. ...

THE CHAIRMAN. And, Mr. Tayler, how much time will you want?

MR. TAYLER. Saturday will do. ...

THE CHAIRMAN. Then that is understood. With that understanding the
committee will stand adjourned. ...

Editor's note

As far as anyone knew at the time, the hearings had come to a long
drawn-out conclusion. Smoot's secretary, Carl Badger, explained to his
wife that there would be "a majority and a minority report from the
Committee; one will recommend that the Senator be unseated, the
other that he retain his seat; but both will agree in their abhorrence of
certain conditions in the State of Utah, and of certain acts of dishonor
on the part of the leaders of the Mormon people."[13]

Eight days following the closing arguments, Badger offered his opinion that Senator Berry of Arkansas "would not make an impartial juror,
because he remembers the day that the children came back bare-footed
from the Mountain Meadow Massacre." Berry had reference to the 1857
atrocity in southern Utah, a prelude to the Utah War, when 120 immi-
grants were killed by the local militia. The only survivors were children
under eight years of age. As Badger wrote, "the emigrants were many of
them from Arkansas."[14] On February 11, 1907, Berry delivered a speech

13. Ibid., 282.
14. Ibid., 250-51.

on the Senate floor opposing Smoot, emphasizing that the perpetrators of the massacre had been Mormons and that although the tragedy "occurred before the Senator from Utah was born," and "he is in no way either directly or indirectly responsible for it," Smoot was "bound to know of this and many other acts of the church in the past" which had been hidden from public view.[15]

In February 1905 Badger informed his wife of a split in the Utah delegation. Senator Thomas Kearns of Utah had decided to endorse a proposed anti-polygamy amendment to the Constitution. According to Badger, Kearns "did his worst with a speech written by Frank J. Cannon," a speech that was nevertheless "well written, as anything which comes from the pen of Cannon is sure to be," but "delivered very poorly." Kearns said "disposed" when he meant "deposed" and otherwise "spoiled the force and emphasis by his lack of understanding of the construction of the sentences." The speech fell on deaf ears in the Senate but "was not meant for th[at] narrow audience." Rather, "it was intended for the country. Kearns has, no doubt, made careful preparations to have his speech printed in detail in the papers; and I am told that the Associated Press is sending it out." Smoot intended to respond to Kearns, but when he stood up to speak, "a number of Senators near him told him not to attempt a reply." In Badger's view, this had been just as well.[16]

In December 1905, Smoot reported to LDS President Joseph F. Smith that there were rumblings of a continuation of the hearings. Smoot's attorney Augustus Worthington assured him that Senator Burrows "had said nothing ... about opening the case. [Burrows] has not [talked] to [Senators] Beveridge or Dillingham [but] still insists to newspaper reporters that it will be opened. He has not said one word to me about the case, nor I to him. I do not intend to mention the case to him."[17] Smoot mentioned that he had been consulted by Senate leaders about who should replace Senator McComas on the Committee on Privileges and Elections. McComas had lost his re-election bid in his home state of Maryland. Without thinking twice, Smoot recommended Senator Dolliver of Iowa. Soon thereafter, Smoot learned that Dolliver was, in fact, opposed to Smoot retaining his seat. Carl Badger found this a "startling ... bit of carelessness on the Senator's part" that could produce "big results" for the prosecution.[18] Predictably Dolliver voted for Smoot's ex-

---

15. *Congressional Record*, 1907, 2681-88.

16. Badger, *Liahona and Iron Rod*, 259.

17. Smoot to Joseph F Smith, Dec. 12, 1905.

18. Badger, *Liahona and Iron Rod*, 290, 292-93.

pulsion in committee, then surprised some observers by reversing himself when it came to a full Senate vote.

Smoot was also discouraged to find he was losing the support of a former staunch ally on the committee, Senator Beveridge, who had become "very unsettled in his mind in regard to my case, and he thought
that he had found, in reading the testimony in my case and in the editorial of the Deseret News ... a disposition on the part of the church to approve of polygamy and a teaching of the same. ... Senator Sutherland has
just called me in relation to the editorial in the News of May 1st, and
informs me that in his opinion this editorial is the most unfortunate
thing that has happened since the hearings in my case began."[19] This
"unfortunate" editorial[20] replied to a Chicago newspaper's criticism of
how the church dismissed the two apostles who refused to testify before
the U.S. Senate. The church did so without publicly airing the evidence
against the two men, and the church membership "obediently" sustained this action.

In the midst of these developments, when public opinion was at its
lowest due to publicity over the continued refusal of Apostles Matthias
F. Cowley and John W. Taylor to appear in Washington, Smoot received
correspondence from a third apostle in hiding, Heber J. Grant, who had
remained in Europe to avoid arrest and the Senate's subpoena. Grant
wrote: "It has been my earnest and constant prayer that Brothers Taylor
and Cowley might be preserved from the shafts of the enemy. I feel sure
that if they were sacrificed that it would only be one more concession
and that in the near future something else would be demanded. It seems
impossible to satisfy a lion when he has once tasted blood and it is
equally as hard to satisfy [such] friends in human form."[21] One month
later, Apostle George Albert Smith stood at the pulpit in the Tabernacle
in Salt Lake City and said the following:

> It becomes my painful duty, and it fills my heart with sorrow, to announce
> to you that, since our last general conference, there have occurred three va-
> cancies in the Quorum of the Twelve. Elder Marriner W. Merrill passed
> from this life on February 6th, 1906. We received from Elders John W. Tay-
> lor and Mathias F. Cowley their written resignations, dated October 28th,
> 1905, of their positions as members of the Quorum of the Twelve, which
> were accepted by the Twelve and the First Presidency of the Church. These

---

19. Smoot to Joseph F. Smith, May 10, 1906.

20. "Wrong and Irrational, *Deseret News,* May 1, 1906.

21. Grant to Smoot, Mar. 7, 1906.

vacancies have been filled, as directed by the Spirit of the Lord through His servant, President Joseph F. Smith.[22]

22. *Conference Reports,* Apr. 1906, 79. The announcement was not made until the final session of conference, and the new apostles, George F. Richards, Orson F. Whitney, and David O. McKay, were not mentioned (even by George Albert Smith) until the end of the last session when the names were read for the sustaining of officers. Five years later Matthias F. Cowley was disfellowshipped and John W. Taylor was excommunicated (Thomas G. Alexander, *Mormonism in Transition: A History of the Latter-day Saints, 1890-1930* [Urbana: University of Illinois Press, 1986], 70).

29.

Additional Witnesses

Walter M. Wolfe, William Jones Thomas, Charles A. Smurthwaite, Henry W. Lawrence, and James H. Linford

Tuesday, Thursday &
Monday, February 6, 8, and March 26

"So little interest is apparent in the Smoot hearing that Senator Burrows finds it impossible to get a quorum of the committee together. ... There was the usual crowd of women and a score of men besides the witnesses, but the testimony was not such as to be of interest." —*Deseret News,* Feb. 8, 1906

Walter M. Wolfe,[1] being duly sworn, was examined and testified as follows ...

MR. CARLISLE. How long have you resided in Utah?

MR. WOLFE. I have resided in Utah since 1890.

MR. CARLISLE. What has been your occupation?

MR. WOLFE. Teaching.

MR. CARLISLE. In the Mormon schools?

MR. WOLFE. Since September, 1892.

MR. CARLISLE. What schools? State to the committee what your position has been and what your duties were.

MR. WOLFE. In the Brigham Young Academy at Provo, Utah, and subsequently in the Brigham Young College at Logan, Utah.

MR. CARLISLE. What was your position in the college?

MR. WOLFE. In the Brigham Young College I was professor of geology. In the academy I had history and Latin.

MR. CARLISLE. You were a member of the Mormon Church?

MR. WOLFE. I was.

---

1. Wolfe (ca. 1868-?) had moved to Utah in 1890 to teach at Brigham Young University, then at the church college in Logan, but left the LDS Church in 1906. Harvard Heath notes: "An interesting twist to Wolfe's testimony before the Committee was that two years previous, he wrote a defense of Smoot's right to be seated which appeared in the Church publication, the *Millennial Star*" (Heath, "Reed Smoot: First Modern Mormon," Ph.D. diss., Brigham Young University 1990, 174).

MR. CARLISLE. For how long?

MR. WOLFE. Practically until the 2d of January, when I severed my relations.

SENATOR OVERMAN. The 2d of January of what year?

MR. WOLFE. Of the present year. I severed my connection not officially, but by refusing to comply with the demand for tithing, which President [Joseph F.] Smith has stated is equivalent to a man withdrawing from the church. ...

MR. CARLISLE. Professor Wolfe, did you ever pass through the Endowment House?

MR. WOLFE. I have been through the Endowment House.

MR. CARLISLE. How many times have you passed through the Endowment House?

MR. WOLFE. Not less than twelve.

MR. CARLISLE. Will you please state to the committee when you first passed through the Endowment House and when you passed through the last time?

MR. WOLFE. Excuse me, secretary.[2] By the Endowment House, I suppose you mean the Temple?

MR. CARLISLE. Yes, the Temple.

MR. WOLFE. Because the old Endowment House is torn down. I was never in that. I first passed through in May, 1894.

MR. CARLISLE. When was the last time?

MR. WOLFE. October, 1902.

MR. CARLISLE. Will you state to the committee whether there is, as part of the ceremonies in the Temple, any oath administered?[3]

---

2. Co-counsel for the prosecution, John Carlisle, had served as Secretary of the Treasury under President Grover Cleveland in the 1890s, thus Professor Wolfe's reference to him as "secretary." In the long run, speculation by the *Deseret News* (Mar. 9, 1904) that Carlisle would abandon the case proved untrue. Aside from Carlisle's ability as an attorney, he had been Speaker of the House throughout most of the 1880s and a Senator prior to his cabinet appointment, making him a well-connected and somewhat formidable opponent ("Carlisle, John G.," *Encyclopedia Britannica Online*, Sept. 16, 2007).

3. The reason the hearings had to be resumed, according to the *Salt Lake Tribune*, was to determine exactly what was said in the LDS temple oaths. Another Salt Lake publication, *Truth*, countered that this would be a "waste of time and money" since the *Tribune's* own editor, Frank J. Cannon, could provide this information himself ("Our Senatorial Representatives," *Truth*, Feb. 3, 1906). Carl Badger suspected that the temple would be the focus of discussion, in particular that Professor Wolfe was "expected to tell about the endowment ceremony in detail. It is said that he has a marvelous memory" (in Harvard Heath, "Reed Smoot: First Modern Mormon," Ph.D. diss., Brigham Young University, 1990, 169). In fact, Wolfe did nothing of the kind. He answered one question

MR. WOLFE. There are several oaths administered.

MR. CARLISLE. Can you state what they are?

MR. WOLFE. There is an oath of chastity, or, I might say, a covenant or law—a law of sacrifice and a law of vengeance.

MR. CARLISLE. When you say a law of vengeance, what do you mean? Do you mean that there is any promise or pledge to avenge a wrong, or do you mean simply that there is some law read to you or some rule read to you?

MR. WOLFE. There is no covenant or agreement on the part of any individual to avenge anything.

MR. CARLISLE. Just state to the committee what it is.

MR. WOLFE. The law of vengeance is this: "You and each of you do covenant and promise that you will pray, and never cease to pray, Almighty God to avenge the blood of the prophets upon this nation, and that you will teach the same to your children and your children's children unto the third and fourth generations." ...

MR. CARLISLE. Was that done?

MR. WOLFE. It was done.

SENATOR OVERMAN. Was that done every time or just one time?

MR. WOLFE. It was done every time I went through.[4]

SENATOR OVERMAN. That was twelve times?

---

about the oath of vengeance and one question about the ritual washing, for which he gave a general answer. However, in reporting on Wolfe's testimony, the *Salt Lake Tribune* reprinted in the same issue an anonymous temple exposé it had originally published twenty-six years earlier, leading to the misconception that Wolfe himself had disclosed these details (*Salt Lake Tribune*, Feb. 12, 1906, Sept. 28, 1879). The author of the exposé was Caroline Owens Miles (Michael W. Homer, "'Similarity of Priesthood in Masonry': The Relationship between Freemasonry and Mormonism," *Dialogue: A Journal of Mormon Thought* 27 (Fall 1994), 62-63).

4. The previous four questions and answers were included in the "View of the Minority" report submitted by Senator Foraker on June 11, 1906 (see *Smoot Hearings*, 4:540).

At a time when Smoot was losing support from such influential Senators as Eugene Hale (R-Maine), Senator Foraker remained constant. Carl Badger wrote that he had "always felt sure about" Foraker. On January 4 the *Washington Post* reported that Senator Bailey had decided to call for Smoot's expulsion. Badger confided to his wife that "the Post is, in my judgment, the weightiest paper in the country, and it seems to have turned its columns over to the opposition," allowing the *Salt Lake Tribune*'s Washington correspondent to submit articles "at the suggestion of Senator Dubois, so I am informed." Badger added that Smoot had "not expressed any but the most hopeful views, but I know that he is greatly worried. I am very sorry for him; he is losing more in this fight than either the Senators or his brethren imagine" (in Rodney J. Badger, *Liahona and Iron Rod: The Biography of Carl A. and Rose J. Badger* [Bountiful, Utah: Family History Publishers, 1985], 294, 296).

MR. WOLFE. Yes, sir.

MR. CARLISLE. Twelve times at different times, he said.

MR. WOLFE. At different times.

[SENATOR] OVERMAN. I understand they were at different times. ...

THE CHAIRMAN. You spoke of John Henry Smith. You know him?

MR. WOLFE. I have met him; yes, sir.

THE CHAIRMAN. What is his position in the church?

MR. WOLFE. He is a member of the quorum of the twelve apostles, the second one on the list, I think.

THE CHAIRMAN. Where is he?

MR. WOLFE. I do not know. I suppose he is in Salt Lake City.

THE CHAIRMAN. Did you have a conversation with him at any time in relation to the [Wilford Woodruff] manifesto?

MR. WOLFE. Yes, sir.

THE CHAIRMAN. State what it was.

MR. WOLFE. Will you allow me, Senator, to give the incidents in connection with it? It will refresh my mind.

THE CHAIRMAN. Yes, sir.

MR. WOLFE. There was a meeting in the Brigham Young Academy, in Provo, Utah, that was addressed by B[enjamin]. F. Grant, a brother of Apostle Heber J. Grant. At that meeting Apostle John Henry Smith was present.

THE CHAIRMAN. On what date was that; what year?

MR. WOLFE. I don't remember, the year. It was in the late nineties, probably.

MR. CARLISLE. It was after the manifesto?

MR. WOLFE. Yes, sir; it was after the manifesto. On my way home I walked several blocks with B. F. Grant and Apostle Smith, and on the way we were talking about the conditions existing, and President Smith used these words to me: "Brother Wolfe, don't you know that the manifesto is only a trick to beat the devil at his own game?"[5] ...

---

5. The following two affidavits—the first from Benjamin F. Grant, the second from John Henry Smith—were subsequently submitted to refute Wolfe's testimony:

B. F. Grant, being first duly sworn, on his oath does say: That he is 49 years of age, and that he is now and has been a resident of Salt Lake City, Utah, most of his life, having been born there; that he is well acquainted with John Henry Smith, one of the twelve apostles of the Church of Jesus Christ of Latter-Day Saints, and that he is slightly acquainted with one Walter M. Wolfe, who was at one time a professor at the Brigham Young Academy at Provo. Affiant further says that he never at any time had any conversation or was present when any conversation was had between the said John Henry Smith and the said Walter M. Wolfe in regard to the matter of plural marriage or the so-called manifesto or anything of a like nature, and affiant posi-

MR. WORTHINGTON. When did your connection with Brigham Young Academy terminate?

MR. WOLFE. In July, 1902. That was the official severance.

MR. WORTHINGTON. Was that severance of your relations with the academy voluntary on your part, or was it involuntary?

MR. WOLFE. It was absolutely voluntary on my part.

MR. WORTHINGTON. There was no request of you to resign?

MR. WOLFE. No, sir.

MR. WORTHINGTON. Were there any charges preferred against you with reference to drunkenness?

MR. WOLFE. Not that I know of, there.[6]

MR. WORTHINGTON. You never heard of that before?

MR. WOLFE. Never.

MR. WORTHINGTON. Before now?

MR. WOLFE. No, sir; I did not. I will not deny that they may have been made, but I never heard of them.

---

tively states that at no time in his presence was there any remark made by the said John Henry Smith or the said Walter M. Wolfe in relation to the so-called manifesto that it was the purpose or intention of the manifesto "to whip the devil at his own game," or any words to that effect or conveying that meaning; and the statement reputed to have been made by said Walter M. Wolfe before the Senate committee in Washington, D.C., that such language was used by either of said persons or any other person in the presence of affiant is absolutely untrue and without any foundation whatever. Affiant further says that he has never met the said Walter M. Wolfe outside of Provo City, and as he remembers it he only met him twice at that place, and he positively knows that on neither occasion was said John Henry Smith present when affiant met said Wolfe (*Smoot Hearings,* 4:367-68).

John Henry Smith being first duly sworn, deposes and says that he is ... an apostle in the Church of Jesus Christ of Latter-Day Saints. Affiant further says that he is sick, being confined to his house with rheumatism, and is unable to go to Washington, D.C., and testify in the investigation now pending before the Committee on Privileges and Elections. Affiant further says that he is acquainted with Walter M. Wolfe, who testified before said Committee on Privileges and Elections in the month of February, 1906; ... Affiant says that he was not present at Provo, Utah, when an address was delivered by B. F. Grant, a brother of Apostle Heber J. Grant, as testified by said Walter M. Wolfe; that he did not walk with the said Walter M. Wolfe and the said B. F. Grant, or either of them, after any such lecture, and that he never, at any time, said to the said Walter M. Wolfe: "Brother Wolfe, don't you know that the manifesto is only a trick to beat the devil at his own game;" nor did affiant say any words to that effect or conveying that meaning, and no such language was ever used by this affiant, or by any other person in the presence of this affiant (*Smoot Hearings,* 4:404-405).

6. Smoot learned from Dillingham a month prior to this testimony that Wolfe was to witness for the prosecution. Smoot immediately asked Joseph F. Smith for an investigation into Wolfe's background even though Dillingham warned Smoot against disclosing this information to anyone for fear of being charged with witness tampering (Smoot to Joseph F. Smith, Jan. 9, 1906).

MR. WORTHINGTON. Do you mean to tell the committee that until now you did not suspect that there had been charges preferred against you of your being a drunkard, and that was the cause of your leaving the institution?

MR. WOLFE. No, sir.

MR. WORTHINGTON. You never heard of it until now?

MR. WOLFE. Never.

MR. WORTHINGTON. You say certain charges might have been preferred against you?

MR. WOLFE. Yes, sir.

MR. WORTHINGTON. What do you mean by that?

MR. WOLFE. I mean that I made myself liable to such charges.

MR. WORTHINGTON. For how long a time?

MR. WOLFE. Why, possibly twenty years.

MR. WORTHINGTON. Had no officer of the institution had any conversation with you about your habits in this regard?

MR. WOLFE. Oh, yes, sir.

MR. WORTHINGTON. Which of them?

MR. WOLFE. President Cluff and Wilson Dusenberry.[7] ...

MR. WORTHINGTON. What about Mr. Linford? What is his position?[8]

MR. WOLFE. Oh, that is an entirely different proposition. You were asking me, as I understood it, about the Brigham Young Academy, at Provo, and, so far as that is concerned and the Logan institution, it is an entirely different matter. If you wish to qualify it by the Logan—

MR. WORTHINGTON. Very well. That is called the Brigham Young College?

MR. WOLFE. Brigham Young College.

MR. WORTHINGTON. When did that terminate?

MR. WOLFE. January 15.

MR. WORTHINGTON. Of this year?

MR. WOLFE. Of this year.

MR. WORTHINGTON. Was that voluntary or involuntary?

MR. WOLFE. It was involuntarily voluntary.

MR. WORTHINGTON. And voluntarily involuntary, I suppose?

MR. WOLFE. Yes, sir; you may take it either way.

MR. WORTHINGTON. Will you tell us all about it so we may understand what that means, because it sounds like an Irishism, some of it.

---

7. Warren N. Dusenberry served as president of Brigham Young Academy in Provo in 1876; Benjamin Cluff was president from 1892 to 1903.

8. Linford was president of Brigham Young College (now Utah State University) in Logan. His full testimony is in *Smoot Hearings,* 4:267-92.

MR. WOLFE. I neglected to pay any tithing during the year 1905, and on the afternoon of New Year's Day I received a telephone message from Bishop Joseph E. Cordon, informing me of the fact that I had paid no tithing, and asking me to call on him. I told him I would be with him at 10 o'clock the next morning at the tithing office. I went up there, and he pulled out his receipt book, and I said, "Bishop, you need not write me a receipt. I am not going to pay any tithing. I would not pay any if I had $10,000." The bishop seemed very much surprised, and ask[ed] if I would explain. I said I did not care to explain in public. We went into a back room. He told me that I could see the books if I wanted to, that that privilege was accorded to every tithe payer. I told him I objected to paying tithing on principle; that I did not believe in it, and I knew what the consequences would be. He said: "That is right; you understand what the consequences are, and you know that a man can not teach in a church school who does not support the church, who is not loyal to all its doctrines." I told him I understood that perfectly. The conversation there ended.

On Saturday evening, by appointment, I visited President James L. Linford, the president of the institution. He said that it had been reported to him that I was drinking during the holidays to a considerable degree. I did not deny the accusation, but I said: "President Linford, have you seen Bishop Cordon since I refused to pay tithing?" He said: "Just as soon as you left the bishop's office he telephoned to me that you had refused to pay tithing, but I did not intend to mention the matter to you." The matter went on until the morning of January 15, when I was called into the president's office, and he said that instead of attending Sunday school the day before I had been in a drug store in an intoxicated condition, and that it would be well if I would resign. I had told him last November that I expected that I might appear before the Senate committee, and that if I did I should not return to Utah. I told the bishop in my conversation with him that if I were summoned to the Senate committee I should probably not return to Utah. They had made up their minds that I had apostasized and they wanted to let me down easy, and I resigned then and there.[9]

SENATOR HOPKINS. Is it a fact that you were drunk in a drug store on Sunday?

MR. WOLFE. No, sir. If the charge had been made the next day it might have been true, but it was not true on that Sunday.

MR. CARLISLE. They missed it one day?

---

9. For Linford's version, see his testimony excerpted below.

MR. WOLFE. They missed it one day. They missed it until after I had handed in my resignation. It is a fact, Senator, that I was in the drug store. It is a fact that I drank whisky in the drug store.

MR. WORTHINGTON. It is a fact, is it not, that you had been on a spree during the holidays?

MR. WOLFE. I had drank all that I ought to; yes, sir.

MR. WORTHINGTON. You had drank a little more, had you not?

MR. WOLFE. I think not; only as it is not good for any man.

MR. WORTHINGTON. Do you mean to say that you were not in an intoxicated condition in the holidays last December?

MR. WOLFE. I will not say I was not in an intoxicated condition.

SENATOR KNOX. Were your habits of drinking practically the same before you refused to pay tithes as they were at the time?[10]

MR. WOLFE. They had been the same for many years.

SENATOR KNOX. They never questioned your standing as a teacher until you refused to pay tithes, then, as I understand?

MR. WOLFE. No, sir.

SENATOR KNOX. Had they made any objection to your habits?

MR. WOLFE. Oh; yes, sir.

SENATOR KNOX. But they had never suggested your removal or the desirability of your resignation?

MR. WOLFE. No, sir.[11] ...

MR. WORTHINGTON. What did you understand to be the meaning of that covenant [of vengeance] which you say you took, then?

MR. WOLFE. I understood the meaning of that covenant to be that the Lord was implored to avenge upon this nation the blood of the prophets. I understood the blood of those prophets to mean Joseph and Hyrum Smith, because they were the only prophets with which this nation had anything to do. In giving that covenant the first time it was gone through with quickly, and it did not impress me until the

---

10. The *Salt Lake Tribune* objected to the tactics used to discredit Wolfe:

In all the annals of self-imposed shame there is nothing else to equal the attack by the Mormon authorities upon [his] character ... They claim now that he was a wicked man all the time ... and seek to convince the world that he was frequently in a state of intoxication. ... In whispers, they accuse him of dishonesty. ... If the Senators ... rightly understand this case they will be to the last degree indignant at the shamelessness with which the Mormon authorities assault this man. ... Prof. Wolfe comes out of the crucial experience a thousand times better than his accusers" ("They Are Shameless," *Salt Lake Tribune*, Feb. 10, 1906).

11. In a letter to his family, Badger gave his opinion that Wolfe was an ineffectual witness due to his "ready admissions of drunkenness" (in Badger, *Liahona and Iron Rod*, 301).

words were spoken what that might mean. I think in that covenant the seed of treason is planted.

SENATOR HOPKINS. When did that thought come to you?

MR. WOLFE. It came to me within an hour after I had taken that oath. I thought it over, because, Senator—

SENATOR HOPKINS. You took that oath twelve times, you say?

MR. WOLFE. Yes; because when I joined the Mormon Church, before I was baptized, I asked the man who baptized me whether there was anything in the Mormon Church that would interfere with a man's politics, with his loyalty, or with his private interests, and the man assured me that there was nothing of the kind.

SENATOR HOPKINS. And you took it with that understanding?

MR. WOLFE. I went in with that understanding.

SENATOR HOPKINS. This man with whom you conversed was one who gave an interpretation to the oaths you were to take, as you understood it?

MR. WOLFE. No; this conversation was some years before, in 1890, with the man who baptized me.

SENATOR HOPKINS. After you took the first oath, if that came to you within an hour, if you were an honest, patriotic citizen, why did you take it the second time?

MR. WOLFE. I did not take it for myself the second time. I went through in the name of some person who was dead.

SENATOR HOPKINS. Why did you permit anybody to take an oath in which you believed the seeds of treason were planted?

MR. WOLFE. Senator, I could not be sure. I was a Mormon at the time. That oath shocked me the first time I heard it.

SENATOR HOPKINS. Did you caution the parties whom you went through with the second time regarding this oath and warn them not to take it?

MR. WOLFE. I had no opportunity to caution anyone. I never mentioned the oath.

SENATOR HOPKINS. But you went through with it, you say, eleven different times after you took it?

MR. WOLFE. I went through over and over again; through the ceremony. There is a great deal in the ceremony that impressed me, that is immaterial here. It was a very impressive ceremony, and there was no going through it without taking that oath, to the best of my knowledge and belief; but a person goes through that ceremony only once in their own name.

THE CHAIRMAN. You took this obligation for yourself the first time?

Mr. Wolfe. Yes, sir.

The Chairman. After that you took it for others. What do you mean by that?

Mr. Wolfe. I mean that the work in the temple is to great extent vicarious work; that under the doctrines of the Latter-Day Saints a certain work must be performed for those that are dead before they can obtain their exaltation; in other words, that baptism is an essential to salvation, and a person alive must be baptized for one who is dead, if the dead has not had an opportunity. In the same way the process of receiving endowments and other things is a vicarious work. ...

William Jones Thomas,[12] being duly sworn, was examined and testified as follows ...

Mr. Carlisle. When did you go to Utah?

Mr. Thomas. In 1861.

Mr. Carlisle. Were you a Mormon at the time you went there, or did you join the church afterwards, or have you joined at all?

Mr. Thomas. I was a Mormon going there.

Mr. Carlisle. Did you ever pass through the Endowment House?

Mr. Thomas. Yes, sir.

Mr. Carlisle. Through the Temple, I believe, they call it now?

Mr. Thomas. Through the Endowment House. I went through the Endowment House in 1869. Did I say 1861?

Mr. Carlisle. You said you went to Utah in 1861.

Mr. Thomas. Oh, yes; that is right.

Mr. Carlisle. How many persons went through the Endowment House with you in 1869, if any more than yourself? About how many?

Mr. Thomas. Well, from 40 to 50, as near as I can remember it.

Mr. Carlisle. Did you take any oath or enter into any covenant, or make a pledge there during those ceremonies?

Mr. Thomas. Yes, sir.

Mr. Carlisle. Will you state to the committee just as nearly as you can what it was in 1869?

Mr. Thomas. I can give you in substance one that was heavy upon my mind, and I remember it pretty well, the substance of it. I couldn't tell it in the words exactly.

Mr. Carlisle. Give it in the words as nearly as you can.

Mr. Thomas. It was, in substance, that I would seek to avenge the blood

---

12. At the time of his testimony, Thomas (1846-1909) was a farmer in Spanish Fork, Utah. He had left the LDS Church in 1880.

of the prophet Joseph Smith upon this nation, and teach my children the same unto the third and fourth generations, as near as I can remember. That was the substance of it.

MR. CARLISLE. By whom was that administered to you, if you can remember?

MR. THOMAS. I think I do. I recognized the man as George Q. Cannon.[13]

MR. CARLISLE. Did any ceremonies take place before that oath was administered to you?

THE CHAIRMAN. Mr. Secretary, may I ask the witness right there what George Q. Cannon's position was in the church?

MR. THOMAS. He was one of the twelve, I believe. Now, I wouldn't be sure.

SENATOR OVERMAN. You say this has weighed heavily on your mind since then?

MR. THOMAS. That one oath did.

SENATOR OVERMAN. Why?

MR. THOMAS. Because it is contrary to the word of God, as understood, and contrary to my feelings. That is all.

SENATOR HOPKINS. In what respect?

MR. THOMAS. Well, I was an American citizen. I swore allegiance and I became an American citizen.

THE CHAIRMAN. Proceed, Mr. Carlisle.

MR. CARLISLE. I have asked you about whether any ceremonies took place before the oath of obligation took place. If so, state what it was.

MR. THOMAS. There were washings and anointings there.

MR. CARLISLE. Describe to the committee what you mean by anointing? Was your whole body anointed or your arm anointed; and, if so, was anything said when that was done?

MR. THOMAS. My head was anointed and my right arm. I do not remember anything else.

MR. CARLISLE. Was anything said by the person who conducted these ceremonies at the time he anointed your right arm? Were you told what it was for?

MR. THOMAS. Yes, sir; he spoke very quick and I couldn't catch it all, but I remember when he anointed my arm to make it strong, and the substance of it was that I would avenge the blood of the prophets—prophet or prophets, I believe it was the plural.[14]

13. The previous two questions and answers were included in Carlisle's closing argument for the protestants (*Smoot Hearings,* 4:424-25).

14. The previous four questions and answers were included in the "View of the Minority" report submitted by Foraker on June 11, 1906 (*Smoot Hearings,* 4:537).

MR. CARLISLE. You say this bore heavily on your mind. Are you now a member of the Mormon Church?

MR. THOMAS. No, sir.

MR. CARLISLE. Well, when did you separate from it?

MR. THOMAS. They dropped me off in 1880—in the year 1880.

MR. CARLISLE. For what?

MR. THOMAS. Because I had spoken too openly against the principle of plural marriage. ...

MR. WORTHINGTON. That ceremony lasted how long—the different ceremonies that you went through when you took the endowments?

MR. THOMAS. The first ceremony, the anointing, didn't take but a few minutes. It might have been not over a minute.

MR. WORTHINGTON. But the whole ceremony?

MR. THOMAS. You mean the whole day?

MR. WORTHINGTON. It took a whole day, did it?

MR. THOMAS. No, sir; not quite all day.

MR. WORTHINGTON. It took several hours?

MR. THOMAS. Yes, sir; it took several hours.

MR. WORTHINGTON. You would go from one room to another and hear various things?

MR. THOMAS. Yes, sir.

MR. WORTHINGTON. Did you repeat anything else you heard that day except this covenant?

MR. THOMAS. There were several covenants or vows with regard to the priesthood—some good counsel.

MR. WORTHINGTON. Can you remember them?

MR. THOMAS. Chastity, and such like.

MR. WORTHINGTON. Do you remember the language of them?

MR. THOMAS. No; I don't remember the language exactly of any of them as correct. They passed from my mind and I never thought of them any more.

MR. WORTHINGTON. You would not undertake to give the exact words of any of them, would you?

MR. THOMAS. No, sir. That one, I can give you the exact meaning that I got.

MR. WORTHINGTON. Did you say anything to Mr. Cannon in regard to it, or to any body else, about its weighing on your mind, and ask for any explanation of it?

MR. THOMAS. At that time?

MR. WORTHINGTON. Yes.

Mr. Thomas. No, sir.

Mr. Worthington. You never did to anybody, to any authorized person in the church?

Mr. Thomas. No, sir.

Mr. Worthington. You just let it prey upon your mind, and did not say anything to anybody about it, did you?

Mr. Thomas. No, sir; it preyed on my mind.

Mr. Worthington. I say you never said anything to anybody about it—any authority in the church?

Mr. Thomas. No, sir.

Mr. Worthington. That is all. ...

Senator Knox. And your right arm was anointed to give you strength that you might do so. Is that correct?

Mr. Thomas. That is the way I understood it.

Senator Knox. What did you ever do in the line of keeping that vow? Did you ever avenge the blood of the martyrs upon this nation?

Mr. Thomas. No, sir; I have enlisted twice to try and defend the nation.

Senator Knox. Were you ever stirred up by the authorities of the church to get busy in that direction of avenging the blood of the martyrs upon this nation?

Mr. Thomas. No.

Mr. Worthington. Do you know of any member of the church who did do anything in the way of using his right arm to avenge the blood of the prophets on this nation?

Mr. Thomas. No, sir.[15]

Mr. Worthington. You never heard anything of the kind, did you?

Mr. Thomas. I have heard something of the kind, but I don't know anything.

Mr. Worthington. I am asking whether anywhere in your neighborhood anything of that kind ever came to your knowledge, by reputation or otherwise?

Mr. Thomas. Not in my neighborhood; no, sir.[16] ...

---

15. This entire exchange, as abridged here, was included in the "View of the Minority" report submitted by Foraker on June 11, 1906 (*Smoot Hearings,* 4:537).

16. On the same day as this testimony from Thomas, Charles M. Owen was recalled to submit and explain several lists he had compiled of Utah state officers over a ten-year period, 1895-1905. Each name was marked "G" for gentile, "M" for Mormon, and "Polyg" for polygamist and indicated whether the individual was a high church officer (*Smoot Hearings,* 4:131-35). This prompted an exchange of insults, Badger writing that "just before one of the sessions began, Senator Smoot leaned over and called Owen a 'liar,' and Owen told the Senator he was no gentleman. This pass took place over the

Charles A. Smurthwaite,[17] being duly sworn, was examined and testified as follows ...

MR. CARLISLE. Are you now a member of the Mormon Church?

MR. SMURTHWAITE. No, sir; I was excommunicated on the 4th day of
April, 1905.

MR. CARLISLE. Were you ever connected in any way with the Beck Salt
Works Company?

MR. SMURTHWAITE. I am a director in that company.

MR. CARLISLE. Will you state to the committee what, if anything, occurred between you and your associates and the presidency of the
Mormon Church in regard to that company and its affairs at the time
of its organization or immediately there after? Just state all the facts.

MR. SMURTHWAITE. The Beck Salt Company was a corporation organized
by John Beck. Sixty per cent of the stock was purchased by a gentleman by the name of Richard J. Taylor, of Ogden [Utah], from Mr.
Beck. I purchased 20 per cent of the stock from Mr. Beck. In the
spring of 1904 we proceeded to build a flume to carry the water from
the Salt Lake to salt-making gardens upon land which we had acquired there to the number of 312 acres. In the month of May, 1904,
Mr. Taylor came to me and said that he had been to see Mr. David
Eccles,[18] of Ogden.

MR. CARLISLE. Did Eccles own any stock in it?

---

list[s] Owen submitted, and which he said did not contain any mistakes. The truth is that
[they] contain many, as will be shown by the evidence the Senator will produce. I have
been making an effort for the last three hours to stand up straight" (in Badger, *Liahona
and Iron Rod,* 303). Smoot's attorneys called witnesses and entered affidavits into the record to challenge the reliability of some of the information on the lists (*Smoot Hearings,*
4: 302-41).

17. Smurthwaite (1862-1929) had joined the LDS Church in Manchester, England.
He was excommunicated in 1905 and lived in Ogden, Utah.

18. David Eccles (1849-1912) testified on January 24, 1905, following testimony by
his post-manifesto plural wife, Margaret Geddes. Margaret's first husband had passed
away in 1891, and after her marriage to David in 1898, she had became pregnant. At the
hearings, she was asked about "the father of the youngest child," to which she responded, "I decline to answer that question." "Is his name Echols?" Tayler asked, and she
responded "No, sir" (*Smoot Hearings,* 2:105). David was asked if Margaret was "reputed to
have a husband now?" to which David responded, "No, sir; she is not." "Since the manifesto, then, you have not taken a plural wife?" "I have not," Eccles replied (ibid., 3:450).
After Eccles's death in 1912, Geddes broke her silence, wanting to see that the couple's
child, Albert, received his share of his father's wealthy estate. She claimed her marriage
was performed by Apostle Marriner W. Merrill and was intentionally called a "union"
rather than a "marriage" to facilitate denials (B. Carmon Hardy, *Solemn Covenant: The
Mormon Polygamous Passage* [Urbana: University of Illinois Press, 1992], 184-85).

MR. SMURTHWAITE. He had some stock in it; yes, sir. Mr. Eccles stated to Mr. Taylor that he had received several letters from Joseph F. Smith, president of the Mormon Church, that he had read these letters, and that in substance they stated that the Inland Crystal Salt Company, of which company Mr. Smith was president—

THE CHAIRMAN. Joseph F. Smith?

MR. SMURTHWAITE. Joseph F. Smith—had never made any money, and that he was very sorry to know that the enterprise had been started.

MR. CARLISLE. That is, your enterprise?

MR. SMURTHWAITE. Our enterprise; and that he was also sorry to know that Mr. Eccles had invested any money in it, because if he desired to invest any money in the salt business they could have sold him any amount of stock that he might have desired to have. Mr. Smith also requested Mr. Eccles to ask Mr. Taylor to visit him at Salt Lake City, and Mr. Taylor came over to my house and asked me if I would go with him, as I was a large stockholder. Mr. Richard J. Taylor, the gentleman to whom I have reference in this statement, is a son of the late John Taylor, president of the Mormon Church in his time. I stated that I would be delighted to go with him, because I had never met Mr. Smith personally; that I had met him on the stand, and would like to meet him personally. Accordingly, I think it was in beginning of June, 1904, Mr. Taylor and myself went to Salt Lake City. We entered the anteroom of the president's office—

MR. CARLISLE. You mean the office of the salt company?

MR. SMURTHWAITE. The office of the first presidency of the church. After waiting there three-quarters of an hour we were finally admitted into the president's room. He was seated at a table similar to the one at which you gentlemen are sitting. I sat, as it were, here, Mr. Taylor at my right, Mr. Anthon H. Lund, the first counselor to President Smith, at my left; next to him, President John R. Winder, the second counselor, and directly in front of me John Henry Smith, one of the quorum of the twelve apostles. We had in the meantime shaken hands.

MR. WORTHINGTON. Was President Smith there, do I understand you to say?

MR. SMURTHWAITE. President Joseph F. Smith sat to my left, a little way distant from Mr. Taylor. Mr. Joseph F. Smith opened the remarks by stating: "Brother, what can we do for you?" Brother Taylor—we refer to our brethren as "brother," and that is my custom; the gentleman I referred to is Richard J. Taylor—stated: "We have come here, Brother

Smith, because of a letter that you have written to David Eccles asking us to come—asking me to come, and I have brought Brother Smurthwaite because he is the next largest stockholder to myself." Then Joseph F. Smith said, looking at Mr. Taylor: "I am surprised, Brother Richard, that a man of your experience would go into business in opposition to us without first coming to consult us. An hour—no; you brethren live in Ogden; two hours, anyway—would have set you brethren right on this matter if you had come to consult us about it. We are very sorry indeed that you have gone into this business. We do not know how much money you brethren have. Of course Mr. Eccles has a lot of money, and if he has to fight us it will be a very serious matter. We don't know how much money you brethren have, but we will ruin you." I replied: "Pardon me, Brother Smith, we grant you have the power. I have the power to crush my child, but I have no right."[19]

Replying, Joseph F. Smith said: "But this is business." I answered: "I have always thought that business meant profit, and I can not believe that you gentlemen will cut off your nose to spite your face. We are not going to fight you. Our policy is already outlined. We shall make salt to the best of our ability. You shall name the prices and we shall sell our salt at the prices which you put upon it." Mr. Smith replied: "Well, if you will not cut prices, we will," and then followed by asking, "Where do you intend to sell your salt?" I said we would sell it anywhere we could and to whomsoever we could persuade to buy it. Mr. Smith then said: "Do you mean to say you will go around persuading people to take the money out of our pockets and put it into yours?" I said: "We don't usually use such terms in discussing competitive business, but if that is the way you prefer to discuss it, that is exactly what we propose to do." He said: "Well, you can't sell your salt outside of a given radius," indicating a circle with the index finger of

---

19. The next day during cross-examination, Senator Knox asked Smurthwaite what Joseph F. Smith had done "in the line of following up his suggestion that they could ruin you; anything?" Smurthwaite answered, "Nothing that I know of," then elaborated:

You must understand, Senator, that we were just building our plant, and, unfortunately, at the end of the building season when the flume was all built it blew down with a very strong canyon wind. It had not been grounded sufficiently strong. It blew down and we had to reconstruct it, and we did reconstruct it at an extra expense of four or five thousand dollars, so that we did not produce any salt that season. In the meantime The Great Western Salt and Soda Company, the only other operating concern on the lake, had made a lot of salt and put it upon the market, and the Inland Crystal Salt Company there and then reduced the price of crude salt from $8 per ton to $2 per ton, and while we made salt last season, we have it piled up, and are not putting it on the market because $2 per ton is practically the cost of production (*Smoot Hearings*, 4:246-47).

his right hand on the table, "because the trust will not permit us to sell it outside of a given territory." I told him that we had nothing to do with the trust; that we proposed to sell our salt anywhere we could and to whomsoever we could get to buy it.

That was in substance and effect the entire interview. I have omitted to state to you in the beginning, when Joseph F. Smith said to Mr. Taylor that he was surprised that we would go into business in opposition to him, Mr. Taylor answered: "We did not know we were in opposition to you. We did not know that the church owns the Inland Crystal Salt Company," and Mr. Smith replied that the church, in connection with a few of the brethren around here, waving his hands, owned a controlling interest in the stock.[20]

Mr. Taylor, at the conclusion of the interview, said to Mr. Smith that we had not started our works for the purpose of selling out to them; that we desired to conduct a legitimate business; to make salt and sell it, and Mr. Smith replied: "Oh, you have started it like all the balance of them," referring to quite a number of other people who started salt works and had been absorbed by the Inland Crystal Salt Company.

I also failed to remark that when I stated to President Joseph Smith that I granted him the power to ruin us, that I had the power to crush my child, but had not the right, Anthon H. Lund, sitting directly at my left, moved away. He rubbed his hands together like this [indicating], as if in discomfort, and moved away and never returned to the table, and after we had gotten through with our conversation he met us at the door, shook our hands, and said, "God bless you, brethren. ..."[21]

---

20. The Inland Salt Company was founded by James Jack, treasurer of the LDS Church, in November 1887, with evidence pointing to church ownership "through a secret trust agreement with the incorporators of the company" (John L. Clark, "History of Utah's Salt Industry, 1847-1970," M.A. thesis, Brigham Young University, Aug. 1971, 69). Inland was sold in 1891 to a Midwestern buyer, who invested heavily in improvements and renamed the company Inland Crystal Salt. The next year the former owners created a rival company, Inter-mountain Salt, with funds they had received from the sale of Inland. They went head-to-head with Inland Crystal, eventually obtaining controlling interest in it, and then combined the two enterprises with Joseph F. Smith as president (68-79). Thereafter the company actively bought up shoreline property to prevent additional competition, and Inland employees blew up the flume of one competitor and filled in the canal of another (84-87).

21. According to his diary, Lund was unsympathetic to the Beck venture. Prior to the meeting with Smurthwaite, Lund recorded that "there is a company at work putting up another works west of the Inland Crystal. They will not be able to make money only

Mr. Smith, in reply to Mr. Taylor, stated that the church, in connection with a few brethren around here, waving his hand as though it was same of the brethren in the immediate vicinity of the table, owned the controlling interest in the stock. ...

MR. CARLISLE. You have said you were excommunicated—I believe that is the word you used—from the Mormon Church. What time was that?

MR. SMURTHWAITE. I was excommunicated on the 4th day of April, 1905.

MR. CARLISLE. Will you state to the committee what led to that? What was the cause of it?

MR. SMURTHWAITE. Following this interview with President Joseph F. Smith and his counselors, on that same day I went home on the noon train, determined to see if there was anything in the church, any law, power, or justice, whereby Joseph F. Smith could be brought to account for so atrocious a thing, as I viewed it. I spent the afternoon at home looking into it, and finally concluded that there was no power in the church to bring him to justice.

On the following morning I met the bishop of my ward, and I told him of the interview and took occasion at that time, as I had on some other occasions, to criticise the church for being in business at all. I stated to my bishop: "My theory is that this is the absolute kingdom of

---

by making the Inland buy them off. The company [Inland] will not be able to do this to all who may want to enter this enterprise, and so" the church had "concluded to let them alone" (in John P. Hatch, ed., *Danish Apostle: The Diaries of Anthon H. Lund, 1890-1921* [Salt Lake City: Signature Books and the Smith-Pettit Foundation, 2006], 280, 283).

In a telegram to Smoot, George F. Gibbs, Secretary to the First Presidency, provided more details from the same perspective:

Smurthwaite visited Inland Salt Company's office [on] several occasions first proposing [to] sell controlling interest in Beck Salt Company for eighty thousand ... [L]ater he reduced this to seventy thousand. Inland ... discovered Beck ... had expended ... twelve thousand all told. When confronted ... Smurthwaite argued it would [benefit] Inland ... to purchase anyway as with controlling interest. Inland ... could close Beck plant and thus shut out competition ... It is now learned Beck ... had authorized him to sell whole thing for thirty five thousand with companys debts amounting ten thousand ... which offer he never definitely made. It is also learned he insisted seeing [Richard] Taylor on deathbed [in 1905] for consent [to] sell his stock for twenty five, he having told ... Taylor he was going offer the whole stock at that figure. It is believed now in Ogden he did this with [the] intent [of] making [a] profitable margin for himself. After this all Salt Companies excepting Inland ... tried [to] consolidate at Smurthwaite instigation to either fight Inland ... or compel Inland [to] buy them out. They failed at consolidation greatly to Smurthwaite disappointment. Their final meeting was held immediately after Smurthwaite interview with President Smith. After meeting he remarked he had something up his sleeve which would prove [a] bombshell against President Smith. ... President Smith never sent for Smurthwaite or Taylor. They came on their own volition neither did he use threat or name of church. He talked with them as president of salt company (Feb. 8, 1906).

God. Joseph F. Smith is the exclusive agent or representative or mouthpiece of God on the earth. When he goes into business it is the equivalent of God being in business, according to our theory, and it is absurd to think that I, a man, a poor weak individual, should hope to compete with God's representative." I put it in that form to show the atrocious character of this church being set up as the Church of Christ being in business at all, because I had been opposed to the commercialism of the church for some years. That was all that took place at that time. In the following November, at the school elections, in the room where the polling booth was located, my wife and I having voted for school trustees—

THE CHAIRMAN. Do you mean last November?

MR. SMURTHWAITE. November, 1904—we met the bishop of my ward as we were going out of the room. I waited until after he got through voting and then I called him to one side and I said: "Bishop, I desire to say to you that I do not believe any longer that Joseph F. Smith is God's prophet. I do not believe that he is worthy to occupy that station, and as I am a visiting teacher in your ward, if you think I should continue to stay in that office, I shall be pleased to do so, but it might be necessary in the discharge of my duties, should matters of this kind arise, to give free expression to my feelings on the subject. If you think under these circumstances I should be released, you are at liberty to release me." Then he said that he was very sorry and that he would release me from further duty in that capacity.

MR. CARLISLE. As a teacher?

MR. SMURTHWAITE. As a teacher. A few days following, perhaps a week, my bishop and his two counselors called upon me at my home and asked me what I was going to do about the matter. I told them I did not know, that I felt very weak and incapable, that I felt it my duty to do something, but that I would not do anything until I felt able to do so; that I hoped that power would some day be given to me to tell the story. At the conclusion of the interview we all shook hands and the bishop went home and nothing was said about it until, I think, one evening in the early part of February, 1905, when Elder Hiram H. Goddard, who had been my fellow teacher on the block on which I reside, called upon me in company with a young man of Ogden with the specific statement that he brought him to my house for the purpose of having his faith built up in the Gospel.

We had two hours conversation. The early part of it was devoted to the discussion of abstract religious questions, such as the existence of God and the necessity for a plan of salvation. Toward the latter end of the conversation, in some unfortunate manner, this matter of my interview with President Joseph [F.] Smith was brought up, and I briefly related the substance of it as I have here to-day. I also substantiated my position or corroborated my position in the matter of the rejection of Joseph F. Smith as a prophet of God, by a quotation from the testimony before this committee, wherein, being asked by a Senator why it was necessary for a man to continue to live with his wives and have issue, he replied it was because his wives were like everybody else's wives, and that was all. I stated that that was a most atrocious thing and the wors[t] thing that had been said in the anti-Mormon period of Utah's unfortunate history. That is the wors[t] thing against the Mormon women, who are fine, beautiful, pure, chaste women. I had not recalled at the moment that this elder, Hiram H. Goddard, himself, was a polygamist, and did not recall that fact until as we were parting, shaking hands, Mrs. Smurthwaite said to me: "Don't you see you have put your foot in it? You have made a mortal enemy for life. That Brother Goddard himself is a polygamist;" and it was at that moment that I first realized what I had done.

The following Sunday I was waited upon by two teachers, one of them Elder Hyrum H. Goddard and the other E. A. Olsen, and Mr. Goddard had a notebook. He said he had come to me for a statement of my position with reference to the church and the authorities thereof, and he desired to put down what I would say. I told him not to put anything down, because he could not put it down correctly. I meant by that that he could not understand my position and that he would unconsciously misinterpret or miswrite what I might say. I stated to him that if the bishop really desired a statement some time, when I felt able, I would write a statement, so that there could be no question as to my attitude upon these matters and there could be no doubt as to my responsibility for the words that I should utter. Notwithstanding that, he continued to use his pencil and paper. I remonstrated with him several times.

I think it was probably about toward the end of February [1905] when that occurred. Well, I did not want to make any statement, as a matter of fact. I was impelled finally to make it. I did not care to make it. I had lived in the community all my life. I had some knowledge of the feeling among the young people as to what an apostate was and what it meant to carry that title through life, and I hesitated a very great deal about making the statement, because I knew beforehand that the moment I made it that moment would my standing in the church be absolutely severed.

Finally I reached the conclusion that I owed a duty to the community to make a statement to the bishop, and I wrote one.

MR. CARLISLE. Addressed to the bishop?

MR. SMURTHWAITE. Addressed to the bishop.

MR. CARLISLE. Bishop Woolley?

MR. SMURTHWAITE. Bishop Woolley.

MR. CARLISLE. Will you state to the committee whether that statement was or was not published; and, if so, under what circumstances and how it was published?

MR. SMURTHWAITE. I sent the original to Bishop Woolley and a copy to the "Deseret News," which is the official organ of the church, with the request that it be published; I think it was on the following evening. I simultaneously sent copies to the "Salt Lake Herald" and to the "Salt Lake Tribune." The letter in question was not published in the "Deseret News."

MR. CARLISLE. Is that the organ of the church?

MR. SMURTHWAITE. That is the official organ of the church. But it was finally published in the "Salt Lake Daily Tribune" and the "Salt Lake Herald" simultaneously on the morning following the day upon which it ought to have appeared, if my request had been granted, in the "Deseret Evening News."

MR. CARLISLE. Will you look at this paper and see if this is the letter to which you refer, and state to the committee whether or not the statements purporting to be statements of facts contained in it are correct and true?

MR. SMURTHWAITE. That is the paper, sir, and the statements of facts therein is true.

MR. CARLISLE. See if this is the letter you addressed to the editor of the "Deseret News," requesting its publication. (Handing witness a letter.)

MR. SMURTHWAITE. That is a copy of the letter, sir.

MR. CARLISLE. We will offer those in evidence ...

OGDEN, UTAH, March 13, 1905.

EDITOR DESERET NEWS, Salt Lake, Utah.

Sir: I shall esteem it a great favor if you will kindly publish in your issue of to-morrow (Tuesday, March 14, 1905) the inclosed copy of letter which I have this day directed to my ward bishop, Elder E. T. Woolley.

Being church business and of general interest to the Latter-day Saints, I desire its publication in the official paper of the church. I therefore thank you in anticipation of this courtesy. ...

[O]n one Sunday evening, during the summer of 1904, at a young people's conference in the tabernacle at Ogden, President Smith, in substance and effect, said: "It is true that the church has had no revelation for many years. I hope to God He will give no more revelation to the church until we learn to live that which He has already given." There were young men in that audience who had been taught to believe all their lives that the church was guided by continuous revelation, who were aghast at this declaration. ... If Joseph Smith, the prophet, was sent of God, then Joseph F. Smith is not, because his teaching on revelation is a complete overthrow of the basic philosophy of the prophet Joseph Smith, on which this church is founded. ...

This church is mine, in common with the other members of the church. I have defended it when it has been assailed. I have supported its doctrine and lived its precepts. I have invested my earthly substance in its physical up building. My children have been born in it. They and my wife look to it for spiritual instruction and consolation. I have no differences with the church whatsoever. My differences are only with individuals who are misusing the church, as I believe (conscientiously, it may be), but still misusing it. My desire only is to see the church take its place as an honored society in this land, consistent with its own doctrines and principles, ... not find[ing] itself inconsistent with the rest of the country, for the plain teaching of the New Testament and of our own doctrine and covenants, as mentioned in another place in this paper, in strict conformity with the spirit and letter of the laws of the United States and the laws of any other land, where we may dwell.[22] ...

MR. CARLISLE. Proceed now and state what occurred thereafter—after the publication of that article.

MR. SMURTHWAITE. On the morning that this was published in the "Salt

---

22. The letter went on to call for "the strict application of the doctrine of common consent," strict adherence to law, separation of church and state, divestiture of commercial holdings—that the church "retire from its commercialism," that "the tithes be accounted for" and "a list of all property holdings of the church and of the leaders of the church ... be read semiannually at each conference," and that members be protected in their right to criticize church leaders. These and a few other proposed reforms, which Smurthwaite characterized as "self-proving doctrines of the church," were enumerated as a list of ten "demands."

Lake Herald" and the "Salt Lake Tribune," at about 11 o'clock in the morning, I was waited upon by the clerk of my ecclesiastical ward in the church with a summons to appear to answer for my fellowship on the charges of unchristianlike conduct and apostasy. ...

This summons was served on me, and then I made a request upon the bishop that he would have the complainant specify the language I had used which he had concluded was unchristianlike and was speaking against the Lord's anointed. The complaint reads that I had spoken very badly against the Lord's anointed, those whom he sustained prophets, seers, and revelators; and I requested that he specify the particular language by which his mind had concluded I had spoken ill of the presidents of the church.

Mr. Carlisle. I will get you to look at these papers and see if this package contains the summons, the charges against you, the proceedings of the two trials, and the correspondence which took place between you and the officials of the church on this subject.

Mr. Smurthwaite. This paper (indicating) is the complaint. This paper (indicating) is my answer to the complaint. It is in the wrong place. The summons should be in the front. This paper (indicating) is a continuance of my answer. That completes my answer to the bishop's court.

Mr. Carlisle. In the first place, right there, the bishop's court is the one which makes the first inquiries, is it, and formulates the charges against you?

Mr. Smurthwaite. No; the custom is, as I discovered in my case, for these special teachers to wait upon you, to comply with some certain technical revelations in the Book of Doctrine and Covenants, whereby you are supposed to be labored with by the teachers before any charge is made against you, in order that you may have an opportunity to repent; and that was complied with by Hyrum H. Goddard and E. A. Olsen upon the Sunday I described. Then, when the complaint is filed and you are summoned to appear, you are supposed to appear before the bishop's court, who either finds you innocent or guilty— generally guilty, of course, because you are never charged unless they have some particular purpose in view on which to find you guilty. Now, I did not appear personally.

Mr. Carlisle. Before the bishop's court?

Mr. Smurthwaite. Before the bishop's court. I thought that it was of the utmost importance that my children, of whom I have seven, as they grew up should understand, without the slightest doubt whatever, the reason their father had been excommunicated from the church. So I would not appear in court; I appeared in writing, so that the writing could speak for itself; and that is the writing.

MR. CARLISLE. That writing is there?

MR. SMURTHWAITE. Yes, sir; this paper (indicating) is the decision of the bishop's court finding me guilty as charged.

MR. CARLISLE. Just state what the papers are.

MR. SMURTHWAITE. This is the decision of the bishop's court, in which he finds me guilty as charged, and states that my case has been referred to the high council of the Weber Stake of Zion. This (indicating) is the letter of the Weber Stake of Zion, officially notifying me of that fact, and asking me to be present at a certain date and show cause why I should not be excommunicated from the church.[23] ...

---

23. According to the *Deseret News,* Senators who had heard the recent testimony wondered why the hearings had been reconvened at all: "The members of the committee are disgusted over the fact that they have been compelled to waste time listening to such statements as [from] ... the 'ruined' salt maker, Mr. Smurthwaite." The *News* applauded Senator Knox's cross-examination of Smurthwaite: "The former attorney-general of the United States demonstrated in 30 minutes how he achieved fame as a lawyer. His questions were shot at the witness like discharges from the guns of the Utah battery in the Philippines" ("The Protestants Close Their Case," Feb. 9, 1906).

For his part, Smoot too was "delighted" to be able to report to Joseph F. Smith that "the reopening of the hearings" had "materially assisted our side. Wolfe was discredited; Holmgren and Thomas amounted to nothing, and Henry Lawrence disproved the very thing they have been trying to prove respecting the obligation taken in the endowment ceremony, for he was compelled to admit that there was no thought of vengeance against 'this nation.'" Smoot thought "Smurthwaite made a great impression the first day," but during the break Smoot had "met a number of my friends in the Senate and told them the history of the salt deal, and they were prepared to ask questions on the cross-examination ... and Senator Knox completely floored Smurthwaite, discrediting him in the eyes of all present." Smoot found it significant and "noticeable during this hearing ... that the Democrats have not been present, but that my friends have been there at every hearing" (Feb. 12, 1906).

The *Salt Lake Tribune* took a different view, claiming Smurthwaite "made a profound impression on the committee. He is a very intelligent man and talked direct. The attorneys for Smoot were so much disconcerted that they announced they would postpone cross-examination till tomorrow" ("Body Blows Are Struck against Apostle Smoot," Feb. 8, 1906). To his wife, Carl Badger admitted Smurthwaite had been "a dangerous witness the first day he was on the stand. He testified that President Smith had said that he would 'ruin' the salt business in which Mr. Smurthwaite and R[ichard] Taylor had embarked their means." However, "Knox showed next morning that Smurthwaite's complaint was a very common one in the business world, and that as far as a business proposition is concerned it is the accepted rule of warfare. As a moral question it might be a bad one, but as a commercial question, it was regular and historical. ... It would have given you an inch of growth to watch Burrows while Knox was questioning Smurthwaite; he is so unfair that he hates an unpleasant truth" (in Badger, *Liahona and Iron Rod,* 302).

Henry W. Lawrence,[24] being duly sworn, was examined and testified as follows ...

MR. CARLISLE. Have you ever passed through the endowment house?

MR. LAWRENCE. Yes, sir.

MR. CARLISLE. Will you state to the committee whether there is any oath or obligation taken there to yield obedience to the priesthood and the church?

MR. WORTHINGTON. Whether there was at that time?

MR. CARLISLE. Yes; whether there was at that time.

MR. LAWRENCE. I do not want to state anything that is not in the public interest, and for the public good, in regard to their affairs like that, because it is held sacred there by them, but so far as I am concerned I do not look upon them as I used to. Whatever is in the public interest I am very willing to state. Outside of that I do not want to say anything about it. I want to simply say that a man has to yield obedience to the priesthood that is over him.

MR. CARLISLE. My question is whether that is taught in the ceremony, or whether any covenant is taken or any promises made that such obedience will be given?

MR. LAWRENCE. It is taught, and covenants are made to that effect.

MR. CARLISLE. In the endowment house?

MR. LAWRENCE. Yes, sir.

MR. CARLISLE. Mr. Lawrence, would you object to stating whether there is any oath, commonly called here the oath of vengeance, taken in the endowment house, and what it is?

MR. LAWRENCE. Yes; there is.

MR. CARLISLE. Can you state it in terms or in substance?

MR. LAWRENCE. "You covenant and agree before God and angels and these witnesses that you will avenge the blood of the prophets, the prophet Joseph Smith, Hyrum Smith, Parley P. Pratt, David Patten"—their names are mentioned.[25]

MR. CARLISLE. Was that the case when you took the endowment?

MR. LAWRENCE. Yes, sir. I do not know whether they were all mentioned when I was there or not, but they have been mentioned when I have been there.

---

24. At the time of his testimony, Lawrence (1838-1924) was seventy years old and lived in Salt Lake City. He had grown up Mormon in Nauvoo, Illinois, worked in Utah's mercantile industry, and left the LDS Church at age thirty-five.

25. This answer was used by Carlisle in his closing argument for the plaintiffs (*Smoot Hearings*, 4:424). This version of the "oath of vengeance" is the only one to mention David W. Patten and Parley P. Pratt.

Mr. Carlisle. You have passed through the endowment a number of times?

Mr. Lawrence. Yes; I have been there a number of times.

Mr. Carlisle. You mean these names have been mentioned some of the times when you passed through? That is what you mean?

Mr. Lawrence. Yes, sir.

Mr. Carlisle. You do not know whether they were all mentioned at the same time or not?

Mr. Lawrence. No, sir.

Senator Dillingham. Do I understand the witness has given the whole of the obligation?

Mr. Carlisle. I will ask him. Do you remember now whether there was anything said about vengeance upon the people or vengeance upon the nation, or what was said of that sort, if you remember?

Mr. Lawrence. I say it has been stated. I can not state it only as I understand it. The word "nation" was not mentioned where I was in regard to that vengeance, but the feeling has always been against the Nation and the State for allowing that deed to be perpetrated. The word "nation" was not mentioned. It is a little ambiguous in regard to that.

Mr. Worthington. You say you are ambiguous or it was ambiguous?

Mr. Lawrence. It was a little ambiguous, there, who it should be executed on. The supposition is it should be executed on the perpetrators of the deed.

The Chairman. Mr. Lawrence, you speak so low that I do not believe you can hear yourself.

Mr. Lawrence. I will try to speak louder.

Mr. Carlisle. Mr. Lawrence, I will get you to state, if you can, whether this covenant, or oath, or whatever it may be called, is always administered by the same person and in the same terms, or whether it is administered at different times by different persons, and whether it is in writing or merely oral.

Mr. Lawrence. It is administered orally by different persons at different times.

Mr. Carlisle. It may be then that there is a different form of the oath?

Mr. Lawrence. It may be administered a little different. Of course the substance is about the same, but there may be some men who administer it a little different from others. I have no doubt that it is from what I have heard.

Mr. Carlisle. You may take the witness.

Senator Knox. Was this vengeance to be executed by the person taking the oath, or vow, or were you to implore the Almighty to avenge the blood of the prophets?

MR. LAWRENCE. As I say, it was a little ambiguous in regard to that. Of course you take an oath to avenge the blood of the prophets and teach the principle to your children and children's children.

SENATOR KNOX. I think you do not understand me. You stated a moment ago that there was some ambiguity in the oath as to whom the vengeance is directed against.

MR. LAWRENCE. Yes.

SENATOR KNOX. Now, I am asking you who was to execute the vengeance. Was the person taking the vow or oath to execute it or were they to implore by prayer that God should take this vengeance?

MR. LAWRENCE. Well, that was not inserted in it for the Lord to do it. They simply took upon themselves the oath to do it; but I say it is almost impossible for them to wreak vengeance, because those men that committed the deed have probably gone years ago.[26]

SENATOR KNOX. My question was based on the exact language used by Professor Wolfe yesterday. He said that he heard the oath taken very recently, and that they vowed or promised that they would pray to Almighty God to avenge the blood of the prophets. I think it is quite material, and I want to know what your recollection is about it.

MR. LAWRENCE. That was not inserted in my day—that is, in regard to asking God to wreak this vengeance.

SENATOR KNOX. Your idea was that the individual who took the oath was to work out a vengeance?

MR. LAWRENCE. That was the wording of the obligation.

SENATOR KNOX. That is all I want to ask.

SENATOR DILLINGHAM. When do I understand you took the obligation?

MR. LAWRENCE. I forgot just when I took the obligation.

SENATOR DILLINGHAM. About when?

MR. LAWRENCE. It was when I was young; but I knew the obligations up to 1869.

MR. CARLISLE. Were you what they call a worker in the temple?

MR. LAWRENCE. I have been there, sir.

MR. CARLISLE. You say you have been there. My question is were you ever a worker in the temple?

MR. LAWRENCE. I have assisted there, sir.

MR. CARLISLE. In what way?

---

26. The previous three questions and answers were used by Worthington in his second closing argument (*Smoot Hearings*, 4:463).

MR. LAWRENCE. I have officiated in different work.

MR. CARLISLE. Officiated in the temple?

MR. LAWRENCE. Yes—not in the temple. It was in the endowment house. ...

MR. WORTHINGTON. On all the occasions when you heard it administered to others, or when it was administered to you, did you ever hear any reference to the nation of the United States as the object of the vengeance?

MR. LAWRENCE. During my administration the word "nation" was not used.

MR. WORTHINGTON. You say in your administration. Do you mean you administered the oath?

MR. LAWRENCE. No, sir—yes, sir. I mean I officiated there with the rest of them.

MR. WORTHINGTON. Then you both administered the covenant and you heard others administer it?

MR. LAWRENCE. Yes, sir.

MR. WORTHINGTON. You administered it hundreds of times and you heard it administered hundreds of times; is that right?

MR. LAWRENCE. I was there off and on for one or two years.

MR. WORTHINGTON. Did you administer it hundreds of times?

MR. LAWRENCE. I will say, yes.[27]

MR. WORTHINGTON. Did you hear it administered to others hundreds of times?

MR. LAWRENCE. I do not know that I did when I was there.

MR. WORTHINGTON. About how many times would you say you heard it administered by others?

MR. LAWRENCE. I do not remember of hearing it administered by others.

MR. WORTHINGTON. Twenty or thirty times?

MR. LAWRENCE. I do not remember hearing it administered.

MR. WORTHINGTON. Who administered it to you?

MR. LAWRENCE. I forget just who administered it to me for the reason that young men and young women are sent through there pretty early in life, and I have forgotten.

MR. WORTHINGTON. How old were you when you took the obligation?

MR. LAWRENCE. That I have forgotten.

MR. WORTHINGTON. Did you take the endowment more than once?

MR. LAWRENCE. No; not myself.

MR. WORTHINGTON. Now, I come back. During all the time you adminis-

---

27. This entire exchange, as abridged here, was included in the "View of the Minority" report submitted by Foraker on June 11, 1906 (*Smoot Hearings*, 4:538-39).

tered the oath, or heard it administered by others, did you ever hear the "nation" or the "United States" or the "Government of the United States" referred to in any way as the object of vengeance that was the subject of that covenant?

MR. LAWRENCE. I will say that at that time it was not connected with the obligation. I say this: That the Government has always been blamed for allowing that deed to be perpetrated. ...

MR. WORTHINGTON. You would not mind telling me whether, as far as financial matters are concerned, you have done very well since you have got out of the church, would you?

MR. LAWRENCE. I had made some money before I came out of the church.

MR. WORTHINGTON. You have made more since, have you not?

MR. LAWRENCE. No; I could not say I have made more. I was in the way of making money when I was in the church.

MR. WORTHINGTON. I do not mean you have made more since than you made while you were in the church, but you have continued to make money?

MR. LAWRENCE. No; I do not. I had a very prosperous business at that time.

MR. WORTHINGTON. And you continued in it for five years after you left the church?

MR. LAWRENCE. I continued in it until 1884.

MR. WORTHINGTON. That is fifteen years.

SENATOR OVERMAN. Did you suffer any loss in business by reason of withdrawing from the church?

MR. LAWRENCE. Yes; I do not make any complaints in that respect. I expected my business would be ruined. My mercantile business was pretty much ruined after I came out of the church. Of course I could not expect it, and did not get it.

THE CHAIRMAN. I could not hear what you said about your business.

MR. LAWRENCE. I said my business at that time was pretty much ruined.

THE CHAIRMAN. At what time?

MR. LAWRENCE. When I came out of the church—my mercantile business. But I say I have no complaints to make on that score; I expected it to be that way and I took the chances.

THE CHAIRMAN. How was it ruined?

MR. LAWRENCE. My former friends and customers did not come into my store. They dared not come into my store.[28] ...

---

28. The *Salt Lake Tribune* reported on February 8 that "only one witness is yet to be heard, Joseph Smith of Lamoni, head of the Reorganized Church of Latter-day Saints,

James H. Linford,[29] being duly sworn, was examined and testified as follows ...

MR. WORTHINGTON. Mr. Wolfe has given testimony here tending to show that he lost his position by reason of the fact that he did not pay his tithing as a member of the church. Have you any personal knowledge of the circumstances which led up to his separation from the position which he held there?

MR. LINFORD. Yes, sir.

MR. WORTHINGTON. I wish you would begin at the beginning and tell us, in the first place, in your own way about that.

MR. LINFORD. The cause for his resignation?

MR. WORTHINGTON. Yes.

MR. LINFORD. Mr. Wolfe acted with us as an able professor in charge of the department of geology and mineralogy from the time he engaged with us until the 15th.

MR. WORTHINGTON. Until when?

MR. LINFORD. Until the 15th of January of the present year.

SENATOR DUBOIS. Mr. Worthington, pardon me a moment. Did he state what ecclesiastical position he holds in the church?

MR. WORTHINGTON. No; he has not stated that. I am going into that later in connection with another matter I want to ask him about.

SENATOR DUBOIS. Very well.[30]

---

who will be put on the stand tomorrow." Two days later the *Deseret News* explained that "Mr. Carlisle decided that he did not care for a doctrinal discussion, and declined to put the Josephites on the stand." A few days later, Smoot elaborated:

> Yesterday I learned a little of the inside history of how the proceedings came to such an abrupt end, and why the Josephites were not given a chance to be heard. Thursday, Charles W. Owen had about fifty volumes of Journals of Discourses, old histories of Utah, and ancient church works placed on the table at which the witnesses sit, with the pages marked for reference. Joseph Smith, Jr., of the Reorganites, was to be placed on the stand, and by all means of his testimony the extracts from these old books were to be put into the record, and he was to explain that the Reorganites did not believe in these doctrines ... The object was to prove that ... polygamy was established by Brigham Young, that they had never been in conflict with the Government, that they have never believed in Temple ordinances ... My friends on the Committee learned of this program, and called an executive meeting of the Committee. They asked Burrows what the thing meant [and said] ... the hearings should be brought to a close, as they did not care to have two factions of a religion—as they designed it—quarreling as to which was right and which was wrong. Even Carlisle said that he did not think it proper. Joseph Smith, Jr., was greatly disappointed, and complained bitterly about being dragged over the county and being advertised as a witness, and then being turned down" (Smoot to Joseph F. Smith, Feb. 12, 1906).

29. Linford (1863-1941) was president of Brigham Young College in Logan. A defense witness, he was expected to rebut Wolfe's and Smurthwaite's testimonies.

30. Smoot was aware that Senator Dubois was working behind the scenes to unseat

MR. LINFORD. I say during the first year Mr. Wolfe rendered us good service as a teacher. Reports came to me, and I was convinced that during that year he drank some. We are fighting very strongly the invasion of the use of liquor among our young people. That is our aim, and it is a matter of constant vigilance on our part. Reports came to me that Professor Wolfe drank some during that year, the school year of 1904-5, beginning September 19, of 1904, and ending in early June of 1905. However, he was not approached directly as to that. The matter had not become serious. During the summer of 1905 Professor Wolfe drank more frequently than during the previous year, and it became evident to the patrons of our school that he was drinking, and it was called to my attention. I referred the matter to him in a delicate way.

MR. WORTHINGTON. Tell us the substance of what took place between you and him, please. ...

MR. LINFORD. In this way: I do not remember the exact wording of it, but we were talking over his work, and said I: "Professor, I am afraid that you have been tampering a little with liquor; doing too much with it." I simply made the suggestion. Said he, in words something to this effect—I don't remember the exact wording—"Well, I have been a little, because of troubles." I can't give you the date, but it was some time during the summer.

MR. WORTHINGTON. The summer of 1905?

MR. LINFORD. Of 1905. Our school ended early in September the 17th or 18th of September. I don't remember the exact date, but it was about that time, and he entered on his work as heretofore, but in my associations with him I found that he had been drinking.

MR. WORTHINGTON. How did you observe it? You state you found he had been drinking. I would like to know how you found it.

MR. LINFORD. From the odor that arose from his breath when coming into connection with him. I don't use it myself, and I can tell very definitely. Reports came to me from the outside calling my attention to his actions. I knew in the meantime that certain of his friends had spoken to him about it; but at various times during the fall that matter

---

him. Shortly before the hearings reopened, he wrote that "Fred Dubois is not idle by any manner of means since his return. ... He is trying to[o] hard to poison the minds of the Republican leaders against me, and all Senators that have been friendly in the past, by telling them that I am a dead duck politically in Utah ... I was in the President's office the other morning when Dubois called and I was pleased to note they were not very cordial. I don't believe the President has much respect for him" (Smoot to Joseph F. Smith, Dec. 12, 1905).

continued. In the early part of our school year I addressed the school, as is usual, against the use of intoxicants.

MR. WORTHINGTON. The school year begins in September, I believe.

MR. LINFORD. In September; yes. I made it very pointed that we could not tolerate the use of liquor, that it was directly opposed to our policy, and especially pointed out the evil effects of the use of that—the dangers that it led up to. I think the professor was present on occasions when that was made very pointed. On one occasion I remember, immediately after our annual reception that we give to the students, Prof. J. C. Jensen, a member of the faculty, and Professor Wolfe and I were standing in the door of my office when attention was called to a certain student who had been drinking the day before, or two days before. I don't recall the exact time of this, but it was within a day or two after the reception, which was held on the 24th or thereabouts.

I there, addressing these two members of the faculty, stated that the matter would have to be looked into; that we could not tolerate the use of liquor in the college among our students—in the college, I put it. Professor Wolfe was present on the occasion, and said, "No, it will not do," or words to that effect. It indicated to me that he knew my policy definitely, and also was in sympathy with that thought. ...

It would have been very humiliating had the student organization come to me with the report that one of our professors was using whisky or liquors, thereby—well, the point is this: He would bring us rather into disrepute. So I decided upon that method of meeting the professor. On the 4th, as I recall, Bishop Cardon, of the First Ward of Logan, called me by telephone and told me he wanted to speak with me. I repaired the same day to his office, to his business house—really, it is a business house—and he there referred to the habits of Professor Wolfe, his habits of drinking, and he referred to some other habits, but especially the habit of drinking, and called my attention to the fact that we could hardly allow a thing of that kind to continue. Before I left he stated that Professor Wolfe was not a tithe payer this year, and related to me the fact that he had been called up.

On the 5th of January, Friday, I called up Professor Wolfe and made an appointment with him at my home, and on that occasion I called his attention to the matter of drinking in something like these words: "Professor Wolfe, I shall have to approach you on a matter that, so far as I am personally concerned, may be none of my business, but so far as my position as president of the institution is concerned, it is decidedly my business." Professor Wolfe said, "Yes; I appreciate that," and anticipated what I was going to refer to. That was the question of drinking. I told the professor that that was the point, and that the conditions that existed were unfortunate; that it would be necessary for him, if he retained his position in the college, to discontinue the use of liquor, and that he must quit associating with those who were using tobacco, because it would not do for him to come repeatedly before his classes, as he had done in the past, with clothes reeking with tobacco fumes and his breath revealing the use of intoxicant liquors.[31]

The members of his class had noticed it and referred the matter to me. Said he: "Well, I know it, and, President Linford, I shall discontinue the use of liquor while I am in the Brigham Young College. I want you to understand that you will not have occasion to refer this matter to me again while I am in the employ of the college." Further he stated that he was willing to ask for forgiveness of the school for what he had done in this respect. I told him that just now I should not make that requirement of him. I did not think it wise. In fact, I should reserve a decision in that matter until later.

After that had occurred, after we had reached an understanding regarding the liquor question, Professor Wolfe said, "Have you seen Bishop Cardon?" Said I, "Yes." Said he, "Then you know my attitude; you know my position," or words to that effect. Said I, "Yes. I am sorry, but," said I, "Professor, I want you to understand that that was not the reason for my calling you in the office on this occasion. I hadn't any idea of calling you up for those matters."

THE CHAIRMAN. You mean for refusal to pay tithes?

MR. LINFORD. Yes, sir. That is what I referred to, and also a statement that he had no longer faith in the Mormon Church. After we had spoken of that just a few minutes together, said I, "I should like to know, Professor, the reasons for your change;" and we entered into a friendly discussion of the question, of the belief in revealed religion. I told him the reason I discussed it with him was not to affect his position, but simply as a matter of personal desire to know the reasons for the change that had occurred. We discussed the matter pro and con in a friendly way, and he said that if there was a revealed religion, said he, "I believe the Latter-Day Saints have that. However, I have no belief in

---

31. In an editorial on this day, the *Salt Lake Tribune* reported that Linford was brought to Washington to refute Wolfe's testimony, which might imply being asked to "deny the treasonable character of the endowment oath," which the *Tribune* thought would be enough to make Linford "scramble" for the tulips ("The Smoot Case," Mar. 26, 1906).

a revealed religion." That was the substance of it. Well, he left my home. School opened on Monday. During the week I watched carefully, and to the best of my knowledge, toward the latter part of the week Professor Wolfe was beginning again to indulge in liquors—not to the excess that he did before, but from evidence that I could gain.

MR. WORTHINGTON. What was the evidence?

MR. LINFORD. The condition of the breath, and at times the general appearance that gives an indication of that. On Sunday morning at 10 o'clock we assembled for a college Sunday school. Professor Wolfe did not appear at his Sunday-school class that morning. I wondered why he was not present. It led me to inquire, and through inquiry I learned that Professor Wolfe was drinking. The report came to me that he was drunk. I did not see him myself, but that was the report. I kept close note of him. On Monday morning he came to the class with his breath heavily loaded with liquor. His actions were rather unsteady, and I knew as positively as I know anything, that he had been drinking—as positively as I would know without having seen him drink.

I called him out of the class and had a conversation with him. I called his attention to the matter somewhat in these words: "Professor, matters seem to be getting very serious." Professor Wolfe said: "Yes, sir; they are serious." Said I: "Faculty members, patrons, are criticising us very severely for allowing you to continue. Now," said I, "you have broken your promise to me, promises that you made on January 5. You were drinking yesterday." "Yes, sir." "You are now more or less under the influence of liquor." "Yes, sir." Said I: "I can't see why, now, you should not offer your resignation." I don't remember the exact words, but I gave him to understand that in view of these broken pledges it would be wise for him to offer his resignation; that we should be glad to settle up with him in full and take his resignation at once. "All right," said Professor Wolfe, "I will offer it and we will settle up." Said I: "Now, Professor, I want you to understand that I have tried to treat you with consideration in all my work here, all my relations with you." He said: "Yes; I appreciate that." Said he, "I want to tell you, Brother Linford, that if I were placed in a similar condition and in similar circumstances I should now be called upon to act in the same way."

MR. WORTHINGTON. He said that?

MR. LINFORD. He said that; yes, sir. ...

MR. WORTHINGTON. Perhaps that covers it, but I will ask you the general question: What was the reason he was requested to resign?

MR. LINFORD. The use of intoxicating liquors. ...

MR. WORTHINGTON. I wish you would tell us a little more particularly what it was the Bishop told you had taken place between him and Mr. Wolfe, which Mr. Wolfe referred to when he said he supposed you knew about it.

MR. LINFORD. As nearly as I can tell, the Bishop referred to it in this way: Said he: "On the 1st," I believe he said the 1st, "I called up Professor Wolfe and stated he had not settled his tithing, and wished he would call." I want to say that is the general policy. All tithing payers—that is, all who have been tithe payers in the past—who have not settled their tithing by that time are called up. That is, it was nothing unusual in Professor Wolfe's case.

THE CHAIRMAN. I did not understand who you said called him up?

MR. LINFORD. Bishop Cardon called me up, Senator.

THE CHAIRMAN. Called you up?

MR. LINFORD. Called me up on the telephone. ...

MR. WORTHINGTON. Did the bishop tell you that in the interview he had had with Mr. Wolfe anything had been said about Mr. Wolfe losing faith in the principles of the church? You said something about that.

MR. LINFORD. Yes.

MR. WORTHINGTON. Aside from tithing?

MR. LINFORD. As I remember, the bishop referred to the fact that he did not have any faith in the church; that he would be likely called on to testify at Washington, and would be compelled to say things that would make him not feel comfortable, or something to that effect, to return to Utah.[32]

MR. WORTHINGTON. Did he speak then about the probability of his coming before this committee?

MR. LINFORD. To the bishop; yes, sir.

MR. WORTHINGTON. Had he said anything to you on that subject before?

MR. LINFORD. Yes, sir.

MR. WORTHINGTON. When?

MR. LINFORD. I am not sure of the date; some time in the latter part of

---

32. During Wolfe's cross-examination, he was asked when he lost his faith. He said it had been gradual, due to "what I considered a violation of the compact with the Federal Government, with the nation. That has been one thing." "That was in 1896?" Worthington asked. "It is since 1896," Wolfe said, adding that it had been because of "the continuation of polygamy, as I have observed it, and the general tone of the church as regards politics and other things. I have been generally dissatisfied, not particularly with tithing, but I have been dissatisfied with the fundamental principles of the religion" in more recent years, "certainly since 1904" (*Smoot Hearings,* 4:28).

November or the first of December. I could not recall the date, but it was somewhere along there.

MR. WORTHINGTON. What had Professor Wolfe said to you then about the probability of his coming here?

MR. LINFORD. That he had been wanted at the investigation before, and that he would more than likely be called upon this time to come to Washington, and he said to me on that occasion that he had already packed up.

MR. WORTHINGTON. Already packed up?

MR. LINFORD. Yes, sir. ...

MR. WORTHINGTON. About this matter of tithe paying. Is it in reference to people employed there in the college of which you are president; that people who do not pay tithes can not stay there that is, members of the church?

MR. LINFORD. We have never yet dismissed a person for nontithe paying.

MR. WORTHINGTON. Do you have any who do not pay tithes?

MR. LINFORD. We have one, to my knowledge, who is not a tithe payer, and we have two at work in the faculty who are not Mormons.[33] ...

MR. CARLISLE. ... [Y]ou have never taken a plural wife?

MR. LINFORD. Yes, sir.

MR. CARLISLE. You do not mean to say you do not believe in the practice of polygamy or plural wives, do you?

MR. LINFORD. I have not made that statement, as I recall.

MR. CARLISLE. Do you or do you not believe in the principle of plural marriage—that is to say, I do not ask you now to state whether you believe in it as lawful or not under the present circumstances; but do you or do you not believe it is right in and of itself?

MR. LINFORD. Is it necessary that I should answer the question?

THE CHAIRMAN. Yes.

MR. CARLISLE. Yes. You said you are not a polygamist.

MR. WORTHINGTON. I understand the committee has ruled that is competent. We have objected to it over and over again on the ground that you have no right to inquire into the operations of a man's mind as to what his beliefs are, but only what he does.

THE CHAIRMAN. I presume the witness has no objection to answering the question.

MR. WORTHINGTON. He does object, as I understand.

---

33. After Linford's testimony, the *Salt Lake Tribune* editorialized that the attempt to "besmirch Prof. Wolfe is, as predicated, not only a failure, but is nauseating in the extreme" ("The Latest Batch," Mar. 27, 1906).

THE CHAIRMAN. The witness may answer.

MR. WORTHINGTON. I would like to state the objection again and put it on the record. I object that it is not competent for the committee to inquire of any man as to merely what his beliefs are unless it is intended to be followed by showing that he has in some way undertaken to carry what he believes into effect.

MR. CARLISLE. If the question were open to argument, the answer to that in this particular case would be that the witness has answered the question in response to counsel for the sitting member of the Senate that he is not a polygamist, and I want to know what he means by that.

MR. WORTHINGTON. He said he meant by that that he had never taken a plural wife.

THE CHAIRMAN. One of the charges by the protestants is that this church teaches, believes in, and practices polygamy.

MR. WORTHINGTON. I do not object to anybody believing it. I object to practicing it.

THE CHAIRMAN. This witness is the head of the Brigham Young College. He is asked what his belief is on that question. I think the question is a proper one. Repeat the question, Mr. Reporter.

The reporter read as follows: "Q. Do you or do you not believe in the principle of plural marriage? That is to say, I do not ask you now to state whether you believe in it as lawful or not under the present circumstances; but do you or do you not believe it is right in and of itself?"

MR. LINFORD. My belief in the principle does not extend to the carrying of the principle into practice under present conditions.

THE CHAIRMAN. That is not an answer.

MR. CARLISLE. That is not an answer to my question.

MR. LINFORD. But so far as the principle, from a sociological point of view or religious point of view is concerned, I believe it would solve many of the difficulties of the present.

MR. CARLISLE. That is not an answer to my question yet. My question is, Do you believe that principle is right in and of itself, without regard to any law or any questions it would solve?

MR. LINFORD. Yes, sir; I do. I believe it is a correct principle. ...

30.

Closing Statements
John G. Carlisle and A. S. Worthington
Thursday & Friday, April 12-13

"Long before 10 o'clock the same party of ladies who have been constant attendants entered the committee room, and at half-past 10 ... there was a flutter among the audience, and whispers passed around, 'That is Mrs. Smoot,' as a lady dressed in a light striped blue-grey gown and becoming hat to match entered and took a seat towards the rear of the room. It is the first time Mrs. Smoot has appeared on the scene." —*Deseret News,* Apr. 13, 1906[1]

Mr. Carlisle [for the prosecution]. It is proper to say in the beginning that, in my opinion, so far as the belief in revelations is confined to those revelations which relate only to religious or spiritual affairs we have no concern with them here and that so far as the priesthood limits the exercise of its authority to purely religious and spiritual affairs we have no concern with them here.

This does not mean, by any means, that the fact of the existence of the belief in revelations—confined exclusively even to religious and spiritual affairs—can be entirely ignored by this committee, because it is evident that if these people believe that the members of their priesthood have received and can and may receive revelations from the Almighty that they may enjoy his personal presence and have personal intercourse with him even in regard to spiritual affairs alone, that belief must very greatly augment the power and influence of the priesthood over the minds and conduct of the people in all matters. It is therefore a matter which the committee can not discard entirely; and the fact is, as disclosed by this testimony, that in the minds of the Mormon people spiritual affairs and temporal affairs are so confused and confounded that they are unable to distinguish between them, and they therefore accept substantially all revelations made, or

---

1. Although there had been closing statements in January 1905, these final statements incorporated the testimony of new witnesses who appeared before the committee in February 1906.

alleged to have been made, to the priesthood as of divine authority, no matter to what subject they relate.

This is shown very clearly by the position which the Mormon hierarchy has always taken upon the subject of marriage. Marriage is a civil institution in this country and belongs exclusively to the domain of the State. In every really civilized country in the world marriage has been the subject of regulation by the law of the State, not by the law or rule or doctrine of the church; and the testimony in this case shows that for years and years the Mormons in Utah and elsewhere have believed that a divine revelation upon the subject of marriage, a civil institution, authorizing or commanding, whichever it may have been, the men of that church to take more wives than the law of the State or the law of the country allows them was and is as binding upon them as any revelation which related purely to a spiritual matter.

They contended that the Government of the United States, while Utah was a Territory, had no power by a solemn enactment of Congress to punish them for complying with the obligations imposed upon them with regard to a civil and temporal matter by the revelation which they claimed Joseph Smith had received; and long after the Supreme Court of the United States had decided the law to be constitutional they resisted it and still claimed that the revelation which they said was binding upon their consciences was superior to this law of the United States, and refused to obey it until the time came when, as a matter of pure policy, for the purpose of avoiding the prosecutions under the law and ultimately succeeding in securing the admission of Utah into the Union as a State, they abandoned not the belief—the belief that the revelation was superior to the law—but merely the practice of polygamy.

Mr. Chairman, the belief in revelations from the Almighty, and the belief that it is the duty of the people to yield implicit obedience to the authority of the priesthood in all matters whatever, as I think the belief is, are so connected with each other that it will be most convenient and will abbreviate the argument to consider them together here; and in endeavoring to ascertain what that belief is, how far it extends in both instances, as to the authority of the revelation and the duty of the people to obey the priesthood, we will have to look to the standard works of the church and to the commentaries upon those works by men who are supposed to be learned in the doctrines of the church; and in order that this evidence may be presented to the committee in a compact form and read hereafter, if my argument is read at all, I propose to read a few extracts which I hope will not be tedious, as they are not very long. ...

It will be remembered by the committee that Mr. Smoot, in his testimony, stated positively that the quorum of apostles exercised no authority in the church, but acted merely in an advisory capacity, and the counsel in his argument emphasized that statement very strongly and said that they had no authority—"absolutely none." And yet here is the creed of the church, which every witness who has testified upon the subject at all has said is the standard authority, which shows that in the distribution of the powers of this organization the quorum of twelve apostles is equal in authority in every respect to the first presidency.

If that be true, and of course all good Mormons accept it as true, the first presidency can do nothing whatever with regard to the affairs of the church, spiritual or temporal, when they exercise temporal power, without the consent and approval of the quorum of the twelve apostles, any more than the House of Representatives could pass a law without the concurrence of the Senate, or the Senate could pass a law without the concurrence of the House. They are of absolutely equal authority in the church.[2]

The only statement contained in the evidence which would tend to limit the authority of the twelve apostles; of which Mr. Smoot is one, is the testimony of Joseph F. Smith, in answer to a question propounded by the counsel on the other side, when he said the apostles exercised no judicial authority in the church. Every other witness and every authority that was read here shows that the quorum of apostles are equal in authority to the presidency.

Mr. Smoot, in his answer, swears that he is not a member of any self-perpetuating body and that there is no such body. Joseph F. Smith and every other witness who testified upon the subject swears distinctly that when a vacancy occurs in the quorum of twelve it is filled by [an individual appointed by] the remaining members; that

---

2. Referring to this testimony, Carl Badger noted:

Carlisle made the mistake of assuming that the Twelve Apostles are a quorum equal in authority to the First Presidency while the First Presidency is organized; when they are so equal only after the dissolution of the First Presidency. This destroyed his first proposition. He then hung too much weight on the oath being "against this nation," and fell down when he went to prove it by Mr. Lawrence. He showed, to my mind, a very wonderful command of strong, weighty English; I enjoyed his speech. He was not rabid and what he said will be all the more powerful from the absence of personal ill will (in Rodney J. Badger, *Liahona and Iron Rod: The Biography of Carl A. and Rose J. Badger* [Bountiful, Utah: Family History Publishers, 1985], 317).

when a vacancy occurs in the office of president—and that is also shown by this authority I have read—the twelve apostles take his place and exercise all the authority vested in him until his successor is elected, and that they nominate and present that successor. If that is not a self-perpetuating body of men, I confess my inability to understand the meaning of the English language.[3] ...

My time is passing, Mr. Chairman, and I want, before discussing another question which I think ought to be presented to the committee, in view of the argument heretofore made, and especially in view of some questions which have been propounded heretofore by Senators; to call attention to the matter of the oaths or covenants which we claim all persons who pass through the old endowment house or who pass through the temple are required to take. I had collected them here and had intended to read them and all the testimony relating to them to the committee, but I will have to refrain from going into the evidence at length.

We do not know, and have not been able to ascertain in this investigation, exactly what the terms of that oath or covenant, whichever it is, are. Naturally most of the witnesses who passed through the old endowment house and the temple many years ago would be unable to repeat verbatim the whole of that long ceremony, which lasted from 8 o'clock in the morning until half past 4 o'clock in the afternoon, or to repeat verbatim any substantial part of it. Forty, fifty, or more people would pass through at a time. These oaths or covenants, whichever they were, were not read to them. No copies were furnished to them, but they were given orally—sometimes by one officiating person and

---

3. Three days earlier, the *Salt Lake Tribune* had reported:

There was much discussion among Senators today of the press reports from Salt Lake City announcing that two apostles [John W. Taylor and Matthias F. Cowley] have been deposed for practicing polygamy since the manifesto. It is generally conceded here [Washington, D.C.] that the action for the hierarchy, instead of having a favorable impression upon sentiment, will have just the opposite. The action is an admission that the law has been defied and the manifesto ignored by men who stood in the highest official relations to the hierarchy. One of Senator Smoot's closest friends in the Senate said today that he considered the action at this time as a mistake from the viewpoint of Smoot's interests. He declared that the Senate would readily understand that it was done to influence action in the case, and it smacked of the hymnal episode which Mr. Carlisle brought out during the recent hearing, when it was disclosed that well-known patriotic hymns had been inserted in the last edition of the book issued since the Smoot case was begun" ("Smoot's Doom Is Sealed," Apr. 9, 1906).

The patriotic songs added to the 1905 edition of the LDS hymnal were *America* and *The Star-Spangled Banner* (*Smoot Hearings*, 283-84).

sometimes by another—and all that could be expected of any witness who had heard this oath administered or this covenant spoken would necessarily be to state it as he remembered it. So we have a variety of statements here as regards the phraseology of this covenant; but upon the question that there was in fact some oath or some covenant of that general character taken or administered during the progress of these ceremonies I think the committee can have no doubt. Some of the witnesses say it was an oath or covenant to seek vengeance upon this nation—I am not giving the exact language—or upon the people of this nation to avenge the blood of the prophets, and they give the form or substance of the oath or covenant in various terms, but all embodying the same idea. Some say it was a covenant that the person would pray the Lord to take this vengeance upon this nation or upon this people on account of the death of the prophet Joseph Smith.

I am willing to accept for the purposes of this argument, because it will obviate the necessity of going into a critical examination of these various oaths or covenants, that the present form of that covenant is as it was stated by Professor [Walter M.] Wolfe, who is a very intelligent man, as members of the committee who happened to be present when he testified could see. He was a professor in the Brigham Young Academy, and he has passed through the endowment house or temple twelve times, once for himself and eleven times afterwards for people who have died; for it is a part of the doctrine of the church that if a person is not able to take or happens to fail to take the endowment during his life, anybody else, whether a relative or not, can, after his death, take the endowment for him, and thus secure his exaltation in the world to come. So Professor Wolfe said he went through once for himself and then he went through eleven times for dead people. ...

SENATOR DILLINGHAM. Does the witness [Wolfe] tell in what way the Government of the United States was responsible for the death of the martyrs and the application of the oath?

MR. CARLISLE. No; he does not, I think, assert anything on that subject. I am not afraid that the Mormon people in Utah or elsewhere will overthrow the Government of the United States. I do not think they will ever be able to do it much injury in any way, or even to successfully resist its laws, and I am referring to this matter simply for the purpose of showing the state of feeling among the Mormon people and the church authorities.

Now, this feeling of hostility to the Government must exist, because a man will not take an oath or enter into a covenant to pray God to take vengeance upon this nation unless he entertains such a feeling of hostility. I submit to the committee that it is far more reasonable to suppose that there is an oath or covenant of this general character administered in the endowment house and in the temple than it is to assume that six or seven witnesses have deliberately perjured themselves here in this investigation about a matter in which they have no personal or pecuniary interest. How does it happen that all of them, while they differ as to the phraseology, give the substance of what took place there, unless they heard it there?

Mr. Worthington attempts to account for it in this way: He says that the evening before his argument he made a discovery which he thinks explains this whole matter. He says he finds in Linn's "Story of the Mormons"[4] a statement that when the Mormons left Nauvoo [Illinois] for Salt Lake, which was then, as we all know, without the limits of the United States, 1,500 of them took this oath, which Mr. Worthington prints in his argument: "You do solemnly swear in the presence of Almighty God, his holy angles, and these witnesses, that you will avenge the blood of Joseph Smith upon this nation, and so teach your children; and that you will, from this day henceforth and forever, begin and carry out hostilities against this nation, and keep the same a profound secret now and forever. So help you God."

His theory is that all these witnesses, some of whom were then unborn and nearly all of whom are now comparatively young men and could have known nothing about the oath taken at Nauvoo, have seen this oath somewhere, and that they are trying to pass it off on the committee as the oath which was taken in the endowment house. The committee will see how similar it is in some respects to the oath or covenant described by the witness, and I think it is far more probable than Mr. Worthington's theory to conclude that when these fifteen hundred men arrived at Salt Lake, having taken this oath, it was incorporated into the ceremony of the endowment house, and was for many years the oath which was there administered. The oath which is given by the witnesses now is not the oath administered at the time of

---

4. William Alexander Linn, *The Story of the Mormons: From the Date of Their Origin to the Year 1901* (New York: Macmillan, 1902). B. H. Roberts called this book "a pretentious work of nearly 650 pages," which went far out of the way for what Linn claimed to be original material and announced as if he had "made a new discovery" when Roberts felt he had covered the same ground years before with better results (B. H. Roberts, *New Witnesses for God* [Salt Lake City: Deseret News, 1909], 3:394-95).

the naturalization cases, and my idea about it—of course I do not assert it as a fact actually proved—is that after those naturalization cases were decided and the Mormon people found that if they continued to take the ceremonies, including the oath, as they then stood they could not be admitted to citizenship, there was a modification of the oath and covenant, whatever it was, and it has been changed by various modifications until it has now assumed the substantial form which Professor Wolfe gives it. That is more probable, I think, than it is to assume that a man who is now only 35 or 40 years old had seen that history and had this form of the oath in his mind from something he had seen or heard outside the endowment house.[5] ...

SENATOR BAILEY. Would it interrupt you, Mr. Carlisle, if I ask you a question?

MR. CARLISLE. Not in the least.

SENATOR BAILEY. ... [I]s it not certain that the men who made the Constitution intended to limit [the extent to which the Senate can] ... make its own rules, and to judge of the elections, returns, and qualifications of its own members? ...

MR. CARLISLE. I will come to that. I concede, Mr. Senator, and Mr. Chairman, that the Constitution has imposed certain limitations ... That is conceded and is undoubtedly correct; but I want to see what those limitations were and what their effect is. I want to see, if we can, to what extent it limits the power of the House and the Senate over this subject.

Undoubtedly the House and the Senate each would have possessed the power to expel a member, without this provision in the Constitution, ... by a majority of one vote. So the framers of the Constitution provided that when they come to expel a member, which is a punishment—and that is the distinction between an expulsion and

---

5. For Worthington's argument referred to here, see chapter 29 in this volume; *Smoot Hearings*, 3:696-98. After the concluding arguments, Carl Badger found "the Senator's case [to be] in a critical condition." The prosecution and defense had both agreed on some embarrassing facts and disagreed only on their interpretation. Senator Depew had been convinced to side with Chairman Burrows. Senator Dolliver seemed concerned about the RLDS vote in his state of Iowa. "It looks as though the Senator will have Foraker, Knox, Dillingham, Hopkins, and Beveridge for him, and the rest of the Committee—eight—against him. Foraker is already working on a report, and is preparing a speech; he has his heart in the matter. The remaining members who will favor the Senator have not got down to work, as far as we can learn. I do not feel to censure them much. It is a mighty unpopular side they are called to defend; and it is not only unpopular, but there are things about our side that cannot be defended" (in Badger, *Liahona and Iron Rod*, 320-21).

the mere vacation of a seat—when they attempt to inflict this punishment upon a Senator or member of the House, by expelling him, there must be a vote of two-thirds. That is the only limitation there is in that clause of the Constitution.

Then comes the great clause around which this controversy revolves. That is that no person—I give it in substance—shall be a Senator who has not attained the age of 30 years, and who has not been a citizen of the United States for nine years, and who was not at the time of his election an inhabitant of the State from which he was chosen. The question is, What is the effect of that limitation?

SENATOR BAILEY. That language is "for which he is chosen," I think.

MR. CARLISLE. From which or for which, whichever it is. Now assuming, as the Senator from Texas [Bailey] and I at least assume, that the Senate would have plenary power [if the Constitution had not imposed limits], then it would have had undoubtedly, upon that theory, which is correct, power to admit a person 21 years old; it would have had power to admit a person who had been a citizen but one day; and it would have had power to admit a person who was not, at the time of his election, an inhabitant of the State for which he was chosen. But the framers of the Constitution said to that body, that in order to secure men of experience, the power should be limited to the admission of persons who have arrived at the age of 30 years; that in order to secure the services of persons who are attached to the institutions of the country and are acquainted with them, it shall be limited to the admission of persons who have been citizens for nine years; and in order to secure persons who properly represent the sentiments and interests of the people for whom they came here to legislate it shall be limited to the admission of persons who were inhabitants of the State for which they were chosen at the time of the election. Does the limitation go a particle beyond that? The Senate can not constitutionally admit a person to a seat on its floor unless he is 30 years old, unless he has been a citizen nine years, unless he was an inhabitant of the State for which he was chosen at the time of the election; but does it follow from this that it is bound to admit every person who is 30 years old, who has been a citizen nine years, and who was an inhabitant of the State at the time he was chosen? It seems to me that would be a manifest non sequitur.

But, it is said, when the Constitution enumerates certain disqualifications—not qualifications, but certain disqualifications—must it not be conclusively presumed that it enumerates all that can be considered? Not at all. If the fundamental proposition which I have stated to the committee is correct, these limitations upon a power which would otherwise exist can extend no further than the enumeration. They must stop there and leave unimpaired all the great mass of power which would have been in the hands of the body without them. Why, it is the common political law of this country that idiots, insane persons, lunatics, and women are not eligible to public office. (Laughter.) I beg the ladies' pardon, but I must state the law correctly, even if the ladies are present. Certainly the constitution of a State may change that political law and admit our lady friends to office, but that is not the common political law of the country. This has been done in many of the States. Perhaps it would be done in more if these ladies could have an opportunity to be heard. The Constitution does not enumerate any of those disqualifications, for it was not necessary. The framers of that instrument knew that these and other disqualifications existed. In the first place, it would have been impossible for them to enumerate all the grounds for disqualification that might arise during the long life of the Republic. They could not foresee, for instance, that there would ever be a Mormon Church organized in this country or that there would ever be such a thing as the practice of polygamy or the taking of plural wives in this country. They could not foresee that within less than seventy-five years after the adoption of the Constitution a great civil war would sweep over the land and create a condition of affairs which alarmed the friends of the Government and that Congress might thereafter, in the exercise of its judgment, consider it necessary to hold that certain persons who had participated in that war, or who were supposed to have participated in it, or who entertained feelings of hostility to the Government or were supposed to entertain such feelings, might not be subject to any one of these constitutional objections, and yet should be excluded.

SENATOR BAILEY. Did not the fourteenth amendment itself assume that it was necessary to adopt the constitutional amendment to exclude them? It does provide that no Senator, Representative, etc., who had taken the oath to support the Constitution and afterwards engaged in the rebellion should be admitted, but that Congress might by a two-thirds vote[6]—

---

6. Section 3 of the 14th Amendment reads: "No person shall be a Senator or Representative in Congress, or elector of President and Vice President, or hold any office, civil or military, under the United States, or under any State, who, having previously taken an oath, as a member of Congress, or as an officer of the United States, or as a member of any State legislature, or as an executive or judicial officer of any State, to support the

MR. CARLISLE. Might remove the disability.

SENATOR BAILEY. Is not that a construction that it became necessary to adopt the constitutional amendment to exclude the man who was engaged in the rebellion?

MR. CARLISLE. Not, Mr. Senator, if you please, in a declaration that it was necessary to adopt it, because they had been excluded before that right along. It was to make the rule permanent in the law, that was all; and it required persons in the South who were supposed to be hostile to the Government to show they were entitled to pardon before they could be qualified.

SENATOR BAILEY. Is it not true, however, that they expelled the Senators who were charged with sympathy with the rebellion, and did not declare their seats vacant, and that where they refused to admit a Senator they did it upon the ground that the State had not been duly reconstructed, as they called it, or duly organized, as we say?

MR. CARLISLE. In some cases; but I will come to the question of expulsion presently.

SENATOR BAILEY. Excuse me for interrupting you.[7] ...

MR. WORTHINGTON [for the defense]. The first case to which I refer is what is known as the Roberts case in the House, where Brigham H. Roberts had been elected as a Representative from the State of Utah and was confessedly a polygamist living in polygamy at the time. Objection was made to his being sworn in, and the question of his qualification was referred to a certain committee, a special committee, as I remember, of which Mr. [Robert W.] Tayler [R-Ohio], who was for a

---

Constitution of the United States, shall have engaged in insurrection or rebellion against the same, or given aid or comfort to the enemies thereof. But Congress may by a vote of two-thirds of each House, remove such disability."

7. Applauding Carlisle's argument, the *Salt Lake Tribune* wrote: "Carlisle appears to have found the great central fact in the Smoot case. His argument yesterday before the committee demonstrates that to him the whole situation has been clarified, and we doubt not that he was able to impress his views upon the understanding of the Senators who were present at the hearings. Is the Mormon hierarchy an alien and a treasonable organization? The testimony in the case answers, Yes. Is Reed Smoot responsible for the treachery and the crime? The testimony in the case answers, Yes. ... Carlisle is to be congratulated upon having fulfilled expectations. He is a great lawyer, and it would not [have been] doubted he would find 'the kernel in the nut'" ("Carlisle's Argument," Apr. 13, 1906). Smoot, on the other hand, wrote that "people expected to hear a great argument from Mr. Carlisle—as some Senators expressed it, 'a great intellectual treat.' He evidently did not know much about the testimony that has been presented, and consequently did not have his case well in hand" (Smoot to Heber J. Grant, April 22, 1906).

long time counsel for those whom we call the protestants here, was the chairman. That committee was composed of nine members of the House. It made two reports, a majority report, which was signed by Mr. Tayler and six other members of the committee, and a minority report, which was signed by Mr. Littlefield [R-Maine] and Mr. De Armond [D-Missouri]. The reports of that committee, both of the majority and of the minority, were in favor of the proposition that, as this case is situated, it would require a two-thirds vote [to expel a member], and, so far as I know, the committee and the House were unanimous on that subject. The majority of the committee said that the House had power to add qualifications to the constitutional qualifications, and that if Roberts was a polygamist he should be excluded from his seat in the House, and they went at great length into a demonstration of the proposition that if he were allowed to take his seat he could not be removed or ousted except by a two-thirds vote. The minority of the committee reported that it was not competent for the House to add anything to the constitutional qualifications, that he should be allowed to take his seat, and, being a polygamist, he should then be expelled, which would of course require a two-thirds vote. ...

The other case in which this matter was thoroughly discussed by the ablest lawyers in the Senate on both sides was what is known as the Roach case. Mr. [William N.] Roach had been the cashier of a bank in this city, and I think I may say without any question—there never was any dispute about it—had embezzled a large sum of money. He of course was deprived of his place in the bank. He was not prosecuted because, as I understand, some of his friends arranged with the bank to make good the amount of the loss. He went out West, and after a while came back as a Senator from North Dakota [Democrat, 1893-99]. After he had been sworn in and had occupied the seat for some time this matter of his crime was bruited in the newspapers and finally came before the Senate in the form of a resolution which was introduced, referring the matter to this committee for investigation and report as to whether he should be allowed to retain his seat. That resolution was discussed very thoroughly, as I say, and the precedents were gone over again as to the power of the Senate in the matter. The case was finally dropped without any action by the Senate. He served out his term, the discussion, I think, showing clearly that if it ever had come to a vote in the Senate the result would have been the same. ...

Mr. Carlisle suggested that perhaps Joseph F. Smith might be sent here. Now, let me say it would not be the first time that a polygamist has been sent to Congress. I do not now refer to the Roberts case; but many years ago, before Utah was a State, George Q. Cannon was sent here as a Delegate from the Territory, and he was admitted and took his seat, and afterwards the question arose as to his expulsion. The matter was investigated and came before the House, and received so little consideration that I believe on the final vote there was not even a call for the yeas and nays. If Joseph F. Smith, polygamist as he is, engaged in violation of the law, as he admits, should be elected a Senator from Utah, I would say that if, after he was elected and when he came here to take his seat, he had given up his unlawful relations and lived only with his lawful wife, he ought to be admitted and ought to be allowed to take his seat, but if, after being sworn in, he remained in that relation, then he should be expelled, which would, of course, require a two-thirds vote.

It should be noted that while the whole argument of Mr. Carlisle was addressed to the proposition that Senator Smoot was disqualified to take his seat, which may accordingly be declared vacant by a mere majority vote, the evidence upon which he relies relates largely to things that have happened since Senator Smoot was admitted to the Senate—his voting to sustain President Smith, for example, after the latter testified before this committee.

SENATOR DUBOIS. Mr. Worthington, would it interrupt you if I make a suggestion? Was not George Q. Cannon's seat declared vacant, he being a Delegate in Congress, and it being avowed that he was a polygamist?

MR. WORTHINGTON. I read last night about that case in the compilation of cases in the House, and that was not the way I read it, Senator.

SENATOR DUBOIS. He was not allowed to serve, was he?

MR. WORTHINGTON. That is as the report reads.

MR. CARLISLE. He was not a member of the House?

MR. WORTHINGTON. No; he was a Delegate; but there was no distinction in the disposition of the case on that ground.

SENATOR DUBOIS. He was excluded, was he not?

MR. WORTHINGTON. Not as I read the report. I read it last night.

SENATOR SMOOT. Not at that time.

SENATOR DUBOIS. Not at that time, but he was excluded as a Delegate in Congress on the ground that he was a polygamist. His seat was contested by a man named Campbell, as I understand it.

MR. WORTHINGTON. Not on that occasion, certainly. On that occasion he served out his term.[8]

---

8. George Q. Cannon was elected to Congress in 1872. As an LDS apostle and favorite of the church's People's Party, he was able to retain his seat for ten years. After he de-

SENATOR DUBOIS.[9] But his status was the same on the second occasion ...

MR. WORTHINGTON. I had referred to the fact that the first charge which is made here is that Senator Smoot actually has the temerity to think he may receive guidance from on high, and that is the ground upon which you are asked to hold that he is not fit to sit by your sides in the Senate Chamber. Mr. Tayler took the same ground when he argued the case, except that he did not make the distinction which Mr. Carlisle now makes between guidance in reference to spiritual mat-

---

feated Allen G. Campbell of the Liberal Party in 1880, the opposition claimed that the English-born Cannon was not a U.S. citizen and that he was a polygamist. According to historian David Buice, "the resolution of the Cannon-Campbell contest was still pending when the Edmunds Bill was introduced," increasing "the likelihood that Cannon's appeal would be denied, which in fact occurred when the House voted on 19 April 1882 against seating either claimant" ("A Stench in the Nostrils of Honest Men: Southern Democrats and the Edmunds Act of 1882," *Dialogue: A Journal of Mormon Thought* 21 [Fall 1988]: 104).

Historian D. Michael Quinn elaborated that "in 1874, when his three plural wives had already borne him eight children, one plural wife was pregnant, and his legal wife was still living, George Q. Cannon sought to maintain his position as Utah's delegate in the U.S. House of Representatives by testifying that he was not living or cohabiting with four wives or any wives in violation of the 1862 Morrill Act; and when again challenged in 1882 he reaffirmed that testimony: 'I denied it then and I can deny it now. I never defiantly or willfully violated any law.' By 1882, his legal wife had died, but his three plural wives were still living, by whom he had now fathered a total of fifteen polygamous children. He had also married two lesser-known wives [and] ... violated the Edmunds Act by marrying his last plural wife in 1884, for which he served five months in the Utah penitentiary" ("LDS Church Authority and New Plural Marriages, 1890-1904," *Dialogue: A Journal of Mormon Thought* 18 [Spring 1985]: 73-74).

9. Senator Dubois had taken an active interest in the Smoot case from the beginning. Smoot shared an anecdote with Joseph F. Smith: "I was in the water closet of the Senate; Fred Dubois was also there having his shoes blacked. Senator Clay, of Georgia, came in while I was in the closet, and Dubois asked him if he was going to make another speech on the rate bill. He replied that he intended to make only one more speech during the present session, and that would be for Smoot, as he intended to vote for him. Dubois knew that I could hear what Clay said, and hushed him up as soon as possible" (May 1, 1906). Heber J. Grant wrote from England that he had heard of a boast Dubois had allegedly made that he had a packed jury "that would convict Jesus Christ." To Grant, this showed the kind of "immoral man" involved "in the fight against our people" (Mar. 7, 1906).

Smoot replied to Grant: "I doubt that there has been a time in the history of our people when the powers of darkness and evil have been arrayed against us as they are at the present time; but there has always been a ray of hope in the fact that President Roosevelt has been brave enough and true enough to stand by the right. He has not allowed the clamor of priests and the pleading of misguided women to swerve him from his duty as President of all the people. He has defended me on all occasions and has spoken of our people as he has understood them to be" (Apr. 22, 1906). Smoot considered Roosevelt the greatest statesman of all political figures he had ever met (Milton R. Merrill, "Theodore Roosevelt and Reed Smoot," *Western Political Quarterly* 4 [September 1951]: 440).

ters and guidance in reference to things temporal, mundane.

It is strange indeed, that this committee should be asked to consider that a disqualification of a man as a Senator or as a member of Congress. I had supposed it was the doctrine of all the Christian churches of this country [and] ... that in every church in this country on every Sabbath Day there go up prayers to the Almighty ... to take care of the sick, to see that those who are upon the sea have a safe voyage, prayers for women who are about to go through the perils of childbirth, prayers for the President of the United States; and I suppose you are asked to decide that those who offer up those prayers and those who believe in them are not fit to go into the Senate of the United States because, perchance, if they get in here they might think the Almighty had instructed them how to vote on the question of railroad rates, or the tariff, or something of that kind.

If there is anything in his argument, that is it. I suppose these ladies who are here will have to go home and tell their children if they have children, or tell the mothers who have children, that when they kneel down at their mother's feet to say the Lord's prayer, it is all right for them to say "Thy Kingdom come, Thy will be done, on earth as it is done in heaven," because that relates to spiritual matters; but when they come to say "Give us this day our daily bread," they must shut their little mouths, because some day they may want to get into the Senate of the United States, and they will be kept out because they are asking the Lord to interfere in things temporal.

I read the other day, having occasion to investigate another matter, that a great man who was President of the United States, in considering perhaps the most momentous event in the history of this country and one of the most momentous in the history of the world, brought his Cabinet before him, in September of 1862, and said he had been considering the question of issuing an emancipation proclamation, and that he had promised himself and promised his God that under certain circumstances he would issue such a proclamation. He had been urged to issue that proclamation long before, but because of the adverse results of the battles around Richmond—he had said it would not do to issue that proclamation then, because it would be said it was a cry of distress—that it was ridiculous to issue such a paper when it was obvious there was no power to enforce it. But he told his advisers that he had promised his God that if there was a victory for the Union arms, he would issue the proclamation; and after Lee had been checked and compelled to retire across the Potomac by the battle of Antietam, on the 17th of September of that year, he, a few days afterwards, called his Cabinet together and complied with the promise he had made to God. I suppose if Abraham Lincoln were still alive and should be elected to the Senate, you would be asked, on the theory that Mr. Carlisle has applied here, to fold your cloaks about you and tell him to stay out because he is not fit to sit by your side. If this means anything, it means that.

Then he referred to the institution of marriage and said the Mormon Church interferes with marriage, which, he says, is purely a civil institution. I have been taught otherwise, and my reading is entirely to the contrary. I understand there is one church, by far the largest in point of membership in this country, which holds that marriage is a religious ceremony and will not recognize the civil law as far as church matters are concerned; that in that church if people want to be married they have to be married by a priest of the church, and if they are divorced the divorce will not be recognized by the church, and that though they may by the civil law obtain a divorce which entitles them to marry again, if they do marry again they are likely to be excommunicated by that church.

Again, during the early sessions of this committee in this hearing, as I remember, a meeting was held here of the ministers of other denominations of the Christian faith for the purpose of having it adopted as a rule of action in all those churches that if the Congress of the United States should see fit to allow in this District divorce for any other cause than adultery, the ministers of those churches would not recognize that edict of the law, but would refuse to marry those who had been divorced and who should seek to be remarried.

SENATOR KNOX. Mr. Worthington, does not the church to which you refer—I presume you refer to the Catholic Church?

MR. WORTHINGTON. Yes.

SENATOR KNOX. Go a little bit further than you have said? You say they regard marriage as a religious ceremony. Do they not teach that marriage is a sacrament, like the Lord's supper, and baptism?

MR. WORTHINGTON. I think they do, Senator.

SENATOR KNOX. I am sure they do. There are the three sacraments of the church—marriage, the supper of the Lord, and baptism.

MR. WORTHINGTON. I will deal no further with that.

The next thing, if I had room left for astonishment about the position that is taken here by those who have opposed Senator Smoot, is the most amazing that I have ever listened to, in view of what had gone before. We had been told, till Mr. Carlisle enlightened us yesterday, that Senator Smoot should not be allowed to retain his seat in the Senate because he belonged to a church the organization of which is such that he was required to obey any order that might come from President Smith, and the intimation is carried—and that is what it means or it means nothing—that if he should be allowed to retain his seat and should be instructed by President Smith to vote this way or the other on some measure that comes before the Senate, he would be bound by the obligations of his church to vote that way even though he believed in his own heart that he should vote the other way; and the picture has been drawn here of President Smith sitting at the head of that church, with all the people assembled around him, upon bended knee, saying "Behold the mouthpiece of God." That is practically the language that has been used here over and over again, that they believe President Smith actually speaks for God and from God, and that they must obey him as they would obey God.

But now we have Mr. Carlisle saying that Senator Smoot should be excluded because he is responsible for everything that President Smith does, and he calls attention to a certain phrase here in the Doctrine and Covenants which reads that the authority of the quorum of the apostles is equal in authority to the quorum of the presidency and that the presidency can not do anything unless the apostles say it may be done. He used almost exactly that language—"the presidency can do nothing without the unanimous consent of the apostles." He is asking you now to exclude Senator Smoot upon the ground that everything that President Smith has done Senator Smoot must have consented to, because he draws the picture of President Smith going around upon his knees to apostle after apostle and saying, "Will you allow me to do this; will you allow me to do that?"

How such diverse conclusions may be reached by two such eminent gentlemen as Brother Tayler and Mr. Carlisle upon the same evidence I do not know. The fact is that neither the apostles nor the presidency are supreme in that church. The evidence here demonstrates beyond all peradventure that it is the most democratic organization, embracing large numbers of people, known to this country. Nothing can be done by the presidency of that church or by the apostles, or all of them put together, that does not either have the authority of the church in convention assembled to warrant it, or that is not subject to be resisted and finally determined to be right or wrong by an assembly of all the quorums and all the people in the tabernacle assembled.

It is not for the quorum of the apostles to say that this man shall be president or that man shall be an apostle. They simply nominate to their people a man for the place, and the nominee must fail of appointment unless the multitude confirms or "sustains" him.

I see the chairman smiling and I know what he will say, what he has in mind—that that is the form they have, but, as a matter of fact, they always ratify. Why do they ratify, Mr. Chairman? Because the men who are at the head of affairs keep their ears to the ground and they know how far they can go and when they must stop. If the president of that church and all the apostles together were to undertake to proclaim to-day a revelation that polygamy should be reestablished, the law to the contrary notwithstanding, and should submit it to their people in the tabernacle to be voted upon, according to the testimony here of the witnesses who know about the situation out there to-day, Mormons and non-Mormons, spread through the pages of the testimony which is here, they would be voted down and put out of their office for attempting to rehabilitate that practice[10] ...

Editor's note

The committee's final vote regarding Smoot's eligibility was taken on

---

10. On March 9, 1906, Charles Penrose advised Smoot to delay the hearings so they would "not terminate until after the holding of April conference. <u>Action may be taken and I believe will then</u> which ought to be placed in a legitimate way upon the record of your case. That record, in my opinion, ought not to be left in the shape in which it will appear without a direct refutation of some things that are now part of it, nor without the benefit of <u>such action as that which I allude to.</u>"

Earlier in the year, Joseph F. Smith had advised Smoot to tell President Roosevelt the two apostles under national media scrutiny, Cowley and Taylor, "had admitted taking plural wives since the Manifesto but it was done not in this country and they never considered the Manifesto applied to any place outside the US." Nevertheless, the two had been asked to "tend their resignations." Smoot was to ask the president's advice about making this public and to "tell him the reason of the delay." Smoot wrote to Smith:

On the train night and day I thought of the subject in every possible way and from every stand point that I was capable of conceiving. The more I studied it and followed the action taken to its logical conclusion the more I became convinced I am either wrong in my conclusions or the Brethren were at home agreeing upon the policy adopted. I could not help but think if I went to President Roosevelt and told him Taylor and Cowley had admitted their guilt, the President in his blunt, honest, and personal way would immediately ask me whether they had been excommunicated, and if not, why not; that the action agreed upon would not have the desired result, but just the opposite. A mere resignation just before the resuming of the case would be looked upon as a mere subterfuge and worthy of the severest condemnation. ... The fact that they had admitted their guilt and the church knowing it and not excommunicating them would be proof positive of our undoing (Draft of letter, ca. Jan. 7, 1906).

June 1, 1906—seven against, five for. The unfavorable report—together with the minority's dissenting report—was submitted to the full Senate ten days later. Carl Badger wrote:

> The action of the Committee yesterday was unexpected; we had thought there would be a tie. Dolliver of Iowa did not vote as had been expected. The Senator felt sure of him. ... Dolliver has certainly played the coward; but I am afraid that the Senator's interests have betrayed him. I know that we are all likely to judge things most favorably to our interests. ... Yesterday Senator Burrows came to Senator Smoot ... and told him what had taken place. He told the Senator that nothing had been said in the Committee against him personally, that all the members of the Committee had the kindliest feelings toward him. This rather exasperated the Senator, and he told Burrows he had heard him say that several times. Burrows asked if the Senator meant to insinuate that he was not telling the truth; and the Senator replied that he would discuss that at some other time.[11]

Later in the year, Smoot told LDS President Joseph F. Smith that he had met with U.S. President Roosevelt:

> The room was filled with strangers, among them a number of Senators, including J. C. Burrows. As soon as the doors were opened the president shook hands with me the first one and asked me to come with him to a seat, and we discussed the situation fully. The President is certainly a great, great big man. Nothing on earth deters him from doing what he thinks is right. He discussed my case in a tone of voice that anybody could hear, and in such a way that nobody could mistake his position. First, in an undertone, he told me that Senator Dolliver had told him personally that he would vote for me ... I had your [Joseph F. Smith's] letter of recent date, to which you had added a postscript in you own handwriting, ... in my pocket, and I read that portion of your letter to the President.

The postscript expressed admiration for President Roosevelt. Smith wrote that he held him "in the highest esteem, as to the President of the United States, of the whole people and not a part of them only. Broad minded, generous, honest, and fearless. God bless him! We pray for him constantly." President Roosevelt said, "I greatly appreciate that, and I wish that you kindly remember me to President Smith, but," he added, "he must, he must stop these new polygamous marriages." Smoot closed: "President Roosevelt remarked in a jocular way to me today, that he did not know how it was, but that someway or other he rather loved me. It does me great good to hear the strong men of the Senate speak of

---

11. In Badger, *Liahona and Iron Rod*, 329.

me in terms of friendship and respect, and I certainly hope that I will always merit the same, and, through their friendship, be able to guard the interest of our people."[12]

Early the next year, Smoot found himself victorious when, on February 20, 1907, the full U.S. Senate voted not to unseat him. Recently called LDS Apostle George F. Richards recorded: "This day after a hard fight for four years Senator Reed Smoot won out & retains his Seat on a vote of 43 to 27. Cost to the Government of $50,000. The Church is vindicated at last. The Devil suffers defeat, Zion prospers. There are more people investigating the Gospel, more tithing being paid, more temple work being done than ever before. We never were so numerous & never so strong before. There is absolute unity with the Presidency and Twelve and the other General Authorities so far as I have been able to discover."[13]

12. Smoot to Joseph F. Smith, June 8, 1906. As time passed, Senators were lobbied from both sides. Senator Joseph Blackburn (D-Ky), "a very popular Democratic senator, the leader of the Senate at present," met the committee chair "and said: 'Brother Burrows, I don't think you will get votes enough to oust Senator Smoot.' 'Well,' said Burrows, 'I have done my duty to the country, and have satisfied my own conscience'" (in Badger, *Liahona and Iron Rod,* 335).

13. Richards, Diary, Feb. 20, 1907, Archives, Historical Department, Church of Jesus Christ of Latter-day Saints, Salt Lake City.

Epilogue
Reed Smoot's Case, 1903-06
Franklin S. Richards

W HEN IT BECAME KNOWN THAT Reed Smoot wanted to be United States Senator, I was opposed in my feelings to having him become a candidate for the office, because I realized that his seat would be contested, on the ground that the church was not sincere in issuing the Manifesto [of 1890], as well as for other reasons, and I felt that it would be a mistake to revive the prejudice which had existed throughout the Country, and had required so much effort to allay. This being the case, I told President [Joseph F.] Smith and other church officials that if Brother Smoot was elected it would result in an investigation, at which some of them would be required to testify, and that President Smith would probably be obliged to admit that he had not only violated the law of the State, against unlawful cohabitation (having pleaded guilty to that offense and paid a fine), but that he had also violated the rules of the church, inasmuch as the Manifesto had been approved by the church at its General Conference, and interpreted by its leaders as including cohabitation. President Smith said he did not think that he would be required to testify, and believing that Reed Smoot should have an opportunity to try to get the office, he would not do anything to prevent his success.

When the Smoot contests were filed, after considerable investigation by the Brethren, as to the best lawyer for him to retain, Mr. [Augustus S.] Worthington, a prominent lawyer at Washington, D.C., was employed as his attorney, to be assisted by Waldemar Van Cott and myself. It was distinctly understood, however, that I should not appear as Smoot's attorney, but be present as counsel for the church and witnesses who might be called to testify. With this understanding, I went to Washington during the holidays of 1903, and commenced consultations with Senator Smoot and his attorneys on the first of January 1904, in relation to the

FRANKLIN SNYDER RICHARDS was a son of LDS Apostle Franklin Dewey Richards and the first of his father's thirteen wives, Jane Snyder. As an attorney, Franklin spent most of his time representing the LDS Church. His short summary of his involvement in the Smoot case resides in typescript in Archives, Historical Department, Church of Jesus Christ of Latter-day Saints, Salt Lake City.

answer which he should file. I remained in Washington on this business till the first of February and then returned home with my wife [Emily], she having been in New York with [our twenty-three-year-old son] Dewey most of the time while I was working in Washington.

February the 24th, 1904, I started for Washington with President Smith and other witnesses. After my arrival, Mr. Van Cott and I were busy examining the witnesses, until the hearing commenced on the 2nd of March. President Smith was on the witness stand till March 7th. We were before the committee during each day and spent the evening with the witnesses. The investigation was adjourned March 12th, and I returned home by way of New York. Upon my arrival I explained the situation to President Smith and the other brethren.

April the 15th, I started for Washington with Van Cott to continue the Smoot investigation, which lasted till May the 2nd, when I returned home with Senator Smoot. (Having contracted a severe case of malaria in Washington, I made my second trip to Europe, where my wife was representing the women of Utah, at an international council held at Berlin.)

December the 7th, started for Washington and after my arrival, spent the time in consultations with Senator Smoot and his attorneys and witnesses, till the investigation was resumed on December the 12th. It lasted till the 20th, when a further adjournment was taken, and I returned home by way of New York, arriving home the 24th. (Mr. [Frederick] Newell [Chief Engineer, U.S. Geological Survey] was with me on the trip from Salt Lake to Washington, and discussed reclamation matters quite fully.)

December 31st, Attorney Worthington and I had an interview with the First Presidency and others, in which we reminded them that the developments had been such as I had predicted before the examination began.

January 17th, 1905, started for Washington with witnesses for the Smoot investigation, which was resumed January 21st, at which time Reed Smoot testified. The hearing was adjourned January 28th and I returned home by New York, after working several days on briefs for Smoot's attorneys. Reached home February 19th. (During this time I also had several interviews with Mr. Newell and others about reclamation matters.)

During October 1905, I spent considerable time with B. H. Roberts preparing matter for Reed Smoot's statement in the investigation of his case. October the 19th, met with the First Presidency and Twelve Apostles in the temple, at which time B. H. Roberts and I explained to them the situation at Washington—Apostles John W. Taylor and M[atthias]. F. Cowley being present.

The chairman of the Senate committee had given President Smith notice that unless these men appeared and testified before the committee, it would be assumed by the committee that they were guilty of marrying plural wives after the Manifesto had been issued, and upon their failure to appear, it would be assumed also that the church had not acted in good faith in issuing the Manifesto, unless Taylor and Cowley were expelled from the quorum and excommunicated from the church. This was done, after an investigation, inasmuch as they positively refused to go and testify.

January 27th 1906, started for Washington again on the Smoot case, with my wife, who was to attend a suffrage convention in Washington. Before starting, I spent considerable time examining witnesses who had been subpoenaed to testify in the investigation. After reaching Washington I had consultations with Smoot and his attorneys, as well as with [attorney and former] Senator [Charles J.] Faulkner, and worked on the case till February the 7th, when the hearing was resumed. February the 9th, the investigation was adjourned and I started for home on the 16th, reaching there February the 20th.

March the 19th, started for Washington again on the Smoot case, having spent many days at work on the case while at home. Reached Washington on the 22nd and worked on the case till March 26th, when the hearing was resumed. March 27th, testimony was closed, but I was detained in Washington, helping to prepare arguments of counsel, and speech for Senator Smoot, till April the 13th, when the hearing was closed by Mr. Worthington's reply to Mr. Carlisle. Arrived home on the 16th.

After my arrival at home, I revised the matter which had been prepared by Brothers [Brigham H.] Roberts, [Charles W.] Penrose and myself, for Senator Smoot to use in his case, which was proved by the Presidency, who were well pleased with the work.

A majority and minority report were filed in the Smoot case on the 11th of June, 1906. The resolution of the chairman of the committee declaring the Senator ineligible for the office was rejected, and he was seated in accordance with the minority report. During the investigation I made seven trips to Washington and was present at every hearing of the committee. I did not appear as counsel for the Senator because of my position as Church Attorney, and it was deemed inadvisable for me to do so, but I did consult with his attorneys, Worthington and Van Cott, at every stage of the proceedings, and examined the witnesses before they testified. Mr. Van Cott and I were the only counsel present at the last hearing.

While the election of the Senator was against my judgment, because I feared the investigation which would follow, I have long since become satisfied that it was providential, because it was the means of bringing to light infractions of the law by prominent officials of the church, which resulted in their excommunication, and conclusively demonstrated the sincerity of the church in the issuing of the Manifesto. If these exposures had not been made at that time the results might have been much more disastrous. ...

Index

About the Editor

Michael Harold Paulos is a graduate of Brigham Young University and recently of the McCombs School of Business, University of Texas at Austin, where he was a Ryoichi Sasakawa Young Fellow. He is now a financial analyst with Kinetic Concepts Inc. (KCI) in San Antonio. He has published on historical subjects in the *LBJ School of Public Affairs Journal*, *Journal of Mormon History*, *Sunstone* magazine, and the *Utah Historical Quarterly*. He and his wife have three boys, whom they are raising to be Utah Jazz fans.

This volume includes an introduction by Harvard Heath, Curator of the Utah and American Archives, Harold B. Lee Library, Brigham Young University, retired. Dr. Heath is the editor of *In the World: The Diaries of Reed Smoot*.

The Mormon Church on Trial
Transcripts of the Reed Smoot Hearings

Printed by Franklin Covey Printing on
Glatfelter Sebago Antique, an acid-free paper.

Bound by Express Solutions Bindery in
Ecological Fibers Rainbow, an archival material.

Dust jacket designed by Ron Stucki.

Interior designed and composed by
Connie Disney in Baskerville, a transitional
typeface created by eighteenth-century
English printer and typographer
John Baskerville.